Garfield
FAT CAT 3-PACK
VOLUME 13

BY
JIM DAVIS

BALLANTINE BOOKS • NEW YORK

Published in the United States by Ballantine Books, an imprint of Random House, a division of
Penguin Random House LLC, New York.

BALLANTINE and the HOUSE colophon are registered trademarks of Penguin Random House LLC.

NICKELODEON is a Trademark of Viacom International, Inc.

ISBN: 978-0-345-46460-6

Printed in China

randomhousebooks.com

First Colorized Edition: September 2006

20 19 18 17

Garfield BEEFS UP

BY JIM DAVIS

Ballantine Books • New York

Garfield's Code of Nevers

NEVER
put off until tomorrow what you can eat today

NEVER
diet on a day ending in "y"

NEVER
swim in the gravy boat

NEVER
lick yourself at the dinner table

NEVER
floss a pit bull

NEVER
buy seafood off a pickup truck with an Iowa license plate

NEVER
snore while the boss is talking

NEVER
eat the "mystery meat"

NEVER
buy used underwear

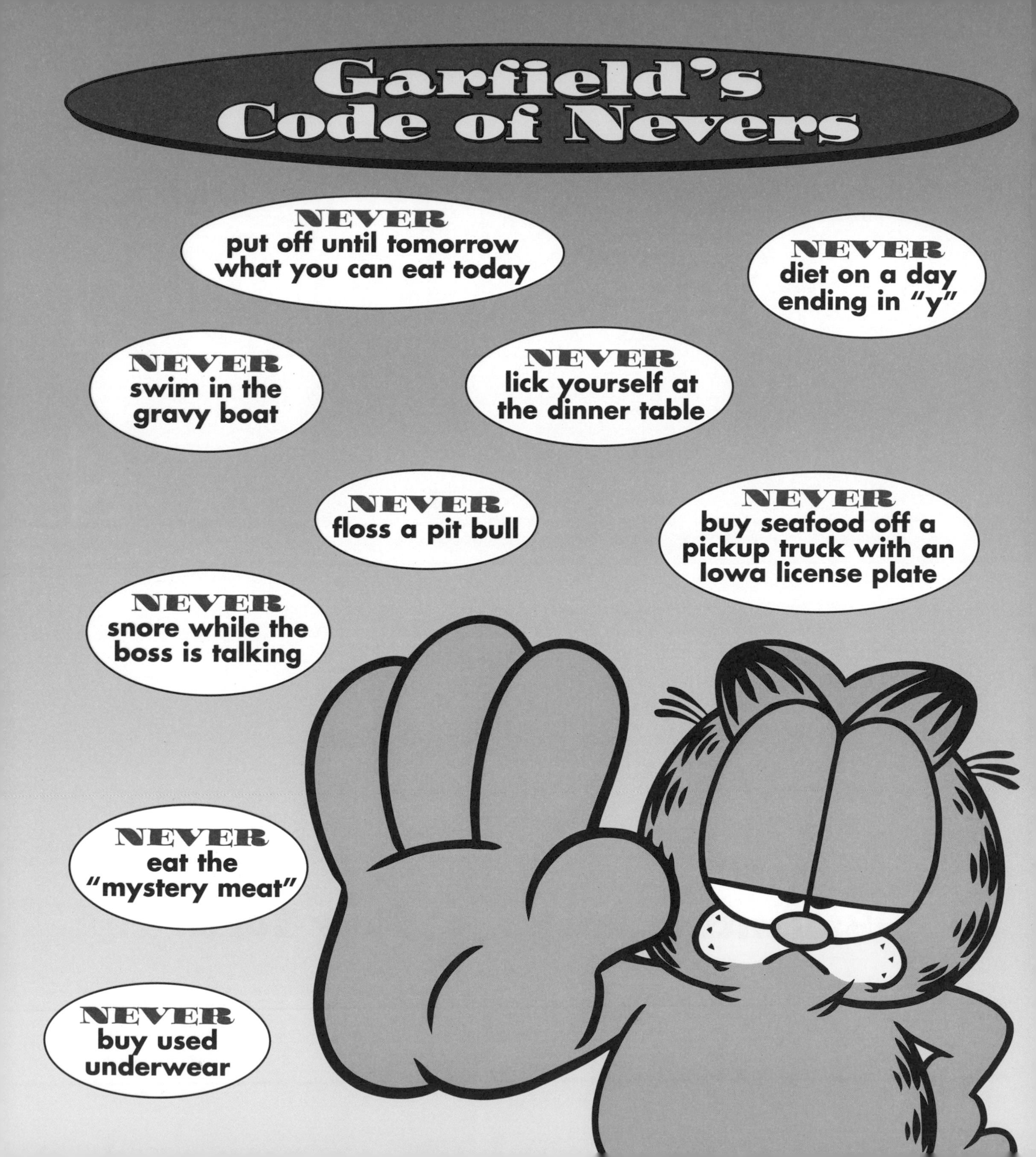

Garfield
FAT CAT 3-PACK
VOLUME 13

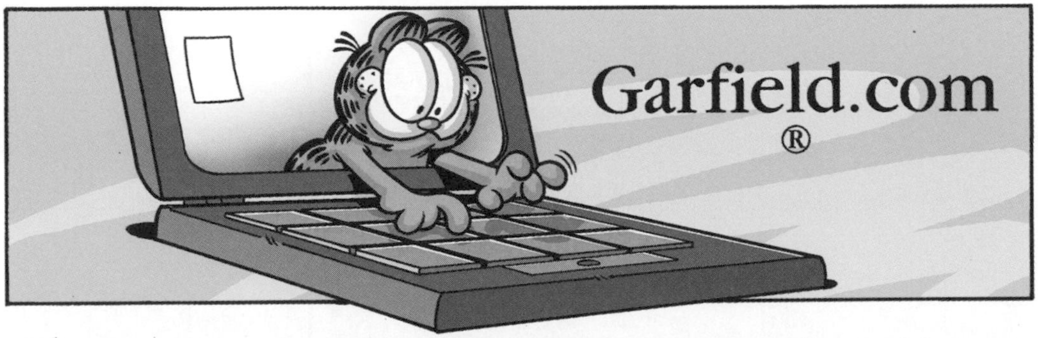
Garfield.com
®

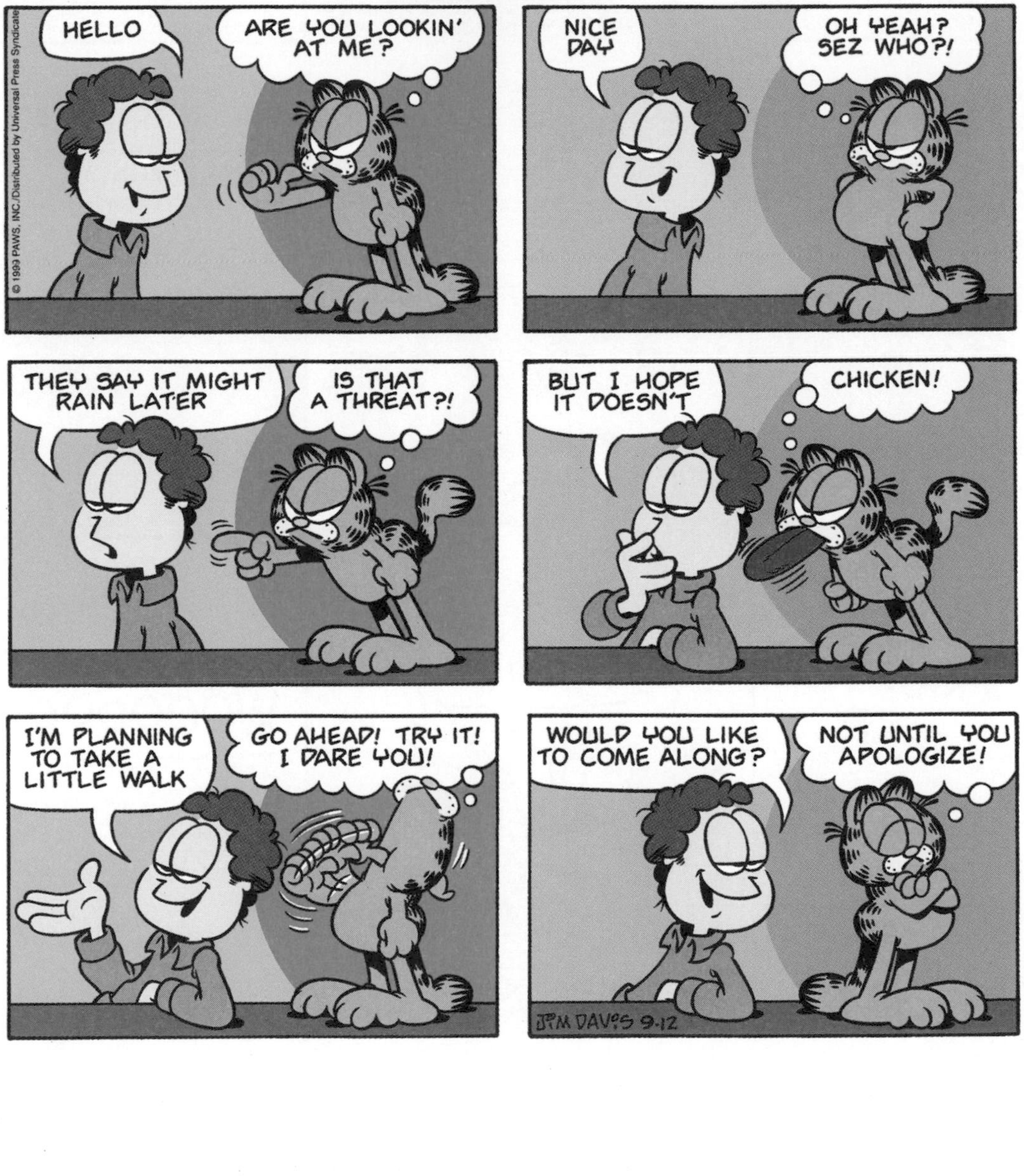
© 1999 PAWS, INC./Distributed by Universal Press Syndicate
HELLO
ARE YOU LOOKIN' AT ME?
NICE DAY
OH YEAH? SEZ WHO?!
THEY SAY IT MIGHT RAIN LATER
IS THAT A THREAT?!
BUT I HOPE IT DOESN'T
CHICKEN!
I'M PLANNING TO TAKE A LITTLE WALK
GO AHEAD! TRY IT! I DARE YOU!
WOULD YOU LIKE TO COME ALONG?
NOT UNTIL YOU APOLOGIZE!
JPM DAVIS 9-12

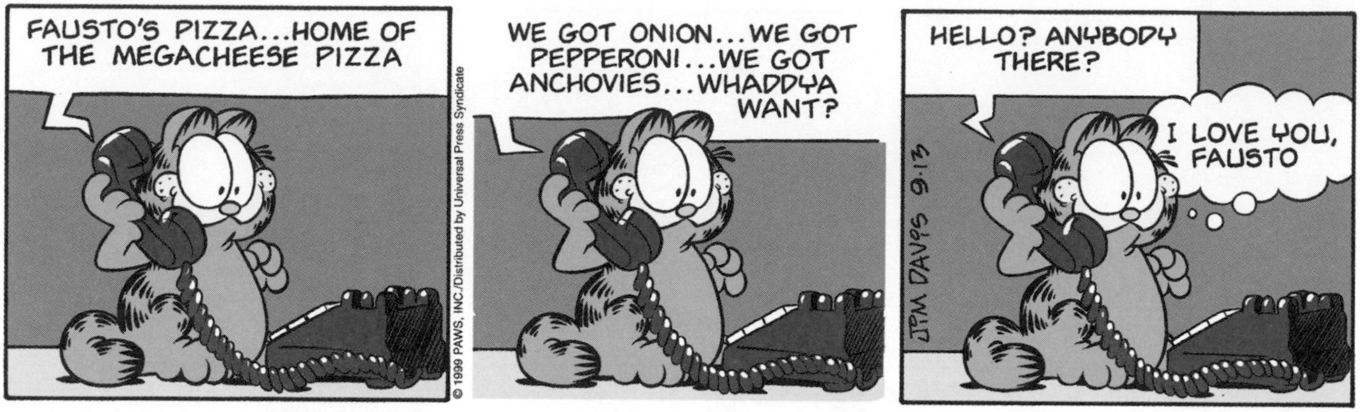
FAUSTO'S PIZZA...HOME OF THE MEGACHEESE PIZZA
WE GOT ONION...WE GOT PEPPERONI...WE GOT ANCHOVIES...WHADDYA WANT?
HELLO? ANYBODY THERE?
I LOVE YOU, FAUSTO
JIM DAVIS 9-13

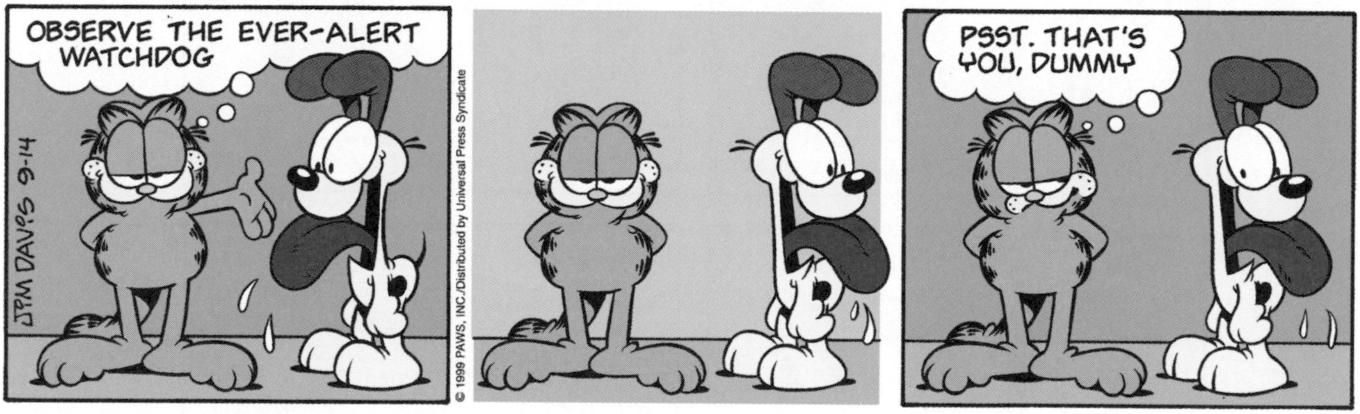
OBSERVE THE EVER-ALERT WATCHDOG
JIM DAVIS 9-14
PSST. THAT'S YOU, DUMMY

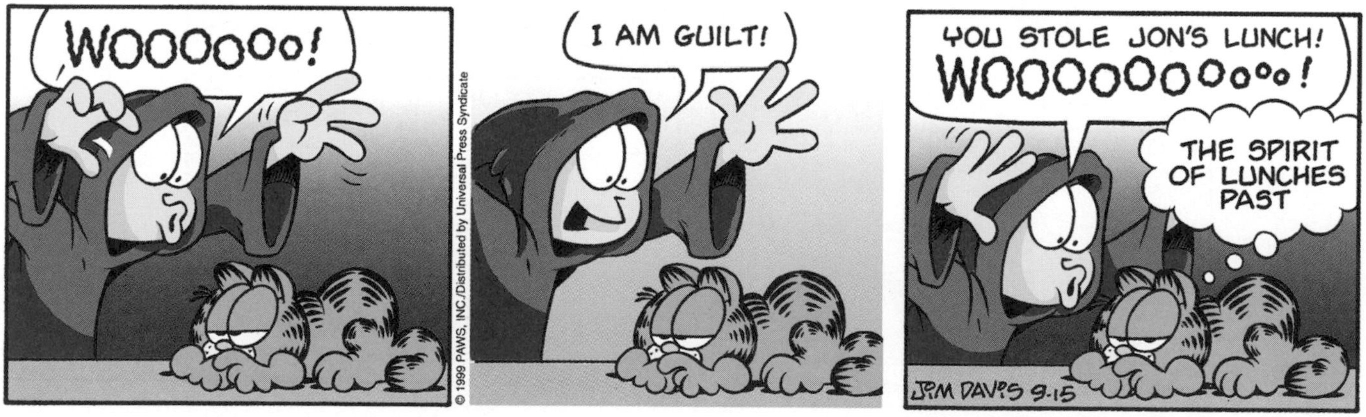
WOOOOOo!
I AM GUILT!
YOU STOLE JON'S LUNCH! WOOOOOOOooo!
THE SPIRIT OF LUNCHES PAST
JIM DAVIS 9-15

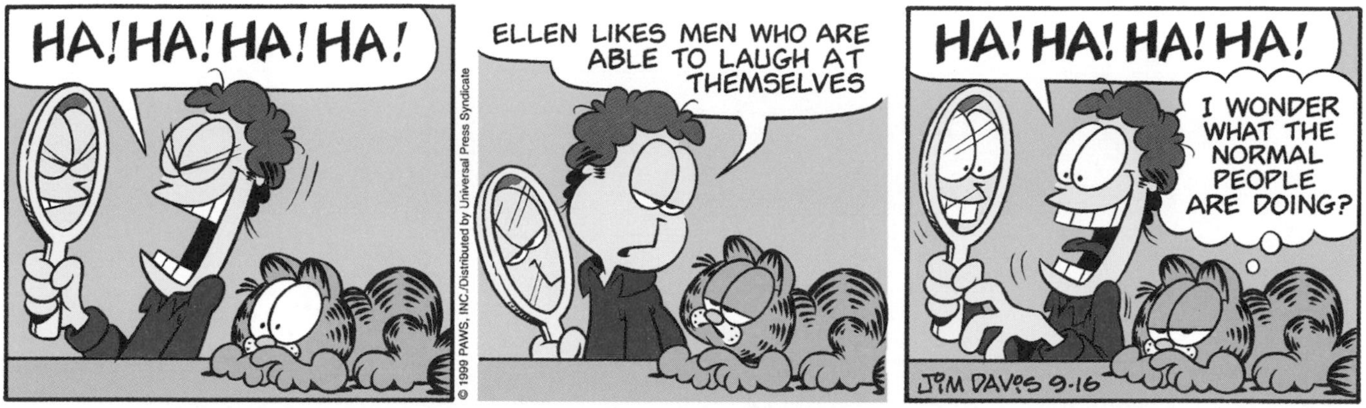
HA! HA! HA! HA!
ELLEN LIKES MEN WHO ARE ABLE TO LAUGH AT THEMSELVES
HA! HA! HA! HA!
I WONDER WHAT THE NORMAL PEOPLE ARE DOING?
JIM DAVIS 9-16
© 1999 PAWS, INC./Distributed by Universal Press Syndicate

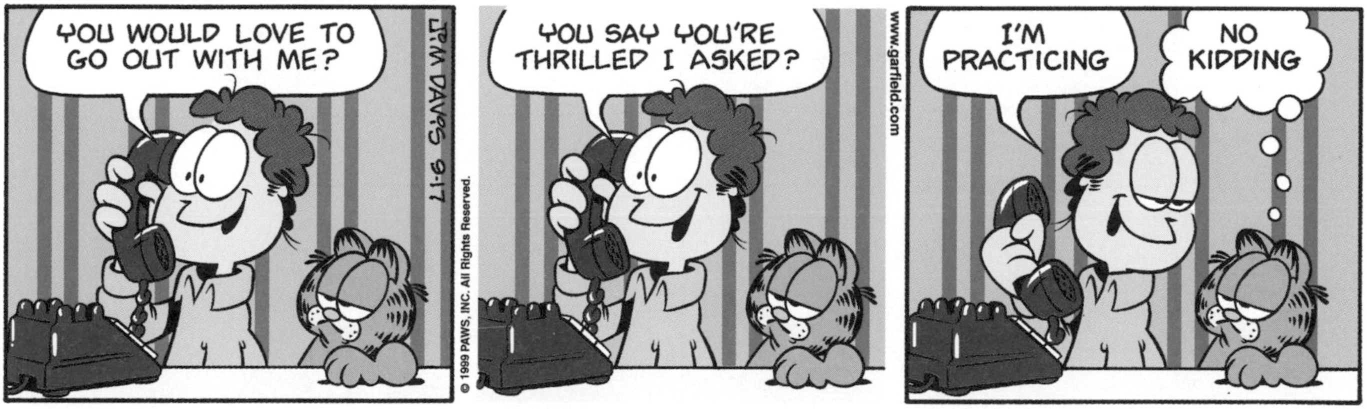
YOU WOULD LOVE TO GO OUT WITH ME?
YOU SAY YOU'RE THRILLED I ASKED?
I'M PRACTICING
NO KIDDING
JIM DAVIS 9-17
© 1999 PAWS, INC. All Rights Reserved.
www.garfield.com

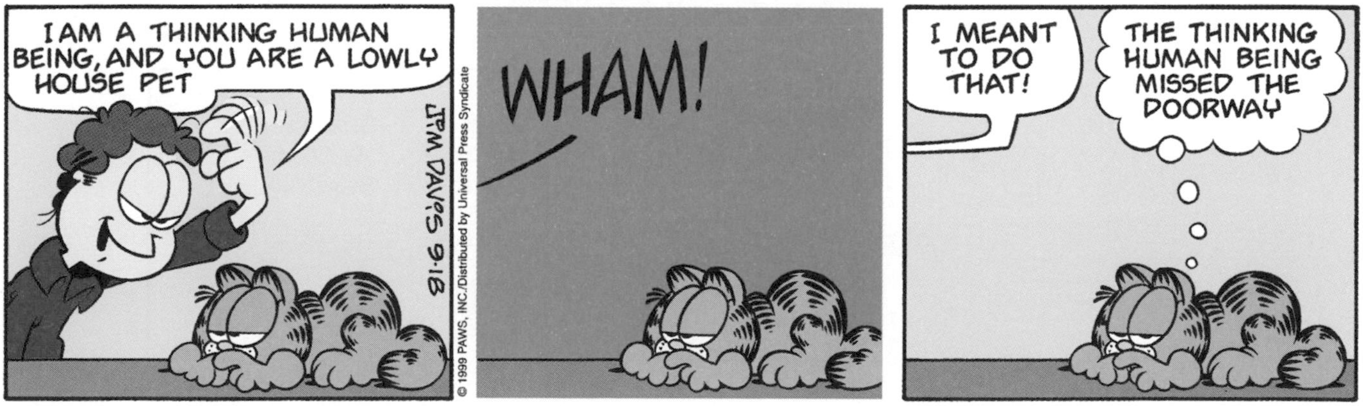
I AM A THINKING HUMAN BEING, AND YOU ARE A LOWLY HOUSE PET
WHAM!
I MEANT TO DO THAT!
THE THINKING HUMAN BEING MISSED THE DOORWAY
JIM DAVIS 9-18
© 1999 PAWS, INC./Distributed by Universal Press Syndicate

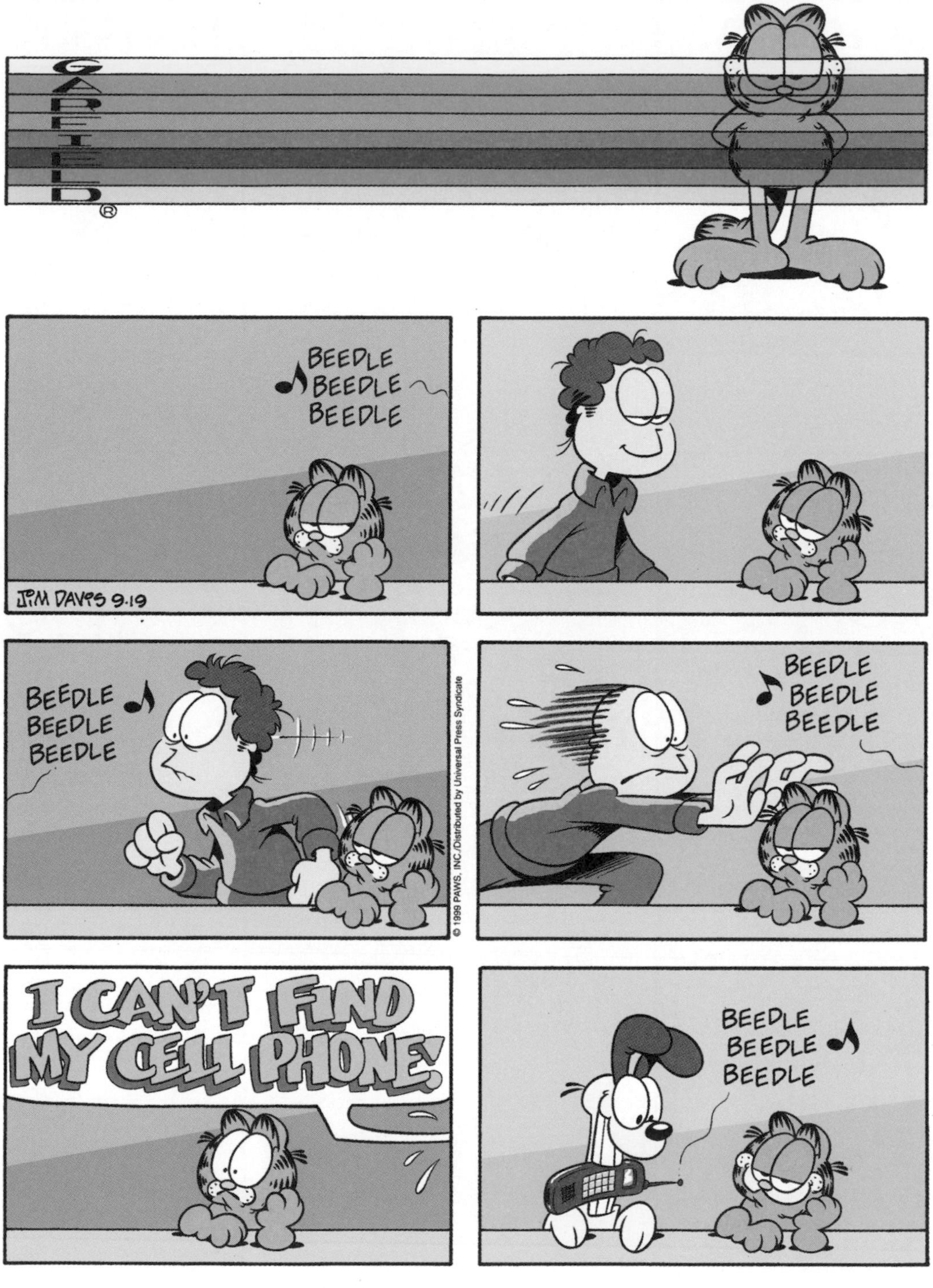
GARFIELD®
JIM DAVIS 9.19
BEEDLE BEEDLE BEEDLE
BEEDLE BEEDLE BEEDLE
BEEDLE BEEDLE BEEDLE
I CAN'T FIND MY CELL PHONE!
BEEDLE BEEDLE BEEDLE
© 1999 PAWS, INC./Distributed by Universal Press Syndicate

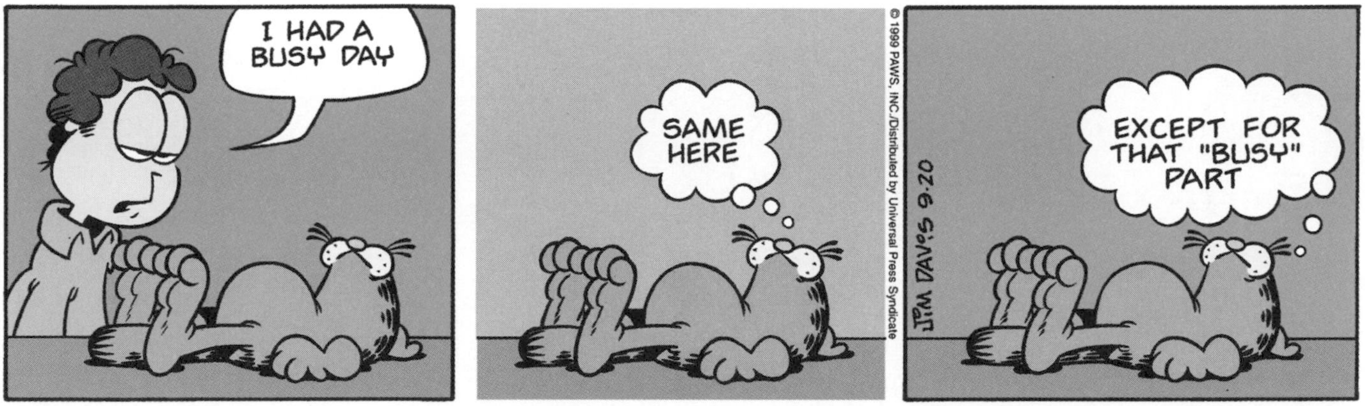
I HAD A BUSY DAY
SAME HERE
EXCEPT FOR THAT "BUSY" PART
JIM DAVIS 9.20
© 1999 PAWS, INC./Distributed by Universal Press Syndicate

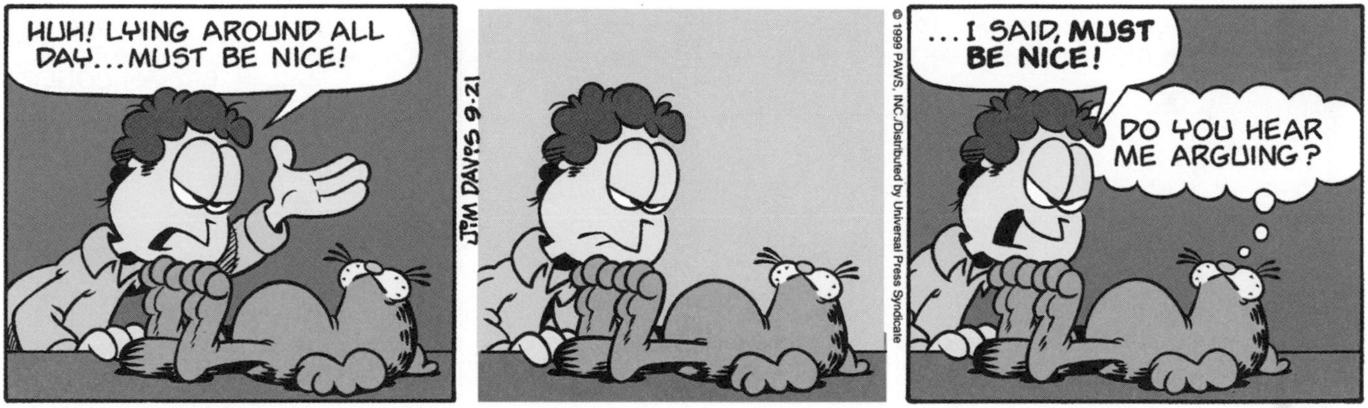
HUH! LYING AROUND ALL DAY...MUST BE NICE!
...I SAID, **MUST BE NICE!**
DO YOU HEAR ME ARGUING?
JIM DAVIS 9.21
© 1999 PAWS, INC./Distributed by Universal Press Syndicate

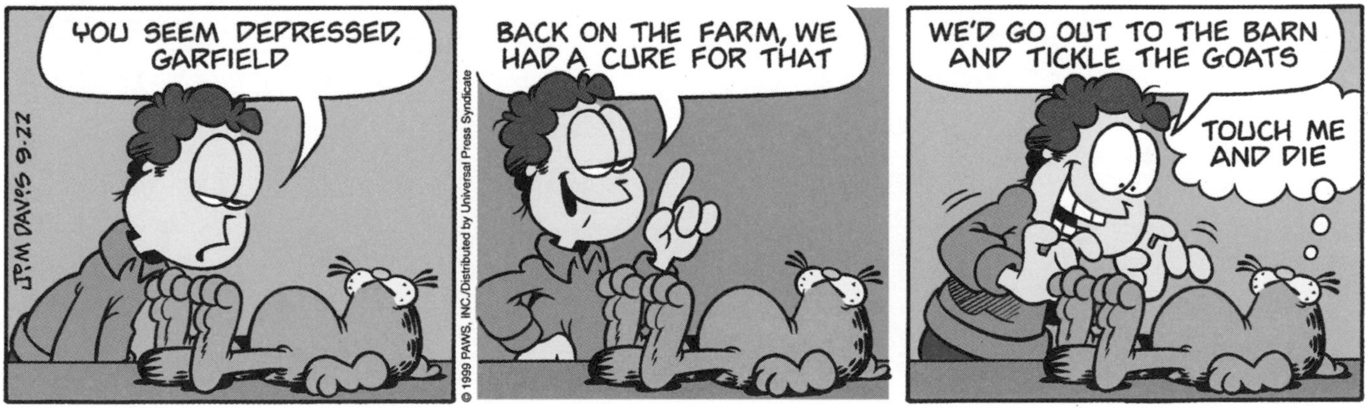
YOU SEEM DEPRESSED, GARFIELD
BACK ON THE FARM, WE HAD A CURE FOR THAT
WE'D GO OUT TO THE BARN AND TICKLE THE GOATS
TOUCH ME AND DIE
JIM DAVIS 9.22
© 1999 PAWS, INC./Distributed by Universal Press Syndicate

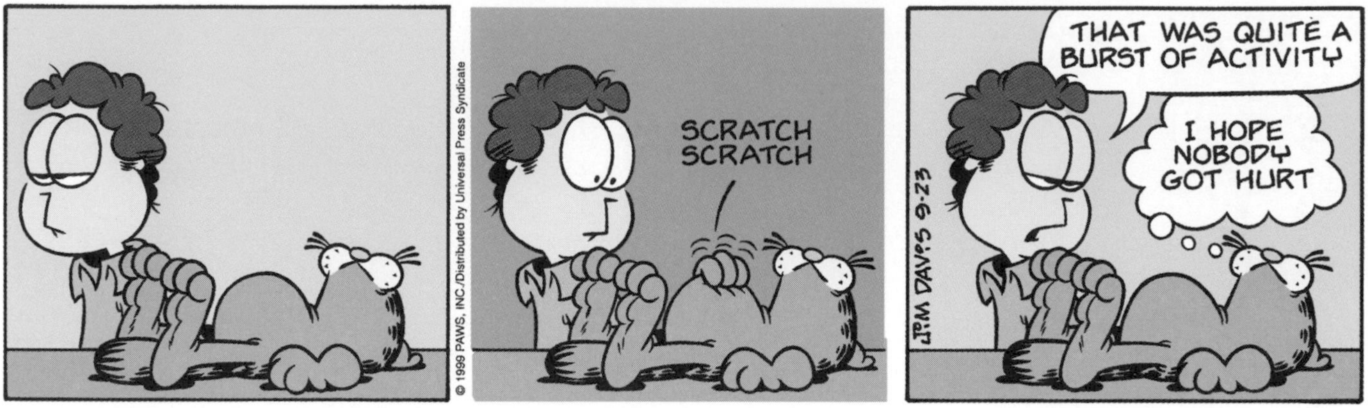
© 1999 PAWS, INC./Distributed by Universal Press Syndicate
SCRATCH SCRATCH
THAT WAS QUITE A BURST OF ACTIVITY
I HOPE NOBODY GOT HURT
JIM DAVIS 9·23

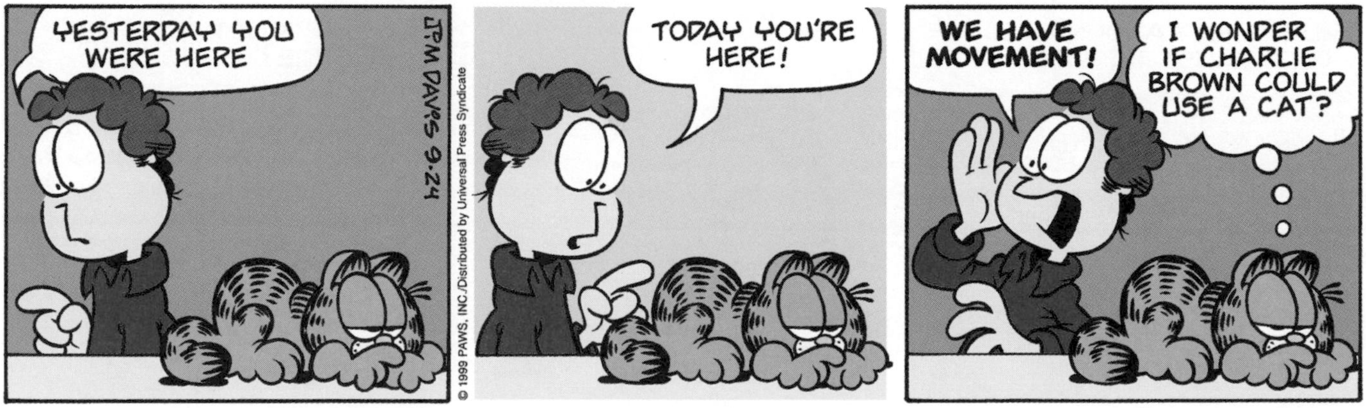
YESTERDAY YOU WERE HERE
JIM DAVIS 9·24
© 1999 PAWS, INC./Distributed by Universal Press Syndicate
TODAY YOU'RE HERE!
WE HAVE MOVEMENT!
I WONDER IF CHARLIE BROWN COULD USE A CAT?

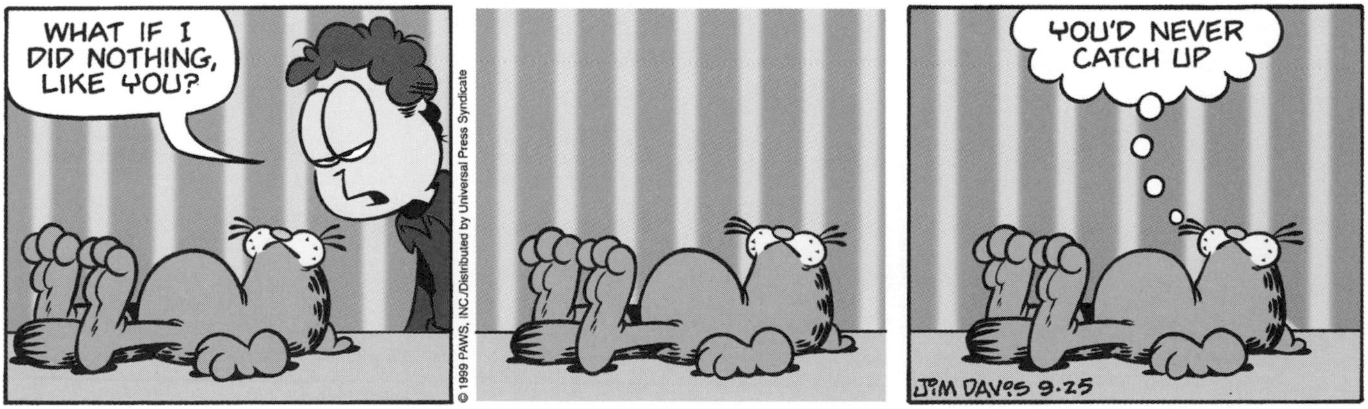
WHAT IF I DID NOTHING, LIKE YOU?
© 1999 PAWS, INC./Distributed by Universal Press Syndicate
YOU'D NEVER CATCH UP
JIM DAVIS 9·25

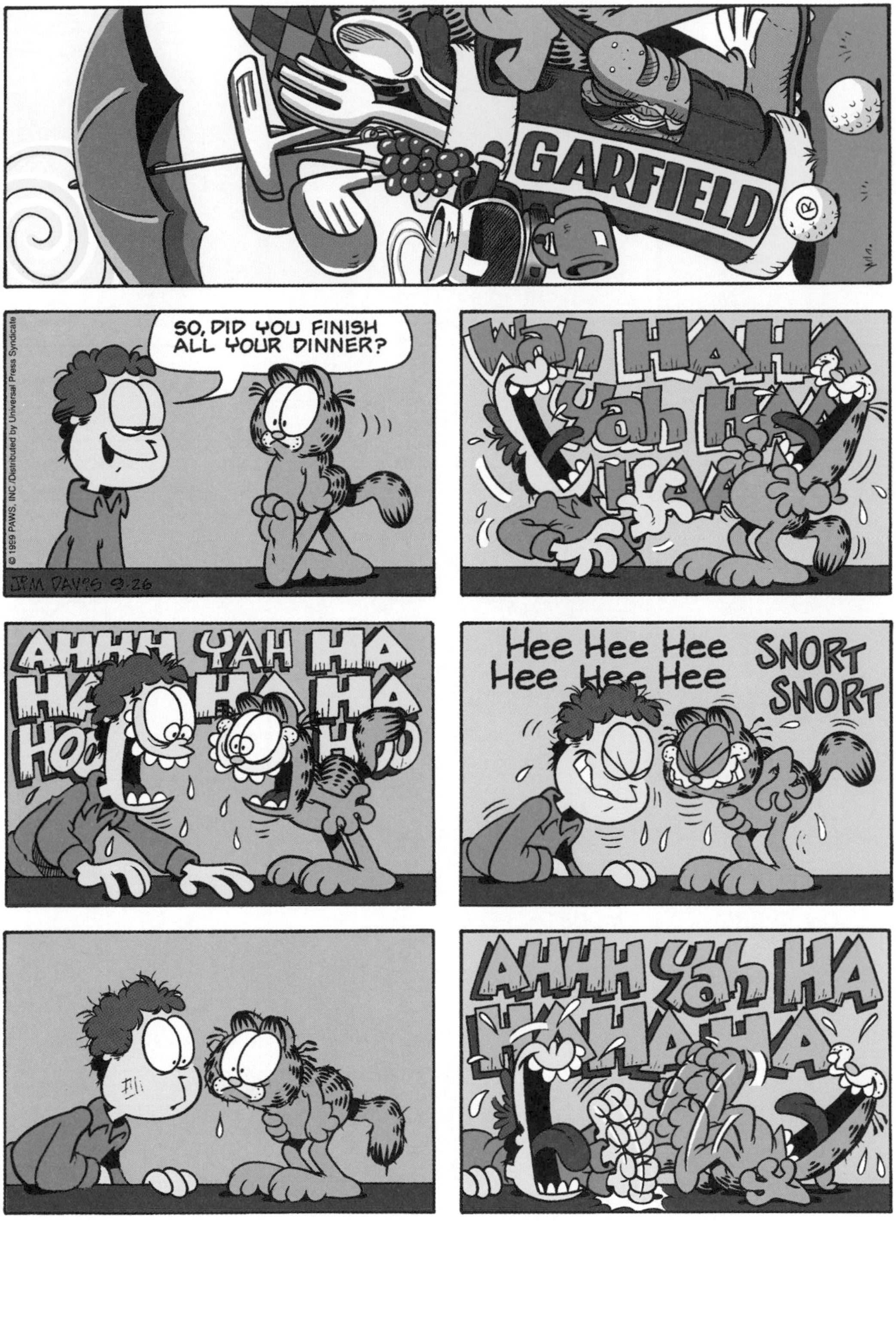
GARFIELD
© 1999 PAWS, INC./Distributed by Universal Press Syndicate
JIM DAVIS 9-26
SO, DID YOU FINISH ALL YOUR DINNER?
Wah HAHA
Yah HA
AHHH YAH HA
HA HA HA
Hee Hee Hee
Hee Hee Hee
SNORT
SNORT
AHHH Yah HA
HAHAHA

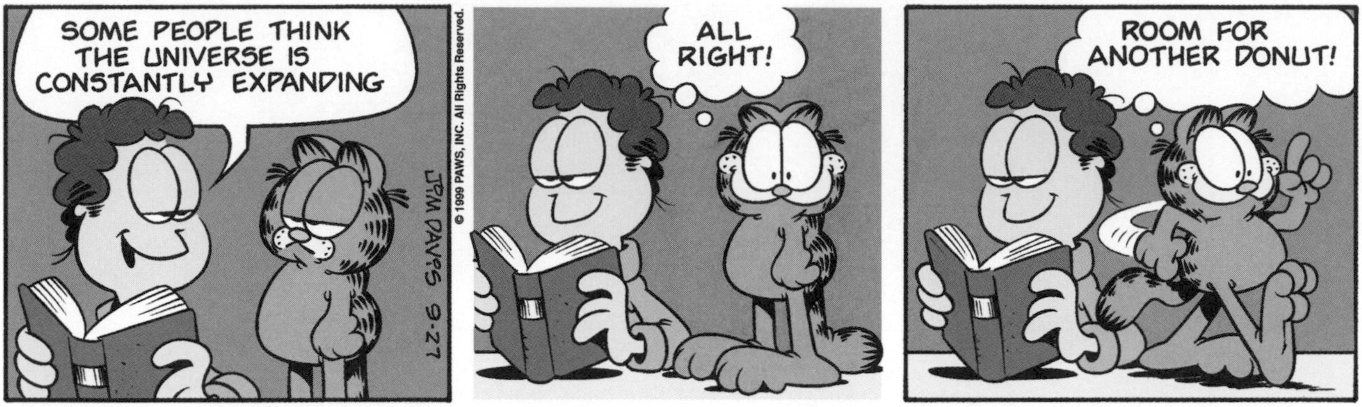
SOME PEOPLE THINK THE UNIVERSE IS CONSTANTLY EXPANDING
JIM DAVIS 9-27
© 1999 PAWS, INC. All Rights Reserved.
ALL RIGHT!
ROOM FOR ANOTHER DONUT!

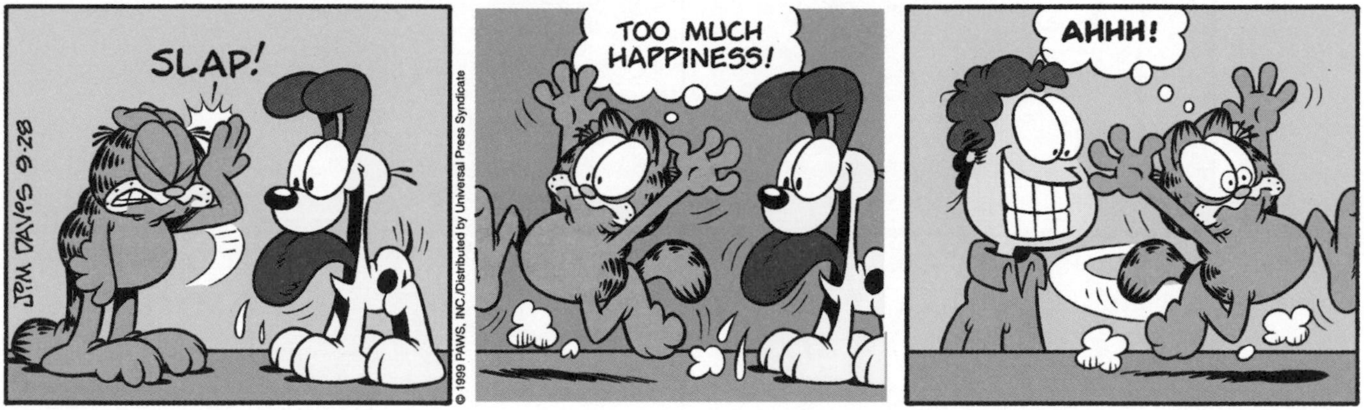
SLAP!
JIM DAVIS 9-28
© 1999 PAWS, INC./Distributed by Universal Press Syndicate
TOO MUCH HAPPINESS!
AHHH!

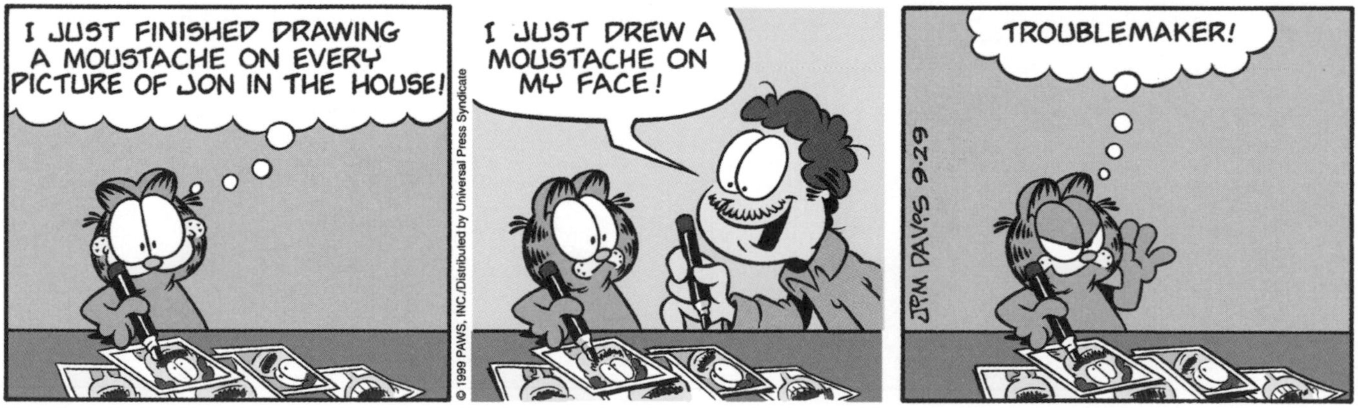
I JUST FINISHED DRAWING A MOUSTACHE ON EVERY PICTURE OF JON IN THE HOUSE!
© 1999 PAWS, INC./Distributed by Universal Press Syndicate
I JUST DREW A MOUSTACHE ON MY FACE!
TROUBLEMAKER!
JIM DAVIS 9-29

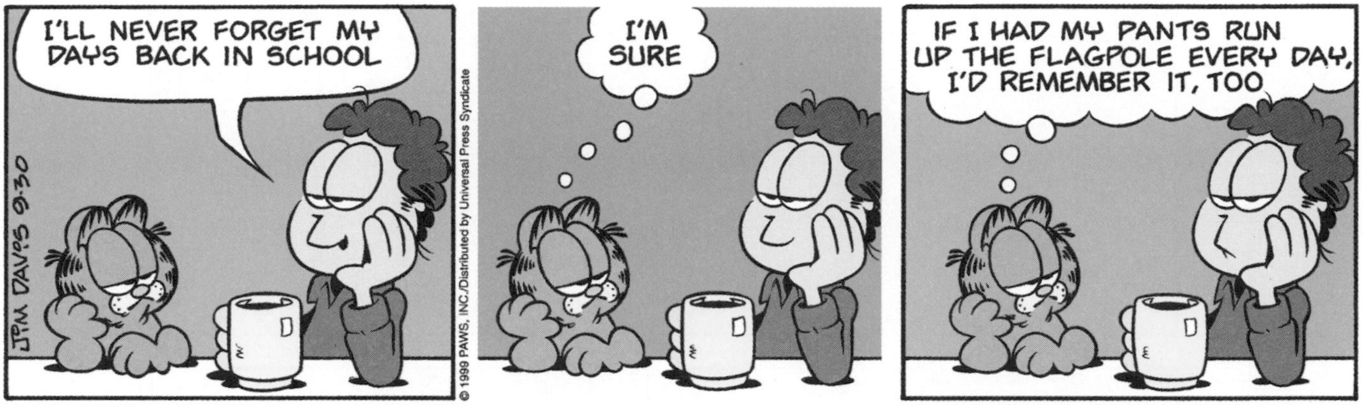
I'LL NEVER FORGET MY DAYS BACK IN SCHOOL
I'M SURE
IF I HAD MY PANTS RUN UP THE FLAGPOLE EVERY DAY, I'D REMEMBER IT, TOO
JIM DAVIS 9-30
© 1999 PAWS, INC./Distributed by Universal Press Syndicate

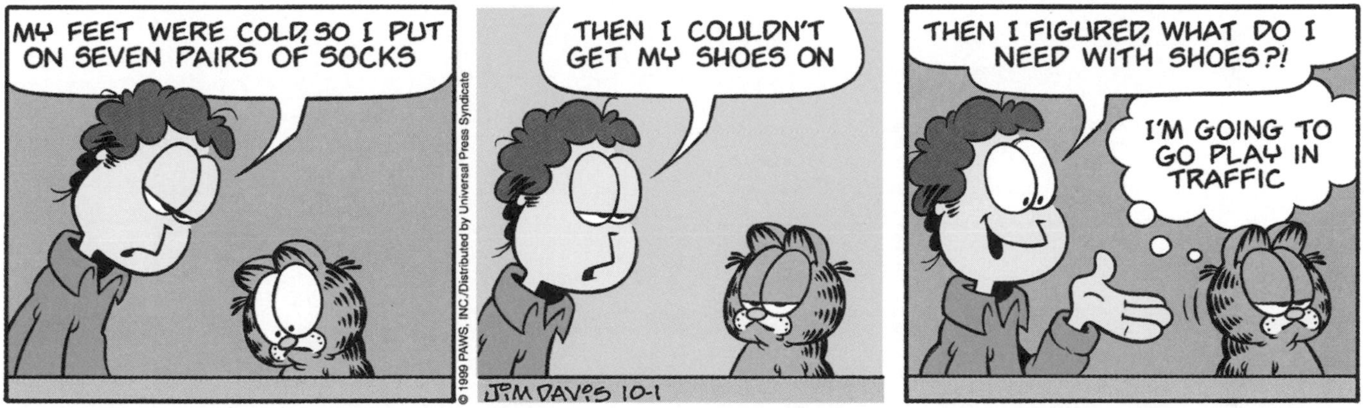
MY FEET WERE COLD, SO I PUT ON SEVEN PAIRS OF SOCKS
THEN I COULDN'T GET MY SHOES ON
THEN I FIGURED, WHAT DO I NEED WITH SHOES?!
I'M GOING TO GO PLAY IN TRAFFIC
JIM DAVIS 10-1
© 1999 PAWS, INC./Distributed by Universal Press Syndicate

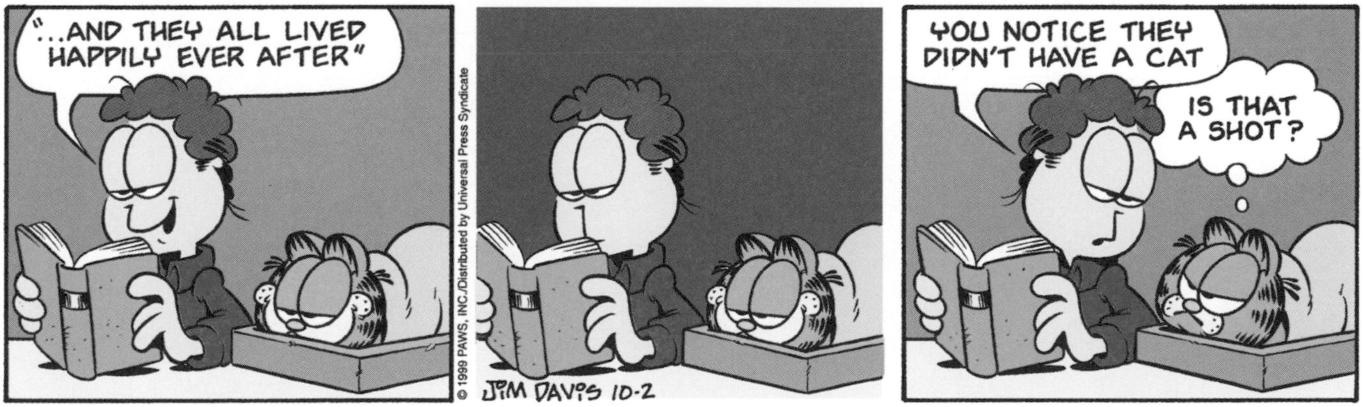
"...AND THEY ALL LIVED HAPPILY EVER AFTER"
YOU NOTICE THEY DIDN'T HAVE A CAT
IS THAT A SHOT?
JIM DAVIS 10-2
© 1999 PAWS, INC./Distributed by Universal Press Syndicate

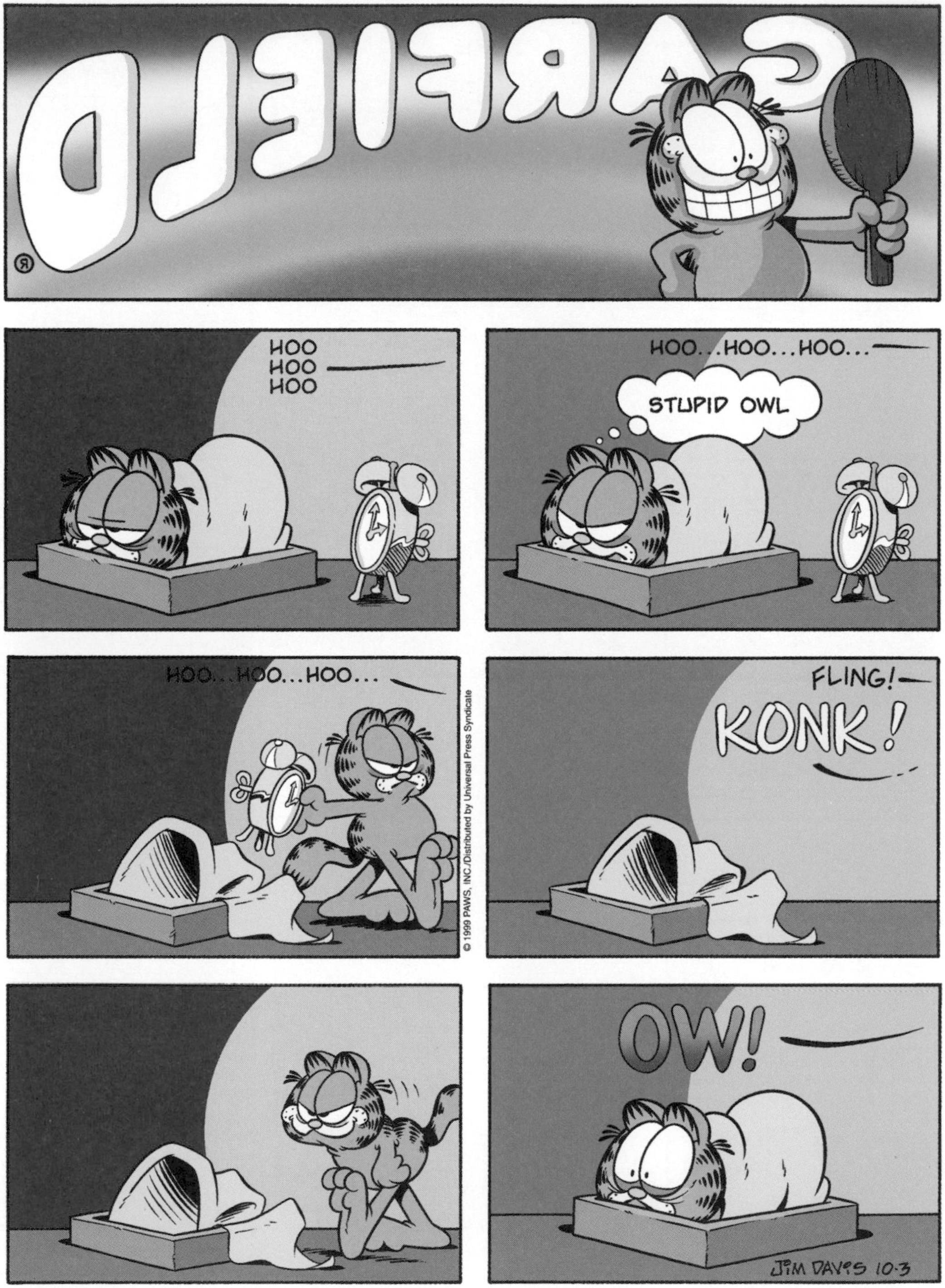
GARFIELD
HOO HOO HOO
HOO...HOO...HOO...
STUPID OWL
HOO...HOO...HOO...
FLING!
KONK!
OW!
JIM DAVIS 10-3
© 1999 PAWS, INC./Distributed by Universal Press Syndicate

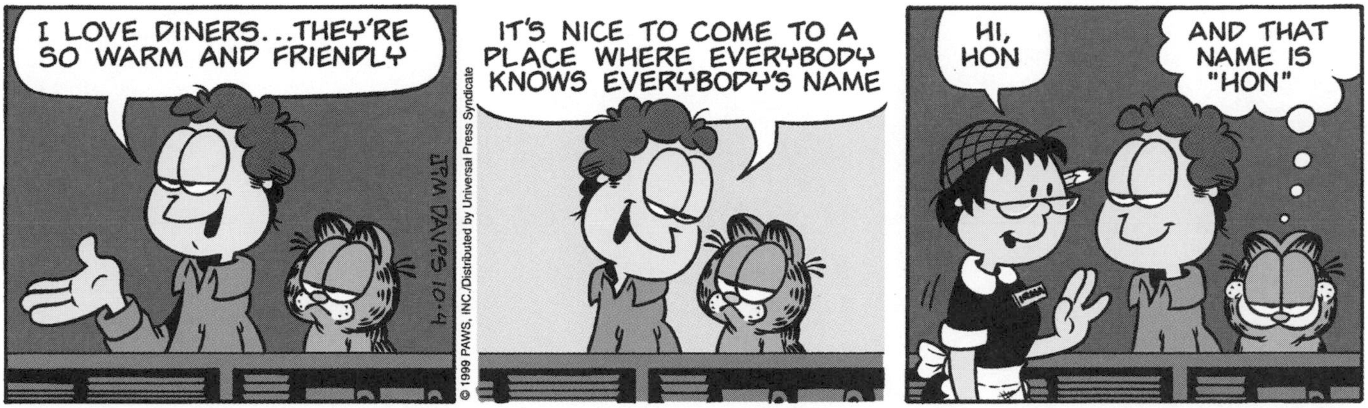
I LOVE DINERS...THEY'RE SO WARM AND FRIENDLY
IT'S NICE TO COME TO A PLACE WHERE EVERYBODY KNOWS EVERYBODY'S NAME
HI, HON
AND THAT NAME IS "HON"
JIM DAVIS 10-4
© 1999 PAWS, INC./Distributed by Universal Press Syndicate

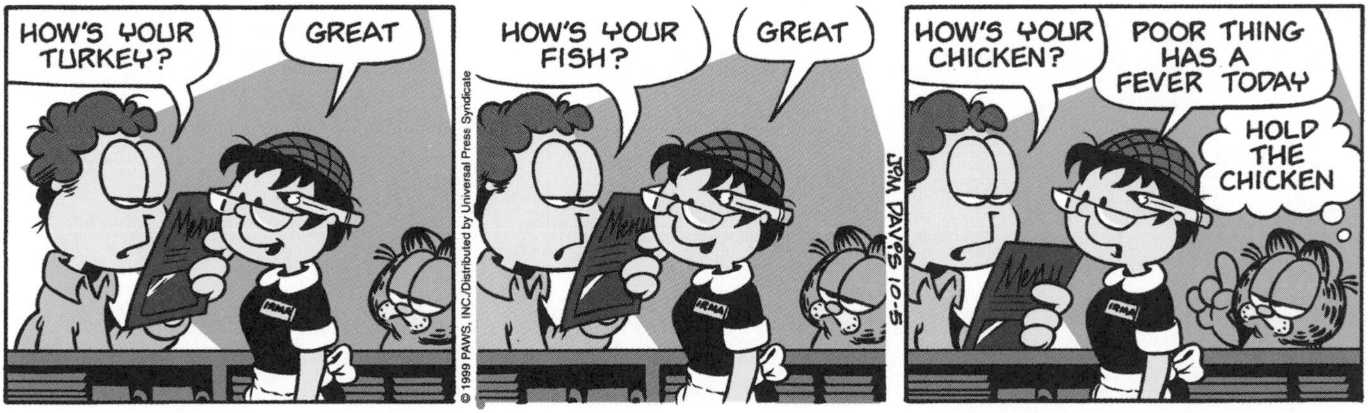
HOW'S YOUR TURKEY?
GREAT
HOW'S YOUR FISH?
GREAT
HOW'S YOUR CHICKEN?
POOR THING HAS A FEVER TODAY
HOLD THE CHICKEN
JIM DAVIS 10-5
© 1999 PAWS, INC./Distributed by Universal Press Syndicate

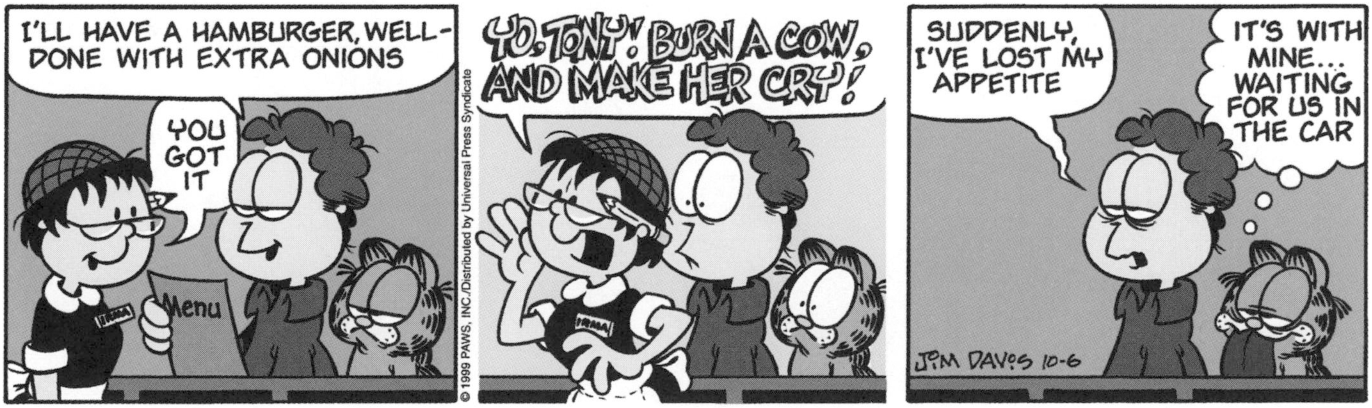
I'LL HAVE A HAMBURGER, WELL-DONE WITH EXTRA ONIONS
YOU GOT IT
Menu
YO, TONY! BURN A COW, AND MAKE HER CRY!
SUDDENLY, I'VE LOST MY APPETITE
IT'S WITH MINE... WAITING FOR US IN THE CAR
JIM DAVIS 10-6
© 1999 PAWS, INC./Distributed by Universal Press Syndicate

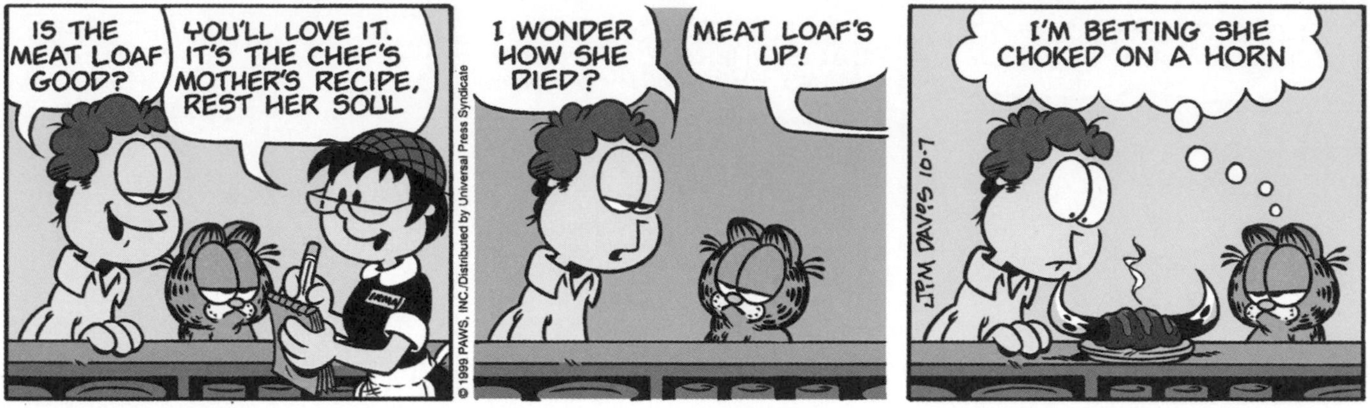
IS THE MEAT LOAF GOOD?
YOU'LL LOVE IT. IT'S THE CHEF'S MOTHER'S RECIPE, REST HER SOUL
I WONDER HOW SHE DIED?
MEAT LOAF'S UP!
I'M BETTING SHE CHOKED ON A HORN
JIM DAVIS 10-7

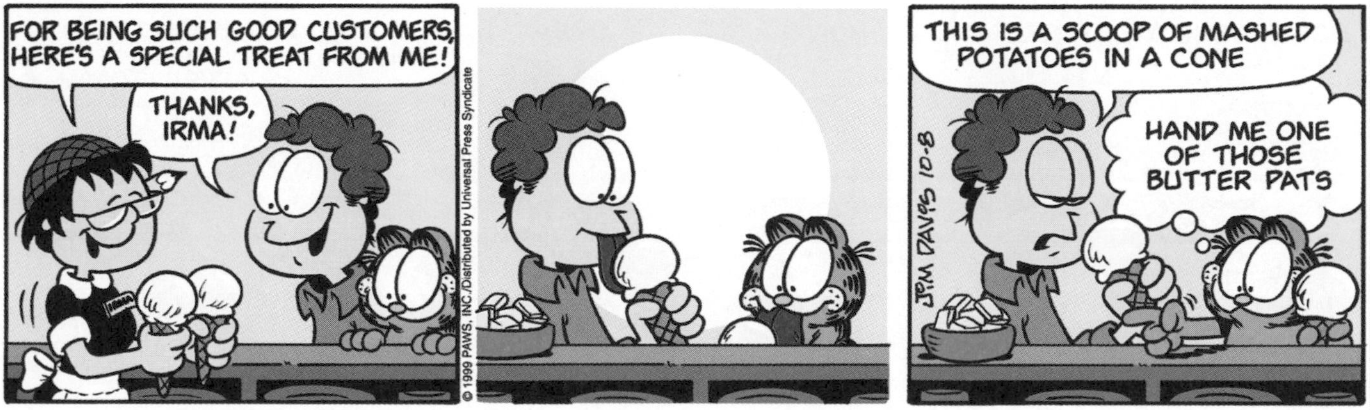
FOR BEING SUCH GOOD CUSTOMERS, HERE'S A SPECIAL TREAT FROM ME!
THANKS, IRMA!
THIS IS A SCOOP OF MASHED POTATOES IN A CONE
HAND ME ONE OF THOSE BUTTER PATS
JIM DAVIS 10-8

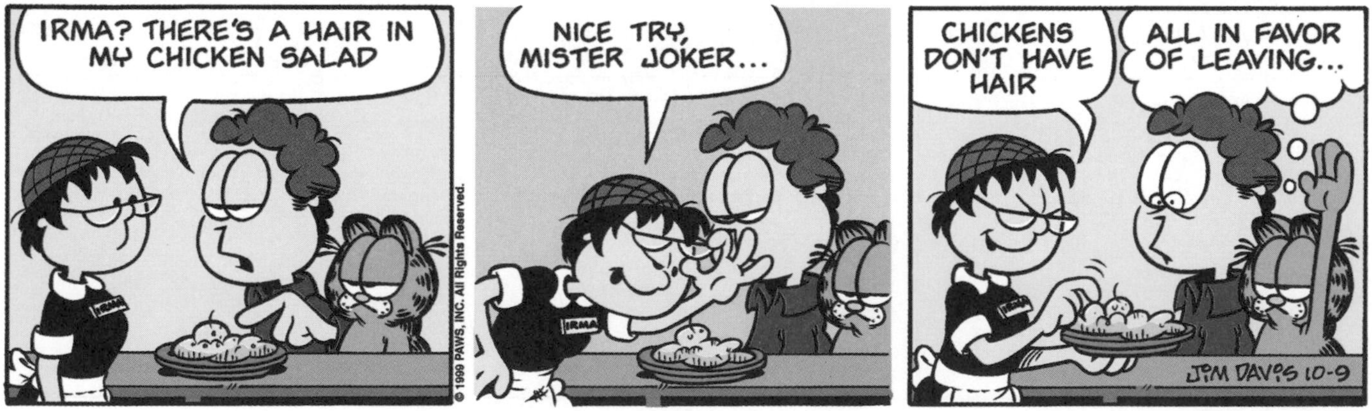
IRMA? THERE'S A HAIR IN MY CHICKEN SALAD
NICE TRY, MISTER JOKER...
CHICKENS DON'T HAVE HAIR
ALL IN FAVOR OF LEAVING...
JIM DAVIS 10-9

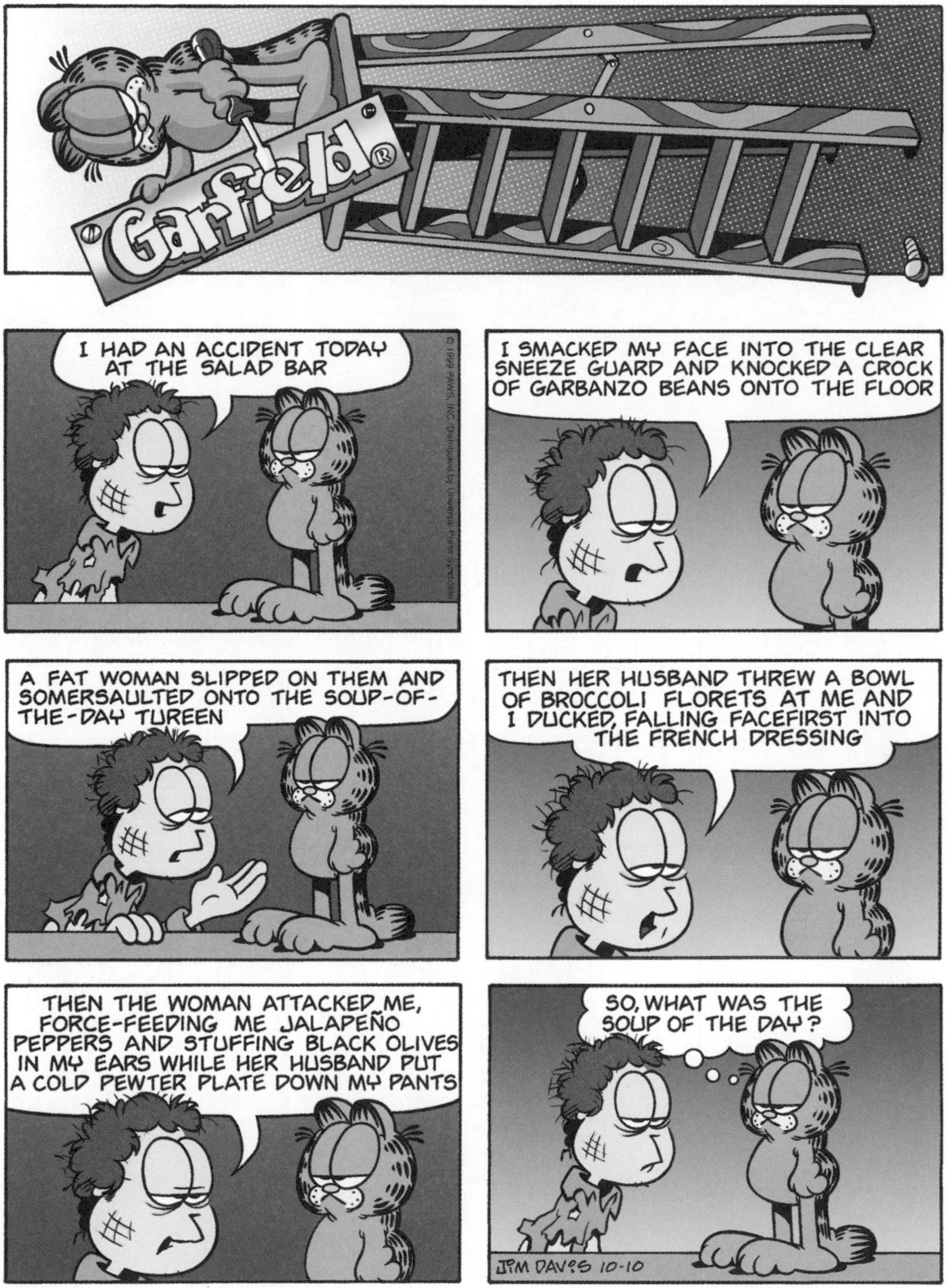
Garfield®
I HAD AN ACCIDENT TODAY AT THE SALAD BAR
© 1999 PAWS, INC. Distributed by Universal Press Syndicate
I SMACKED MY FACE INTO THE CLEAR SNEEZE GUARD AND KNOCKED A CROCK OF GARBANZO BEANS ONTO THE FLOOR
A FAT WOMAN SLIPPED ON THEM AND SOMERSAULTED ONTO THE SOUP-OF-THE-DAY TUREEN
THEN HER HUSBAND THREW A BOWL OF BROCCOLI FLORETS AT ME AND I DUCKED, FALLING FACEFIRST INTO THE FRENCH DRESSING
THEN THE WOMAN ATTACKED ME, FORCE-FEEDING ME JALAPEÑO PEPPERS AND STUFFING BLACK OLIVES IN MY EARS WHILE HER HUSBAND PUT A COLD PEWTER PLATE DOWN MY PANTS
SO, WHAT WAS THE SOUP OF THE DAY?
JIM DAVIS 10-10

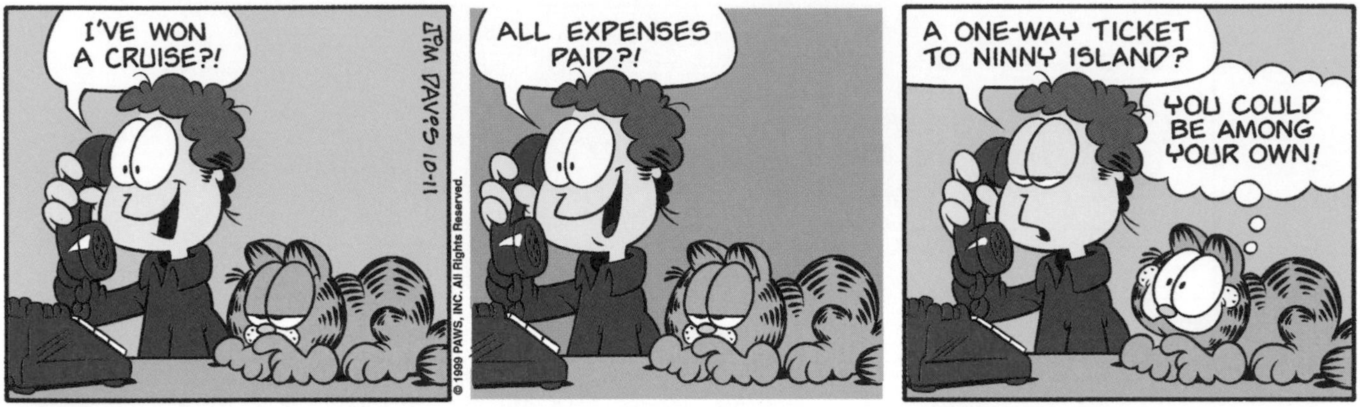
I'VE WON A CRUISE?!
JIM DAVIS 10-11
© 1999 PAWS, INC. All Rights Reserved.
ALL EXPENSES PAID?!
A ONE-WAY TICKET TO NINNY ISLAND?
YOU COULD BE AMONG YOUR OWN!

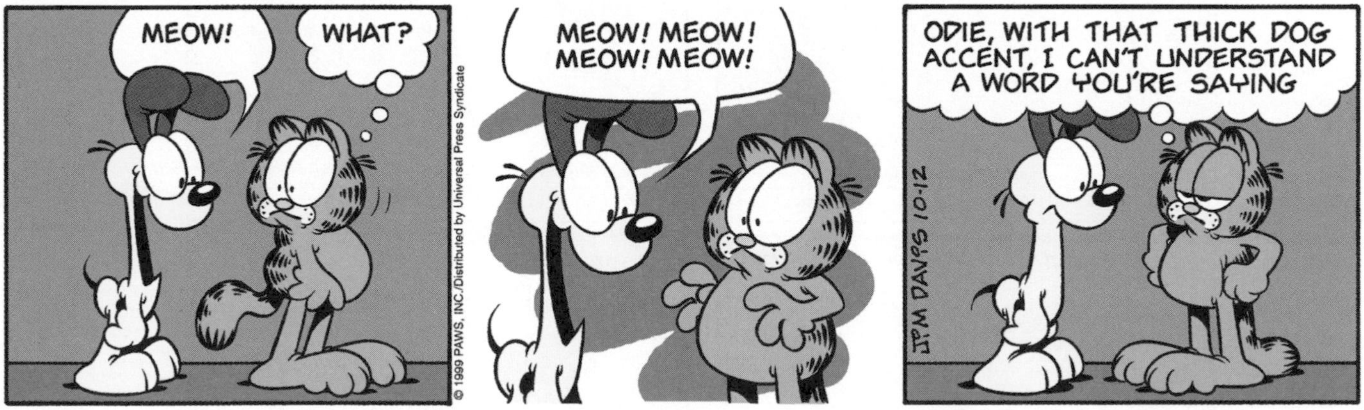
MEOW!
WHAT?
© 1999 PAWS, INC./Distributed by Universal Press Syndicate
MEOW! MEOW! MEOW! MEOW!
ODIE, WITH THAT THICK DOG ACCENT, I CAN'T UNDERSTAND A WORD YOU'RE SAYING
JIM DAVIS 10-12

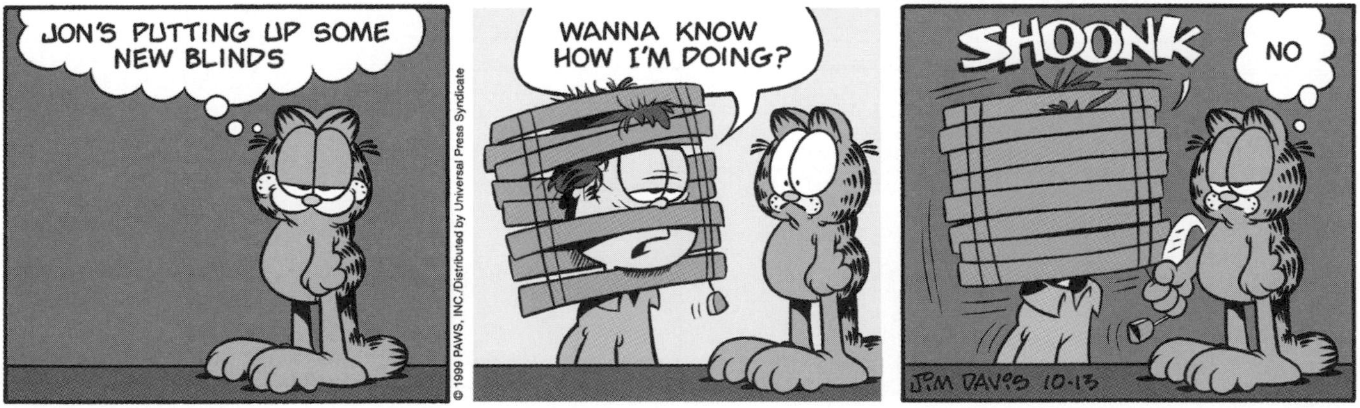
JON'S PUTTING UP SOME NEW BLINDS
© 1999 PAWS, INC./Distributed by Universal Press Syndicate
WANNA KNOW HOW I'M DOING?
SHOONK
NO
JIM DAVIS 10-13

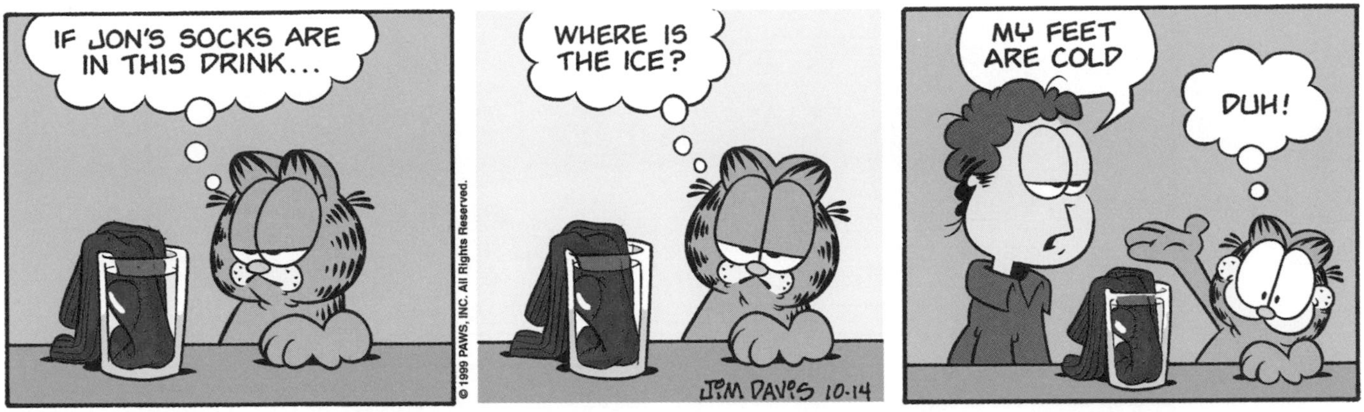
IF JON'S SOCKS ARE IN THIS DRINK...
WHERE IS THE ICE?
MY FEET ARE COLD
DUH!
© 1999 PAWS, INC. All Rights Reserved.
JIM DAVIS 10-14

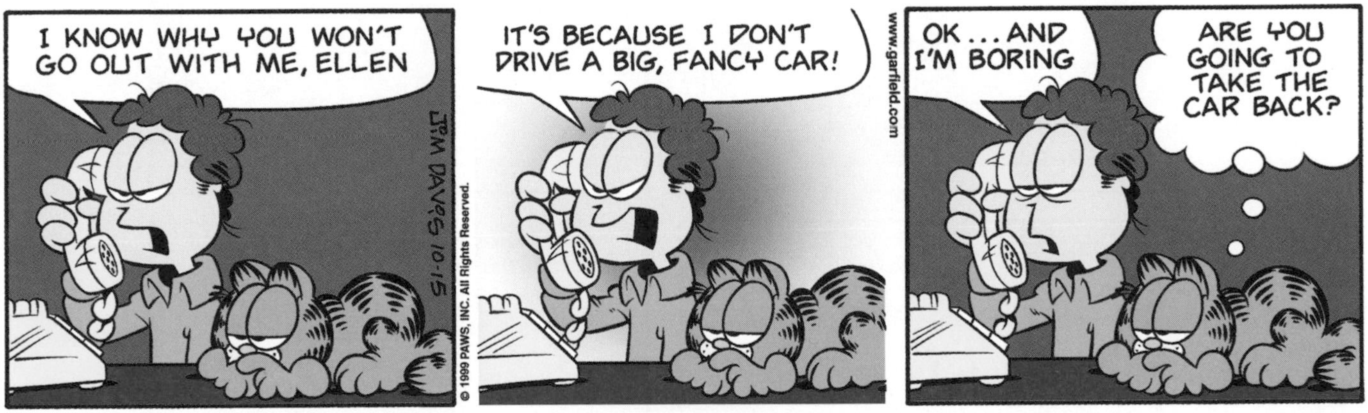
I KNOW WHY YOU WON'T GO OUT WITH ME, ELLEN
IT'S BECAUSE I DON'T DRIVE A BIG, FANCY CAR!
OK . . . AND I'M BORING
ARE YOU GOING TO TAKE THE CAR BACK?
JIM DAVIS 10-15
© 1999 PAWS, INC. All Rights Reserved.
www.garfield.com

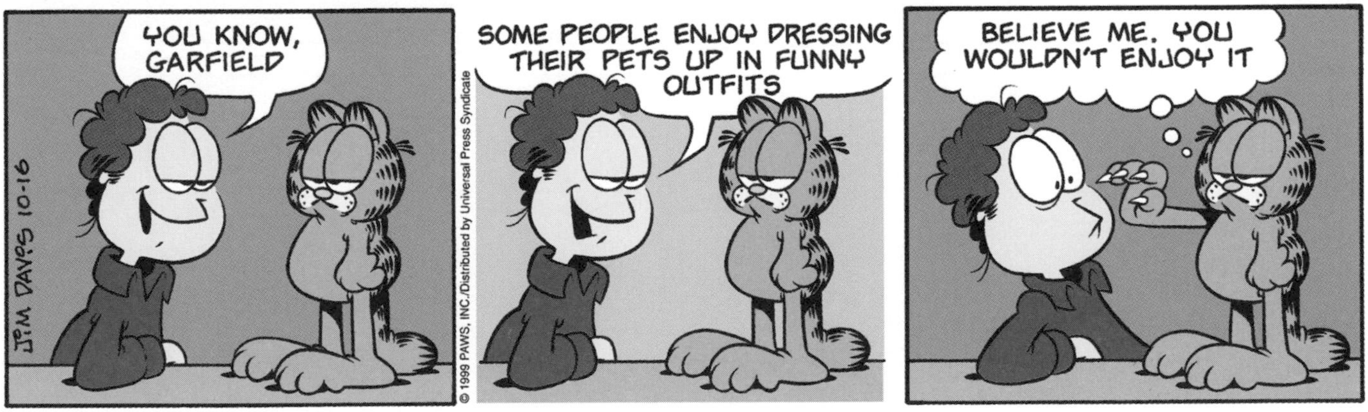
YOU KNOW, GARFIELD
SOME PEOPLE ENJOY DRESSING THEIR PETS UP IN FUNNY OUTFITS
BELIEVE ME. YOU WOULDN'T ENJOY IT
JIM DAVIS 10-16
© 1999 PAWS, INC./Distributed by Universal Press Syndicate

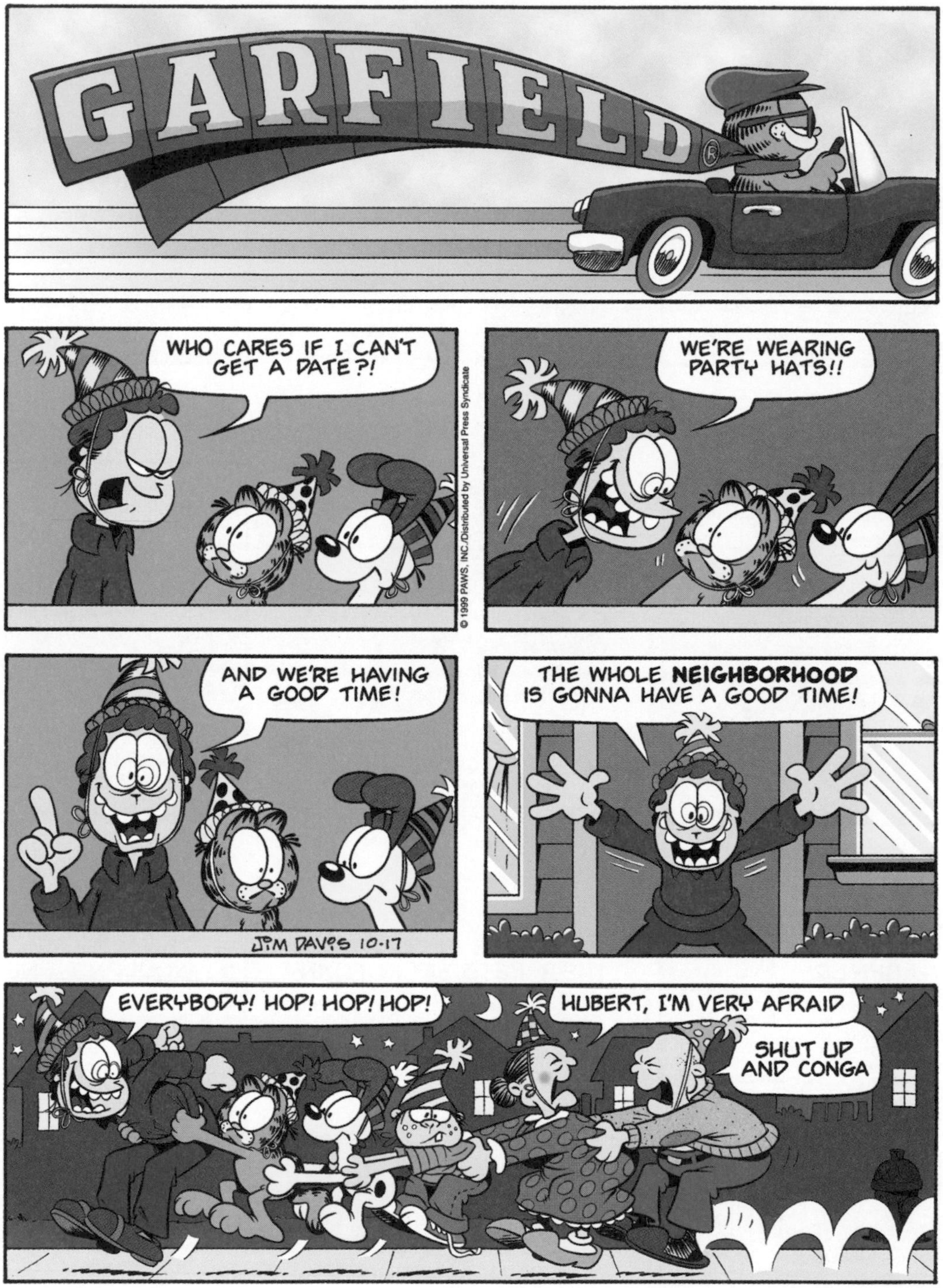
GARFIELD®
WHO CARES IF I CAN'T GET A DATE?!
© 1999 PAWS, INC./Distributed by Universal Press Syndicate
WE'RE WEARING PARTY HATS!!
AND WE'RE HAVING A GOOD TIME!
JIM DAVIS 10-17
THE WHOLE **NEIGHBORHOOD** IS GONNA HAVE A GOOD TIME!
EVERYBODY! HOP! HOP! HOP!
HUBERT, I'M VERY AFRAID
SHUT UP AND CONGA

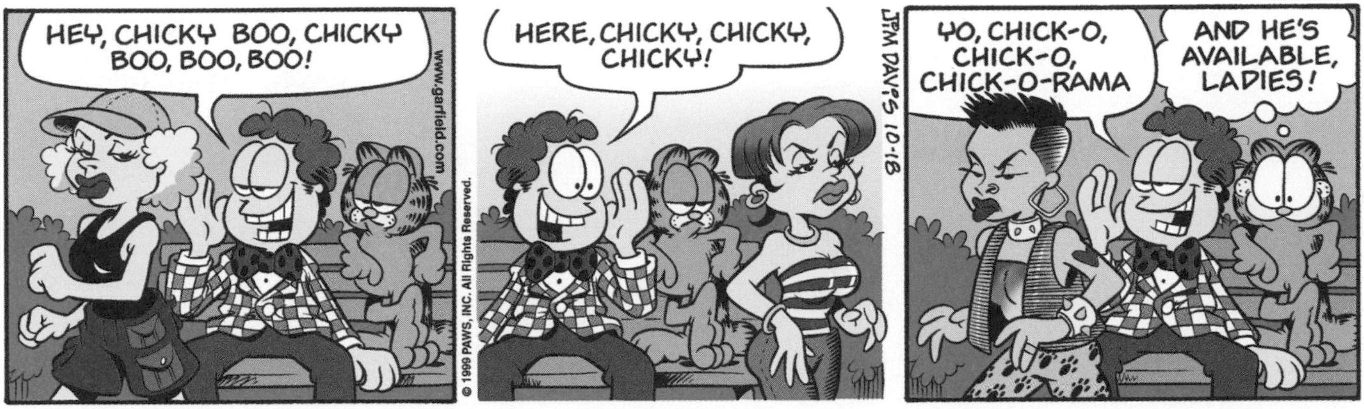
HEY, CHICKY BOO, CHICKY BOO, BOO, BOO!
www.garfield.com
© 1999 PAWS, INC. All Rights Reserved.
HERE, CHICKY, CHICKY, CHICKY!
YO, CHICK-O, CHICK-O, CHICK-O-RAMA
AND HE'S AVAILABLE, LADIES!

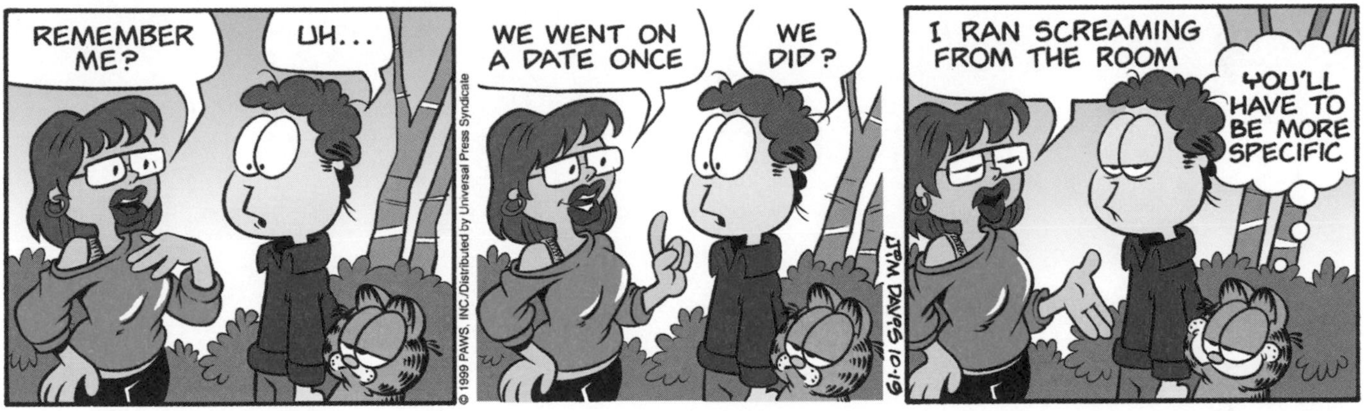
REMEMBER ME?
UH...
© 1999 PAWS, INC./Distributed by Universal Press Syndicate
WE WENT ON A DATE ONCE
WE DID?
I RAN SCREAMING FROM THE ROOM
YOU'LL HAVE TO BE MORE SPECIFIC

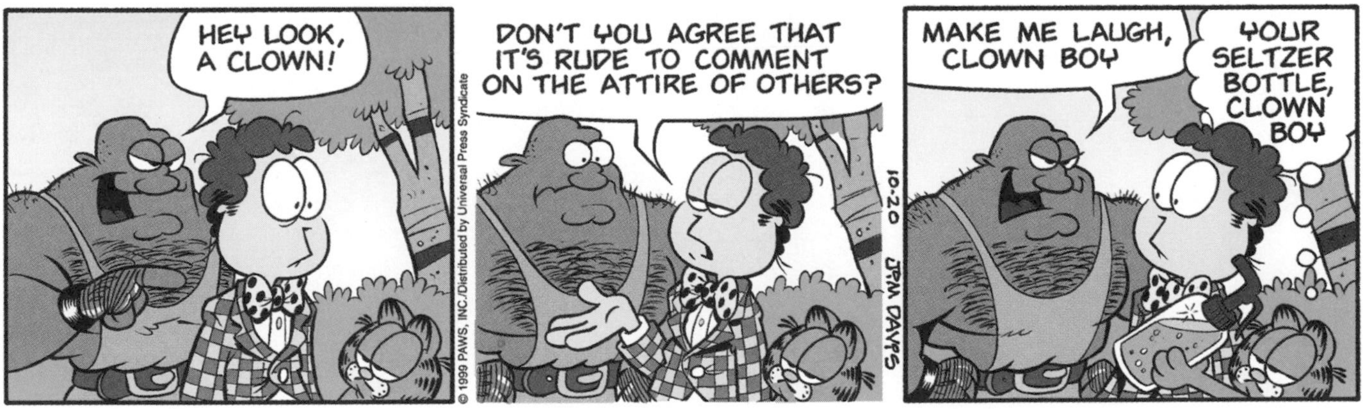
HEY LOOK, A CLOWN!
© 1999 PAWS, INC./Distributed by Universal Press Syndicate
DON'T YOU AGREE THAT IT'S RUDE TO COMMENT ON THE ATTIRE OF OTHERS?
MAKE ME LAUGH, CLOWN BOY
YOUR SELTZER BOTTLE, CLOWN BOY

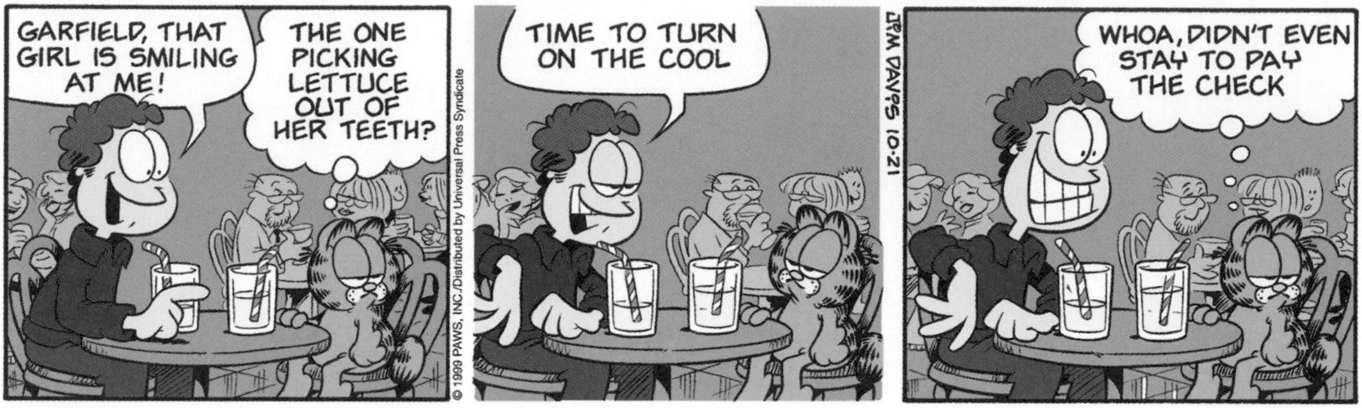
GARFIELD, THAT GIRL IS SMILING AT ME!
THE ONE PICKING LETTUCE OUT OF HER TEETH?
© 1999 PAWS, INC./Distributed by Universal Press Syndicate
TIME TO TURN ON THE COOL
JIM DAVIS 10-21
WHOA, DIDN'T EVEN STAY TO PAY THE CHECK

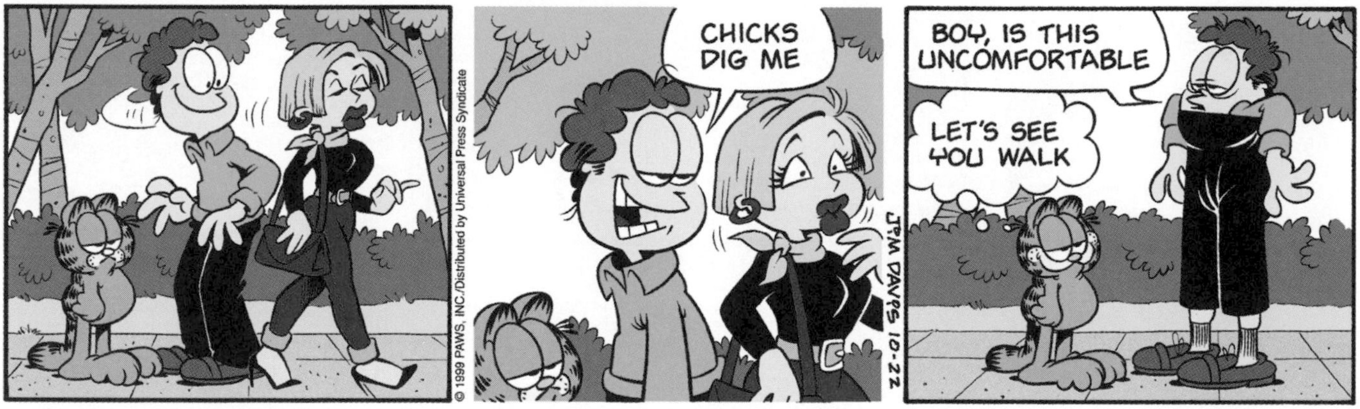
© 1999 PAWS, INC./Distributed by Universal Press Syndicate
CHICKS DIG ME
JIM DAVIS 10-22
BOY, IS THIS UNCOMFORTABLE
LET'S SEE YOU WALK

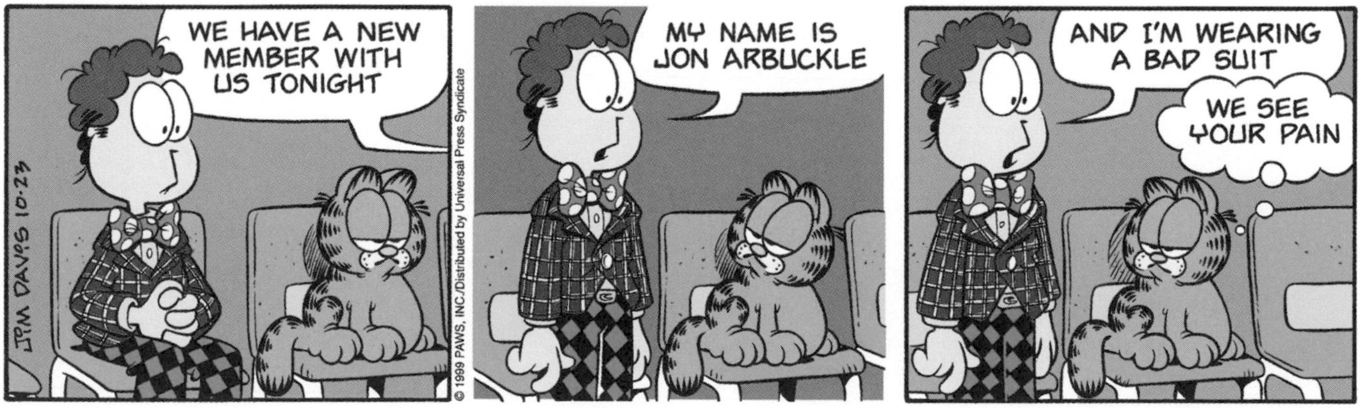
JIM DAVIS 10-23
WE HAVE A NEW MEMBER WITH US TONIGHT
© 1999 PAWS, INC./Distributed by Universal Press Syndicate
MY NAME IS JON ARBUCKLE
AND I'M WEARING A BAD SUIT
WE SEE YOUR PAIN

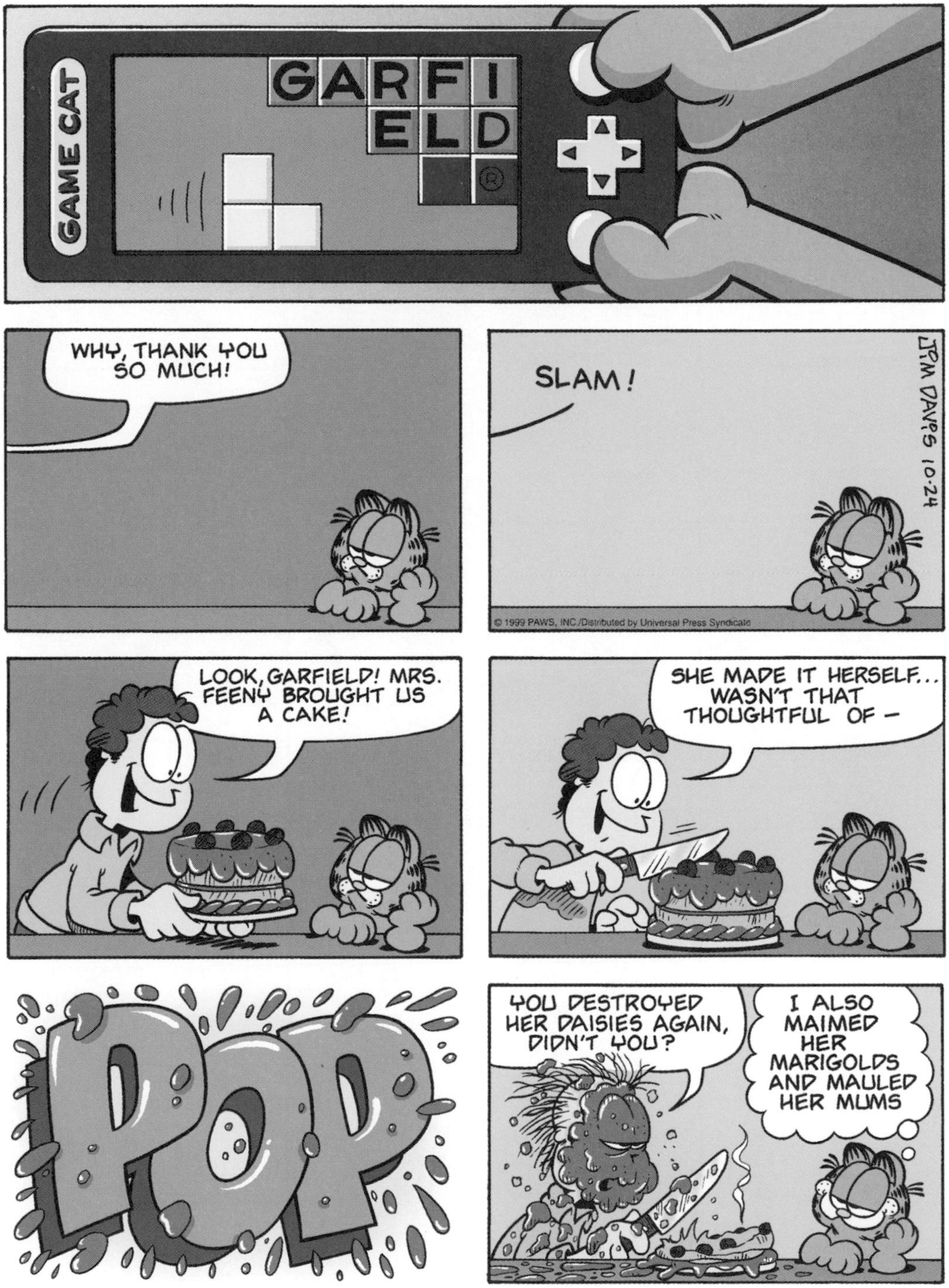
GAME CAT
GARFIELD®
WHY, THANK YOU SO MUCH!
SLAM!
JPM DAVPS 10·24
© 1999 PAWS, INC./Distributed by Universal Press Syndicate
LOOK, GARFIELD! MRS. FEENY BROUGHT US A CAKE!
SHE MADE IT HERSELF... WASN'T THAT THOUGHTFUL OF –
POP
YOU DESTROYED HER DAISIES AGAIN, DIDN'T YOU?
I ALSO MAIMED HER MARIGOLDS AND MAULED HER MUMS

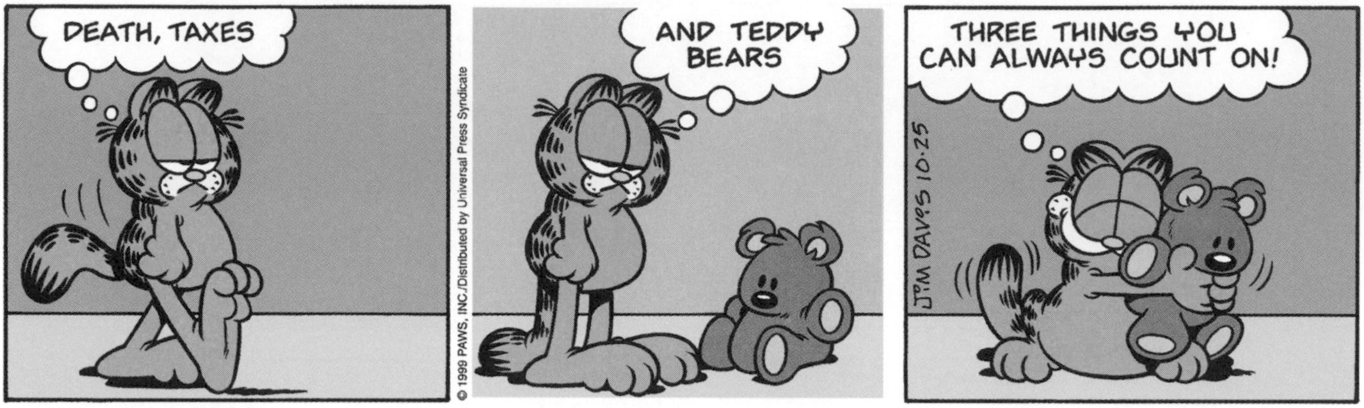
DEATH, TAXES
AND TEDDY BEARS
THREE THINGS YOU CAN ALWAYS COUNT ON!
© 1999 PAWS, INC./Distributed by Universal Press Syndicate
JIM DAVIS 10-25

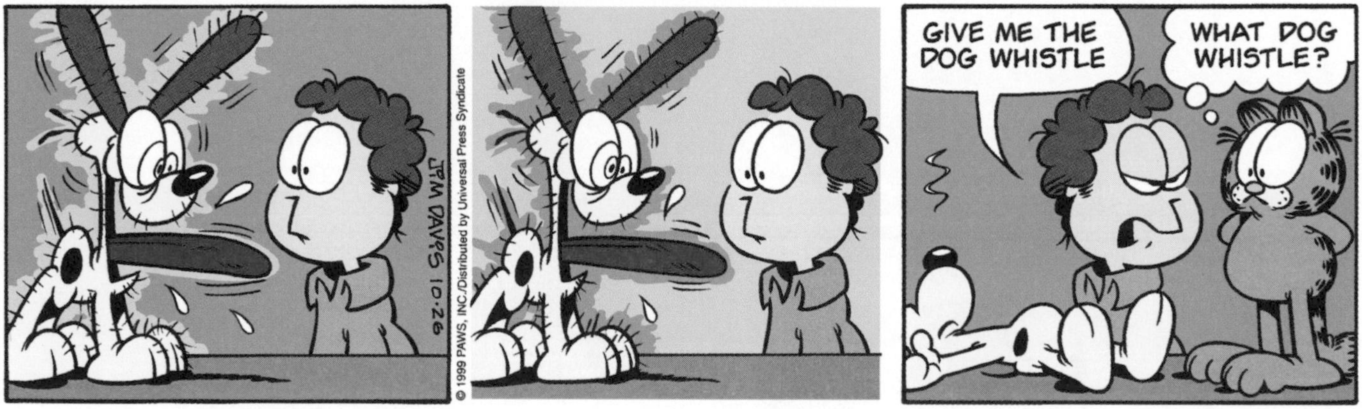
JIM DAVIS 10-26
© 1999 PAWS, INC./Distributed by Universal Press Syndicate
GIVE ME THE DOG WHISTLE
WHAT DOG WHISTLE?

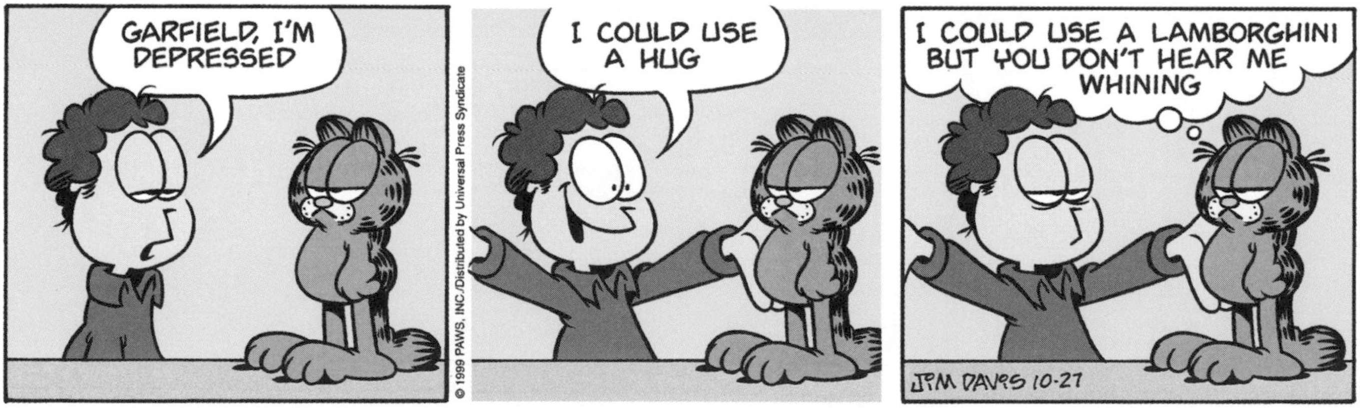
GARFIELD, I'M DEPRESSED
I COULD USE A HUG
© 1999 PAWS, INC./Distributed by Universal Press Syndicate
I COULD USE A LAMBORGHINI BUT YOU DON'T HEAR ME WHINING
JIM DAVIS 10-27

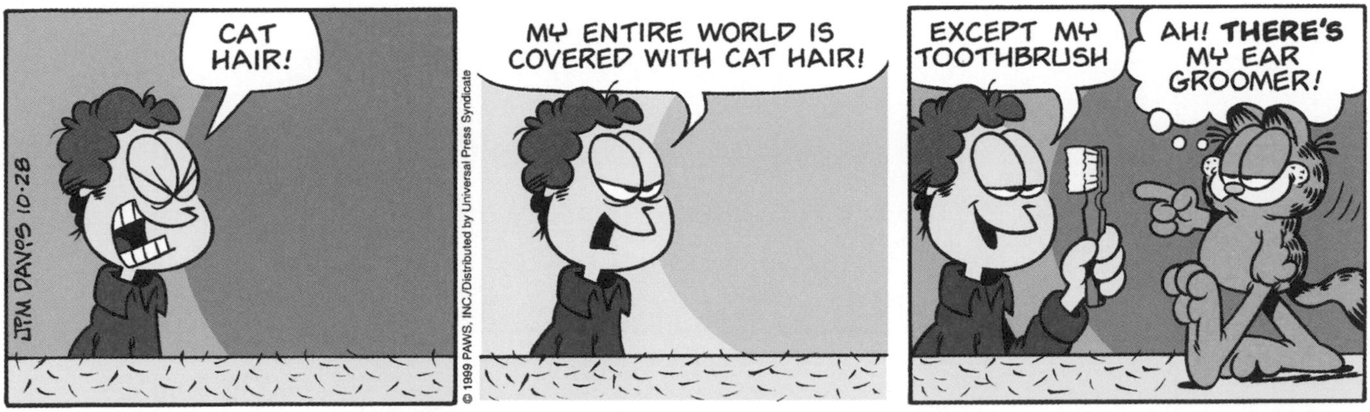
CAT HAIR!
JIM DAVIS 10-28
MY ENTIRE WORLD IS COVERED WITH CAT HAIR!
© 1999 PAWS, INC./Distributed by Universal Press Syndicate
EXCEPT MY TOOTHBRUSH
AH! **THERE'S** MY EAR GROOMER!

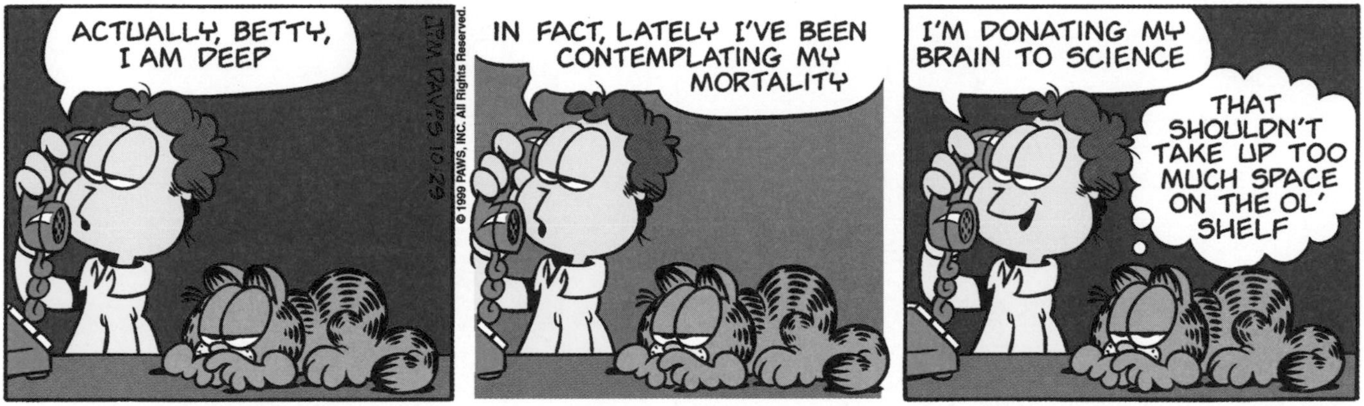
ACTUALLY, BETTY, I AM DEEP
JIM DAVIS 10-29
© 1999 PAWS, INC. All Rights Reserved.
IN FACT, LATELY I'VE BEEN CONTEMPLATING MY MORTALITY
I'M DONATING MY BRAIN TO SCIENCE
THAT SHOULDN'T TAKE UP TOO MUCH SPACE ON THE OL' SHELF

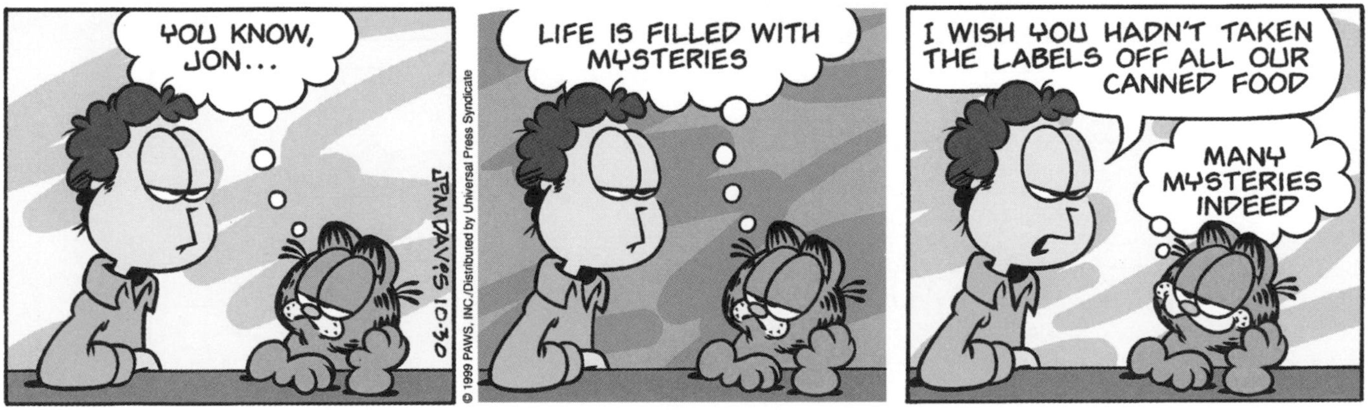
YOU KNOW, JON...
JIM DAVIS 10-30
© 1999 PAWS, INC./Distributed by Universal Press Syndicate
LIFE IS FILLED WITH MYSTERIES
I WISH YOU HADN'T TAKEN THE LABELS OFF ALL OUR CANNED FOOD
MANY MYSTERIES INDEED

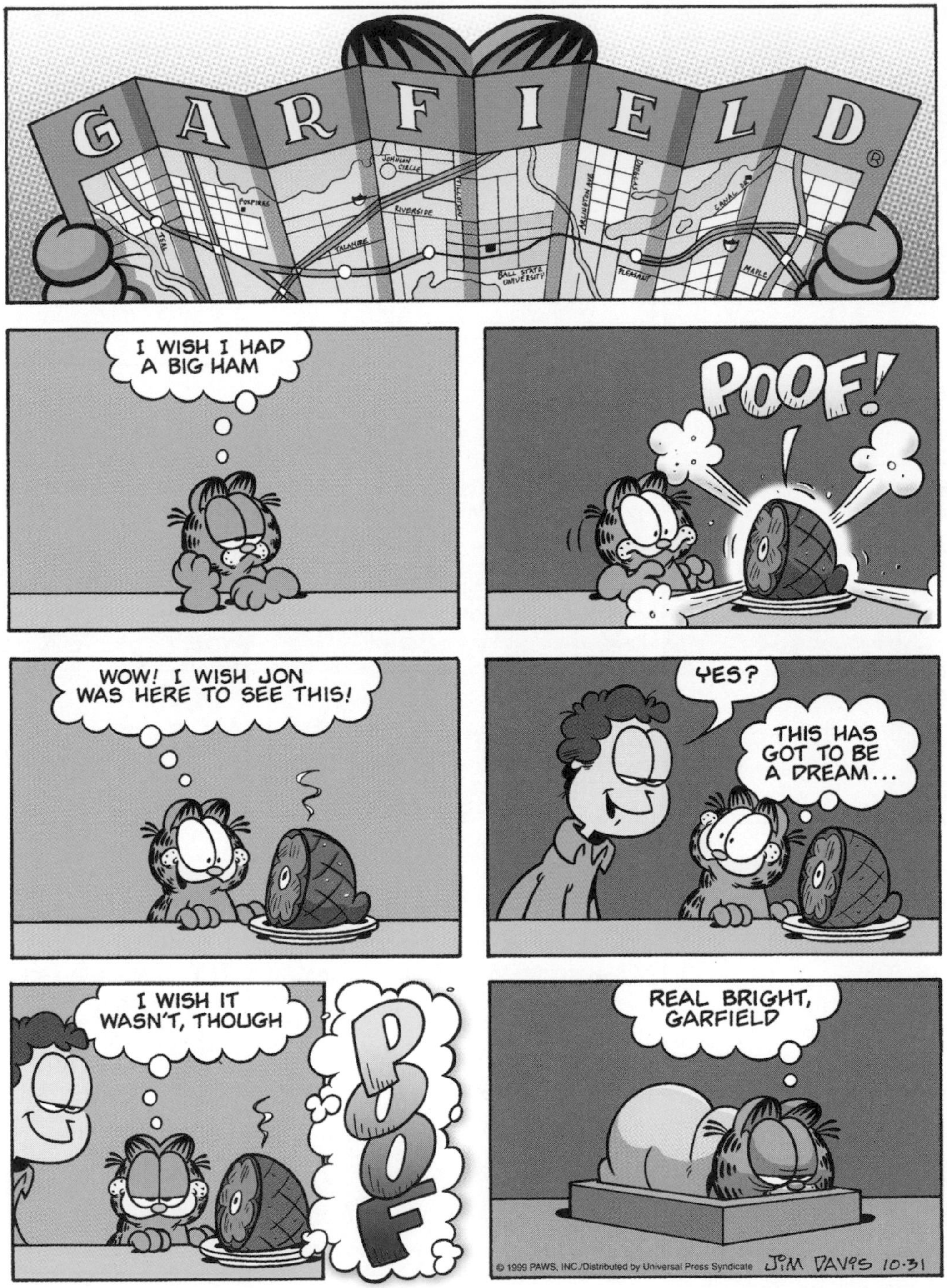
GARFIELD®
I WISH I HAD A BIG HAM
POOF!
WOW! I WISH JON WAS HERE TO SEE THIS!
YES?
THIS HAS GOT TO BE A DREAM...
I WISH IT WASN'T, THOUGH
POOF
REAL BRIGHT, GARFIELD
© 1999 PAWS, INC./Distributed by Universal Press Syndicate
JIM DAVIS 10-31

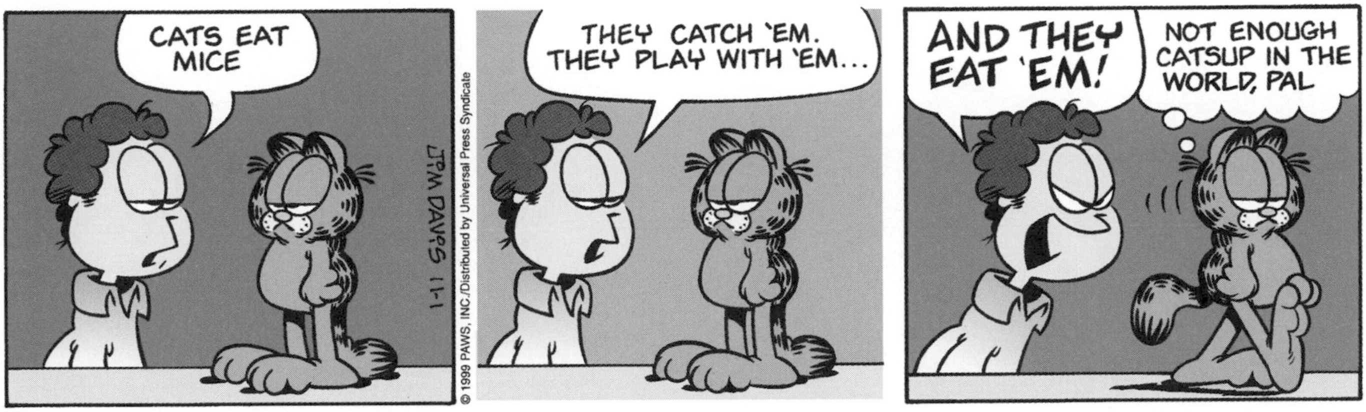
CATS EAT MICE
JIM DAVIS 11-1
© 1999 PAWS, INC./Distributed by Universal Press Syndicate
THEY CATCH 'EM. THEY PLAY WITH 'EM...
AND THEY EAT 'EM!
NOT ENOUGH CATSUP IN THE WORLD, PAL

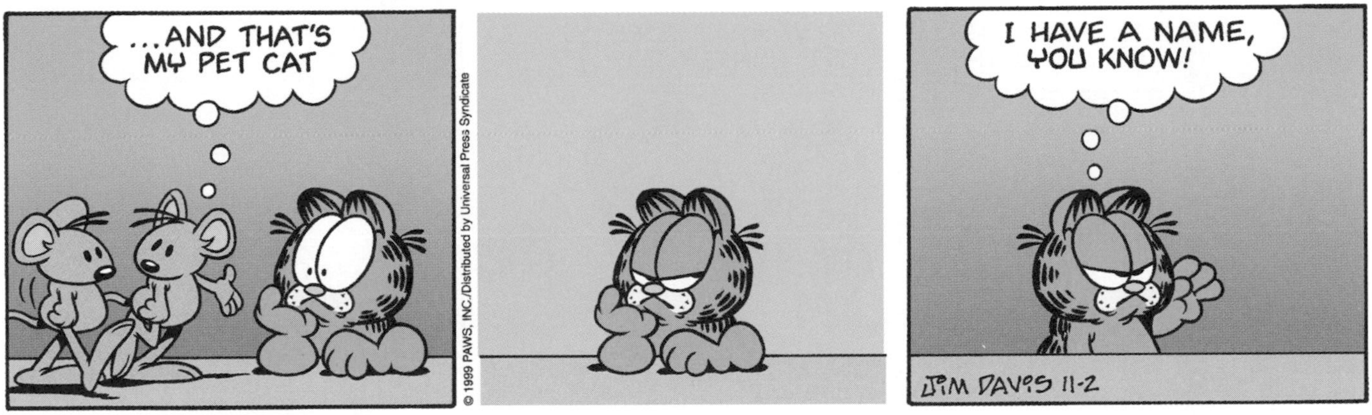
...AND THAT'S MY PET CAT
© 1999 PAWS, INC./Distributed by Universal Press Syndicate
I HAVE A NAME, YOU KNOW!
JIM DAVIS 11-2

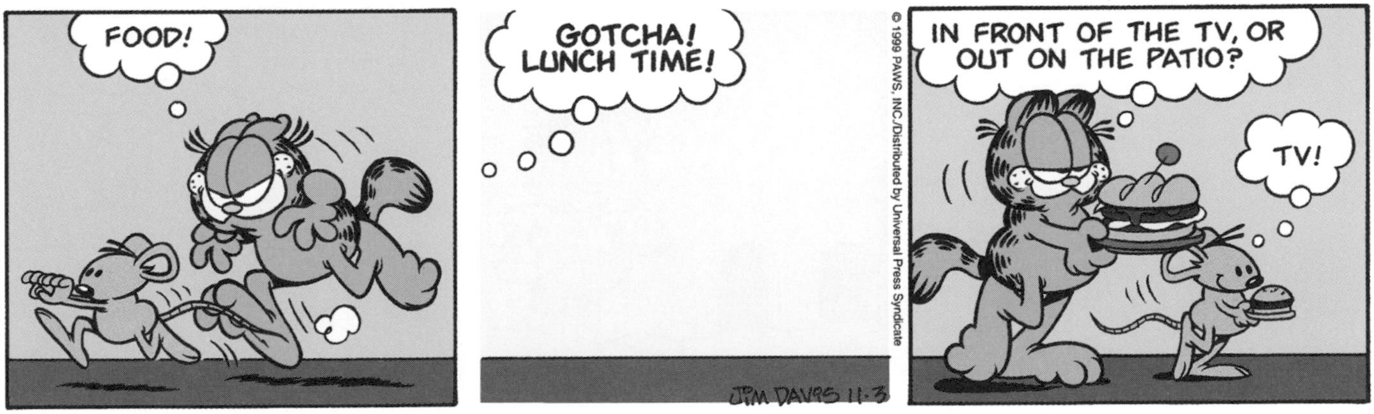
FOOD!
GOTCHA! LUNCH TIME!
JIM DAVIS 11-3
© 1999 PAWS, INC./Distributed by Universal Press Syndicate
IN FRONT OF THE TV, OR OUT ON THE PATIO?
TV!

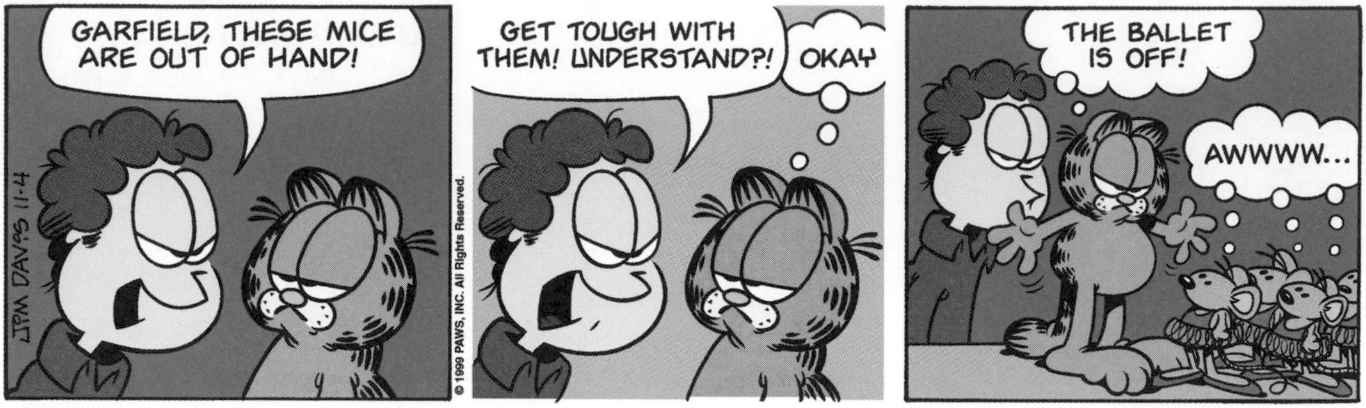
GARFIELD, THESE MICE ARE OUT OF HAND!
JPM DAVPS 11-4
GET TOUGH WITH THEM! UNDERSTAND?!
OKAY
THE BALLET IS OFF!
AWWWW...

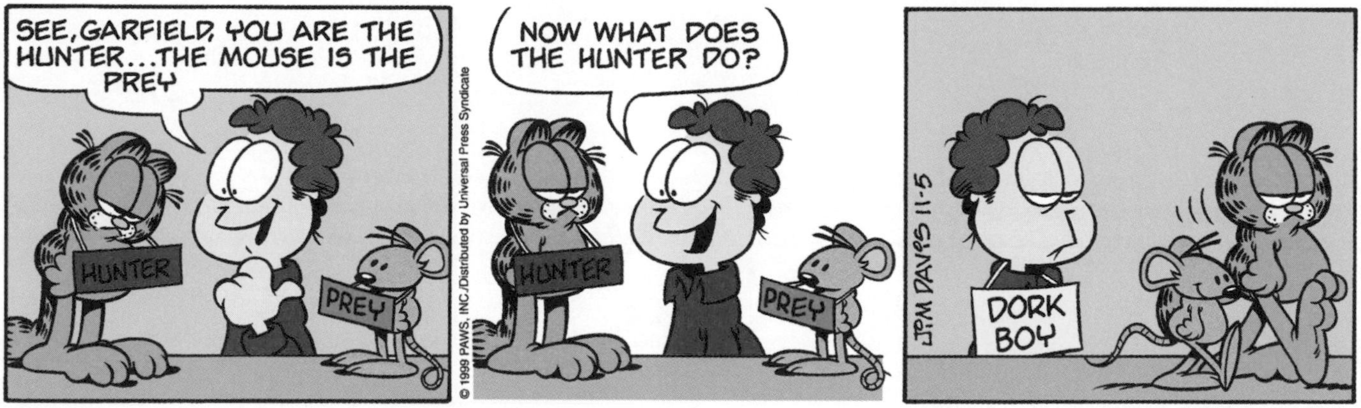
SEE, GARFIELD, YOU ARE THE HUNTER...THE MOUSE IS THE PREY
HUNTER
PREY
NOW WHAT DOES THE HUNTER DO?
HUNTER
PREY
JPM DAVPS 11-5
DORK BOY

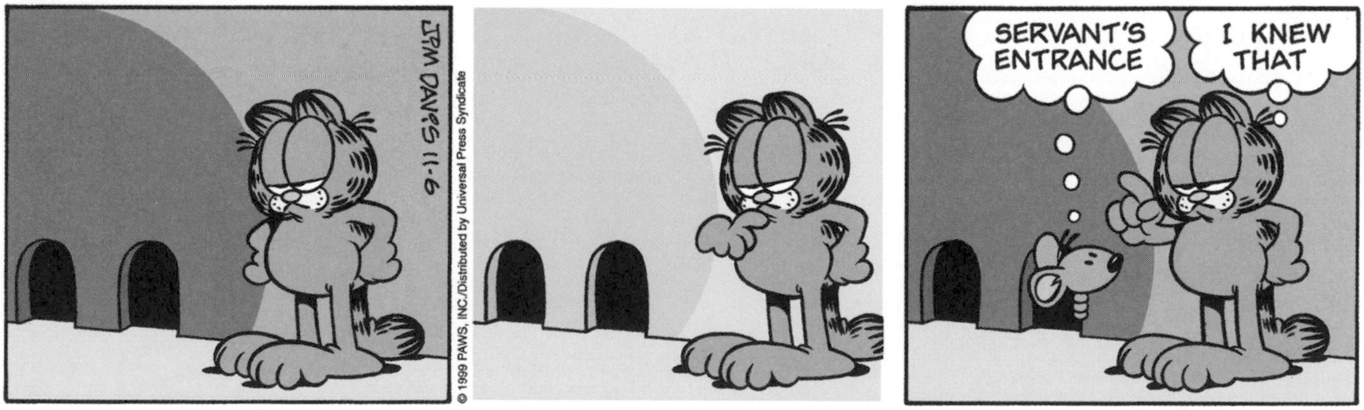
JPM DAVPS 11-6
SERVANT'S ENTRANCE
I KNEW THAT

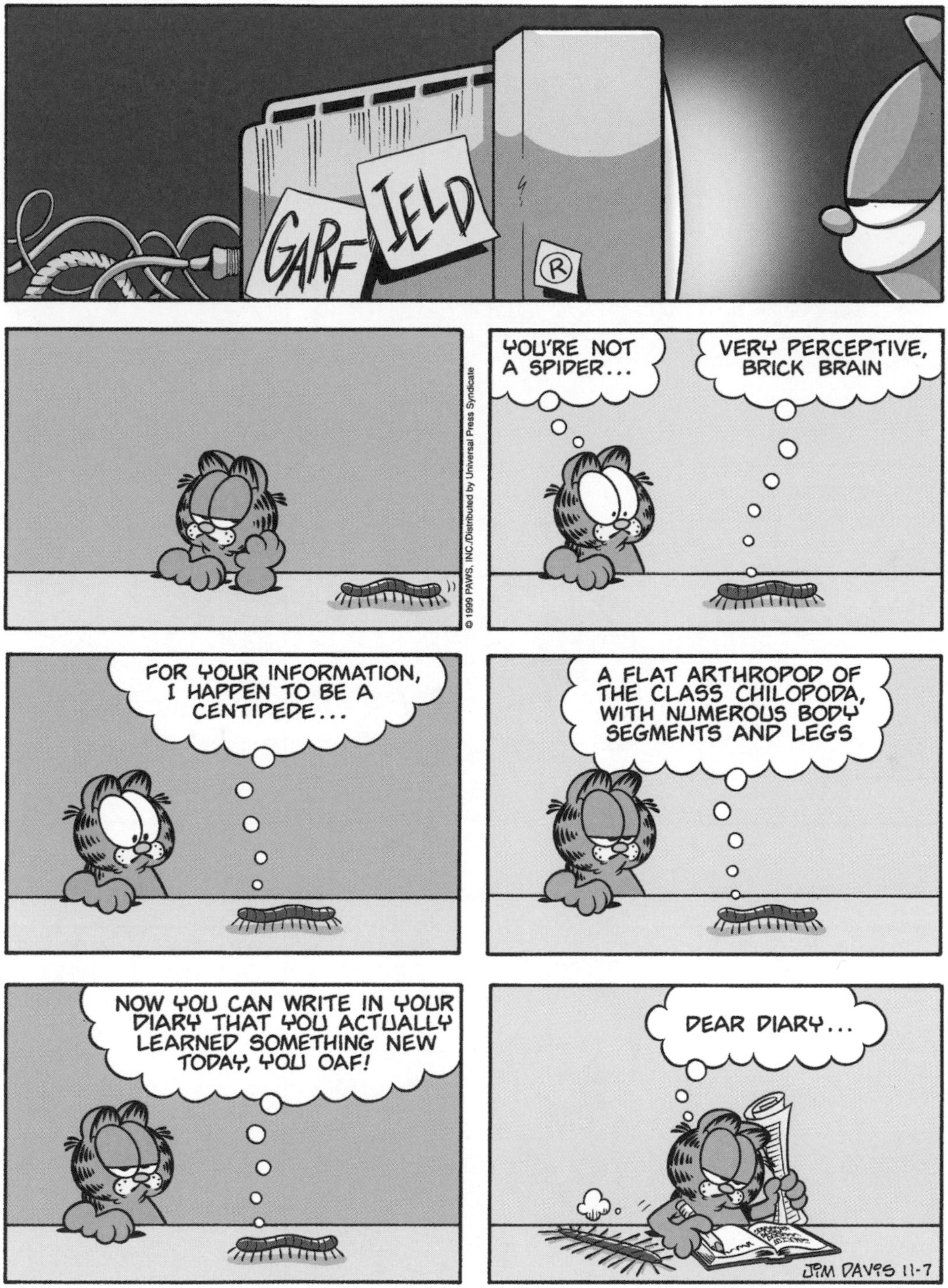
GARFIELD
®
© 1999 PAWS, INC./Distributed by Universal Press Syndicate
YOU'RE NOT A SPIDER...
VERY PERCEPTIVE, BRICK BRAIN
FOR YOUR INFORMATION, I HAPPEN TO BE A CENTIPEDE...
A FLAT ARTHROPOD OF THE CLASS CHILOPODA, WITH NUMEROUS BODY SEGMENTS AND LEGS
NOW YOU CAN WRITE IN YOUR DIARY THAT YOU ACTUALLY LEARNED SOMETHING NEW TODAY, YOU OAF!
DEAR DIARY...
JIM DAVIS 11-7

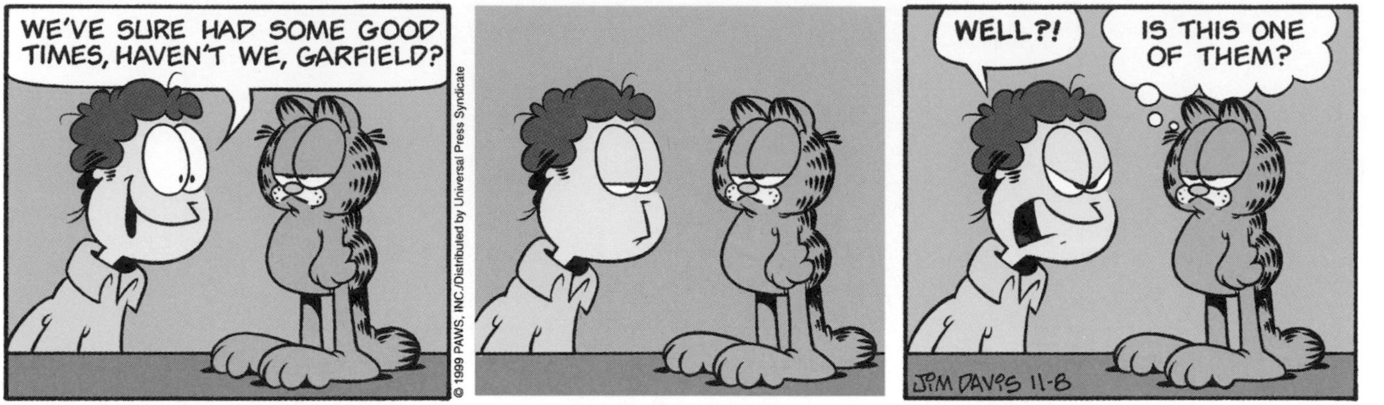
WE'VE SURE HAD SOME GOOD TIMES, HAVEN'T WE, GARFIELD?
© 1999 PAWS, INC./Distributed by Universal Press Syndicate
WELL?!
IS THIS ONE OF THEM?
JIM DAVIS 11-8

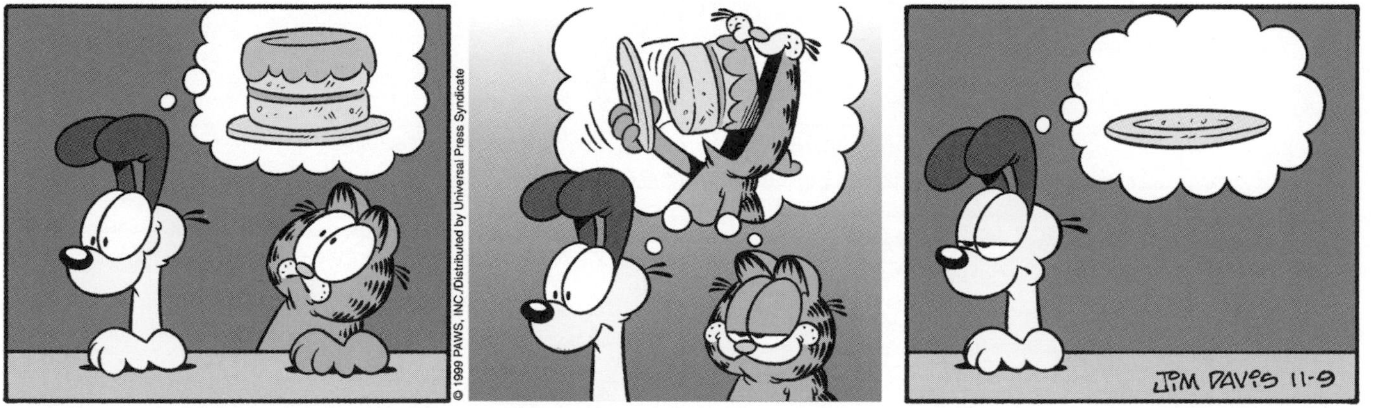
© 1999 PAWS, INC./Distributed by Universal Press Syndicate
JIM DAVIS 11-9

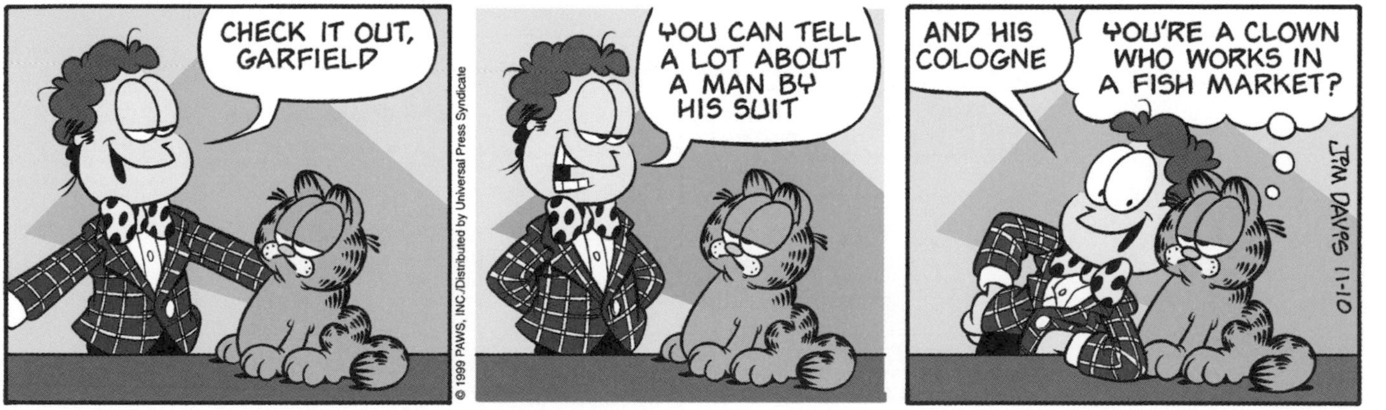
CHECK IT OUT, GARFIELD
© 1999 PAWS, INC./Distributed by Universal Press Syndicate
YOU CAN TELL A LOT ABOUT A MAN BY HIS SUIT
AND HIS COLOGNE
YOU'RE A CLOWN WHO WORKS IN A FISH MARKET?
JIM DAVIS 11-10

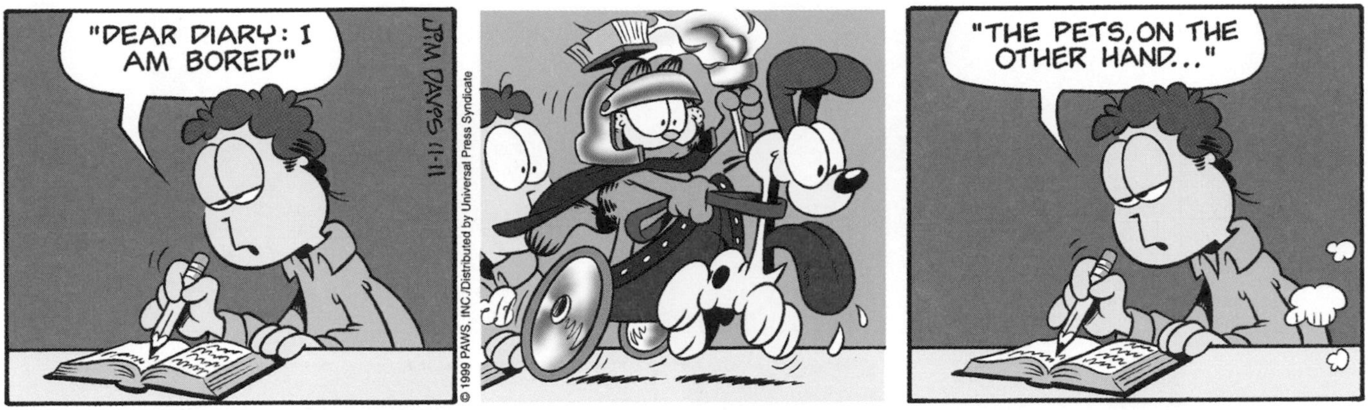
"DEAR DIARY: I AM BORED"
JIM DAVIS 11-11
© 1999 PAWS, INC./Distributed by Universal Press Syndicate
"THE PETS, ON THE OTHER HAND..."

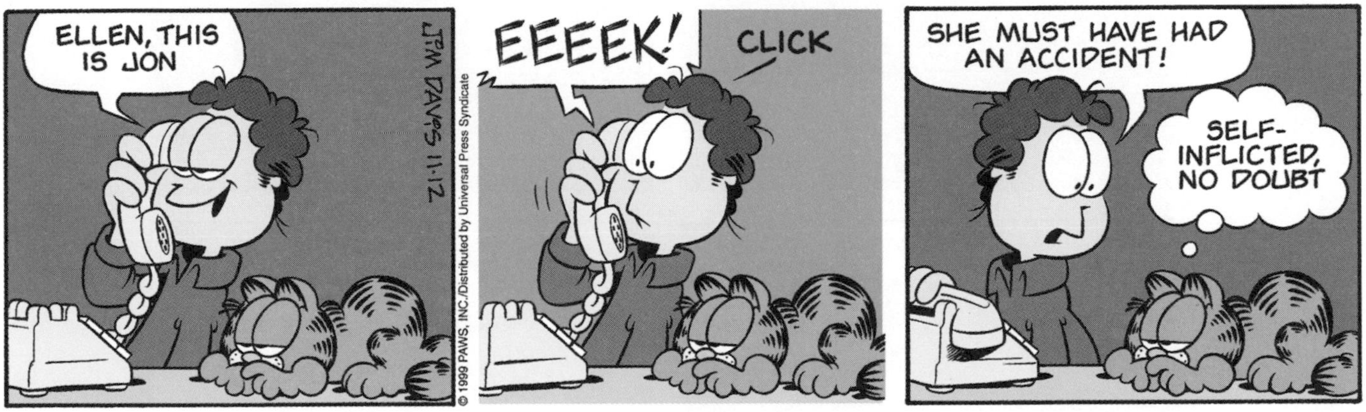
ELLEN, THIS IS JON
JIM DAVIS 11-12
© 1999 PAWS, INC./Distributed by Universal Press Syndicate
EEEEK!
CLICK
SHE MUST HAVE HAD AN ACCIDENT!
SELF-INFLICTED, NO DOUBT

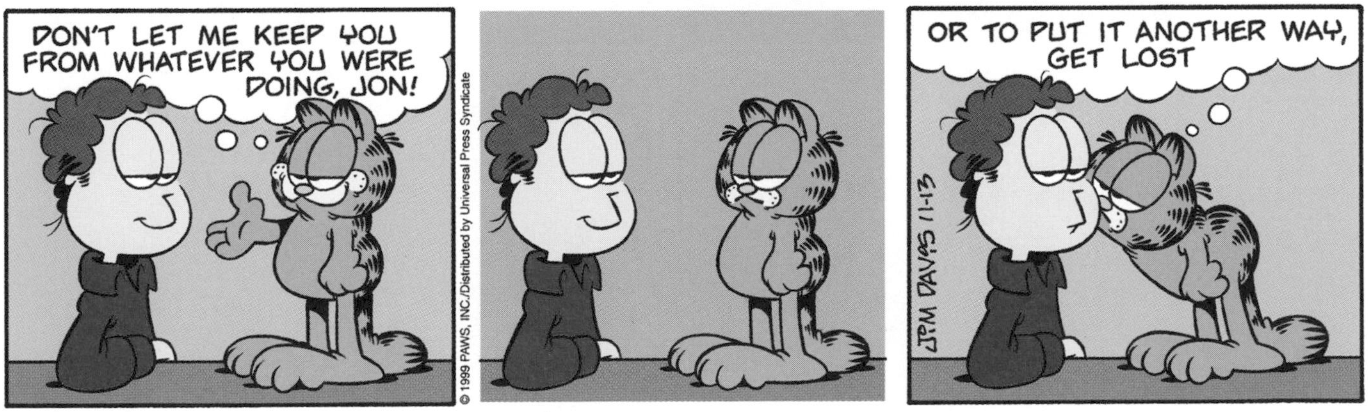
DON'T LET ME KEEP YOU FROM WHATEVER YOU WERE DOING, JON!
© 1999 PAWS, INC./Distributed by Universal Press Syndicate
OR TO PUT IT ANOTHER WAY, GET LOST
JIM DAVIS 11-13

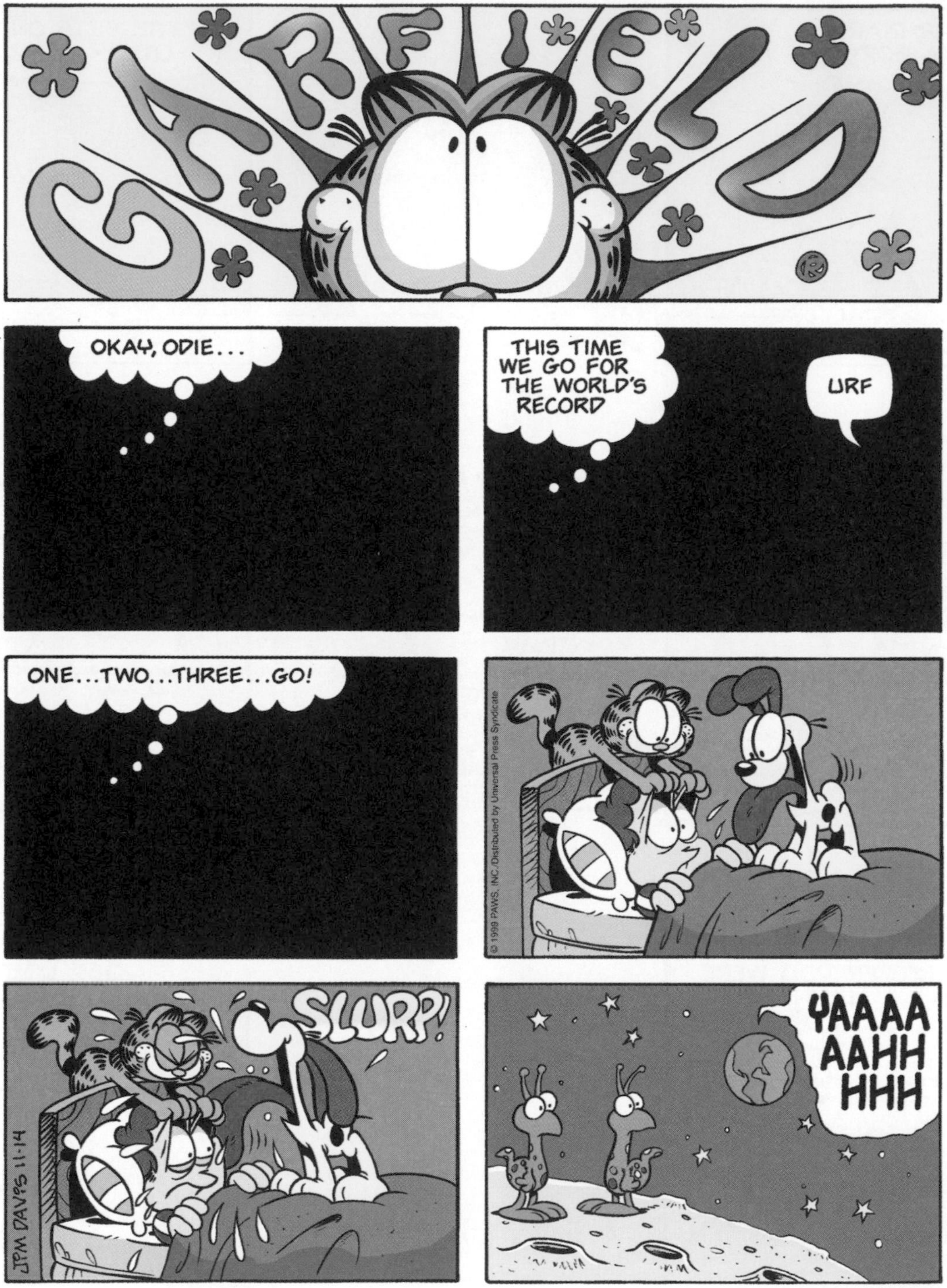
GARFIELD
OKAY, ODIE...
THIS TIME WE GO FOR THE WORLD'S RECORD
URF
ONE...TWO...THREE...GO!
© 1999 PAWS, INC./Distributed by Universal Press Syndicate
SLURP!
JPM DAVIS 11-14
YAAAA AAHH HHH

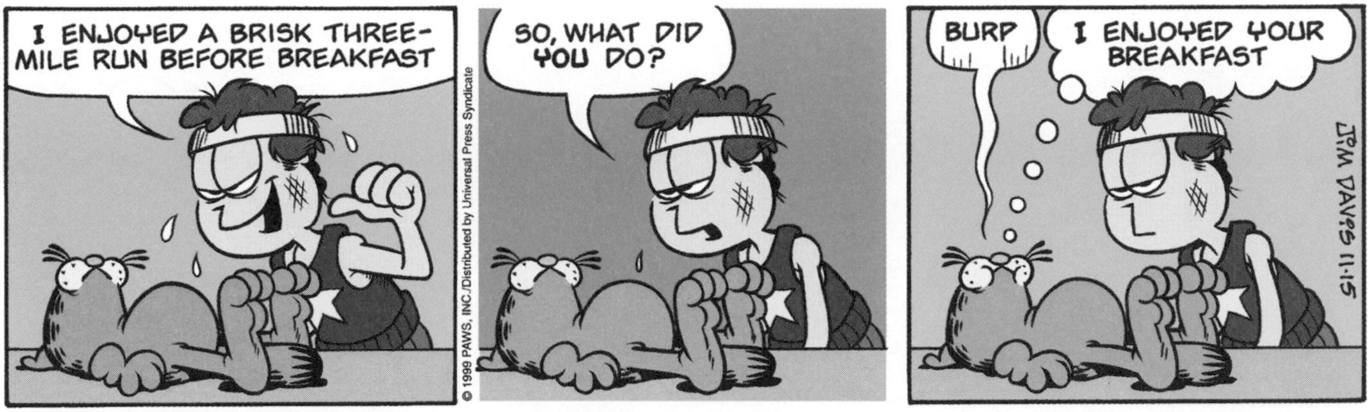
I ENJOYED A BRISK THREE-MILE RUN BEFORE BREAKFAST
© 1999 PAWS, INC./Distributed by Universal Press Syndicate
SO, WHAT DID YOU DO?
BURP
I ENJOYED YOUR BREAKFAST
JIM DAVIS 11-15

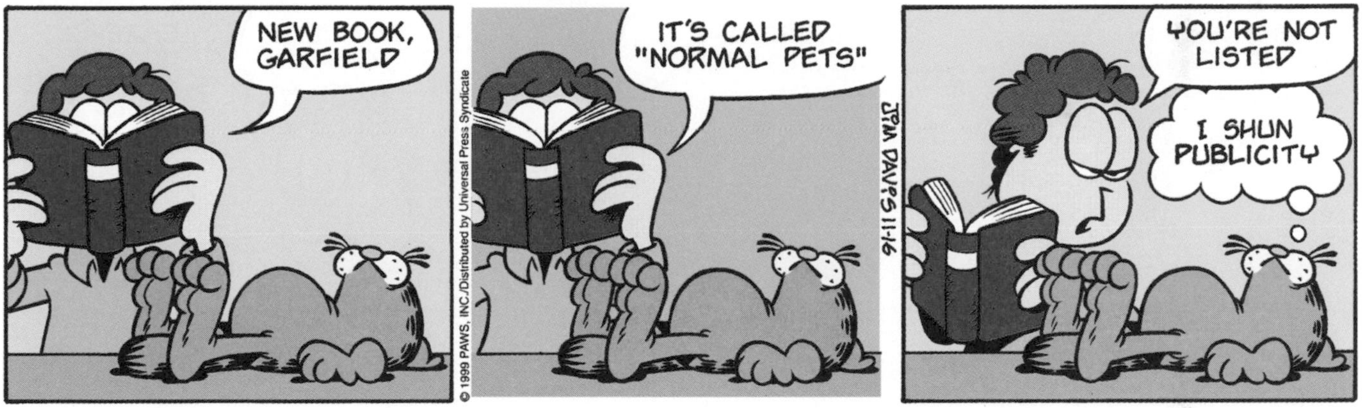
NEW BOOK, GARFIELD
© 1999 PAWS, INC./Distributed by Universal Press Syndicate
IT'S CALLED "NORMAL PETS"
JIM DAVIS 11-16
YOU'RE NOT LISTED
I SHUN PUBLICITY

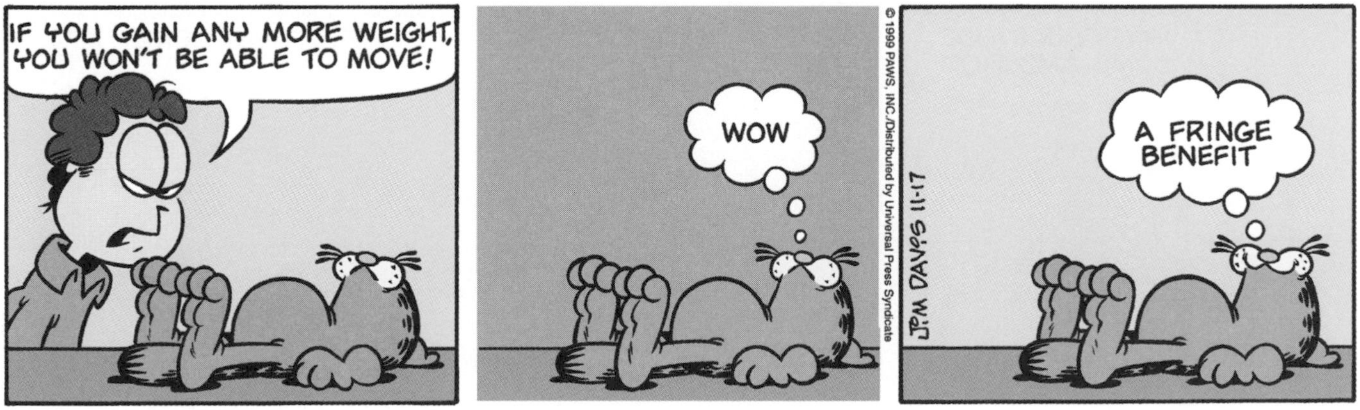
IF YOU GAIN ANY MORE WEIGHT, YOU WON'T BE ABLE TO MOVE!
WOW
© 1999 PAWS, INC./Distributed by Universal Press Syndicate
JIM DAVIS 11-17
A FRINGE BENEFIT

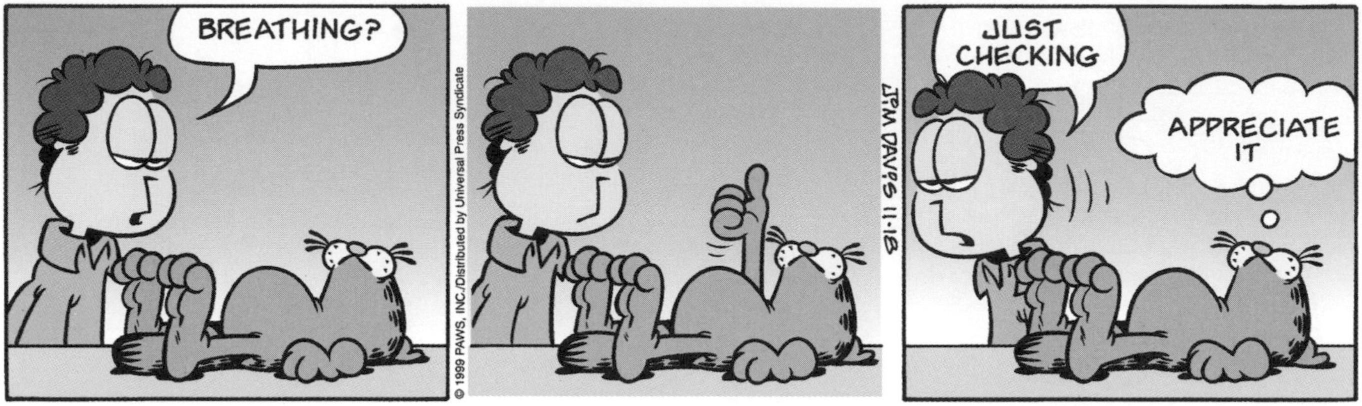
BREATHING?
© 1999 PAWS, INC./Distributed by Universal Press Syndicate
JIM DAVIS 11-18
JUST CHECKING
APPRECIATE IT

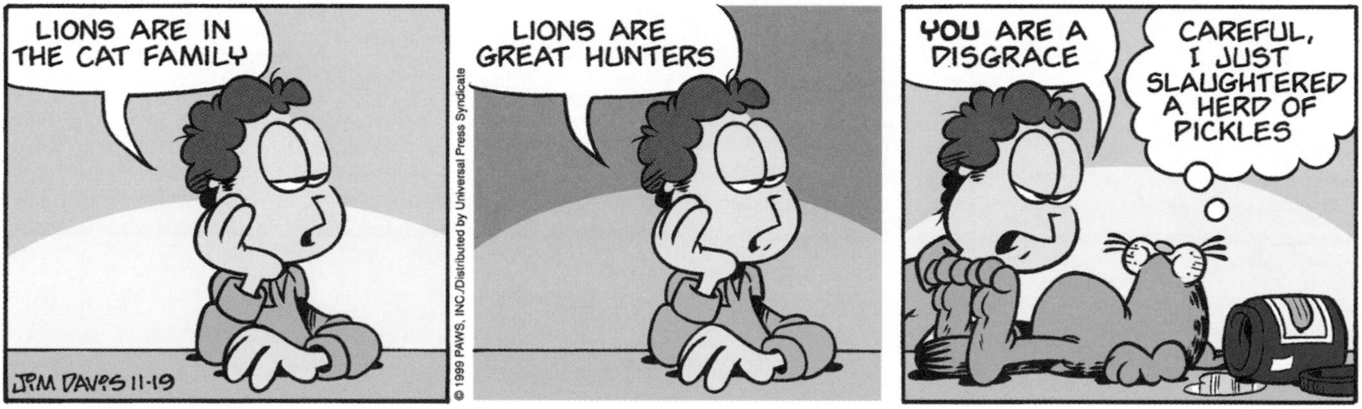
LIONS ARE IN THE CAT FAMILY
JIM DAVIS 11-19
© 1999 PAWS, INC./Distributed by Universal Press Syndicate
LIONS ARE GREAT HUNTERS
YOU ARE A DISGRACE
CAREFUL, I JUST SLAUGHTERED A HERD OF PICKLES

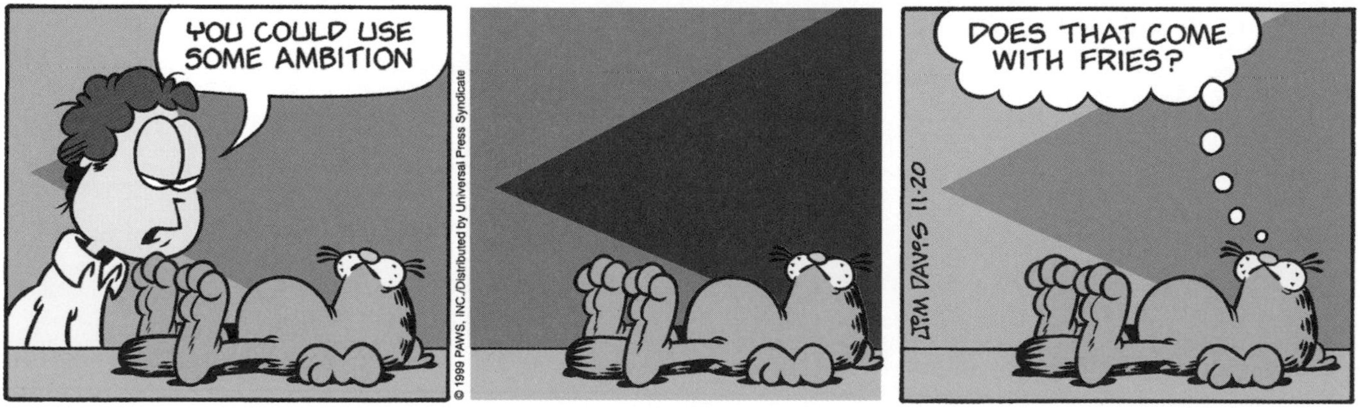
YOU COULD USE SOME AMBITION
© 1999 PAWS, INC./Distributed by Universal Press Syndicate
JIM DAVIS 11-20
DOES THAT COME WITH FRIES?

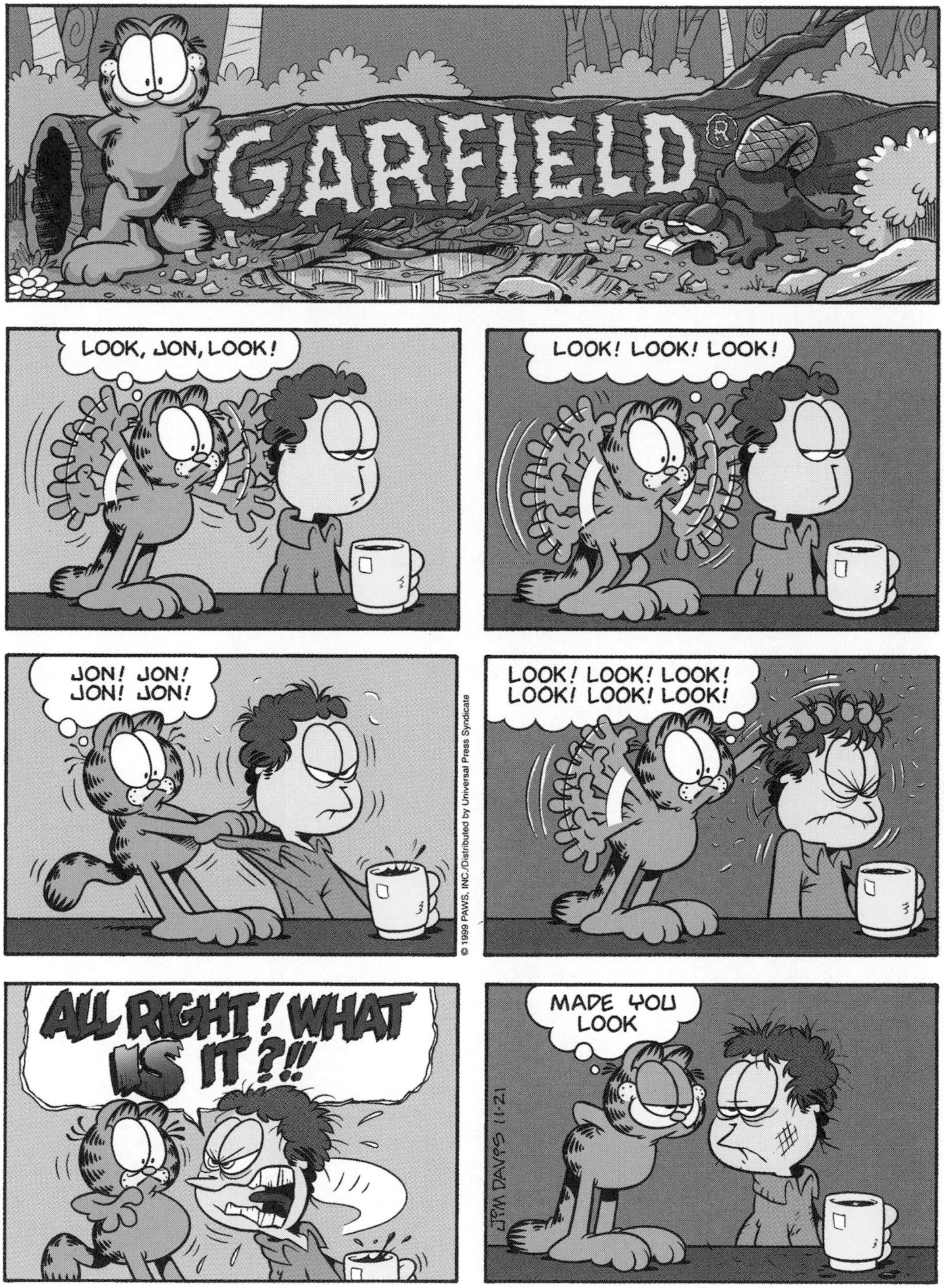
GARFIELD®
LOOK, JON, LOOK!
LOOK! LOOK! LOOK!
JON! JON! JON! JON!
LOOK! LOOK! LOOK! LOOK! LOOK! LOOK!
ALL RIGHT! WHAT IS IT?!!
MADE YOU LOOK
JPM DAVPS 11-21
© 1999 PAWS, INC./Distributed by Universal Press Syndicate

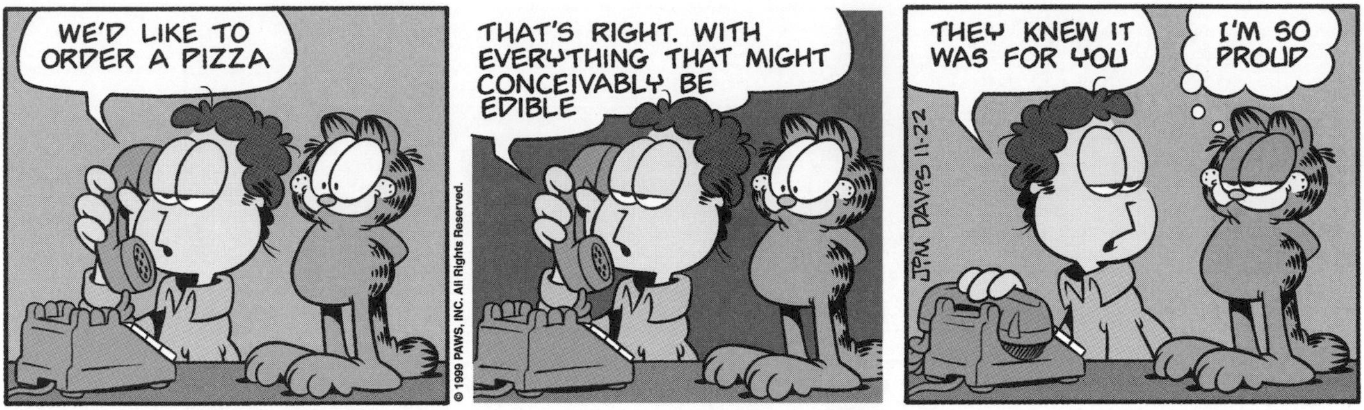
WE'D LIKE TO ORDER A PIZZA
© 1999 PAWS, INC. All Rights Reserved.
THAT'S RIGHT. WITH EVERYTHING THAT MIGHT CONCEIVABLY BE EDIBLE
THEY KNEW IT WAS FOR YOU
I'M SO PROUD
JIM DAVIS 11-22

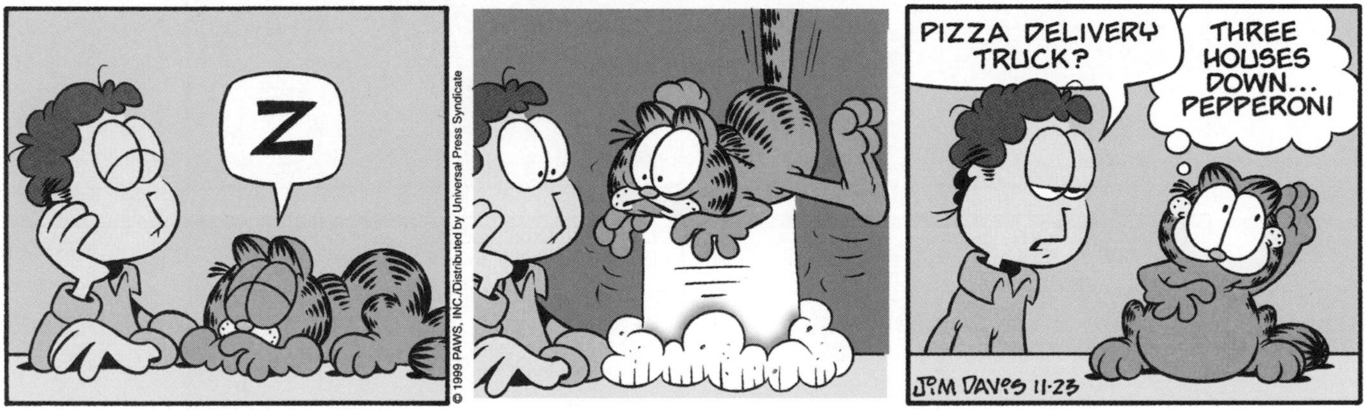
Z
© 1999 PAWS, INC./Distributed by Universal Press Syndicate
PIZZA DELIVERY TRUCK?
THREE HOUSES DOWN... PEPPERONI
JIM DAVIS 11-23

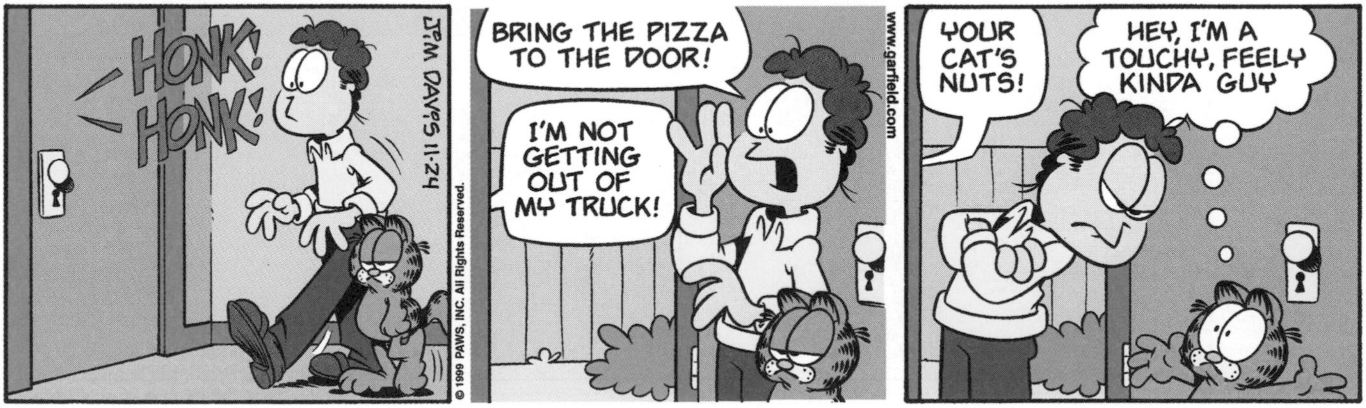
HONK! HONK!
JIM DAVIS 11-24
© 1999 PAWS, INC. All Rights Reserved.
BRING THE PIZZA TO THE DOOR!
I'M NOT GETTING OUT OF MY TRUCK!
www.garfield.com
YOUR CAT'S NUTS!
HEY, I'M A TOUCHY, FEELY KINDA GUY

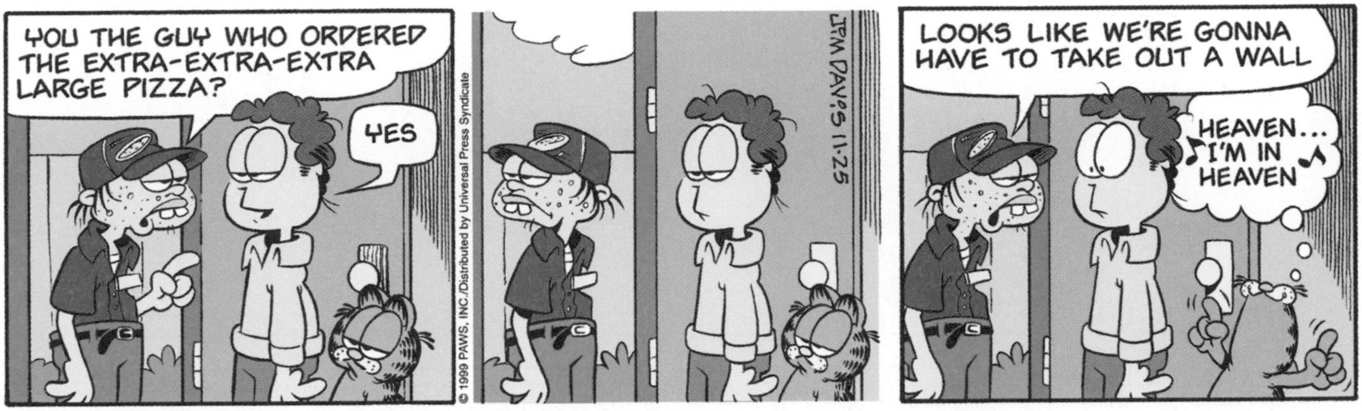
YOU THE GUY WHO ORDERED THE EXTRA-EXTRA-EXTRA LARGE PIZZA?
YES
© 1999 PAWS, INC./Distributed by Universal Press Syndicate
JIM DAVIS 11-25
LOOKS LIKE WE'RE GONNA HAVE TO TAKE OUT A WALL
HEAVEN... I'M IN HEAVEN

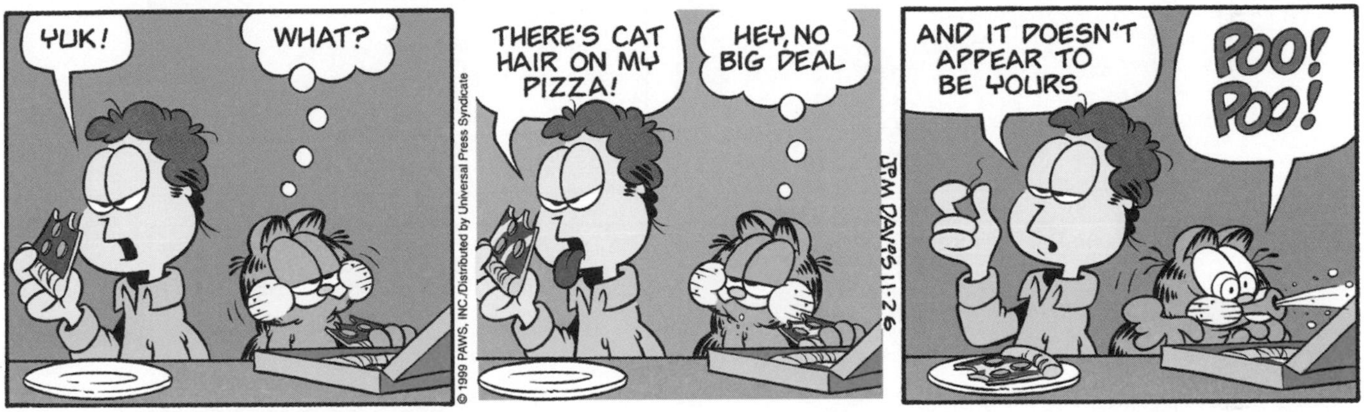
YUK!
WHAT?
© 1999 PAWS, INC./Distributed by Universal Press Syndicate
THERE'S CAT HAIR ON MY PIZZA!
HEY, NO BIG DEAL
JIM DAVIS 11-26
AND IT DOESN'T APPEAR TO BE YOURS
POO! POO!

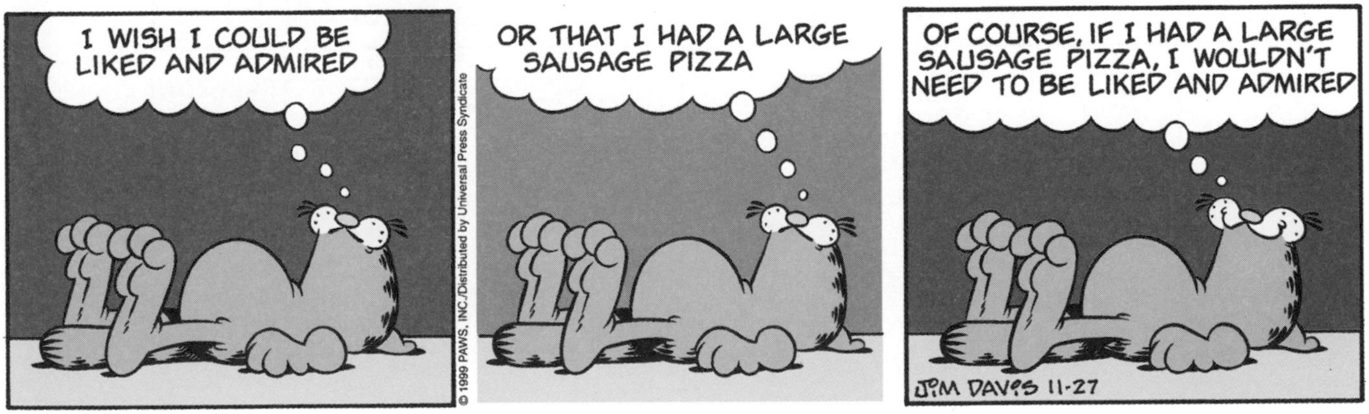
I WISH I COULD BE LIKED AND ADMIRED
© 1999 PAWS, INC./Distributed by Universal Press Syndicate
OR THAT I HAD A LARGE SAUSAGE PIZZA
OF COURSE, IF I HAD A LARGE SAUSAGE PIZZA, I WOULDN'T NEED TO BE LIKED AND ADMIRED
JIM DAVIS 11-27

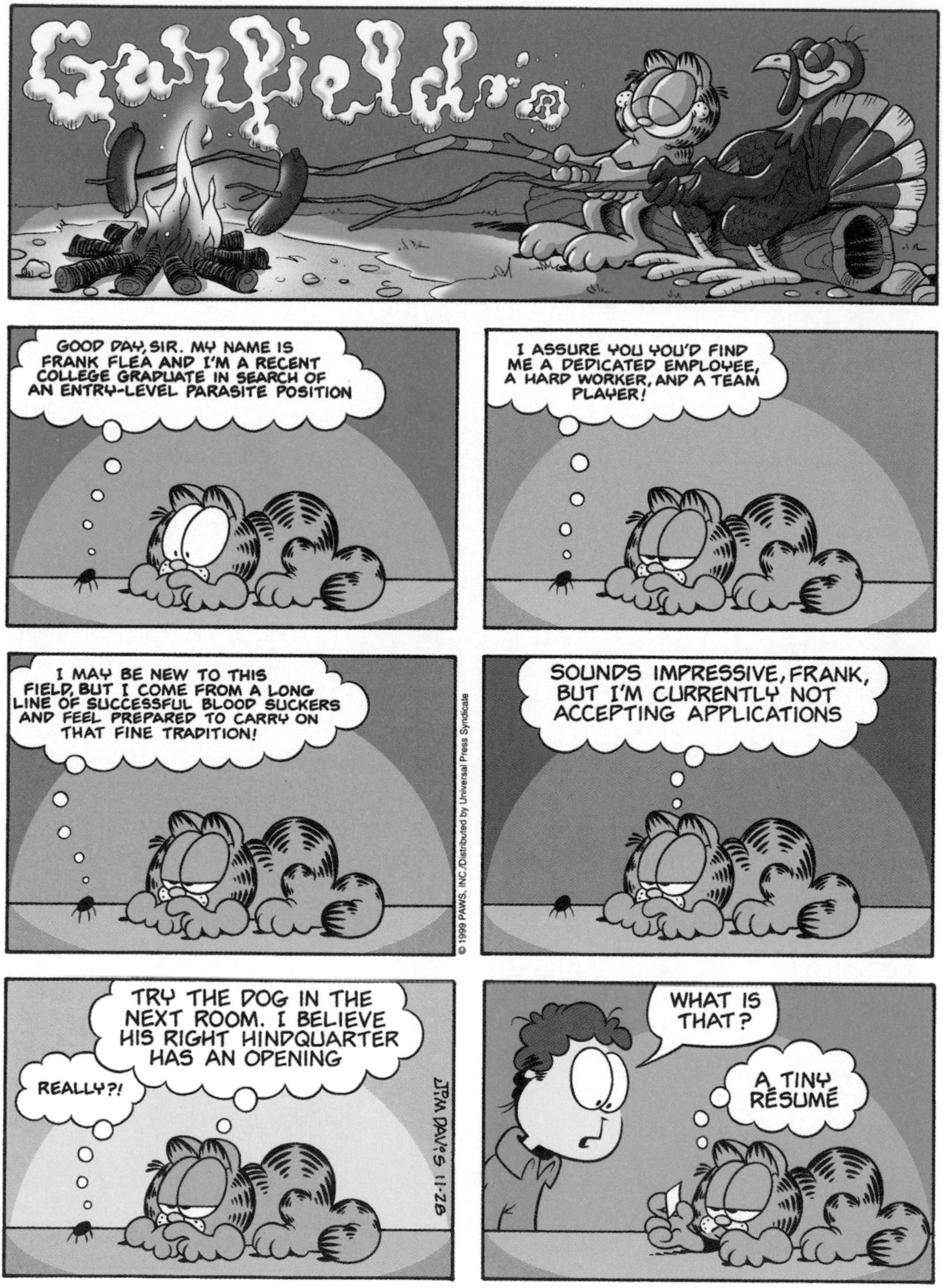
GARFIELD®
GOOD DAY, SIR. MY NAME IS FRANK FLEA AND I'M A RECENT COLLEGE GRADUATE IN SEARCH OF AN ENTRY-LEVEL PARASITE POSITION
I ASSURE YOU YOU'D FIND ME A DEDICATED EMPLOYEE, A HARD WORKER, AND A TEAM PLAYER!
I MAY BE NEW TO THIS FIELD, BUT I COME FROM A LONG LINE OF SUCCESSFUL BLOOD SUCKERS AND FEEL PREPARED TO CARRY ON THAT FINE TRADITION!
SOUNDS IMPRESSIVE, FRANK, BUT I'M CURRENTLY NOT ACCEPTING APPLICATIONS
TRY THE DOG IN THE NEXT ROOM. I BELIEVE HIS RIGHT HINDQUARTER HAS AN OPENING
REALLY?!
JPM DAVIS 11-28
WHAT IS THAT?
A TINY RÉSUMÉ
© 1999 PAWS, INC./Distributed by Universal Press Syndicate

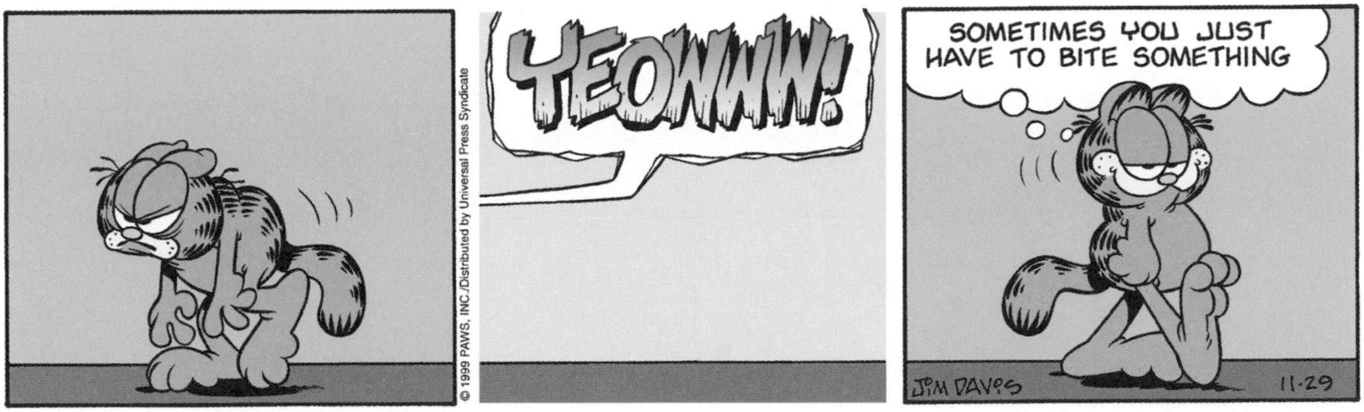
YEOWWW!
© 1999 PAWS, INC./Distributed by Universal Press Syndicate
SOMETIMES YOU JUST HAVE TO BITE SOMETHING
JIM DAVIS
11-29

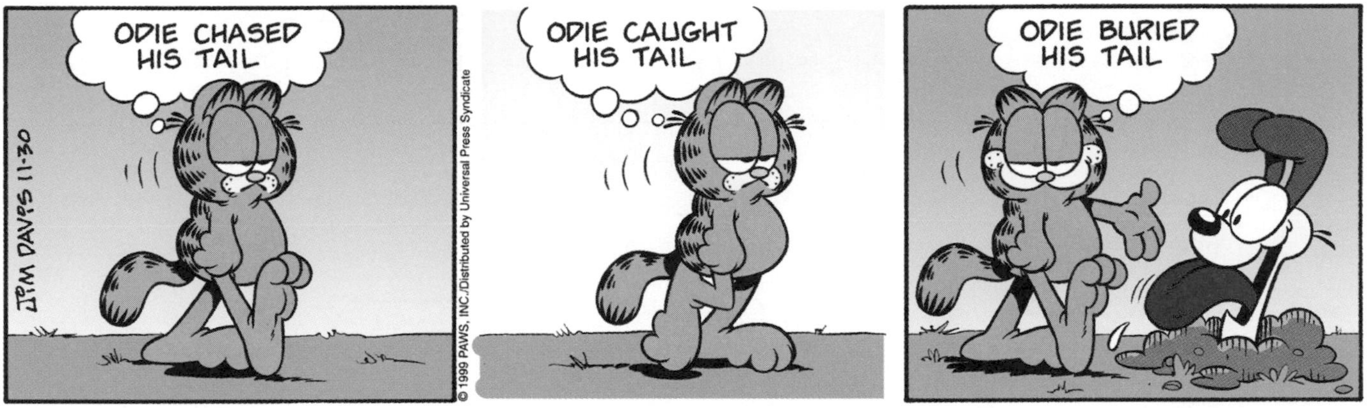
ODIE CHASED HIS TAIL
JIM DAVIS 11-30
© 1999 PAWS, INC./Distributed by Universal Press Syndicate
ODIE CAUGHT HIS TAIL
ODIE BURIED HIS TAIL

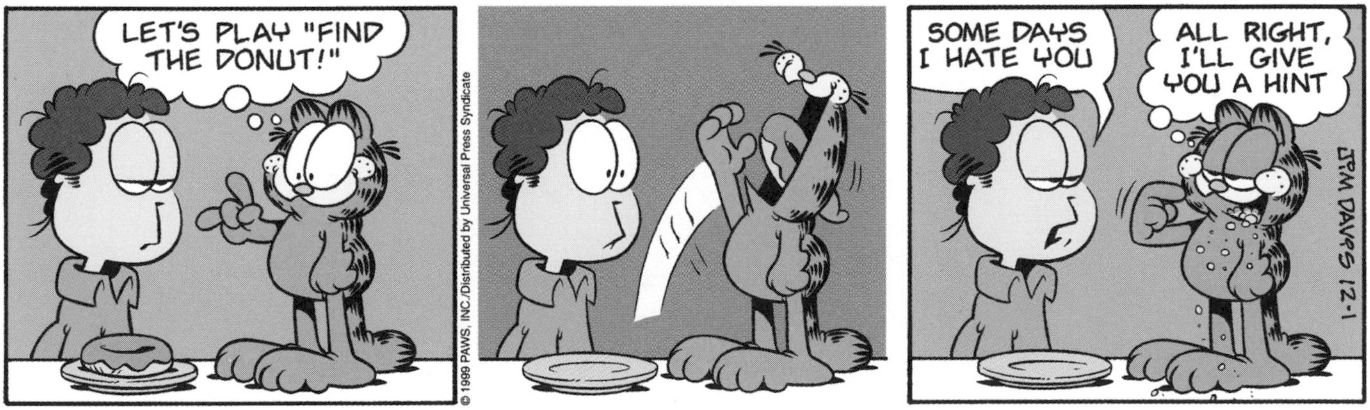
LET'S PLAY "FIND THE DONUT!"
© 1999 PAWS, INC./Distributed by Universal Press Syndicate
SOME DAYS I HATE YOU
ALL RIGHT, I'LL GIVE YOU A HINT
JIM DAVIS 12-1

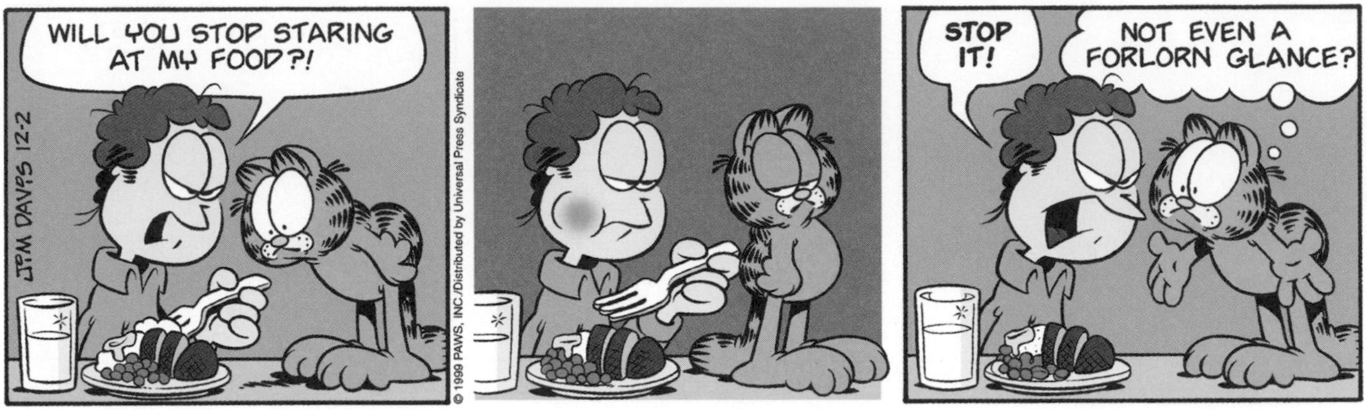
WILL YOU STOP STARING AT MY FOOD?!
JIM DAVIS 12-2
© 1999 PAWS, INC./Distributed by Universal Press Syndicate
STOP IT!
NOT EVEN A FORLORN GLANCE?

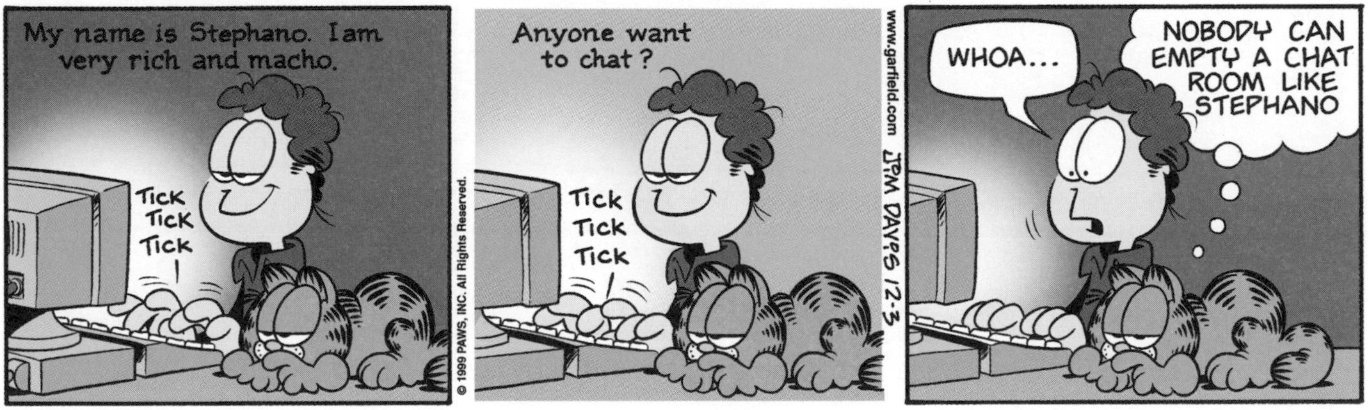
My name is Stephano. I am very rich and macho.
Tick Tick Tick
© 1999 PAWS, INC. All Rights Reserved.
Anyone want to chat?
Tick Tick Tick
www.garfield.com
JIM DAVIS 12-3
WHOA...
NOBODY CAN EMPTY A CHAT ROOM LIKE STEPHANO

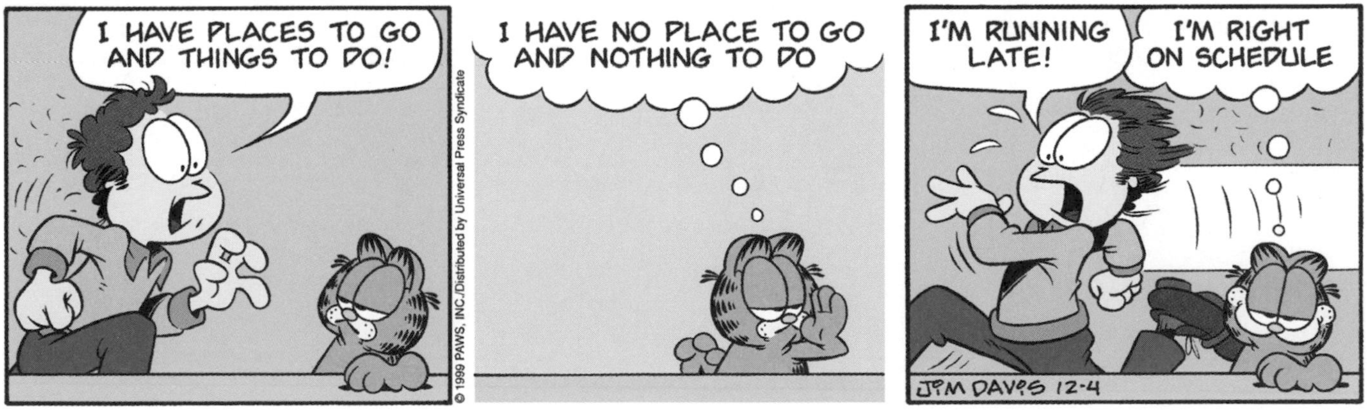
I HAVE PLACES TO GO AND THINGS TO DO!
© 1999 PAWS, INC./Distributed by Universal Press Syndicate
I HAVE NO PLACE TO GO AND NOTHING TO DO
I'M RUNNING LATE!
I'M RIGHT ON SCHEDULE
JIM DAVIS 12-4

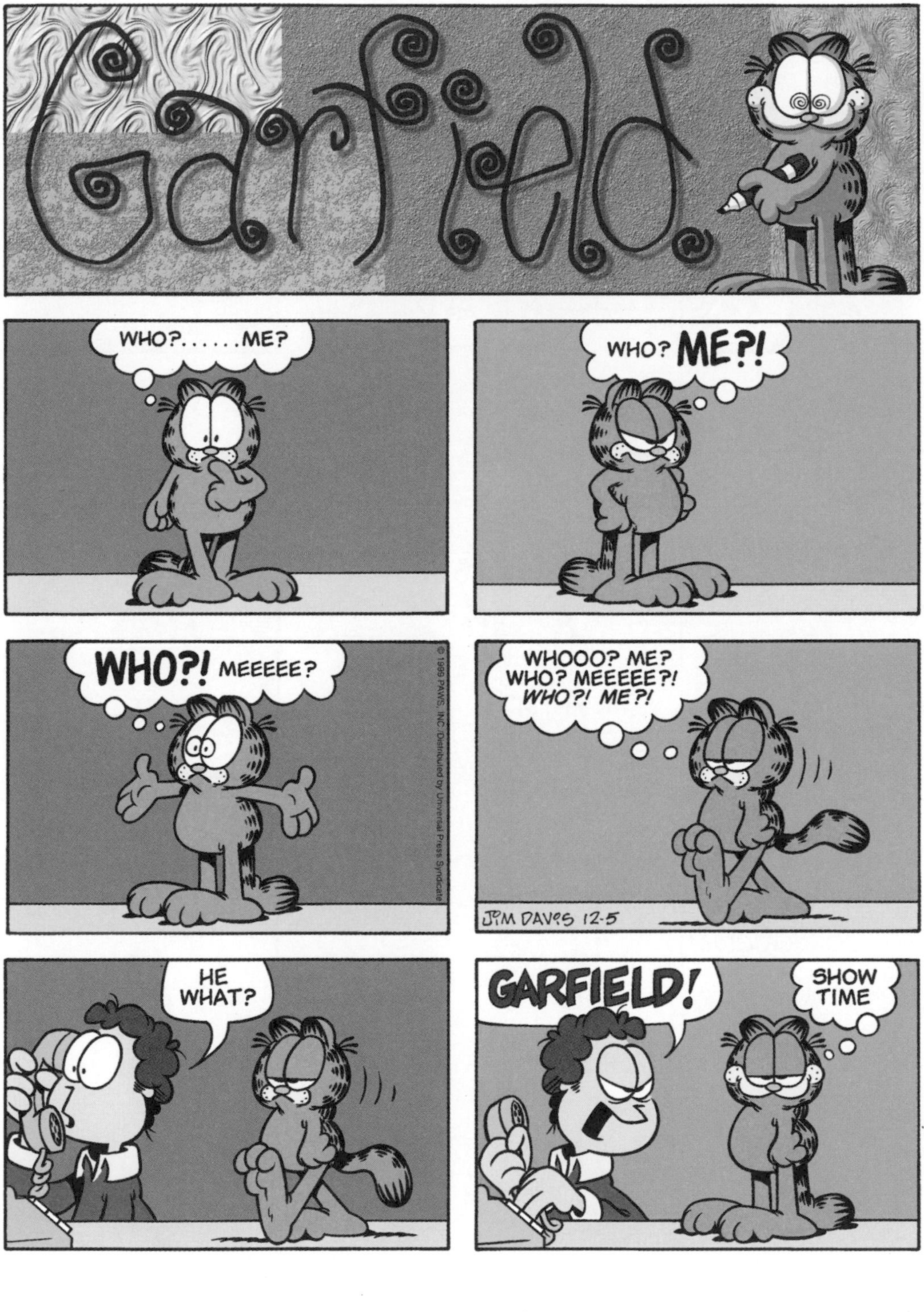
Garfield
WHO?......ME?
WHO? ME?!
WHO?! MEEEEE?
© 1999 PAWS, INC./Distributed by Universal Press Syndicate
WHOOO? ME?
WHO? MEEEEE?!
WHO?! ME?!
JIM DAVIS 12-5
HE WHAT?
GARFIELD!
SHOW TIME

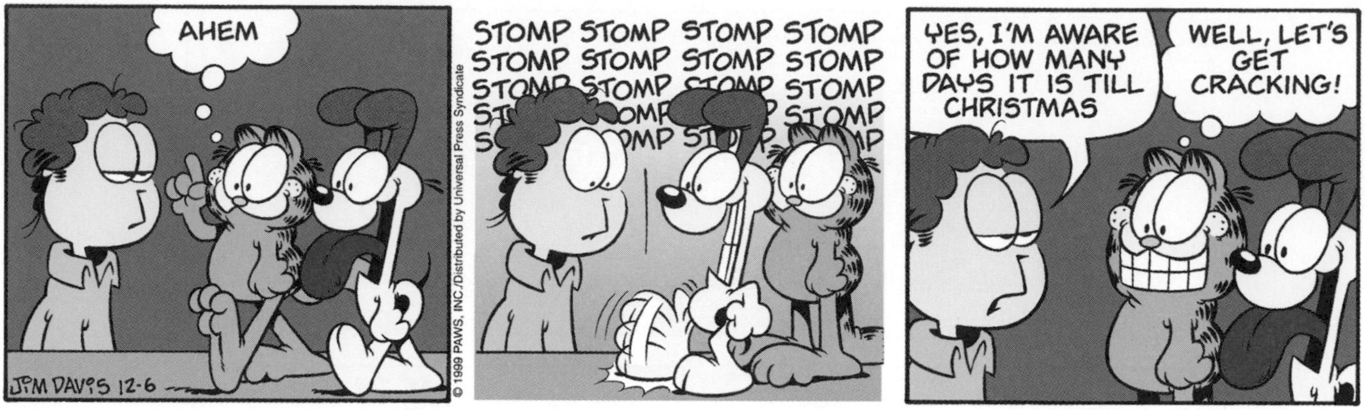
AHEM
JIM DAVIS 12-6
© 1999 PAWS, INC./Distributed by Universal Press Syndicate
STOMP STOMP STOMP STOMP
STOMP STOMP STOMP STOMP
YES, I'M AWARE OF HOW MANY DAYS IT IS TILL CHRISTMAS
WELL, LET'S GET CRACKING!

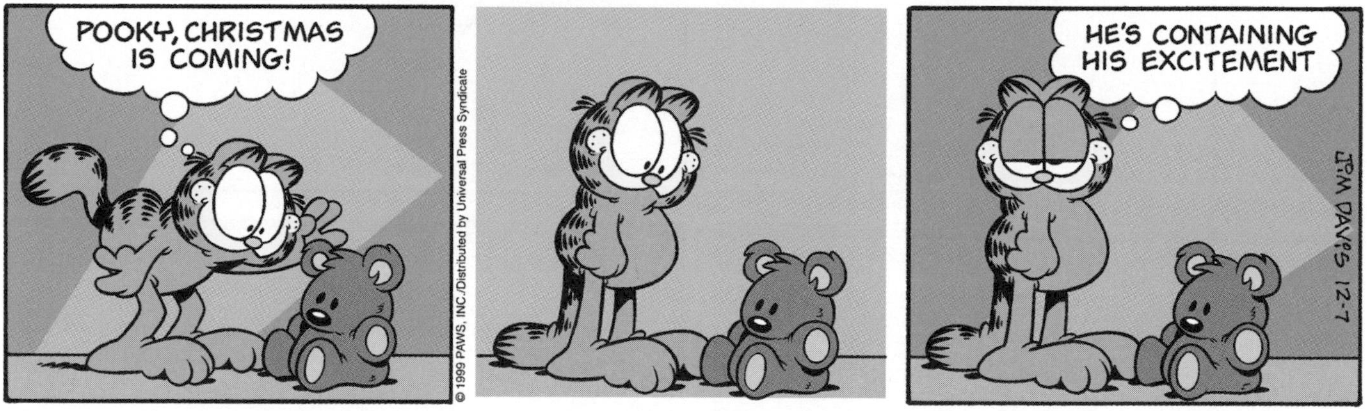
POOKY, CHRISTMAS IS COMING!
© 1999 PAWS, INC./Distributed by Universal Press Syndicate
HE'S CONTAINING HIS EXCITEMENT
JIM DAVIS 12-7

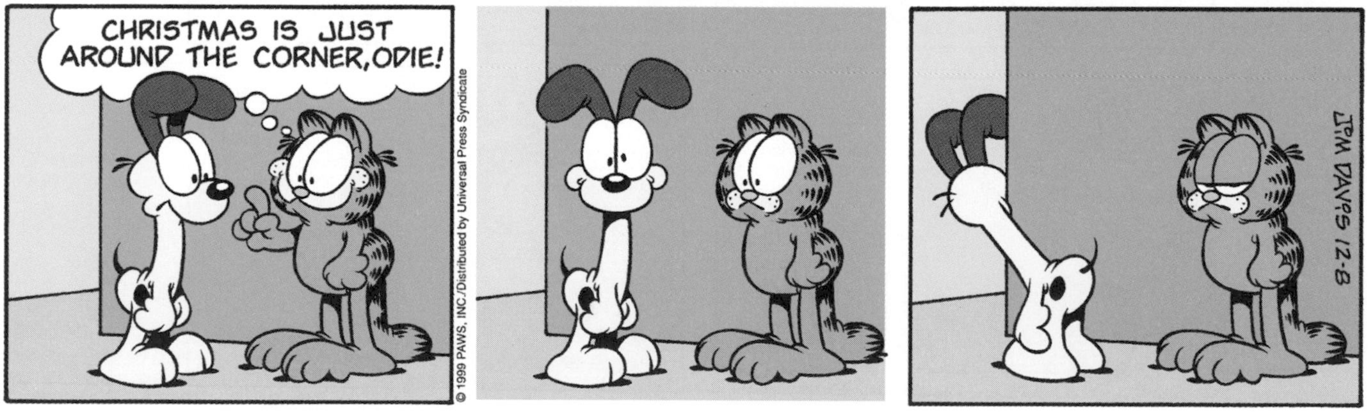
CHRISTMAS IS JUST AROUND THE CORNER, ODIE!
© 1999 PAWS, INC./Distributed by Universal Press Syndicate
JIM DAVIS 12-8

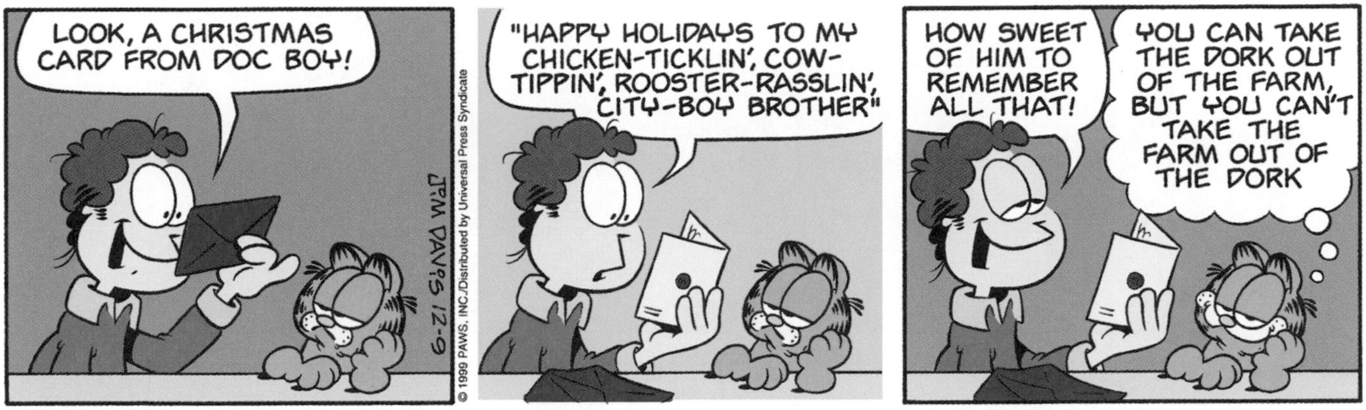
LOOK, A CHRISTMAS CARD FROM DOC BOY!
JPM DAVPS 12-9
© 1999 PAWS, INC./Distributed by Universal Press Syndicate
"HAPPY HOLIDAYS TO MY CHICKEN-TICKLIN', COW-TIPPIN', ROOSTER-RASSLIN', CITY-BOY BROTHER"
HOW SWEET OF HIM TO REMEMBER ALL THAT!
YOU CAN TAKE THE DORK OUT OF THE FARM, BUT YOU CAN'T TAKE THE FARM OUT OF THE DORK

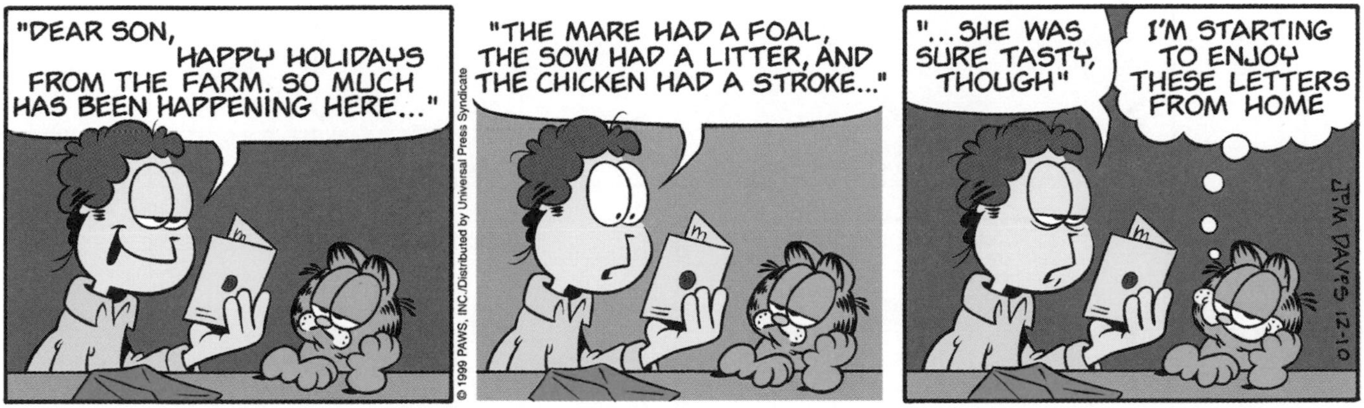
"DEAR SON, HAPPY HOLIDAYS FROM THE FARM. SO MUCH HAS BEEN HAPPENING HERE..."
© 1999 PAWS, INC./Distributed by Universal Press Syndicate
"THE MARE HAD A FOAL, THE SOW HAD A LITTER, AND THE CHICKEN HAD A STROKE..."
"...SHE WAS SURE TASTY, THOUGH"
I'M STARTING TO ENJOY THESE LETTERS FROM HOME
JPM DAVPS 12-10

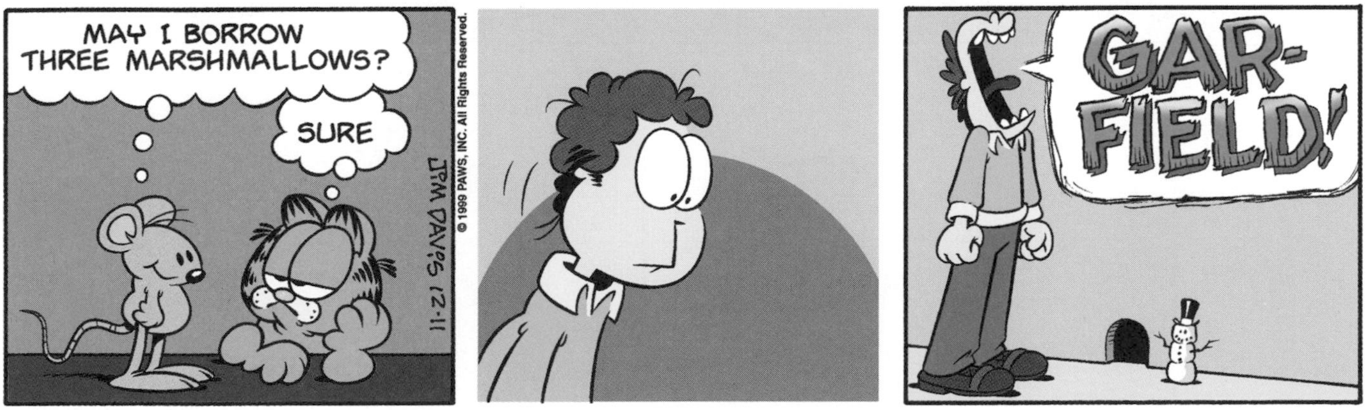
MAY I BORROW THREE MARSHMALLOWS?
SURE
JPM DAVPS 12-11
© 1999 PAWS, INC. All Rights Reserved.
GAR-FIELD!

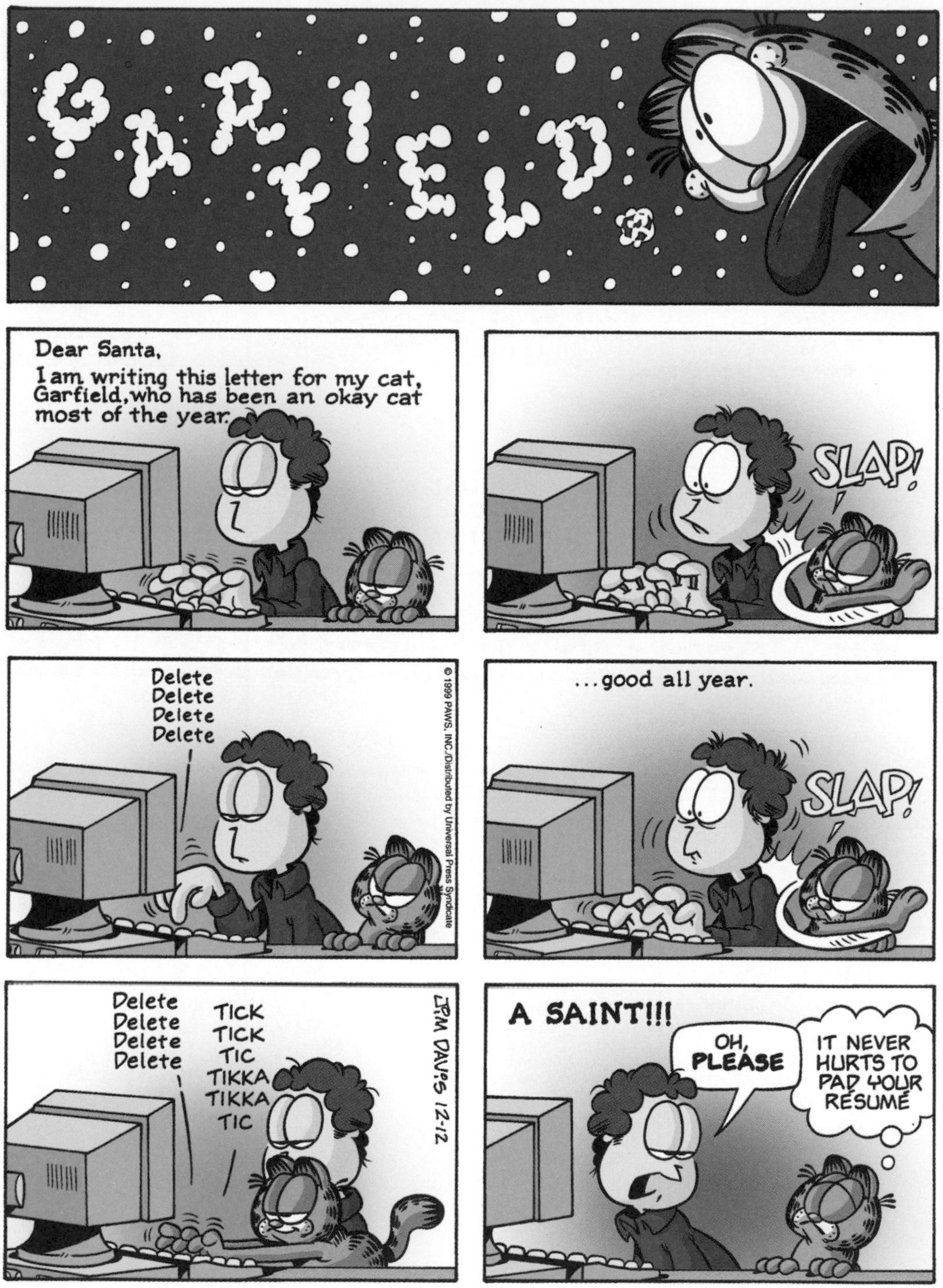
GARFIELD
Dear Santa,
I am writing this letter for my cat, Garfield, who has been an okay cat most of the year.
SLAP!
Delete
Delete
Delete
Delete
© 1999 PAWS, INC./Distributed by Universal Press Syndicate
...good all year.
SLAP!
Delete
Delete
Delete
Delete
TICK
TICK
TIC
TIKKA
TIKKA
TIC
JIM DAVIS 12-12
A SAINT!!!
OH, PLEASE
IT NEVER HURTS TO PAD YOUR RESUME

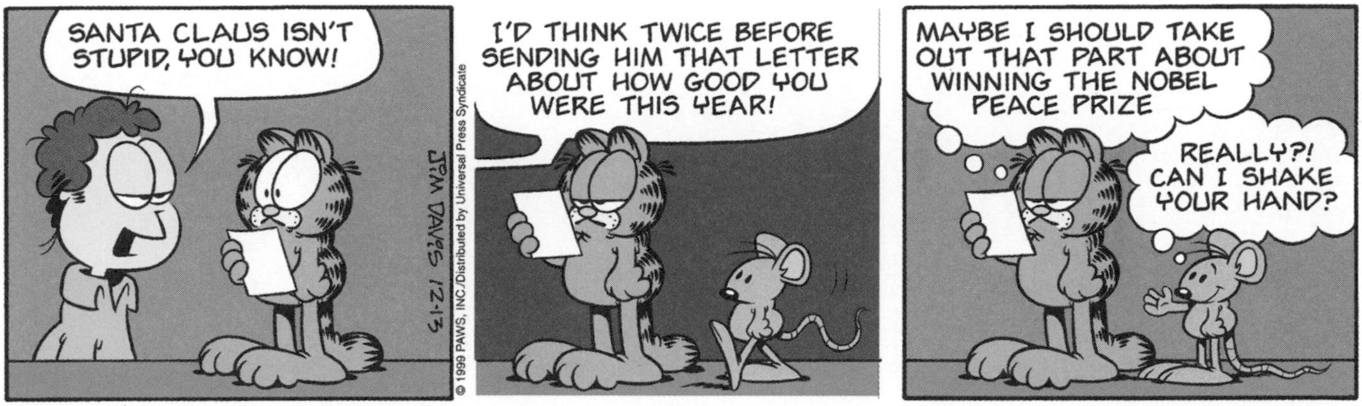
SANTA CLAUS ISN'T STUPID, YOU KNOW!
JIM DAVIS 12-13
© 1999 PAWS, INC./Distributed by Universal Press Syndicate
I'D THINK TWICE BEFORE SENDING HIM THAT LETTER ABOUT HOW GOOD YOU WERE THIS YEAR!
MAYBE I SHOULD TAKE OUT THAT PART ABOUT WINNING THE NOBEL PEACE PRIZE
REALLY?! CAN I SHAKE YOUR HAND?

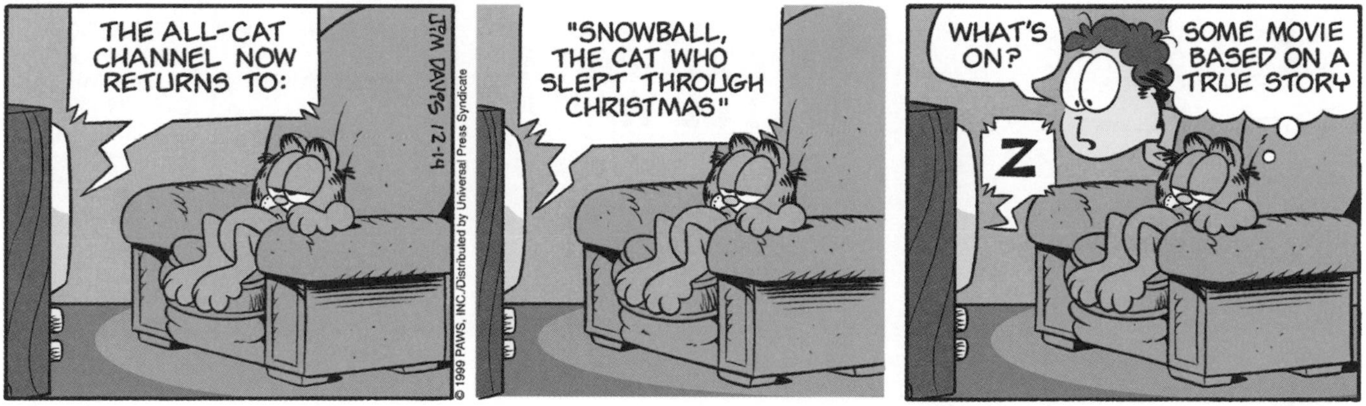
THE ALL-CAT CHANNEL NOW RETURNS TO:
JIM DAVIS 12-14
© 1999 PAWS, INC./Distributed by Universal Press Syndicate
"SNOWBALL, THE CAT WHO SLEPT THROUGH CHRISTMAS"
WHAT'S ON?
Z
SOME MOVIE BASED ON A TRUE STORY

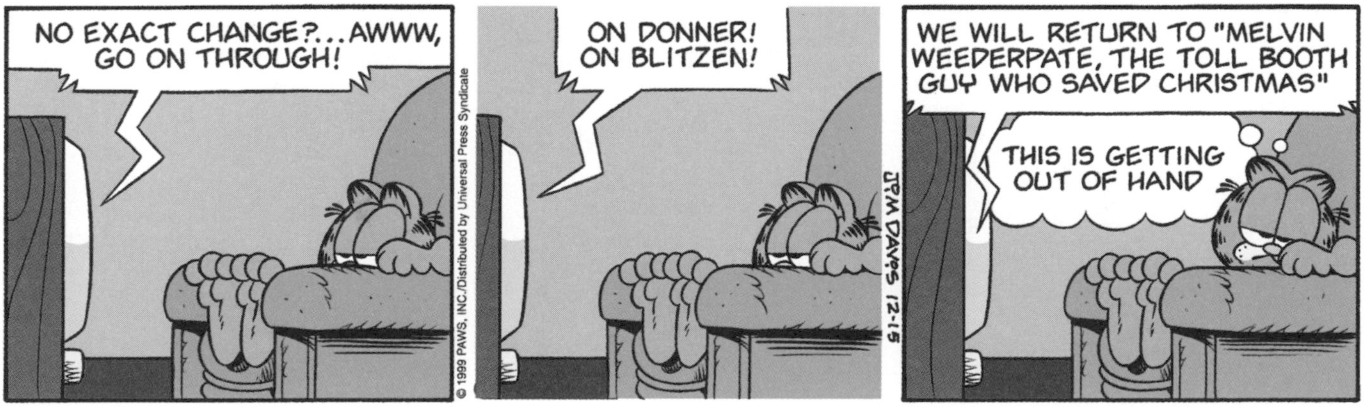
NO EXACT CHANGE?...AWWW, GO ON THROUGH!
© 1999 PAWS, INC./Distributed by Universal Press Syndicate
ON DONNER! ON BLITZEN!
JIM DAVIS 12-15
WE WILL RETURN TO "MELVIN WEEDERPATE, THE TOLL BOOTH GUY WHO SAVED CHRISTMAS"
THIS IS GETTING OUT OF HAND

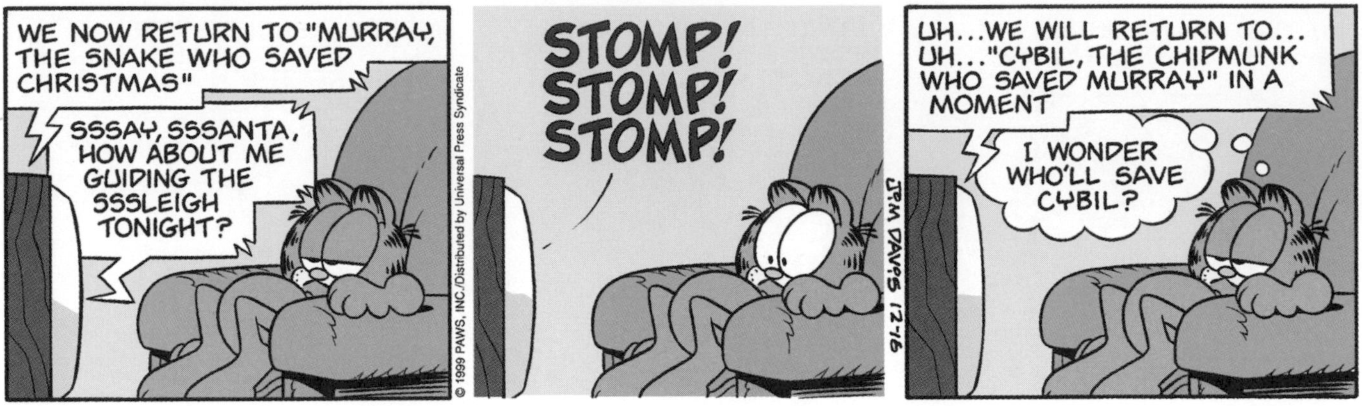
WE NOW RETURN TO "MURRAY, THE SNAKE WHO SAVED CHRISTMAS"
SSSAY, SSSANTA, HOW ABOUT ME GUIDING THE SSSLEIGH TONIGHT?
© 1999 PAWS, INC./Distributed by Universal Press Syndicate
STOMP! STOMP! STOMP!
JIM DAVIS 12-16
UH...WE WILL RETURN TO... UH..."CYBIL, THE CHIPMUNK WHO SAVED MURRAY" IN A MOMENT
I WONDER WHO'LL SAVE CYBIL?

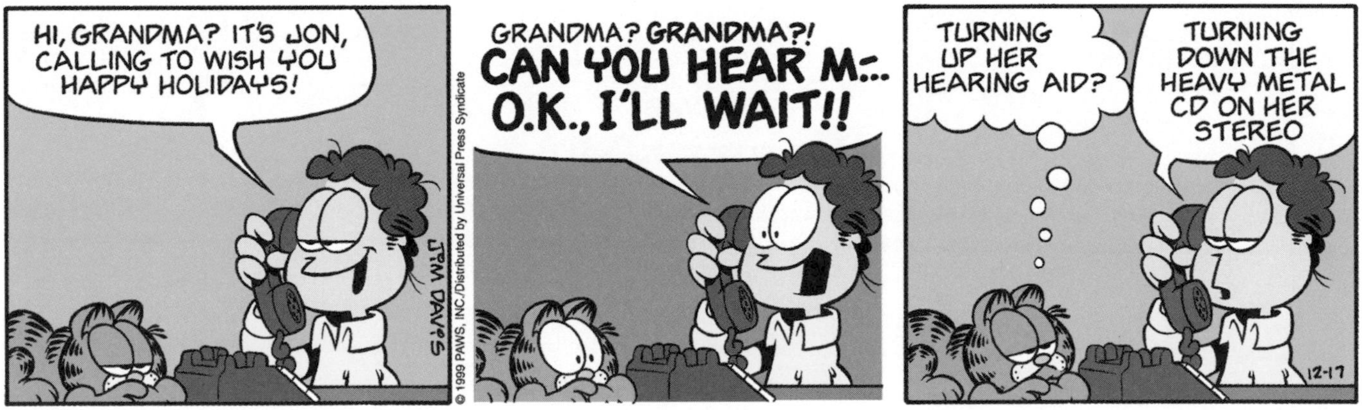
HI, GRANDMA? IT'S JON, CALLING TO WISH YOU HAPPY HOLIDAYS!
JIM DAVIS
© 1999 PAWS, INC./Distributed by Universal Press Syndicate
GRANDMA? GRANDMA?! CAN YOU HEAR M:.. O.K., I'LL WAIT!!
TURNING UP HER HEARING AID?
TURNING DOWN THE HEAVY METAL CD ON HER STEREO
12-17

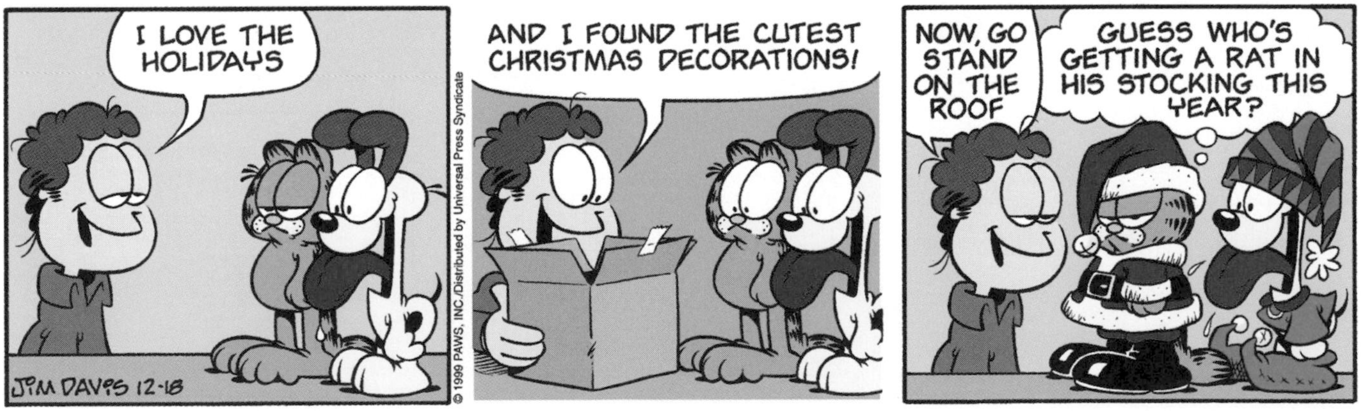
I LOVE THE HOLIDAYS
JIM DAVIS 12-18
© 1999 PAWS, INC./Distributed by Universal Press Syndicate
AND I FOUND THE CUTEST CHRISTMAS DECORATIONS!
NOW, GO STAND ON THE ROOF
GUESS WHO'S GETTING A RAT IN HIS STOCKING THIS YEAR?

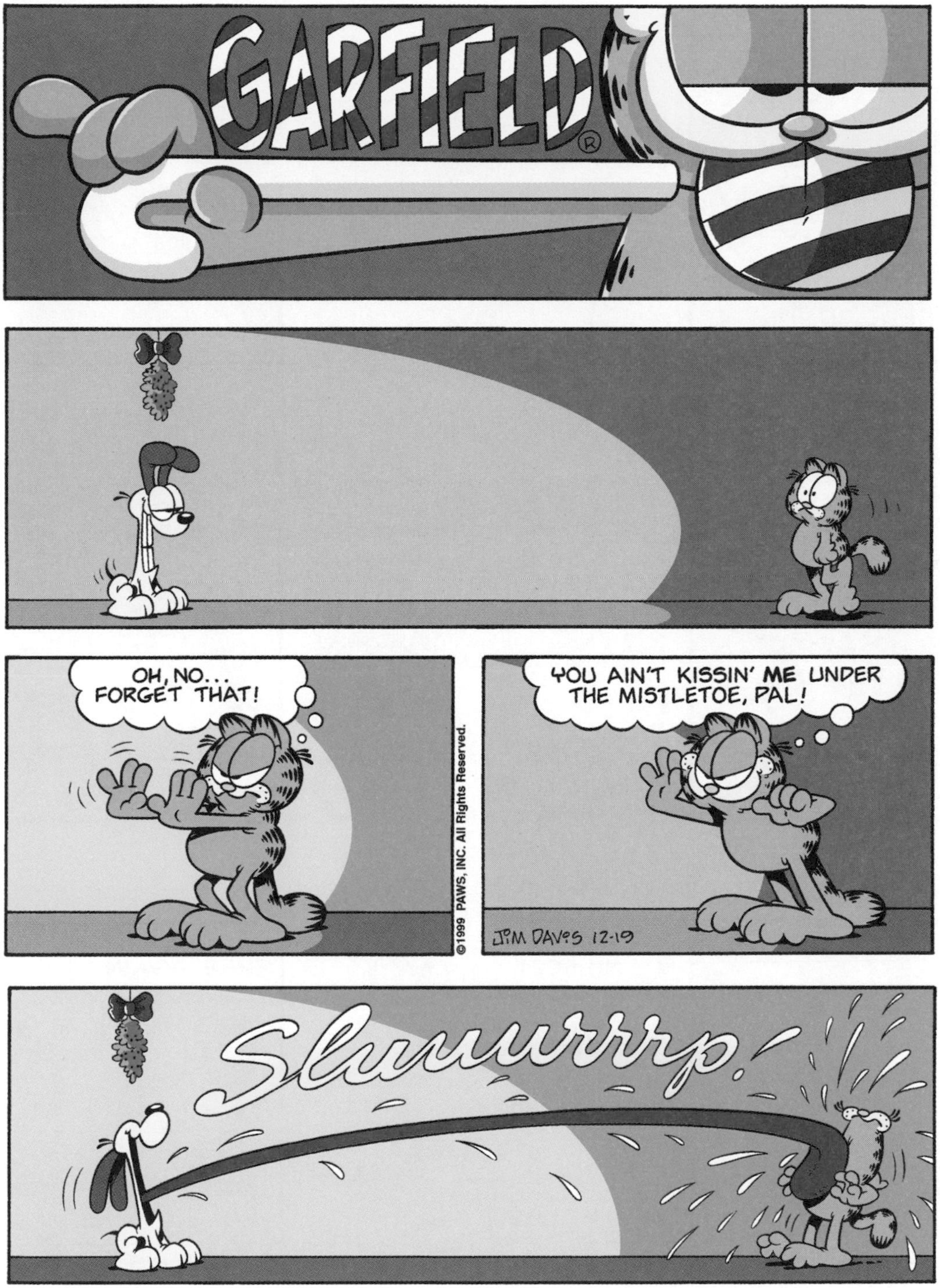
GARFIELD
OH, NO... FORGET THAT!
YOU AIN'T KISSIN' ME UNDER THE MISTLETOE, PAL!
©1999 PAWS, INC. All Rights Reserved.
JIM DAVIS 12-19
Sluuurrrp!

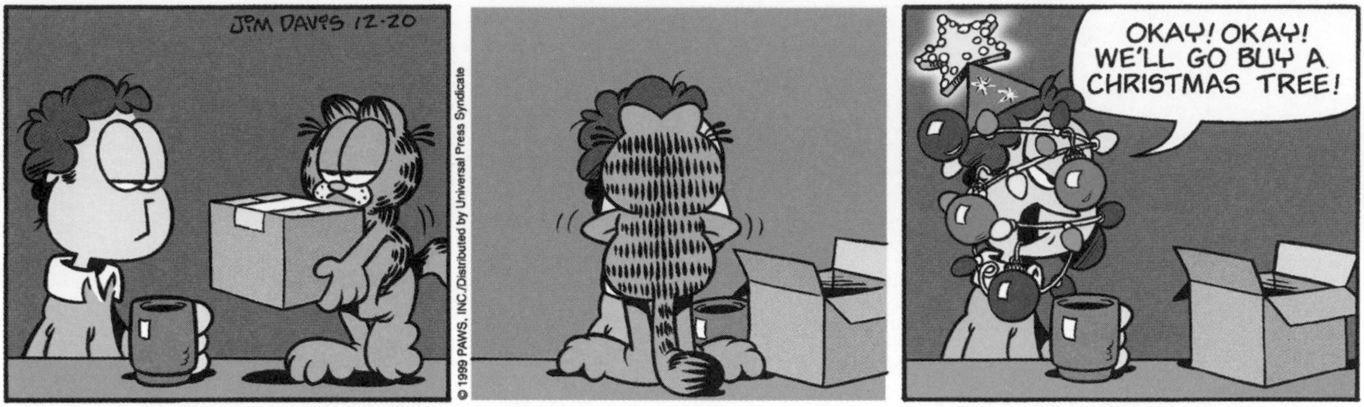
JIM DAVIS 12-20
© 1999 PAWS, INC./Distributed by Universal Press Syndicate
OKAY! OKAY! WE'LL GO BUY A CHRISTMAS TREE!

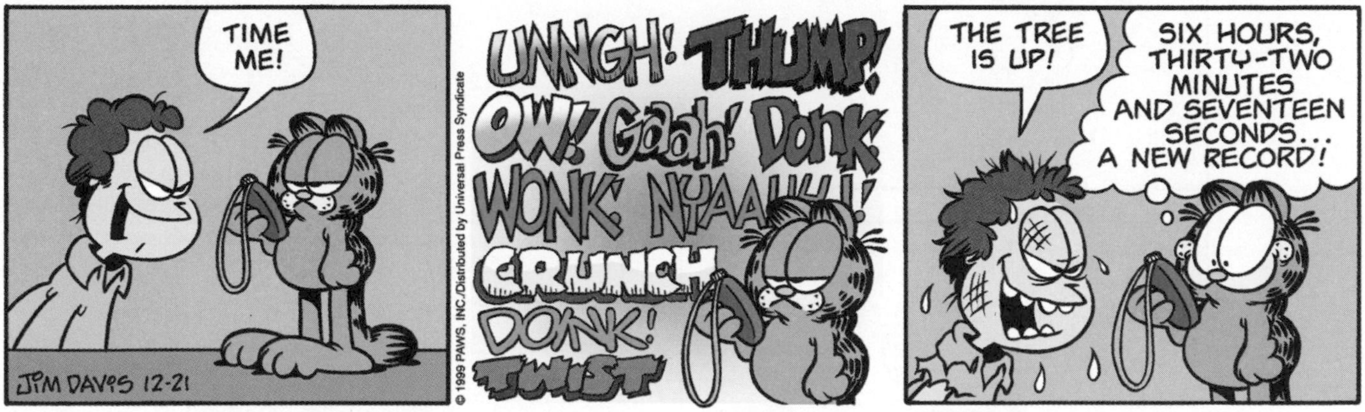
TIME ME!
JIM DAVIS 12-21
© 1999 PAWS, INC./Distributed by Universal Press Syndicate
UNNGH! THUMP! OW! Gaah! Donk! WONK! NYAA
CRUNCH
DONK!
TWIST
THE TREE IS UP!
SIX HOURS, THIRTY-TWO MINUTES AND SEVENTEEN SECONDS... A NEW RECORD!

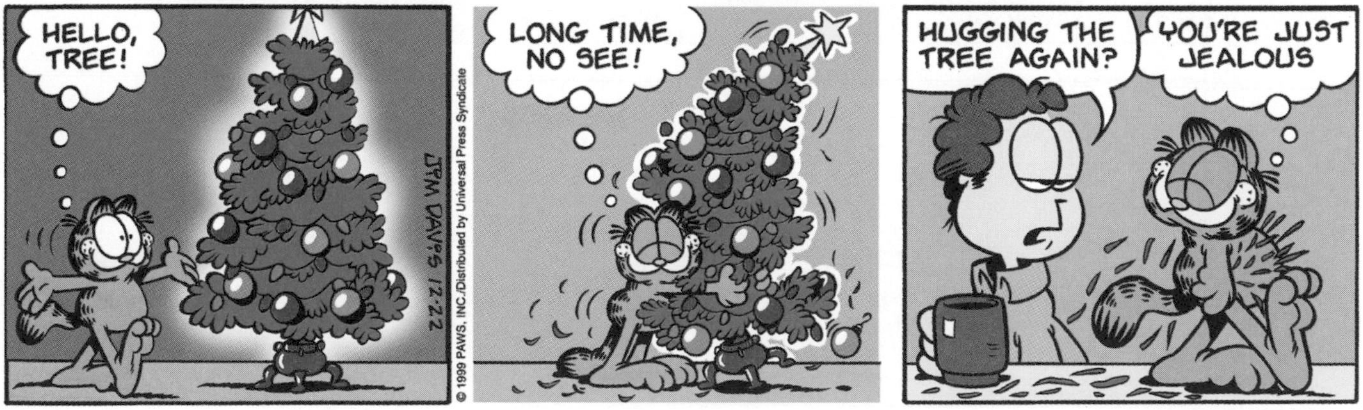
HELLO, TREE!
JIM DAVIS 12-22
© 1999 PAWS, INC./Distributed by Universal Press Syndicate
LONG TIME, NO SEE!
HUGGING THE TREE AGAIN?
YOU'RE JUST JEALOUS

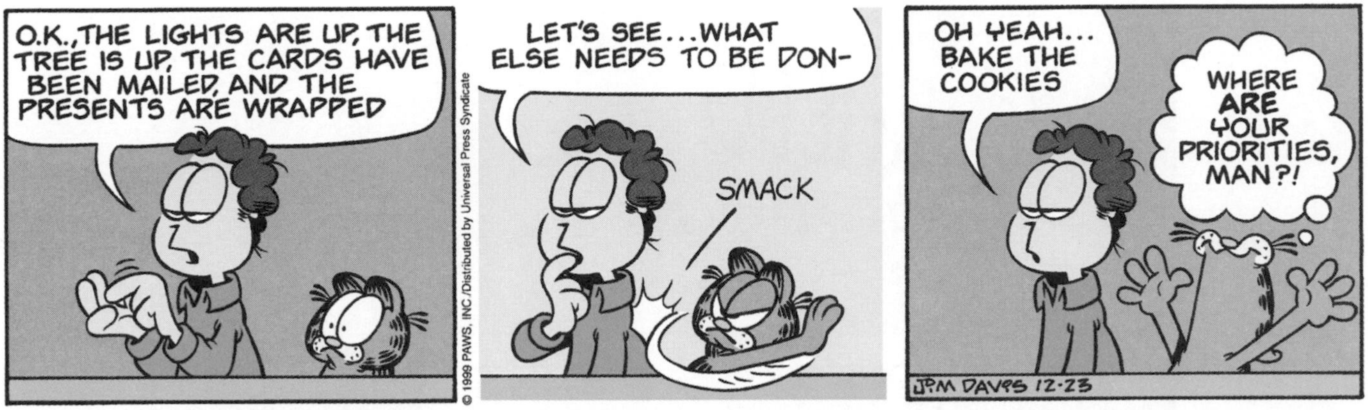
O.K., THE LIGHTS ARE UP, THE TREE IS UP, THE CARDS HAVE BEEN MAILED, AND THE PRESENTS ARE WRAPPED
© 1999 PAWS, INC./Distributed by Universal Press Syndicate
LET'S SEE...WHAT ELSE NEEDS TO BE DON-
SMACK
OH YEAH... BAKE THE COOKIES
WHERE **ARE** YOUR PRIORITIES, MAN?!
JIM DAVIS 12·23

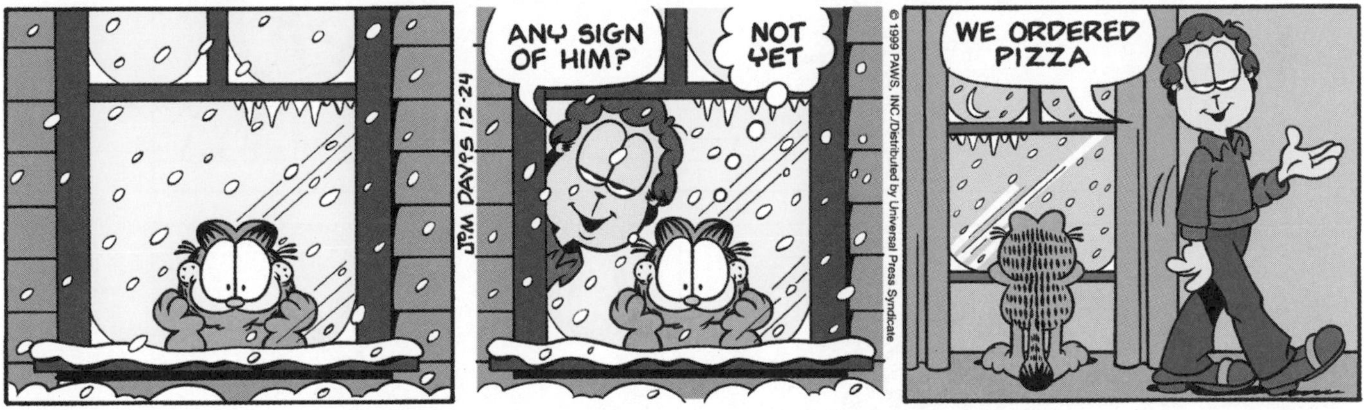
JIM DAVIS 12·24
ANY SIGN OF HIM?
NOT YET
© 1999 PAWS, INC./Distributed by Universal Press Syndicate
WE ORDERED PIZZA

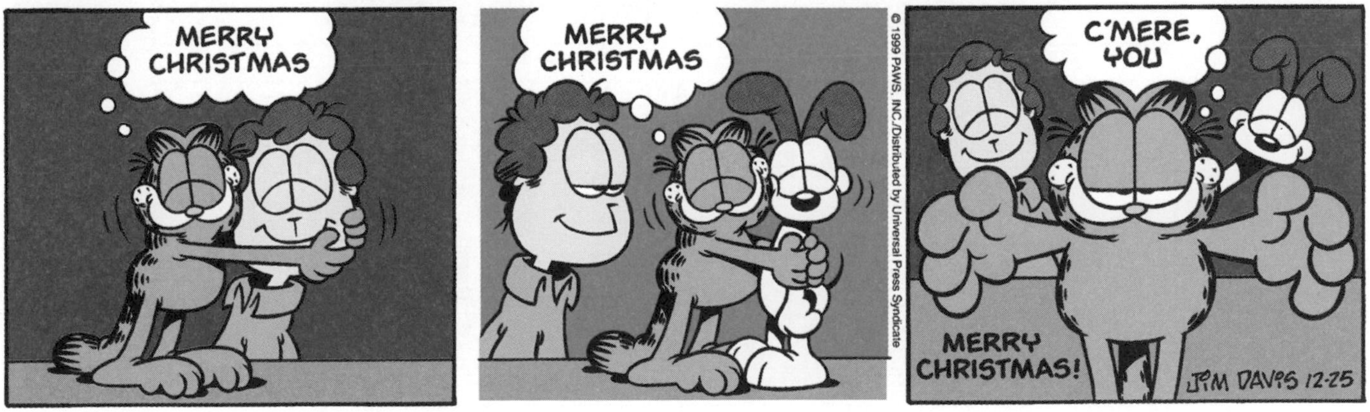
MERRY CHRISTMAS
MERRY CHRISTMAS
© 1999 PAWS, INC./Distributed by Universal Press Syndicate
C'MERE, YOU
MERRY CHRISTMAS!
JIM DAVIS 12·25

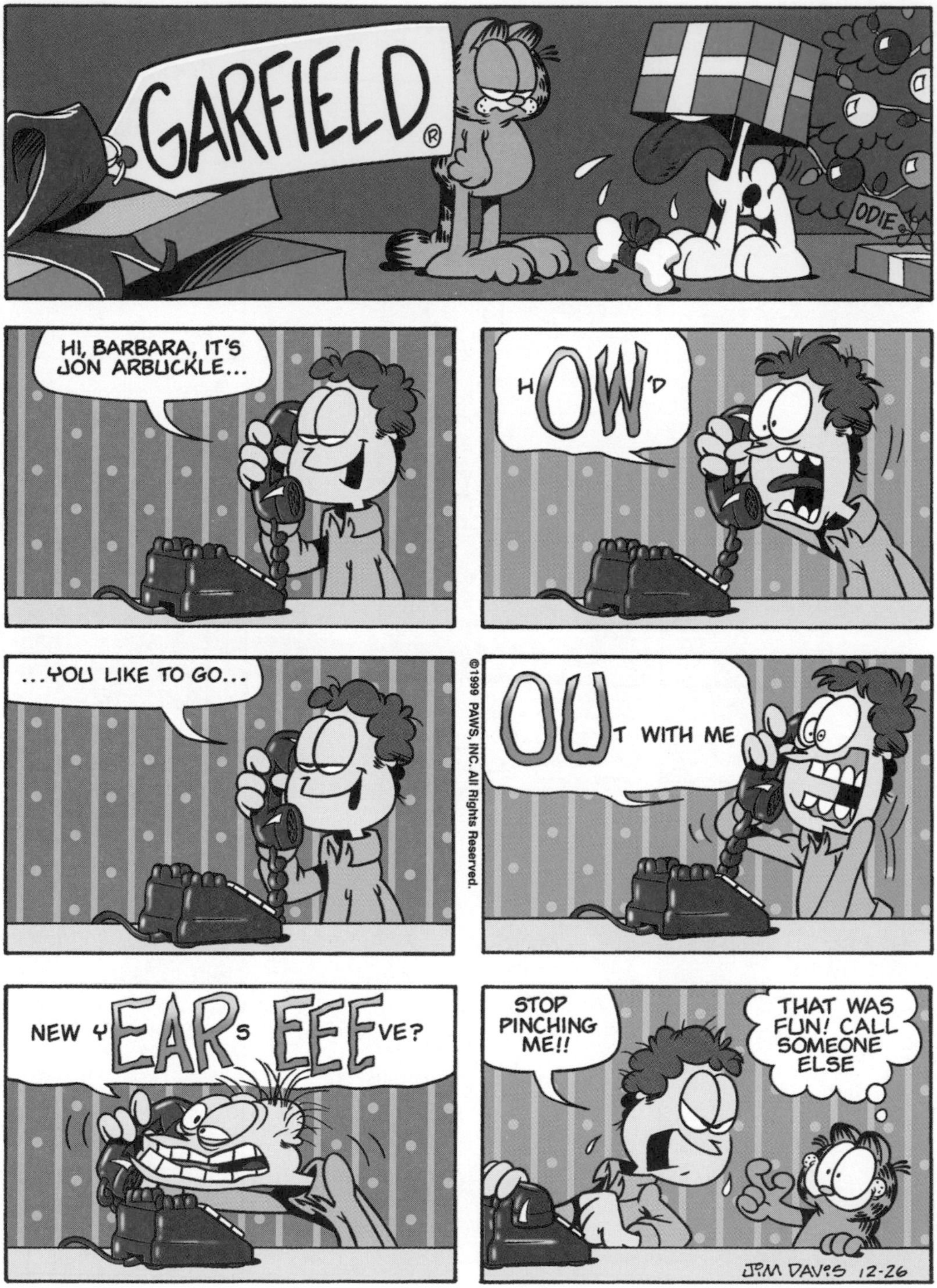
GARFIELD®
ODIE
HI, BARBARA, IT'S JON ARBUCKLE...
HOW'D
...YOU LIKE TO GO...
OUT WITH ME
NEW YEARS EEEVE?
STOP PINCHING ME!!
THAT WAS FUN! CALL SOMEONE ELSE
JIM DAVIS 12-26

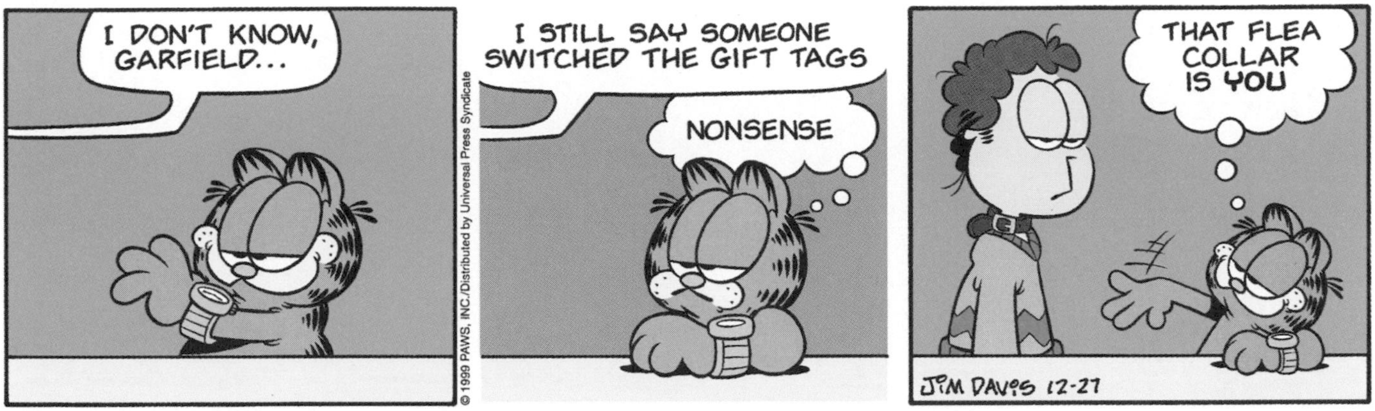
I DON'T KNOW, GARFIELD...
I STILL SAY SOMEONE SWITCHED THE GIFT TAGS
NONSENSE
THAT FLEA COLLAR IS **YOU**
© 1999 PAWS, INC./Distributed by Universal Press Syndicate
JIM DAVIS 12-27

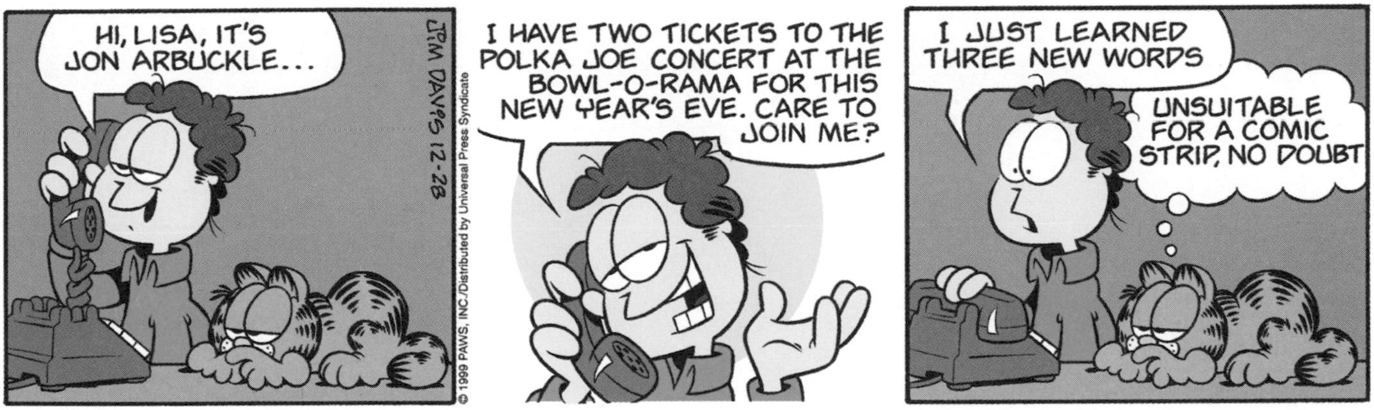
HI, LISA, IT'S JON ARBUCKLE...
I HAVE TWO TICKETS TO THE POLKA JOE CONCERT AT THE BOWL-O-RAMA FOR THIS NEW YEAR'S EVE. CARE TO JOIN ME?
I JUST LEARNED THREE NEW WORDS
UNSUITABLE FOR A COMIC STRIP, NO DOUBT
© 1999 PAWS, INC./Distributed by Universal Press Syndicate
JIM DAVIS 12-28

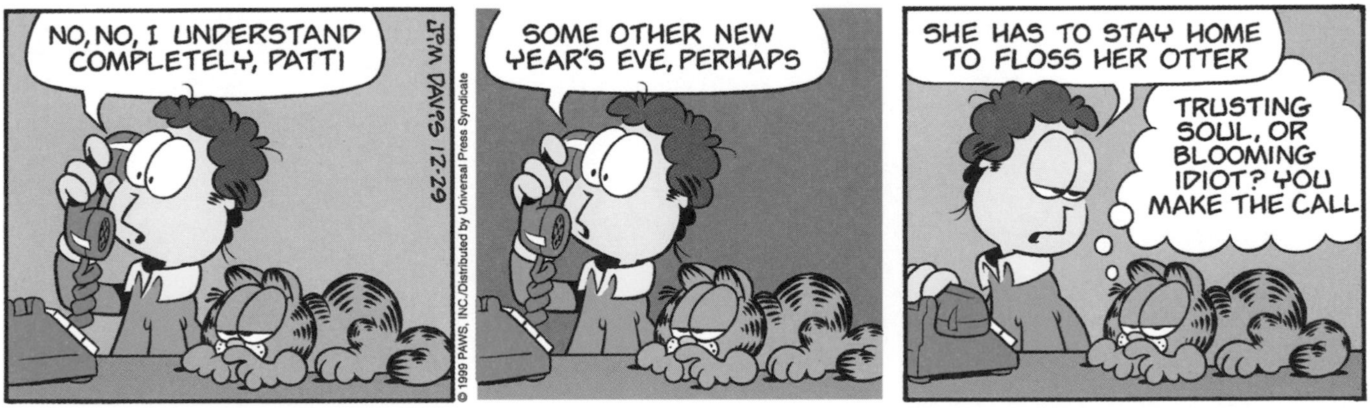
NO, NO, I UNDERSTAND COMPLETELY, PATTI
SOME OTHER NEW YEAR'S EVE, PERHAPS
SHE HAS TO STAY HOME TO FLOSS HER OTTER
TRUSTING SOUL, OR BLOOMING IDIOT? YOU MAKE THE CALL
© 1999 PAWS, INC./Distributed by Universal Press Syndicate
JIM DAVIS 12-29

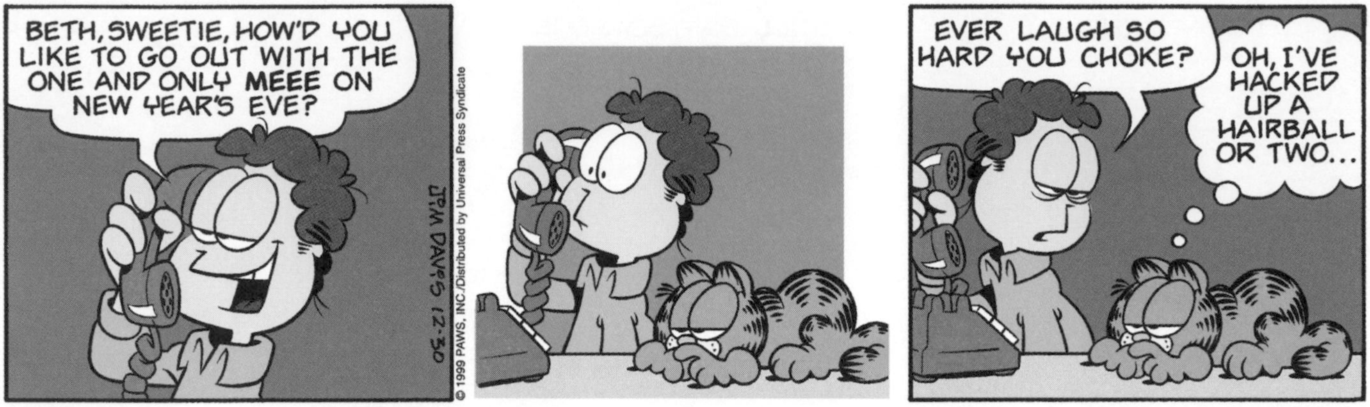
BETH, SWEETIE, HOW'D YOU LIKE TO GO OUT WITH THE ONE AND ONLY **MEEE** ON NEW YEAR'S EVE?
JIM DAVIS 12-30
© 1999 PAWS, INC./Distributed by Universal Press Syndicate
EVER LAUGH SO HARD YOU CHOKE?
OH, I'VE HACKED UP A HAIRBALL OR TWO...

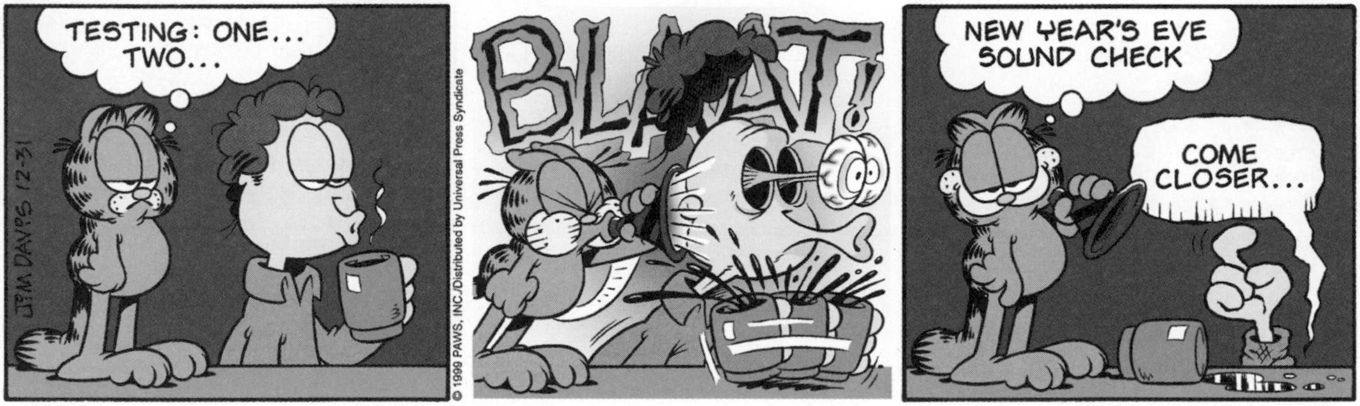
TESTING: ONE... TWO...
JIM DAVIS 12-31
© 1999 PAWS, INC./Distributed by Universal Press Syndicate
BLAAT!
NEW YEAR'S EVE SOUND CHECK
COME CLOSER...

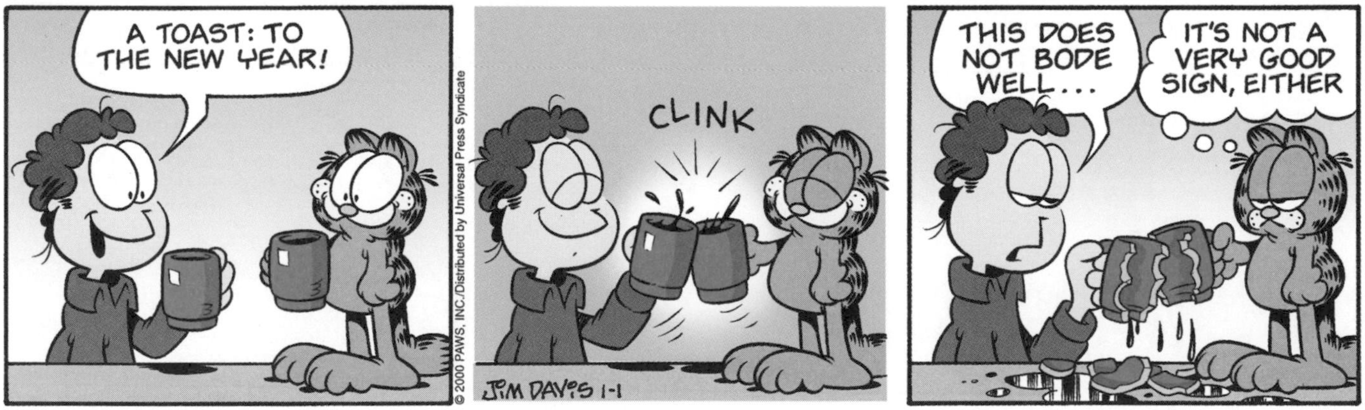
A TOAST: TO THE NEW YEAR!
© 2000 PAWS, INC./Distributed by Universal Press Syndicate
CLINK
JIM DAVIS 1-1
THIS DOES NOT BODE WELL...
IT'S NOT A VERY GOOD SIGN, EITHER

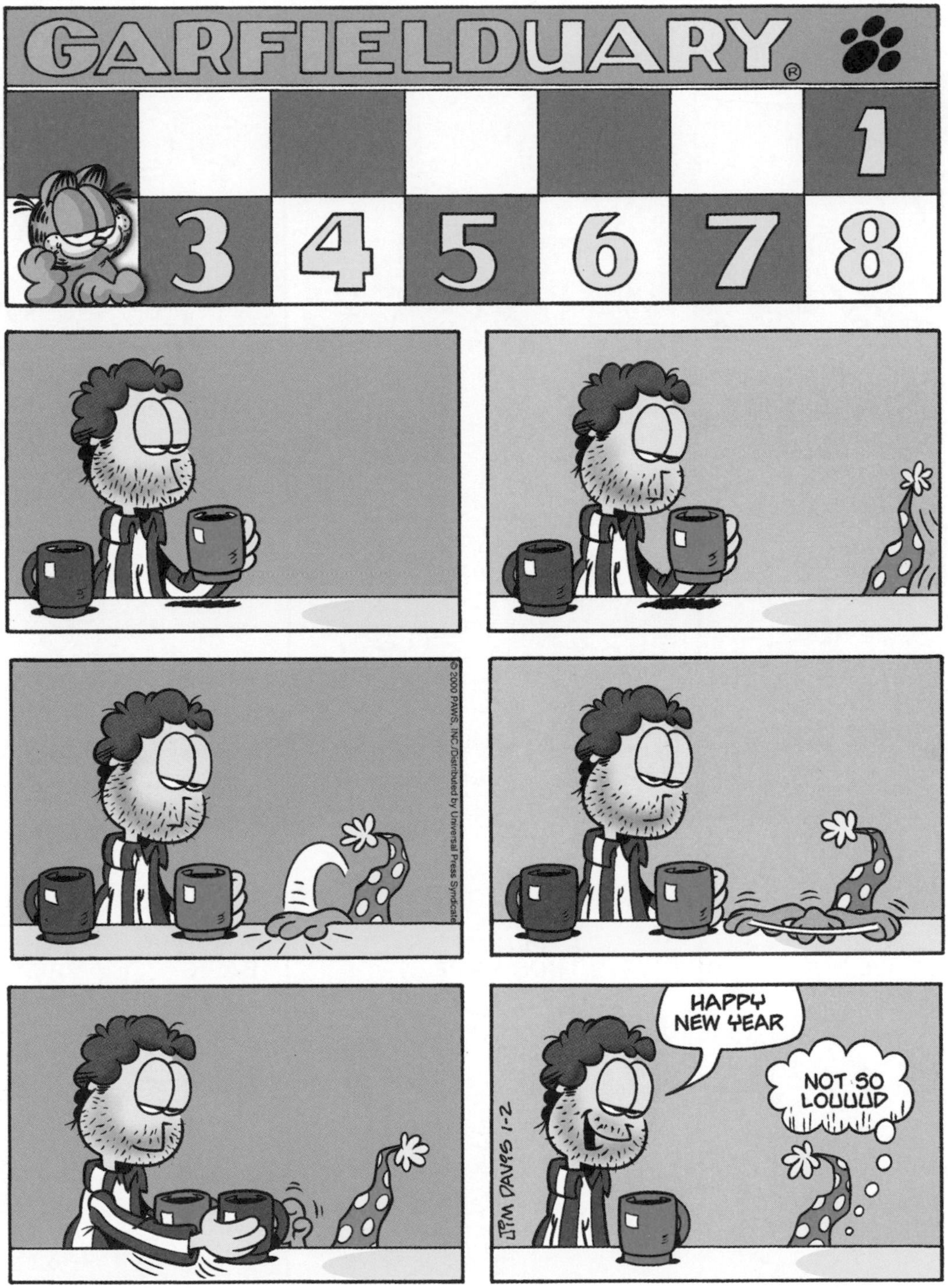
GARFIELDUARY®
1
3 4 5 6 7 8
© 2000 PAWS, INC./Distributed by Universal Press Syndicate
JIM DAVIS 1-2
HAPPY NEW YEAR
NOT SO LOUUUD

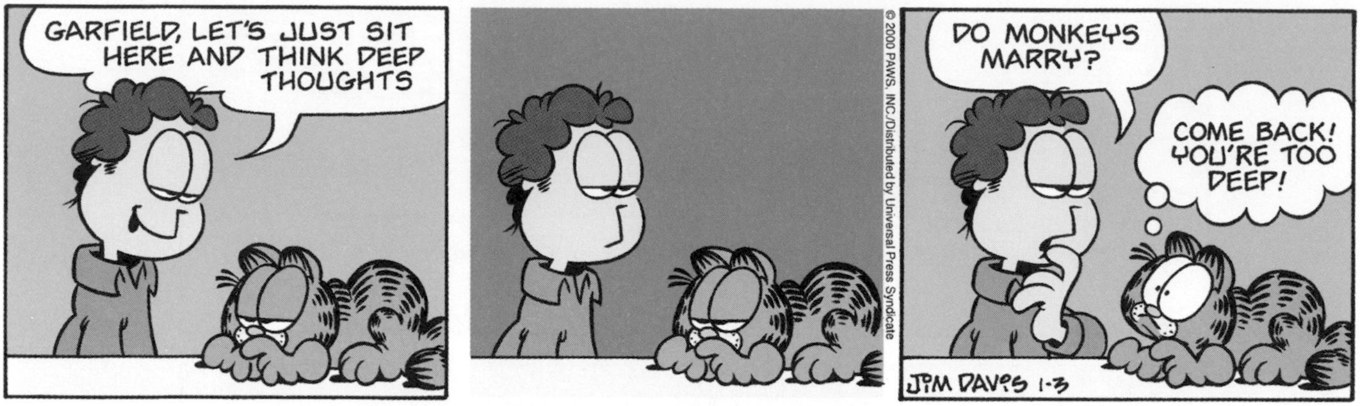
GARFIELD, LET'S JUST SIT HERE AND THINK DEEP THOUGHTS
DO MONKEYS MARRY?
COME BACK! YOU'RE TOO DEEP!
JIM DAVIS 1-3
© 2000 PAWS, INC./Distributed by Universal Press Syndicate

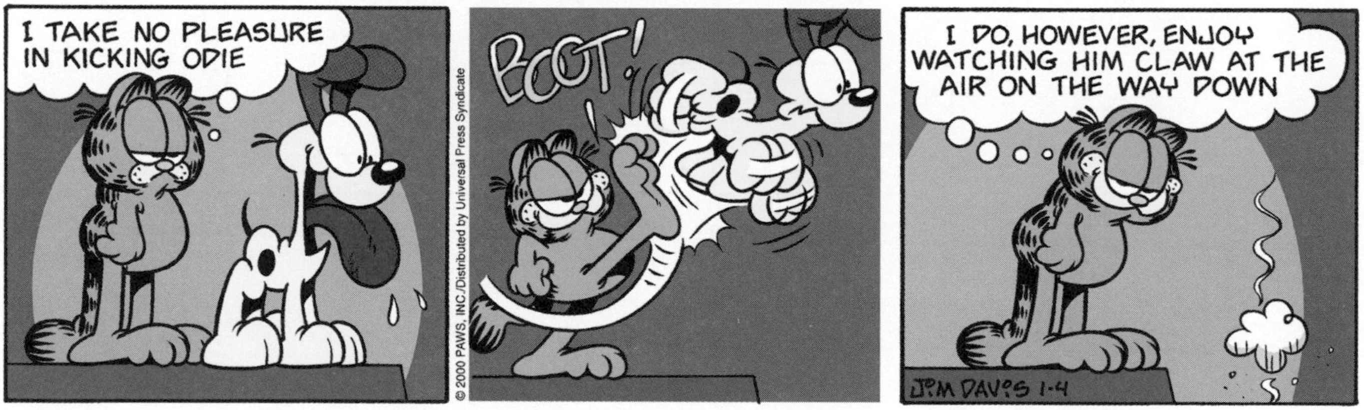
I TAKE NO PLEASURE IN KICKING ODIE
BOOT!
I DO, HOWEVER, ENJOY WATCHING HIM CLAW AT THE AIR ON THE WAY DOWN
JIM DAVIS 1-4
© 2000 PAWS, INC./Distributed by Universal Press Syndicate

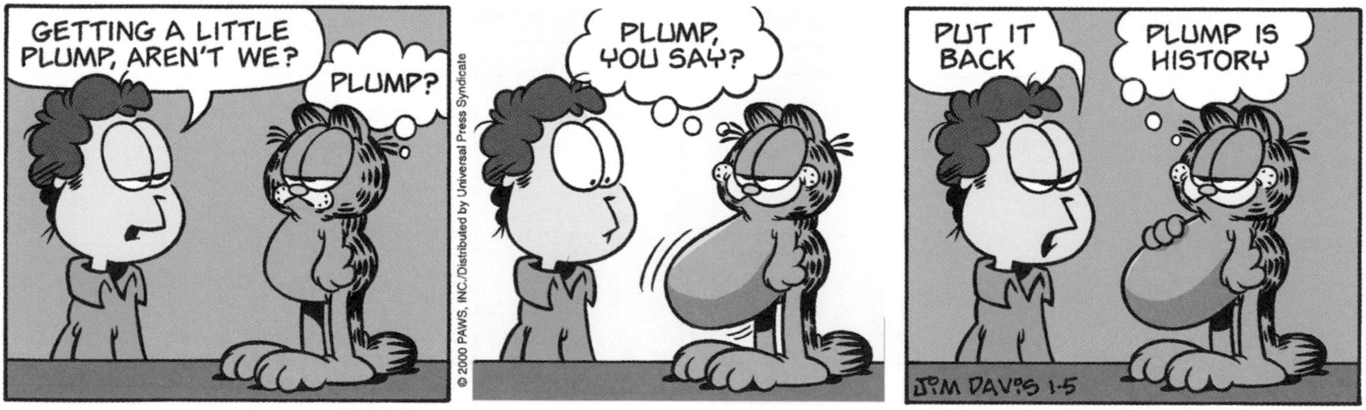
GETTING A LITTLE PLUMP, AREN'T WE?
PLUMP?
PLUMP, YOU SAY?
PUT IT BACK
PLUMP IS HISTORY
JIM DAVIS 1-5
© 2000 PAWS, INC./Distributed by Universal Press Syndicate

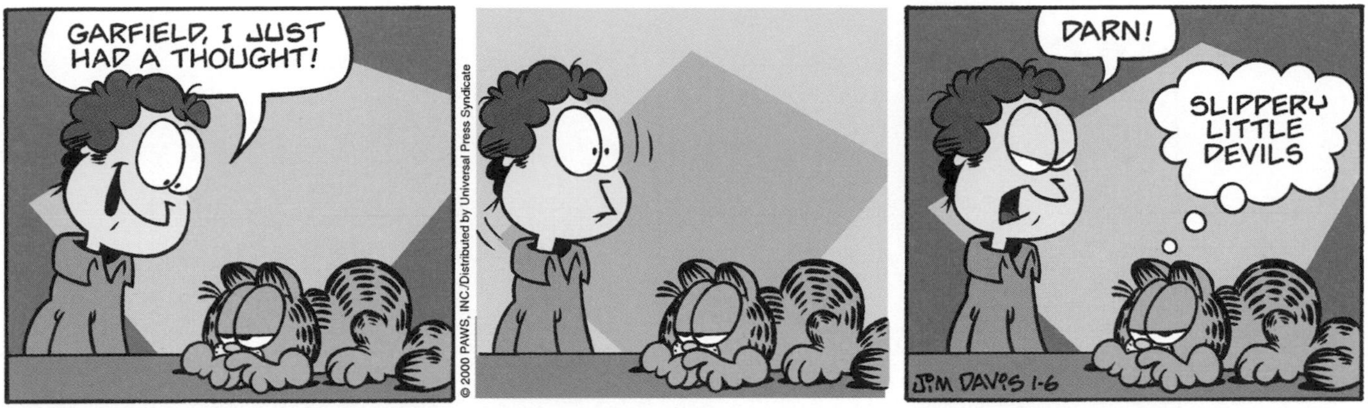
GARFIELD, I JUST HAD A THOUGHT!
© 2000 PAWS, INC./Distributed by Universal Press Syndicate
DARN!
SLIPPERY LITTLE DEVILS
JIM DAVIS 1-6

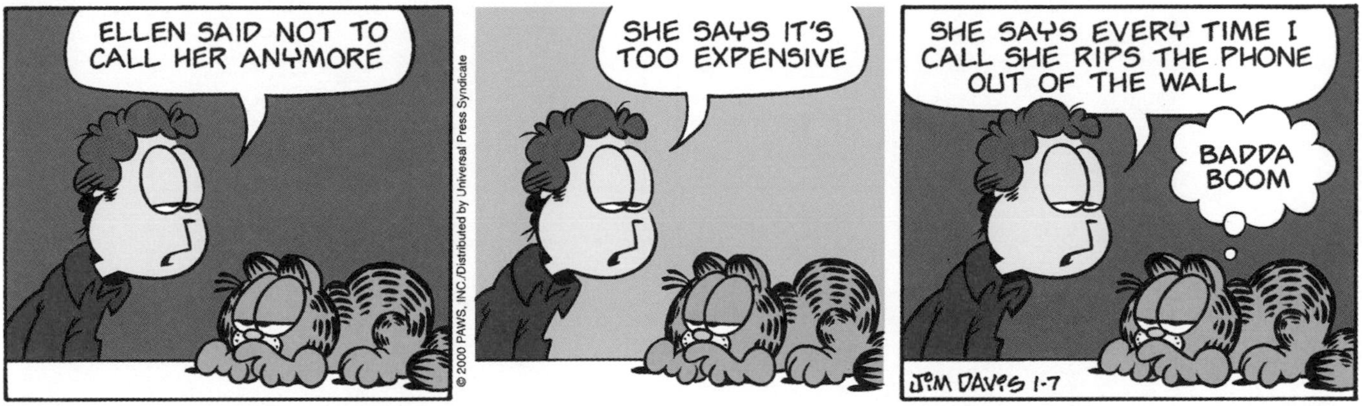
ELLEN SAID NOT TO CALL HER ANYMORE
© 2000 PAWS, INC./Distributed by Universal Press Syndicate
SHE SAYS IT'S TOO EXPENSIVE
SHE SAYS EVERY TIME I CALL SHE RIPS THE PHONE OUT OF THE WALL
BADDA BOOM
JIM DAVIS 1-7

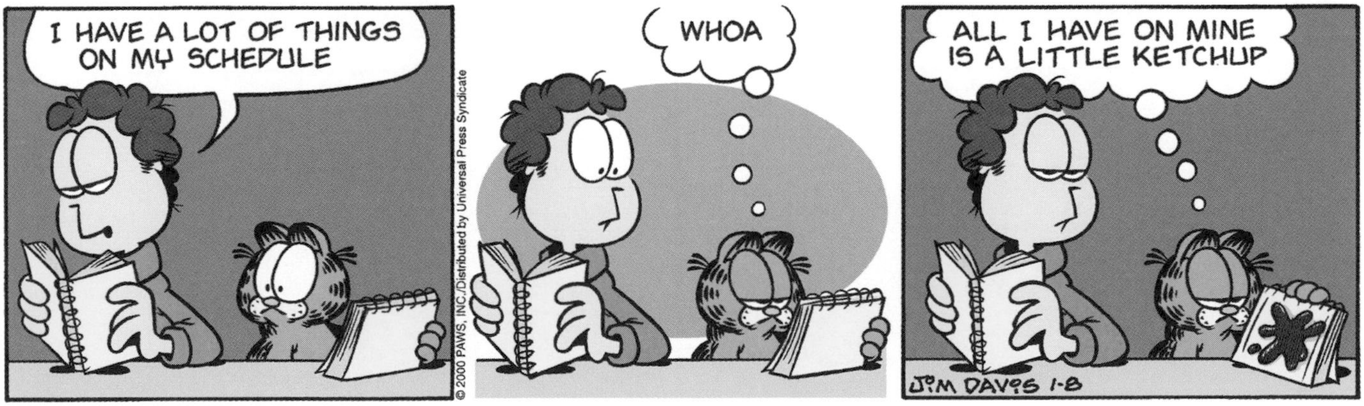
I HAVE A LOT OF THINGS ON MY SCHEDULE
© 2000 PAWS, INC./Distributed by Universal Press Syndicate
WHOA
ALL I HAVE ON MINE IS A LITTLE KETCHUP
JIM DAVIS 1-8

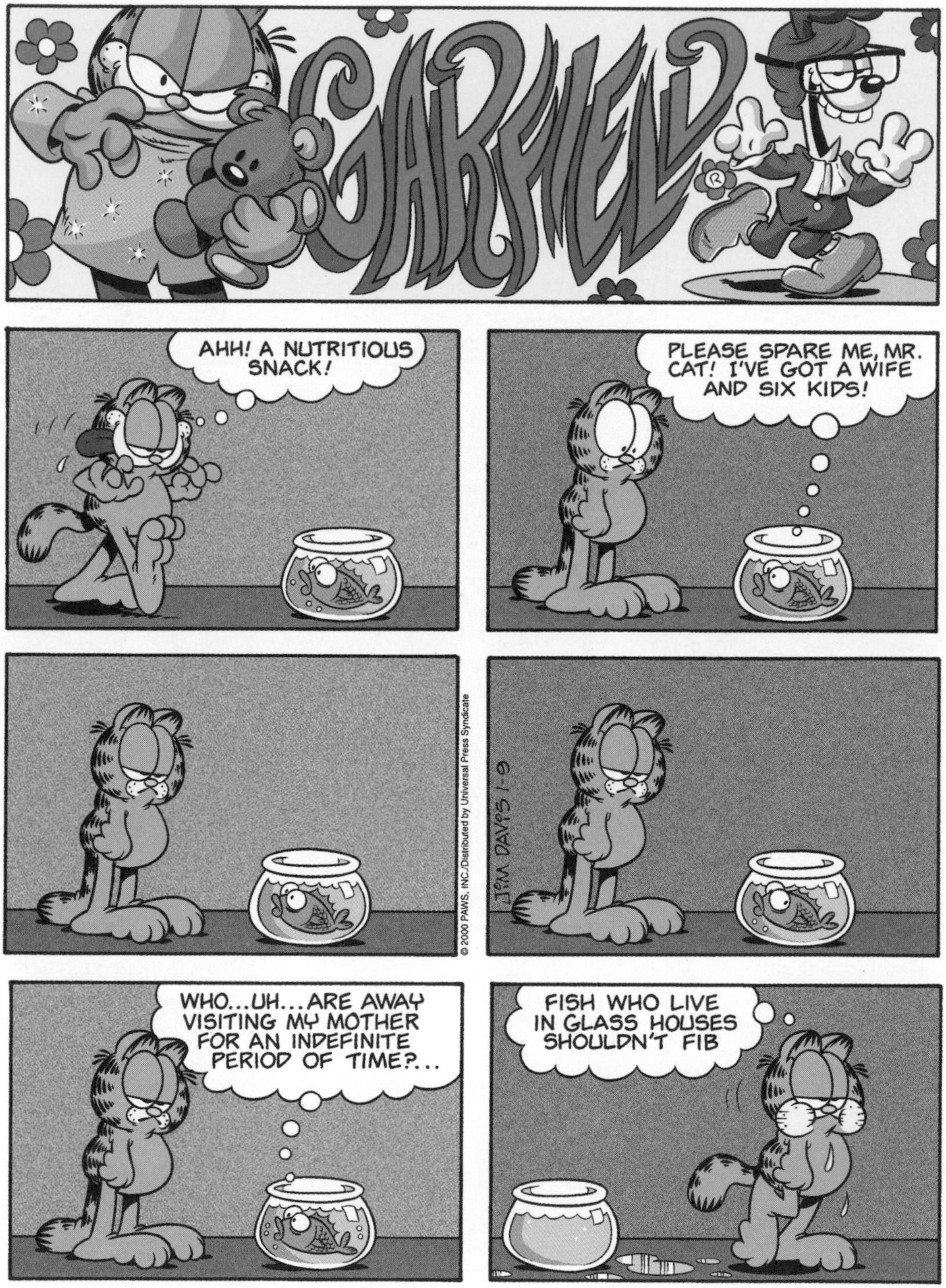
GARFIELD
AHH! A NUTRITIOUS SNACK!
PLEASE SPARE ME, MR. CAT! I'VE GOT A WIFE AND SIX KIDS!
© 2000 PAWS, INC./Distributed by Universal Press Syndicate
JIM DAVIS 1-9
WHO...UH...ARE AWAY VISITING MY MOTHER FOR AN INDEFINITE PERIOD OF TIME?...
FISH WHO LIVE IN GLASS HOUSES SHOULDN'T FIB

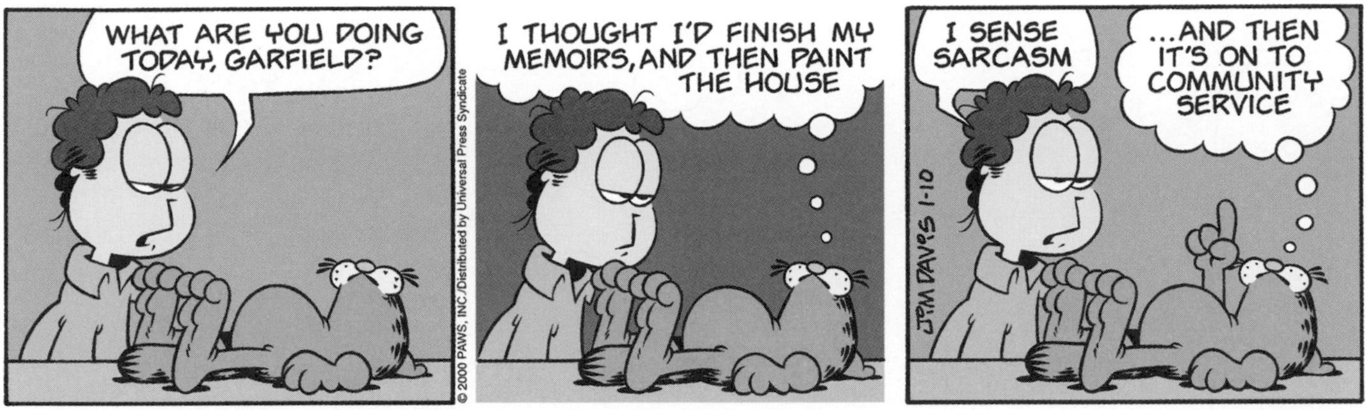
WHAT ARE YOU DOING TODAY, GARFIELD?
I THOUGHT I'D FINISH MY MEMOIRS, AND THEN PAINT THE HOUSE
I SENSE SARCASM
...AND THEN IT'S ON TO COMMUNITY SERVICE
JIM DAVIS 1-10
© 2000 PAWS, INC./Distributed by Universal Press Syndicate

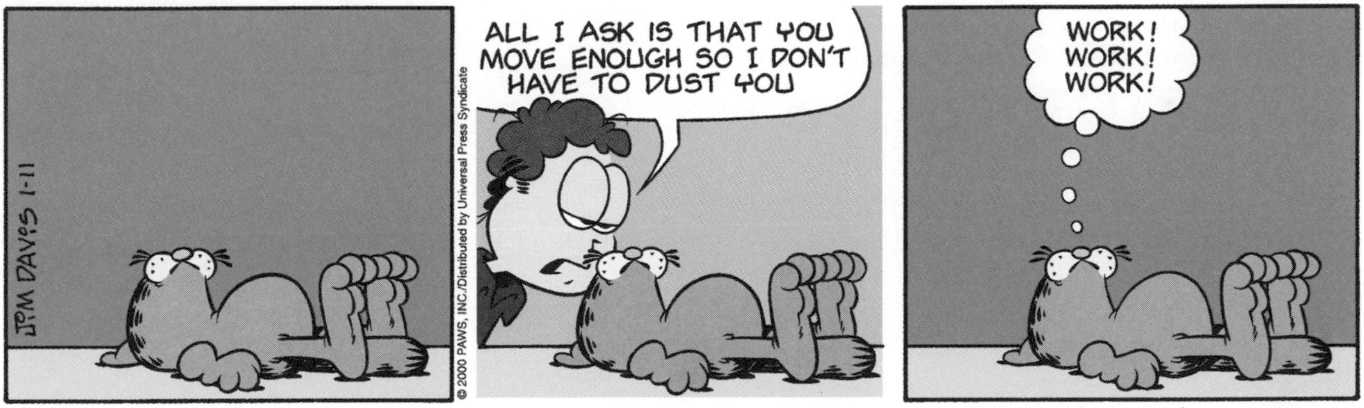
JIM DAVIS 1-11
ALL I ASK IS THAT YOU MOVE ENOUGH SO I DON'T HAVE TO DUST YOU
WORK! WORK! WORK!
© 2000 PAWS, INC./Distributed by Universal Press Syndicate

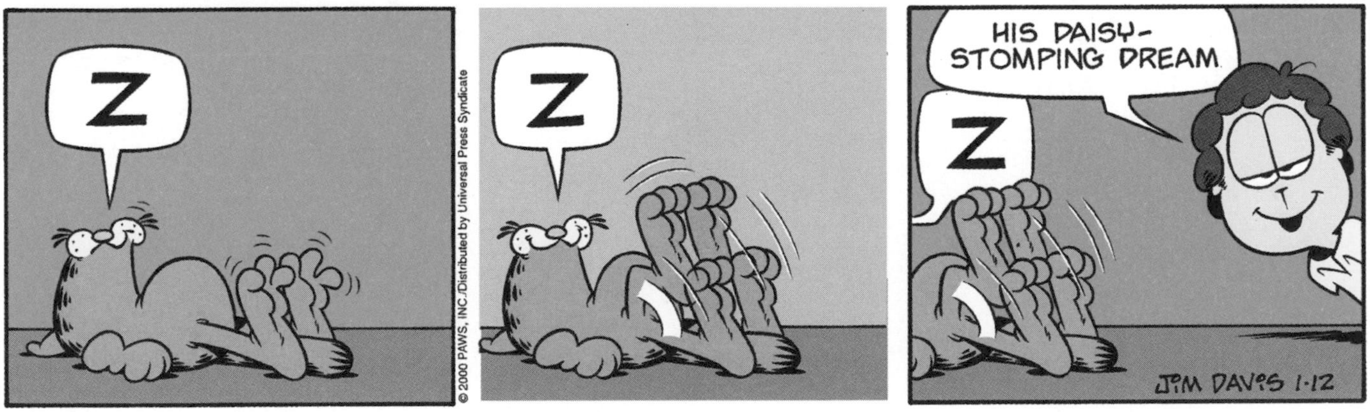
Z
Z
Z
HIS DAISY-STOMPING DREAM
JIM DAVIS 1-12
© 2000 PAWS, INC./Distributed by Universal Press Syndicate

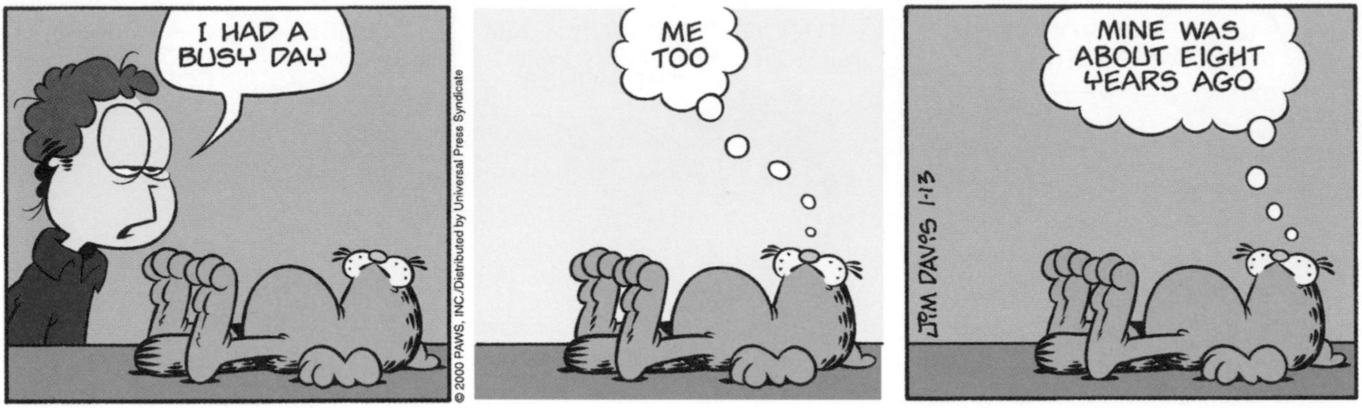
I HAD A BUSY DAY
ME TOO
MINE WAS ABOUT EIGHT YEARS AGO
JIM DAVIS 1-13
© 2000 PAWS, INC./Distributed by Universal Press Syndicate

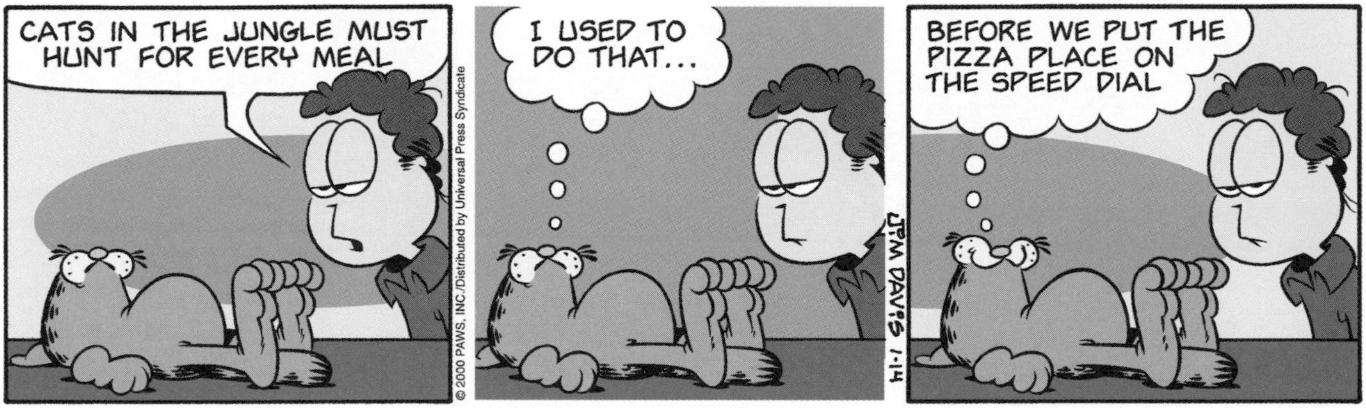
CATS IN THE JUNGLE MUST HUNT FOR EVERY MEAL
I USED TO DO THAT...
BEFORE WE PUT THE PIZZA PLACE ON THE SPEED DIAL
JIM DAVIS 1-14
© 2000 PAWS, INC./Distributed by Universal Press Syndicate

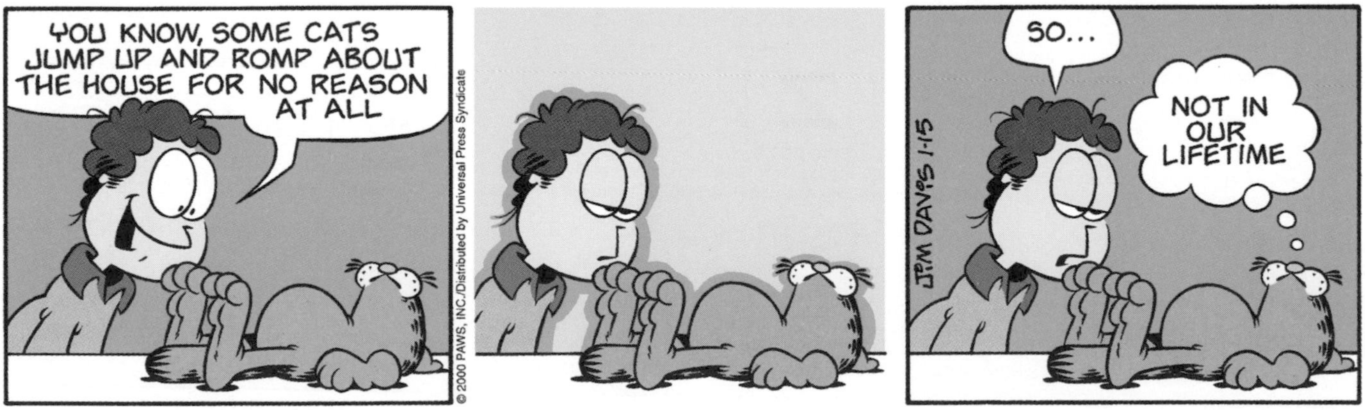
YOU KNOW, SOME CATS JUMP UP AND ROMP ABOUT THE HOUSE FOR NO REASON AT ALL
SO...
NOT IN OUR LIFETIME
JIM DAVIS 1-15
© 2000 PAWS, INC./Distributed by Universal Press Syndicate

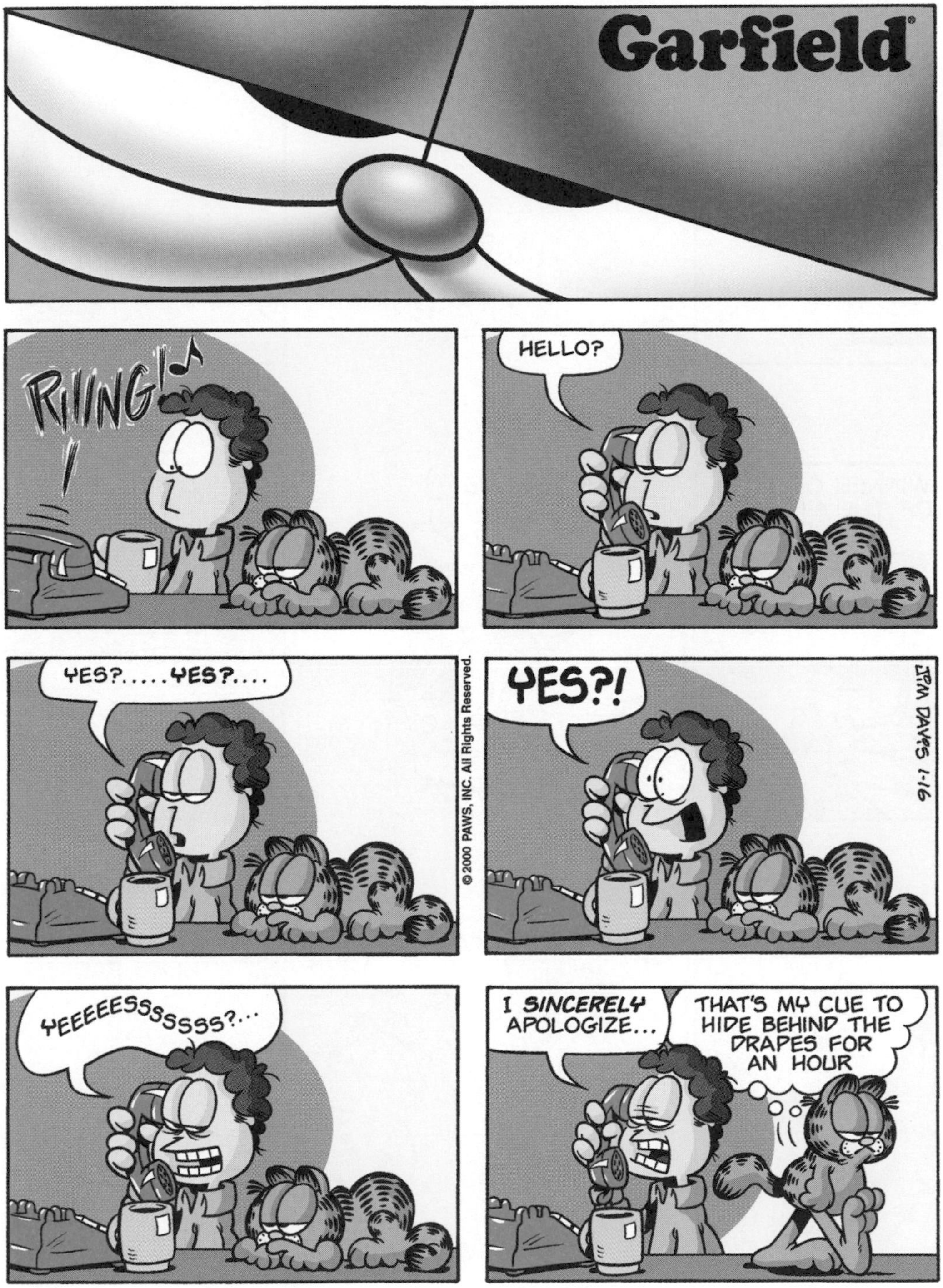
Garfield
RIIING!
HELLO?
YES?.....YES?....
YES?!
JIM DAVIS 1-16
YEEEEESSSSSSS?...
I SINCERELY APOLOGIZE...
THAT'S MY CUE TO HIDE BEHIND THE DRAPES FOR AN HOUR

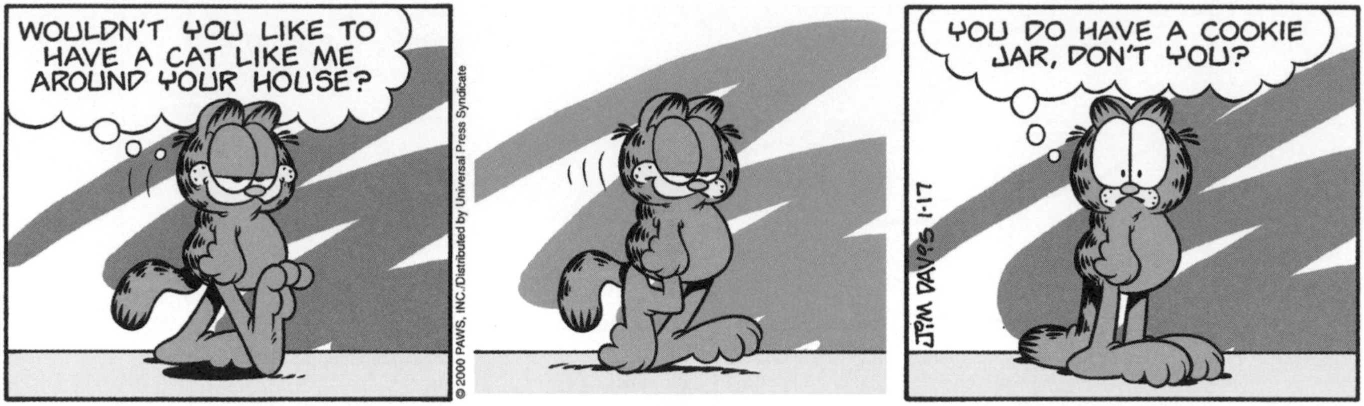
WOULDN'T YOU LIKE TO HAVE A CAT LIKE ME AROUND YOUR HOUSE?
© 2000 PAWS, INC./Distributed by Universal Press Syndicate
JIM DAVIS 1-17
YOU DO HAVE A COOKIE JAR, DON'T YOU?

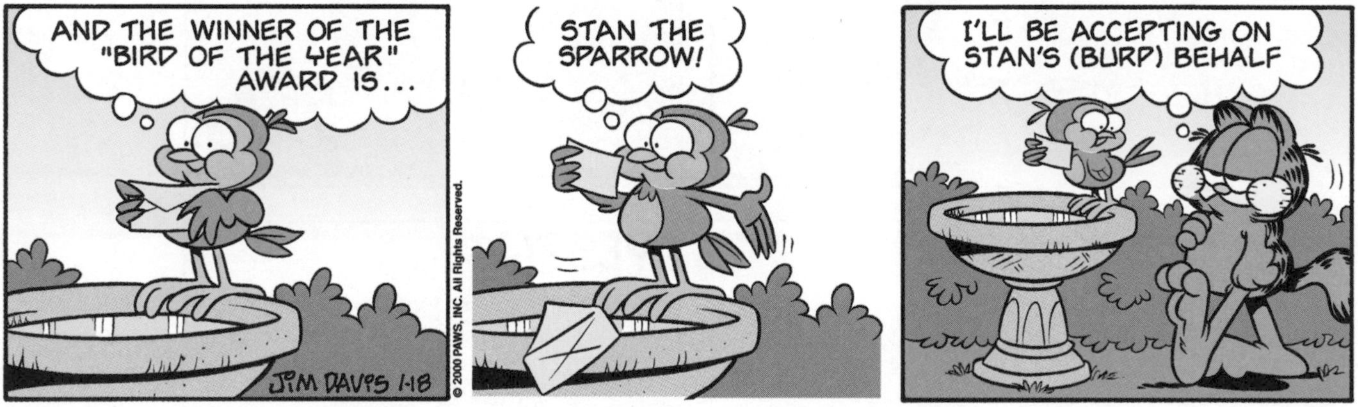
AND THE WINNER OF THE "BIRD OF THE YEAR" AWARD IS...
JIM DAVIS 1-18
© 2000 PAWS, INC. All Rights Reserved.
STAN THE SPARROW!
I'LL BE ACCEPTING ON STAN'S (BURP) BEHALF

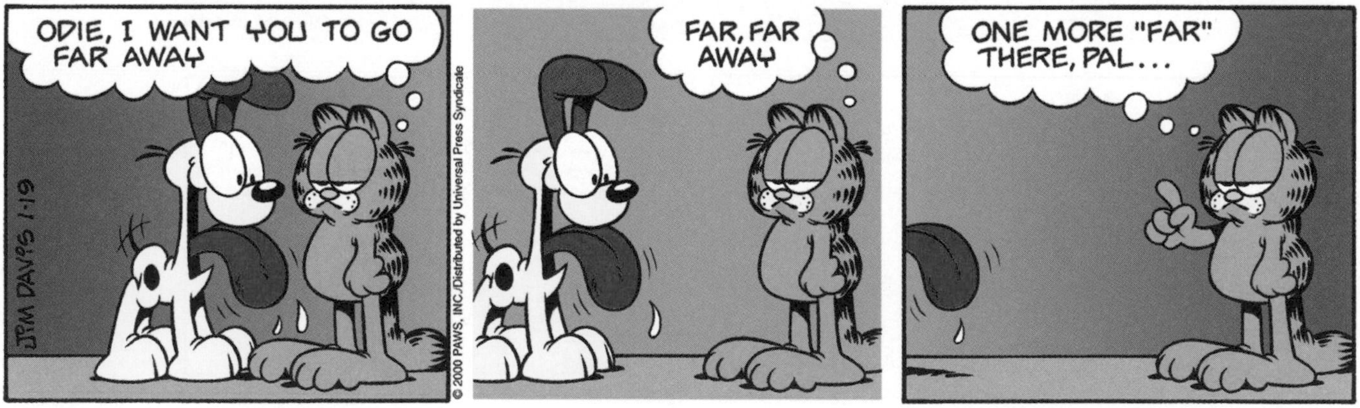
ODIE, I WANT YOU TO GO FAR AWAY
JIM DAVIS 1-19
© 2000 PAWS, INC./Distributed by Universal Press Syndicate
FAR, FAR AWAY
ONE MORE "FAR" THERE, PAL...

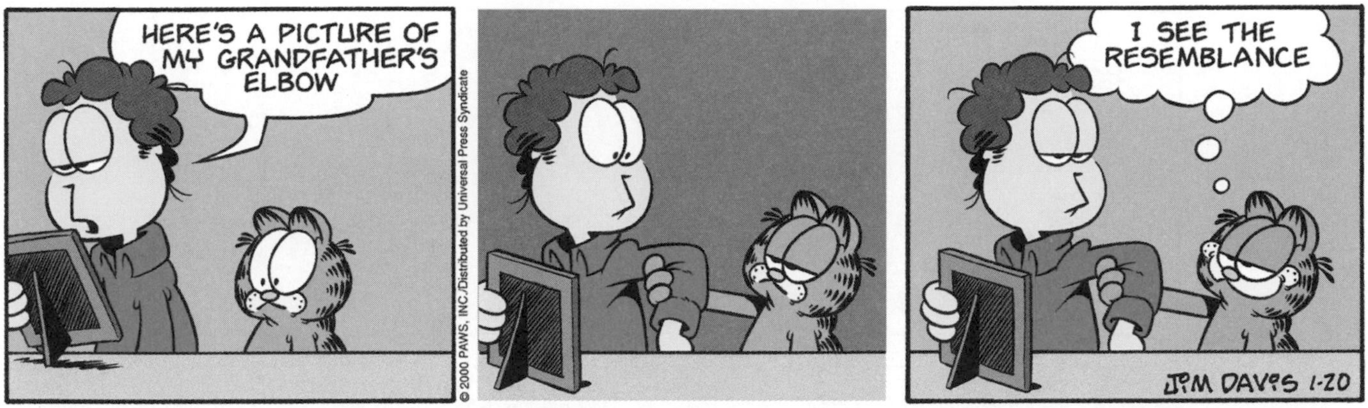
HERE'S A PICTURE OF MY GRANDFATHER'S ELBOW
© 2000 PAWS, INC./Distributed by Universal Press Syndicate
I SEE THE RESEMBLANCE
JIM DAVIS 1-20

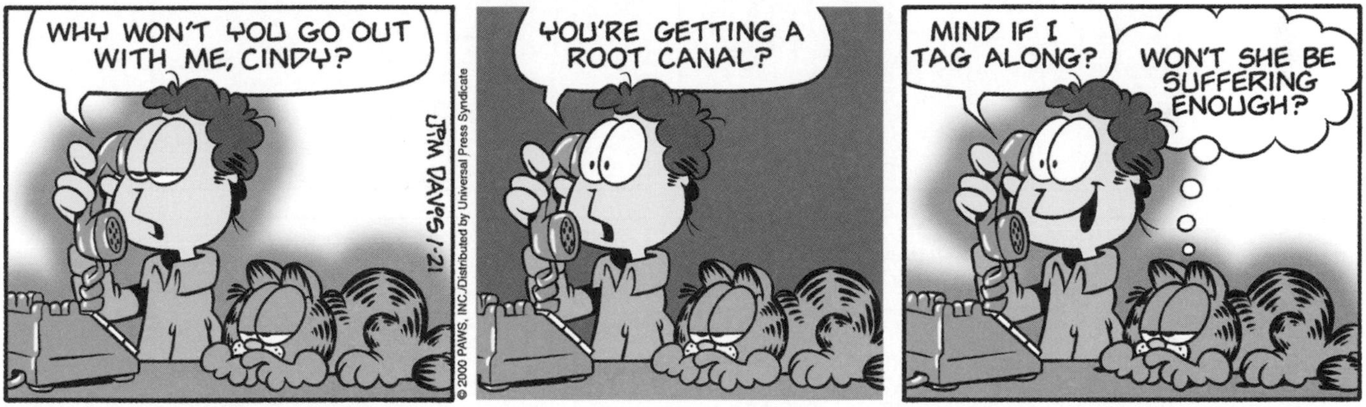
WHY WON'T YOU GO OUT WITH ME, CINDY?
JIM DAVIS 1-21
© 2000 PAWS, INC./Distributed by Universal Press Syndicate
YOU'RE GETTING A ROOT CANAL?
MIND IF I TAG ALONG?
WON'T SHE BE SUFFERING ENOUGH?

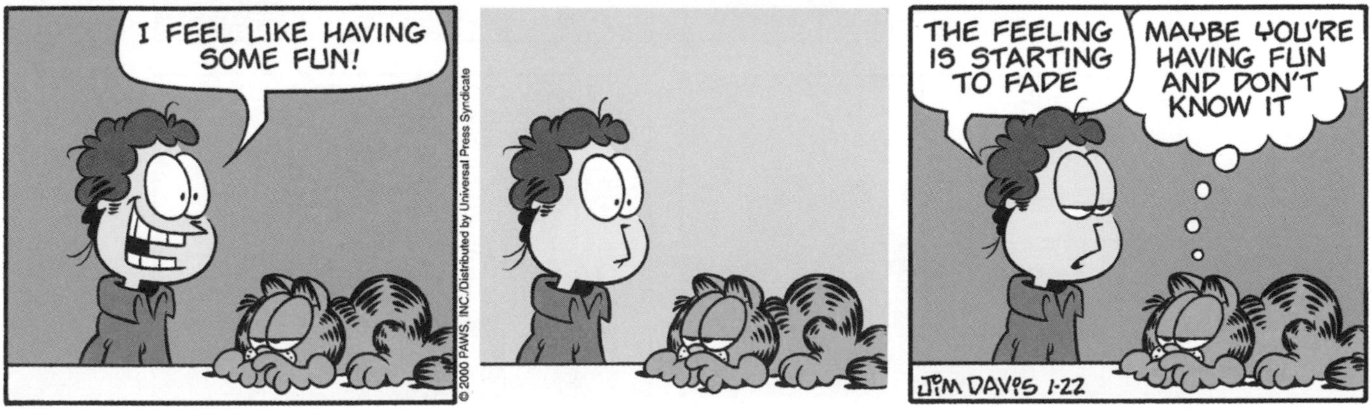
I FEEL LIKE HAVING SOME FUN!
© 2000 PAWS, INC./Distributed by Universal Press Syndicate
THE FEELING IS STARTING TO FADE
MAYBE YOU'RE HAVING FUN AND DON'T KNOW IT
JIM DAVIS 1-22

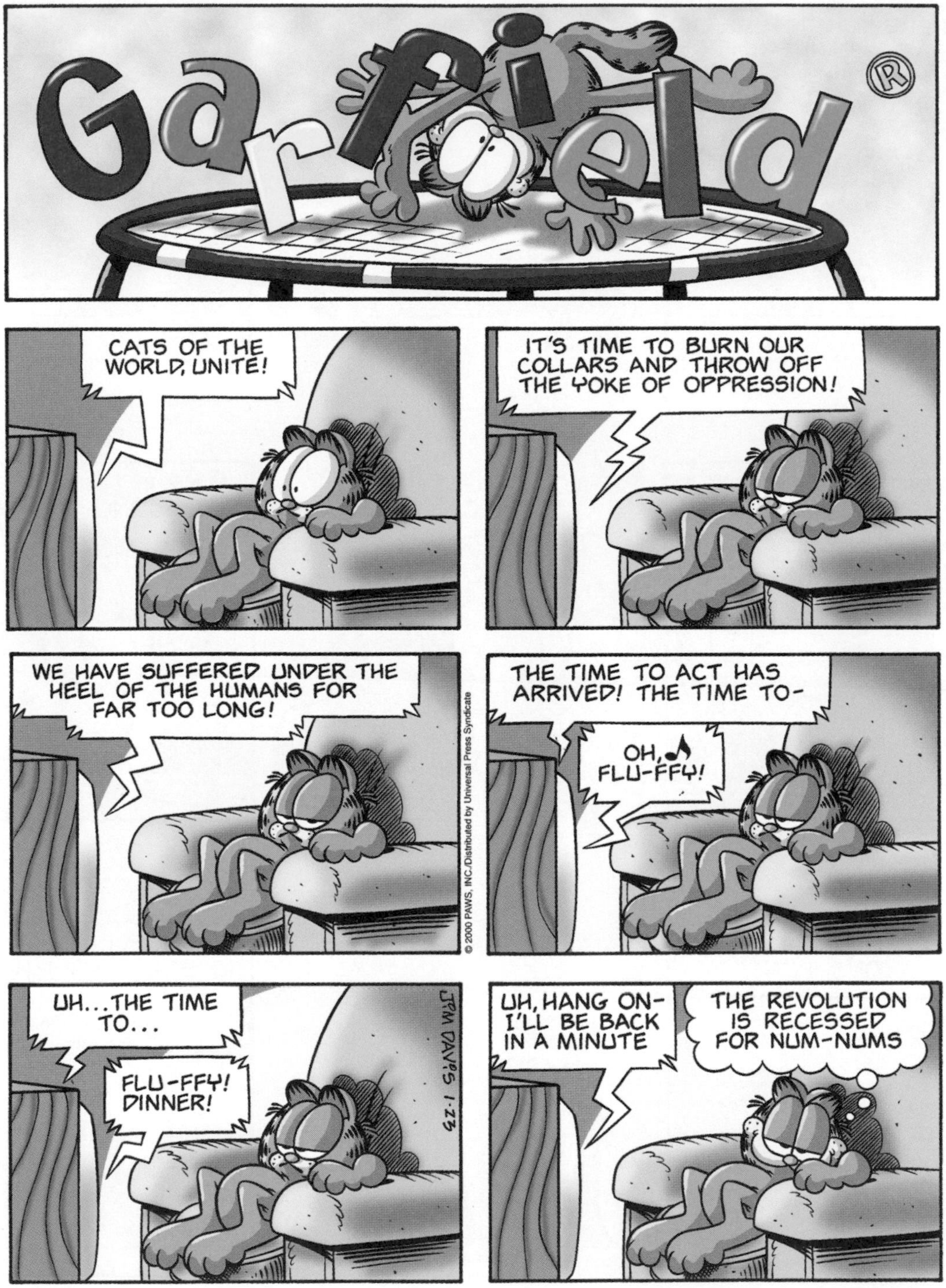
Garfield®
CATS OF THE WORLD, UNITE!
IT'S TIME TO BURN OUR COLLARS AND THROW OFF THE YOKE OF OPPRESSION!
WE HAVE SUFFERED UNDER THE HEEL OF THE HUMANS FOR FAR TOO LONG!
THE TIME TO ACT HAS ARRIVED! THE TIME TO-
OH, ♪ FLU-FFY!
UH... THE TIME TO...
FLU-FFY! DINNER!
UH, HANG ON- I'LL BE BACK IN A MINUTE
THE REVOLUTION IS RECESSED FOR NUM-NUMS
JPM DAVPS 1-23
© 2000 PAWS, INC./Distributed by Universal Press Syndicate

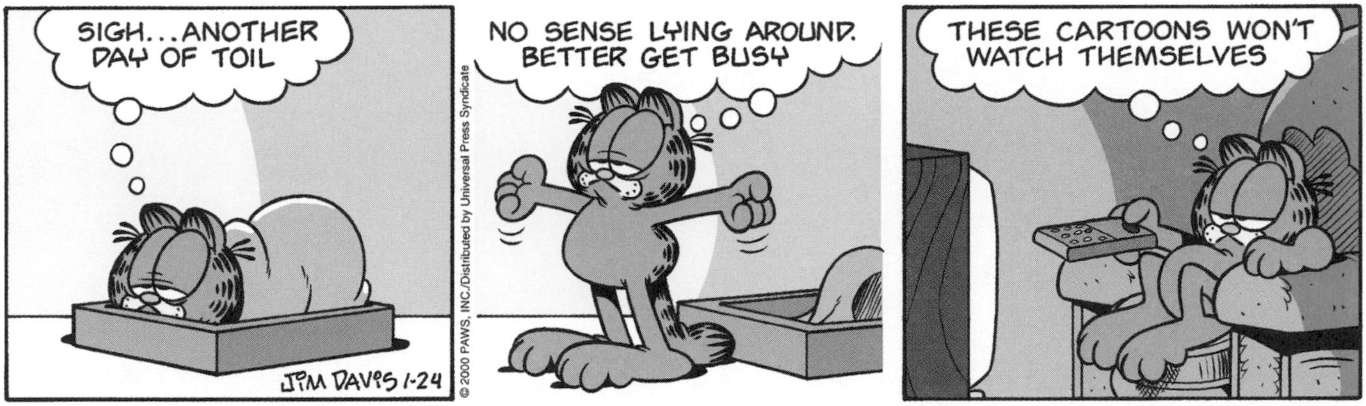
SIGH...ANOTHER DAY OF TOIL
JIM DAVIS 1-24
NO SENSE LYING AROUND. BETTER GET BUSY
THESE CARTOONS WON'T WATCH THEMSELVES

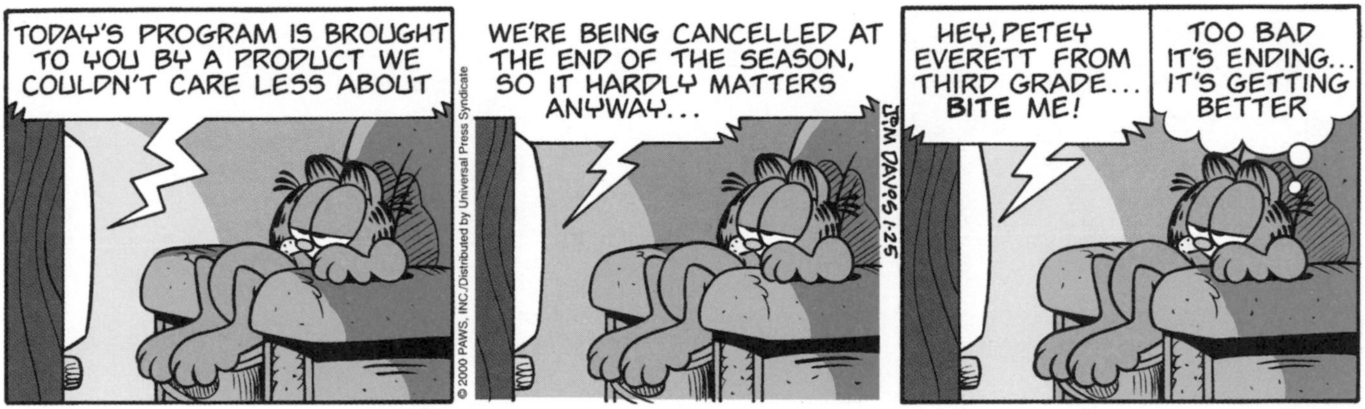
TODAY'S PROGRAM IS BROUGHT TO YOU BY A PRODUCT WE COULDN'T CARE LESS ABOUT
WE'RE BEING CANCELLED AT THE END OF THE SEASON, SO IT HARDLY MATTERS ANYWAY...
JIM DAVIS 1-25
HEY, PETEY EVERETT FROM THIRD GRADE... **BITE ME!**
TOO BAD IT'S ENDING... IT'S GETTING BETTER

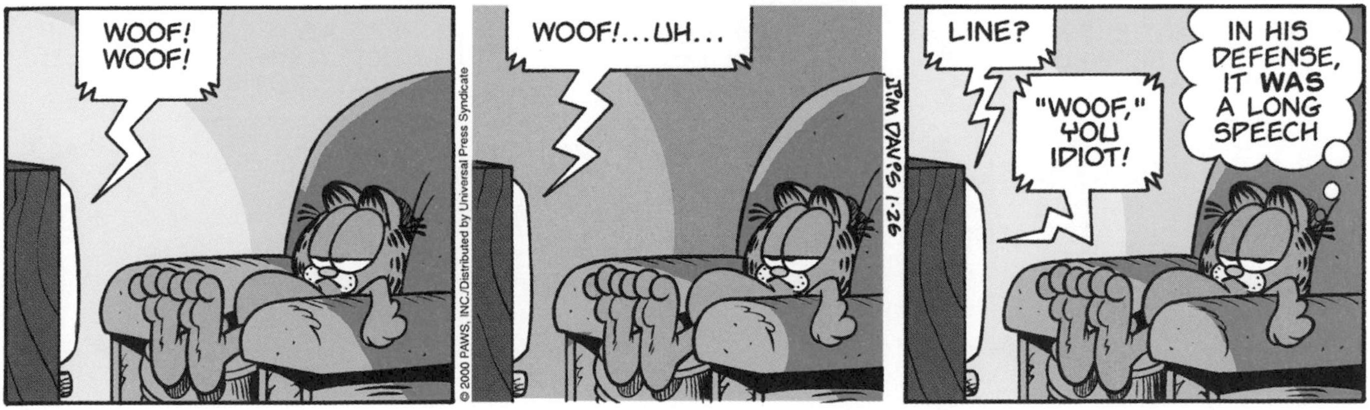
WOOF! WOOF!
WOOF!...UH...
JIM DAVIS 1-26
LINE?
"WOOF," YOU IDIOT!
IN HIS DEFENSE, IT **WAS** A LONG SPEECH

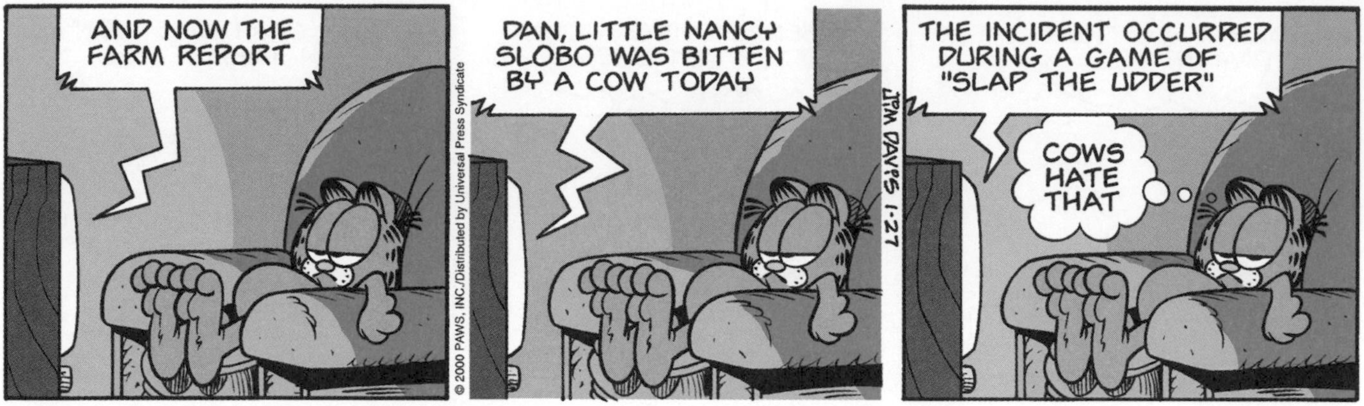
AND NOW THE FARM REPORT
DAN, LITTLE NANCY SLOBO WAS BITTEN BY A COW TODAY
THE INCIDENT OCCURRED DURING A GAME OF "SLAP THE UDDER"
COWS HATE THAT
© 2000 PAWS, INC./Distributed by Universal Press Syndicate
JIM DAVIS 1-27

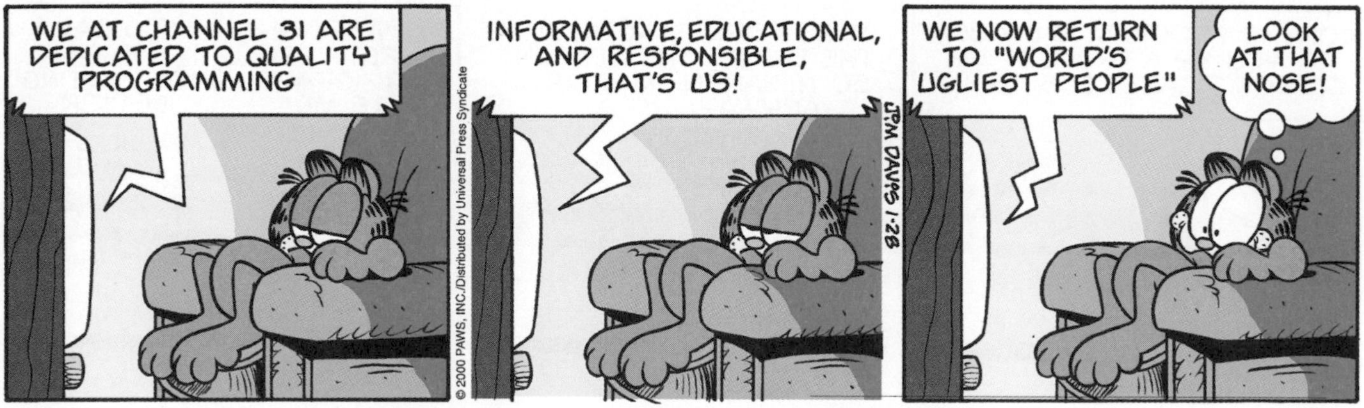
WE AT CHANNEL 31 ARE DEDICATED TO QUALITY PROGRAMMING
INFORMATIVE, EDUCATIONAL, AND RESPONSIBLE, THAT'S US!
WE NOW RETURN TO "WORLD'S UGLIEST PEOPLE"
LOOK AT THAT NOSE!
© 2000 PAWS, INC./Distributed by Universal Press Syndicate
JIM DAVIS 1-28

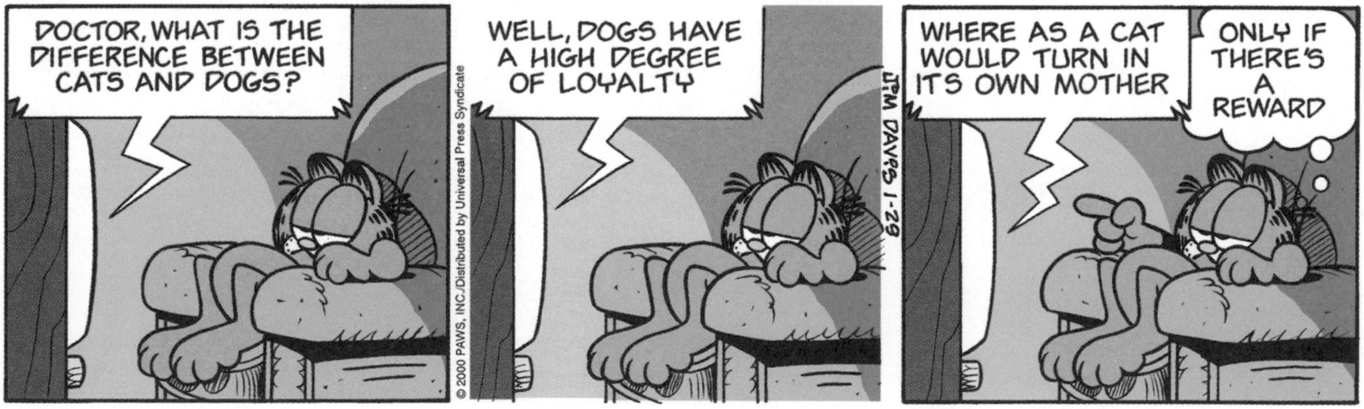
DOCTOR, WHAT IS THE DIFFERENCE BETWEEN CATS AND DOGS?
WELL, DOGS HAVE A HIGH DEGREE OF LOYALTY
WHERE AS A CAT WOULD TURN IN ITS OWN MOTHER
ONLY IF THERE'S A REWARD
© 2000 PAWS, INC./Distributed by Universal Press Syndicate
JIM DAVIS 1-29

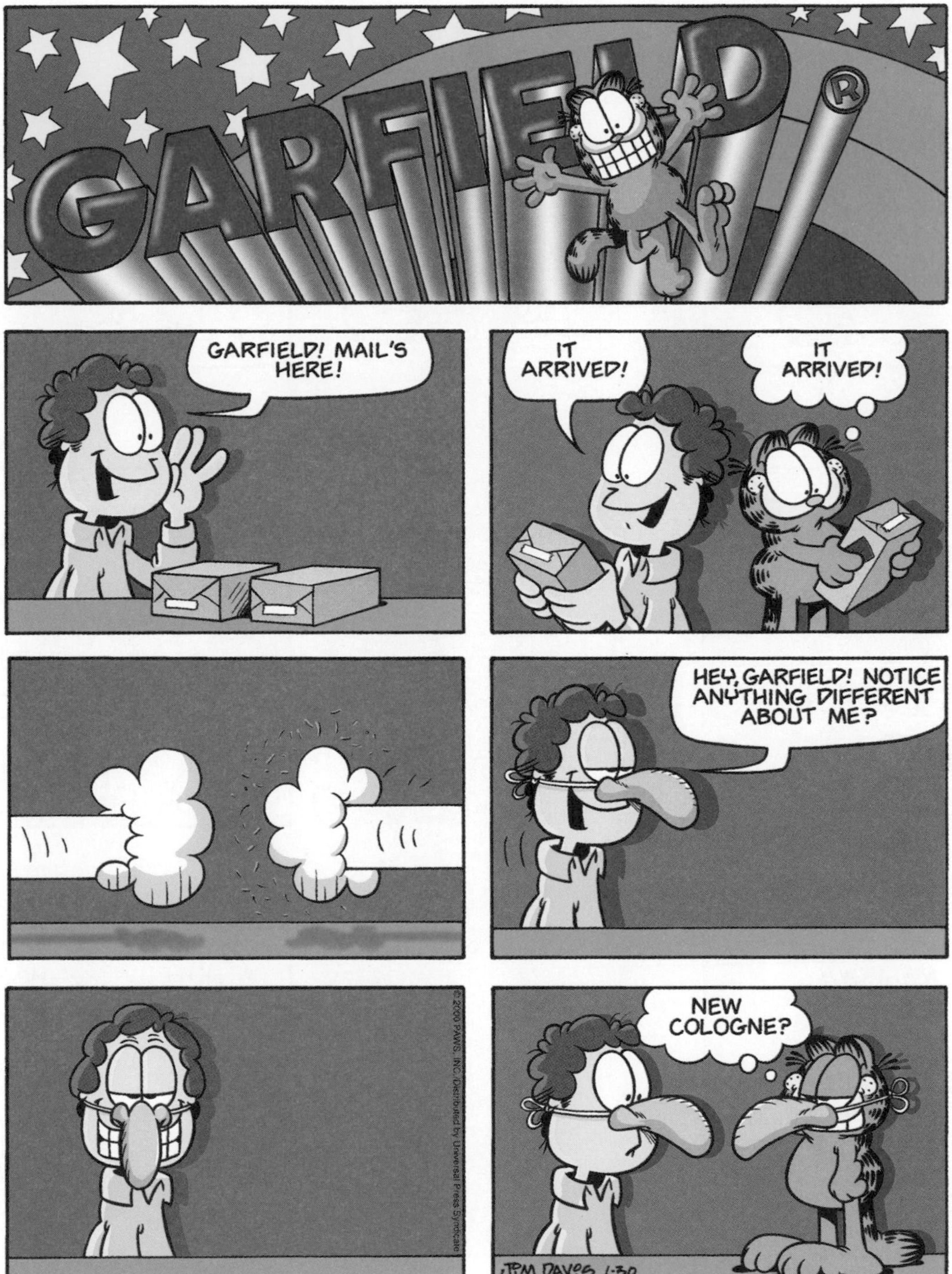
GARFIELD®
GARFIELD! MAIL'S HERE!
IT ARRIVED!
IT ARRIVED!
HEY, GARFIELD! NOTICE ANYTHING DIFFERENT ABOUT ME?
NEW COLOGNE?
© 2000 PAWS, INC./Distributed by Universal Press Syndicate
JIM DAVIS 1-30

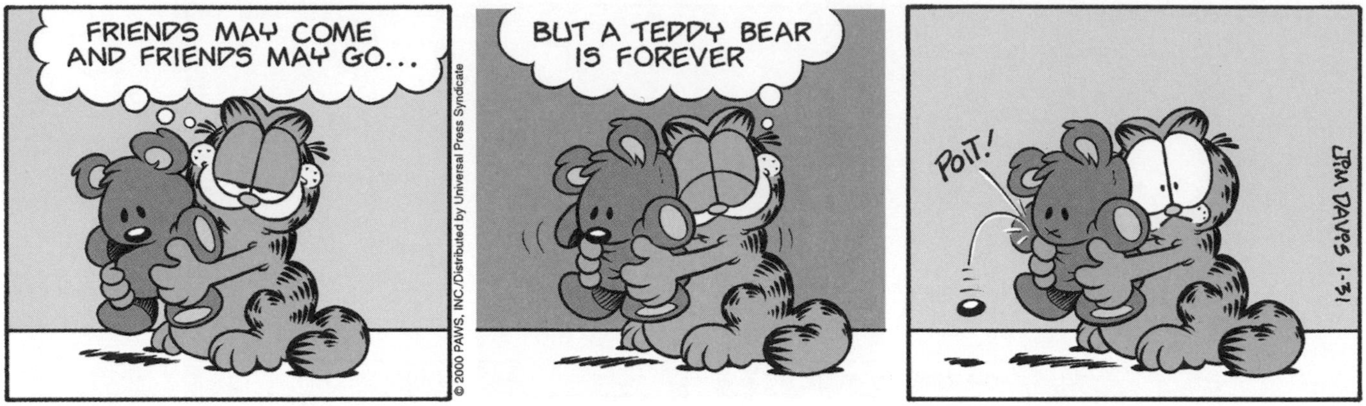
FRIENDS MAY COME AND FRIENDS MAY GO...
© 2000 PAWS, INC./Distributed by Universal Press Syndicate
BUT A TEDDY BEAR IS FOREVER
POIT!
JIM DAVIS 1-31

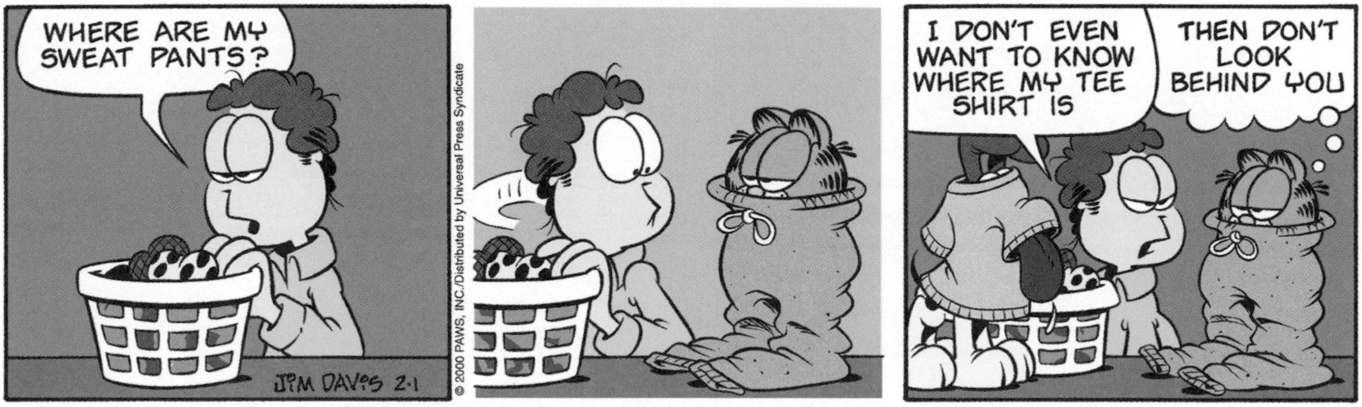
WHERE ARE MY SWEAT PANTS?
JIM DAVIS 2-1
© 2000 PAWS, INC./Distributed by Universal Press Syndicate
I DON'T EVEN WANT TO KNOW WHERE MY TEE SHIRT IS
THEN DON'T LOOK BEHIND YOU

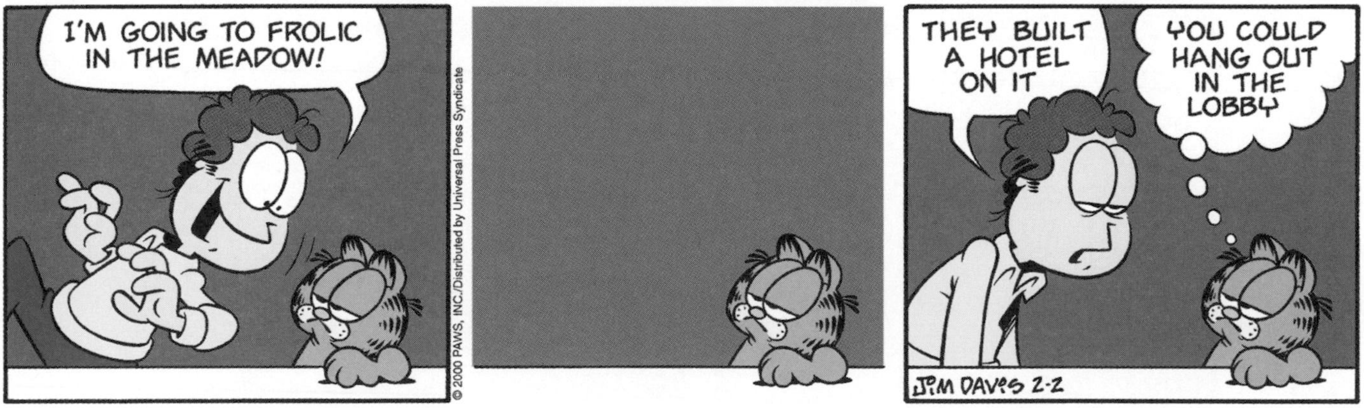
I'M GOING TO FROLIC IN THE MEADOW!
© 2000 PAWS, INC./Distributed by Universal Press Syndicate
THEY BUILT A HOTEL ON IT
YOU COULD HANG OUT IN THE LOBBY
JIM DAVIS 2-2

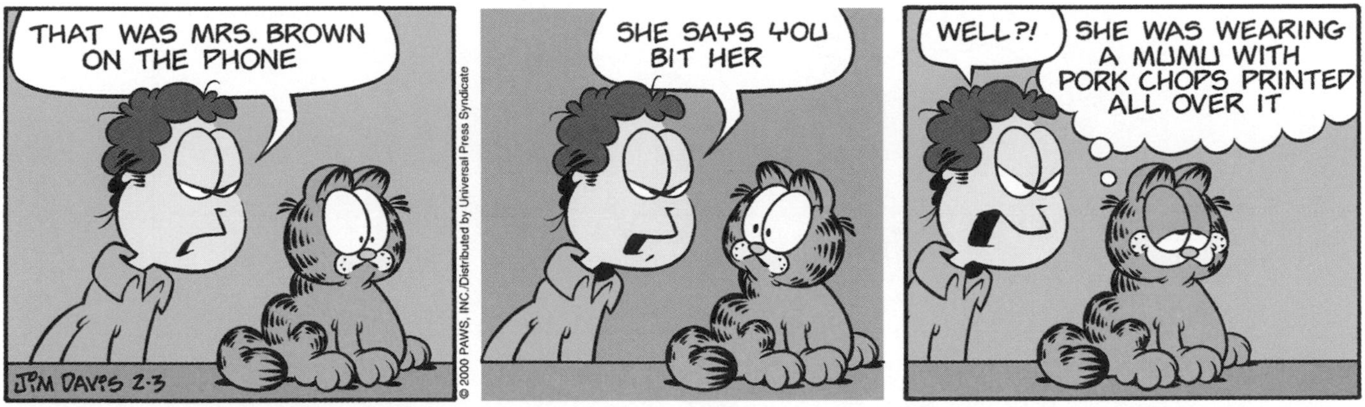
THAT WAS MRS. BROWN ON THE PHONE
JIM DAVIS 2-3
© 2000 PAWS, INC./Distributed by Universal Press Syndicate
SHE SAYS YOU BIT HER
WELL?!
SHE WAS WEARING A MUMU WITH PORK CHOPS PRINTED ALL OVER IT

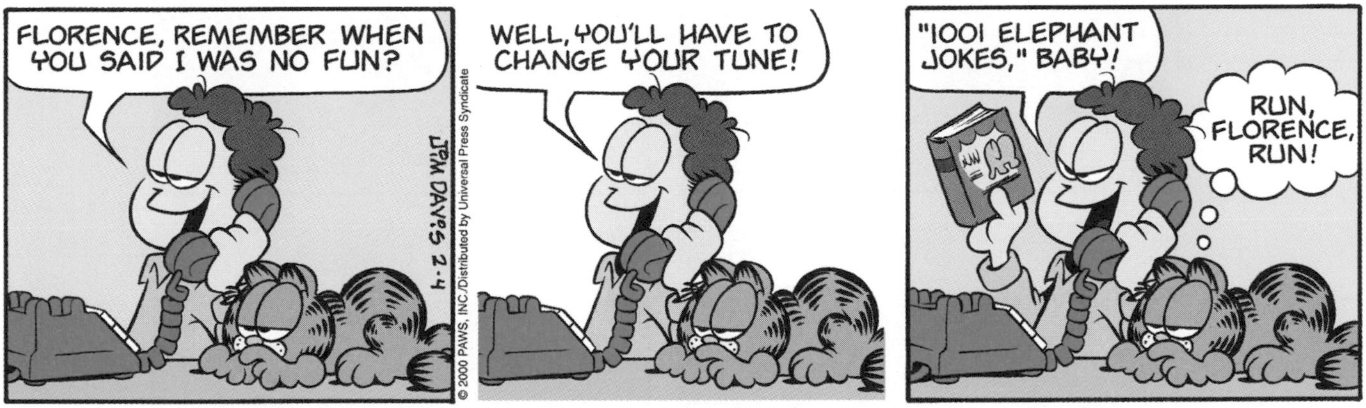
FLORENCE, REMEMBER WHEN YOU SAID I WAS NO FUN?
JIM DAVIS 2-4
© 2000 PAWS, INC./Distributed by Universal Press Syndicate
WELL, YOU'LL HAVE TO CHANGE YOUR TUNE!
"1001 ELEPHANT JOKES," BABY!
RUN, FLORENCE, RUN!

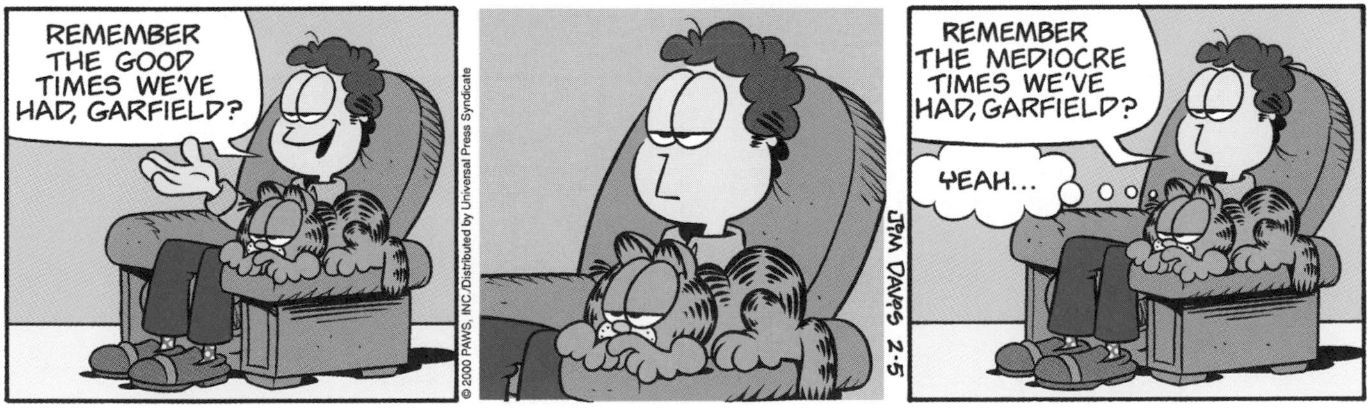
REMEMBER THE GOOD TIMES WE'VE HAD, GARFIELD?
© 2000 PAWS, INC./Distributed by Universal Press Syndicate
JIM DAVIS 2-5
REMEMBER THE MEDIOCRE TIMES WE'VE HAD, GARFIELD?
YEAH...

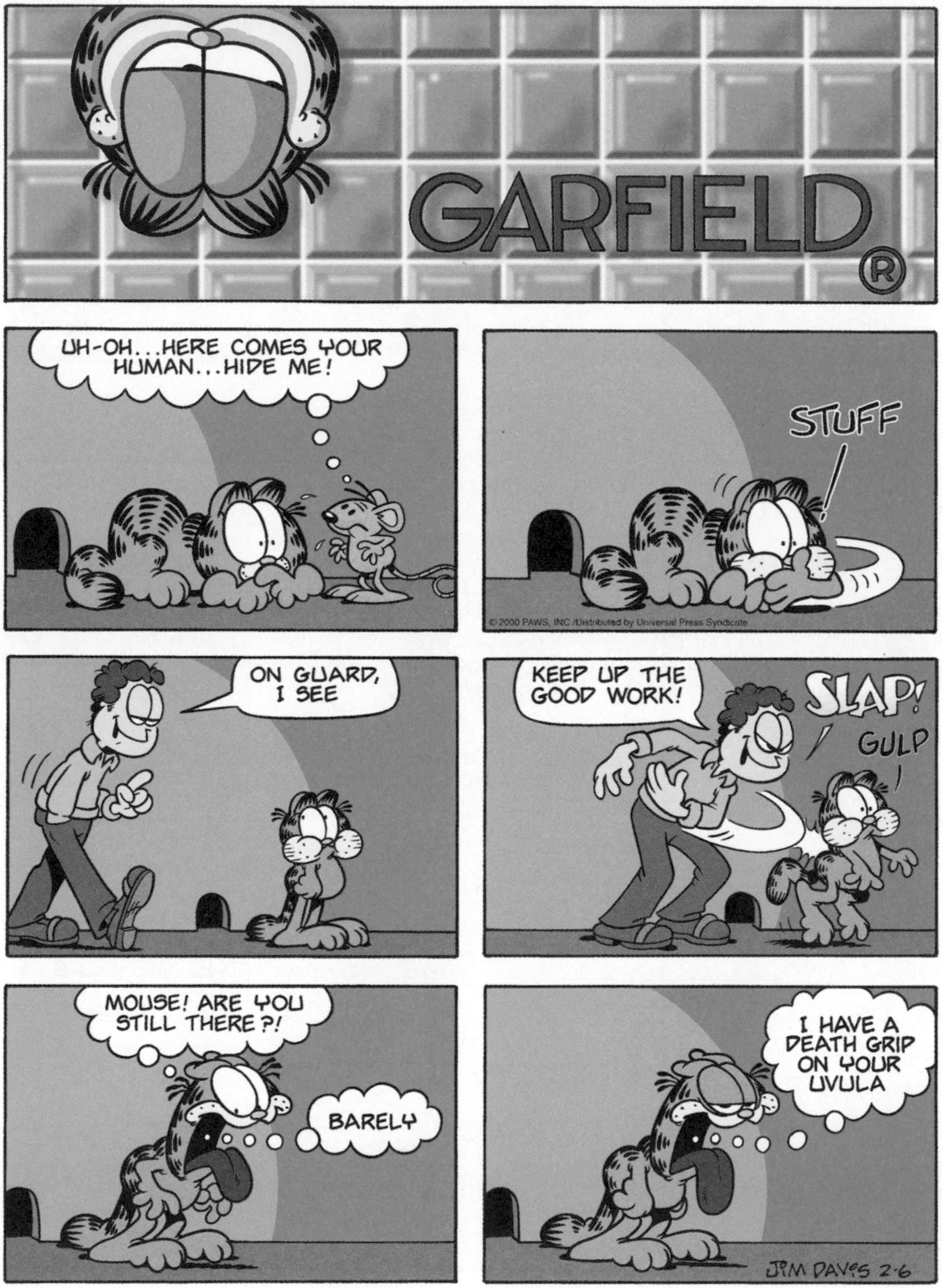
GARFIELD®
UH-OH...HERE COMES YOUR HUMAN...HIDE ME!
STUFF
© 2000 PAWS, INC./Distributed by Universal Press Syndicate
ON GUARD, I SEE
KEEP UP THE GOOD WORK!
SLAP!
GULP
MOUSE! ARE YOU STILL THERE?!
BARELY
I HAVE A DEATH GRIP ON YOUR UVULA
JIM DAVIS 2-6

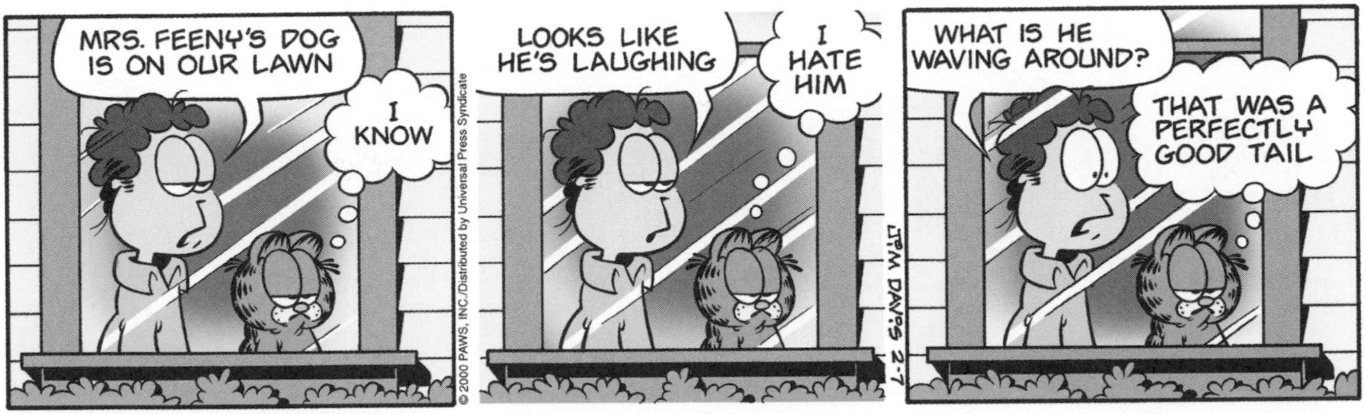
MRS. FEENY'S DOG IS ON OUR LAWN
I KNOW
LOOKS LIKE HE'S LAUGHING
I HATE HIM
WHAT IS HE WAVING AROUND?
THAT WAS A PERFECTLY GOOD TAIL
JIM DAVIS 2-7

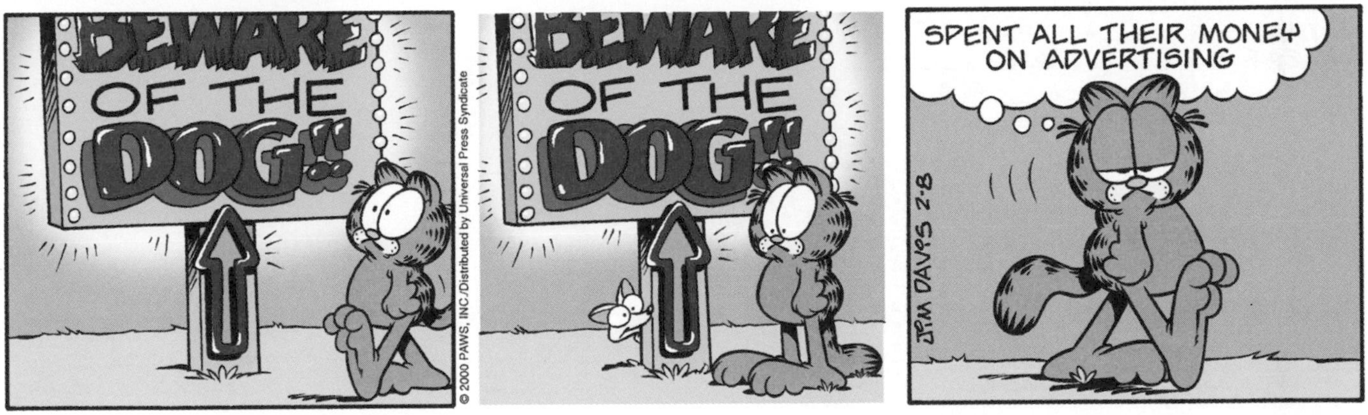
BEWARE OF THE DOG!!
SPENT ALL THEIR MONEY ON ADVERTISING
JIM DAVIS 2-8

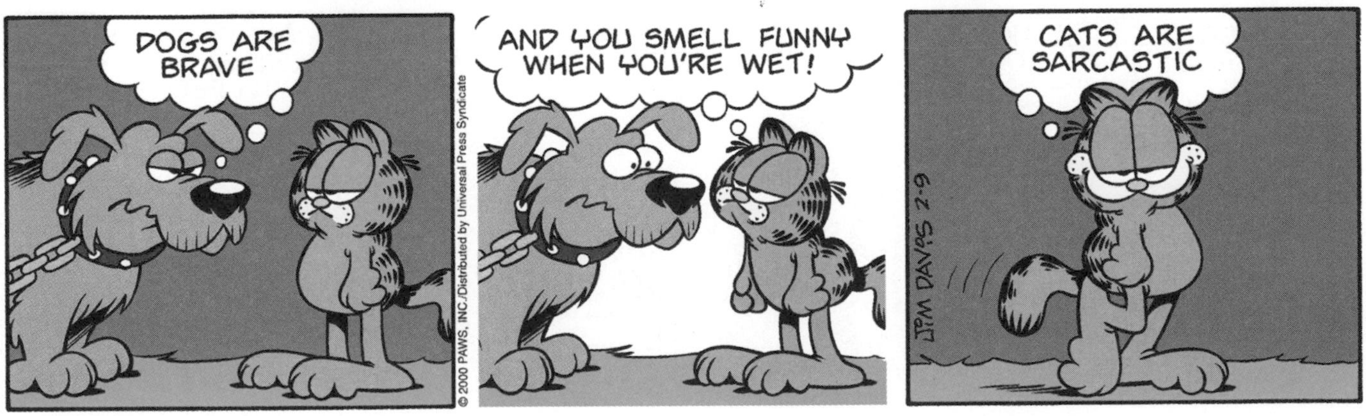
DOGS ARE BRAVE
AND YOU SMELL FUNNY WHEN YOU'RE WET!
CATS ARE SARCASTIC
JIM DAVIS 2-9

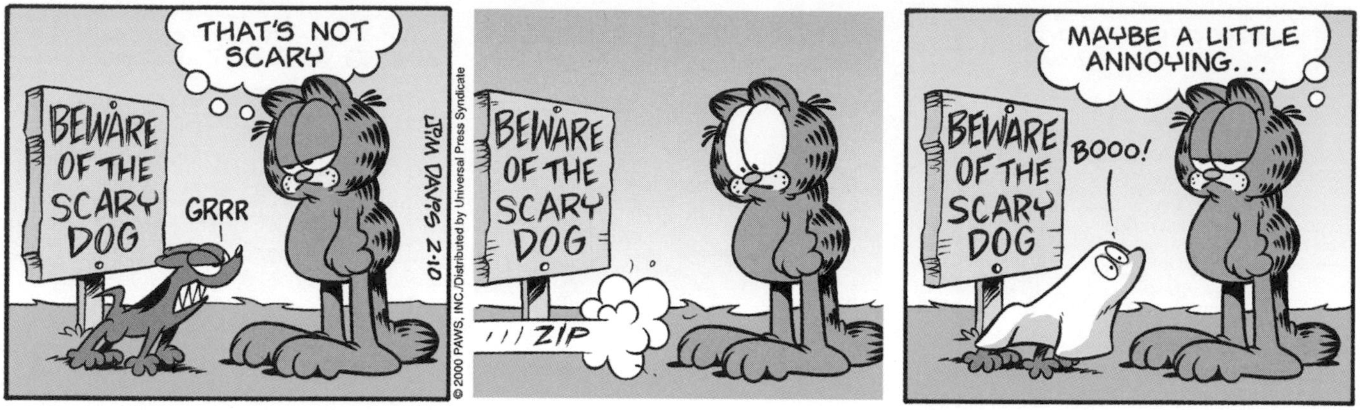
THAT'S NOT SCARY
BEWARE OF THE SCARY DOG
GRRR
JIM DAVIS 2-10
ZIP
MAYBE A LITTLE ANNOYING...
BOOO!

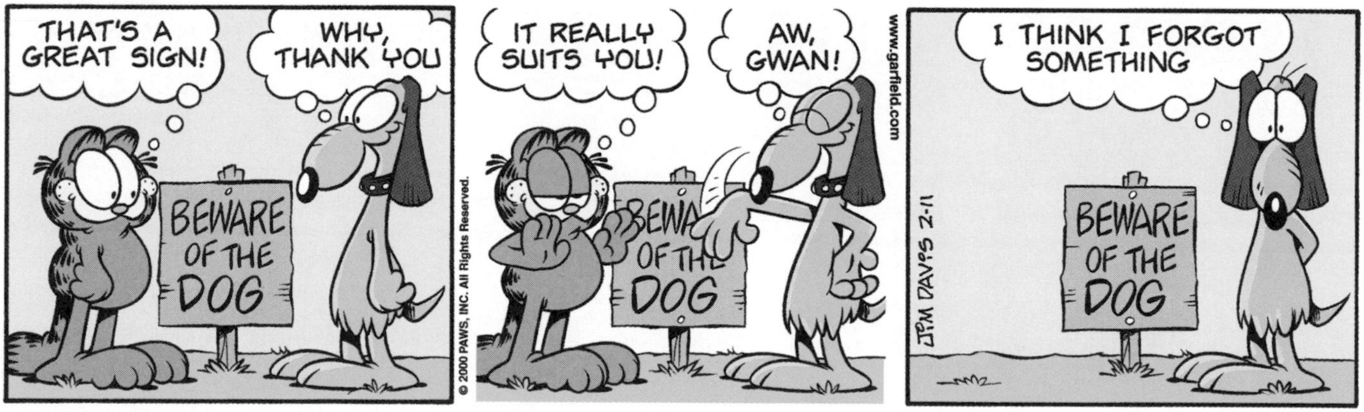
THAT'S A GREAT SIGN!
WHY, THANK YOU
BEWARE OF THE DOG
IT REALLY SUITS YOU!
AW, GWAN!
www.garfield.com
I THINK I FORGOT SOMETHING
JIM DAVIS 2-11

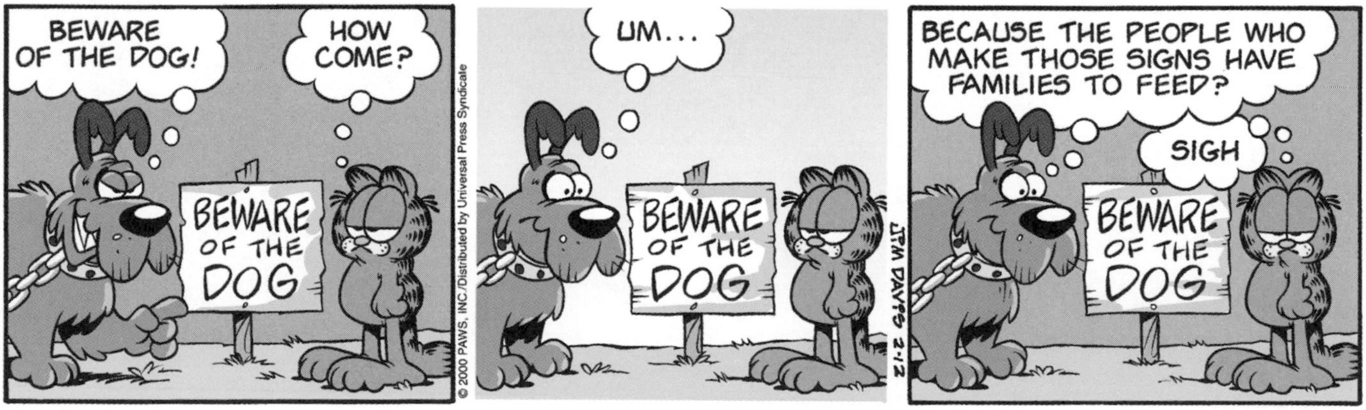
BEWARE OF THE DOG!
HOW COME?
BEWARE OF THE DOG
UM...
JIM DAVIS 2-12
BECAUSE THE PEOPLE WHO MAKE THOSE SIGNS HAVE FAMILIES TO FEED?
SIGH

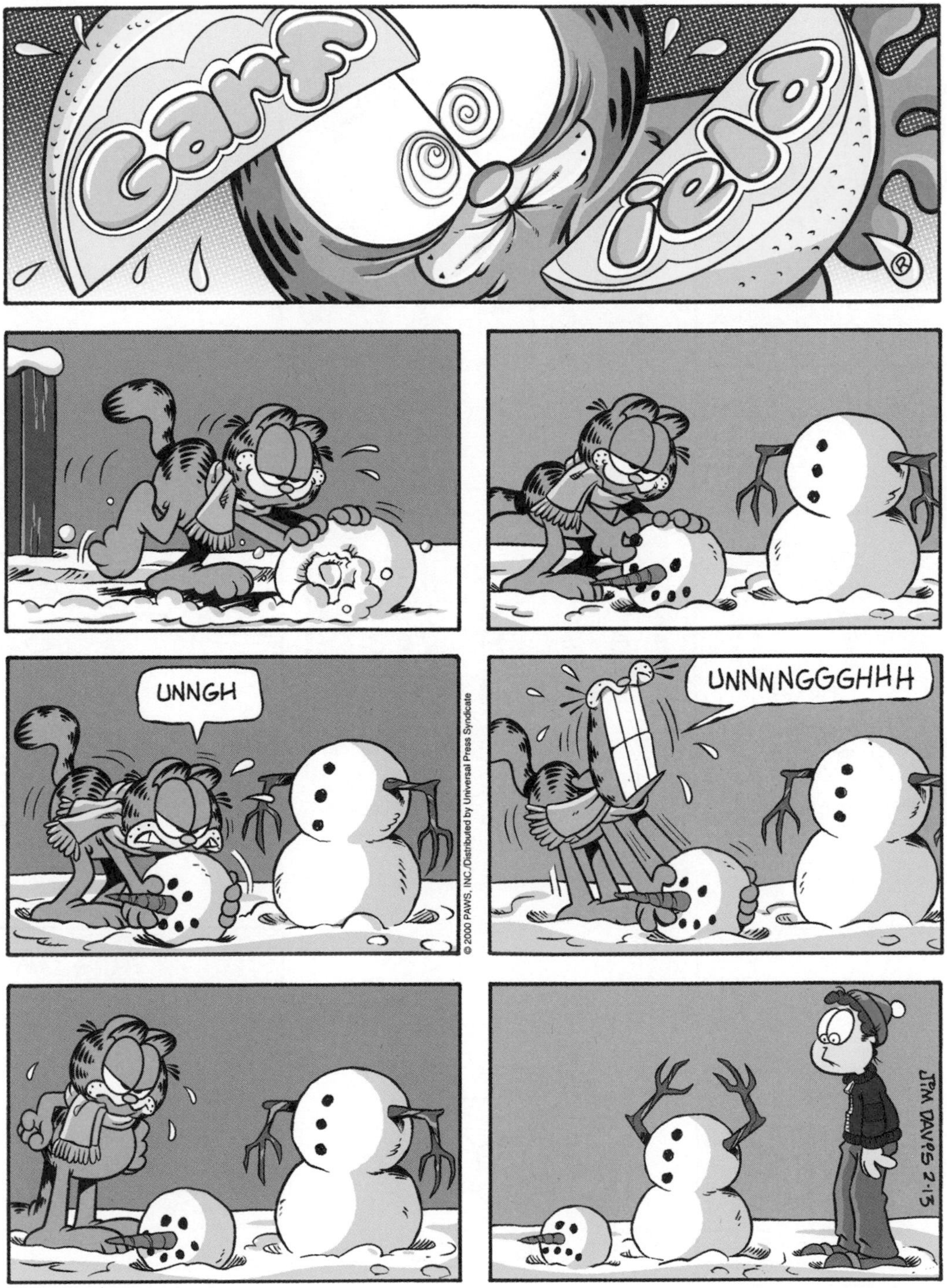
Garfield
© 2000 PAWS, INC./Distributed by Universal Press Syndicate
UNNGH
UNNNNGGGHHH
JIM DAVIS 2-13

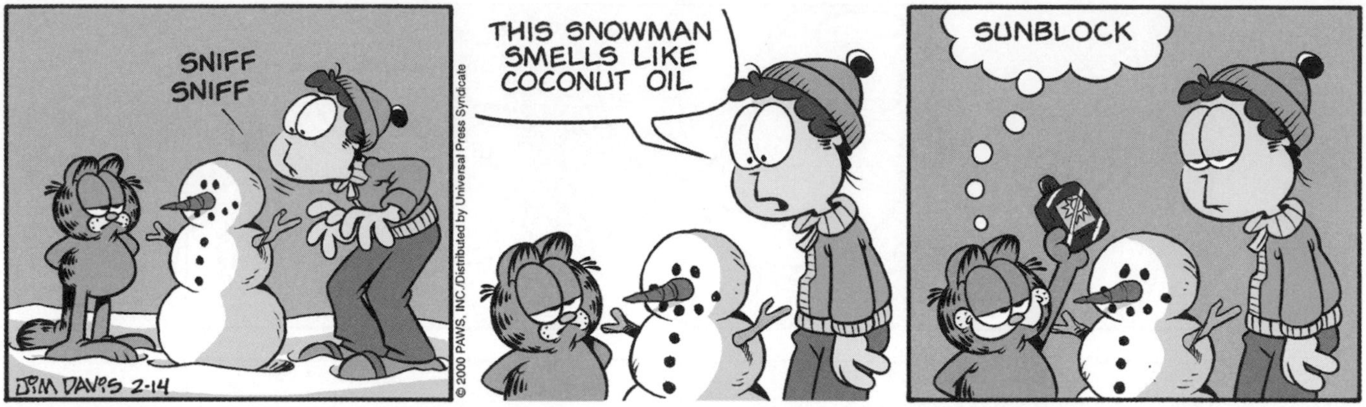
SNIFF SNIFF
JIM DAVIS 2-14
© 2000 PAWS, INC./Distributed by Universal Press Syndicate
THIS SNOWMAN SMELLS LIKE COCONUT OIL
SUNBLOCK

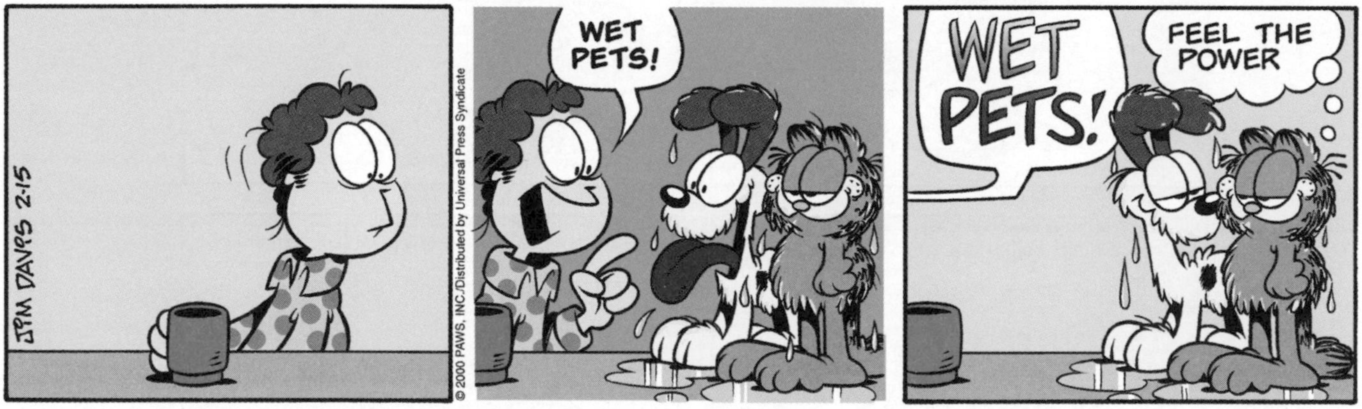
JIM DAVIS 2-15
© 2000 PAWS, INC./Distributed by Universal Press Syndicate
WET PETS!
WET PETS!
FEEL THE POWER

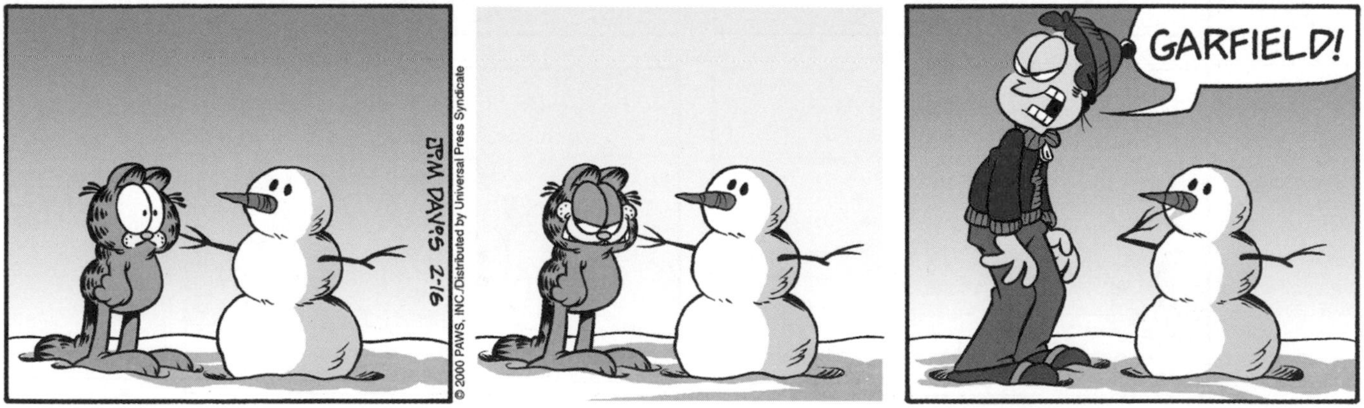
JIM DAVIS 2-16
© 2000 PAWS, INC./Distributed by Universal Press Syndicate
GARFIELD!

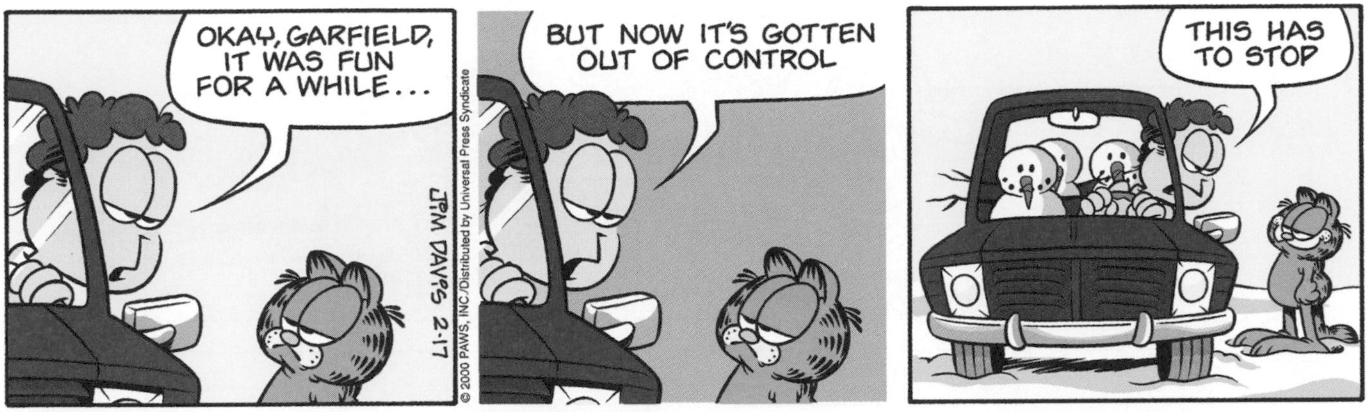
OKAY, GARFIELD, IT WAS FUN FOR A WHILE...
JIM DAVIS 2-17
© 2000 PAWS, INC./Distributed by Universal Press Syndicate
BUT NOW IT'S GOTTEN OUT OF CONTROL
THIS HAS TO STOP

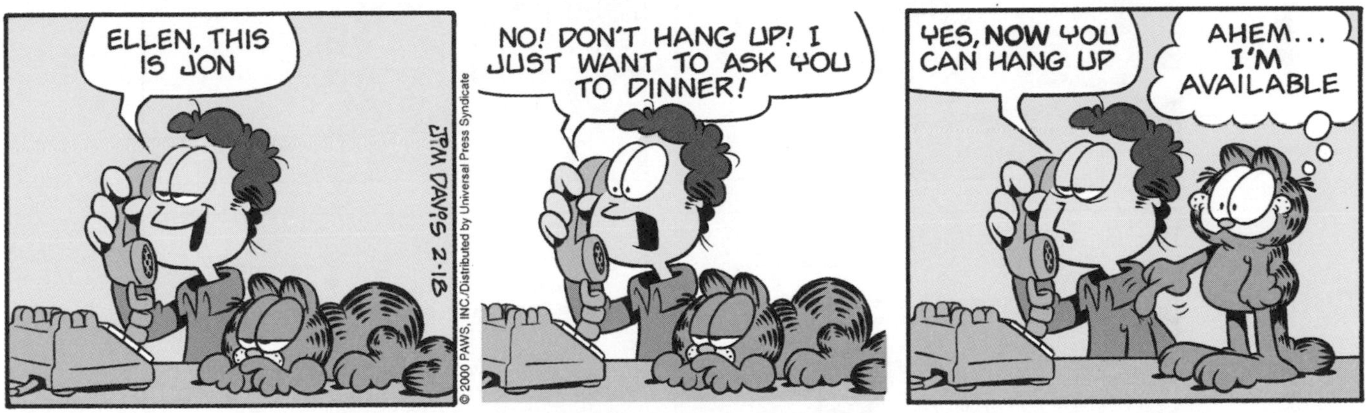
ELLEN, THIS IS JON
JIM DAVIS 2-18
© 2000 PAWS, INC./Distributed by Universal Press Syndicate
NO! DON'T HANG UP! I JUST WANT TO ASK YOU TO DINNER!
YES, **NOW** YOU CAN HANG UP
AHEM... **I'M** AVAILABLE

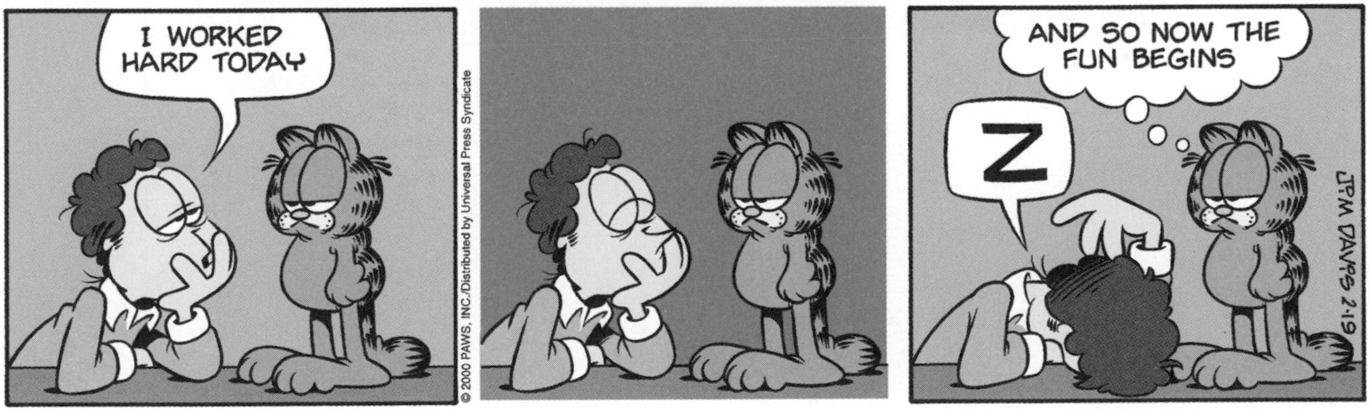
I WORKED HARD TODAY
© 2000 PAWS, INC./Distributed by Universal Press Syndicate
AND SO NOW THE FUN BEGINS
Z
JIM DAVIS 2-19

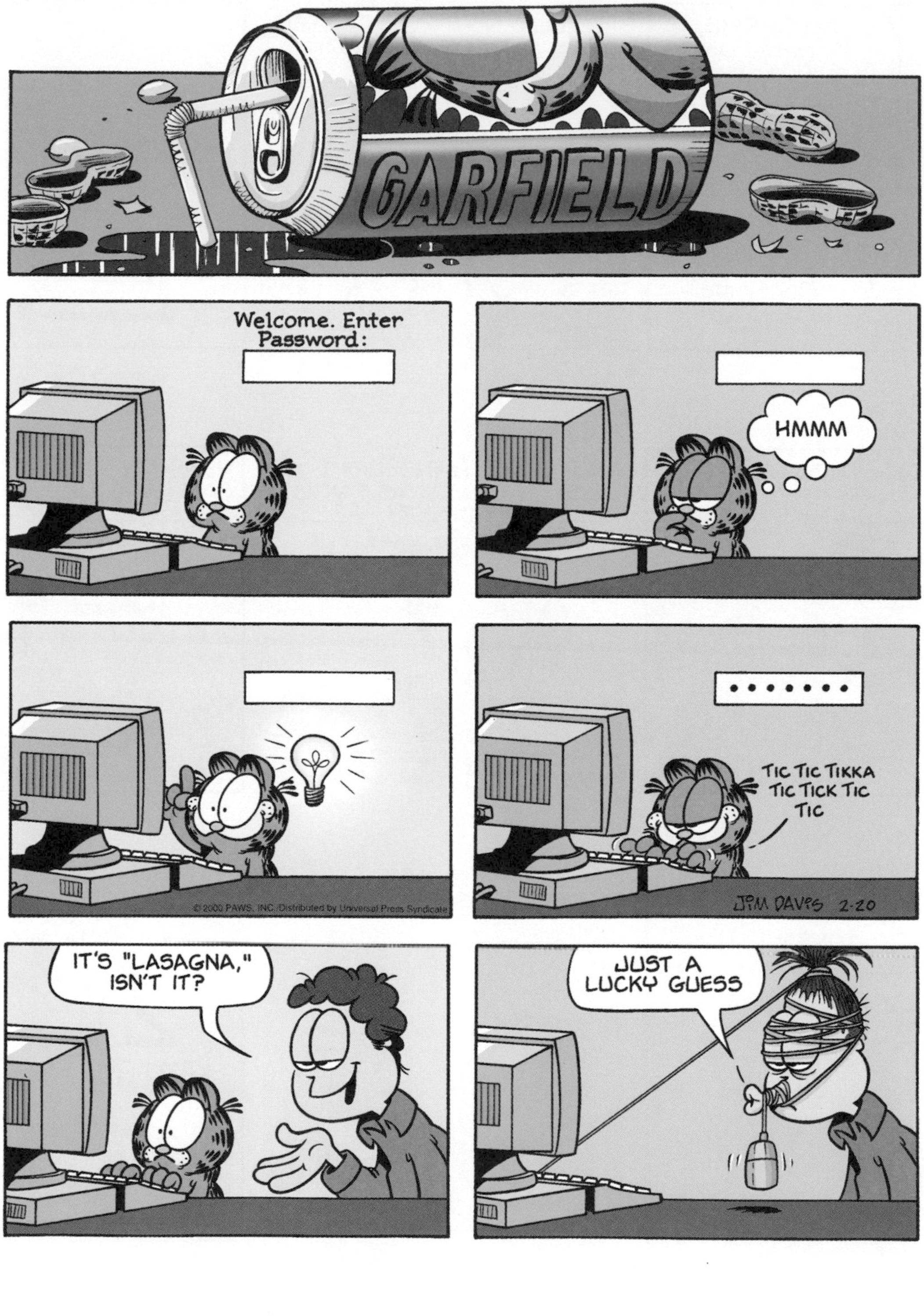
GARFIELD
Welcome. Enter Password:
HMMM
TIC TIC TIKKA TIC TICK TIC TIC
© 2000 PAWS, INC./Distributed by Universal Press Syndicate
JIM DAVIS 2-20
IT'S "LASAGNA," ISN'T IT?
JUST A LUCKY GUESS

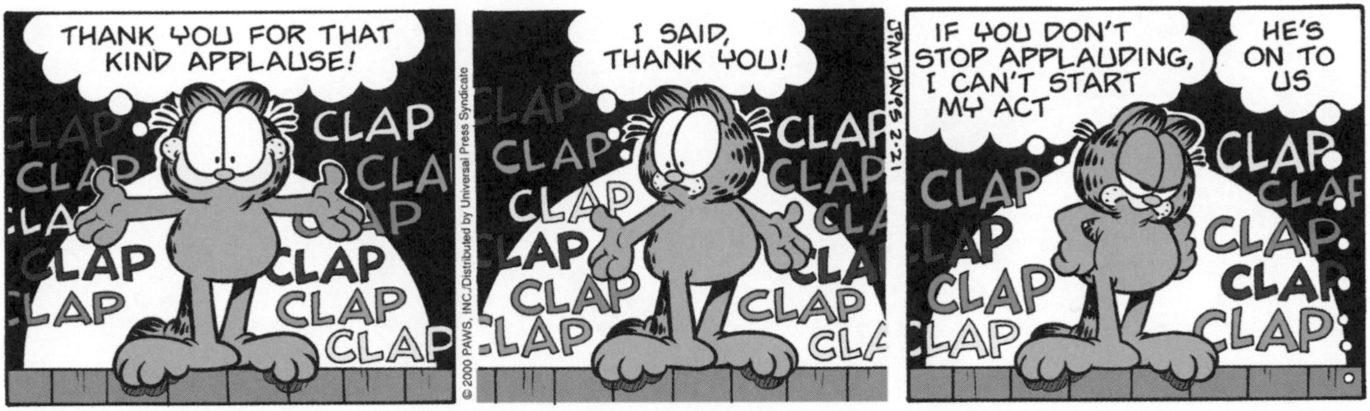
THANK YOU FOR THAT KIND APPLAUSE!
CLAP CLAP CLAP CLAP CLAP CLAP CLAP CLAP CLAP
I SAID, THANK YOU!
© 2000 PAWS, INC./Distributed by Universal Press Syndicate
JIM DAVIS 2-21
IF YOU DON'T STOP APPLAUDING, I CAN'T START MY ACT
HE'S ON TO US

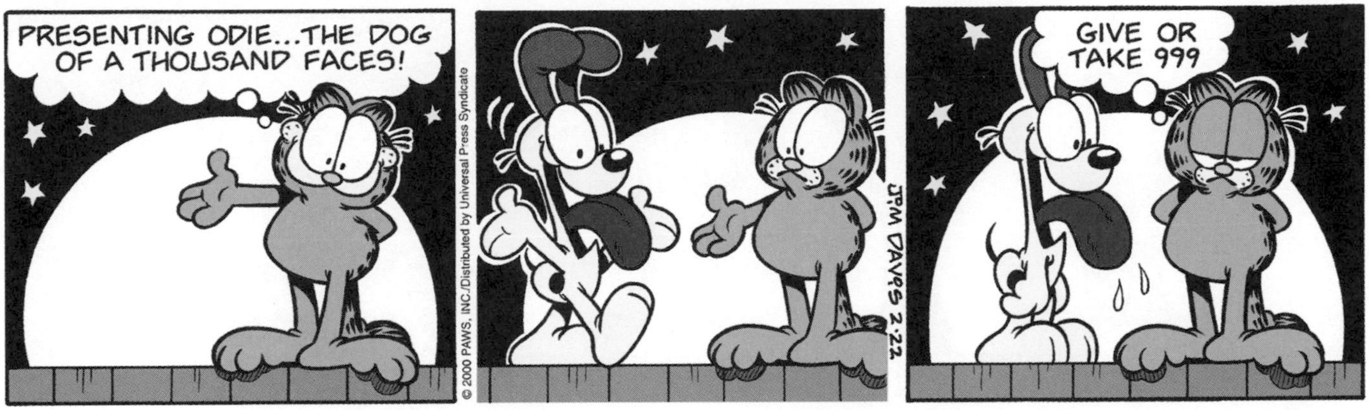
PRESENTING ODIE... THE DOG OF A THOUSAND FACES!
© 2000 PAWS, INC./Distributed by Universal Press Syndicate
JIM DAVIS 2-22
GIVE OR TAKE 999

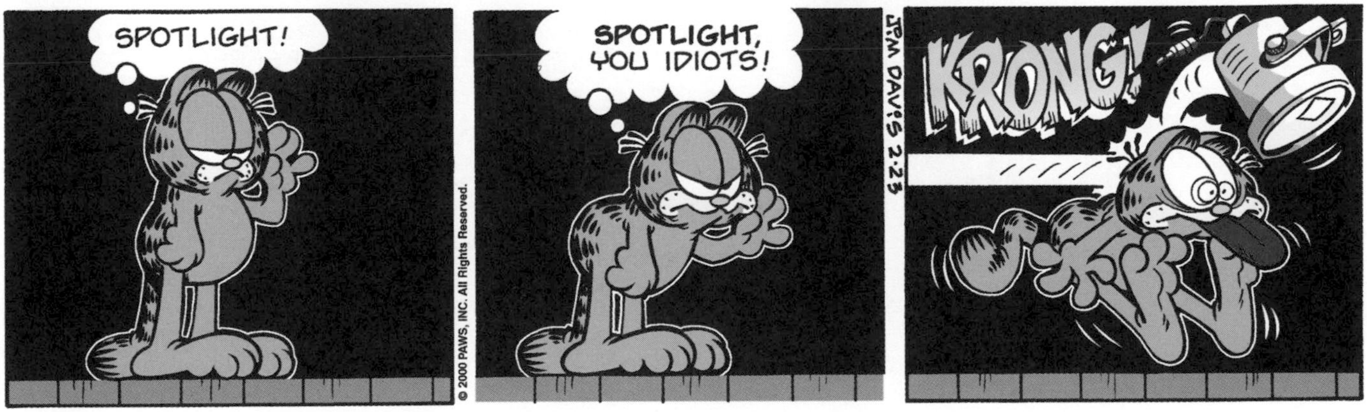
SPOTLIGHT!
© 2000 PAWS, INC. All Rights Reserved.
SPOTLIGHT, YOU IDIOTS!
JIM DAVIS 2-23
KRONG!

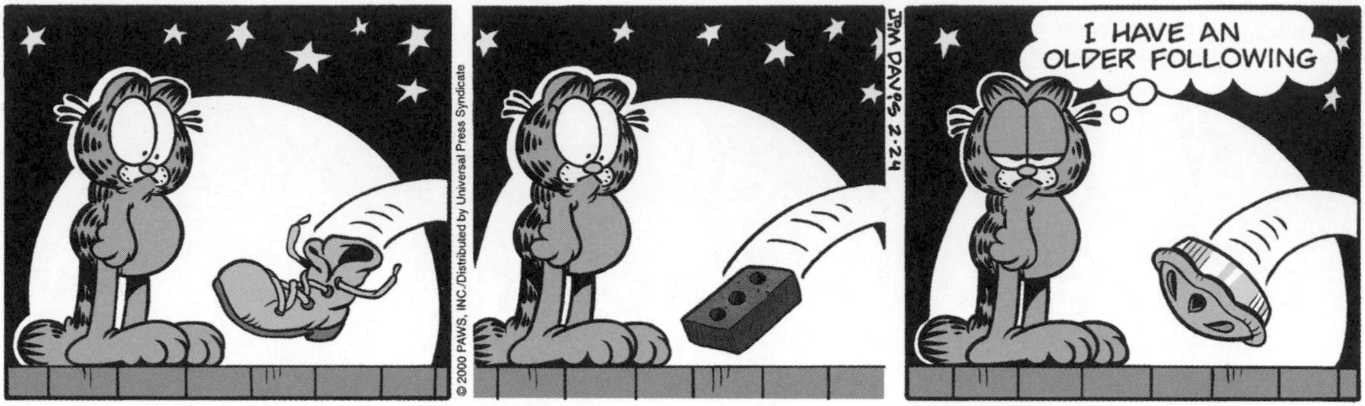
I HAVE AN OLDER FOLLOWING

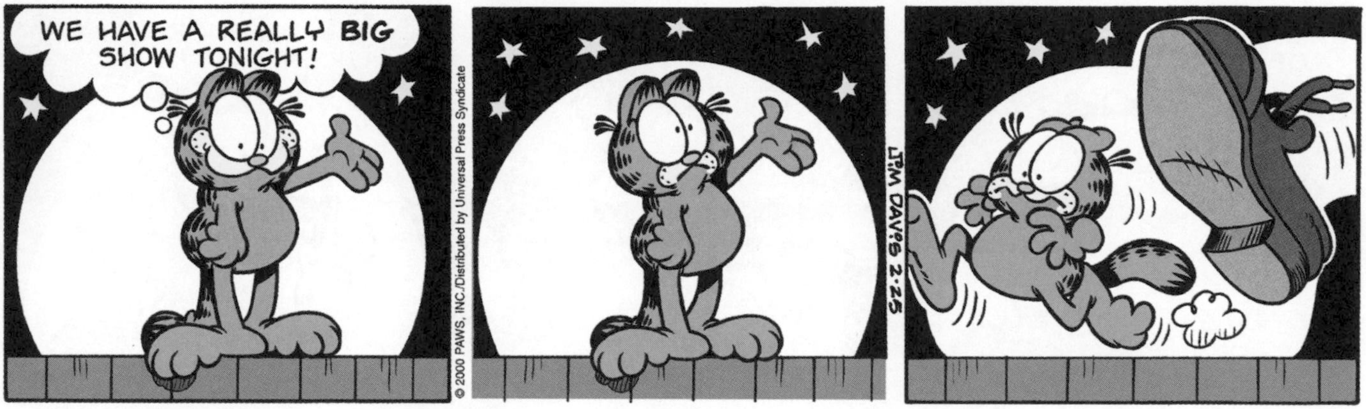
WE HAVE A REALLY BIG SHOW TONIGHT!

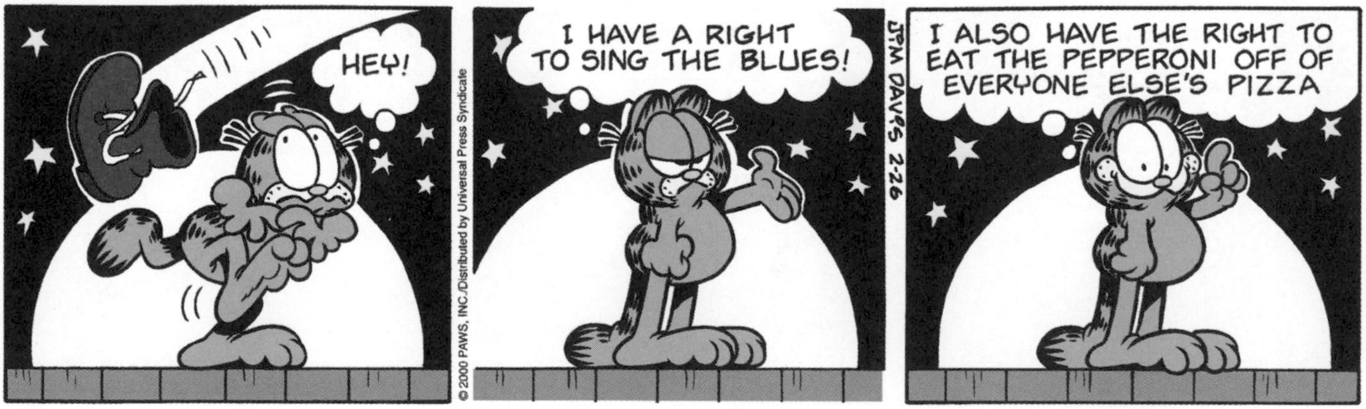
HEY!
I HAVE A RIGHT TO SING THE BLUES!
I ALSO HAVE THE RIGHT TO EAT THE PEPPERONI OFF OF EVERYONE ELSE'S PIZZA

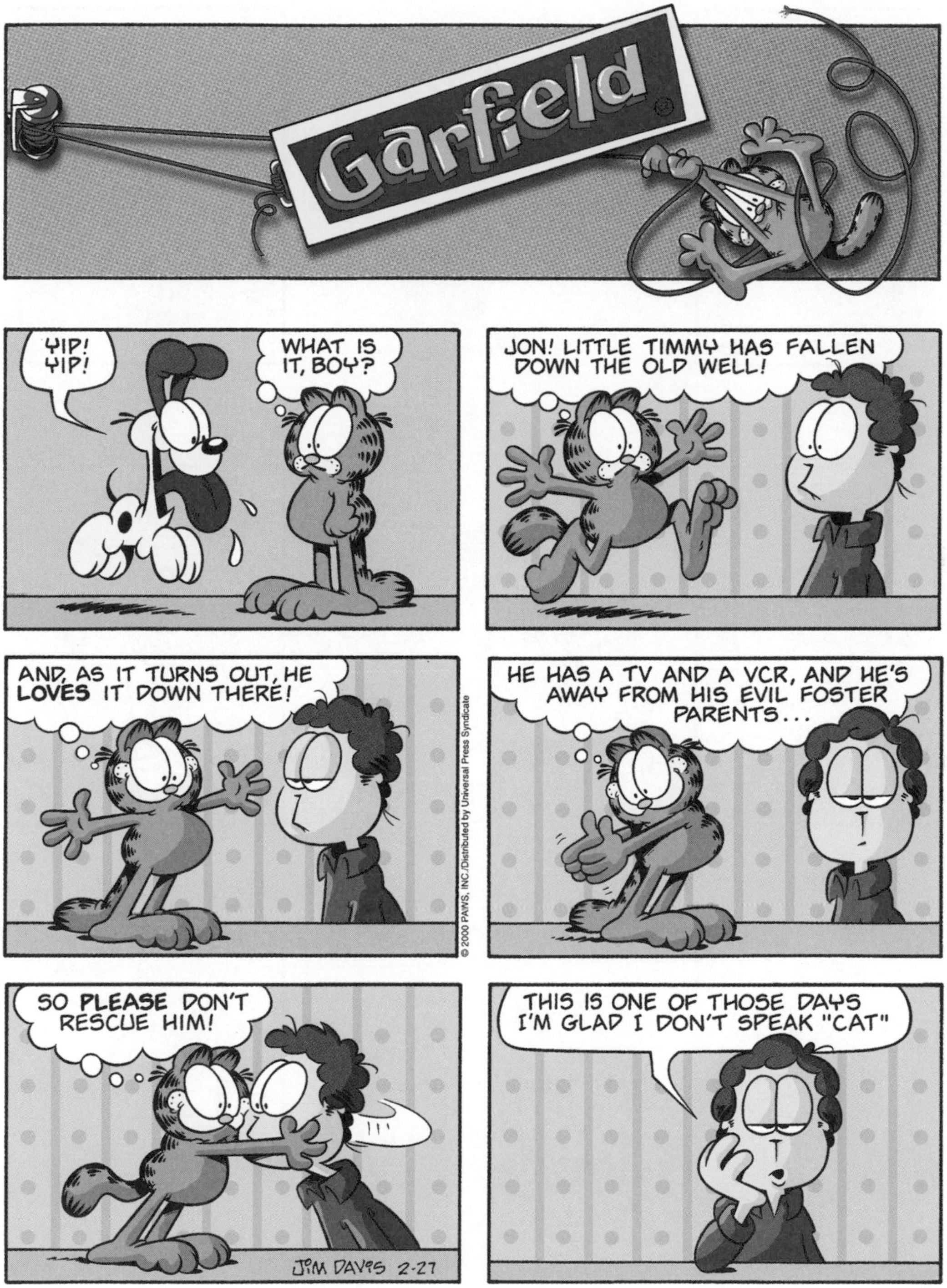
Garfield
YIP! YIP!
WHAT IS IT, BOY?
JON! LITTLE TIMMY HAS FALLEN DOWN THE OLD WELL!
AND, AS IT TURNS OUT, HE **LOVES** IT DOWN THERE!
HE HAS A TV AND A VCR, AND HE'S AWAY FROM HIS EVIL FOSTER PARENTS...
SO **PLEASE** DON'T RESCUE HIM!
THIS IS ONE OF THOSE DAYS I'M GLAD I DON'T SPEAK "CAT"
JIM DAVIS 2-27
© 2000 PAWS, INC./Distributed by Universal Press Syndicate

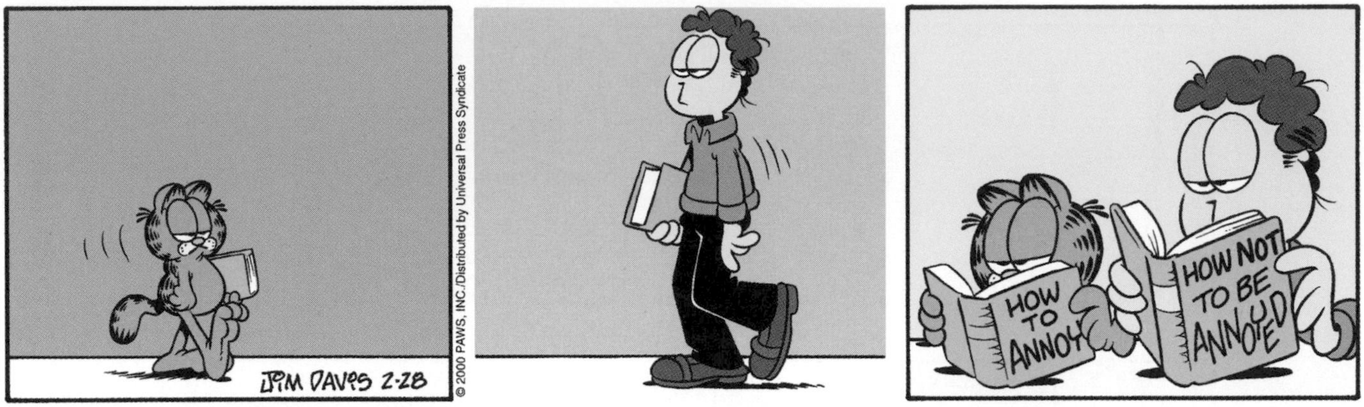
JIM DAVIS 2-28
© 2000 PAWS, INC./Distributed by Universal Press Syndicate
HOW TO ANNOY
HOW NOT TO BE ANNOYED

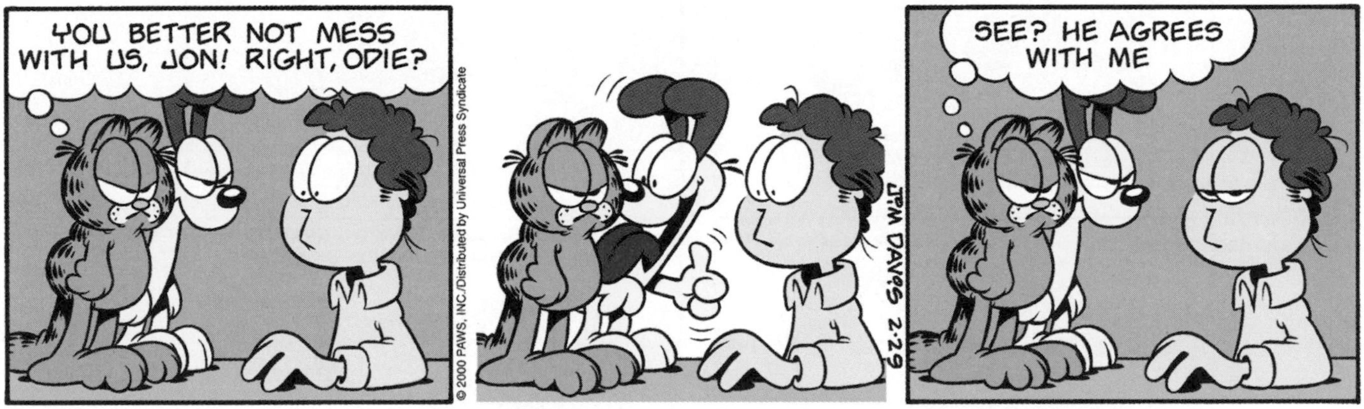
YOU BETTER NOT MESS WITH US, JON! RIGHT, ODIE?
© 2000 PAWS, INC./Distributed by Universal Press Syndicate
JIM DAVIS 2-29
SEE? HE AGREES WITH ME

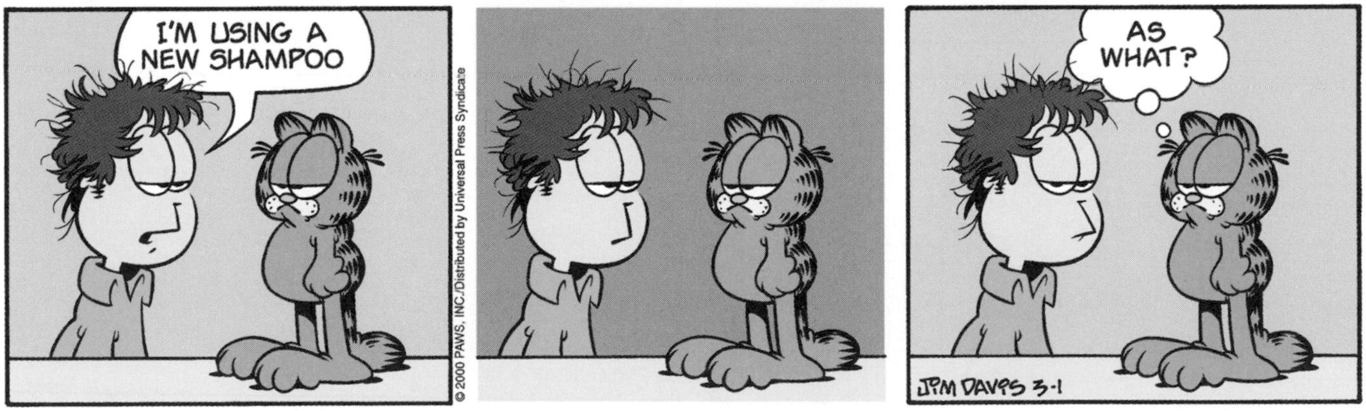
I'M USING A NEW SHAMPOO
© 2000 PAWS, INC./Distributed by Universal Press Syndicate
AS WHAT?
JIM DAVIS 3-1

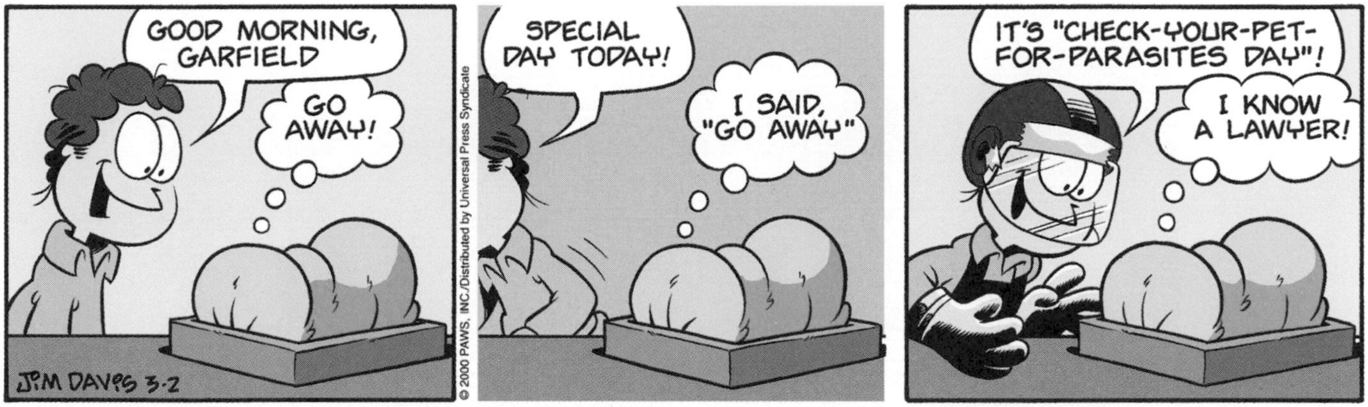
GOOD MORNING, GARFIELD
GO AWAY!
JIM DAVIS 3-2
© 2000 PAWS, INC./Distributed by Universal Press Syndicate
SPECIAL DAY TODAY!
I SAID, "GO AWAY"
IT'S "CHECK-YOUR-PET-FOR-PARASITES DAY"!
I KNOW A LAWYER!

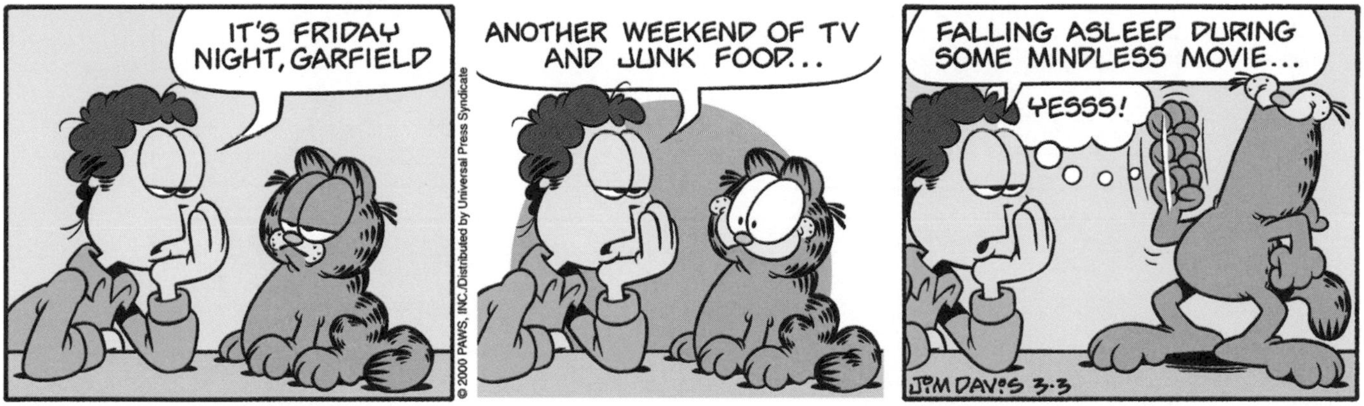
IT'S FRIDAY NIGHT, GARFIELD
© 2000 PAWS, INC./Distributed by Universal Press Syndicate
ANOTHER WEEKEND OF TV AND JUNK FOOD...
FALLING ASLEEP DURING SOME MINDLESS MOVIE...
YESSS!
JIM DAVIS 3-3

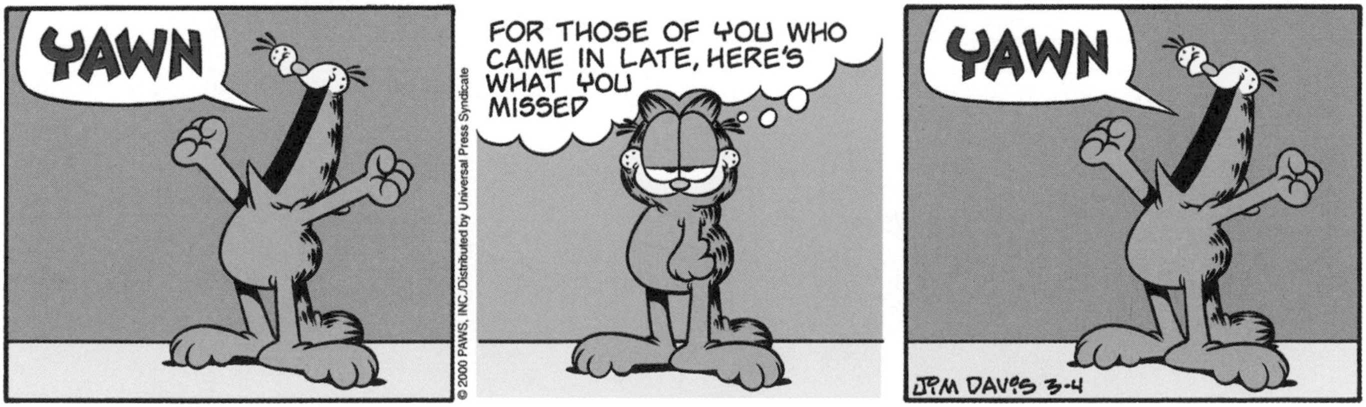
YAWN
© 2000 PAWS, INC./Distributed by Universal Press Syndicate
FOR THOSE OF YOU WHO CAME IN LATE, HERE'S WHAT YOU MISSED
YAWN
JIM DAVIS 3-4

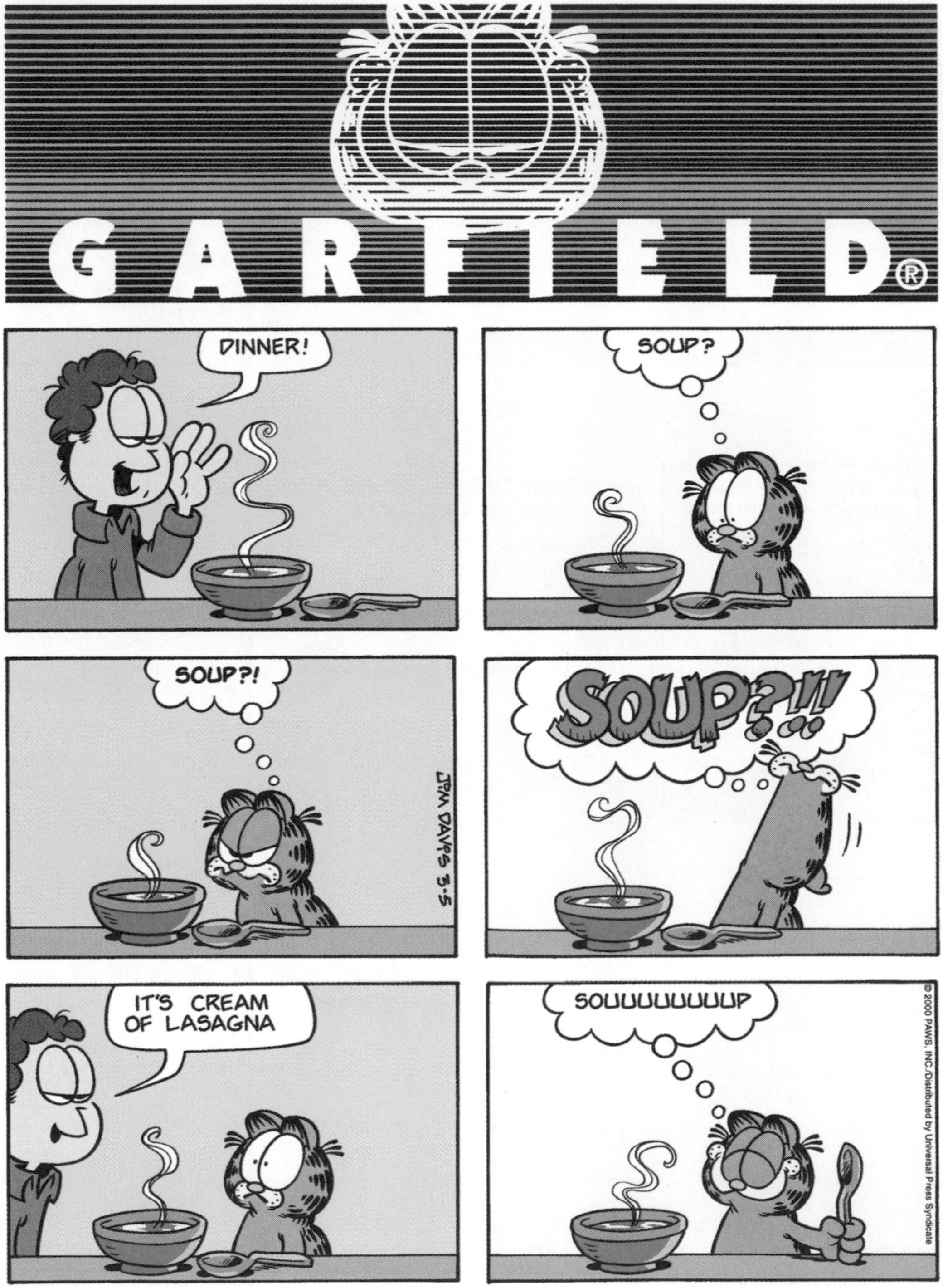
GARFIELD®
DINNER!
SOUP?
SOUP?!
JIM DAVIS 3-5
SOUP?!!
IT'S CREAM OF LASAGNA
SOUUUUUUUUP
© 2000 PAWS, INC./Distributed by Universal Press Syndicate

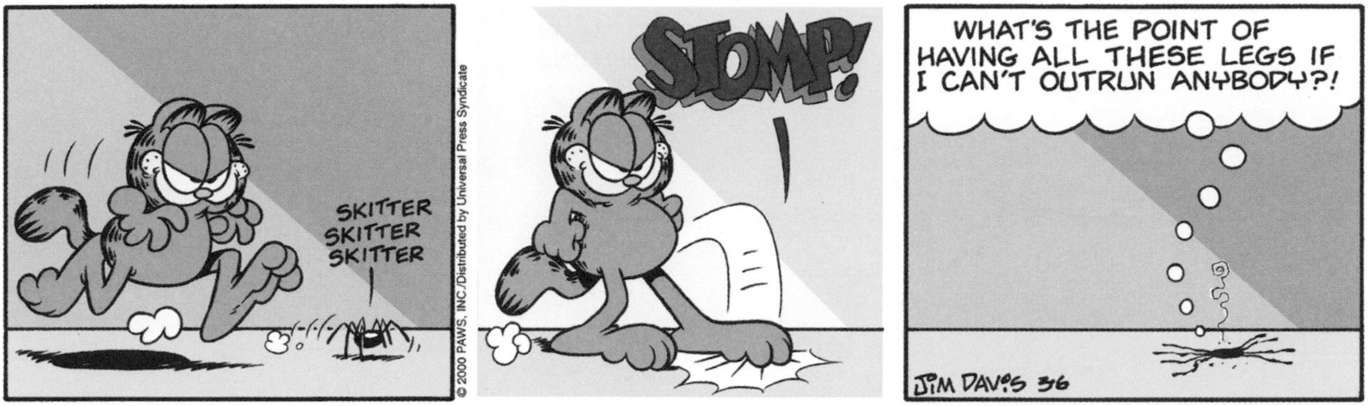
SKITTER
SKITTER
SKITTER
STOMP!
WHAT'S THE POINT OF HAVING ALL THESE LEGS IF I CAN'T OUTRUN ANYBODY?!
JIM DAVIS 3-6
© 2000 PAWS, INC./Distributed by Universal Press Syndicate

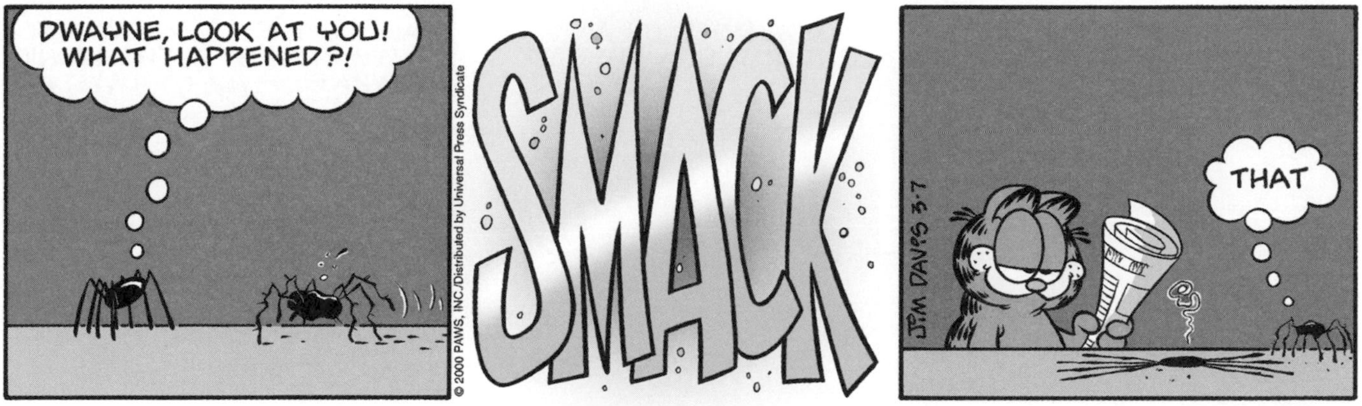
DWAYNE, LOOK AT YOU! WHAT HAPPENED?!
SMACK
THAT
JIM DAVIS 3-7
© 2000 PAWS, INC./Distributed by Universal Press Syndicate

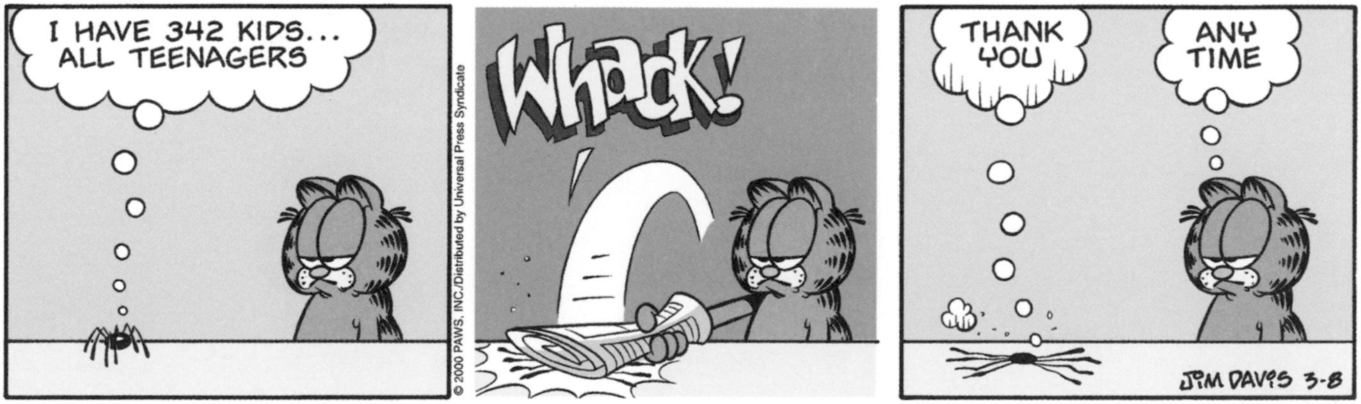
I HAVE 342 KIDS... ALL TEENAGERS
Whack!
THANK YOU
ANY TIME
JIM DAVIS 3-8
© 2000 PAWS, INC./Distributed by Universal Press Syndicate

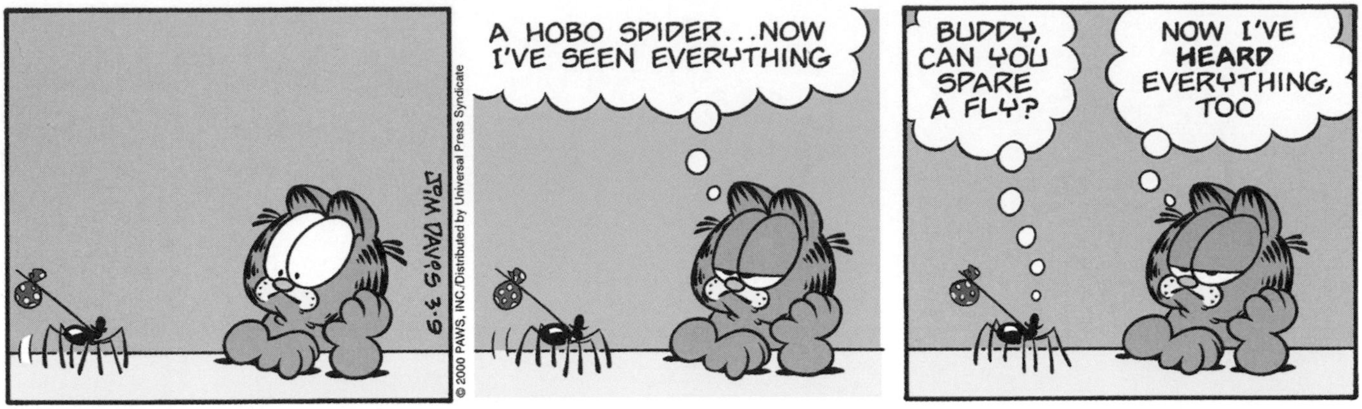
JIM DAVIS 3-9
© 2000 PAWS, INC./Distributed by Universal Press Syndicate
A HOBO SPIDER...NOW I'VE SEEN EVERYTHING
BUDDY, CAN YOU SPARE A FLY?
NOW I'VE **HEARD** EVERYTHING, TOO

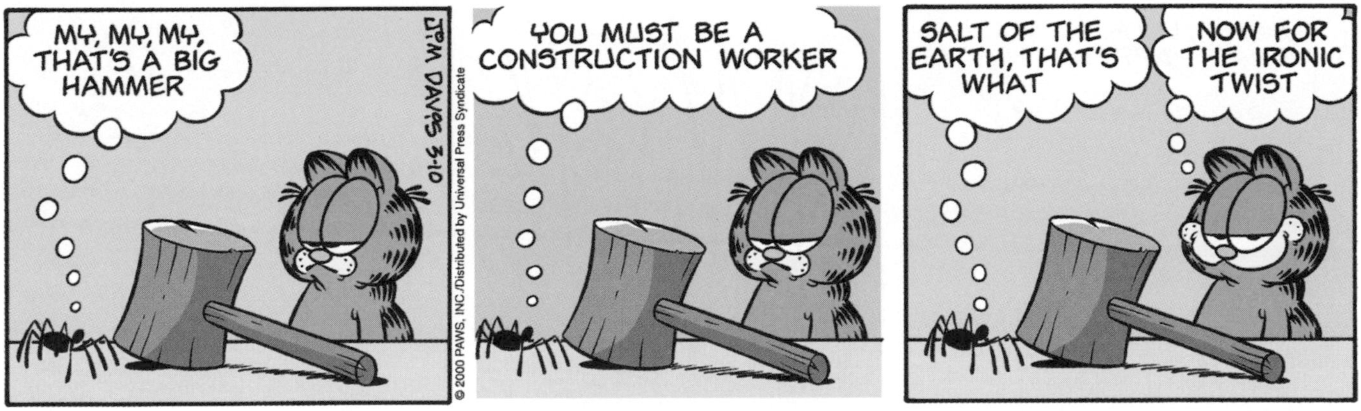
MY, MY, MY, THAT'S A BIG HAMMER
JIM DAVIS 3-10
© 2000 PAWS, INC./Distributed by Universal Press Syndicate
YOU MUST BE A CONSTRUCTION WORKER
SALT OF THE EARTH, THAT'S WHAT
NOW FOR THE IRONIC TWIST

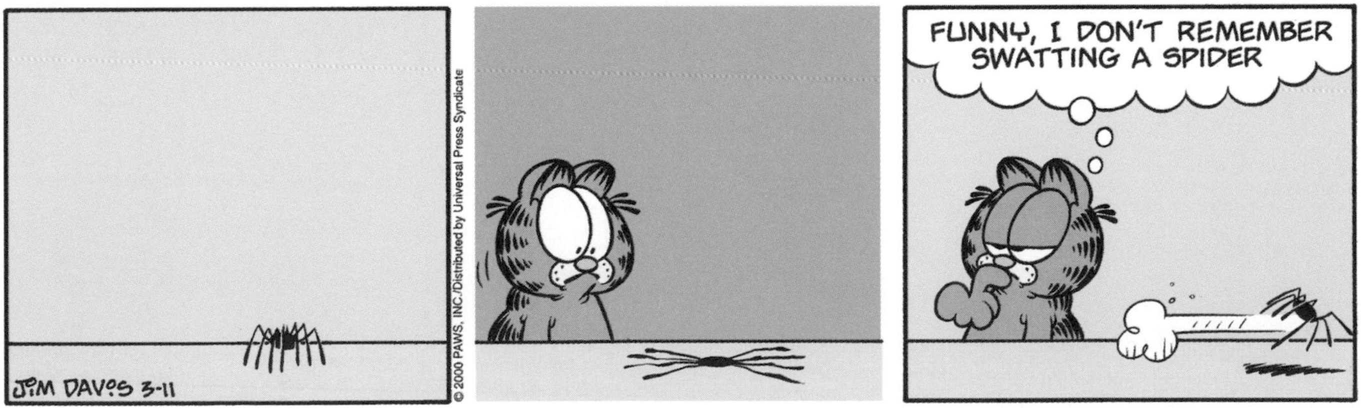
JIM DAVIS 3-11
© 2000 PAWS, INC./Distributed by Universal Press Syndicate
FUNNY, I DON'T REMEMBER SWATTING A SPIDER

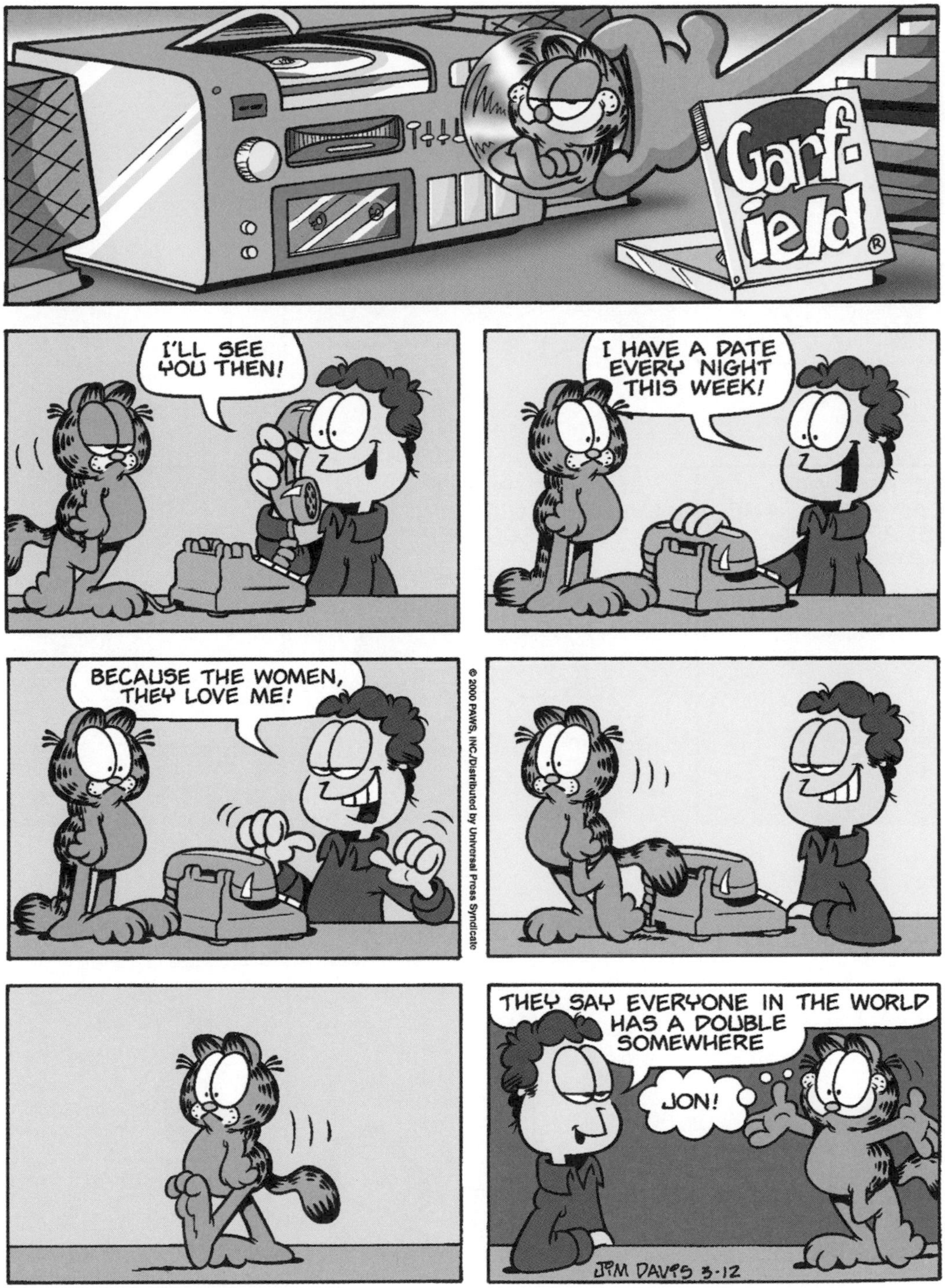
Garfield®
I'LL SEE YOU THEN!
I HAVE A DATE EVERY NIGHT THIS WEEK!
BECAUSE THE WOMEN, THEY LOVE ME!
THEY SAY EVERYONE IN THE WORLD HAS A DOUBLE SOMEWHERE
JON!
JIM DAVIS 3-12

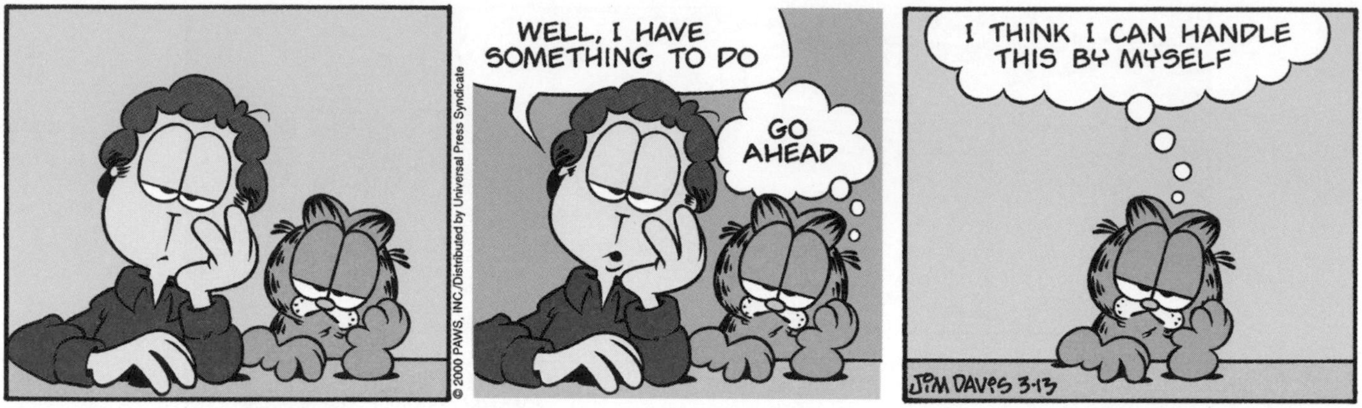
WELL, I HAVE SOMETHING TO DO
GO AHEAD
I THINK I CAN HANDLE THIS BY MYSELF
© 2000 PAWS, INC./Distributed by Universal Press Syndicate
JIM DAVIS 3-13

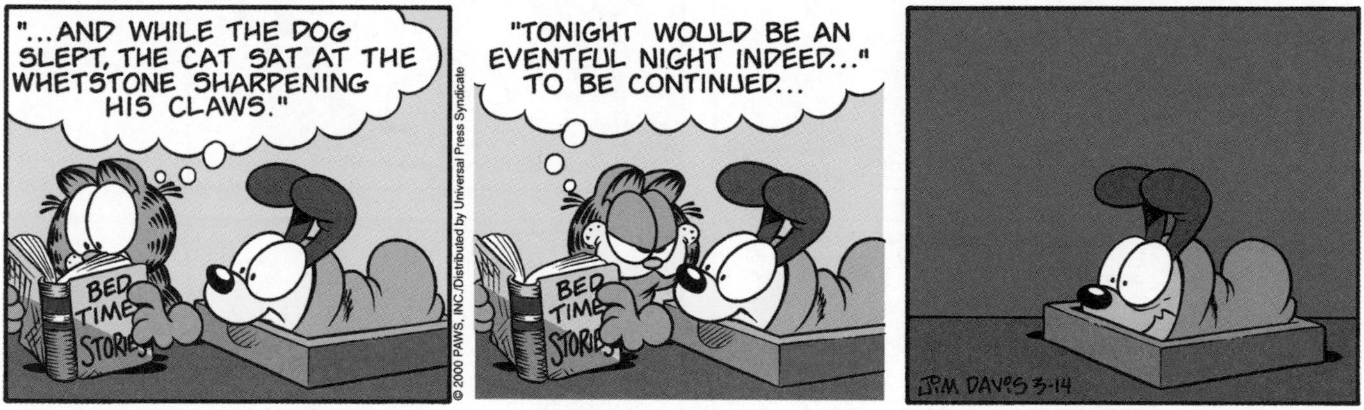
"...AND WHILE THE DOG SLEPT, THE CAT SAT AT THE WHETSTONE SHARPENING HIS CLAWS."
BED TIME STORIES
"TONIGHT WOULD BE AN EVENTFUL NIGHT INDEED..." TO BE CONTINUED...
© 2000 PAWS, INC./Distributed by Universal Press Syndicate
JIM DAVIS 3-14

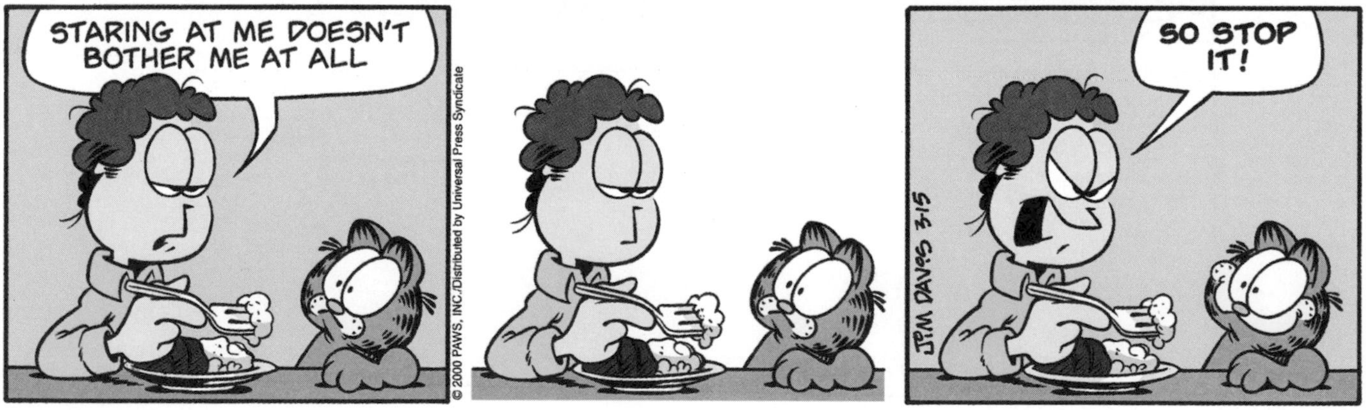
STARING AT ME DOESN'T BOTHER ME AT ALL
SO STOP IT!
© 2000 PAWS, INC./Distributed by Universal Press Syndicate
JIM DAVIS 3-15

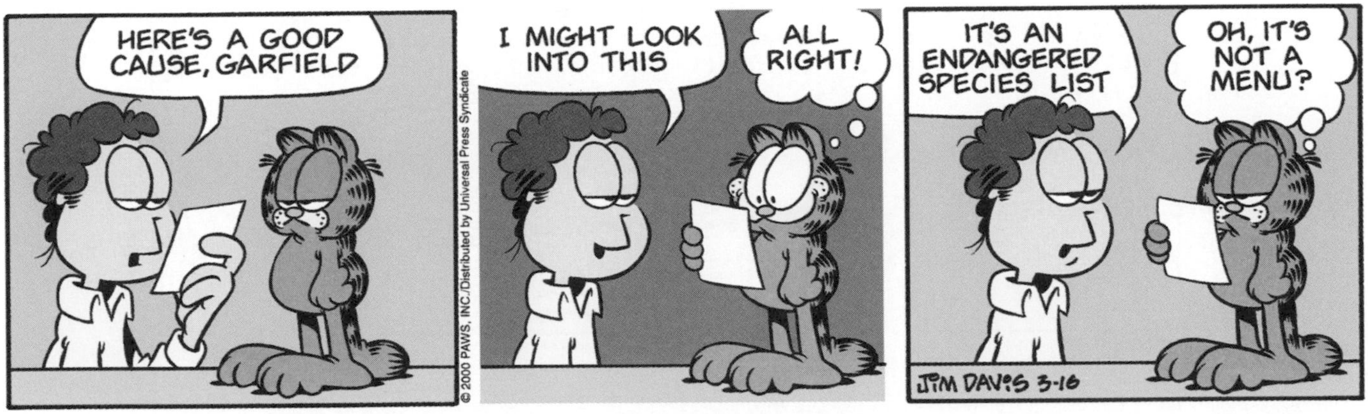
HERE'S A GOOD CAUSE, GARFIELD
I MIGHT LOOK INTO THIS
ALL RIGHT!
IT'S AN ENDANGERED SPECIES LIST
OH, IT'S NOT A MENU?
JIM DAVIS 3-16

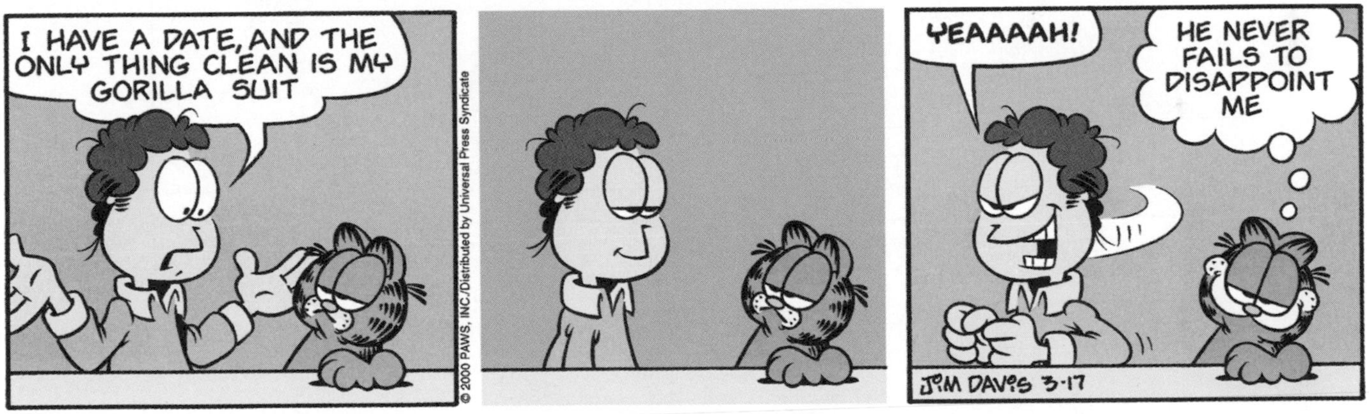
I HAVE A DATE, AND THE ONLY THING CLEAN IS MY GORILLA SUIT
YEAAAAH!
HE NEVER FAILS TO DISAPPOINT ME
JIM DAVIS 3-17

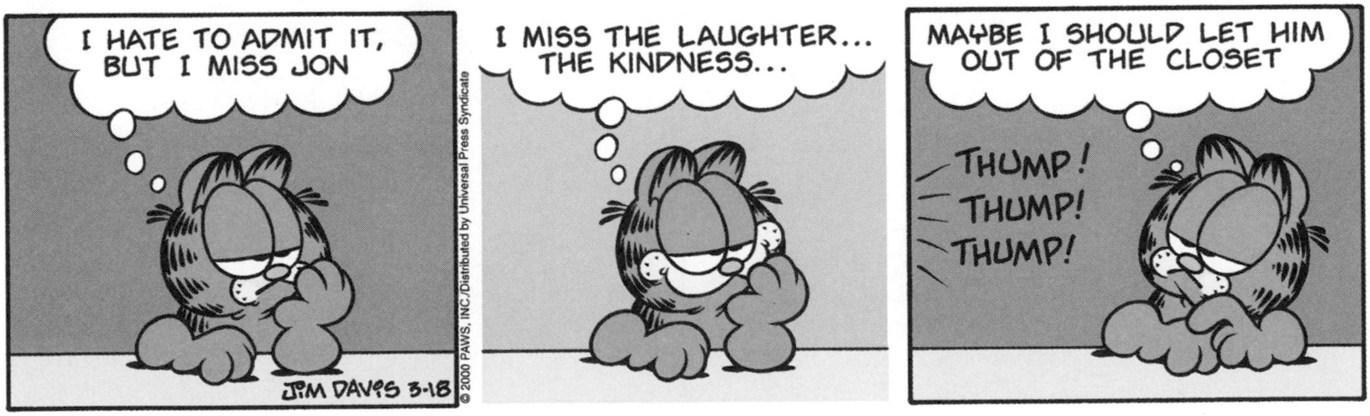
I HATE TO ADMIT IT, BUT I MISS JON
JIM DAVIS 3-18
I MISS THE LAUGHTER... THE KINDNESS...
MAYBE I SHOULD LET HIM OUT OF THE CLOSET
THUMP!
THUMP!
THUMP!

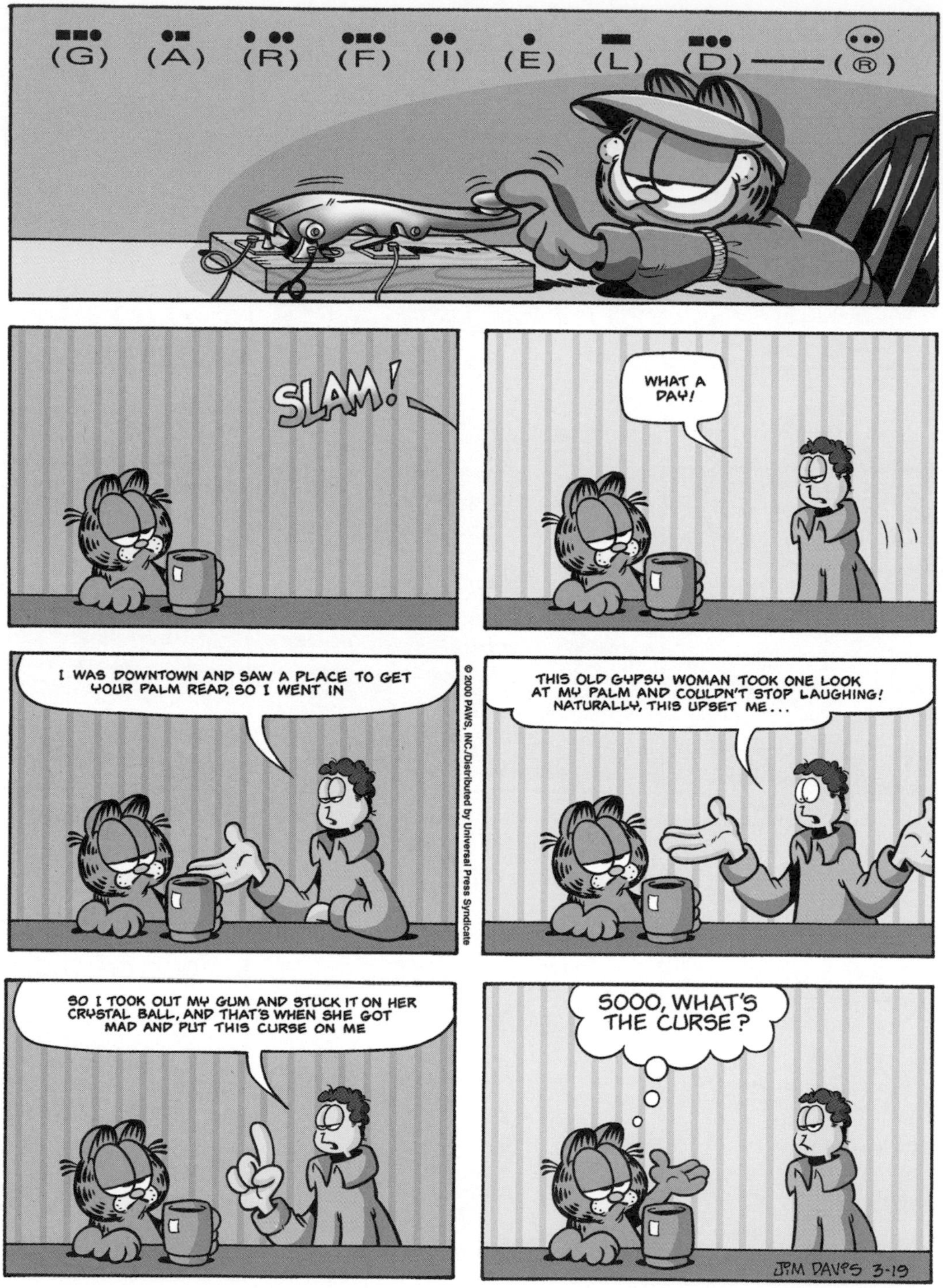
(G) (A) (R) (F) (I) (E) (L) (D) —— (®)
SLAM!
WHAT A DAY!
I WAS DOWNTOWN AND SAW A PLACE TO GET YOUR PALM READ, SO I WENT IN
THIS OLD GYPSY WOMAN TOOK ONE LOOK AT MY PALM AND COULDN'T STOP LAUGHING! NATURALLY, THIS UPSET ME...
SO I TOOK OUT MY GUM AND STUCK IT ON HER CRYSTAL BALL, AND THAT'S WHEN SHE GOT MAD AND PUT THIS CURSE ON ME
SOOO, WHAT'S THE CURSE?
JIM DAVIS 3-19
© 2000 PAWS, INC./Distributed by Universal Press Syndicate

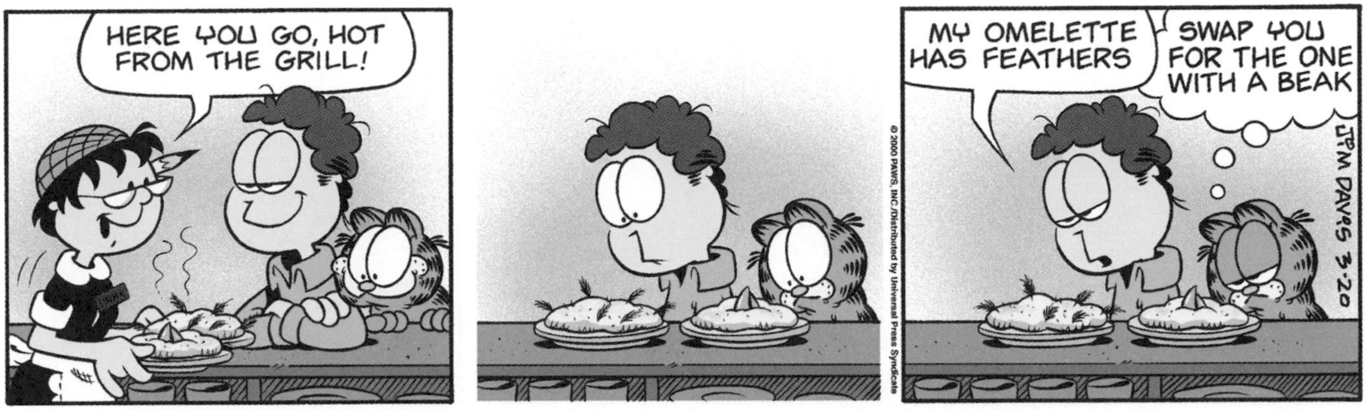
HERE YOU GO, HOT FROM THE GRILL!
© 2000 PAWS, INC./Distributed by Universal Press Syndicate
MY OMELETTE HAS FEATHERS
SWAP YOU FOR THE ONE WITH A BEAK
JIM DAVIS 3-20

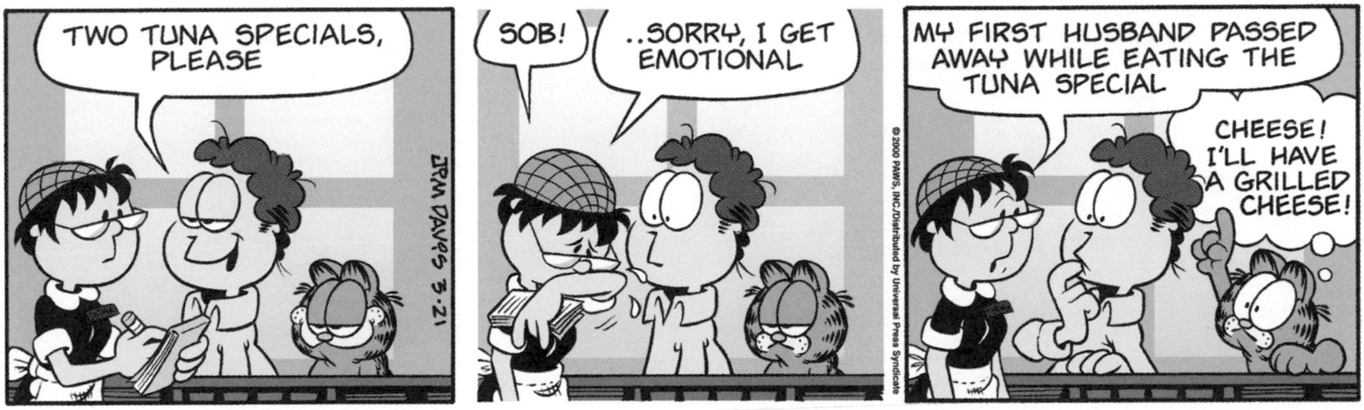
TWO TUNA SPECIALS, PLEASE
JIM DAVIS 3-21
SOB!
..SORRY, I GET EMOTIONAL
© 2000 PAWS, INC./Distributed by Universal Press Syndicate
MY FIRST HUSBAND PASSED AWAY WHILE EATING THE TUNA SPECIAL
CHEESE! I'LL HAVE A GRILLED CHEESE!

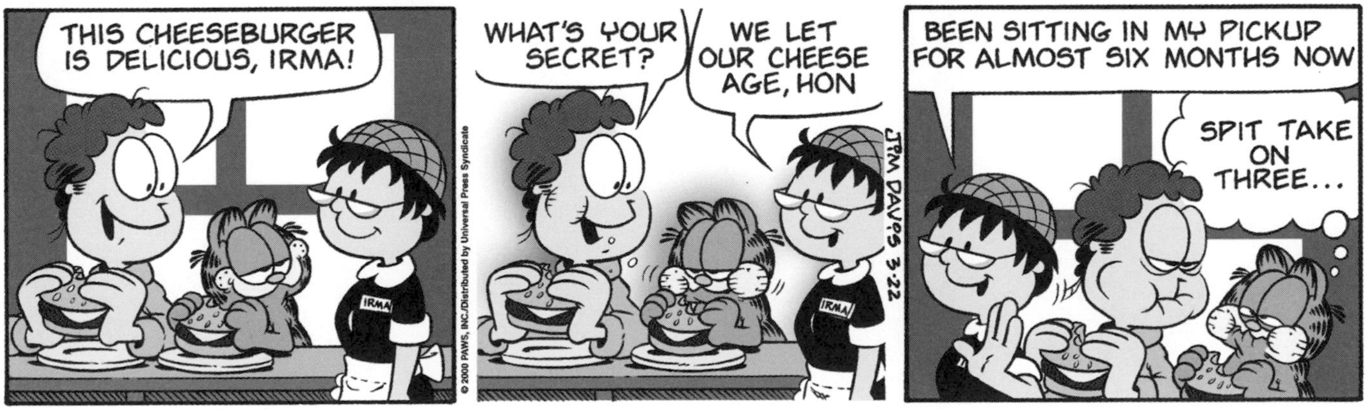
THIS CHEESEBURGER IS DELICIOUS, IRMA!
IRMA
© 2000 PAWS, INC./Distributed by Universal Press Syndicate
WHAT'S YOUR SECRET?
WE LET OUR CHEESE AGE, HON
JIM DAVIS 3-22
IRMA
BEEN SITTING IN MY PICKUP FOR ALMOST SIX MONTHS NOW
SPIT TAKE ON THREE...

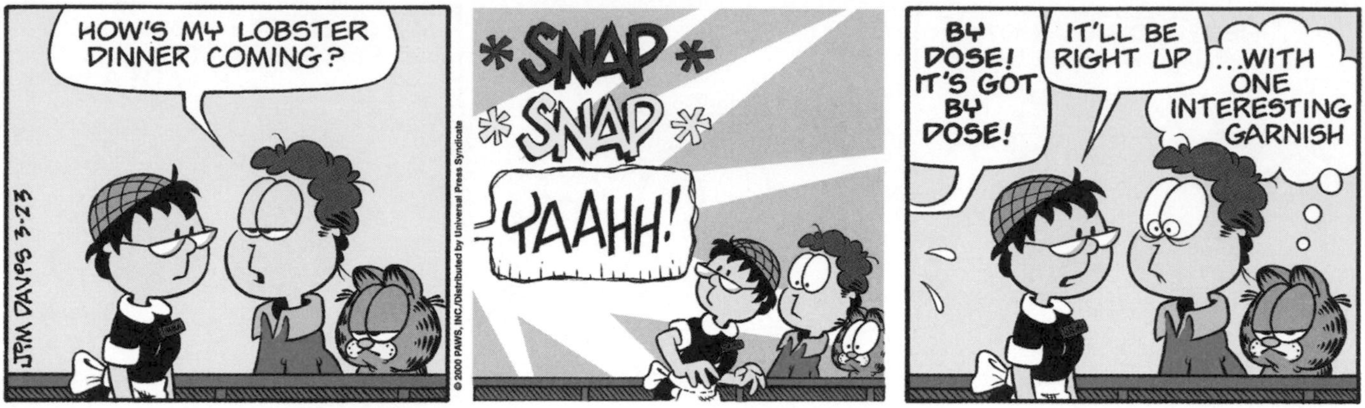
HOW'S MY LOBSTER DINNER COMING?
SNAP
SNAP
YAAHH!
BY DOSE! IT'S GOT BY DOSE!
IT'LL BE RIGHT UP
...WITH ONE INTERESTING GARNISH
JIM DAVIS 3-23
© 2000 PAWS, INC./Distributed by Universal Press Syndicate

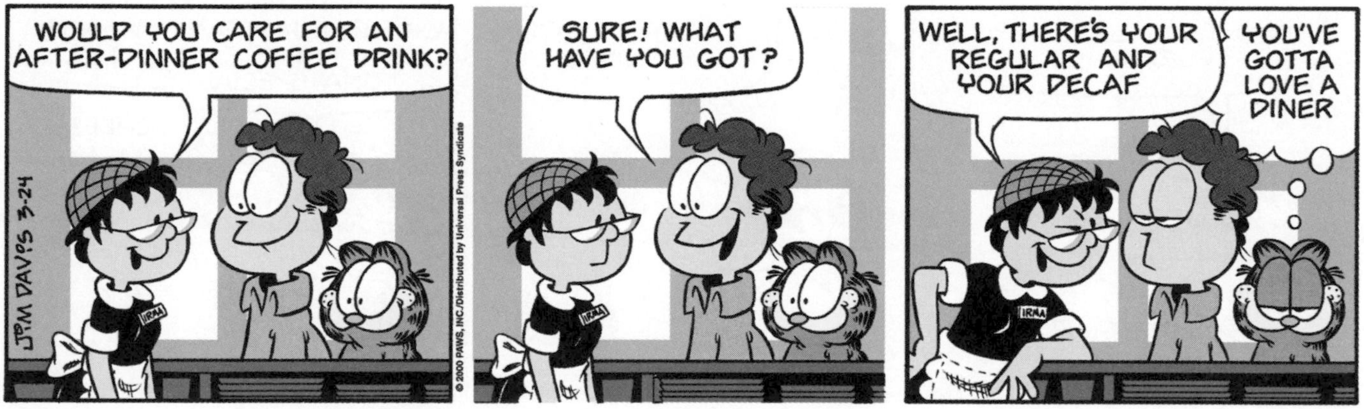
WOULD YOU CARE FOR AN AFTER-DINNER COFFEE DRINK?
SURE! WHAT HAVE YOU GOT?
WELL, THERE'S YOUR REGULAR AND YOUR DECAF
YOU'VE GOTTA LOVE A DINER
IRMA
JIM DAVIS 3-24
© 2000 PAWS, INC./Distributed by Universal Press Syndicate

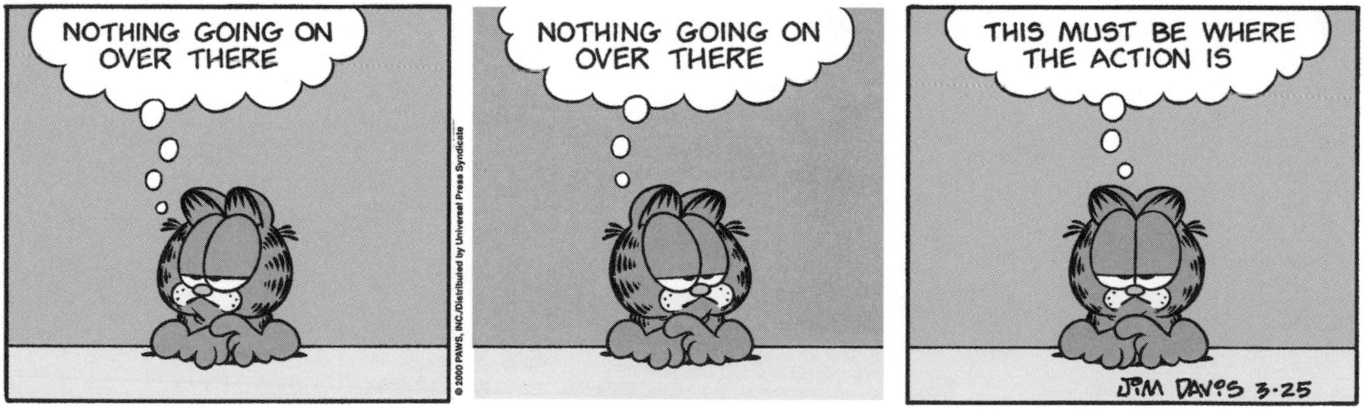
NOTHING GOING ON OVER THERE
NOTHING GOING ON OVER THERE
THIS MUST BE WHERE THE ACTION IS
JIM DAVIS 3-25
© 2000 PAWS, INC./Distributed by Universal Press Syndicate

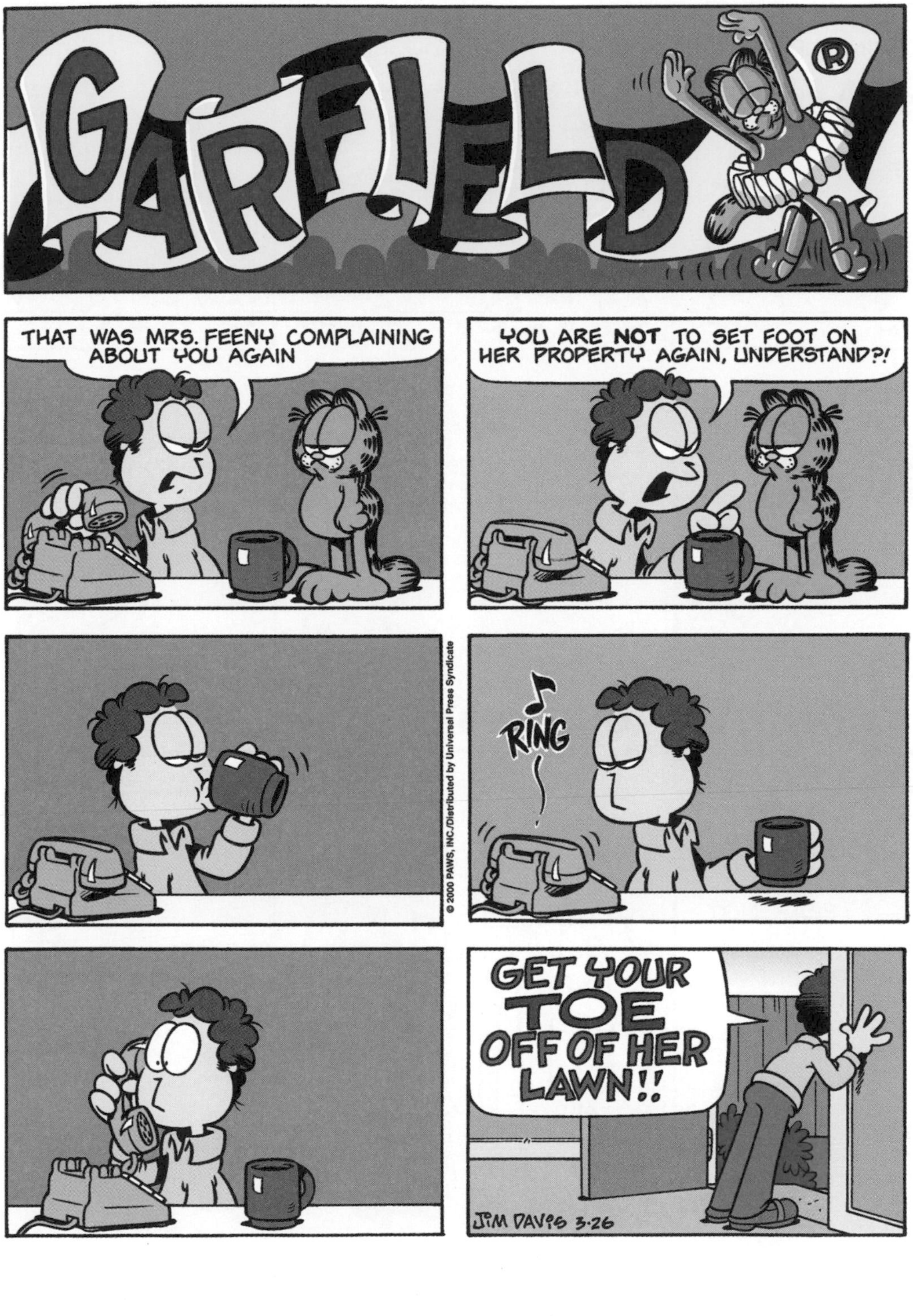

GARFIELD®
THAT WAS MRS. FEENY COMPLAINING ABOUT YOU AGAIN
YOU ARE **NOT** TO SET FOOT ON HER PROPERTY AGAIN, UNDERSTAND?!
© 2000 PAWS, INC./Distributed by Universal Press Syndicate
RING
GET YOUR TOE OFF OF HER LAWN!!
JIM DAVIS 3-26

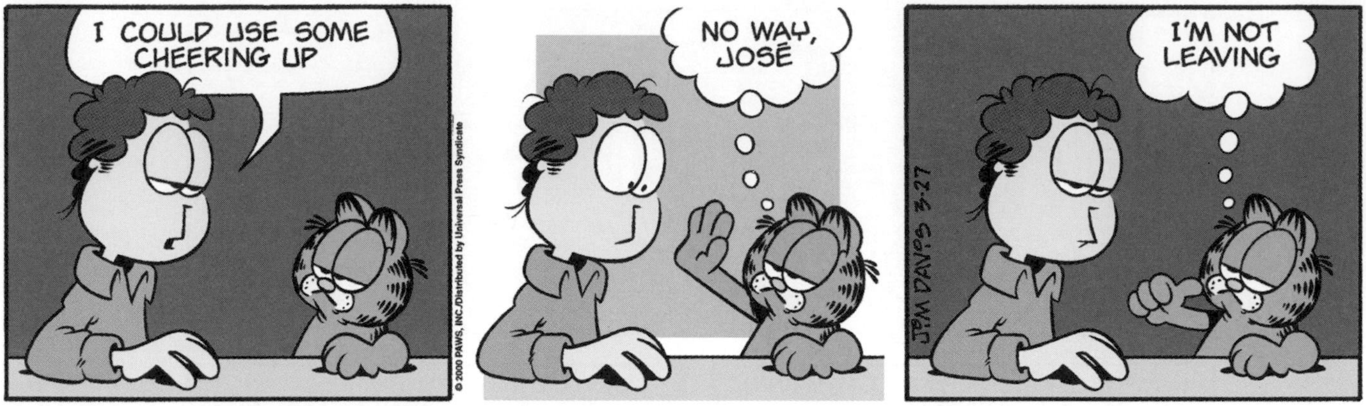
I COULD USE SOME CHEERING UP
NO WAY, JOSÉ
I'M NOT LEAVING
© 2000 PAWS, INC./Distributed by Universal Press Syndicate
JIM DAVIS 3-27

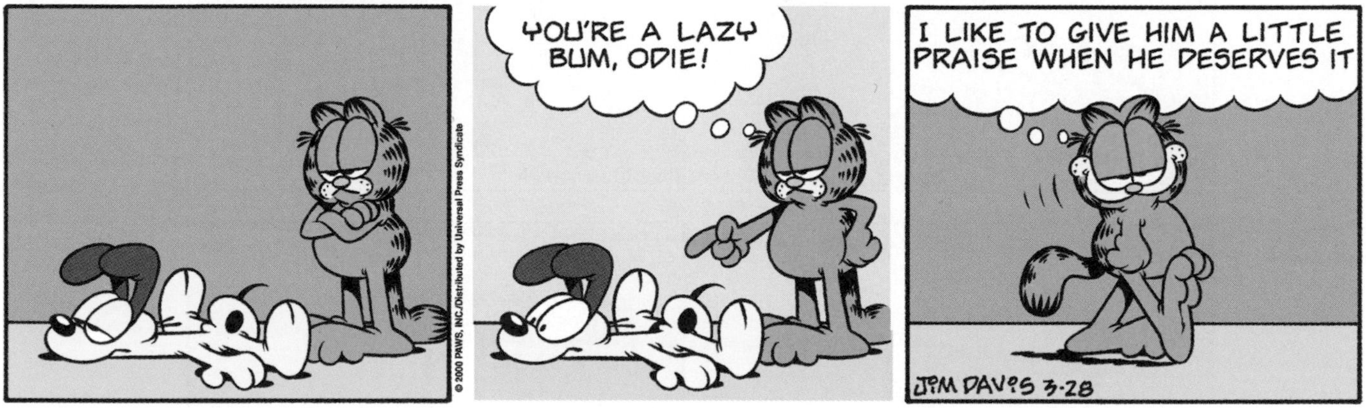
YOU'RE A LAZY BUM, ODIE!
I LIKE TO GIVE HIM A LITTLE PRAISE WHEN HE DESERVES IT
© 2000 PAWS, INC./Distributed by Universal Press Syndicate
JIM DAVIS 3-28

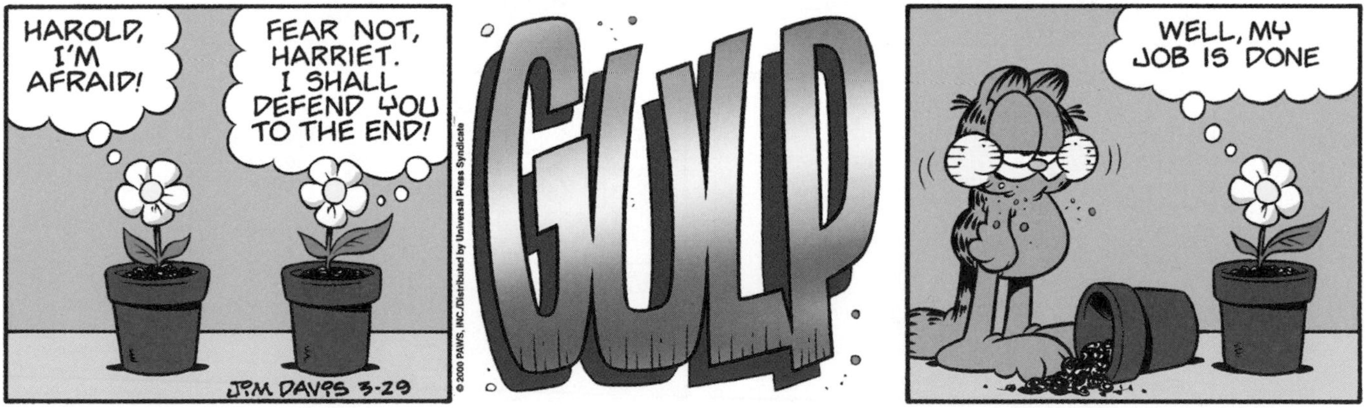
HAROLD, I'M AFRAID!
FEAR NOT, HARRIET. I SHALL DEFEND YOU TO THE END!
GULP
WELL, MY JOB IS DONE
© 2000 PAWS, INC./Distributed by Universal Press Syndicate
JIM DAVIS 3-29

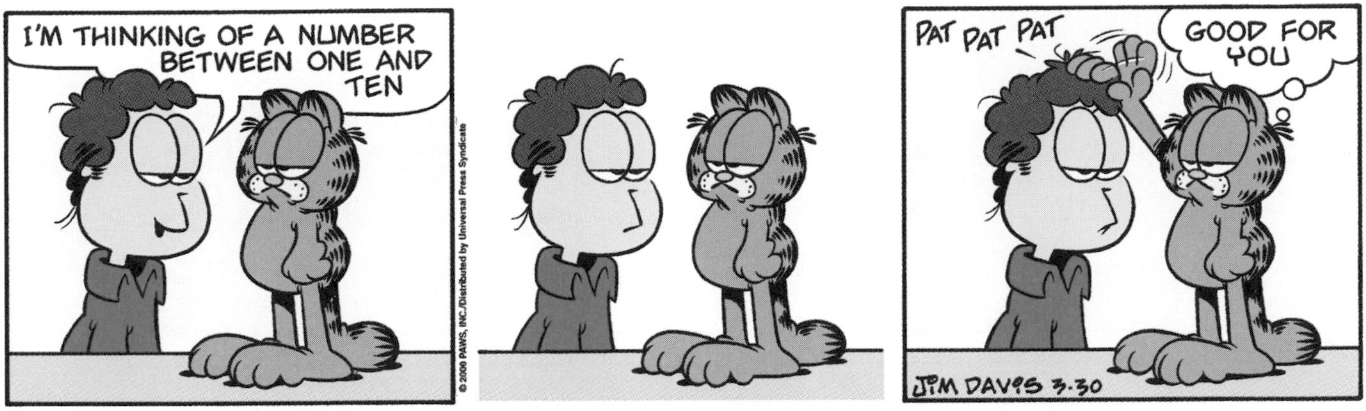
I'M THINKING OF A NUMBER BETWEEN ONE AND TEN
PAT PAT PAT
GOOD FOR YOU
JIM DAVIS 3-30

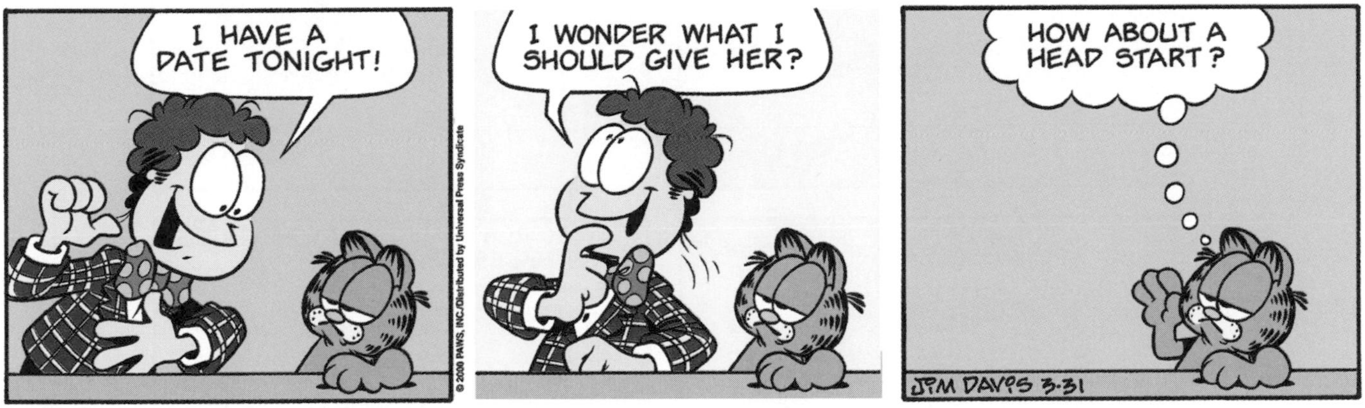
I HAVE A DATE TONIGHT!
I WONDER WHAT I SHOULD GIVE HER?
HOW ABOUT A HEAD START?
JIM DAVIS 3-31

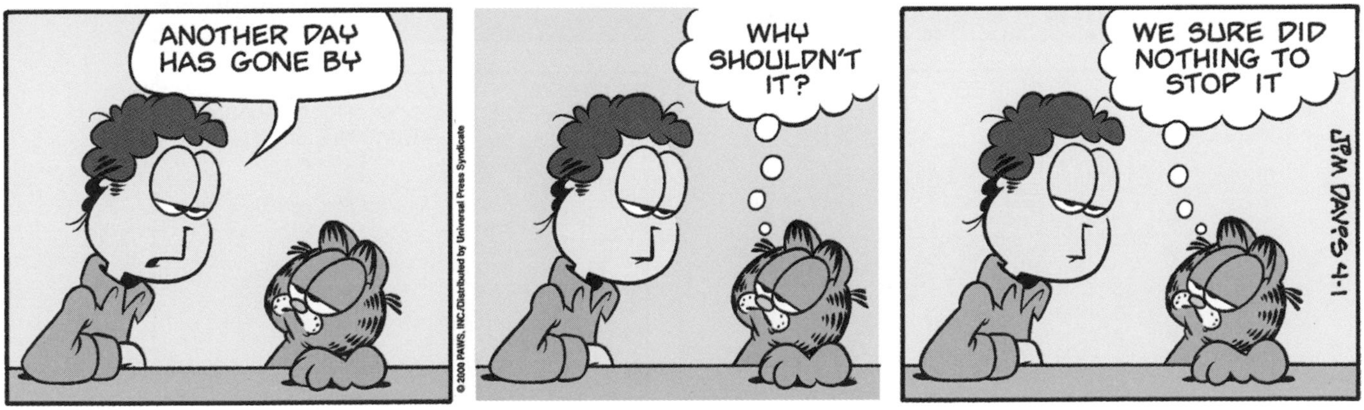
ANOTHER DAY HAS GONE BY
WHY SHOULDN'T IT?
WE SURE DID NOTHING TO STOP IT
JIM DAVIS 4-1

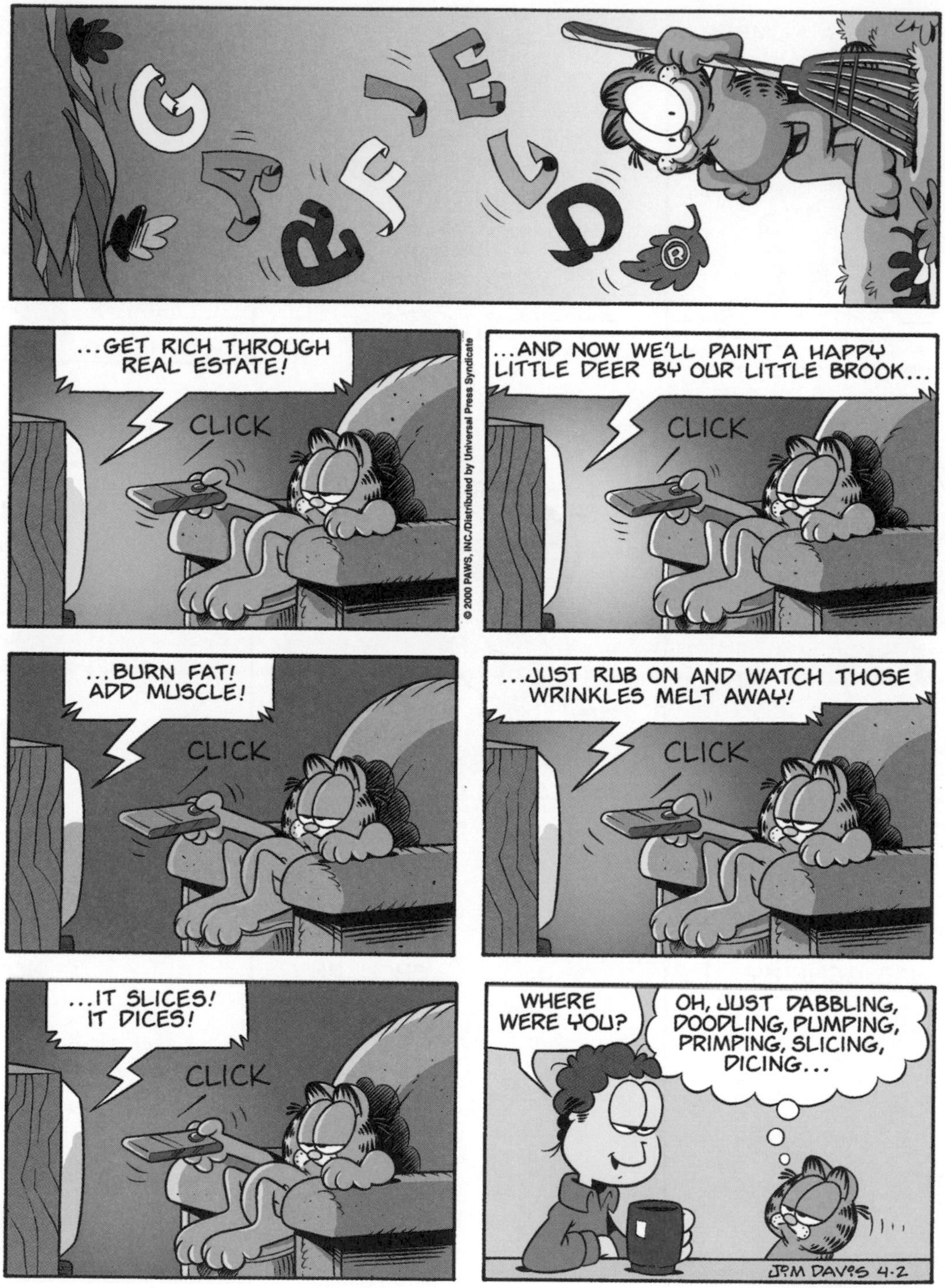
GARFIELD ®
...GET RICH THROUGH REAL ESTATE!
CLICK
...AND NOW WE'LL PAINT A HAPPY LITTLE DEER BY OUR LITTLE BROOK...
CLICK
...BURN FAT! ADD MUSCLE!
CLICK
...JUST RUB ON AND WATCH THOSE WRINKLES MELT AWAY!
CLICK
...IT SLICES! IT DICES!
CLICK
WHERE WERE YOU?
OH, JUST DABBLING, DOODLING, PUMPING, PRIMPING, SLICING, DICING...
JIM DAVIS 4-2
© 2000 PAWS, INC./Distributed by Universal Press Syndicate

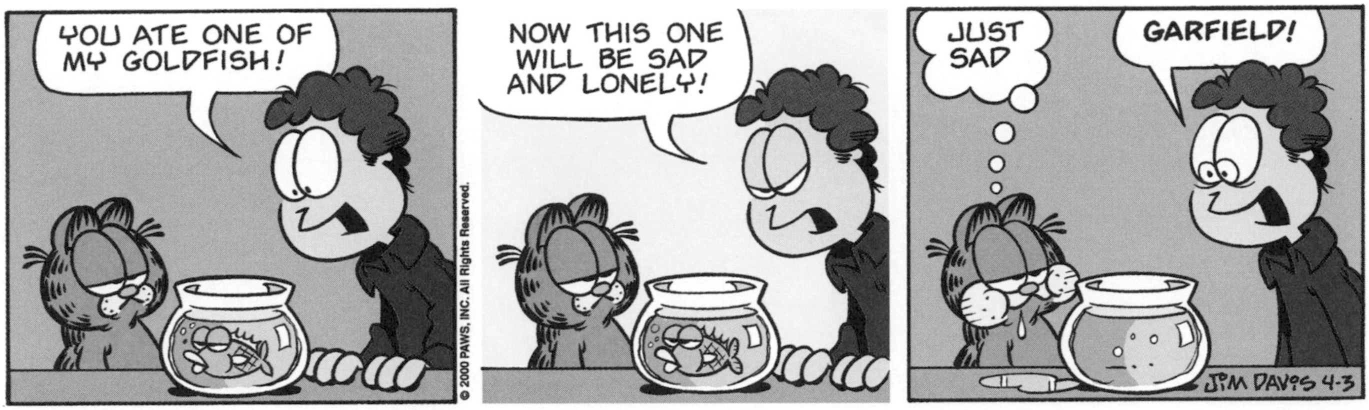
YOU ATE ONE OF MY GOLDFISH!
NOW THIS ONE WILL BE SAD AND LONELY!
JUST SAD
GARFIELD!
© 2000 PAWS, INC. All Rights Reserved.
JIM DAVIS 4-3

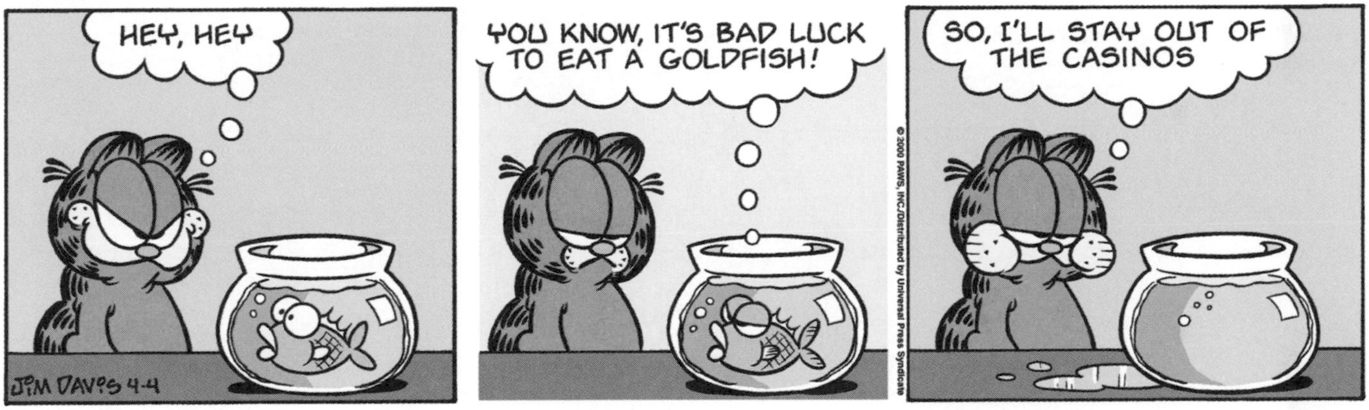
HEY, HEY
YOU KNOW, IT'S BAD LUCK TO EAT A GOLDFISH!
SO, I'LL STAY OUT OF THE CASINOS
JIM DAVIS 4-4
© 2000 PAWS, INC./Distributed by Universal Press Syndicate

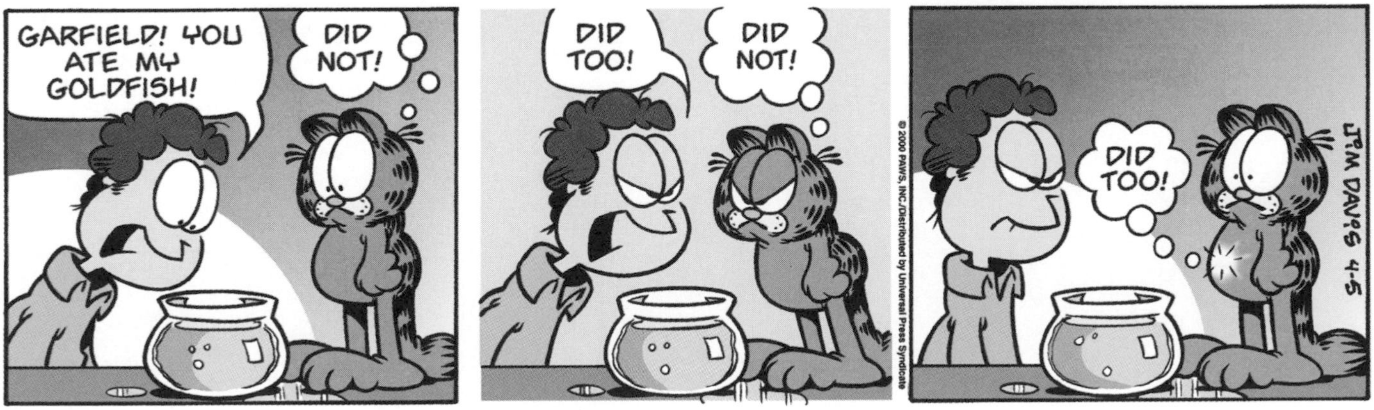
GARFIELD! YOU ATE MY GOLDFISH!
DID NOT!
DID TOO!
DID NOT!
DID TOO!
JIM DAVIS 4-5
© 2000 PAWS, INC./Distributed by Universal Press Syndicate

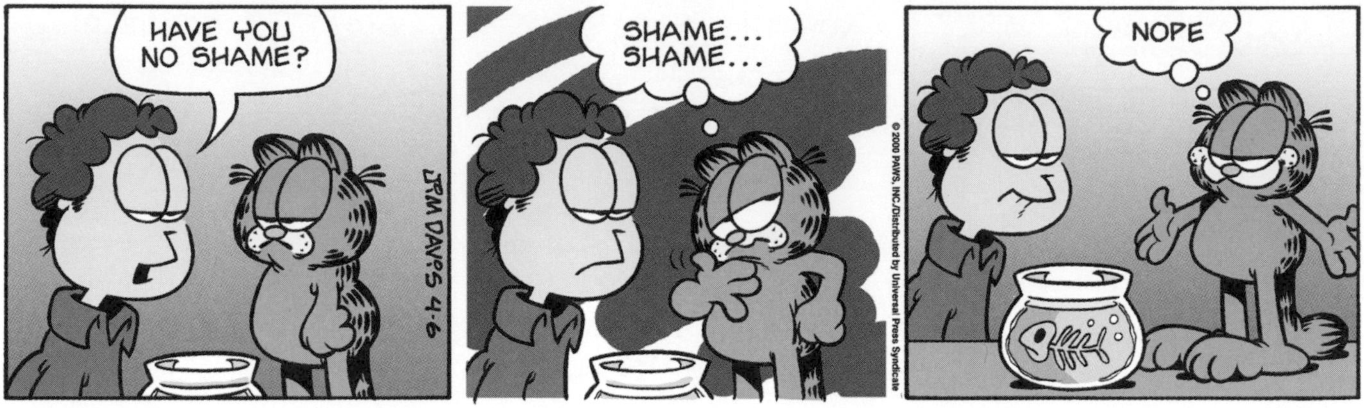
HAVE YOU NO SHAME?
JIM DAVIS 4-6
SHAME... SHAME...
© 2000 PAWS, INC./Distributed by Universal Press Syndicate
NOPE

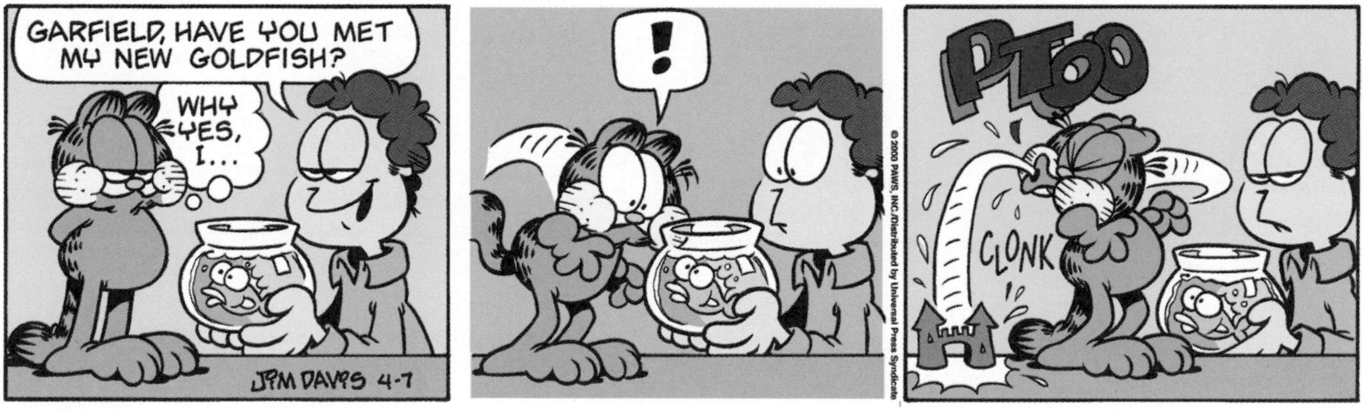
GARFIELD, HAVE YOU MET MY NEW GOLDFISH?
WHY YES, I...
JIM DAVIS 4-7
!
© 2000 PAWS, INC./Distributed by Universal Press Syndicate
PTOO
CLONK

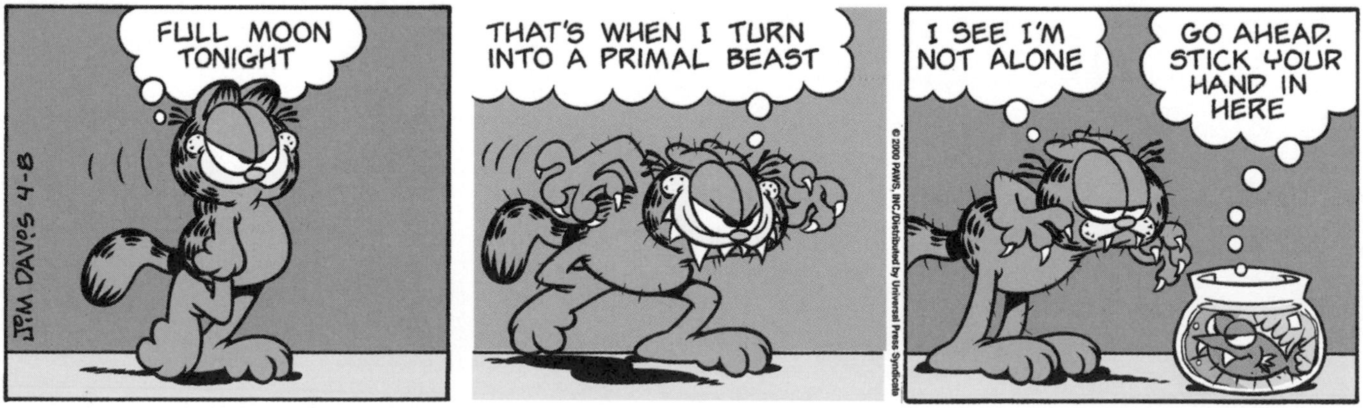
FULL MOON TONIGHT
JIM DAVIS 4-8
THAT'S WHEN I TURN INTO A PRIMAL BEAST
© 2000 PAWS, INC./Distributed by Universal Press Syndicate
I SEE I'M NOT ALONE
GO AHEAD. STICK YOUR HAND IN HERE

GARFIELD'S
TOP TEN SUGGESTIONS
FOR NEW ATHLETIC EVENTS

10 The dogput

9 Synchronized snoring

8 Speedsnacking

7 Mice hockey

6 Demolition bobsleds

5 90-meter ski jump onto unsuspecting grandma

4 Long jump over a pit of rabid wolverines

3 Fridge lift

2 Hairball hack

1 Eat till you explode!

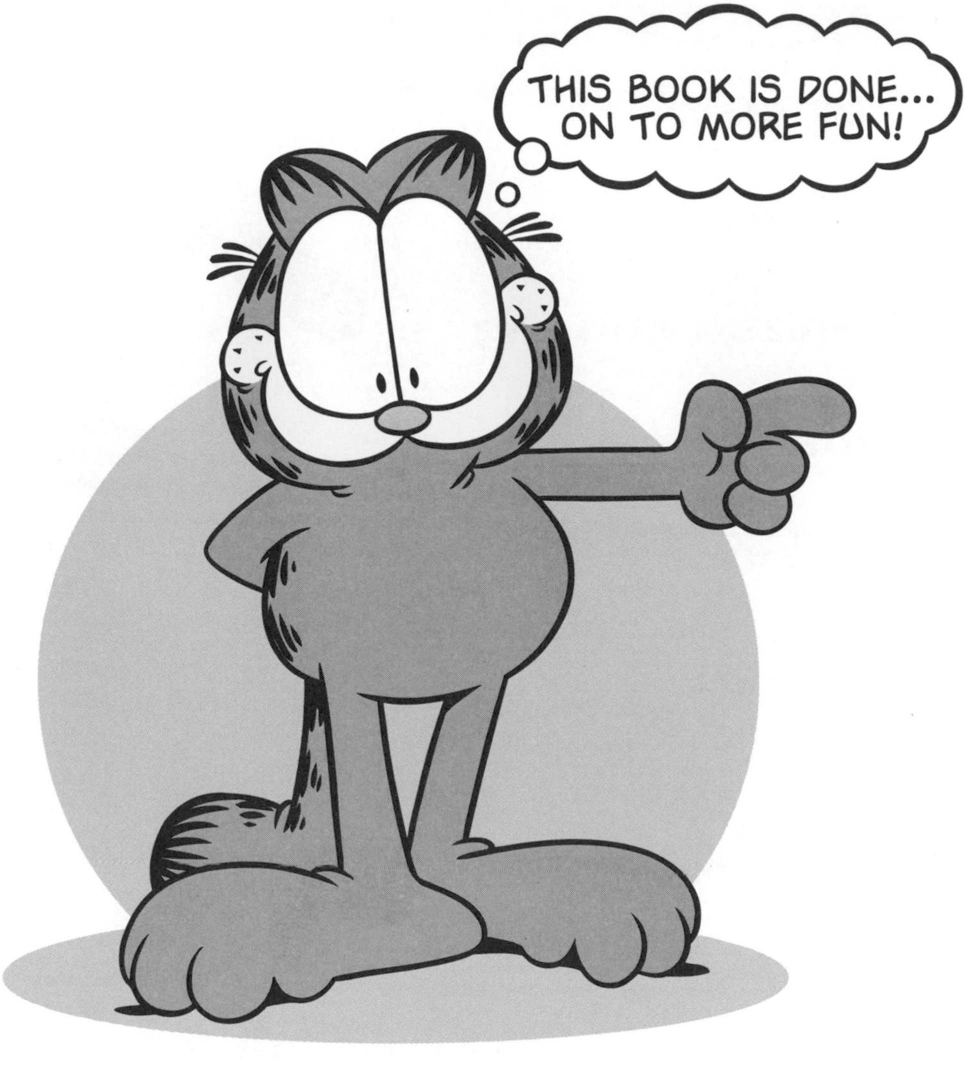
THIS BOOK IS DONE...
ON TO MORE FUN!

Garfield gets cookin'

BY JIM DAVIS

Ballantine Books • New York

Top Ten Dating Dodges Women Use On Jon

10. "Sorry, I Don't Date Outside My Species."

9. "I'll Be Washing My hair All That Week. Each One. Individually."

8. "I'm Getting a Sex-change Operation."

7. "I Came Down With a Severe Case of Toe Jam."

6. "Darn, I have to Pick Up My Wombat From the Taxidermist that Night."

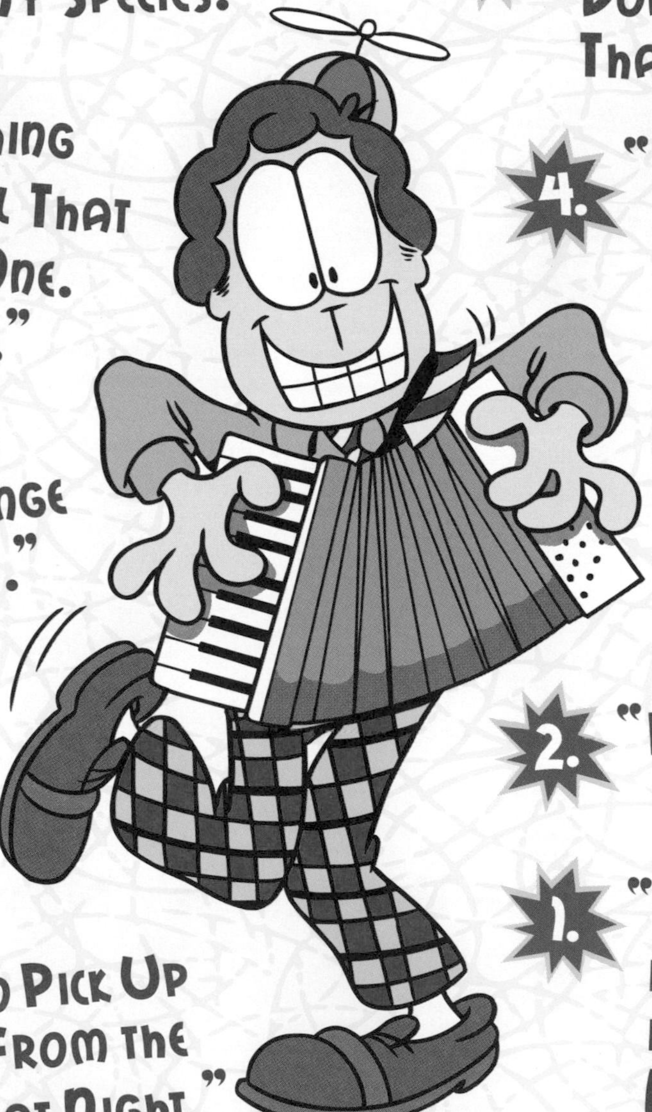

5. "No Can Do. I'm Donating My Kidne That Weekend."

4. "That's the Night I Wax My Grandmother's Mustache."

3. "I have to Stay hom and Floss My Otter.

2. "I'm Allergic to Geeks."

1. "I'd Rather Swim in Piranha-infested Waters Dressed as a Meat Loaf."

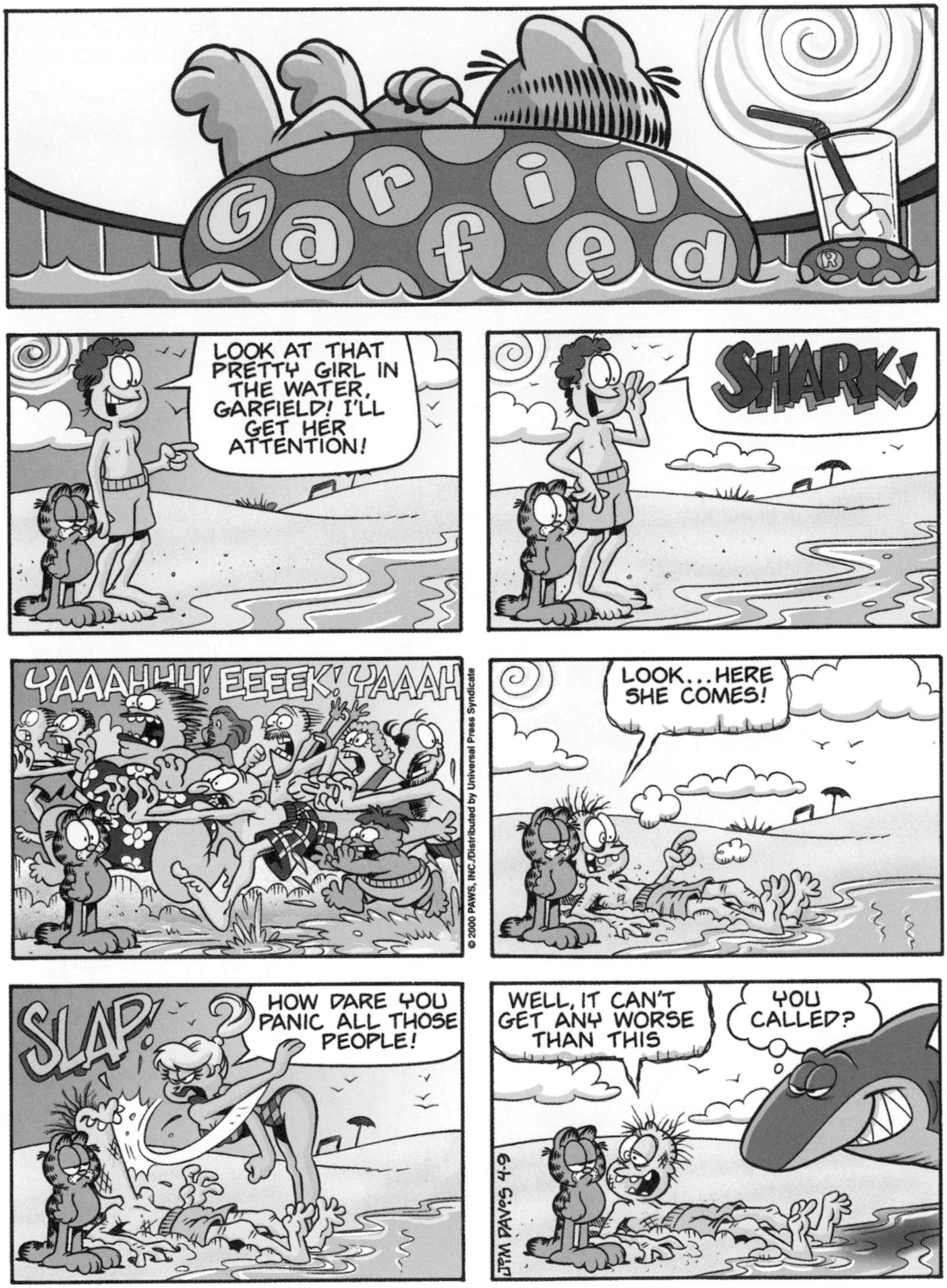
Garfield
LOOK AT THAT PRETTY GIRL IN THE WATER, GARFIELD! I'LL GET HER ATTENTION!
SHARK!
YAAAHHH! EEEEK! YAAAH
© 2000 PAWS, INC./Distributed by Universal Press Syndicate
LOOK...HERE SHE COMES!
SLAP
HOW DARE YOU PANIC ALL THOSE PEOPLE!
WELL, IT CAN'T GET ANY WORSE THAN THIS
YOU CALLED?
JPM DAVIS 4-9

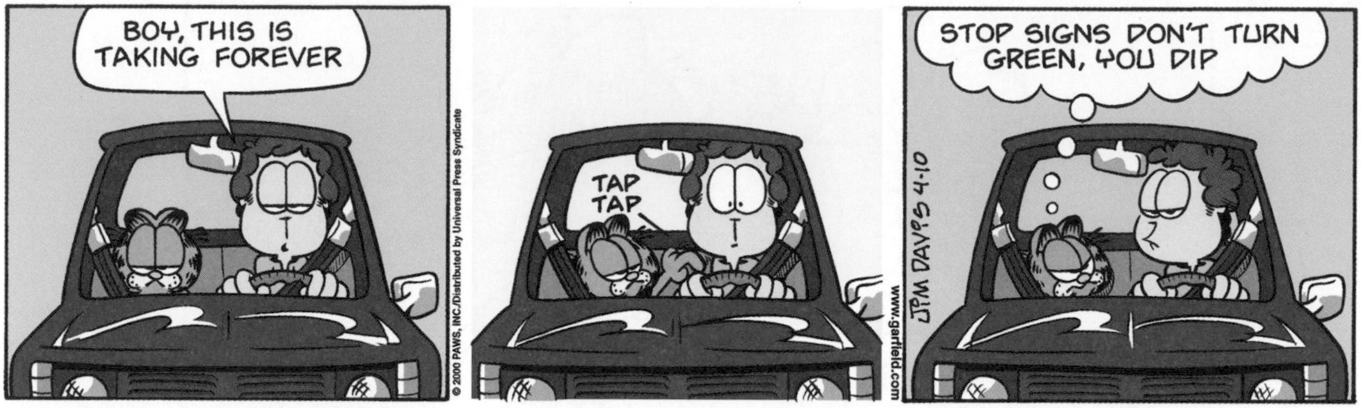
BOY, THIS IS TAKING FOREVER
TAP TAP
STOP SIGNS DON'T TURN GREEN, YOU DIP
© 2000 PAWS, INC./Distributed by Universal Press Syndicate
www.garfield.com
JIM DAVIS 4·10

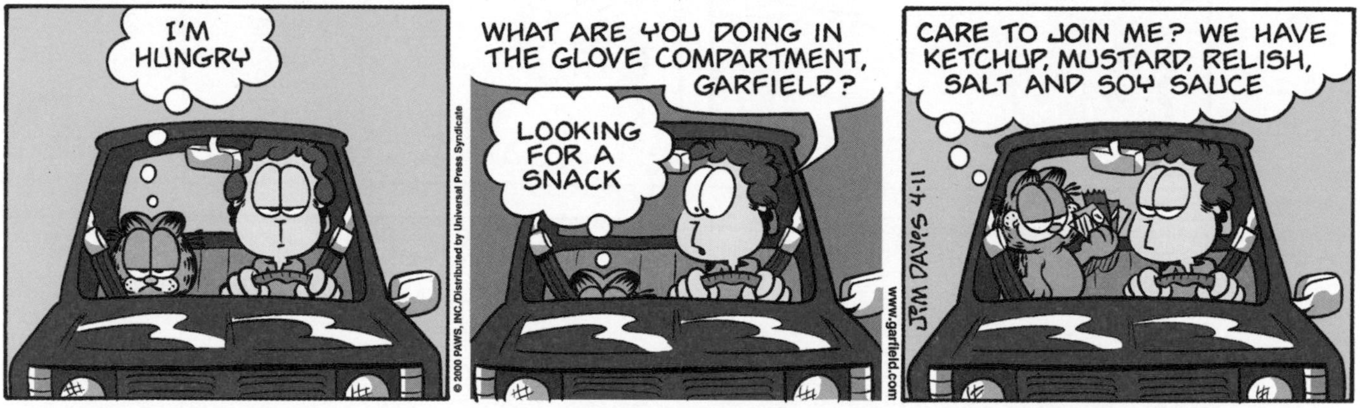
I'M HUNGRY
WHAT ARE YOU DOING IN THE GLOVE COMPARTMENT, GARFIELD?
LOOKING FOR A SNACK
CARE TO JOIN ME? WE HAVE KETCHUP, MUSTARD, RELISH, SALT AND SOY SAUCE
© 2000 PAWS, INC./Distributed by Universal Press Syndicate
www.garfield.com
JIM DAVIS 4·11

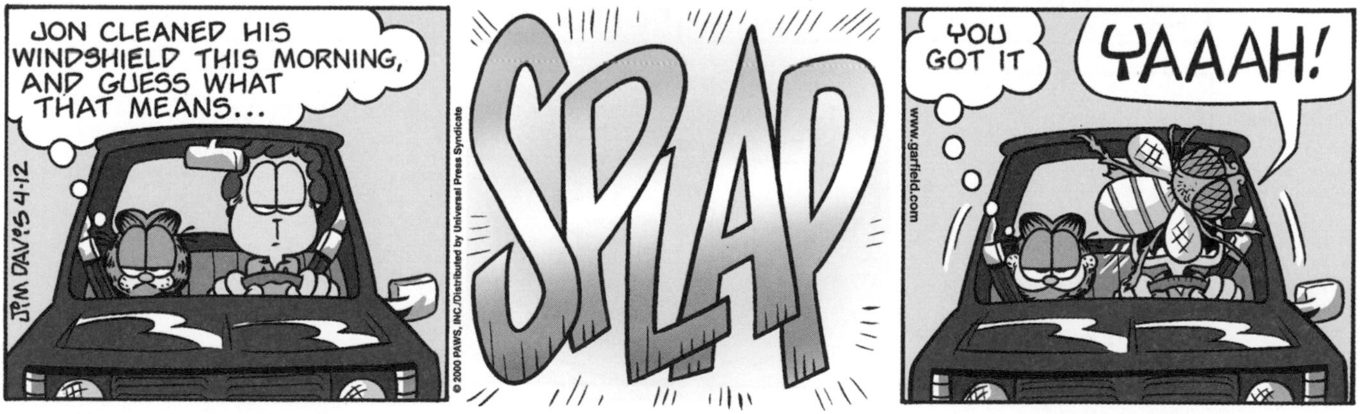
JON CLEANED HIS WINDSHIELD THIS MORNING, AND GUESS WHAT THAT MEANS...
SPLAP
YOU GOT IT
YAAAH!
© 2000 PAWS, INC./Distributed by Universal Press Syndicate
www.garfield.com
JIM DAVIS 4·12

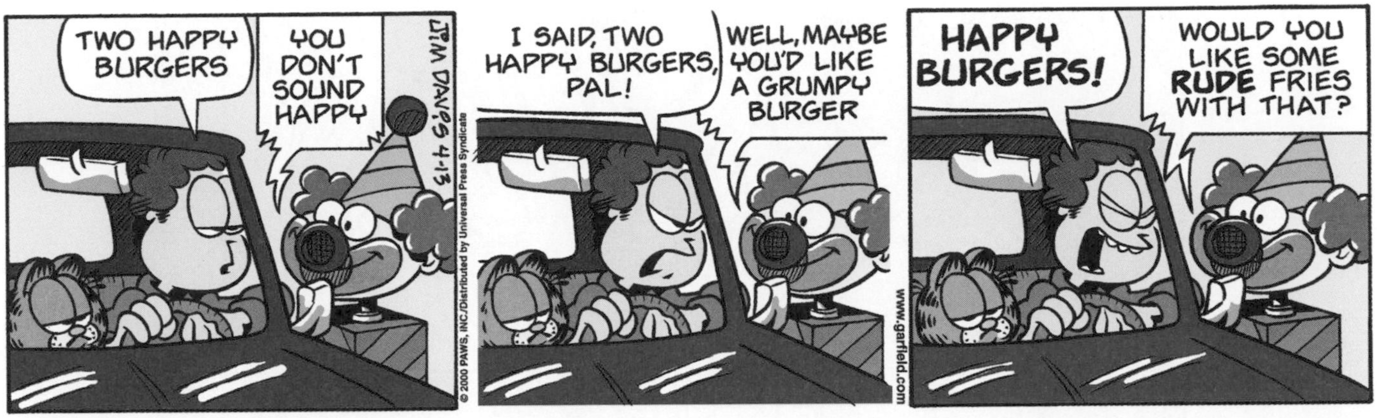
TWO HAPPY BURGERS
YOU DON'T SOUND HAPPY
JIM DAVIS 4-13
© 2000 PAWS, INC./Distributed by Universal Press Syndicate
I SAID, TWO HAPPY BURGERS, PAL!
WELL, MAYBE YOU'D LIKE A GRUMPY BURGER
www.garfield.com
HAPPY BURGERS!
WOULD YOU LIKE SOME **RUDE** FRIES WITH THAT?

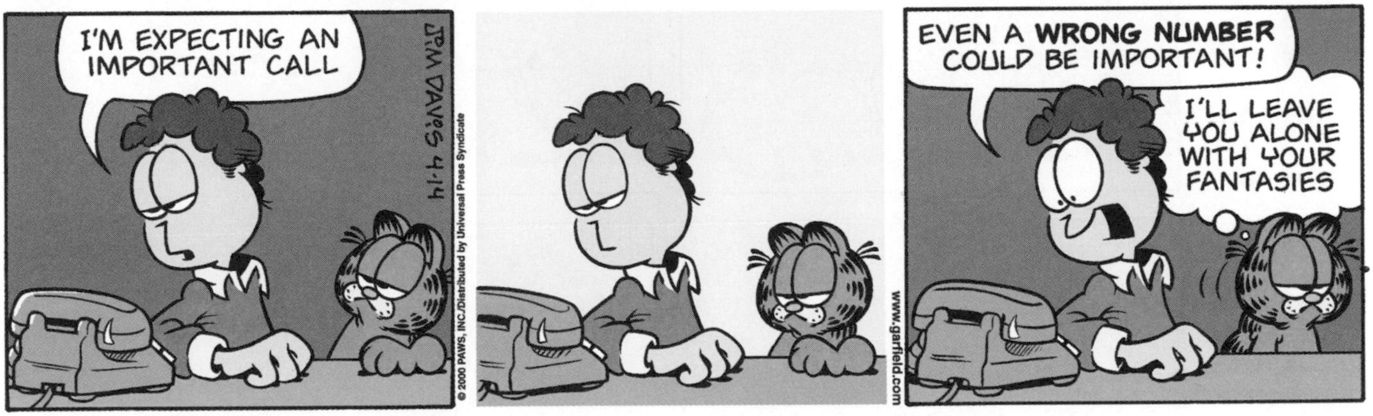
I'M EXPECTING AN IMPORTANT CALL
JIM DAVIS 4-14
© 2000 PAWS, INC./Distributed by Universal Press Syndicate
www.garfield.com
EVEN A **WRONG NUMBER** COULD BE IMPORTANT!
I'LL LEAVE YOU ALONE WITH YOUR FANTASIES

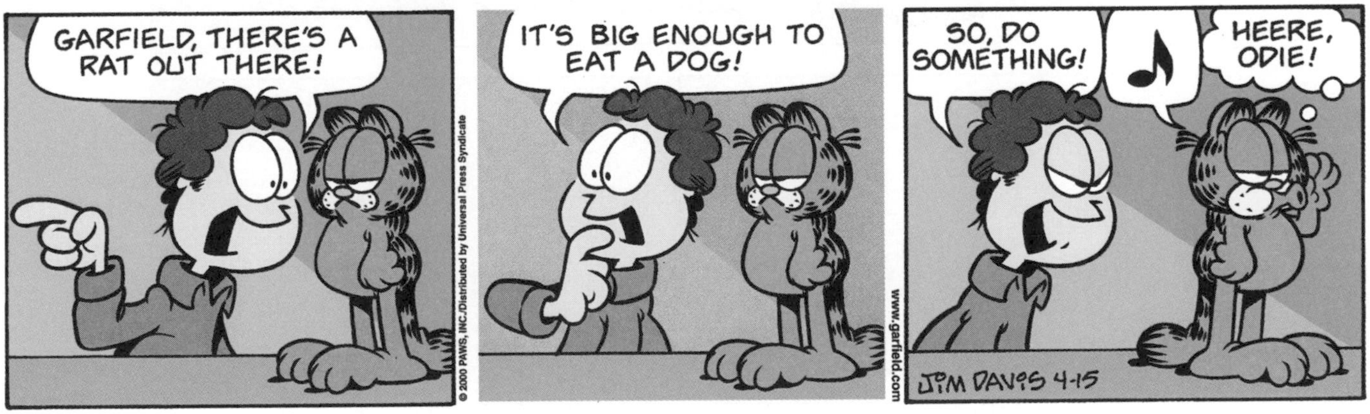
GARFIELD, THERE'S A RAT OUT THERE!
© 2000 PAWS, INC./Distributed by Universal Press Syndicate
IT'S BIG ENOUGH TO EAT A DOG!
www.garfield.com
SO, DO SOMETHING!
HEERE, ODIE!
JIM DAVIS 4-15

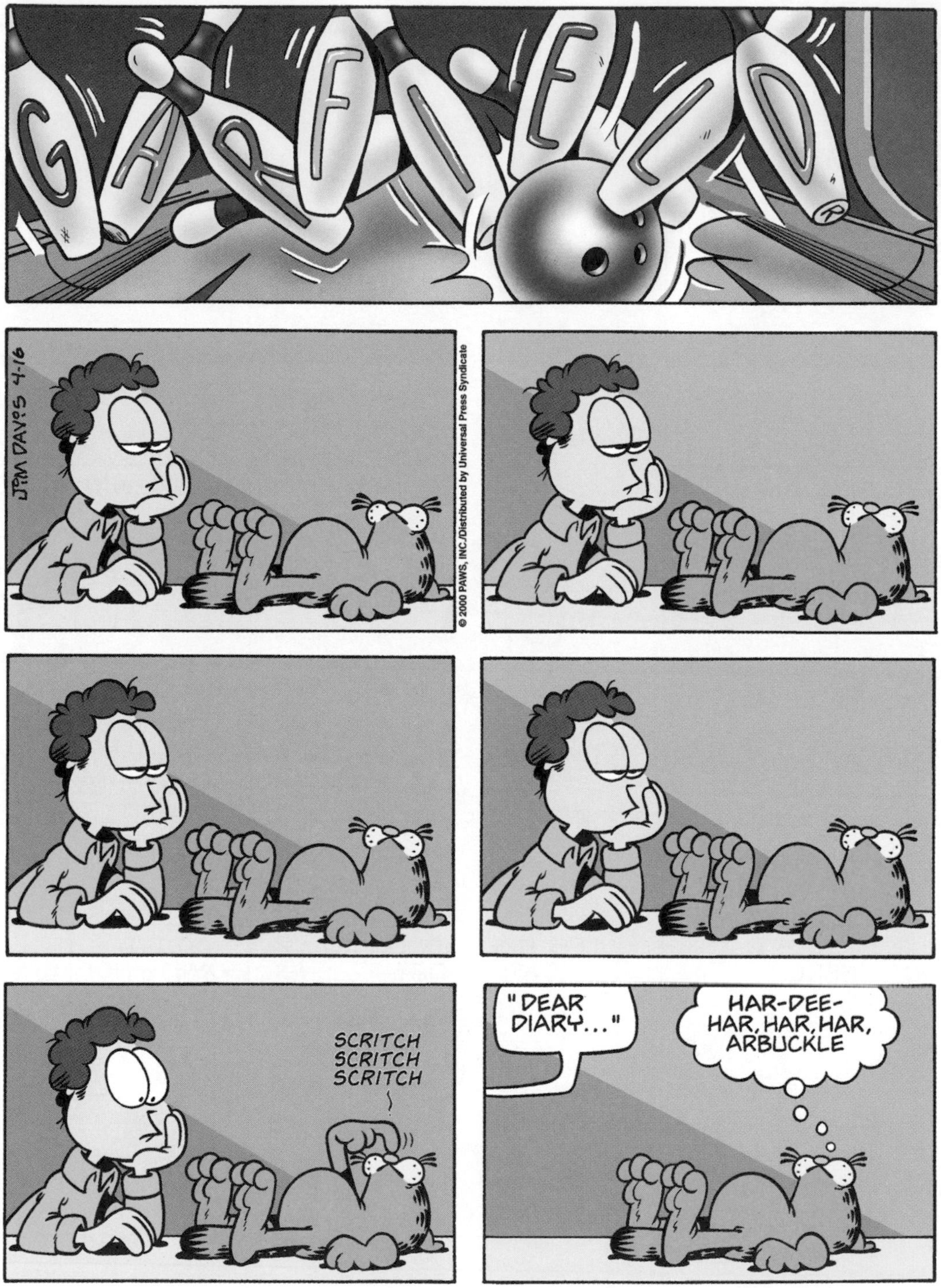
GARFIELD
JIM DAVIS 4-16
© 2000 PAWS, INC./Distributed by Universal Press Syndicate
SCRITCH SCRITCH SCRITCH
"DEAR DIARY..."
HAR-DEE-HAR, HAR, HAR, ARBUCKLE

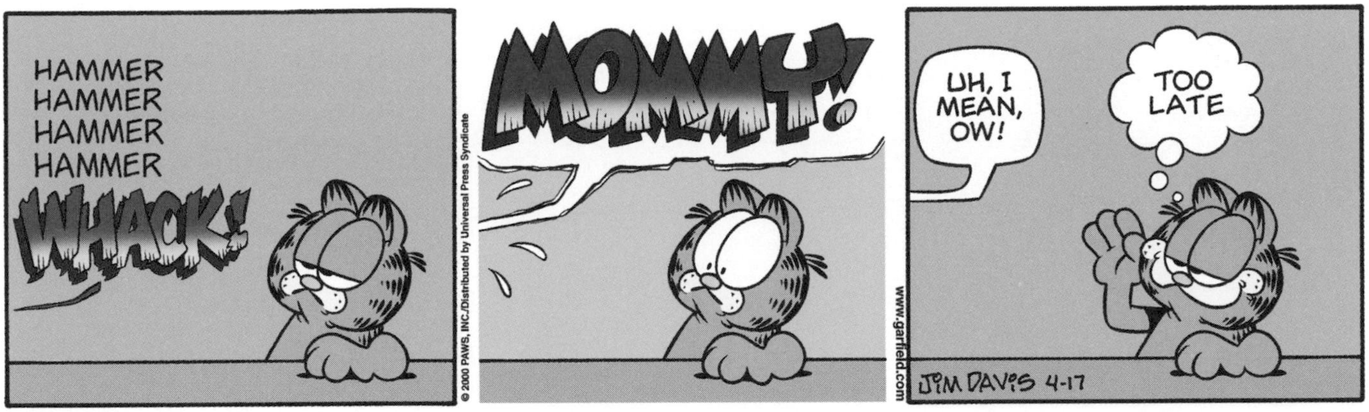
HAMMER
HAMMER
HAMMER
HAMMER
WHACK!
MOMMY!
UH, I MEAN, OW!
TOO LATE
© 2000 PAWS, INC./Distributed by Universal Press Syndicate
www.garfield.com
JIM DAVIS 4-17

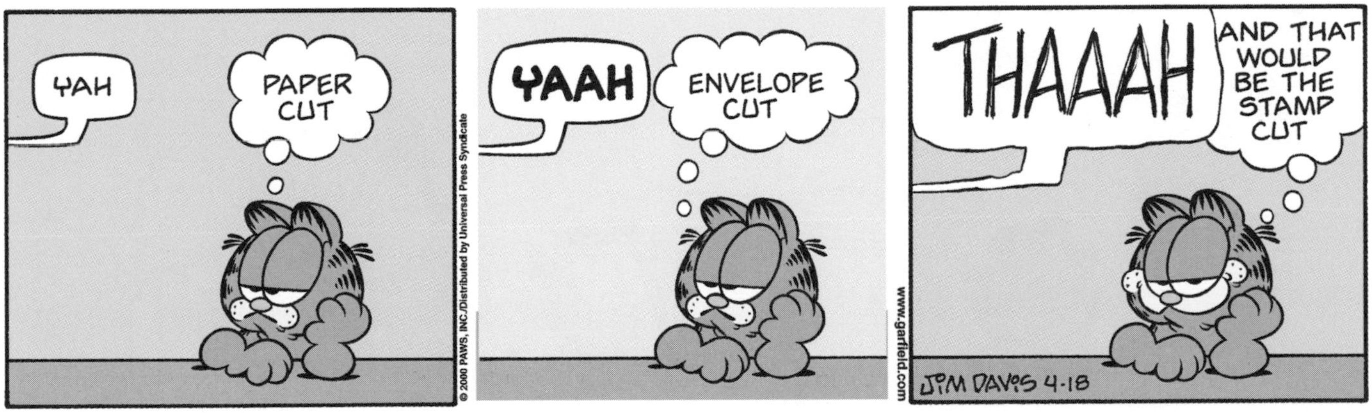
YAH
PAPER CUT
YAAH
ENVELOPE CUT
THAAAH
AND THAT WOULD BE THE STAMP CUT
© 2000 PAWS, INC./Distributed by Universal Press Syndicate
www.garfield.com
JIM DAVIS 4-18

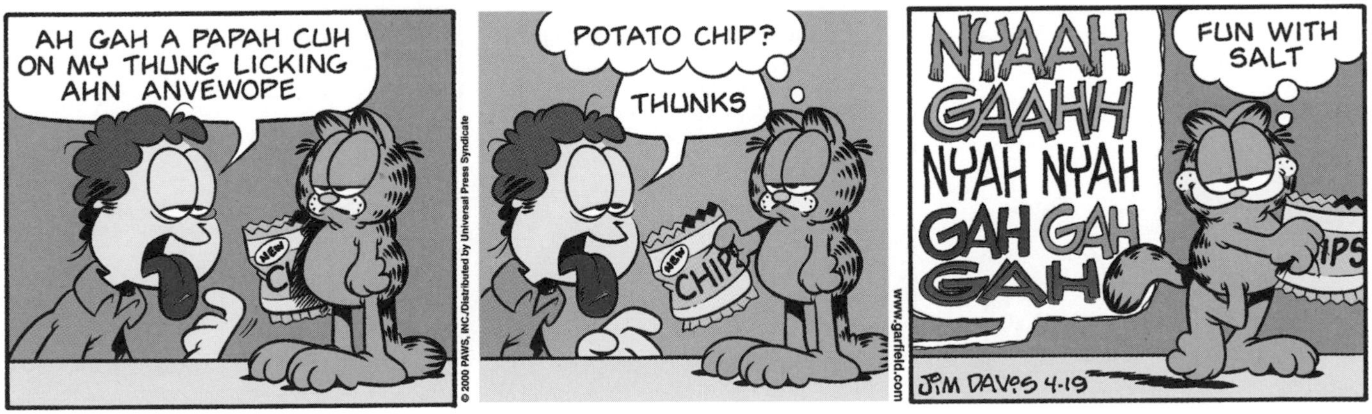
AH GAH A PAPAH CUH ON MY THUNG LICKING AHN ANVEWOPE
POTATO CHIP?
THUNKS
NYAAH
GAAHH
NYAH NYAH
GAH GAH
GAH
FUN WITH SALT
© 2000 PAWS, INC./Distributed by Universal Press Syndicate
www.garfield.com
JIM DAVIS 4-19

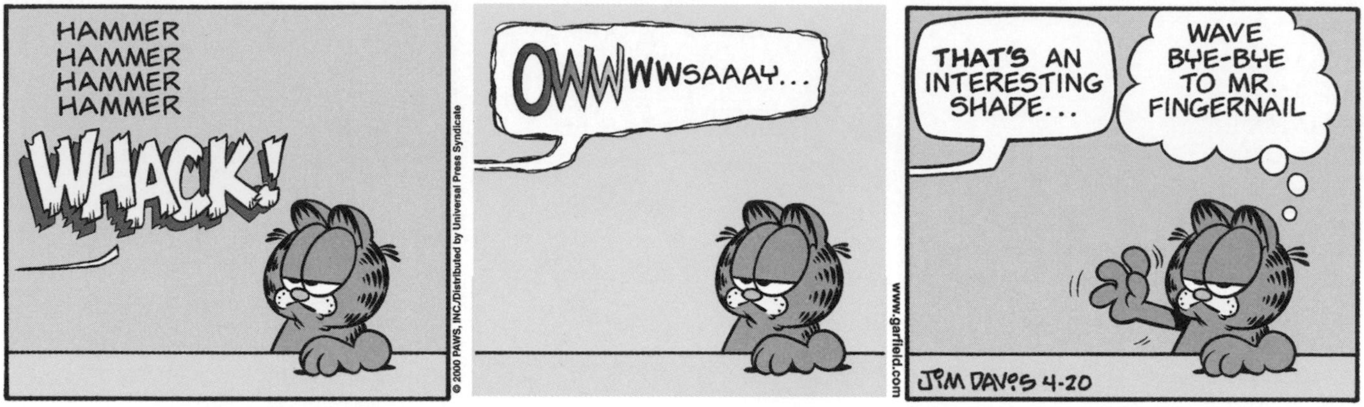
HAMMER
HAMMER
HAMMER
HAMMER
WHACK!
OWWWWWSAAAAY...
THAT'S AN INTERESTING SHADE...
WAVE BYE-BYE TO MR. FINGERNAIL
© 2000 PAWS, INC./Distributed by Universal Press Syndicate
www.garfield.com
JIM DAVIS 4-20

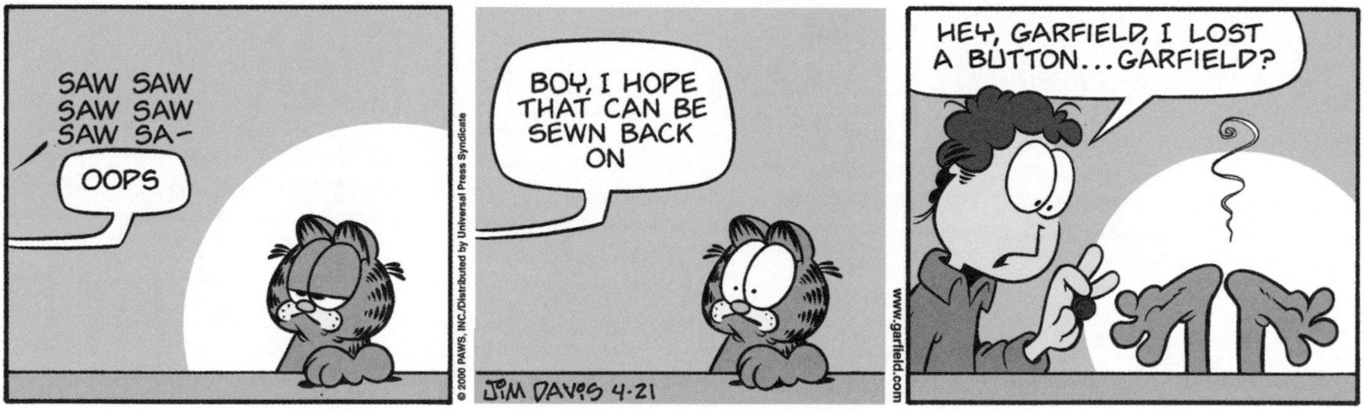
SAW SAW
SAW SAW
SAW SA-
OOPS
BOY, I HOPE THAT CAN BE SEWN BACK ON
HEY, GARFIELD, I LOST A BUTTON...GARFIELD?
© 2000 PAWS, INC./Distributed by Universal Press Syndicate
www.garfield.com
JIM DAVIS 4-21

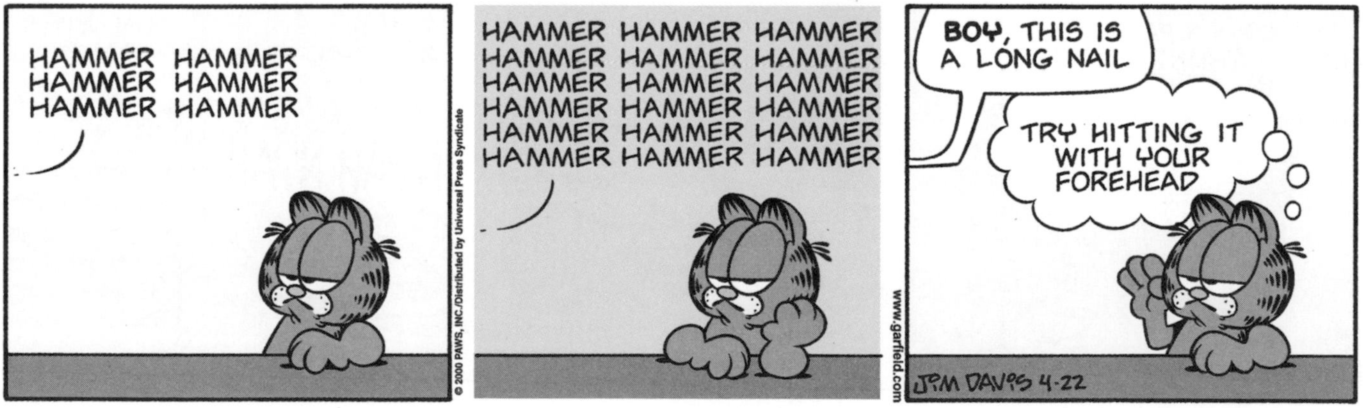
HAMMER HAMMER
HAMMER HAMMER
HAMMER HAMMER
HAMMER HAMMER HAMMER
HAMMER HAMMER HAMMER
HAMMER HAMMER HAMMER
HAMMER HAMMER HAMMER
HAMMER HAMMER HAMMER
HAMMER HAMMER HAMMER
BOY, THIS IS A LONG NAIL
TRY HITTING IT WITH YOUR FOREHEAD
© 2000 PAWS, INC./Distributed by Universal Press Syndicate
www.garfield.com
JIM DAVIS 4-22

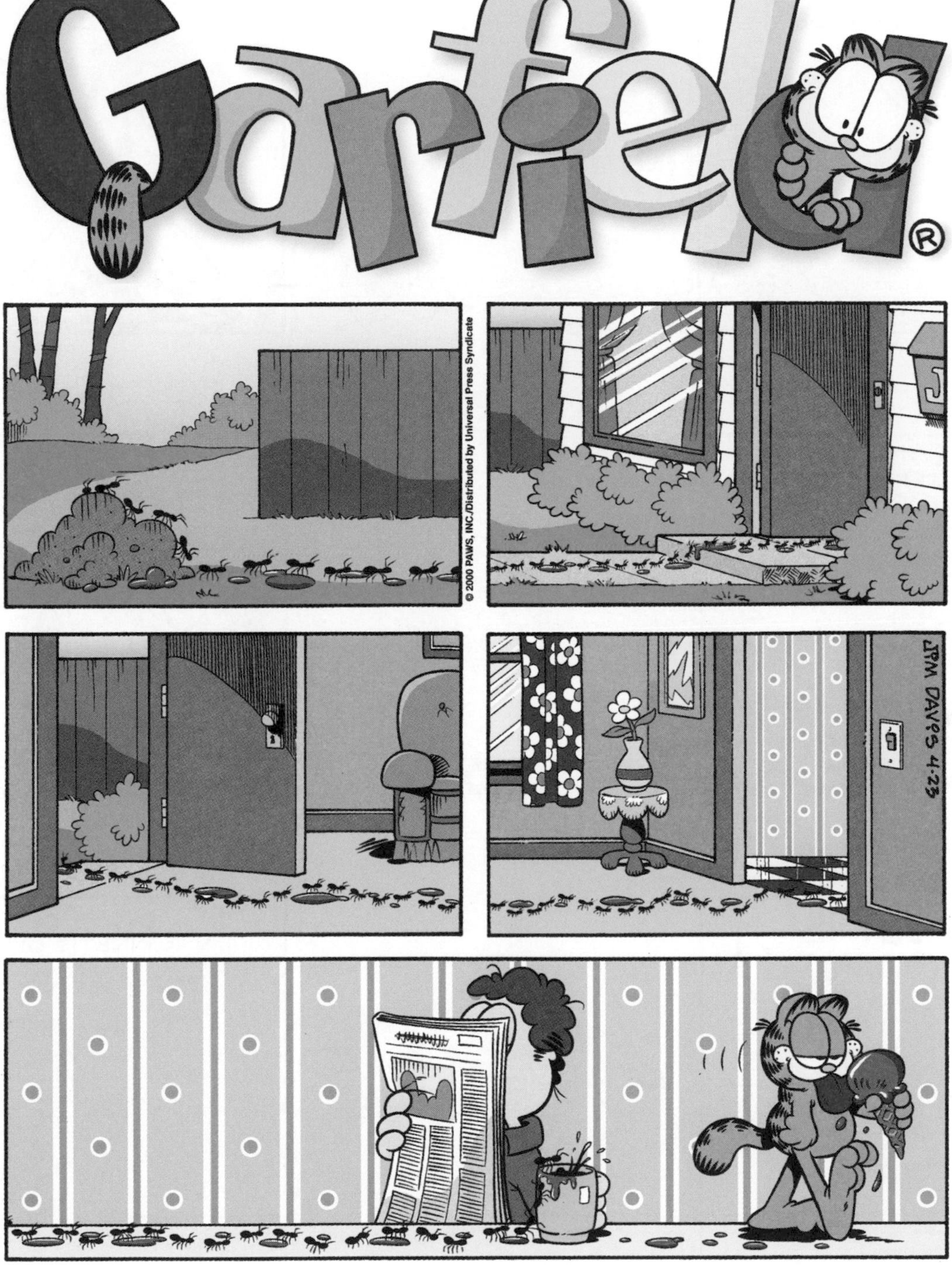
Garfield®
© 2000 PAWS, INC./Distributed by Universal Press Syndicate
JIM DAVIS 4-23

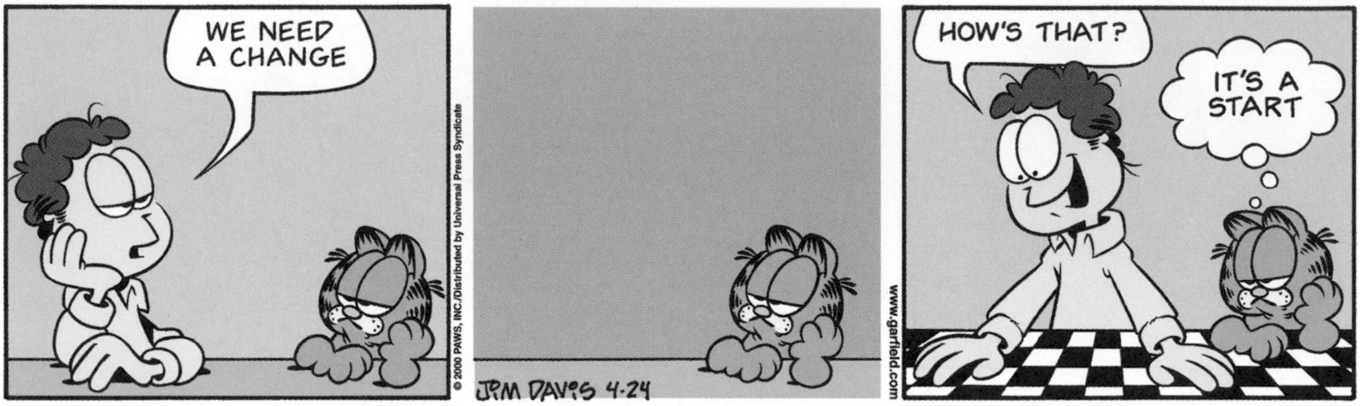
WE NEED A CHANGE
© 2000 PAWS, INC./Distributed by Universal Press Syndicate
JIM DAVIS 4-24
www.garfield.com
HOW'S THAT?
IT'S A START

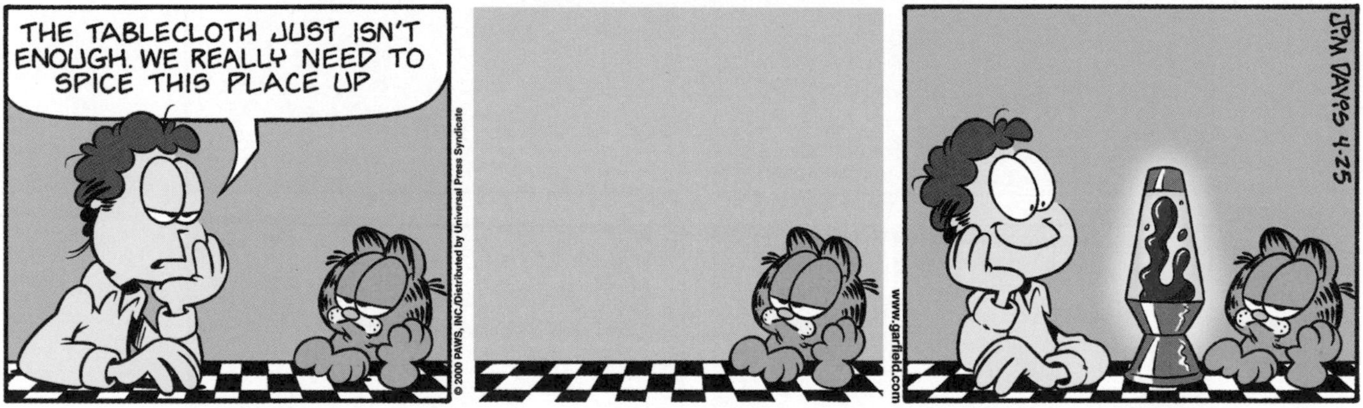
THE TABLECLOTH JUST ISN'T ENOUGH. WE REALLY NEED TO SPICE THIS PLACE UP
© 2000 PAWS, INC./Distributed by Universal Press Syndicate
www.garfield.com
JIM DAVIS 4-25

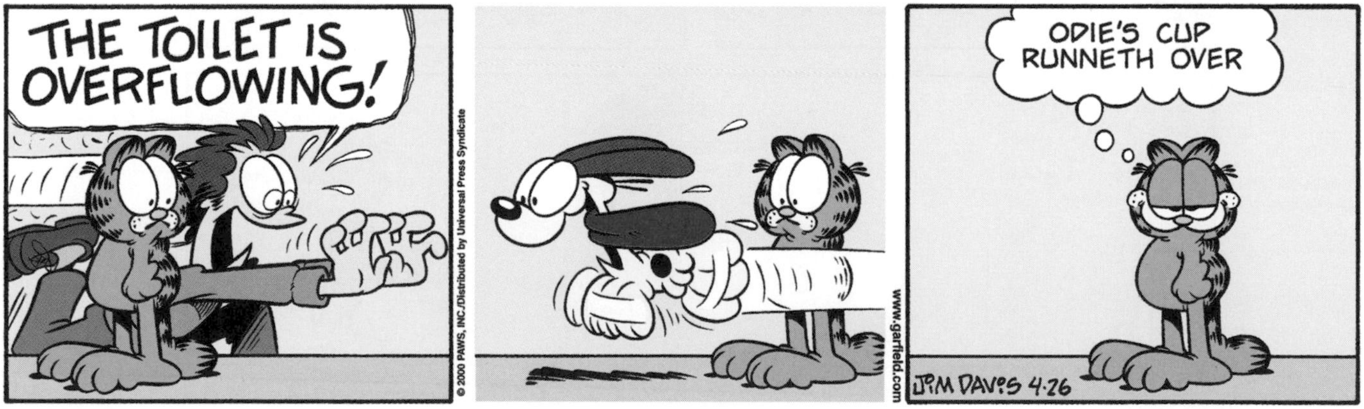
THE TOILET IS OVERFLOWING!
© 2000 PAWS, INC./Distributed by Universal Press Syndicate
www.garfield.com
JIM DAVIS 4-26
ODIE'S CUP RUNNETH OVER

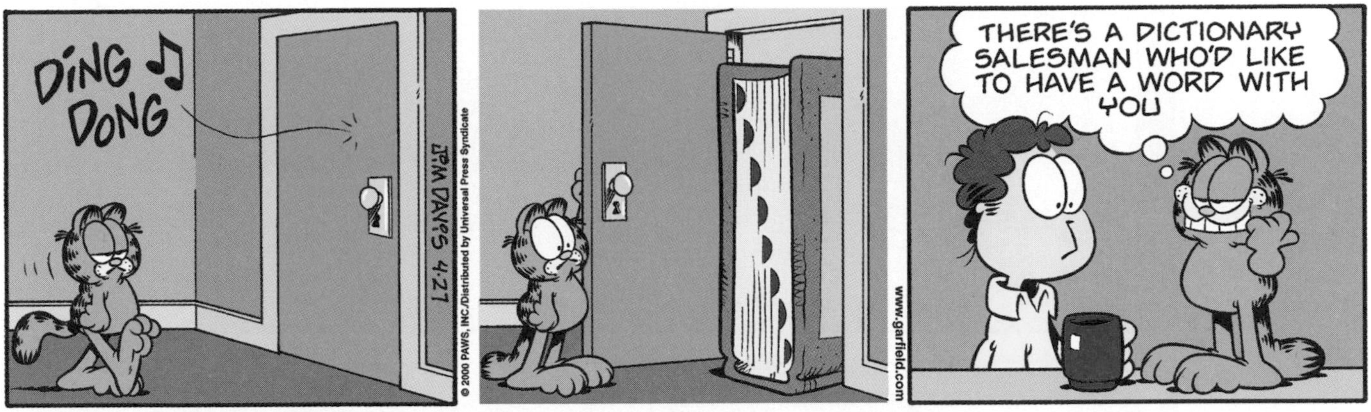
DING DONG
JIM DAVIS 4-27
© 2000 PAWS, INC./Distributed by Universal Press Syndicate
www.garfield.com
THERE'S A DICTIONARY SALESMAN WHO'D LIKE TO HAVE A WORD WITH YOU

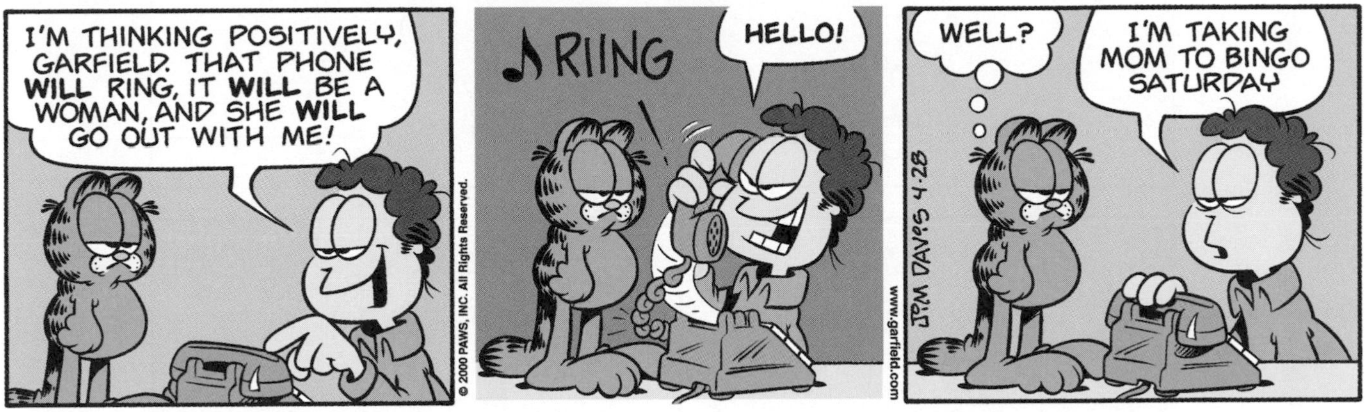
I'M THINKING POSITIVELY, GARFIELD. THAT PHONE **WILL** RING, IT **WILL** BE A WOMAN, AND SHE **WILL** GO OUT WITH ME!
© 2000 PAWS, INC. All Rights Reserved.
RIING
HELLO!
www.garfield.com
JIM DAVIS 4-28
WELL?
I'M TAKING MOM TO BINGO SATURDAY

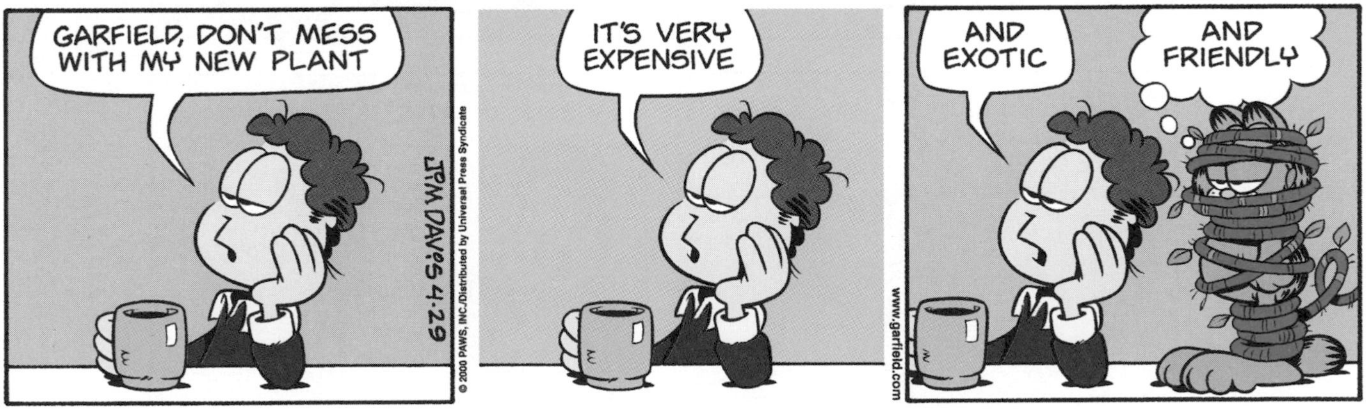
GARFIELD, DON'T MESS WITH MY NEW PLANT
JIM DAVIS 4-29
© 2000 PAWS, INC./Distributed by Universal Press Syndicate
IT'S VERY EXPENSIVE
www.garfield.com
AND EXOTIC
AND FRIENDLY

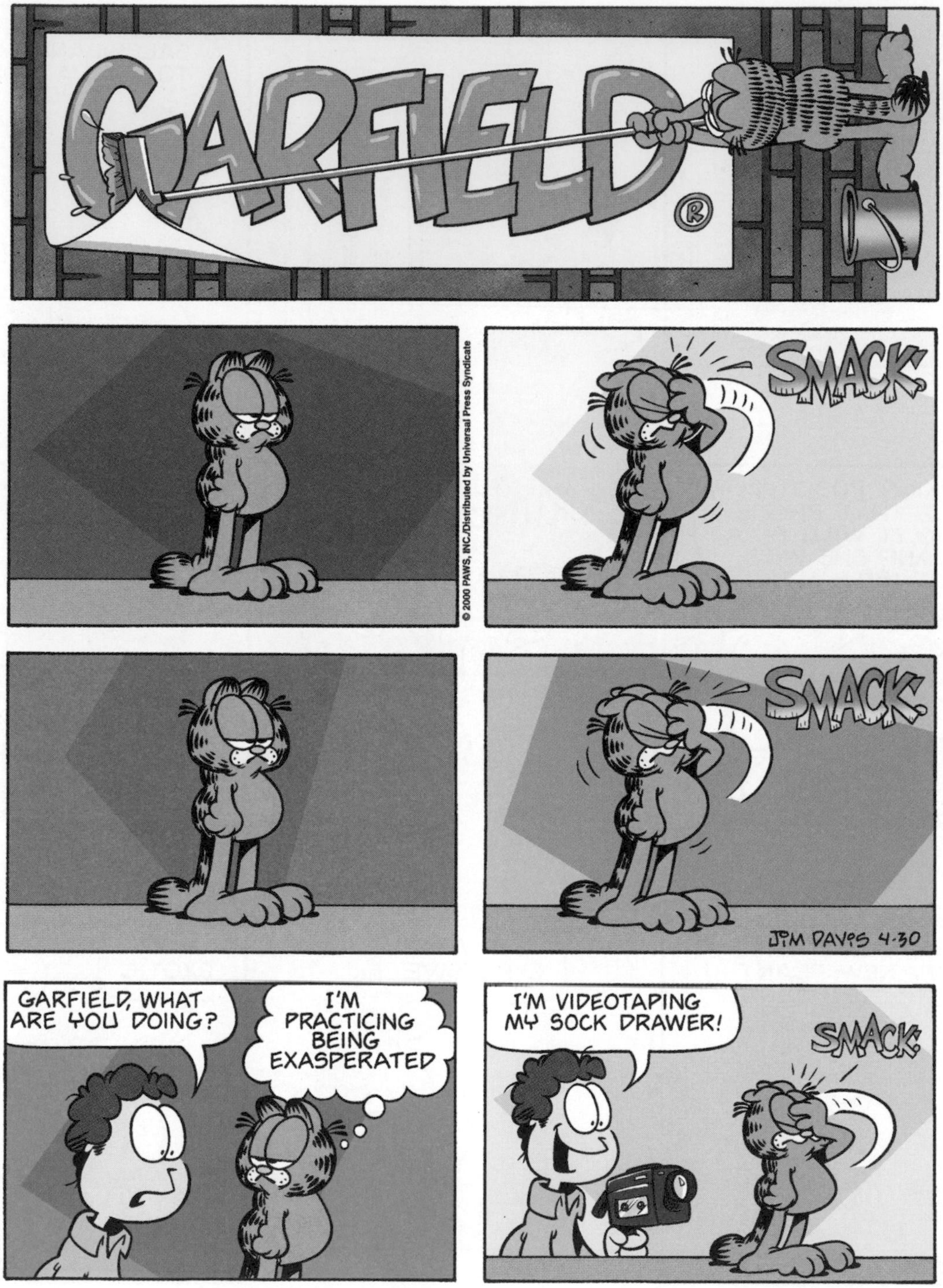
GARFIELD
© 2000 PAWS, INC./Distributed by Universal Press Syndicate
SMACK!
SMACK!
JIM DAVIS 4-30
GARFIELD, WHAT ARE YOU DOING?
I'M PRACTICING BEING EXASPERATED
I'M VIDEOTAPING MY SOCK DRAWER!
SMACK!

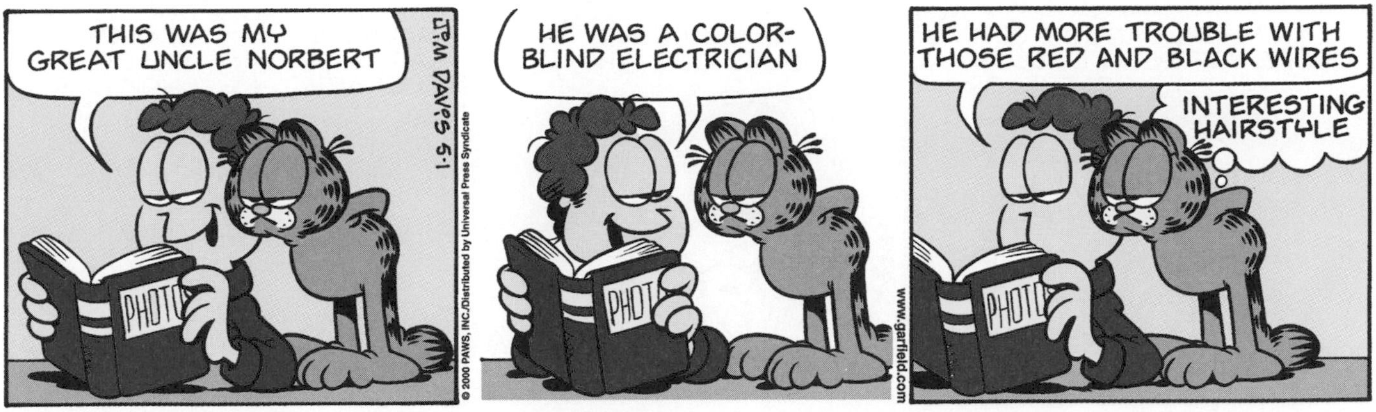
THIS WAS MY GREAT UNCLE NORBERT
JIM DAVIS 5-1
© 2000 PAWS, INC./Distributed by Universal Press Syndicate
HE WAS A COLOR-BLIND ELECTRICIAN
PHOTO
www.garfield.com
HE HAD MORE TROUBLE WITH THOSE RED AND BLACK WIRES
INTERESTING HAIRSTYLE

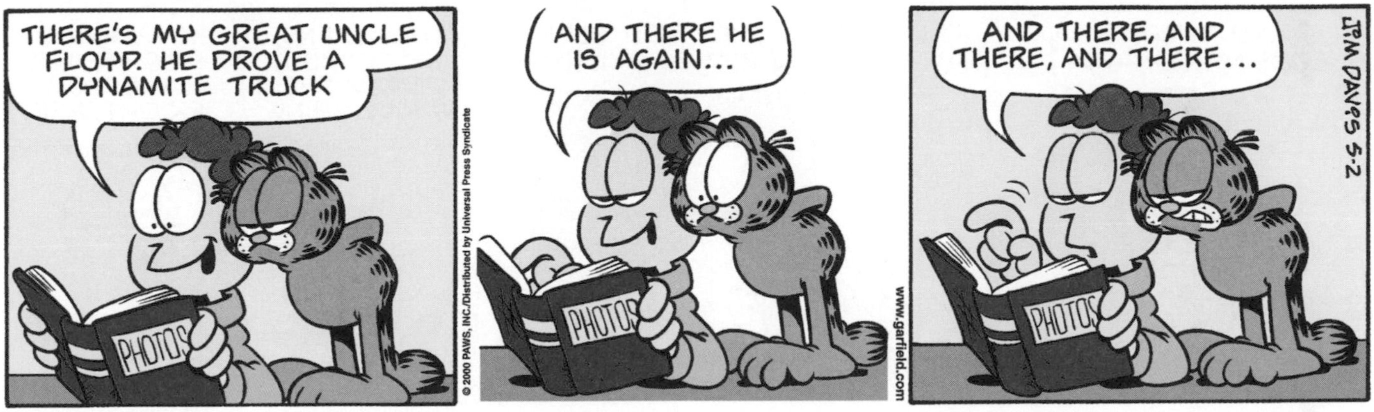
THERE'S MY GREAT UNCLE FLOYD. HE DROVE A DYNAMITE TRUCK
PHOTOS
© 2000 PAWS, INC./Distributed by Universal Press Syndicate
AND THERE HE IS AGAIN...
www.garfield.com
AND THERE, AND THERE, AND THERE...
JIM DAVIS 5-2

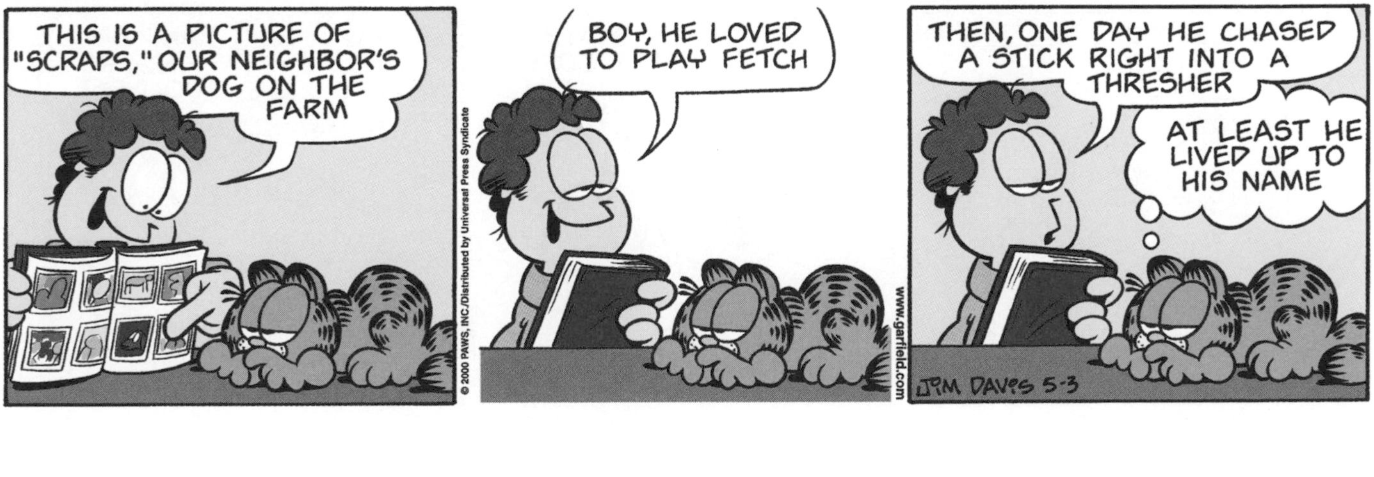
THIS IS A PICTURE OF "SCRAPS," OUR NEIGHBOR'S DOG ON THE FARM
© 2000 PAWS, INC./Distributed by Universal Press Syndicate
BOY, HE LOVED TO PLAY FETCH
www.garfield.com
THEN, ONE DAY HE CHASED A STICK RIGHT INTO A THRESHER
AT LEAST HE LIVED UP TO HIS NAME
JIM DAVIS 5-3

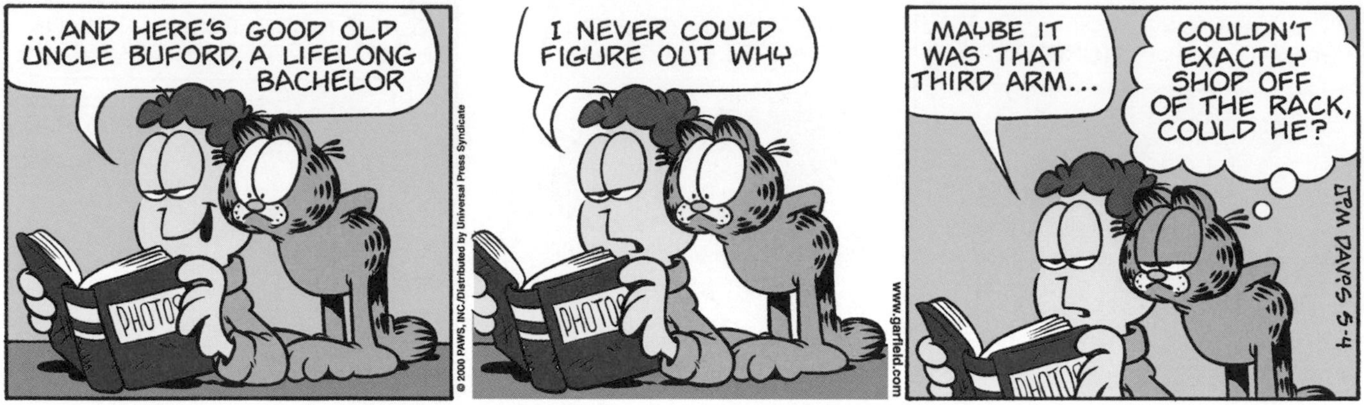
...AND HERE'S GOOD OLD UNCLE BUFORD, A LIFELONG BACHELOR
I NEVER COULD FIGURE OUT WHY
MAYBE IT WAS THAT THIRD ARM...
COULDN'T EXACTLY SHOP OFF OF THE RACK, COULD HE?
JIM DAVIS 5-4
© 2000 PAWS, INC./Distributed by Universal Press Syndicate
www.garfield.com

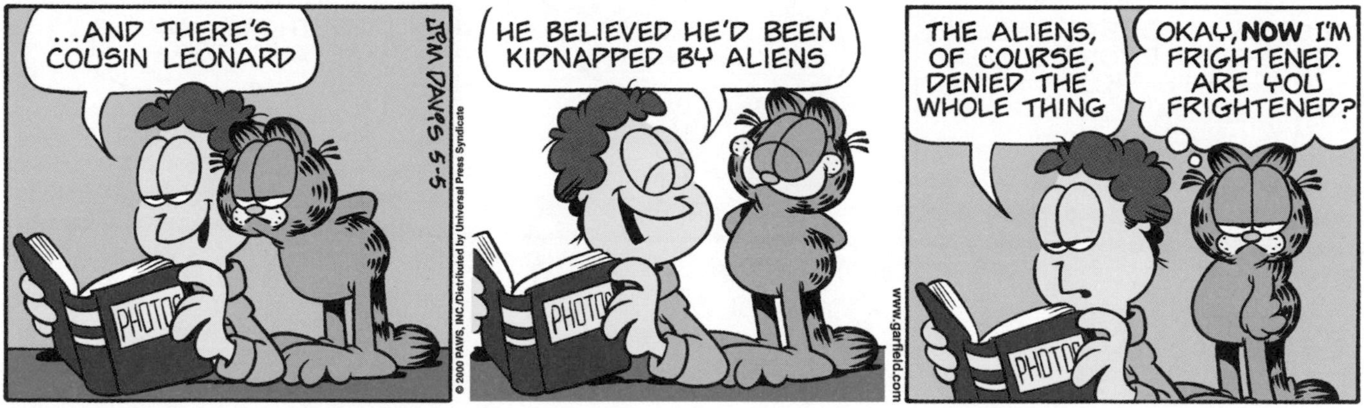
...AND THERE'S COUSIN LEONARD
HE BELIEVED HE'D BEEN KIDNAPPED BY ALIENS
THE ALIENS, OF COURSE, DENIED THE WHOLE THING
OKAY, **NOW** I'M FRIGHTENED. ARE YOU FRIGHTENED?
JIM DAVIS 5-5
© 2000 PAWS, INC./Distributed by Universal Press Syndicate
www.garfield.com

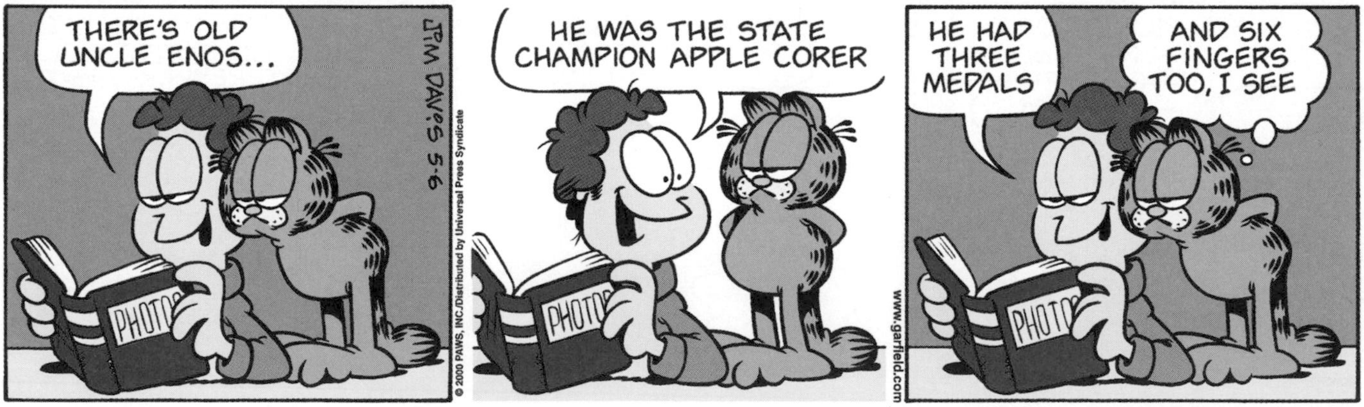
THERE'S OLD UNCLE ENOS...
HE WAS THE STATE CHAMPION APPLE CORER
HE HAD THREE MEDALS
AND SIX FINGERS TOO, I SEE
JIM DAVIS 5-6
© 2000 PAWS, INC./Distributed by Universal Press Syndicate
www.garfield.com

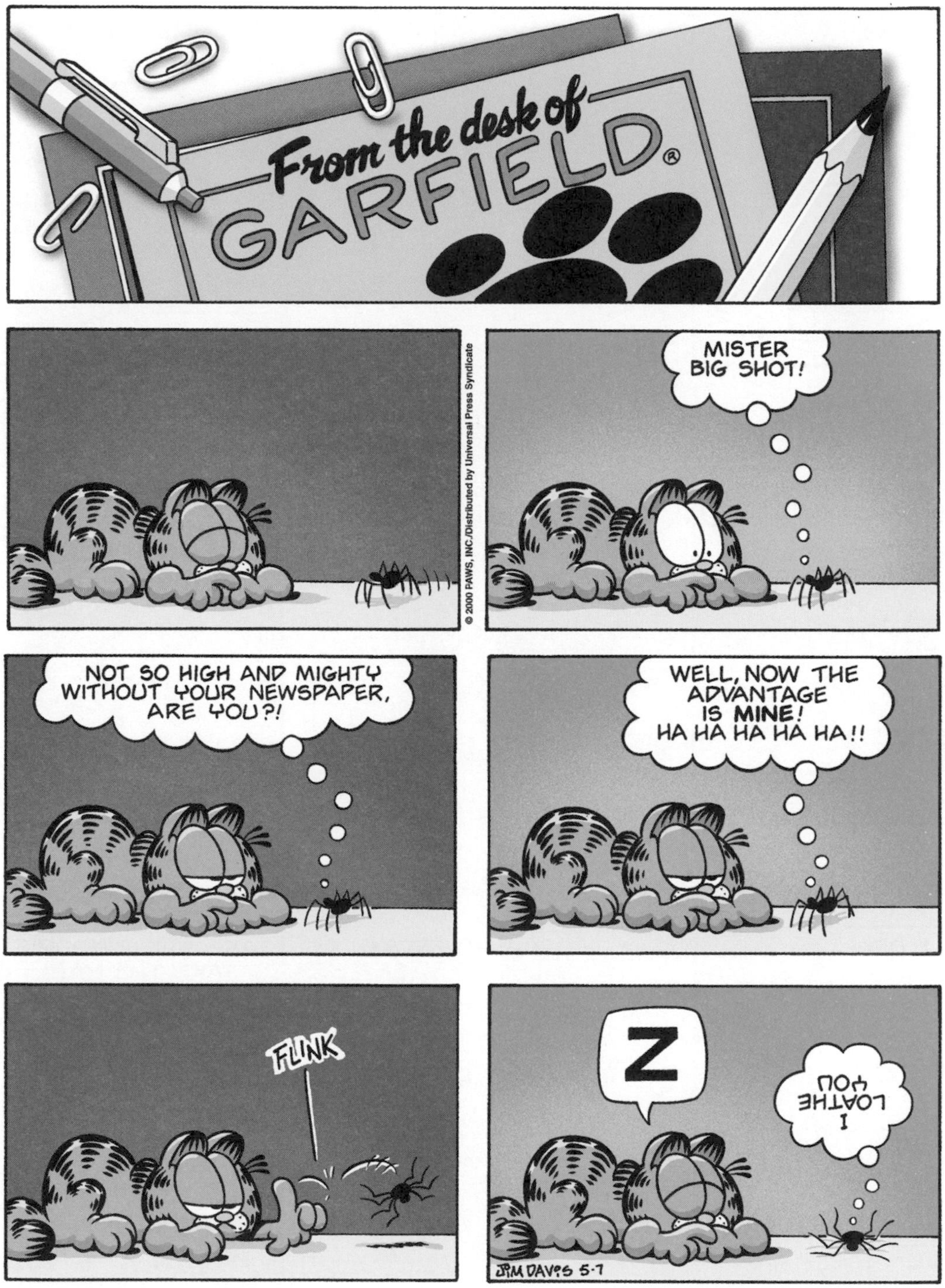
From the desk of
GARFIELD®
© 2000 PAWS, INC./Distributed by Universal Press Syndicate
MISTER BIG SHOT!
NOT SO HIGH AND MIGHTY WITHOUT YOUR NEWSPAPER, ARE YOU?!
WELL, NOW THE ADVANTAGE IS **MINE**! HA HA HA HA HA!!
FLINK
Z
I LOATHE YOU
JIM DAVIS 5-7

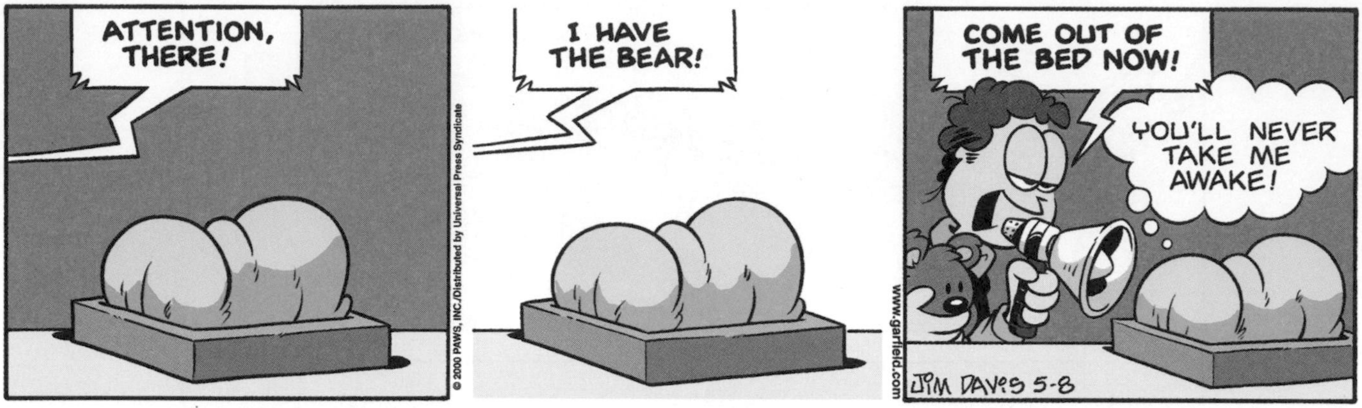
ATTENTION, THERE!
I HAVE THE BEAR!
COME OUT OF THE BED NOW!
YOU'LL NEVER TAKE ME AWAKE!
© 2000 PAWS, INC./Distributed by Universal Press Syndicate
www.garfield.com
JIM DAVIS 5-8

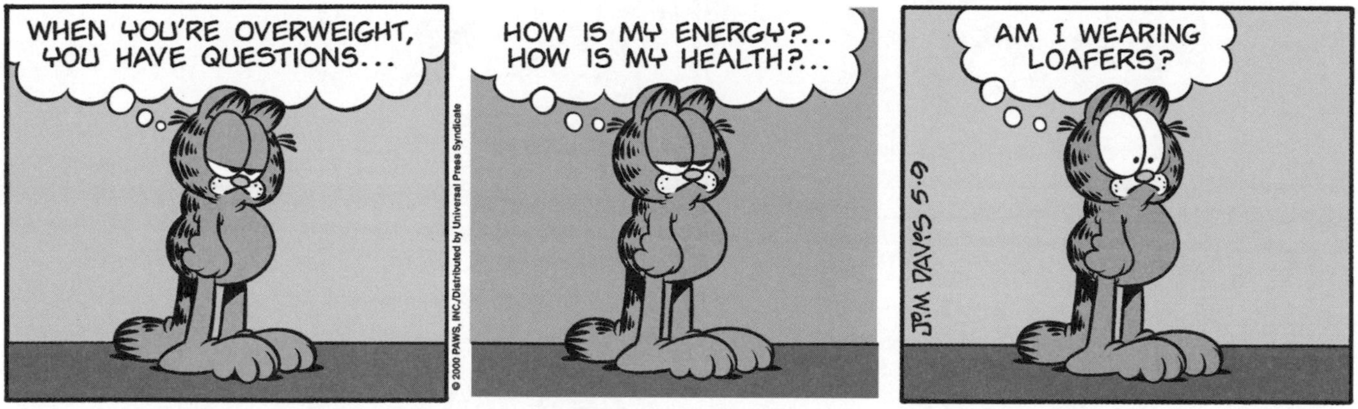
WHEN YOU'RE OVERWEIGHT, YOU HAVE QUESTIONS...
HOW IS MY ENERGY?... HOW IS MY HEALTH?...
AM I WEARING LOAFERS?
© 2000 PAWS, INC./Distributed by Universal Press Syndicate
JIM DAVIS 5-9

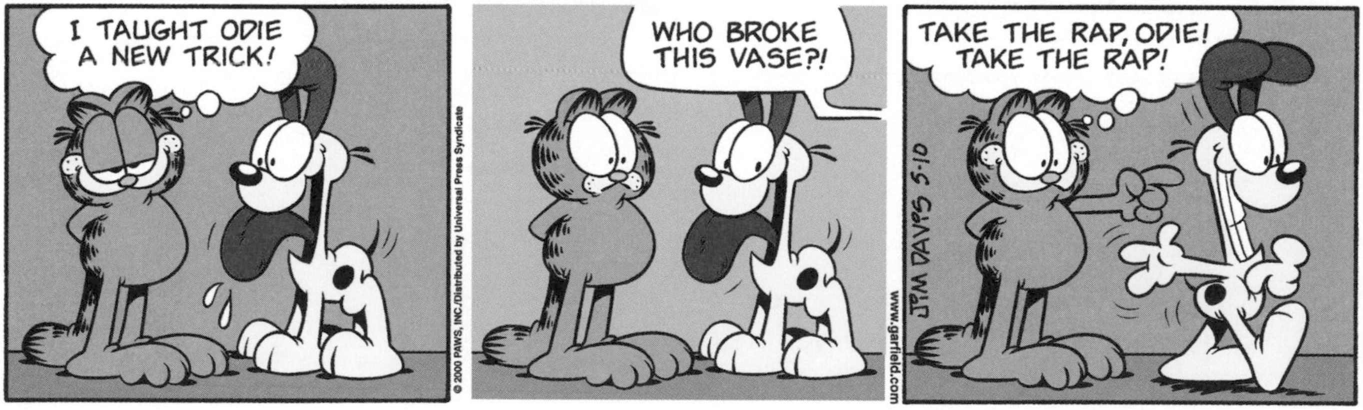
I TAUGHT ODIE A NEW TRICK!
WHO BROKE THIS VASE?!
TAKE THE RAP, ODIE! TAKE THE RAP!
© 2000 PAWS, INC./Distributed by Universal Press Syndicate
www.garfield.com
JIM DAVIS 5-10

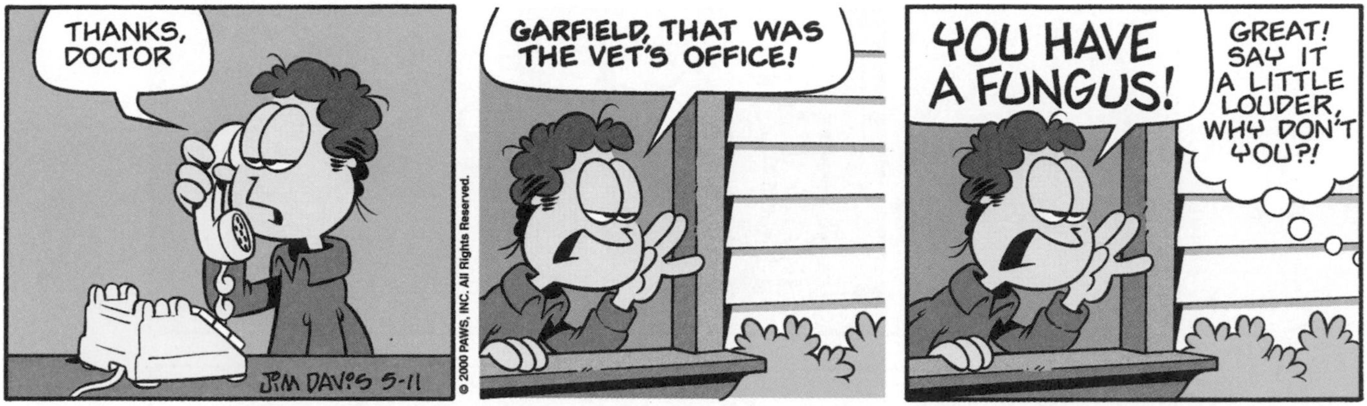
THANKS, DOCTOR
JIM DAVIS 5-11
© 2000 PAWS, INC. All Rights Reserved.
GARFIELD, THAT WAS THE VET'S OFFICE!
YOU HAVE A FUNGUS!
GREAT! SAY IT A LITTLE LOUDER, WHY DON'T YOU?!

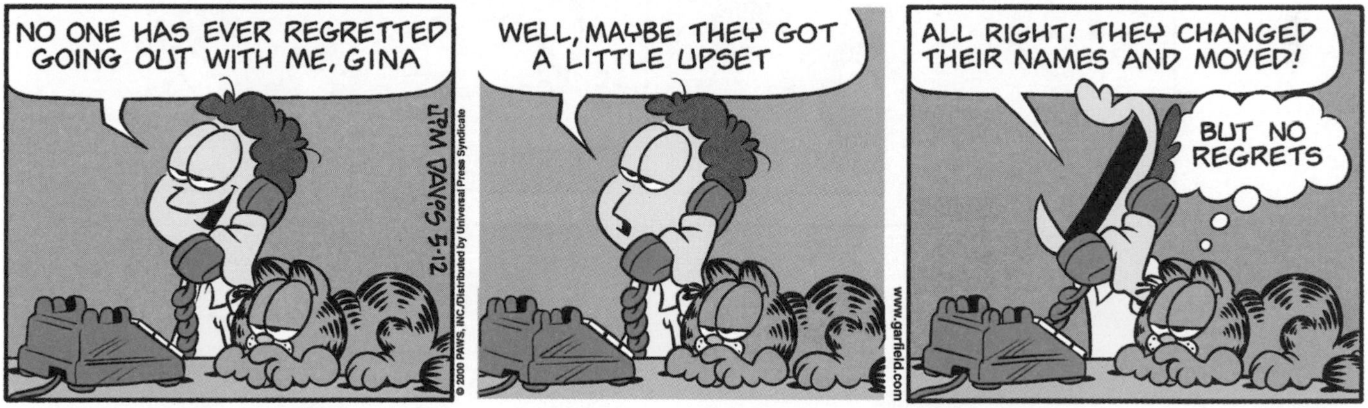
NO ONE HAS EVER REGRETTED GOING OUT WITH ME, GINA
JIM DAVIS 5-12
© 2000 PAWS, INC./Distributed by Universal Press Syndicate
WELL, MAYBE THEY GOT A LITTLE UPSET
www.garfield.com
ALL RIGHT! THEY CHANGED THEIR NAMES AND MOVED!
BUT NO REGRETS

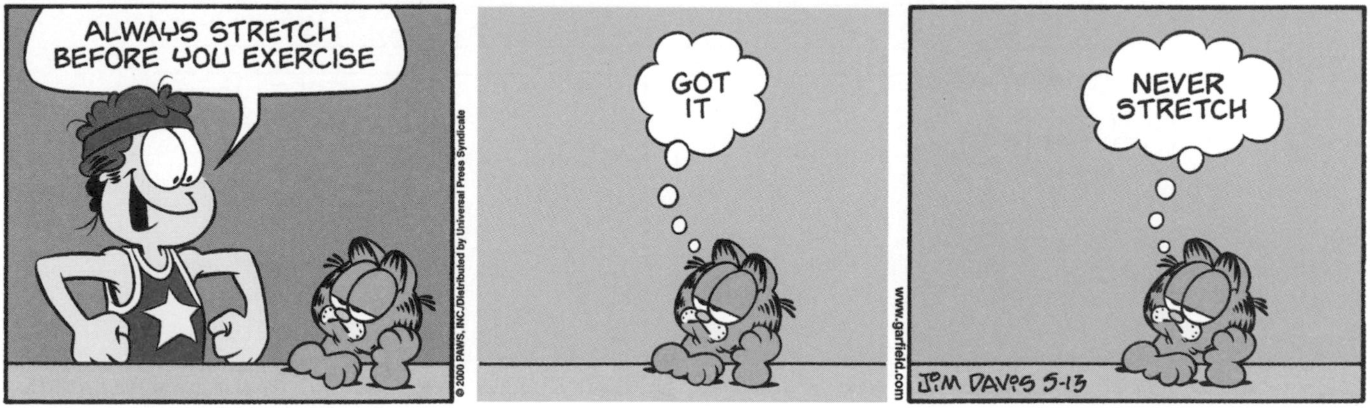
ALWAYS STRETCH BEFORE YOU EXERCISE
© 2000 PAWS, INC./Distributed by Universal Press Syndicate
GOT IT
www.garfield.com
NEVER STRETCH
JIM DAVIS 5-13

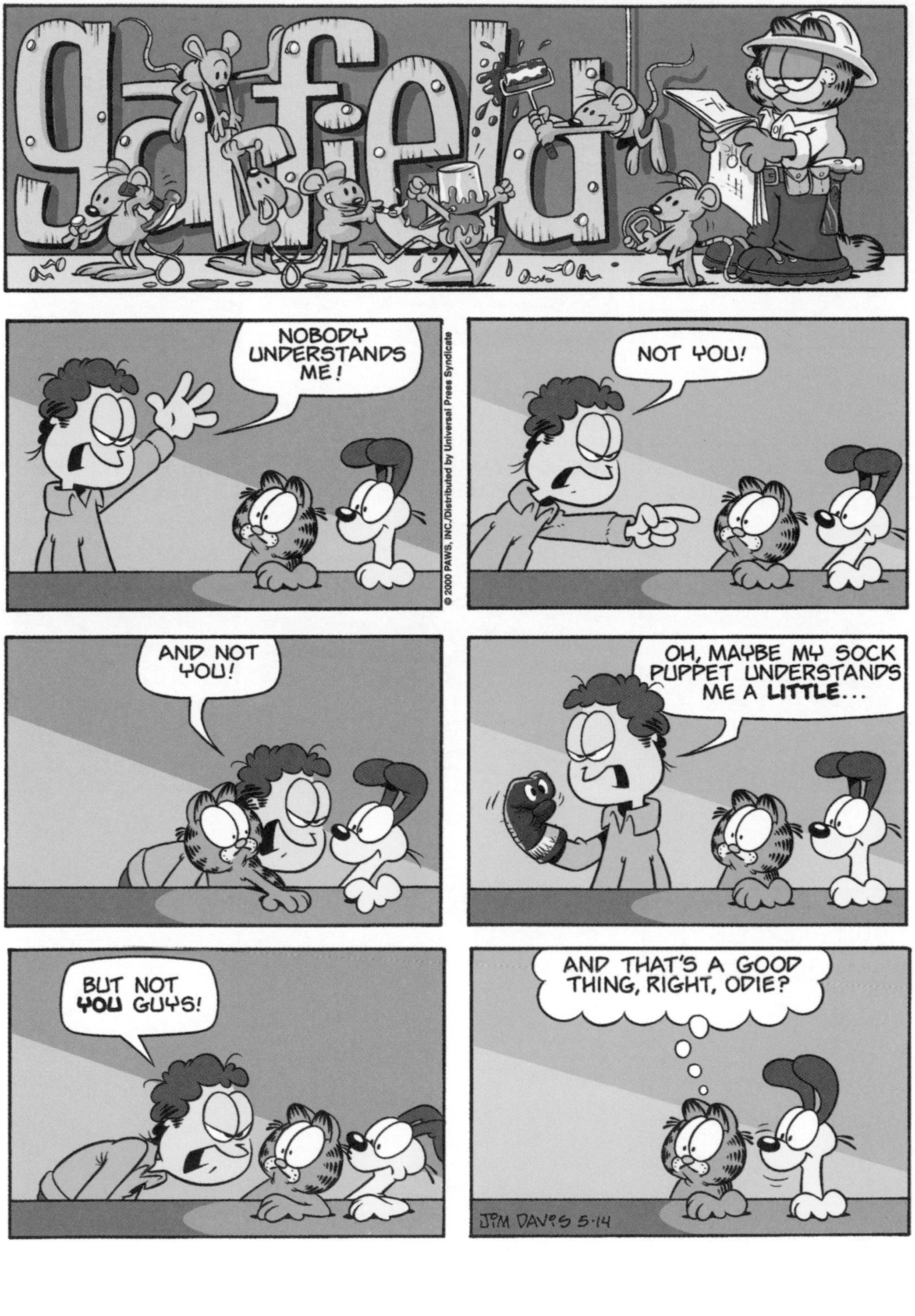
garfield
© 2000 PAWS, INC./Distributed by Universal Press Syndicate
NOBODY UNDERSTANDS ME!
NOT YOU!
AND NOT YOU!
OH, MAYBE MY SOCK PUPPET UNDERSTANDS ME A **LITTLE**...
BUT NOT **YOU** GUYS!
AND THAT'S A GOOD THING, RIGHT, ODIE?
JIM DAVIS 5-14

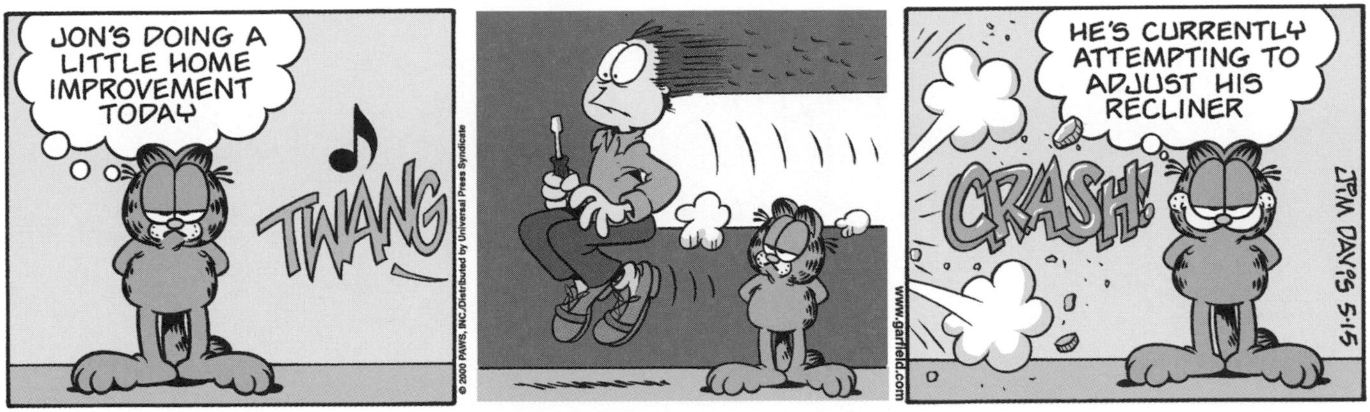
JON'S DOING A LITTLE HOME IMPROVEMENT TODAY
TWANG
© 2000 PAWS, INC./Distributed by Universal Press Syndicate
www.garfield.com
CRASH!
HE'S CURRENTLY ATTEMPTING TO ADJUST HIS RECLINER
JIM DAVIS 5-15

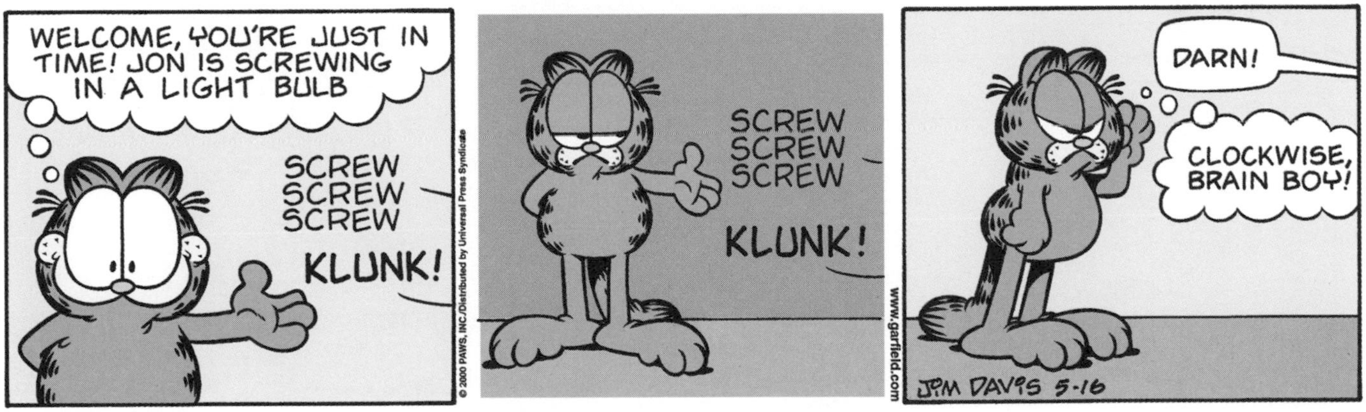
WELCOME, YOU'RE JUST IN TIME! JON IS SCREWING IN A LIGHT BULB
SCREW SCREW SCREW
KLUNK!
© 2000 PAWS, INC./Distributed by Universal Press Syndicate
SCREW SCREW SCREW
KLUNK!
www.garfield.com
DARN!
CLOCKWISE, BRAIN BOY!
JIM DAVIS 5-16

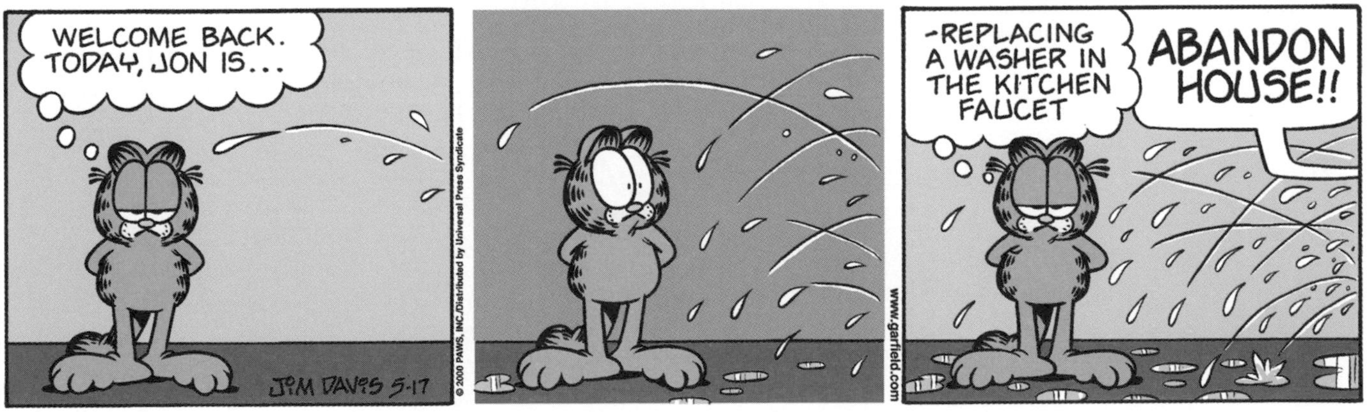
WELCOME BACK. TODAY, JON IS...
JIM DAVIS 5-17
© 2000 PAWS, INC./Distributed by Universal Press Syndicate
www.garfield.com
-REPLACING A WASHER IN THE KITCHEN FAUCET
ABANDON HOUSE!!

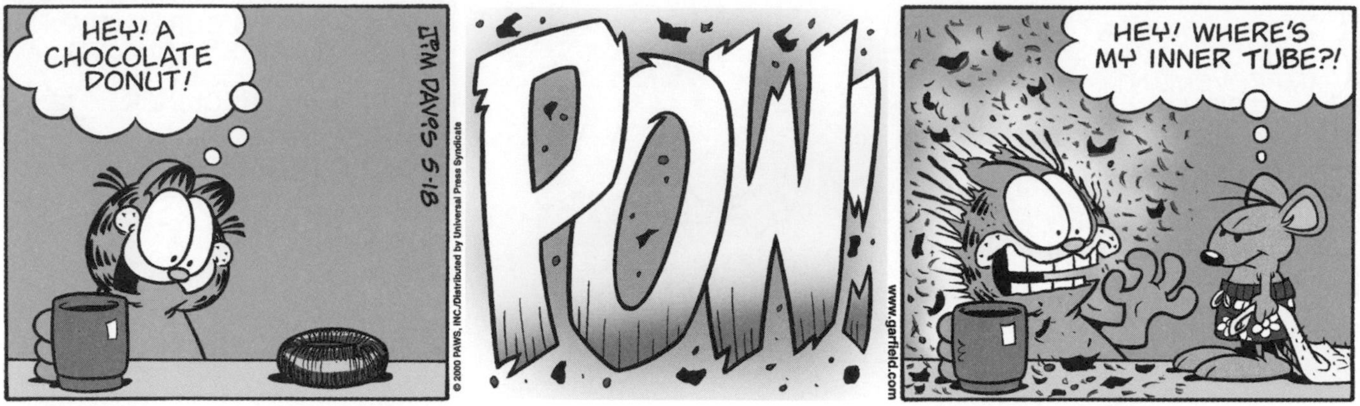
HEY! A CHOCOLATE DONUT!
JIM DAVIS 5-18
© 2000 PAWS, INC./Distributed by Universal Press Syndicate
POW!
www.garfield.com
HEY! WHERE'S MY INNER TUBE?!

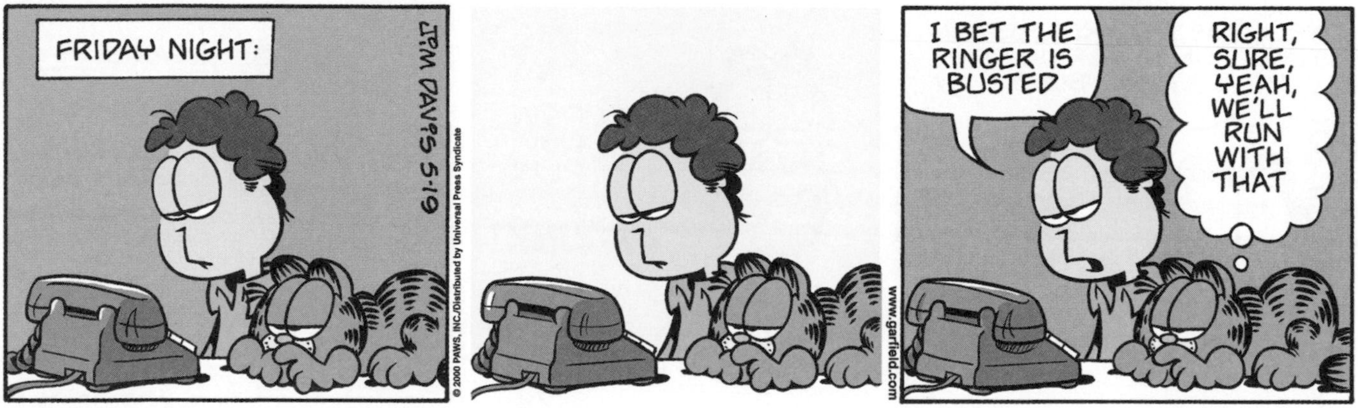
FRIDAY NIGHT:
JIM DAVIS 5-19
© 2000 PAWS, INC./Distributed by Universal Press Syndicate
www.garfield.com
I BET THE RINGER IS BUSTED
RIGHT, SURE, YEAH, WE'LL RUN WITH THAT

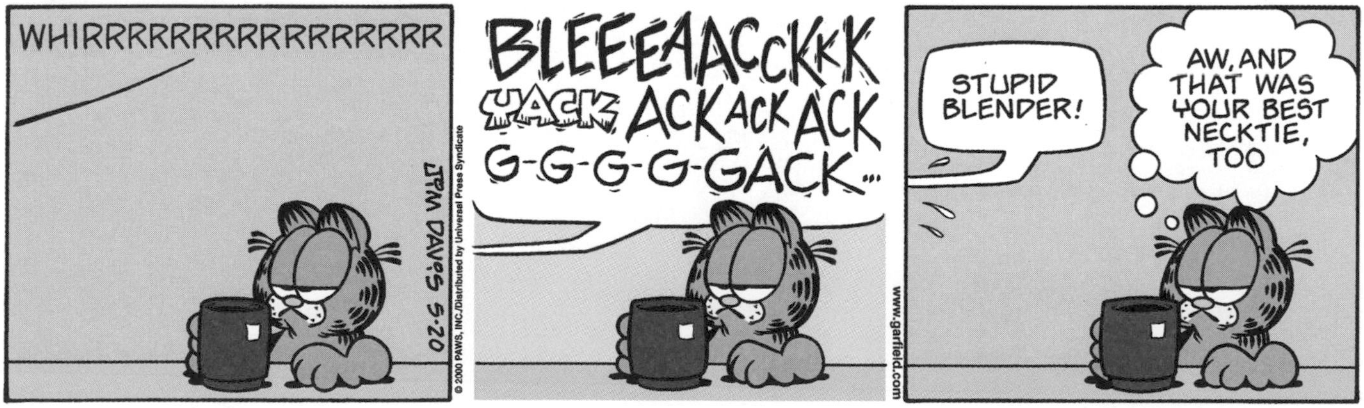
WHIRRRRRRRRRRRRRRRR
JIM DAVIS 5-20
© 2000 PAWS, INC./Distributed by Universal Press Syndicate
BLEEEAACCKKK YACK ACK ACK ACK G-G-G-G-GACK...
www.garfield.com
STUPID BLENDER!
AW, AND THAT WAS YOUR BEST NECKTIE, TOO

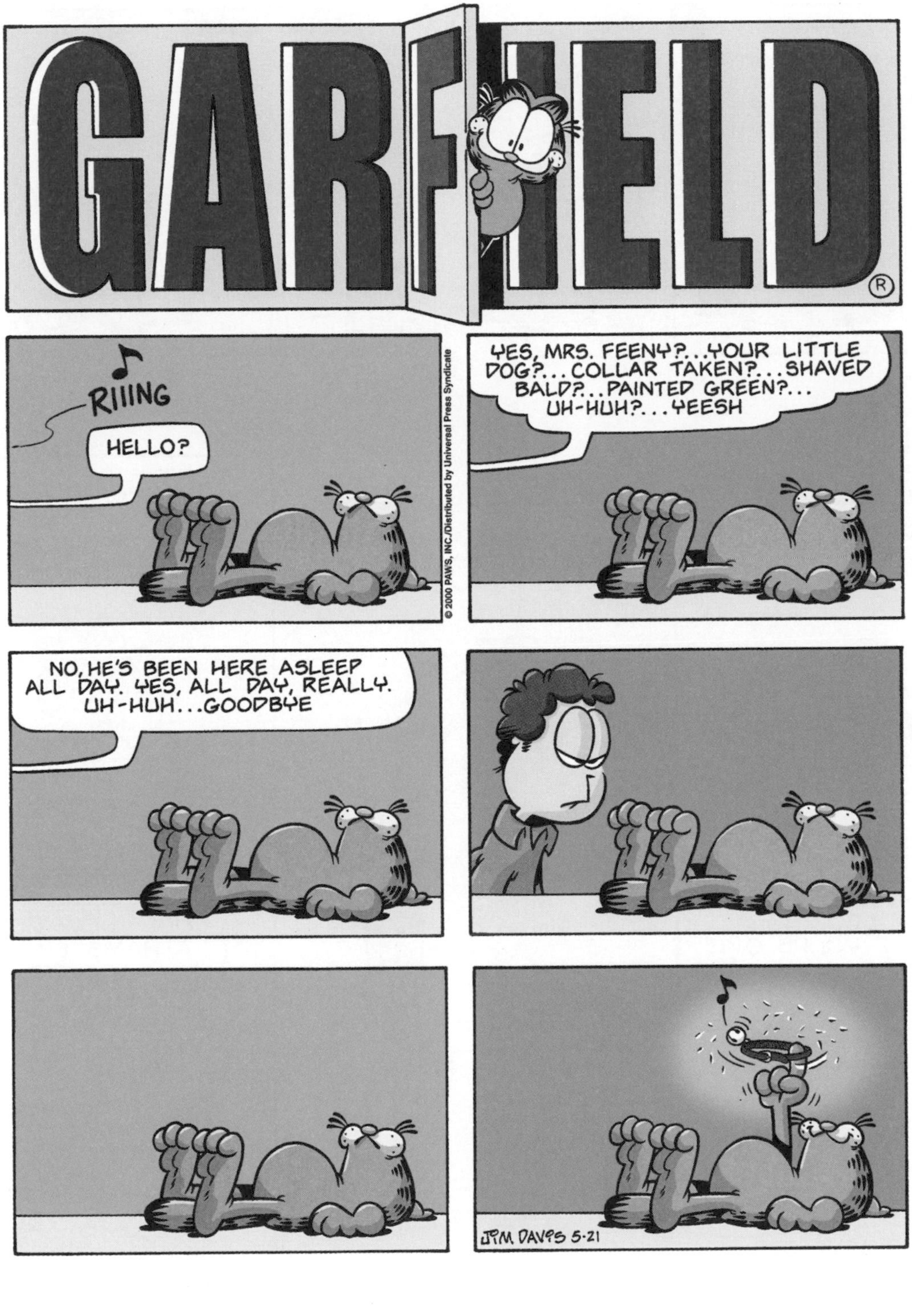
GARFIELD ®
© 2000 PAWS, INC./Distributed by Universal Press Syndicate
RIIING
HELLO?
YES, MRS. FEENY?...YOUR LITTLE DOG?...COLLAR TAKEN?...SHAVED BALD?...PAINTED GREEN?... UH-HUH?...YEESH
NO, HE'S BEEN HERE ASLEEP ALL DAY. YES, ALL DAY, REALLY. UH-HUH...GOODBYE
JIM DAVIS 5-21

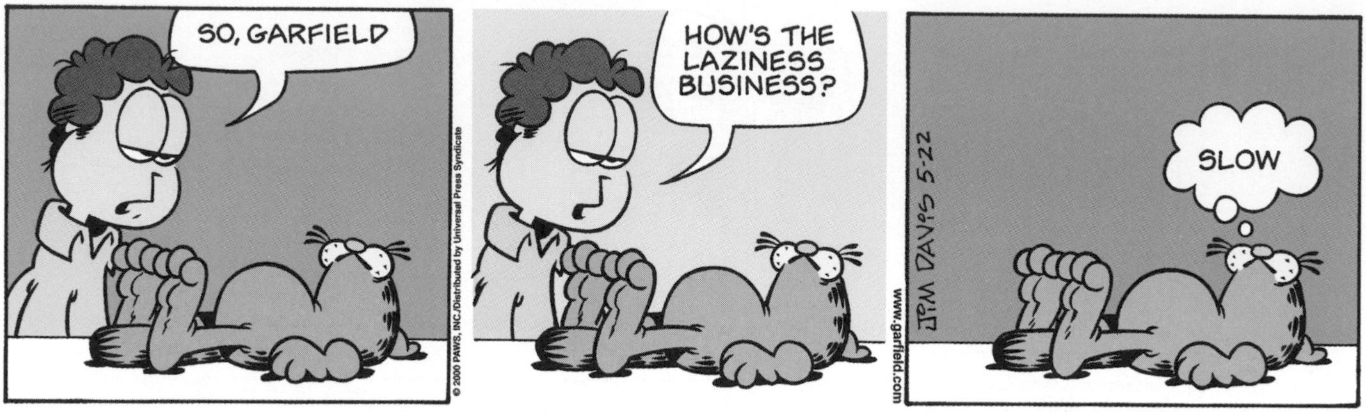
SO, GARFIELD
HOW'S THE LAZINESS BUSINESS?
SLOW
JIM DAVIS 5-22
© 2000 PAWS, INC./Distributed by Universal Press Syndicate
www.garfield.com

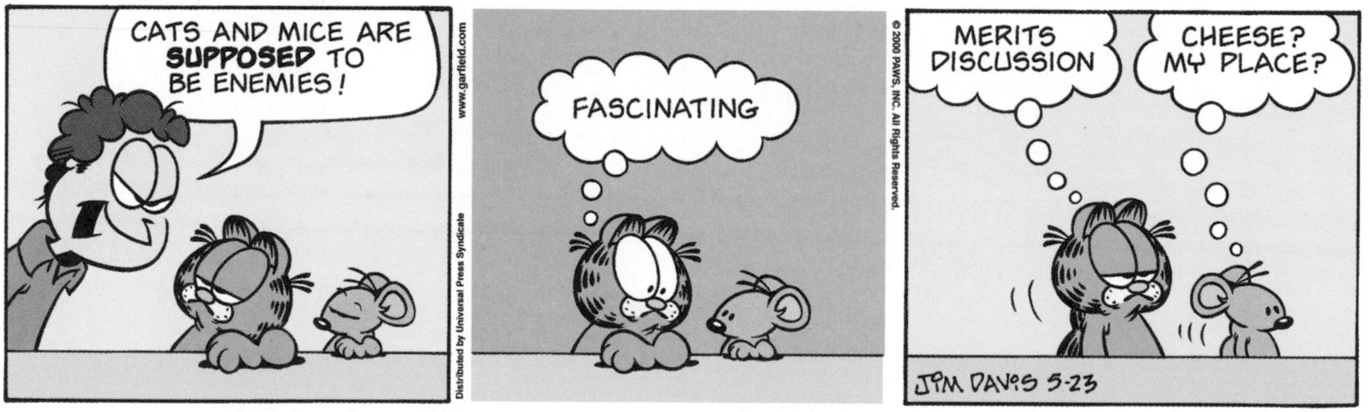
CATS AND MICE ARE **SUPPOSED** TO BE ENEMIES!
FASCINATING
MERITS DISCUSSION
CHEESE? MY PLACE?
JIM DAVIS 5-23
www.garfield.com
Distributed by Universal Press Syndicate
© 2000 PAWS, INC. All Rights Reserved.

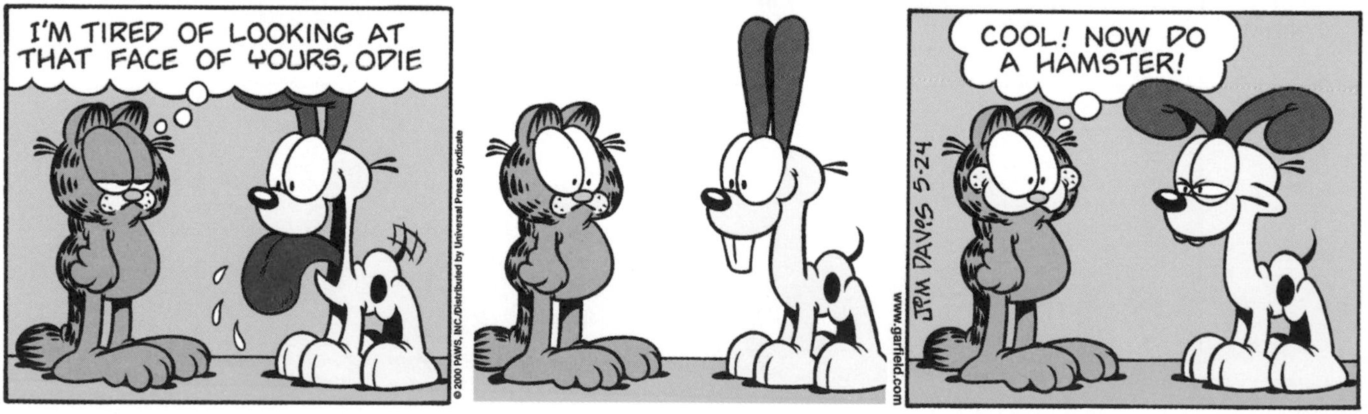
I'M TIRED OF LOOKING AT THAT FACE OF YOURS, ODIE
COOL! NOW DO A HAMSTER!
JIM DAVIS 5-24
© 2000 PAWS, INC./Distributed by Universal Press Syndicate
www.garfield.com

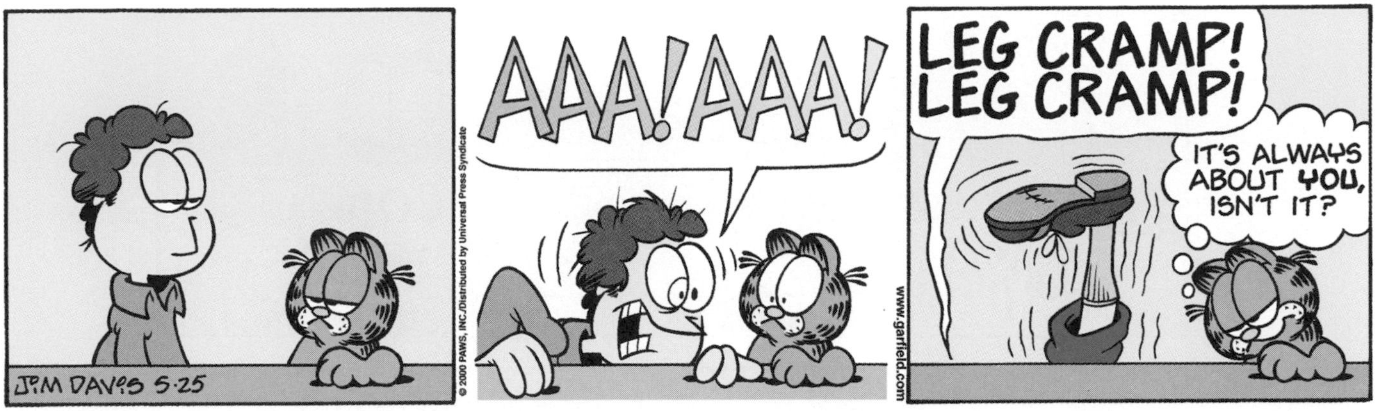
JIM DAVIS 5·25
© 2000 PAWS, INC./Distributed by Universal Press Syndicate
AAA! AAA!
www.garfield.com
LEG CRAMP! LEG CRAMP!
IT'S ALWAYS ABOUT **YOU**, ISN'T IT?

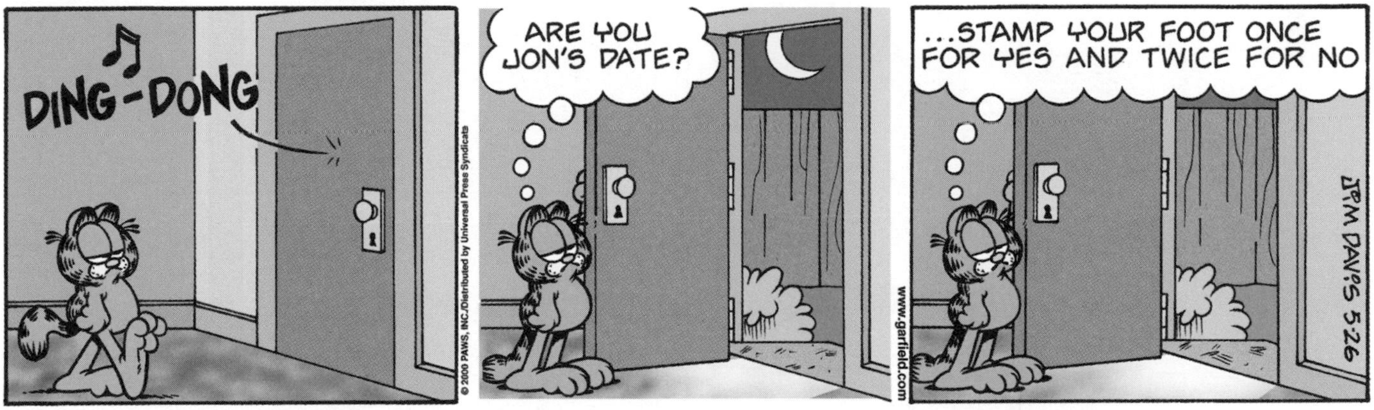
DING-DONG
© 2000 PAWS, INC./Distributed by Universal Press Syndicate
ARE YOU JON'S DATE?
www.garfield.com
...STAMP YOUR FOOT ONCE FOR YES AND TWICE FOR NO
JIM DAVIS 5·26

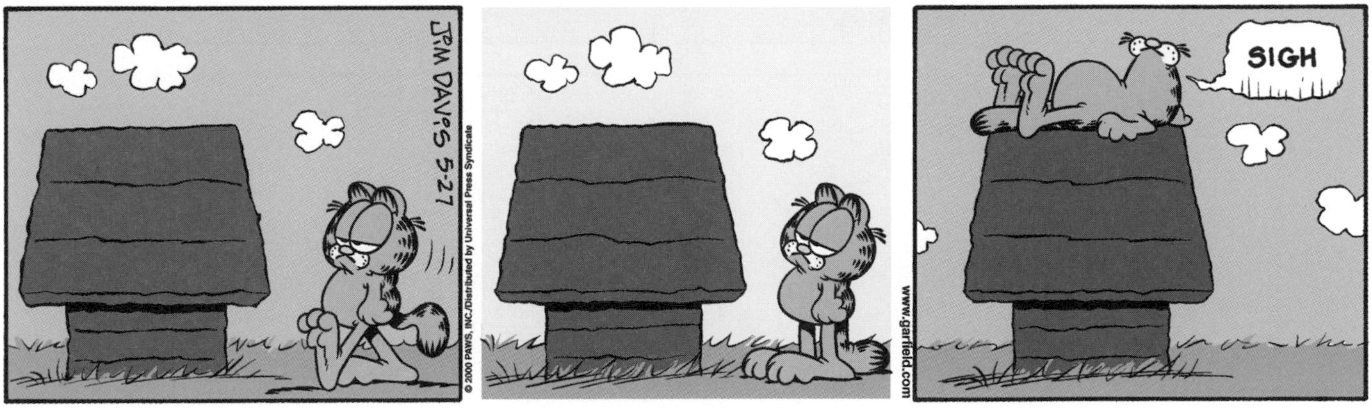
JIM DAVIS 5·27
© 2000 PAWS, INC./Distributed by Universal Press Syndicate
www.garfield.com
SIGH

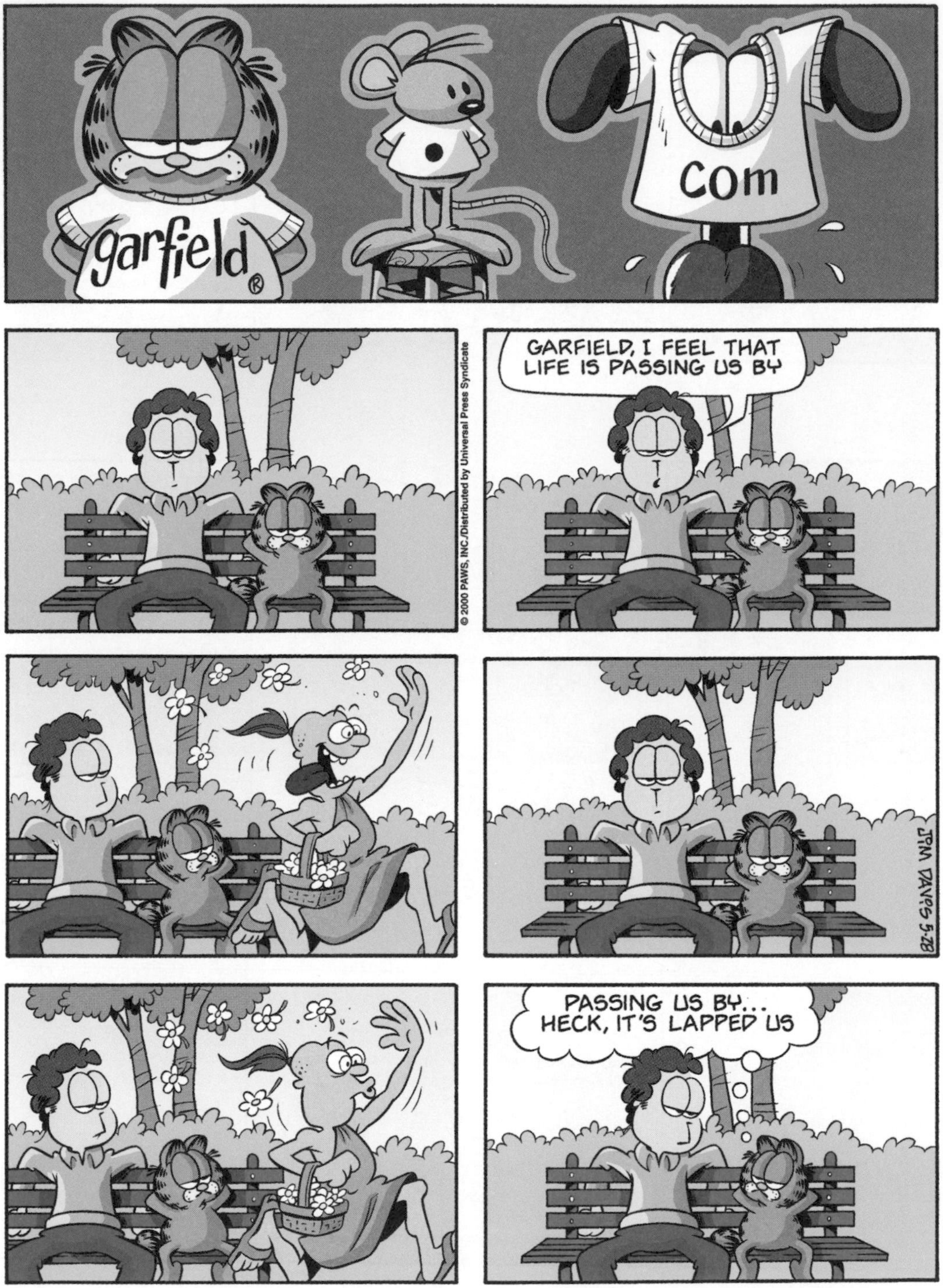
garfield®
com
© 2000 PAWS, INC./Distributed by Universal Press Syndicate
GARFIELD, I FEEL THAT LIFE IS PASSING US BY
JIM DAVIS 5-28
PASSING US BY... HECK, IT'S LAPPED US

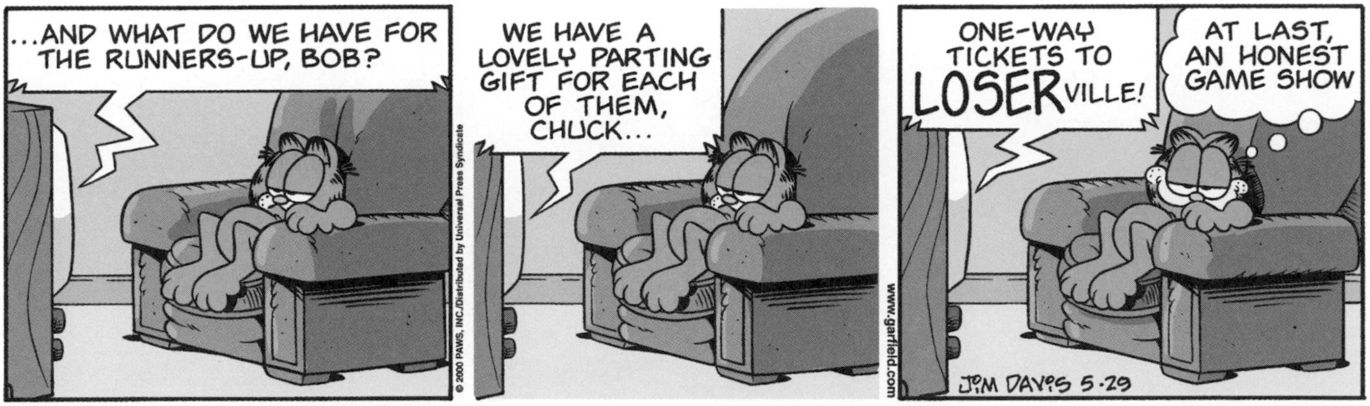
...AND WHAT DO WE HAVE FOR THE RUNNERS-UP, BOB?
© 2000 PAWS, INC./Distributed by Universal Press Syndicate
WE HAVE A LOVELY PARTING GIFT FOR EACH OF THEM, CHUCK...
www.garfield.com
ONE-WAY TICKETS TO LOSERVILLE!
AT LAST, AN HONEST GAME SHOW
JIM DAVIS 5-29

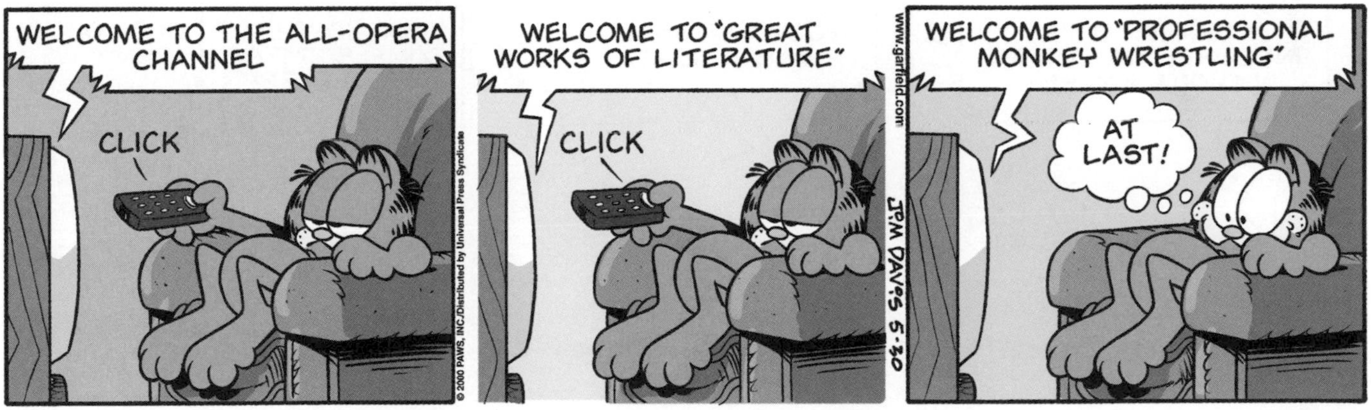
WELCOME TO THE ALL-OPERA CHANNEL
CLICK
© 2000 PAWS, INC./Distributed by Universal Press Syndicate
WELCOME TO "GREAT WORKS OF LITERATURE"
CLICK
www.garfield.com
JIM DAVIS 5-30
WELCOME TO "PROFESSIONAL MONKEY WRESTLING"
AT LAST!

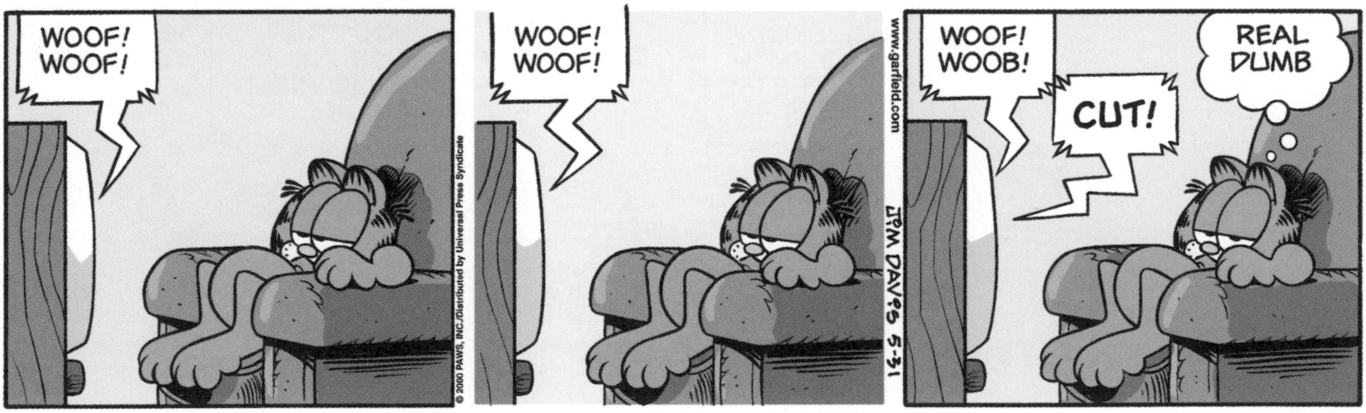
WOOF! WOOF!
© 2000 PAWS, INC./Distributed by Universal Press Syndicate
WOOF! WOOF!
www.garfield.com
JIM DAVIS 5-31
WOOF! WOOB!
CUT!
REAL DUMB

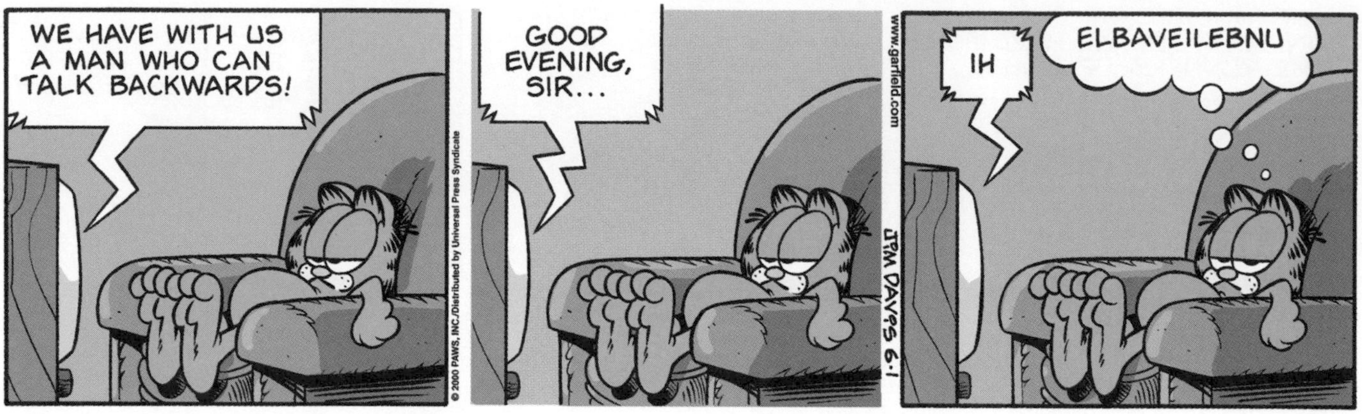
WE HAVE WITH US A MAN WHO CAN TALK BACKWARDS!
GOOD EVENING, SIR...
IH
ELBAVEILEBNU
JPM DAVIS 6-1
© 2000 PAWS, INC./Distributed by Universal Press Syndicate
www.garfield.com

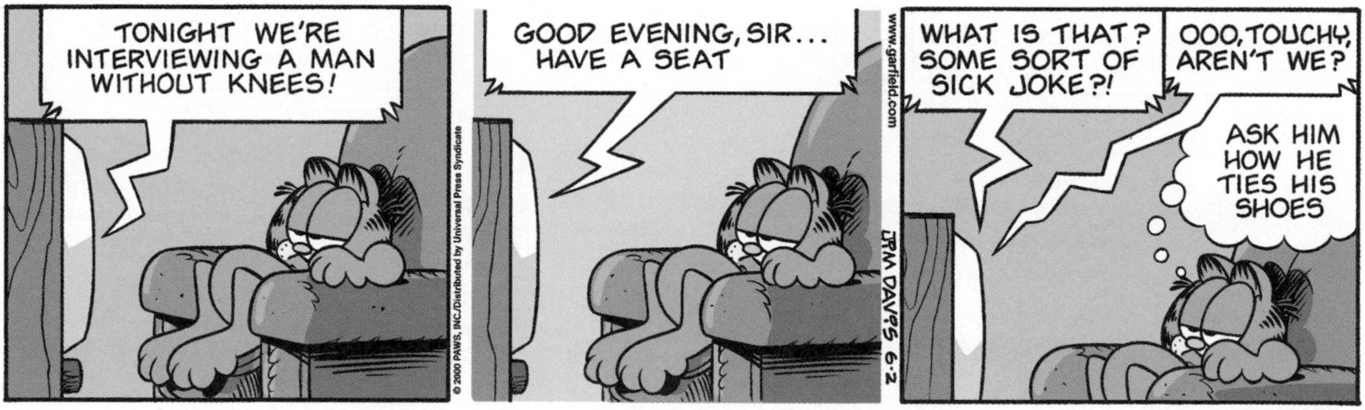
TONIGHT WE'RE INTERVIEWING A MAN WITHOUT KNEES!
GOOD EVENING, SIR... HAVE A SEAT
WHAT IS THAT? SOME SORT OF SICK JOKE?!
OOO, TOUCHY, AREN'T WE?
ASK HIM HOW HE TIES HIS SHOES
JPM DAVIS 6-2
© 2000 PAWS, INC./Distributed by Universal Press Syndicate
www.garfield.com

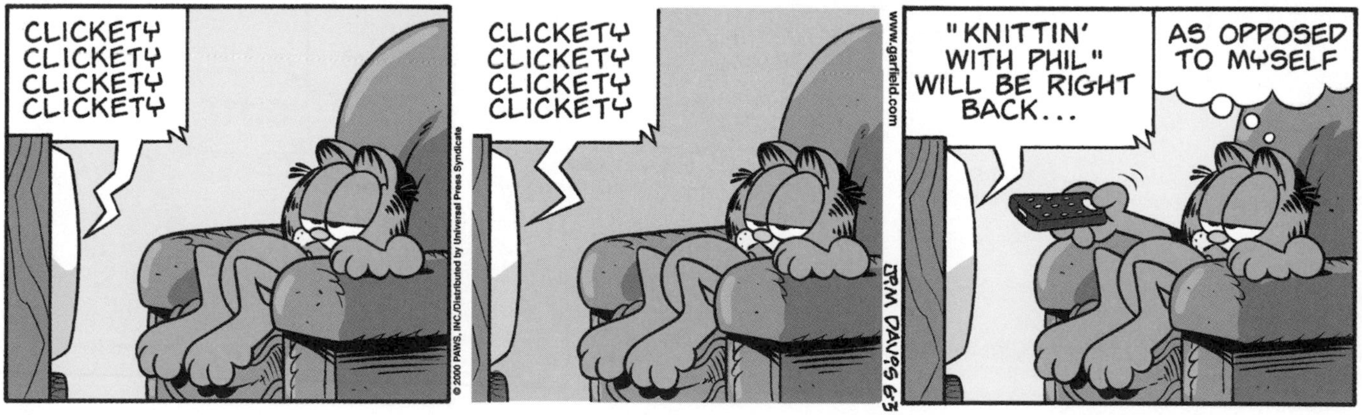
CLICKETY CLICKETY CLICKETY CLICKETY
CLICKETY CLICKETY CLICKETY CLICKETY
"KNITTIN' WITH PHIL" WILL BE RIGHT BACK...
AS OPPOSED TO MYSELF
JPM DAVIS 6-3
© 2000 PAWS, INC./Distributed by Universal Press Syndicate
www.garfield.com

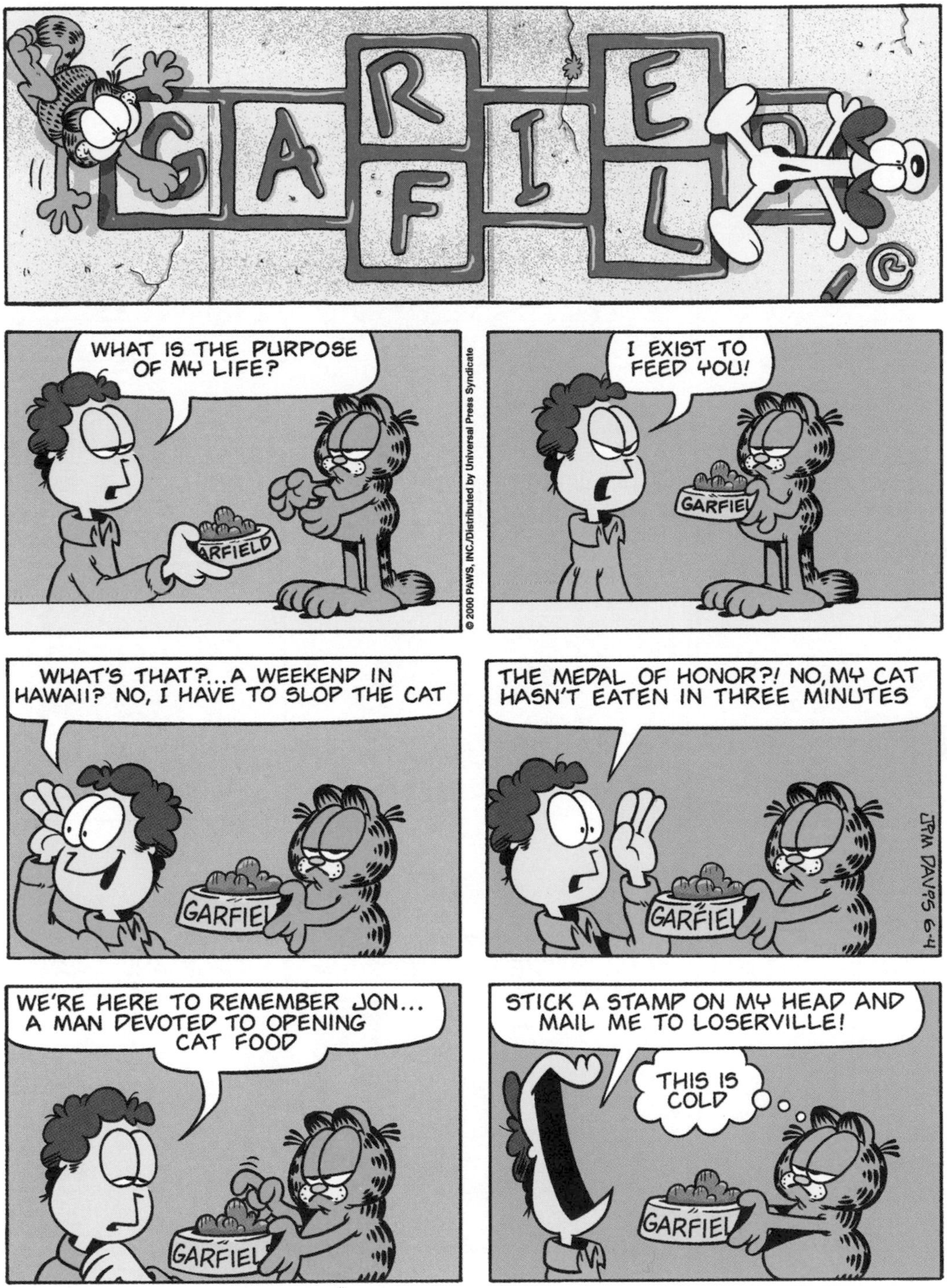
GARFIELD ®
WHAT IS THE PURPOSE OF MY LIFE?
GARFIELD
© 2000 PAWS, INC./Distributed by Universal Press Syndicate
I EXIST TO FEED YOU!
GARFIEL
WHAT'S THAT?...A WEEKEND IN HAWAII? NO, I HAVE TO SLOP THE CAT
GARFIEL
THE MEDAL OF HONOR?! NO, MY CAT HASN'T EATEN IN THREE MINUTES
GARFIEL
JPM DAVPS 6-4
WE'RE HERE TO REMEMBER JON... A MAN DEVOTED TO OPENING CAT FOOD
GARFIEL
STICK A STAMP ON MY HEAD AND MAIL ME TO LOSERVILLE!
THIS IS COLD
GARFIEL

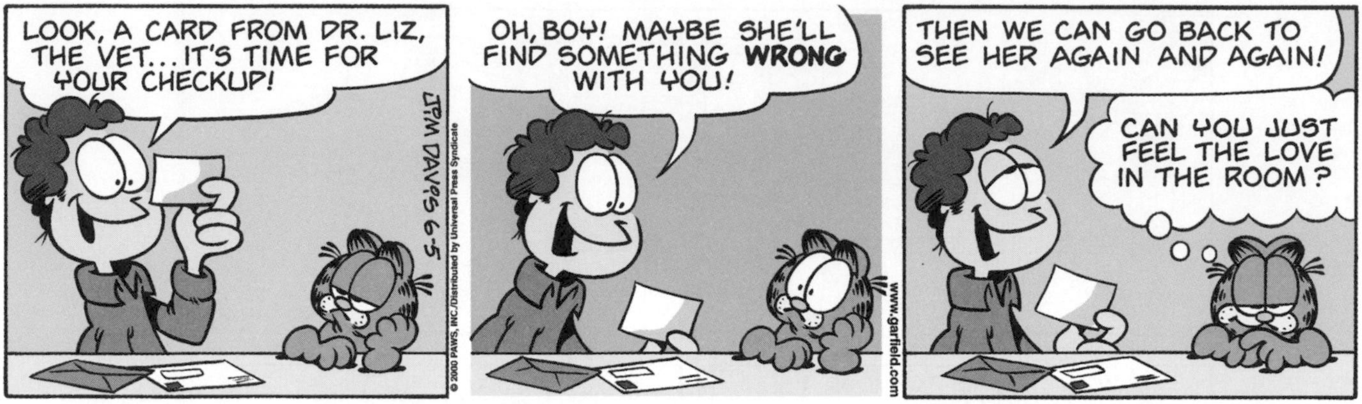
LOOK, A CARD FROM DR. LIZ, THE VET... IT'S TIME FOR YOUR CHECKUP!
JIM DAVIS 6-5
© 2000 PAWS, INC./Distributed by Universal Press Syndicate
OH, BOY! MAYBE SHE'LL FIND SOMETHING **WRONG** WITH YOU!
www.garfield.com
THEN WE CAN GO BACK TO SEE HER AGAIN AND AGAIN!
CAN YOU JUST FEEL THE LOVE IN THE ROOM?

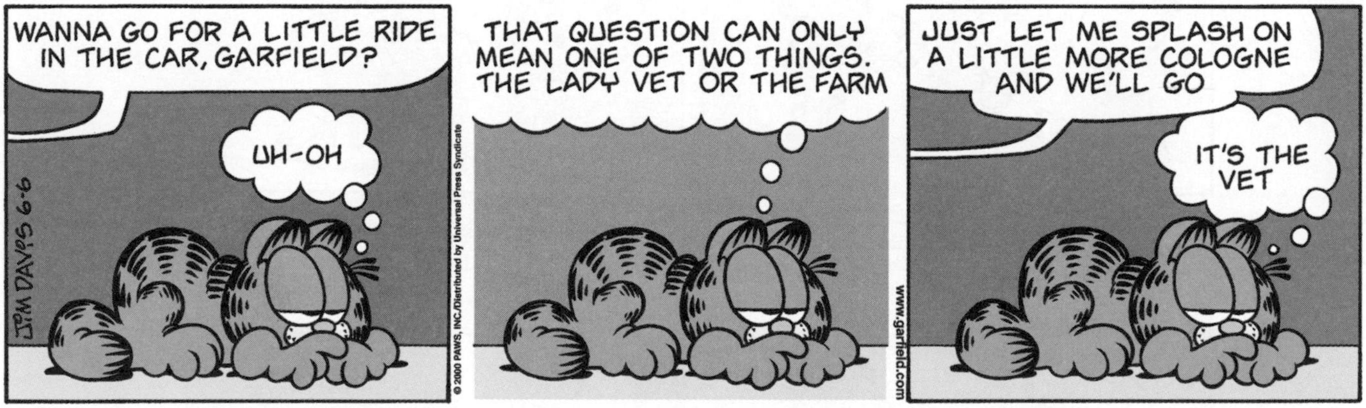
WANNA GO FOR A LITTLE RIDE IN THE CAR, GARFIELD?
UH-OH
JIM DAVIS 6-6
© 2000 PAWS, INC./Distributed by Universal Press Syndicate
THAT QUESTION CAN ONLY MEAN ONE OF TWO THINGS. THE LADY VET OR THE FARM
www.garfield.com
JUST LET ME SPLASH ON A LITTLE MORE COLOGNE AND WE'LL GO
IT'S THE VET

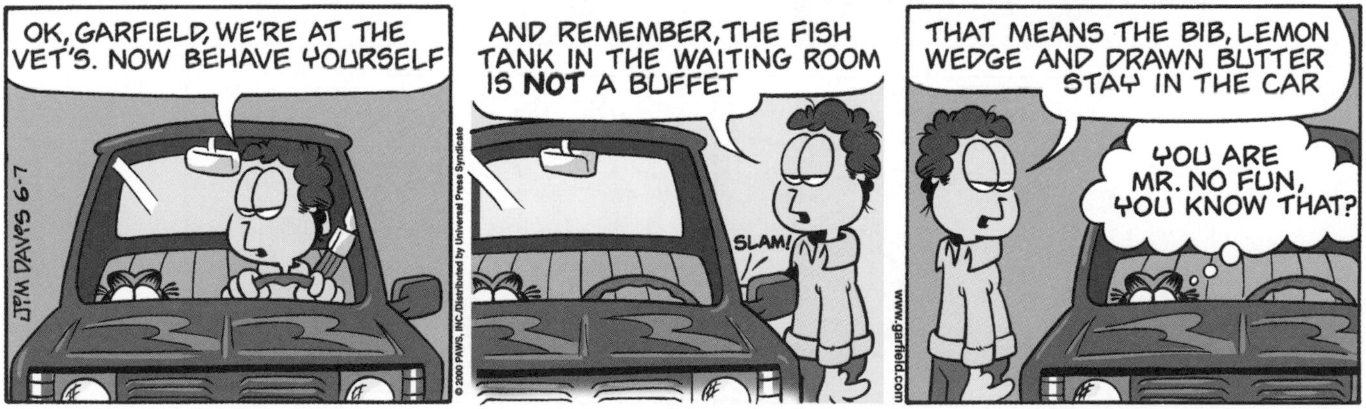
OK, GARFIELD, WE'RE AT THE VET'S. NOW BEHAVE YOURSELF
JIM DAVIS 6-7
© 2000 PAWS, INC./Distributed by Universal Press Syndicate
AND REMEMBER, THE FISH TANK IN THE WAITING ROOM IS **NOT** A BUFFET
SLAM!
www.garfield.com
THAT MEANS THE BIB, LEMON WEDGE AND DRAWN BUTTER STAY IN THE CAR
YOU ARE MR. NO FUN, YOU KNOW THAT?

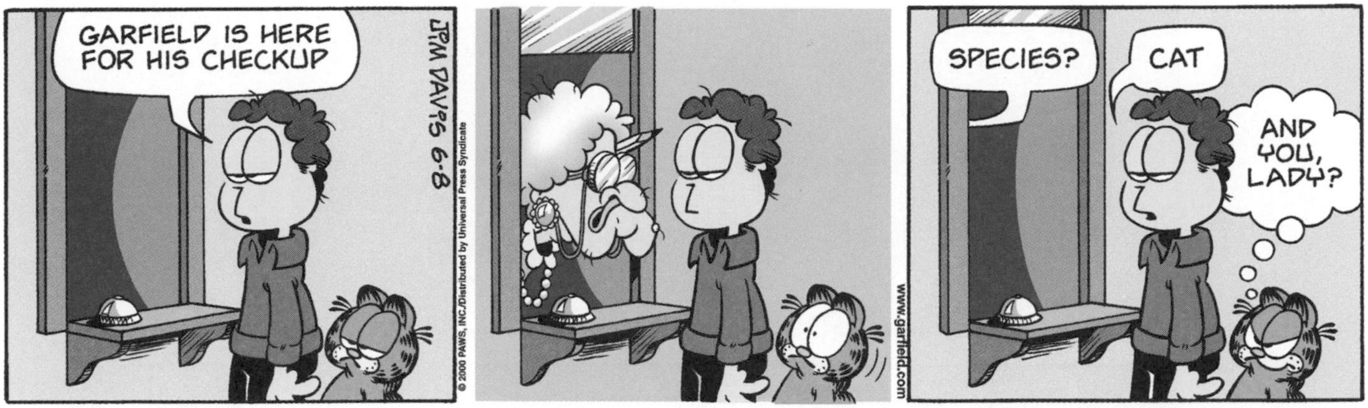
GARFIELD IS HERE FOR HIS CHECKUP
JIM DAVIS 6-8
© 2000 PAWS, INC./Distributed by Universal Press Syndicate
www.garfield.com
SPECIES?
CAT
AND YOU, LADY?

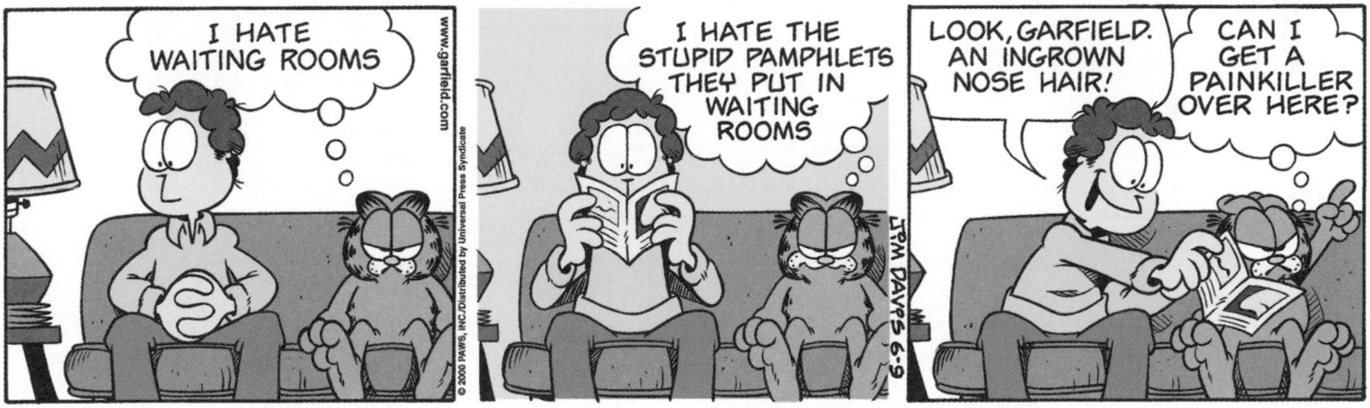
I HATE WAITING ROOMS
www.garfield.com
© 2000 PAWS, INC./Distributed by Universal Press Syndicate
I HATE THE STUPID PAMPHLETS THEY PUT IN WAITING ROOMS
JIM DAVIS 6-9
LOOK, GARFIELD. AN INGROWN NOSE HAIR!
CAN I GET A PAINKILLER OVER HERE?

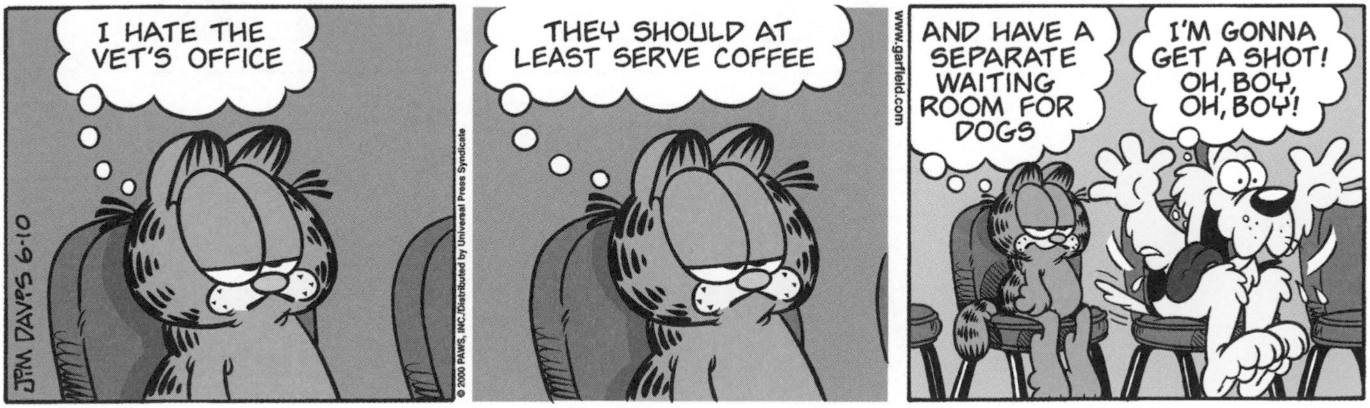
I HATE THE VET'S OFFICE
JIM DAVIS 6-10
THEY SHOULD AT LEAST SERVE COFFEE
© 2000 PAWS, INC./Distributed by Universal Press Syndicate
www.garfield.com
AND HAVE A SEPARATE WAITING ROOM FOR DOGS
I'M GONNA GET A SHOT! OH, BOY, OH, BOY!

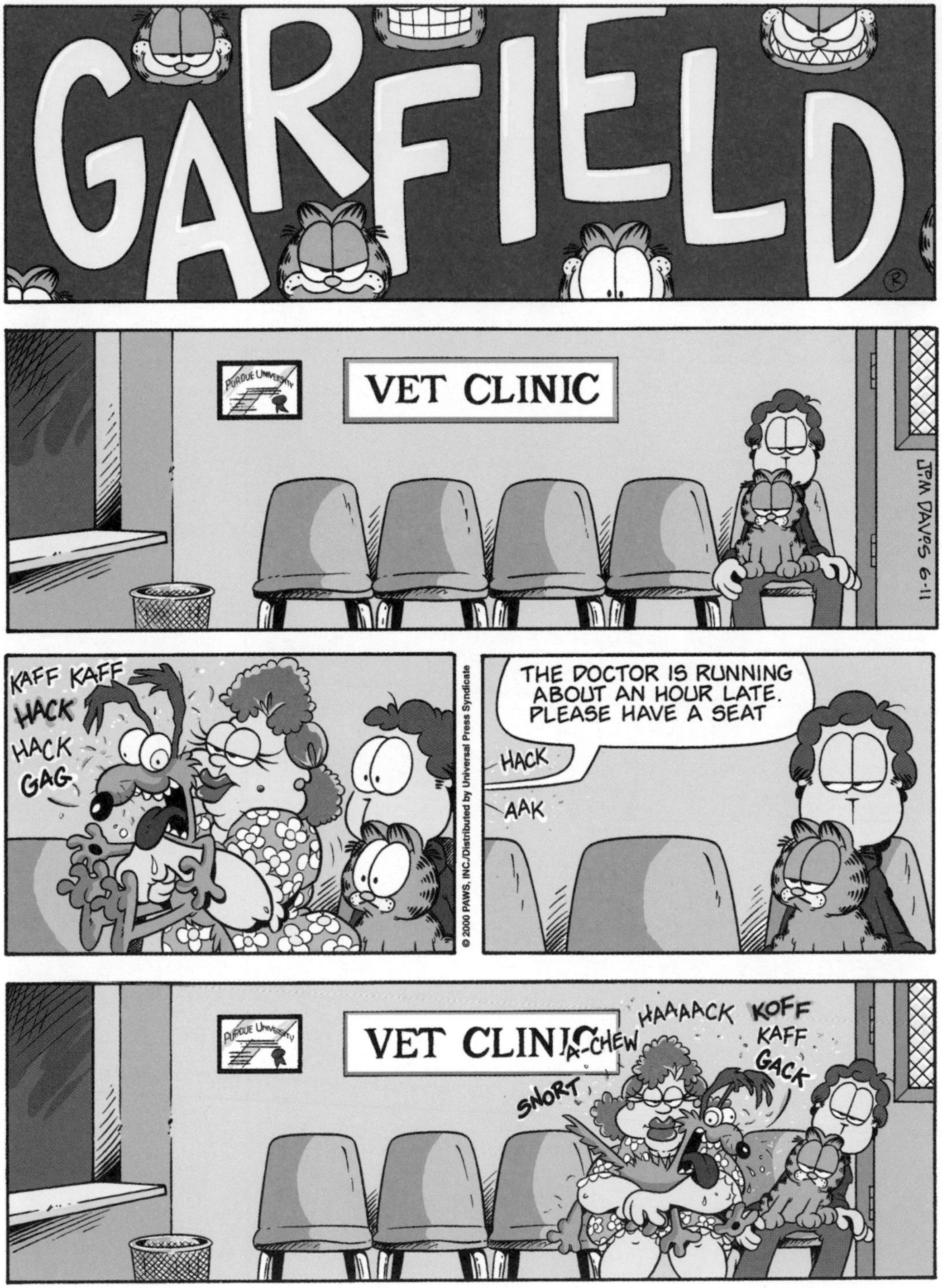
GARFIELD
PURDUE UNIVERSITY
VET CLINIC
JIM DAVIS 6-11
KAFF KAFF
HACK
HACK
GAG
© 2000 PAWS, INC./Distributed by Universal Press Syndicate
THE DOCTOR IS RUNNING ABOUT AN HOUR LATE. PLEASE HAVE A SEAT
HACK
AAK
PURDUE UNIVERSITY
VET CLINIC
A-CHEW
HAAAACK
KOFF
KAFF
GACK
SNORT

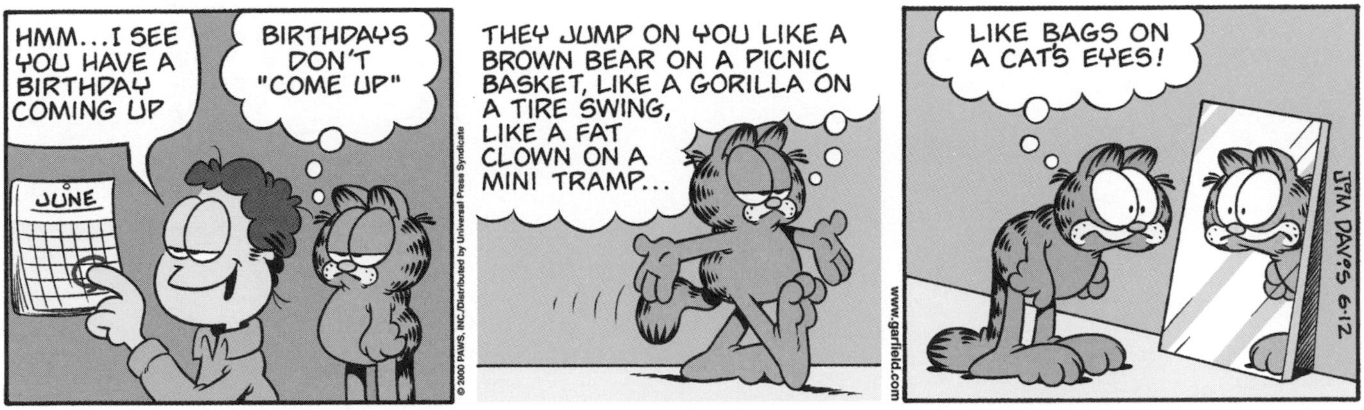
HMM...I SEE YOU HAVE A BIRTHDAY COMING UP
BIRTHDAYS DON'T "COME UP"
JUNE
THEY JUMP ON YOU LIKE A BROWN BEAR ON A PICNIC BASKET, LIKE A GORILLA ON A TIRE SWING, LIKE A FAT CLOWN ON A MINI TRAMP...
LIKE BAGS ON A CAT'S EYES!
JIM DAVIS 6-12
© 2000 PAWS, INC./Distributed by Universal Press Syndicate
www.garfield.com

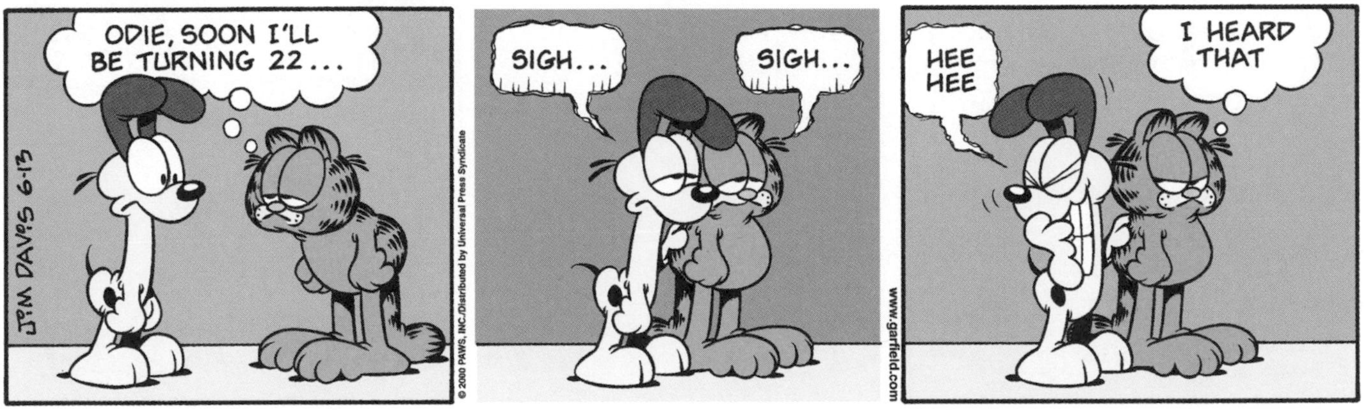
ODIE, SOON I'LL BE TURNING 22...
JIM DAVIS 6-13
SIGH...
SIGH...
HEE HEE
I HEARD THAT
© 2000 PAWS, INC./Distributed by Universal Press Syndicate
www.garfield.com

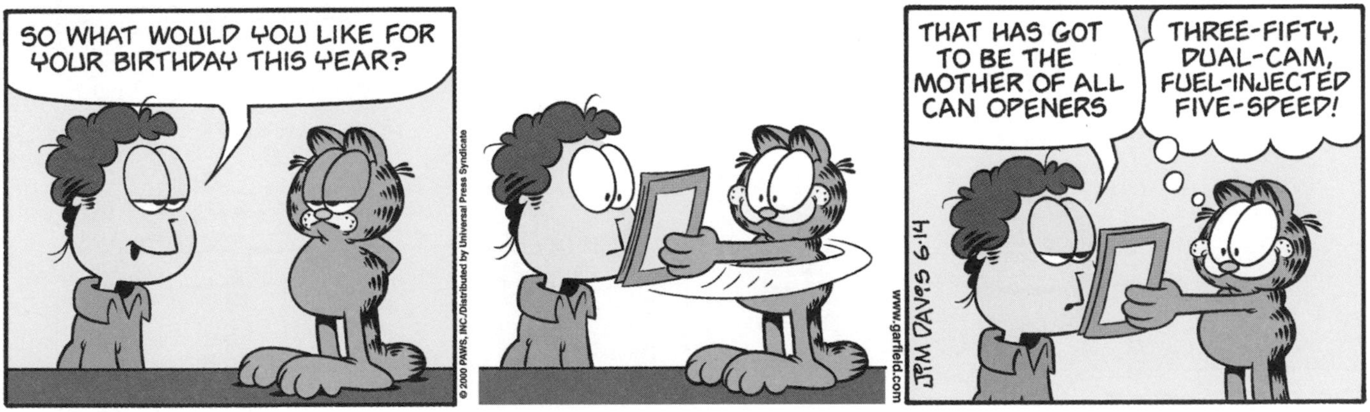
SO WHAT WOULD YOU LIKE FOR YOUR BIRTHDAY THIS YEAR?
THAT HAS GOT TO BE THE MOTHER OF ALL CAN OPENERS
THREE-FIFTY, DUAL-CAM, FUEL-INJECTED FIVE-SPEED!
JIM DAVIS 6-14
© 2000 PAWS, INC./Distributed by Universal Press Syndicate
www.garfield.com

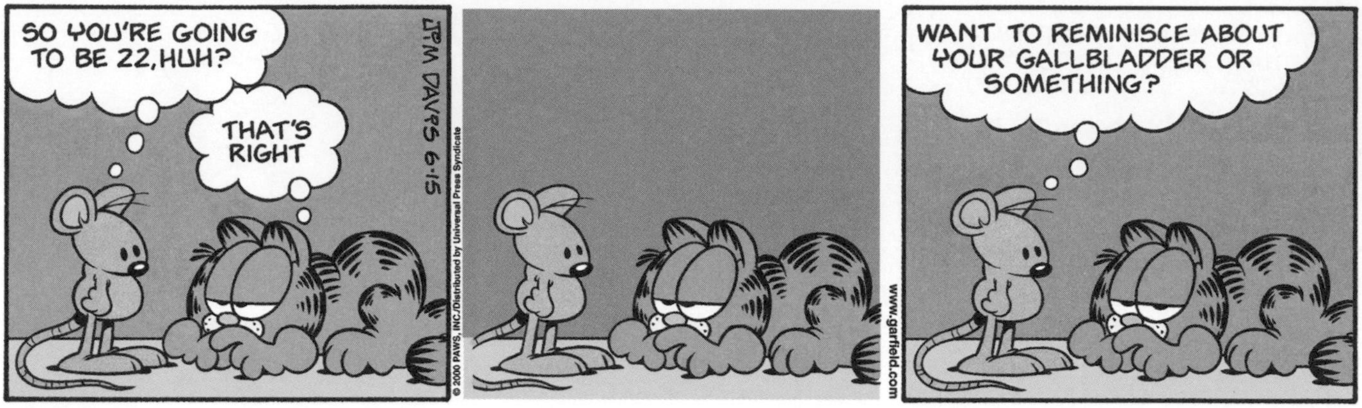
SO YOU'RE GOING TO BE 22, HUH?
THAT'S RIGHT
JIM DAVIS 6-15
© 2000 PAWS, INC./Distributed by Universal Press Syndicate
www.garfield.com
WANT TO REMINISCE ABOUT YOUR GALLBLADDER OR SOMETHING?

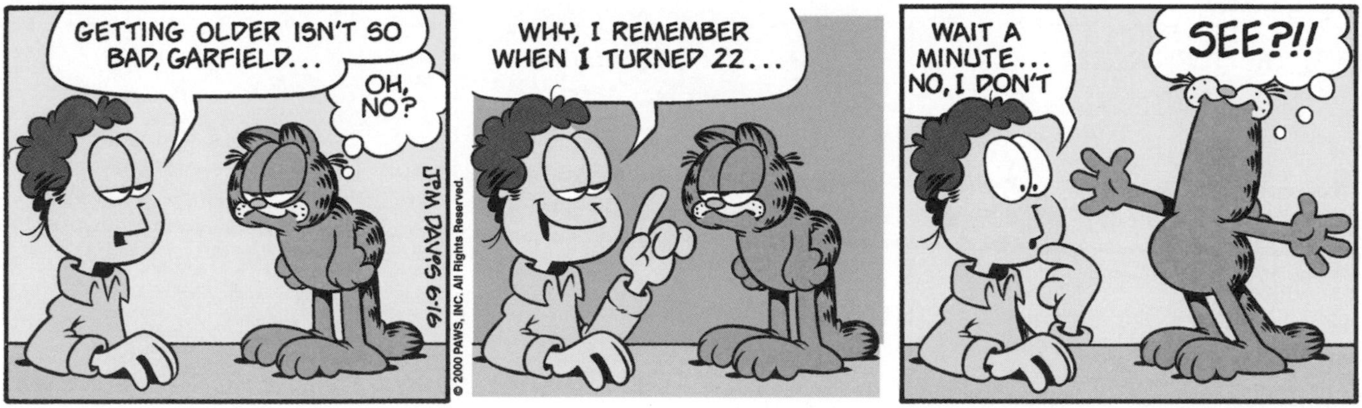
GETTING OLDER ISN'T SO BAD, GARFIELD...
OH, NO?
JIM DAVIS 6-16
© 2000 PAWS, INC. All Rights Reserved.
WHY, I REMEMBER WHEN I TURNED 22...
WAIT A MINUTE... NO, I DON'T
SEE?!!

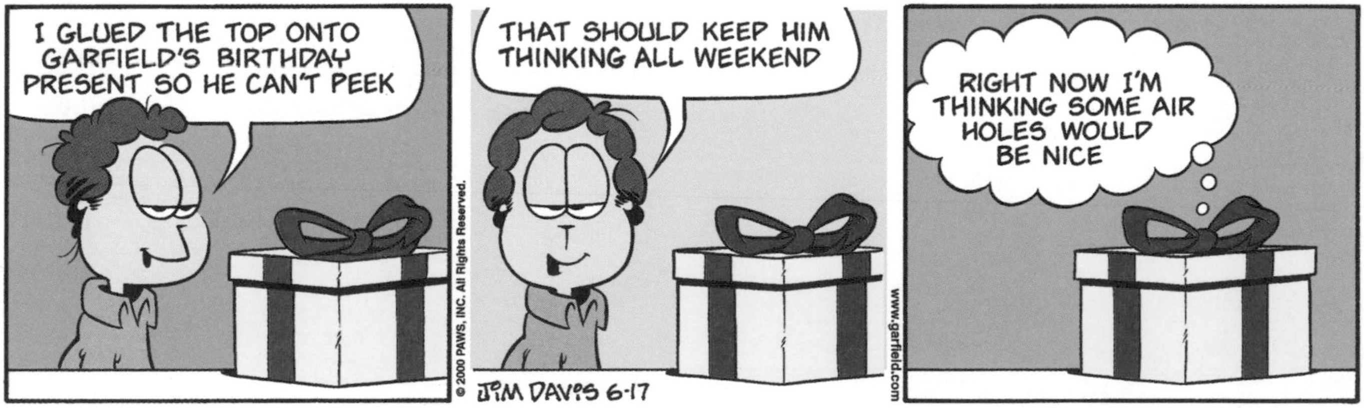
I GLUED THE TOP ONTO GARFIELD'S BIRTHDAY PRESENT SO HE CAN'T PEEK
© 2000 PAWS, INC. All Rights Reserved.
THAT SHOULD KEEP HIM THINKING ALL WEEKEND
JIM DAVIS 6-17
www.garfield.com
RIGHT NOW I'M THINKING SOME AIR HOLES WOULD BE NICE

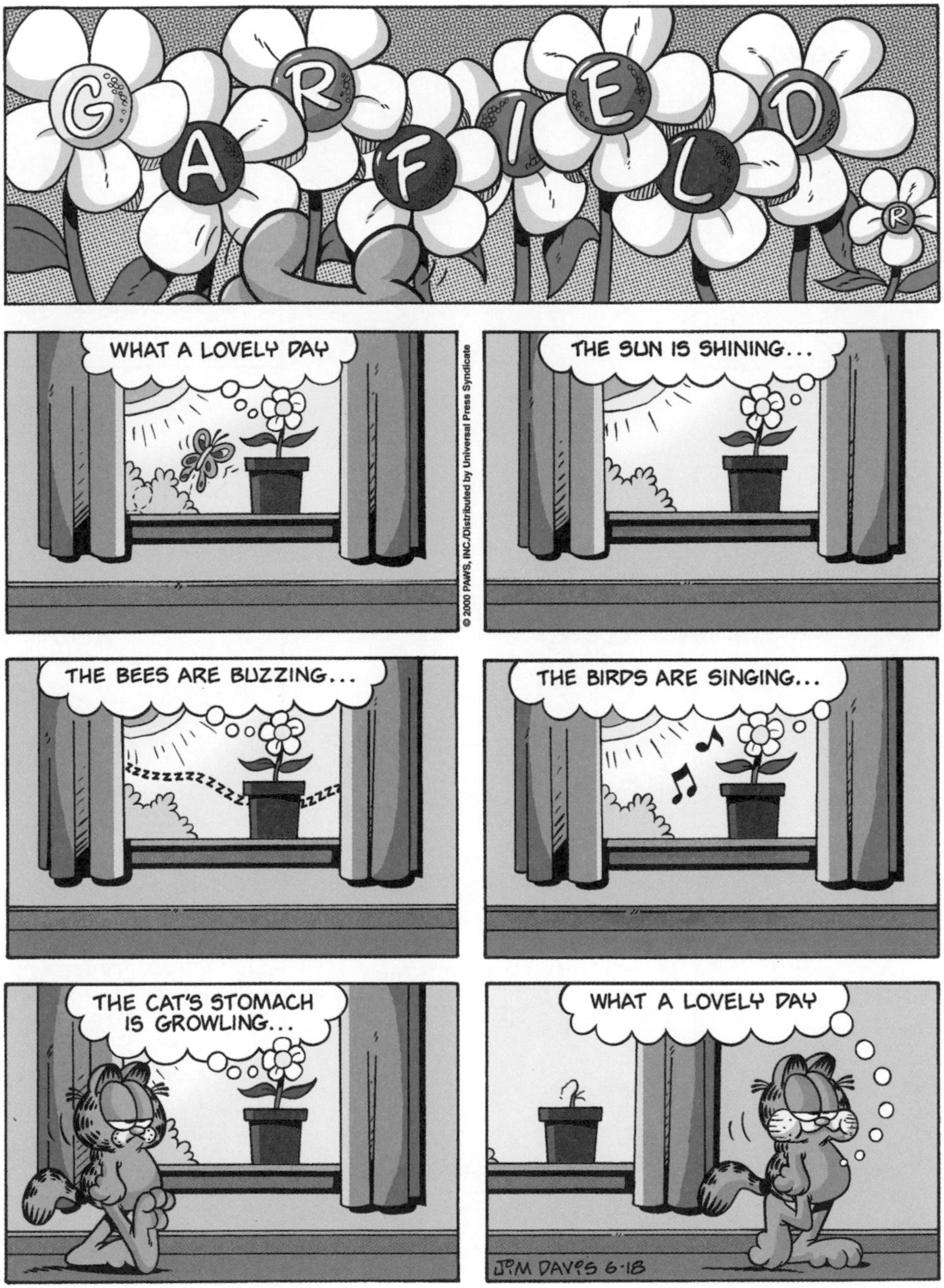
GARFIELD
WHAT A LOVELY DAY
THE SUN IS SHINING...
THE BEES ARE BUZZING...
zzzzzzzzzzzz
THE BIRDS ARE SINGING...
THE CAT'S STOMACH IS GROWLING...
WHAT A LOVELY DAY
JIM DAVIS 6-18
© 2000 PAWS, INC./Distributed by Universal Press Syndicate

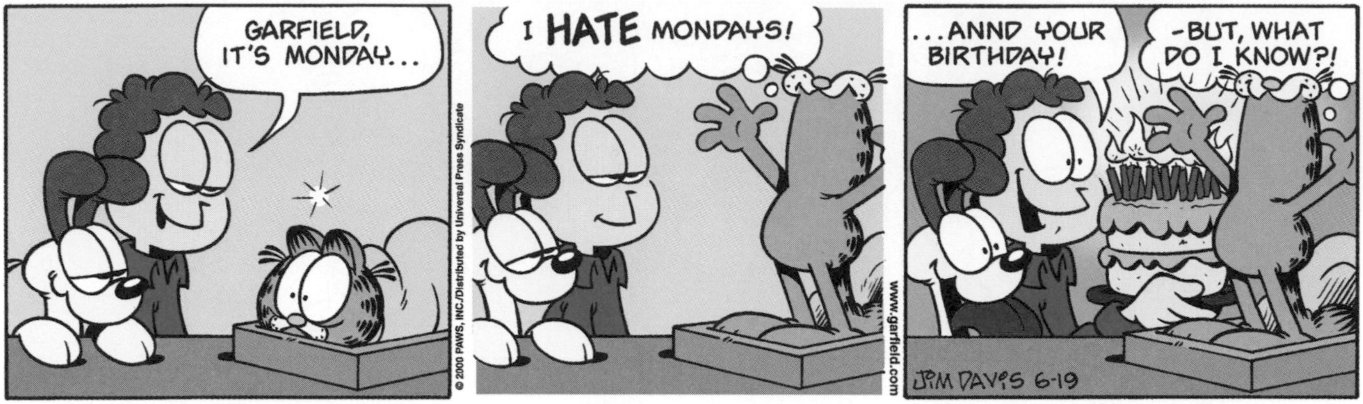
GARFIELD, IT'S MONDAY...
I HATE MONDAYS!
...ANND YOUR BIRTHDAY!
-BUT, WHAT DO I KNOW?!
JIM DAVIS 6-19
www.garfield.com

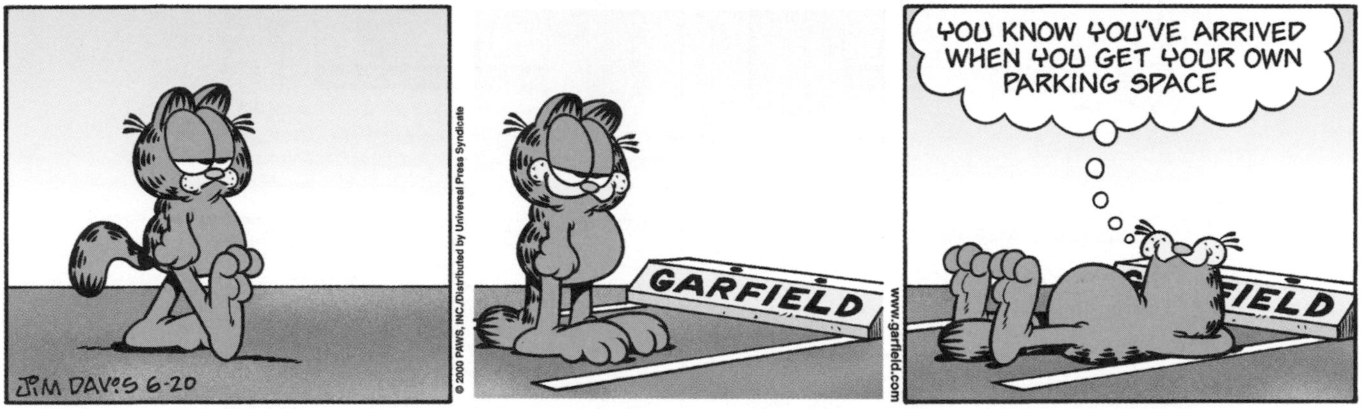
JIM DAVIS 6-20
GARFIELD
YOU KNOW YOU'VE ARRIVED WHEN YOU GET YOUR OWN PARKING SPACE
FIELD
www.garfield.com

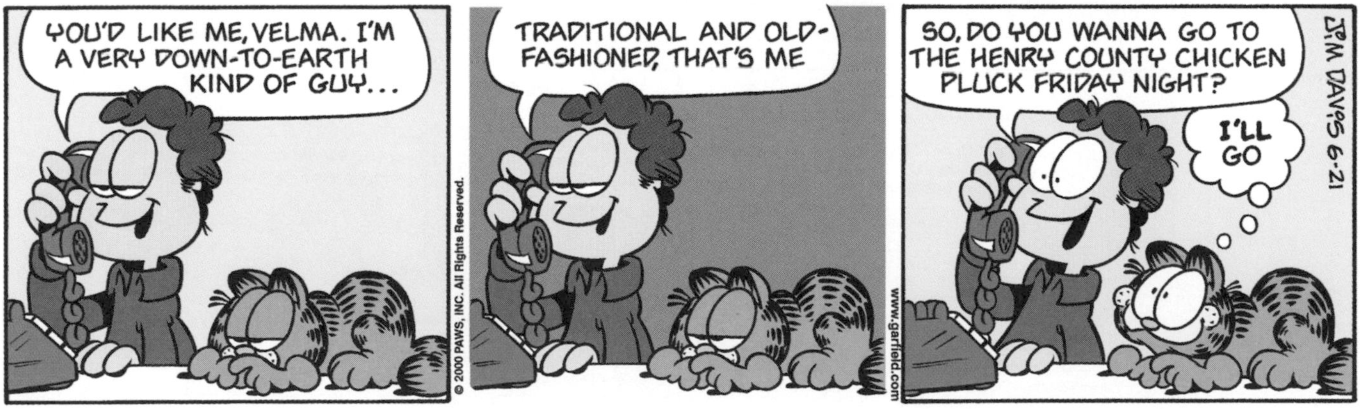
YOU'D LIKE ME, VELMA. I'M A VERY DOWN-TO-EARTH KIND OF GUY...
TRADITIONAL AND OLD-FASHIONED, THAT'S ME
SO, DO YOU WANNA GO TO THE HENRY COUNTY CHICKEN PLUCK FRIDAY NIGHT?
I'LL GO
JIM DAVIS 6-21
www.garfield.com

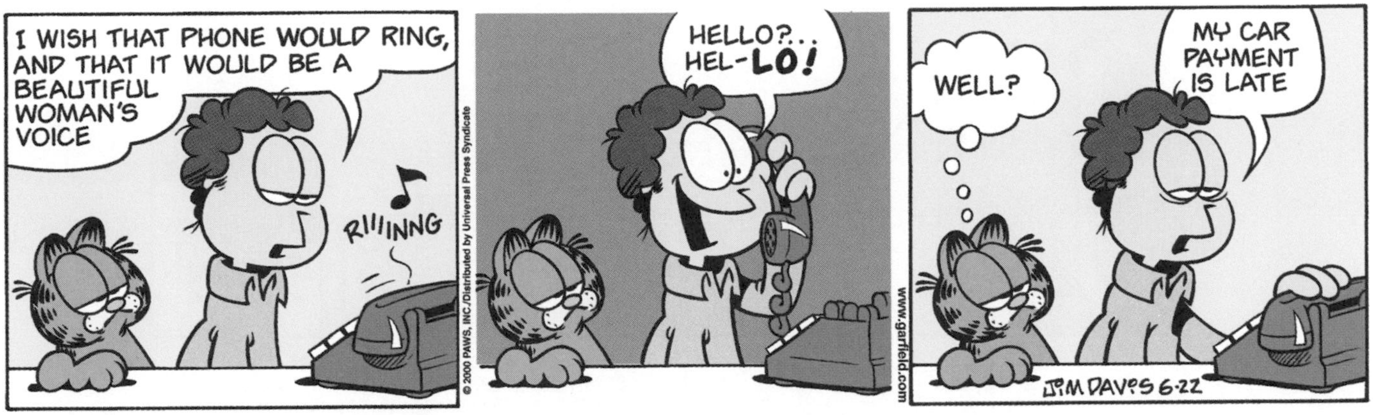
I WISH THAT PHONE WOULD RING, AND THAT IT WOULD BE A BEAUTIFUL WOMAN'S VOICE
RIIIINNG
© 2000 PAWS, INC./Distributed by Universal Press Syndicate
HELLO?... HEL-LO!
www.garfield.com
WELL?
MY CAR PAYMENT IS LATE
JIM DAVIS 6-22

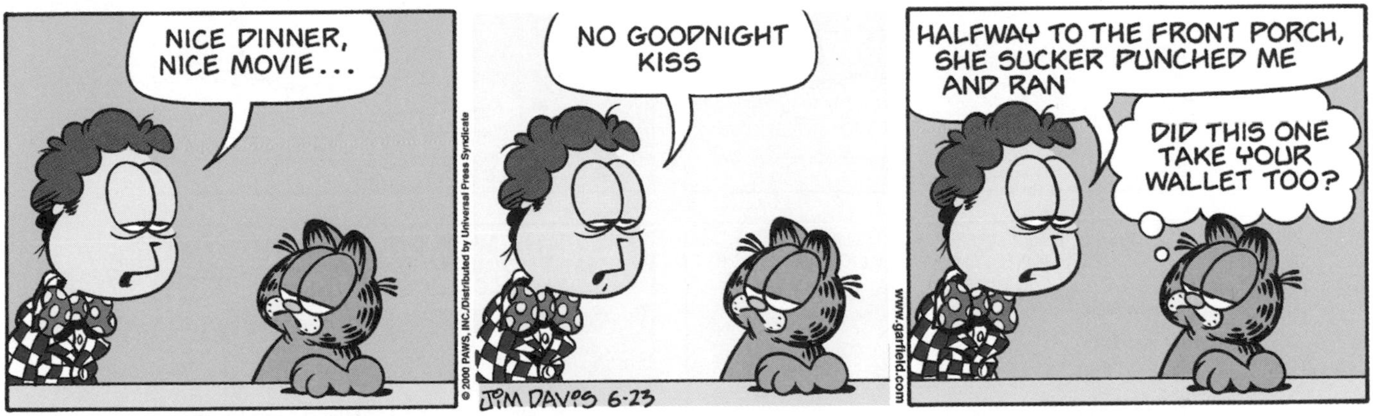
NICE DINNER, NICE MOVIE...
© 2000 PAWS, INC./Distributed by Universal Press Syndicate
NO GOODNIGHT KISS
JIM DAVIS 6-23
www.garfield.com
HALFWAY TO THE FRONT PORCH, SHE SUCKER PUNCHED ME AND RAN
DID THIS ONE TAKE YOUR WALLET TOO?

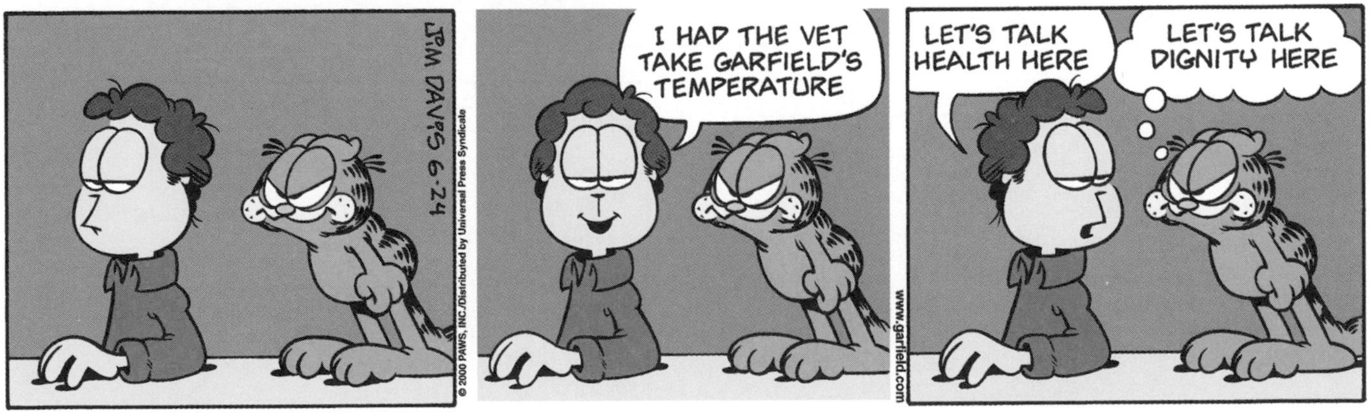
JIM DAVIS 6-24
© 2000 PAWS, INC./Distributed by Universal Press Syndicate
I HAD THE VET TAKE GARFIELD'S TEMPERATURE
www.garfield.com
LET'S TALK HEALTH HERE
LET'S TALK DIGNITY HERE

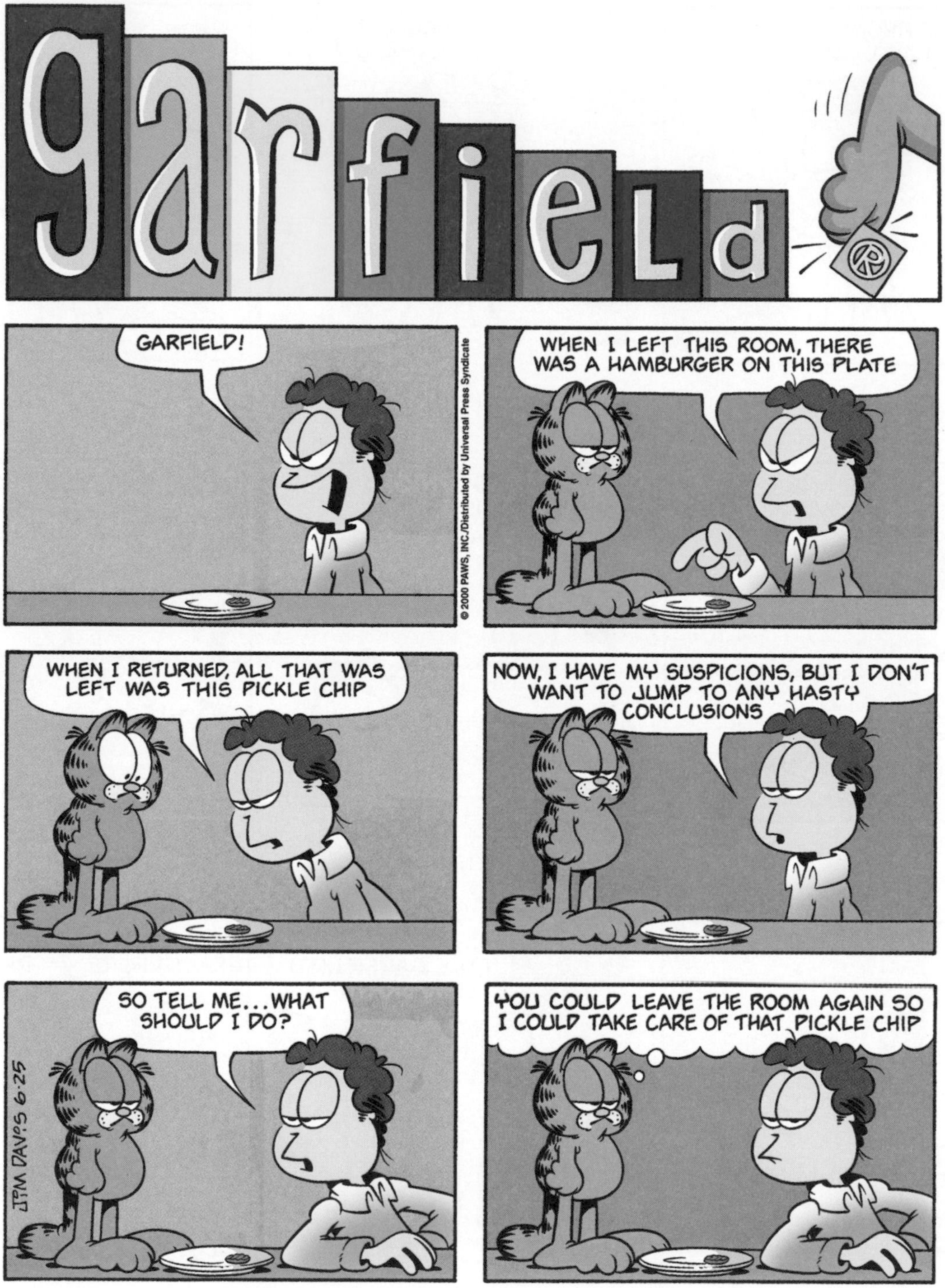
garfield
GARFIELD!
© 2000 PAWS, INC./Distributed by Universal Press Syndicate
WHEN I LEFT THIS ROOM, THERE WAS A HAMBURGER ON THIS PLATE
WHEN I RETURNED, ALL THAT WAS LEFT WAS THIS PICKLE CHIP
NOW, I HAVE MY SUSPICIONS, BUT I DON'T WANT TO JUMP TO ANY HASTY CONCLUSIONS
JIM DAVIS 6-25
SO TELL ME... WHAT SHOULD I DO?
YOU COULD LEAVE THE ROOM AGAIN SO I COULD TAKE CARE OF THAT PICKLE CHIP

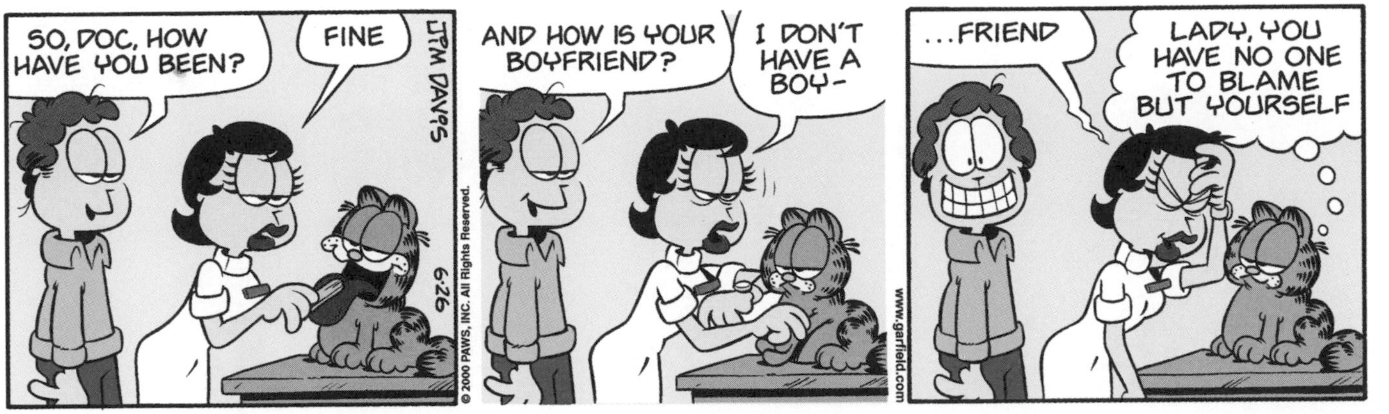
SO, DOC, HOW HAVE YOU BEEN?
FINE
JIM DAVIS 6-26
© 2000 PAWS, INC. All Rights Reserved.
AND HOW IS YOUR BOYFRIEND?
I DON'T HAVE A BOY-
...FRIEND
LADY, YOU HAVE NO ONE TO BLAME BUT YOURSELF
www.garfield.com

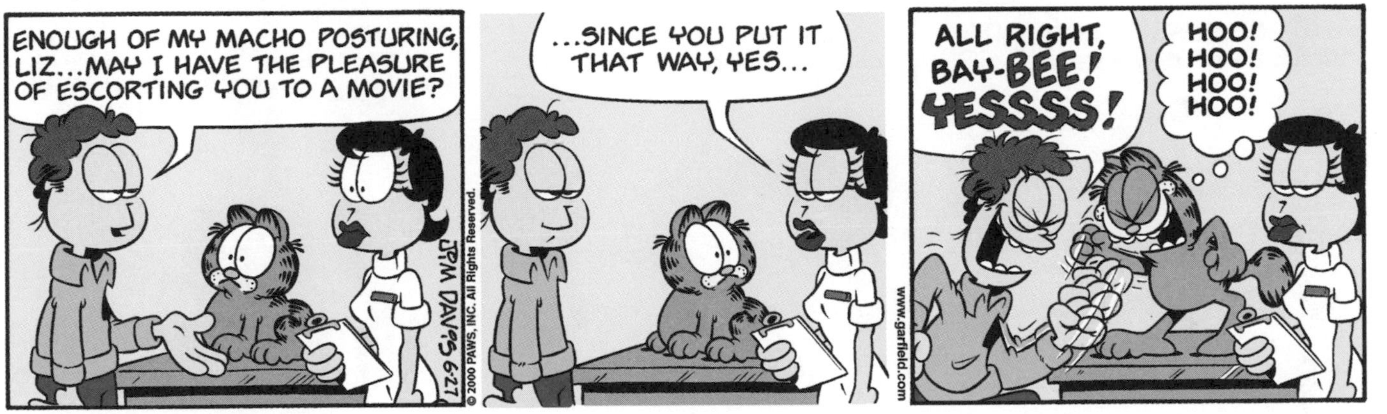
ENOUGH OF MY MACHO POSTURING, LIZ...MAY I HAVE THE PLEASURE OF ESCORTING YOU TO A MOVIE?
JIM DAVIS 6-27
© 2000 PAWS, INC. All Rights Reserved.
...SINCE YOU PUT IT THAT WAY, YES...
ALL RIGHT, BAY-BEE! YESSSS!
HOO! HOO! HOO! HOO!
www.garfield.com

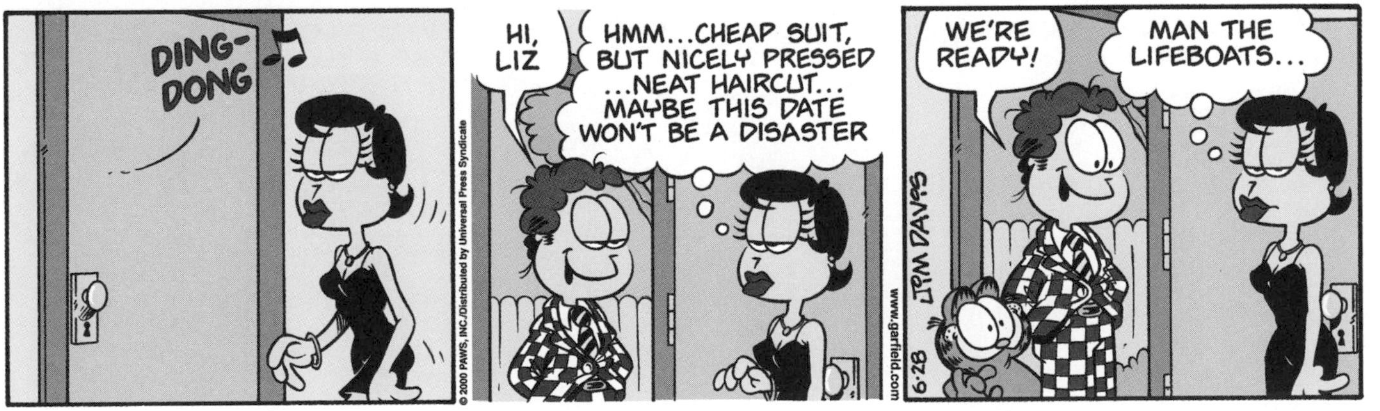
DING-DONG
© 2000 PAWS, INC./Distributed by Universal Press Syndicate
HI, LIZ
HMM...CHEAP SUIT, BUT NICELY PRESSED ...NEAT HAIRCUT... MAYBE THIS DATE WON'T BE A DISASTER
JIM DAVIS 6-28
www.garfield.com
WE'RE READY!
MAN THE LIFEBOATS...

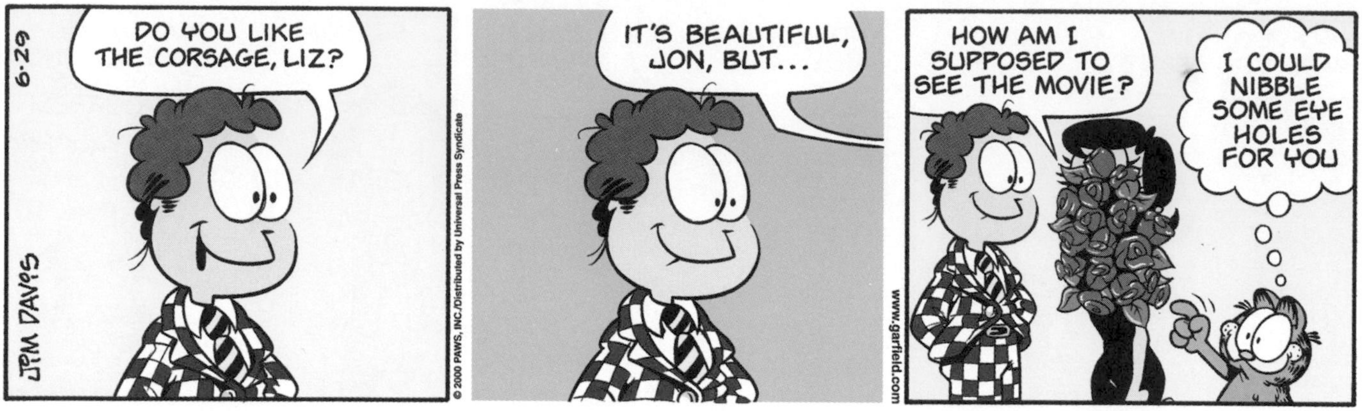
6·29
JIM DAVIS
DO YOU LIKE THE CORSAGE, LIZ?
IT'S BEAUTIFUL, JON, BUT...
© 2000 PAWS, INC./Distributed by Universal Press Syndicate
HOW AM I SUPPOSED TO SEE THE MOVIE?
I COULD NIBBLE SOME EYE HOLES FOR YOU
www.garfield.com

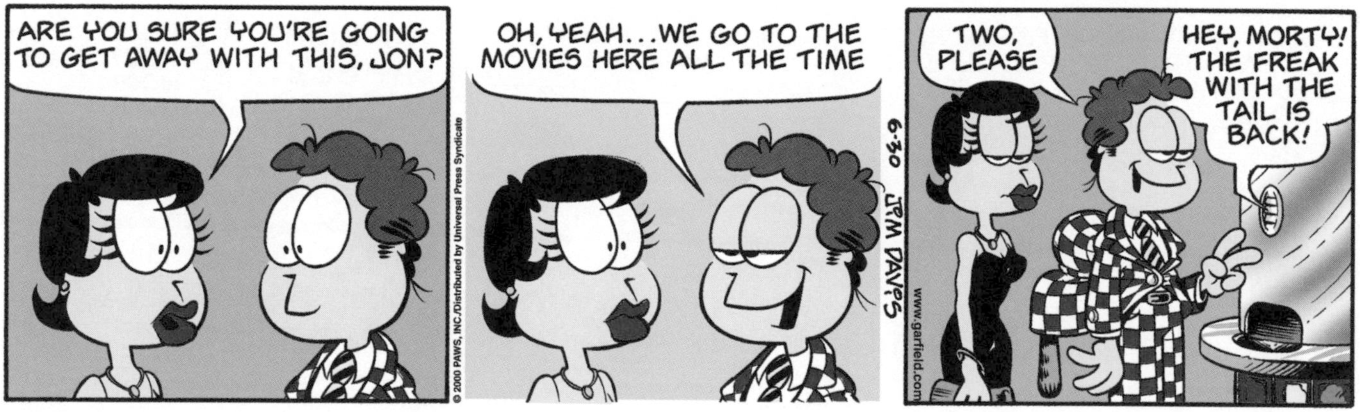
ARE YOU SURE YOU'RE GOING TO GET AWAY WITH THIS, JON?
OH, YEAH...WE GO TO THE MOVIES HERE ALL THE TIME
© 2000 PAWS, INC./Distributed by Universal Press Syndicate
6·30
JIM DAVIS
TWO, PLEASE
HEY, MORTY! THE FREAK WITH THE TAIL IS BACK!
www.garfield.com

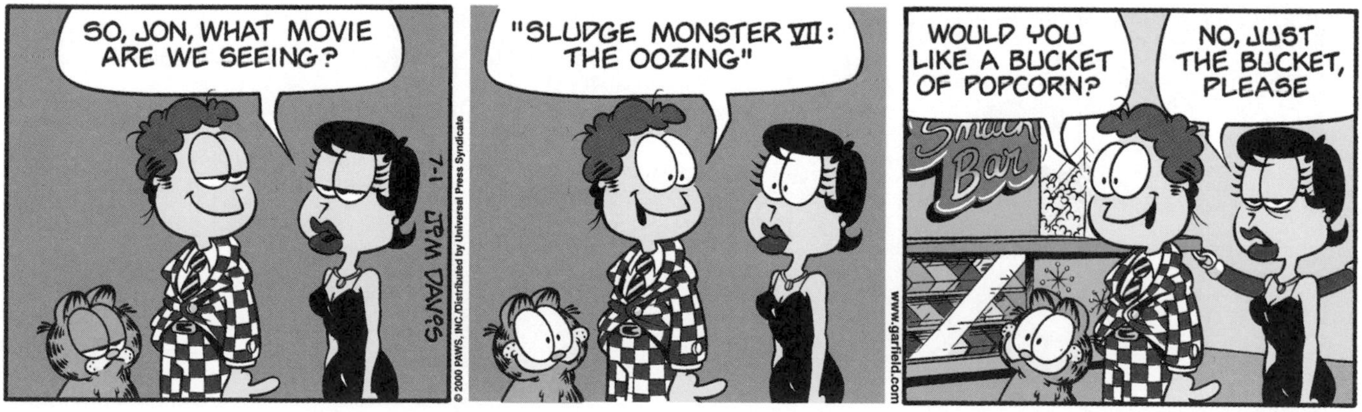
SO, JON, WHAT MOVIE ARE WE SEEING?
7·1
JIM DAVIS
"SLUDGE MONSTER VII: THE OOZING"
© 2000 PAWS, INC./Distributed by Universal Press Syndicate
WOULD YOU LIKE A BUCKET OF POPCORN?
NO, JUST THE BUCKET, PLEASE
Snack Bar
www.garfield.com

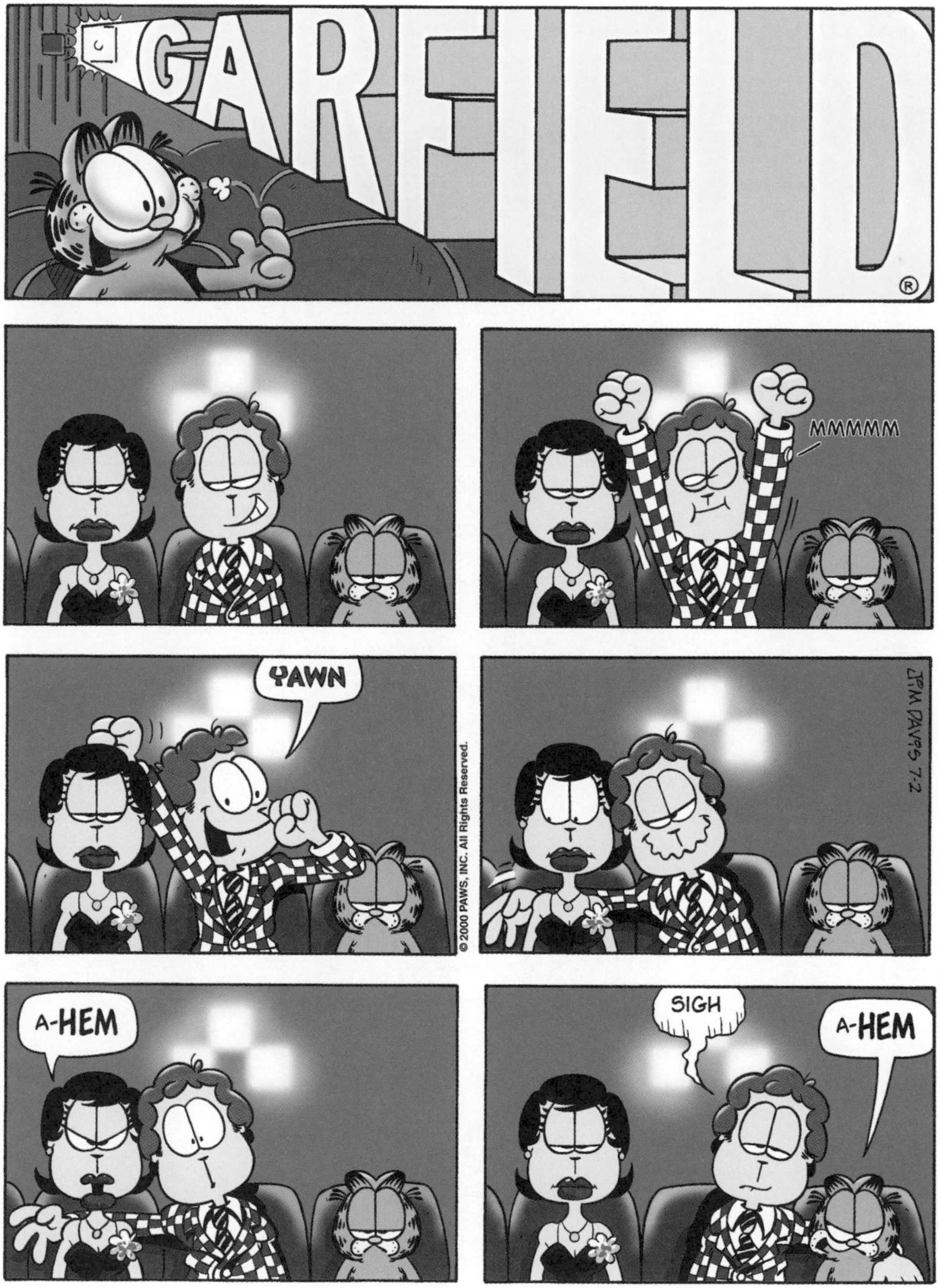
GARFIELD®
MMMMM
YAWN
JIM DAVIS 7-2
© 2000 PAWS, INC. All Rights Reserved.
A-HEM
SIGH
A-HEM

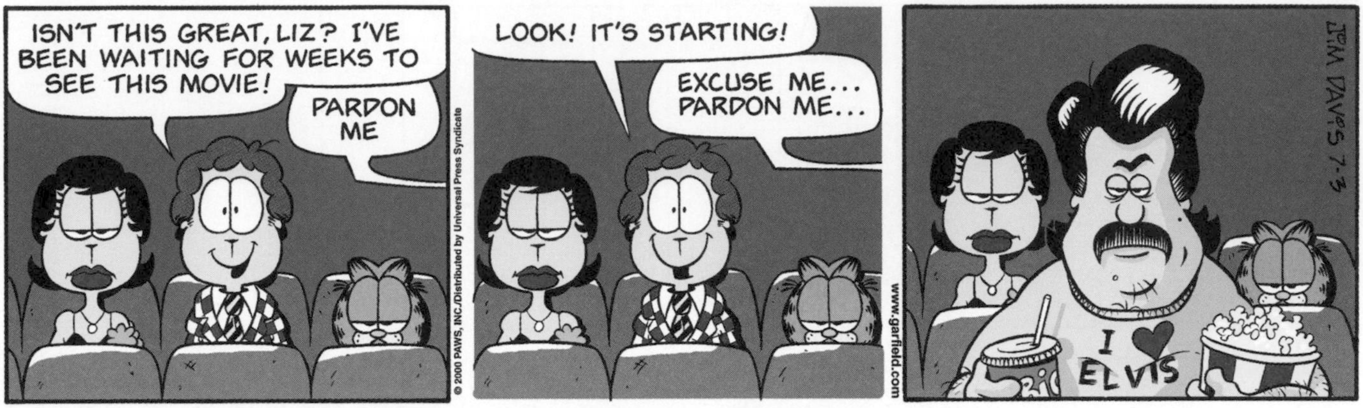
ISN'T THIS GREAT, LIZ? I'VE BEEN WAITING FOR WEEKS TO SEE THIS MOVIE!
PARDON ME
© 2000 PAWS, INC./Distributed by Universal Press Syndicate
LOOK! IT'S STARTING!
EXCUSE ME... PARDON ME...
www.garfield.com
JIM DAVIS 7-3
I ♥ ELVIS

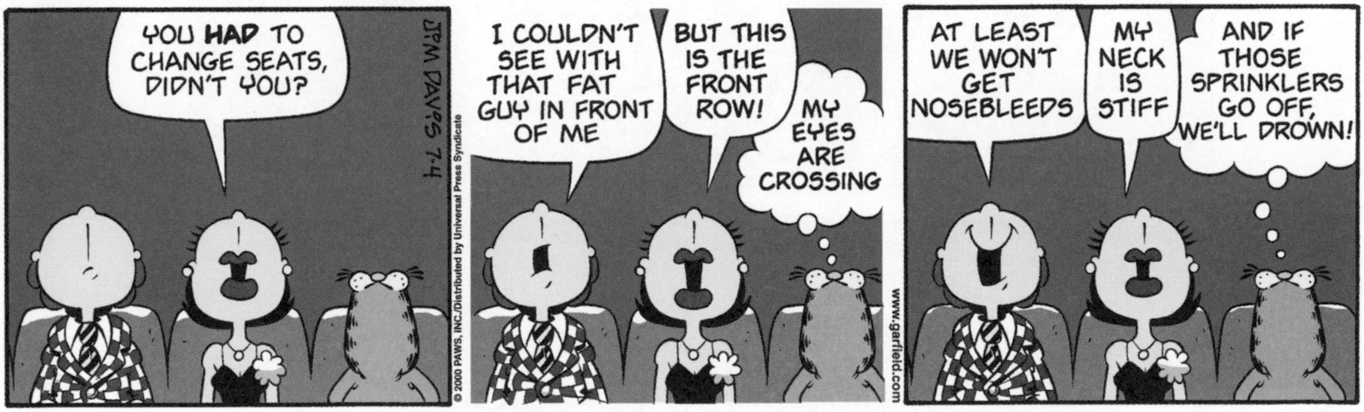
YOU **HAD** TO CHANGE SEATS, DIDN'T YOU?
JIM DAVIS 7-4
© 2000 PAWS, INC./Distributed by Universal Press Syndicate
I COULDN'T SEE WITH THAT FAT GUY IN FRONT OF ME
BUT THIS IS THE FRONT ROW!
MY EYES ARE CROSSING
www.garfield.com
AT LEAST WE WON'T GET NOSEBLEEDS
MY NECK IS STIFF
AND IF THOSE SPRINKLERS GO OFF, WE'LL DROWN!

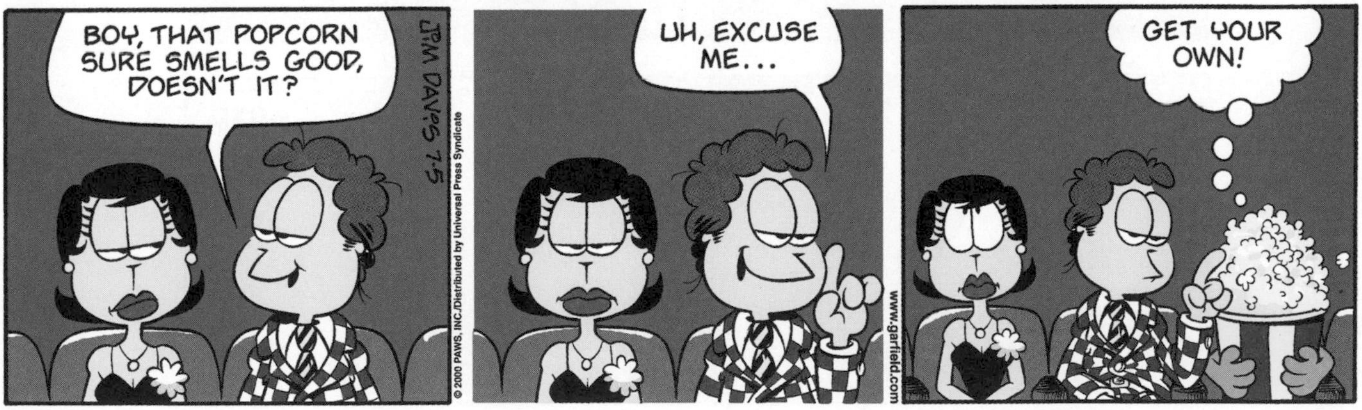
BOY, THAT POPCORN SURE SMELLS GOOD, DOESN'T IT?
JIM DAVIS 7-5
© 2000 PAWS, INC./Distributed by Universal Press Syndicate
UH, EXCUSE ME...
www.garfield.com
GET YOUR OWN!

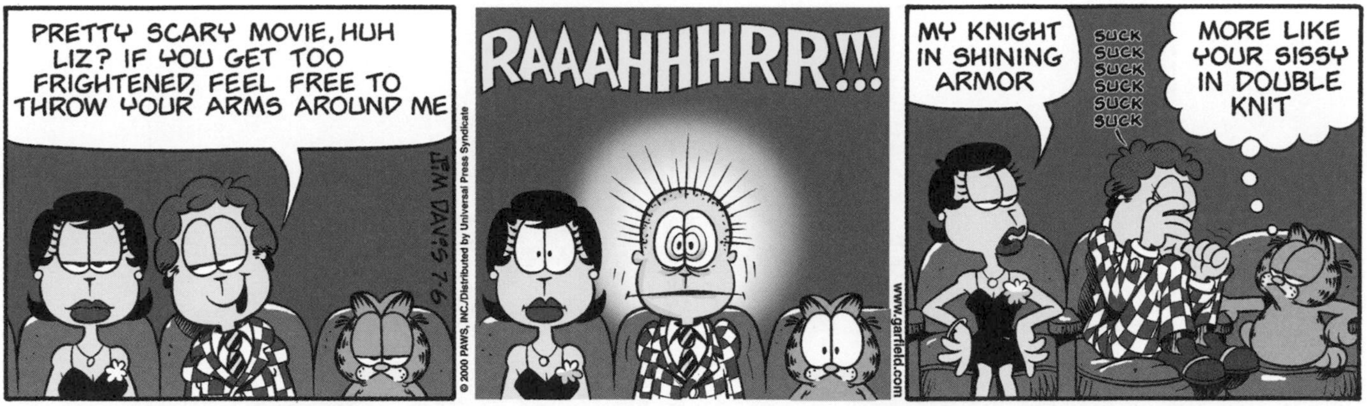
PRETTY SCARY MOVIE, HUH LIZ? IF YOU GET TOO FRIGHTENED, FEEL FREE TO THROW YOUR ARMS AROUND ME
JPM DAVIS 7-6
© 2000 PAWS, INC./Distributed by Universal Press Syndicate
RAAAHHHRR!!!
www.garfield.com
MY KNIGHT IN SHINING ARMOR
SUCK SUCK SUCK SUCK SUCK SUCK
MORE LIKE YOUR SISSY IN DOUBLE KNIT

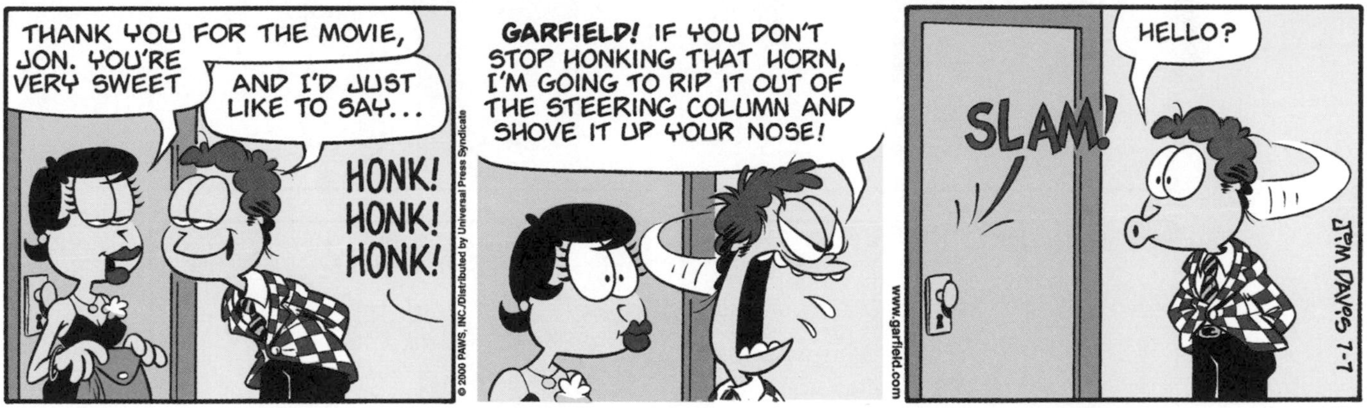
THANK YOU FOR THE MOVIE, JON. YOU'RE VERY SWEET
AND I'D JUST LIKE TO SAY...
HONK! HONK! HONK!
© 2000 PAWS, INC./Distributed by Universal Press Syndicate
GARFIELD! IF YOU DON'T STOP HONKING THAT HORN, I'M GOING TO RIP IT OUT OF THE STEERING COLUMN AND SHOVE IT UP YOUR NOSE!
www.garfield.com
SLAM!
HELLO?
JPM DAVIS 7-7

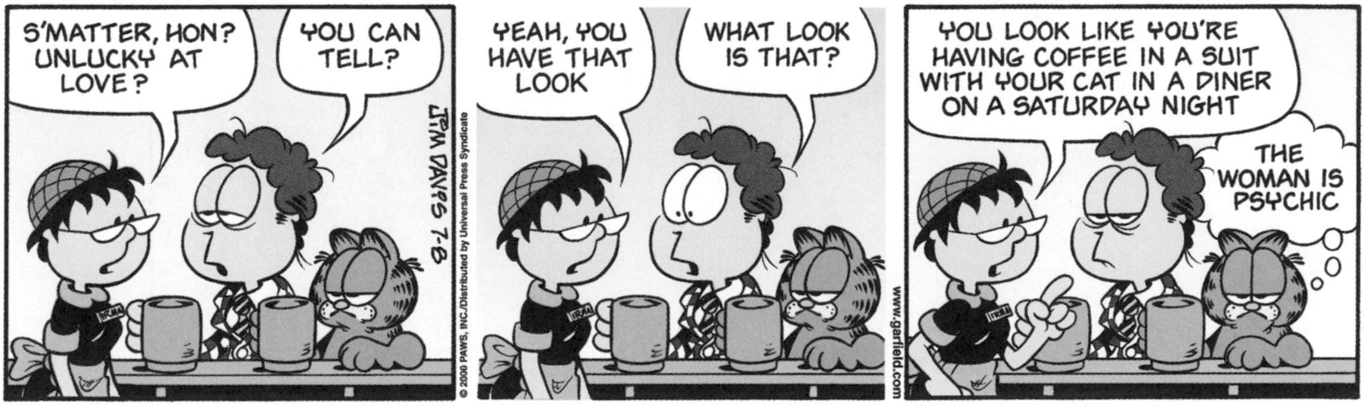
S'MATTER, HON? UNLUCKY AT LOVE?
YOU CAN TELL?
JPM DAVIS 7-8
© 2000 PAWS, INC./Distributed by Universal Press Syndicate
YEAH, YOU HAVE THAT LOOK
WHAT LOOK IS THAT?
www.garfield.com
YOU LOOK LIKE YOU'RE HAVING COFFEE IN A SUIT WITH YOUR CAT IN A DINER ON A SATURDAY NIGHT
THE WOMAN IS PSYCHIC

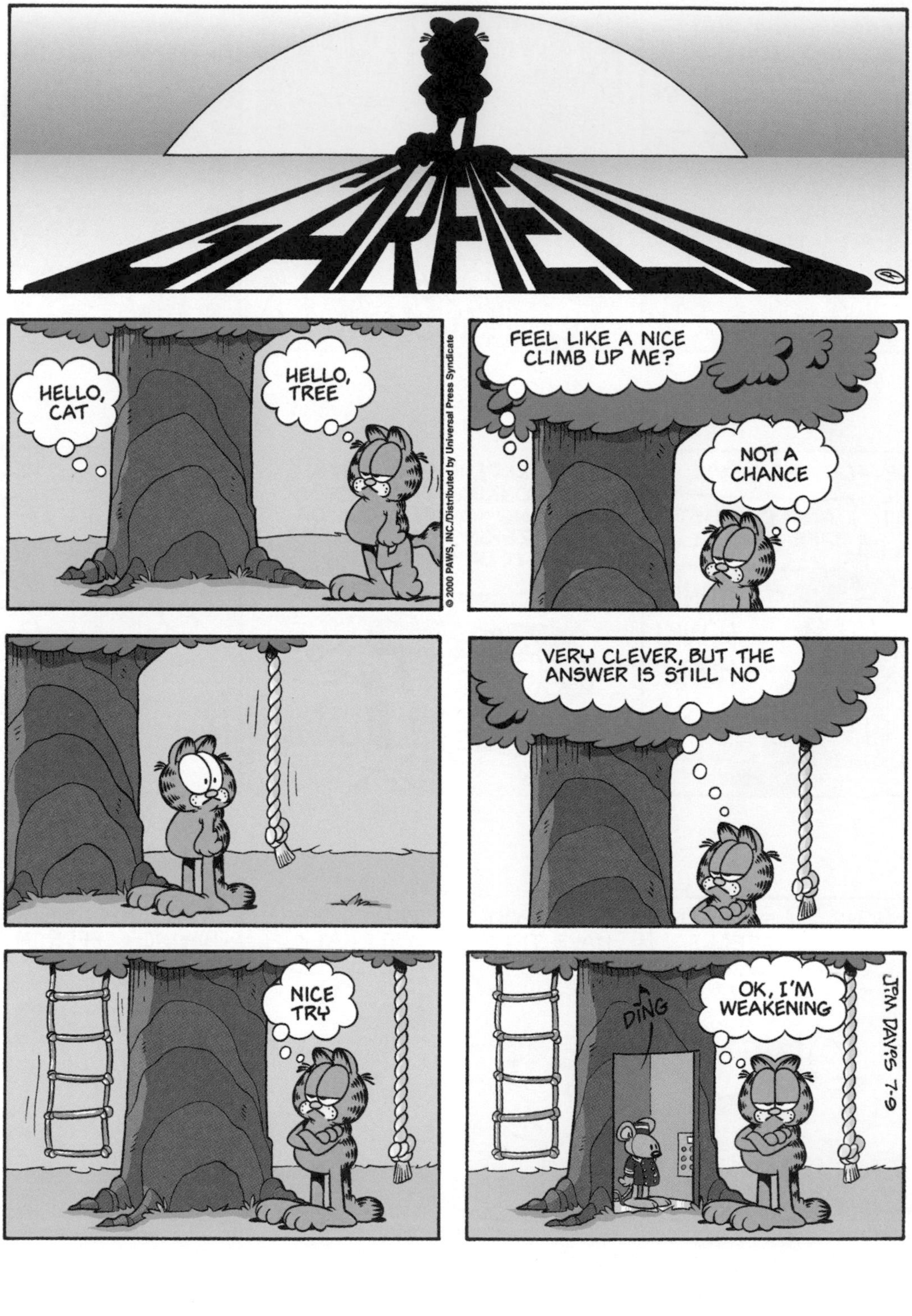
GARFIELD
HELLO, CAT
HELLO, TREE
© 2000 PAWS, INC./Distributed by Universal Press Syndicate
FEEL LIKE A NICE CLIMB UP ME?
NOT A CHANCE
VERY CLEVER, BUT THE ANSWER IS STILL NO
NICE TRY
DING
OK, I'M WEAKENING
JIM DAVIS 7-9

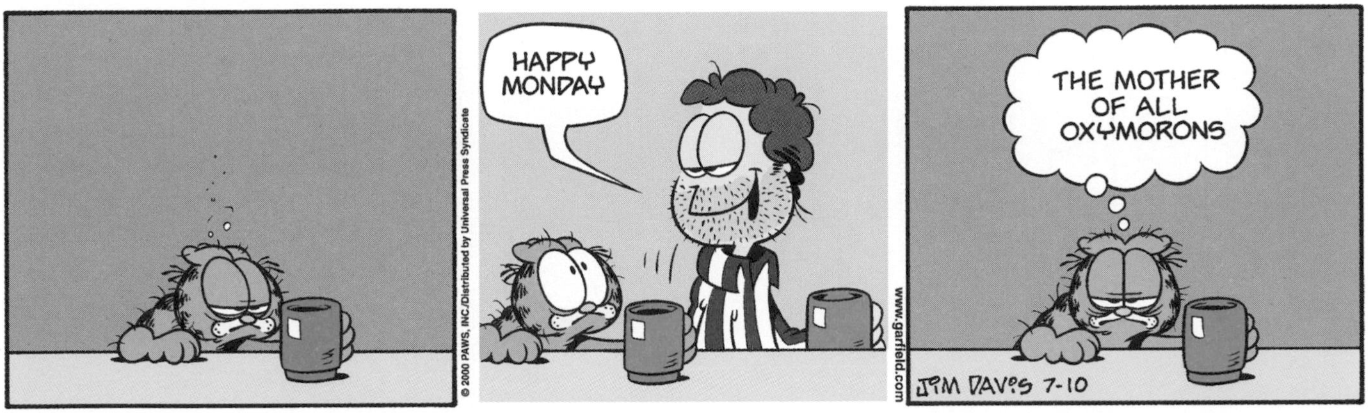
HAPPY MONDAY
THE MOTHER OF ALL OXYMORONS
© 2000 PAWS, INC./Distributed by Universal Press Syndicate
www.garfield.com
JIM DAVIS 7-10

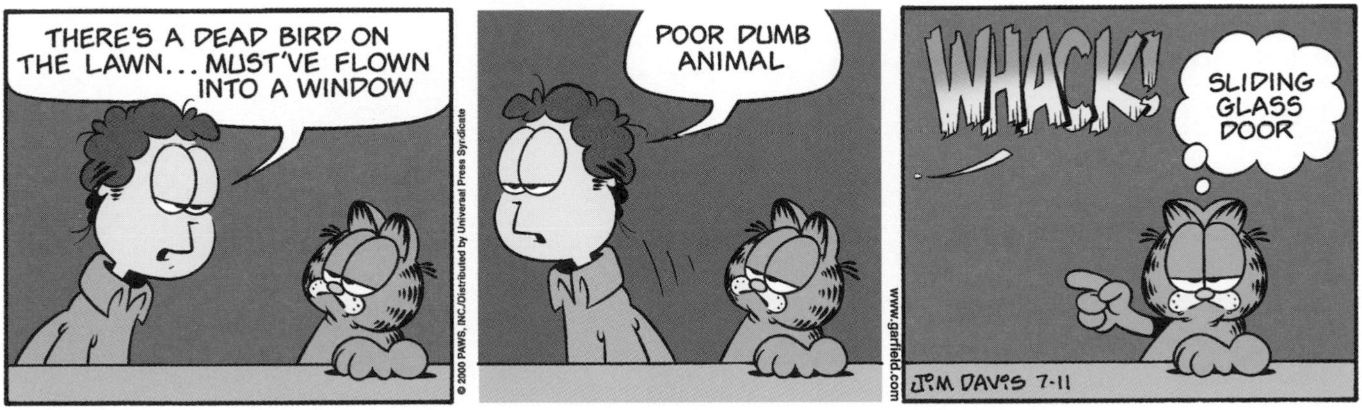
THERE'S A DEAD BIRD ON THE LAWN... MUST'VE FLOWN INTO A WINDOW
POOR DUMB ANIMAL
WHACK!
SLIDING GLASS DOOR
© 2000 PAWS, INC./Distributed by Universal Press Syndicate
www.garfield.com
JIM DAVIS 7-11

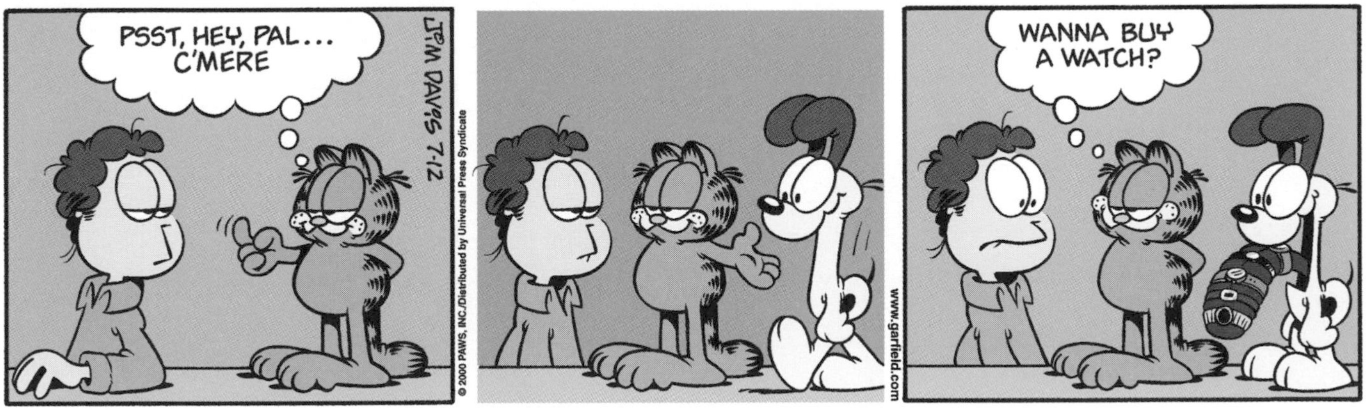
PSST, HEY, PAL... C'MERE
JIM DAVIS 7-12
WANNA BUY A WATCH?
© 2000 PAWS, INC./Distributed by Universal Press Syndicate
www.garfield.com

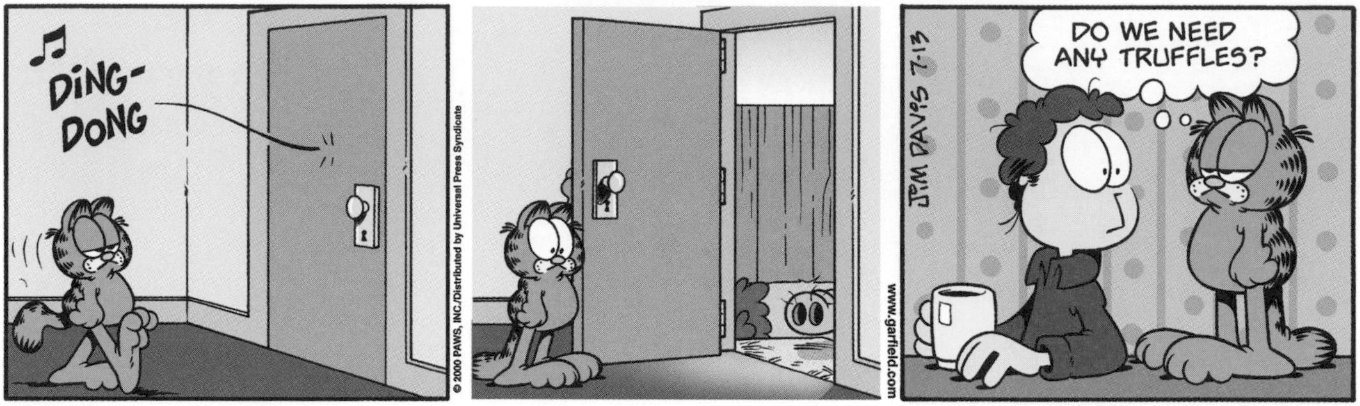
DING-DONG
© 2000 PAWS, INC./Distributed by Universal Press Syndicate
JIM DAVIS 7-13
www.garfield.com
DO WE NEED ANY TRUFFLES?

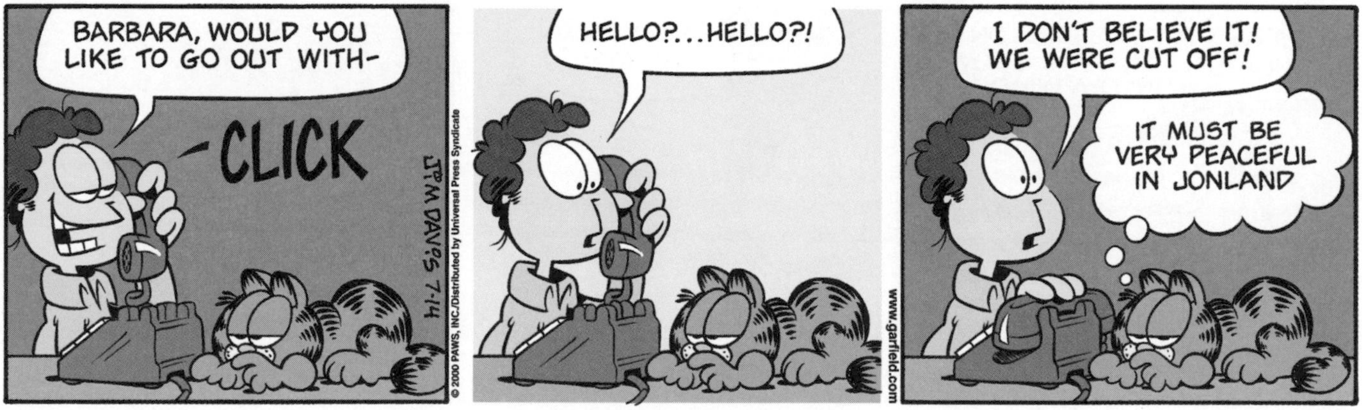
BARBARA, WOULD YOU LIKE TO GO OUT WITH-
-CLICK
JIM DAVIS 7-14
© 2000 PAWS, INC./Distributed by Universal Press Syndicate
HELLO?...HELLO?!
www.garfield.com
I DON'T BELIEVE IT! WE WERE CUT OFF!
IT MUST BE VERY PEACEFUL IN JONLAND

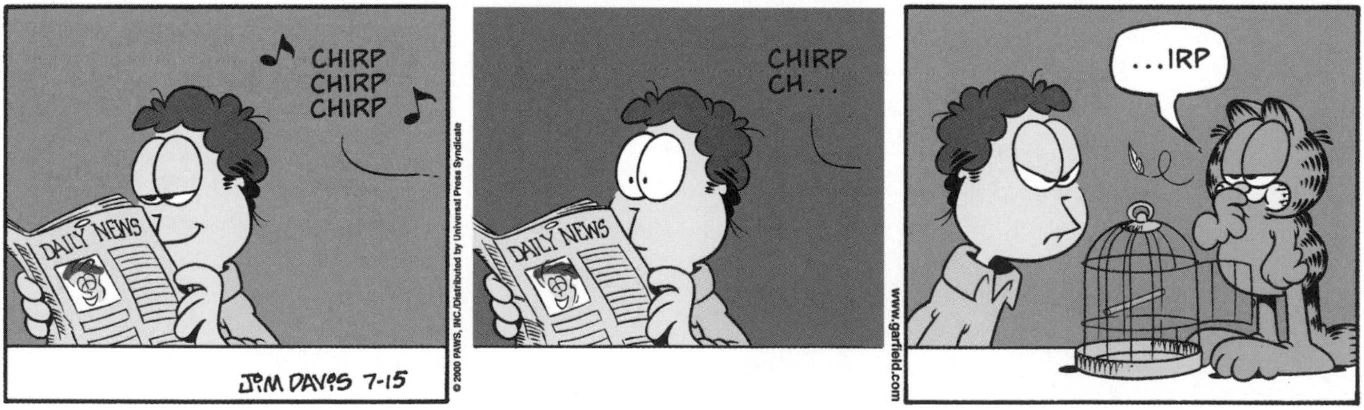
CHIRP CHIRP CHIRP
DAILY NEWS
JIM DAVIS 7-15
© 2000 PAWS, INC./Distributed by Universal Press Syndicate
CHIRP CH...
DAILY NEWS
www.garfield.com
...IRP

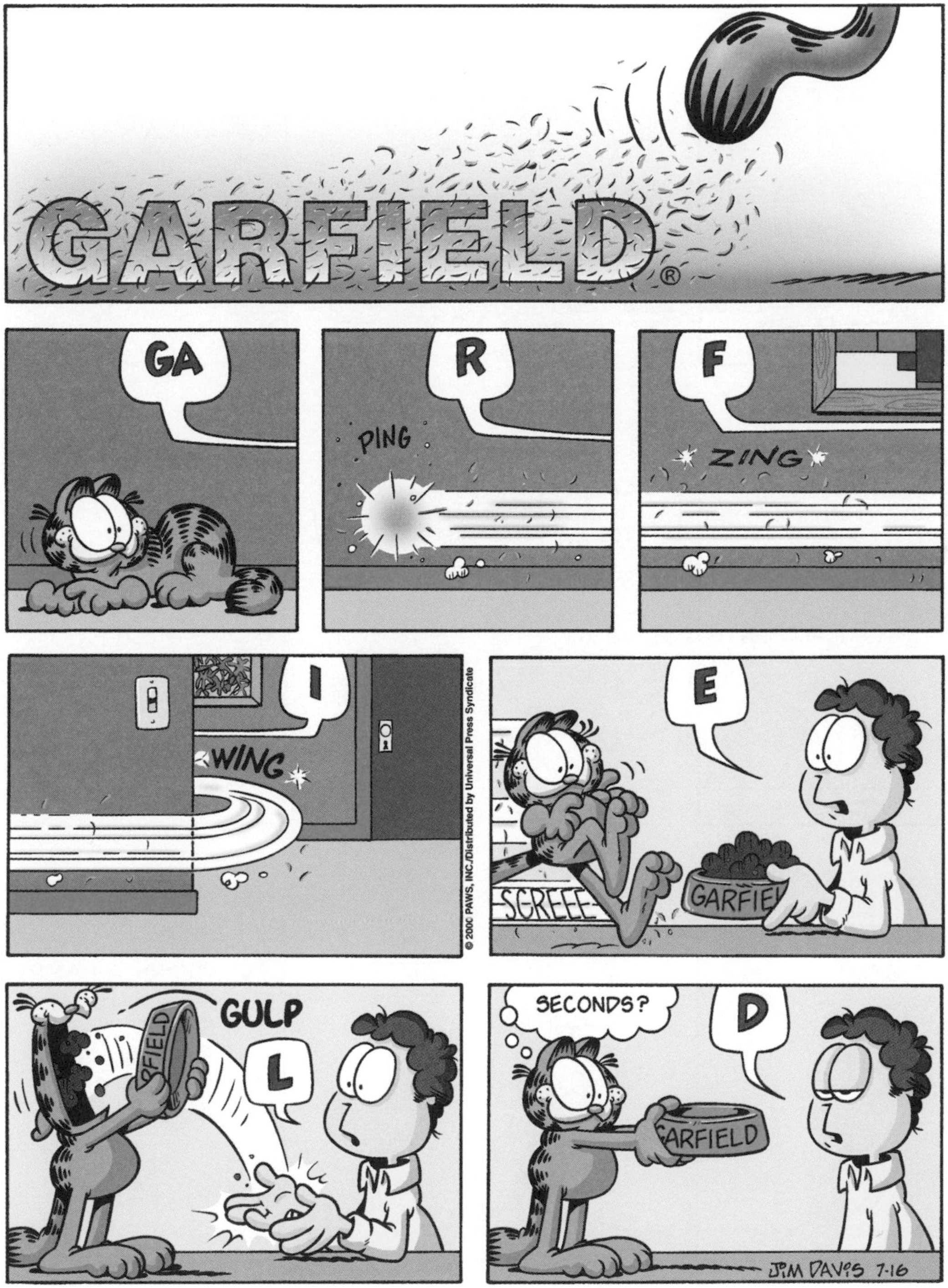
GARFIELD®
GA
R
PING
F
ZING
I
WING
© 2000 PAWS, INC./Distributed by Universal Press Syndicate
E
SCREEE
GARFIEL
GULP
FIELD
L
SECONDS?
D
GARFIELD
JIM DAVIS 7-16

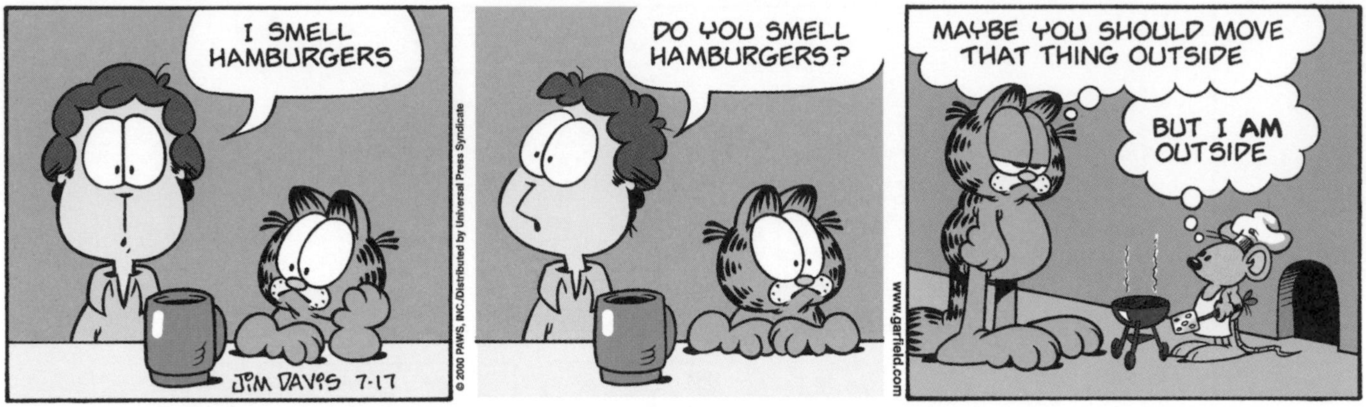
I SMELL HAMBURGERS
JIM DAVIS 7-17
© 2000 PAWS, INC./Distributed by Universal Press Syndicate
DO YOU SMELL HAMBURGERS?
www.garfield.com
MAYBE YOU SHOULD MOVE THAT THING OUTSIDE
BUT I AM OUTSIDE

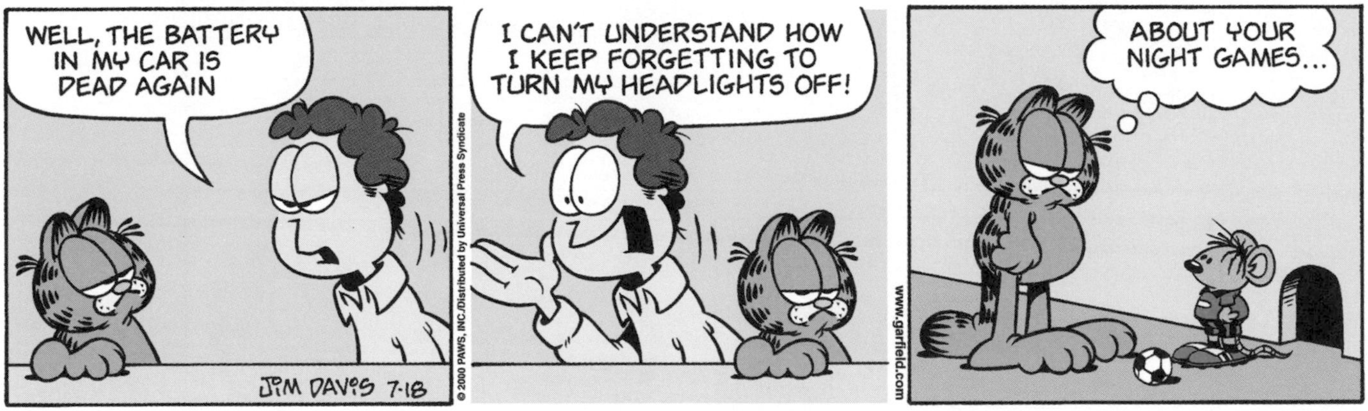
WELL, THE BATTERY IN MY CAR IS DEAD AGAIN
JIM DAVIS 7-18
© 2000 PAWS, INC./Distributed by Universal Press Syndicate
I CAN'T UNDERSTAND HOW I KEEP FORGETTING TO TURN MY HEADLIGHTS OFF!
www.garfield.com
ABOUT YOUR NIGHT GAMES...

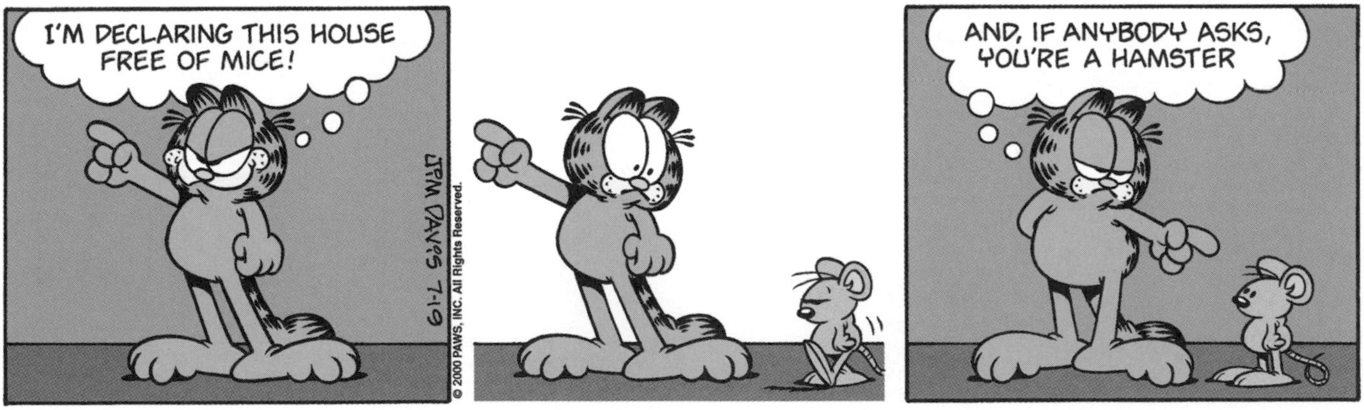
I'M DECLARING THIS HOUSE FREE OF MICE!
JIM DAVIS 7-19
© 2000 PAWS, INC. All Rights Reserved.
AND, IF ANYBODY ASKS, YOU'RE A HAMSTER

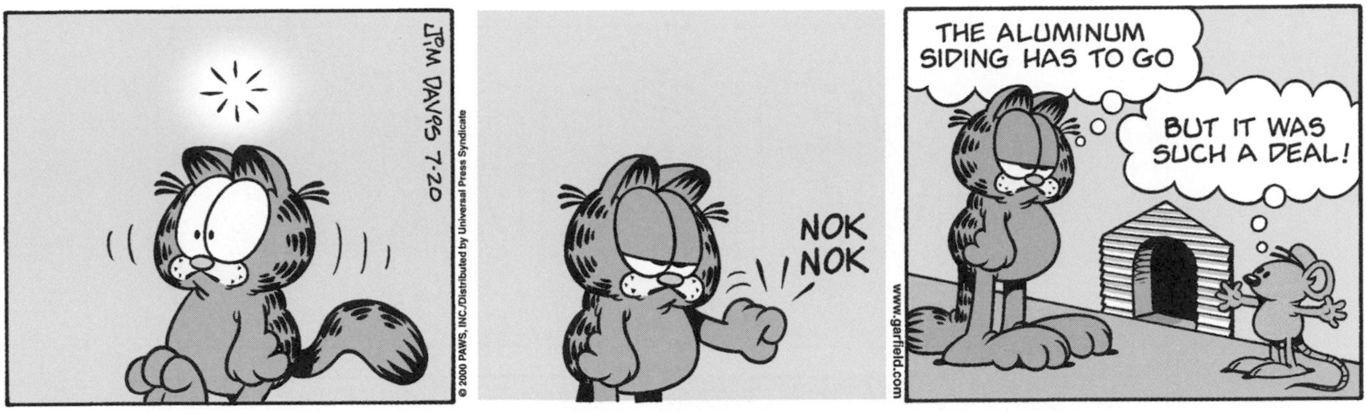
JIM DAVIS 7-20
© 2000 PAWS, INC./Distributed by Universal Press Syndicate
NOK NOK
www.garfield.com
THE ALUMINUM SIDING HAS TO GO
BUT IT WAS SUCH A DEAL!

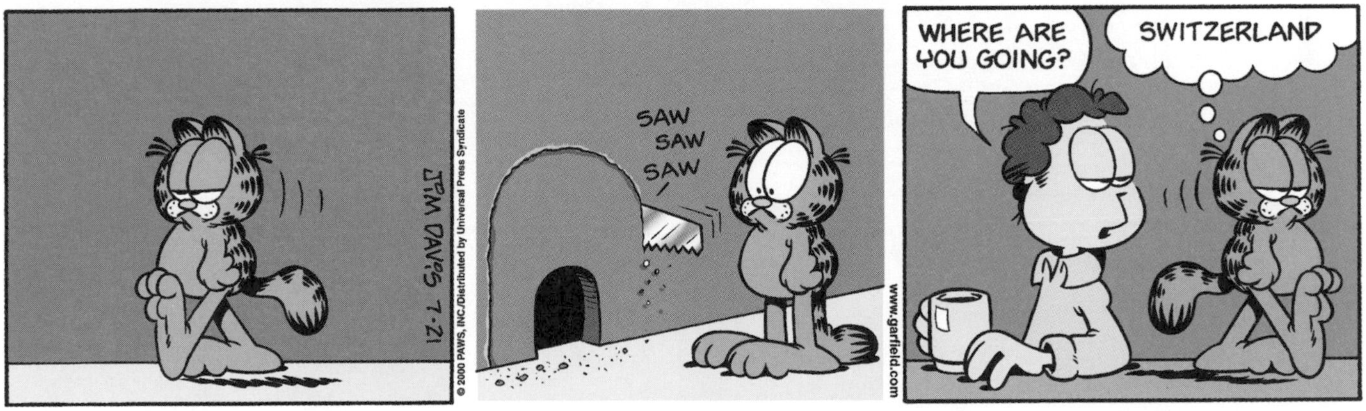
JIM DAVIS 7-21
© 2000 PAWS, INC./Distributed by Universal Press Syndicate
SAW SAW SAW
www.garfield.com
WHERE ARE YOU GOING?
SWITZERLAND

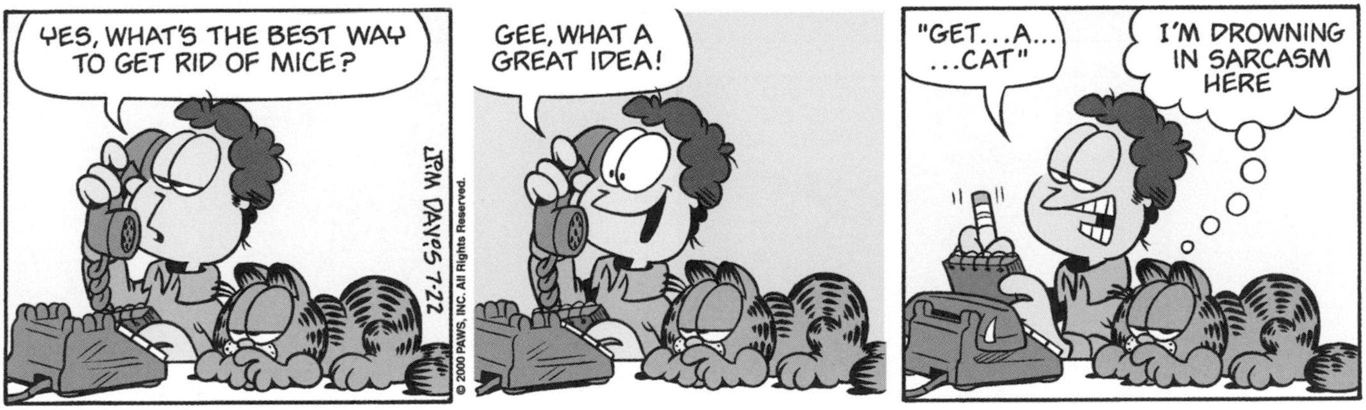
YES, WHAT'S THE BEST WAY TO GET RID OF MICE?
JIM DAVIS 7-22
© 2000 PAWS, INC. All Rights Reserved.
GEE, WHAT A GREAT IDEA!
"GET...A... ...CAT"
I'M DROWNING IN SARCASM HERE

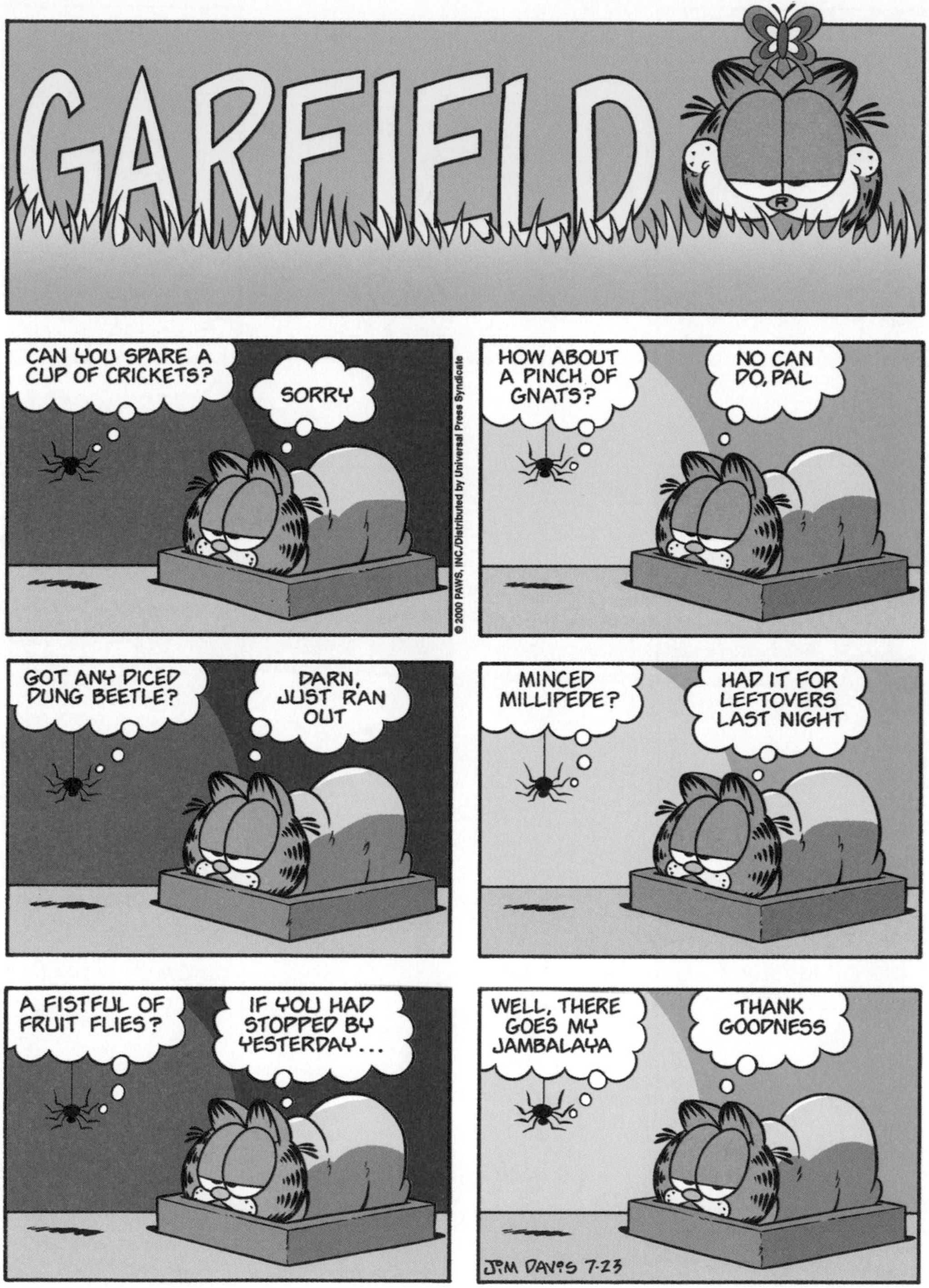
GARFIELD
CAN YOU SPARE A CUP OF CRICKETS?
SORRY
HOW ABOUT A PINCH OF GNATS?
NO CAN DO, PAL
GOT ANY DICED DUNG BEETLE?
DARN, JUST RAN OUT
MINCED MILLIPEDE?
HAD IT FOR LEFTOVERS LAST NIGHT
A FISTFUL OF FRUIT FLIES?
IF YOU HAD STOPPED BY YESTERDAY...
WELL, THERE GOES MY JAMBALAYA
THANK GOODNESS
JIM DAVIS 7-23

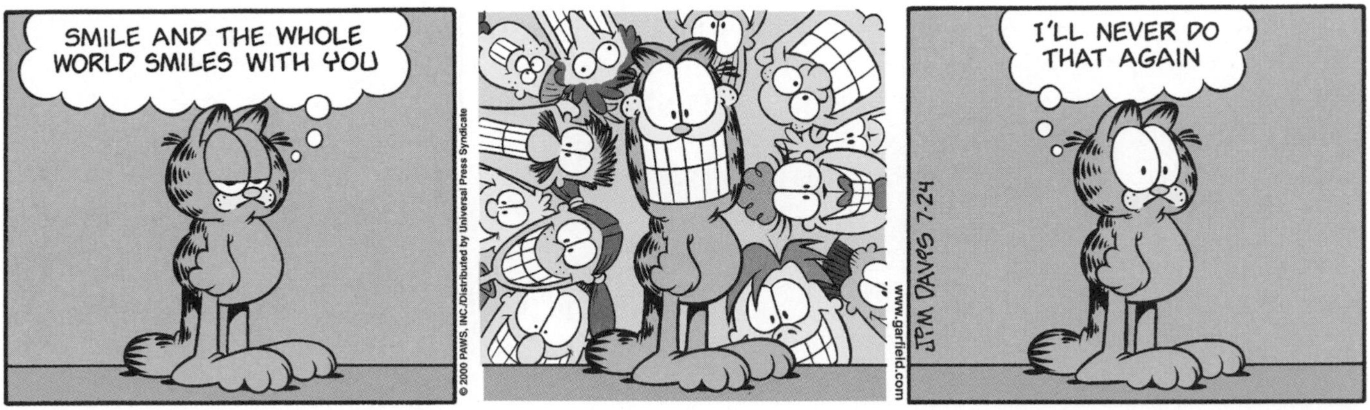
SMILE AND THE WHOLE WORLD SMILES WITH YOU
© 2000 PAWS, INC./Distributed by Universal Press Syndicate
JIM DAVIS 7-24
www.garfield.com
I'LL NEVER DO THAT AGAIN

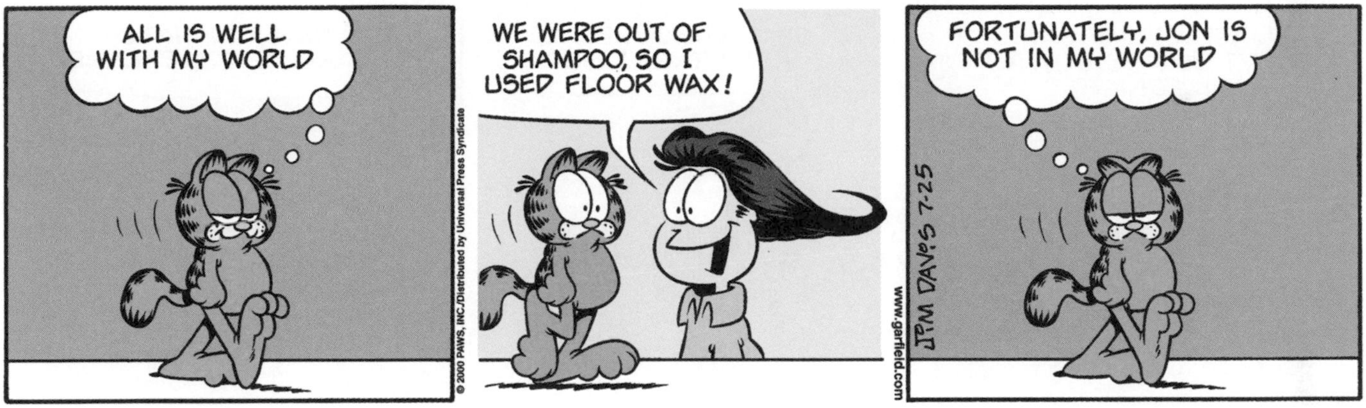
ALL IS WELL WITH MY WORLD
© 2000 PAWS, INC./Distributed by Universal Press Syndicate
WE WERE OUT OF SHAMPOO, SO I USED FLOOR WAX!
JIM DAVIS 7-25
www.garfield.com
FORTUNATELY, JON IS NOT IN MY WORLD

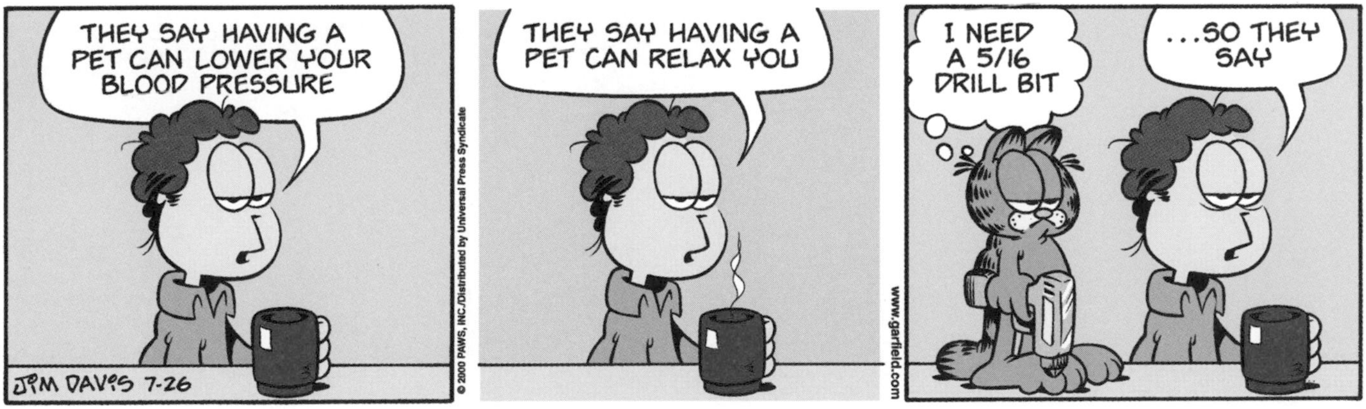
THEY SAY HAVING A PET CAN LOWER YOUR BLOOD PRESSURE
JIM DAVIS 7-26
© 2000 PAWS, INC./Distributed by Universal Press Syndicate
THEY SAY HAVING A PET CAN RELAX YOU
www.garfield.com
I NEED A 5/16 DRILL BIT
...SO THEY SAY

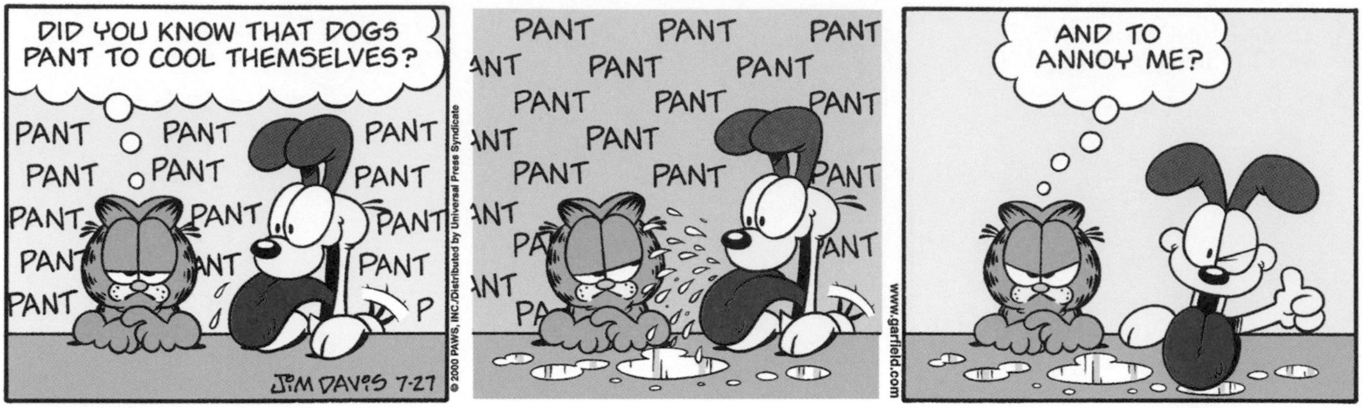
DID YOU KNOW THAT DOGS PANT TO COOL THEMSELVES?
PANT PANT PANT PANT PANT PANT PANT PANT PANT PANT PANT P
JIM DAVIS 7-27
© 2000 PAWS, INC./Distributed by Universal Press Syndicate
PANT PANT PANT PANT PANT PANT PANT PANT PANT PANT PANT
www.garfield.com
AND TO ANNOY ME?

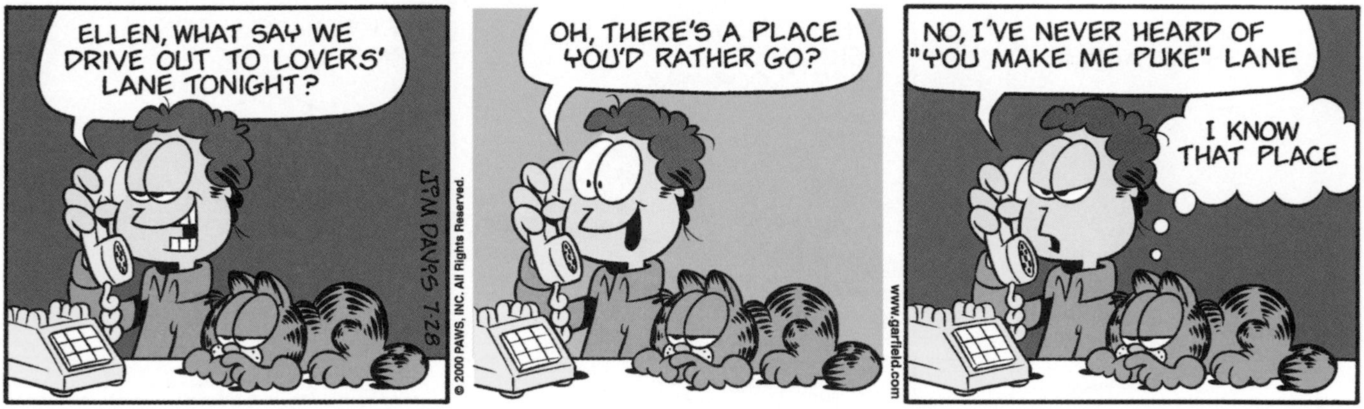
ELLEN, WHAT SAY WE DRIVE OUT TO LOVERS' LANE TONIGHT?
JIM DAVIS 7-28
© 2000 PAWS, INC. All Rights Reserved.
OH, THERE'S A PLACE YOU'D RATHER GO?
www.garfield.com
NO, I'VE NEVER HEARD OF "YOU MAKE ME PUKE" LANE
I KNOW THAT PLACE

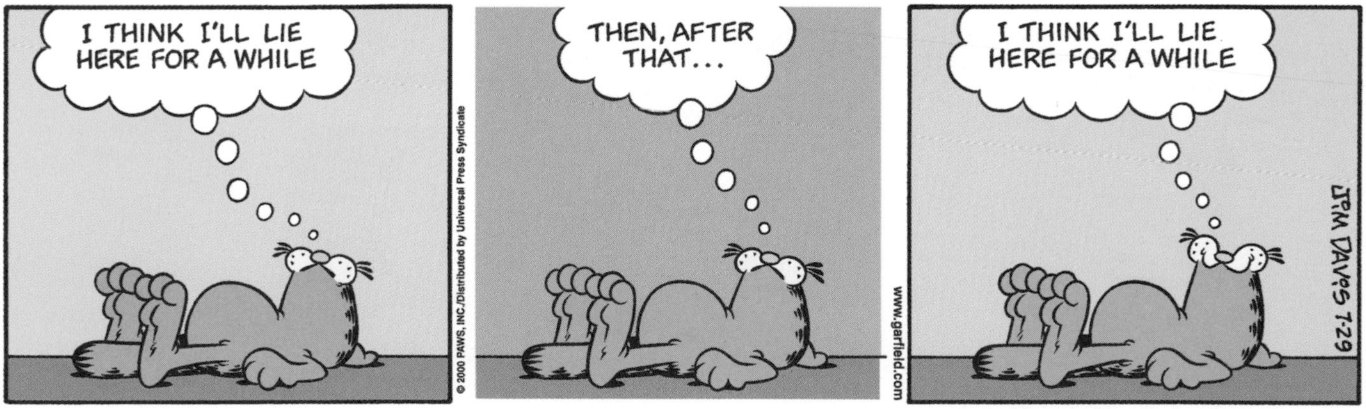
I THINK I'LL LIE HERE FOR A WHILE
© 2000 PAWS, INC./Distributed by Universal Press Syndicate
THEN, AFTER THAT...
www.garfield.com
I THINK I'LL LIE HERE FOR A WHILE
JIM DAVIS 7-29

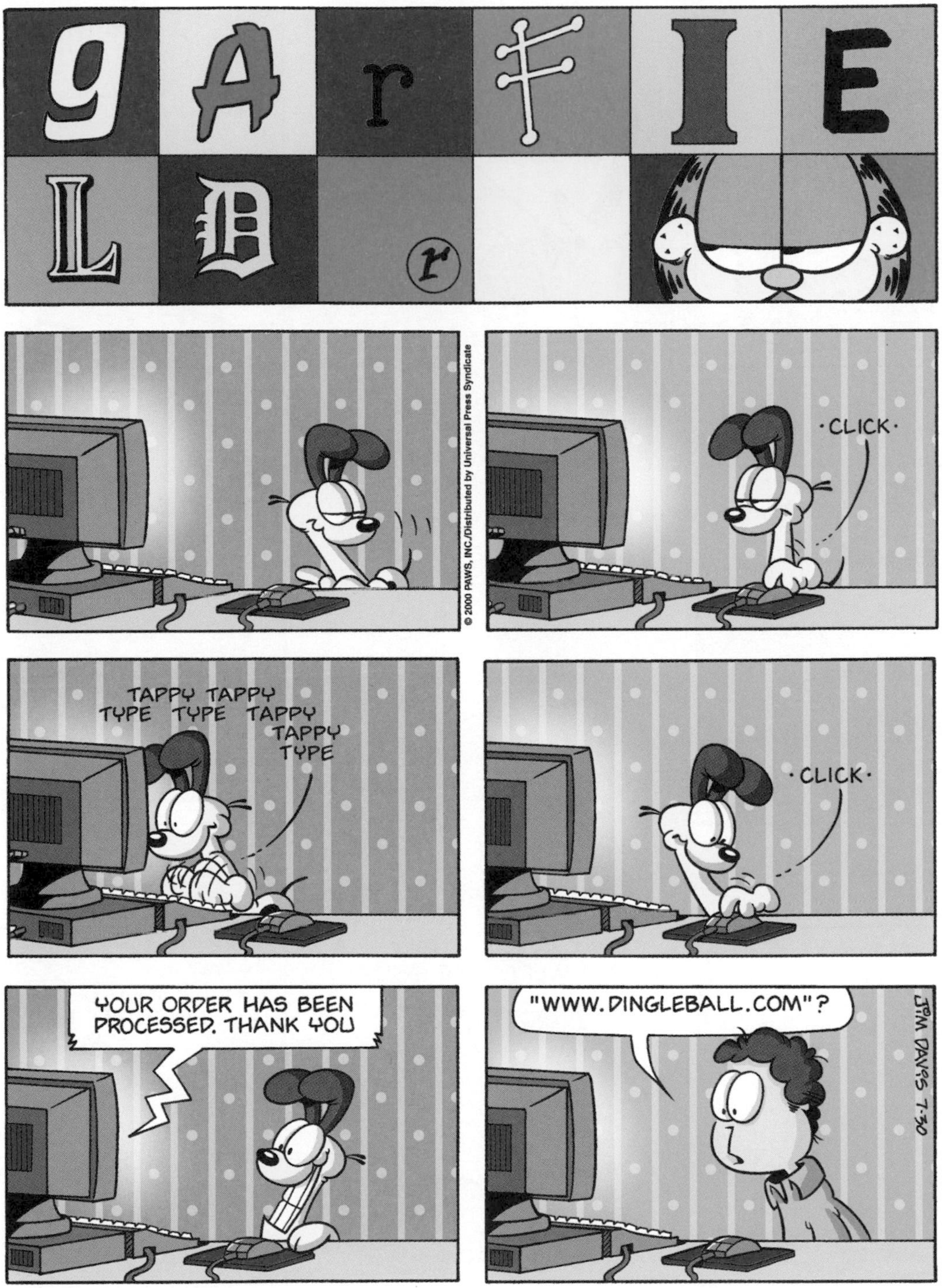
GARFIELD
© 2000 PAWS, INC./Distributed by Universal Press Syndicate
·CLICK·
TAPPY TAPPY TYPE TYPE TAPPY TAPPY TYPE
·CLICK·
YOUR ORDER HAS BEEN PROCESSED. THANK YOU
"WWW.DINGLEBALL.COM"?
JIM DAVIS 7-30

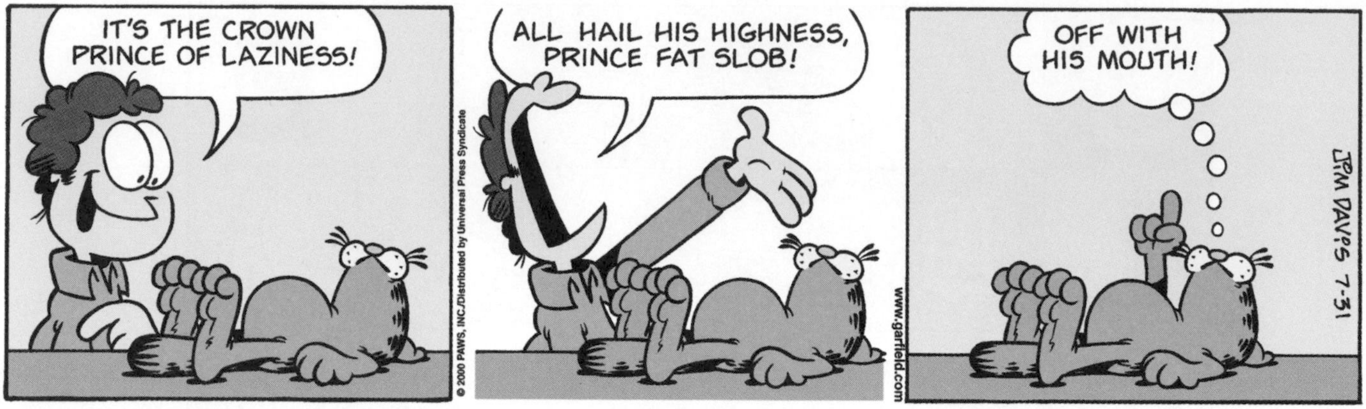
IT'S THE CROWN PRINCE OF LAZINESS!
ALL HAIL HIS HIGHNESS, PRINCE FAT SLOB!
OFF WITH HIS MOUTH!
© 2000 PAWS, INC./Distributed by Universal Press Syndicate
www.garfield.com
JIM DAVIS 7-31

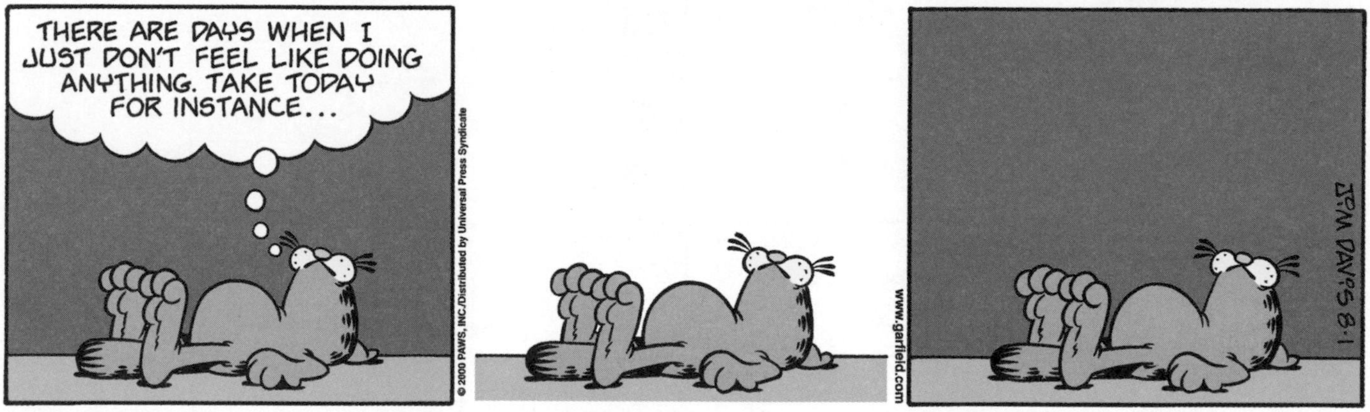
THERE ARE DAYS WHEN I JUST DON'T FEEL LIKE DOING ANYTHING. TAKE TODAY FOR INSTANCE...
© 2000 PAWS, INC./Distributed by Universal Press Syndicate
www.garfield.com
JIM DAVIS 8-1

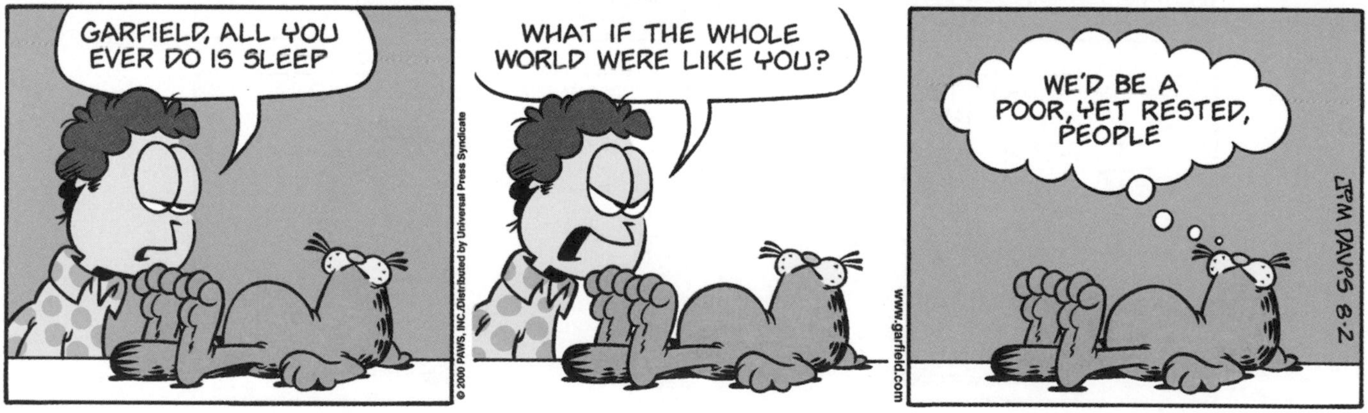
GARFIELD, ALL YOU EVER DO IS SLEEP
WHAT IF THE WHOLE WORLD WERE LIKE YOU?
WE'D BE A POOR, YET RESTED, PEOPLE
© 2000 PAWS, INC./Distributed by Universal Press Syndicate
www.garfield.com
JIM DAVIS 8-2

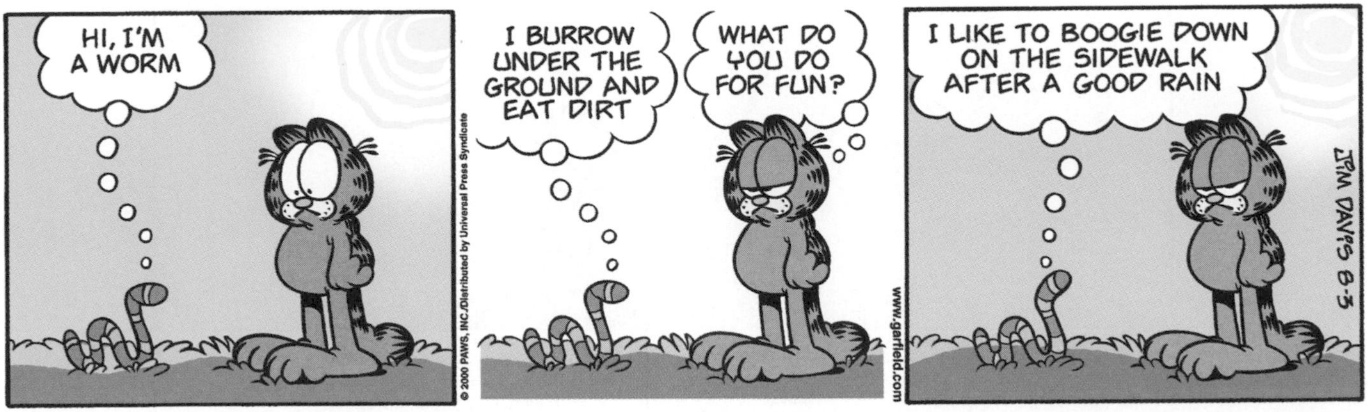
HI, I'M A WORM
I BURROW UNDER THE GROUND AND EAT DIRT
WHAT DO YOU DO FOR FUN?
I LIKE TO BOOGIE DOWN ON THE SIDEWALK AFTER A GOOD RAIN
© 2000 PAWS, INC./Distributed by Universal Press Syndicate
www.garfield.com
JIM DAVIS 8-3

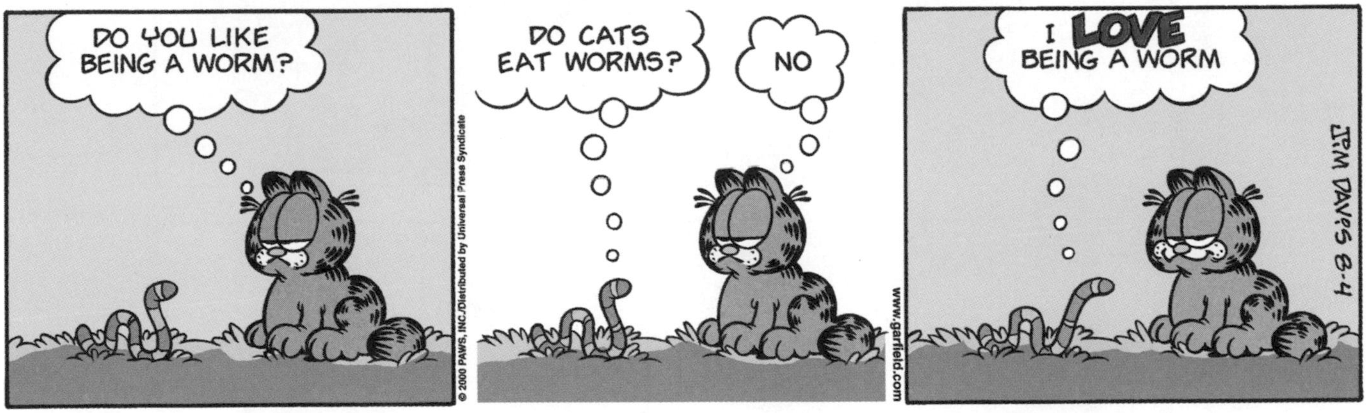
DO YOU LIKE BEING A WORM?
DO CATS EAT WORMS?
NO
I LOVE BEING A WORM
© 2000 PAWS, INC./Distributed by Universal Press Syndicate
www.garfield.com
JIM DAVIS 8-4

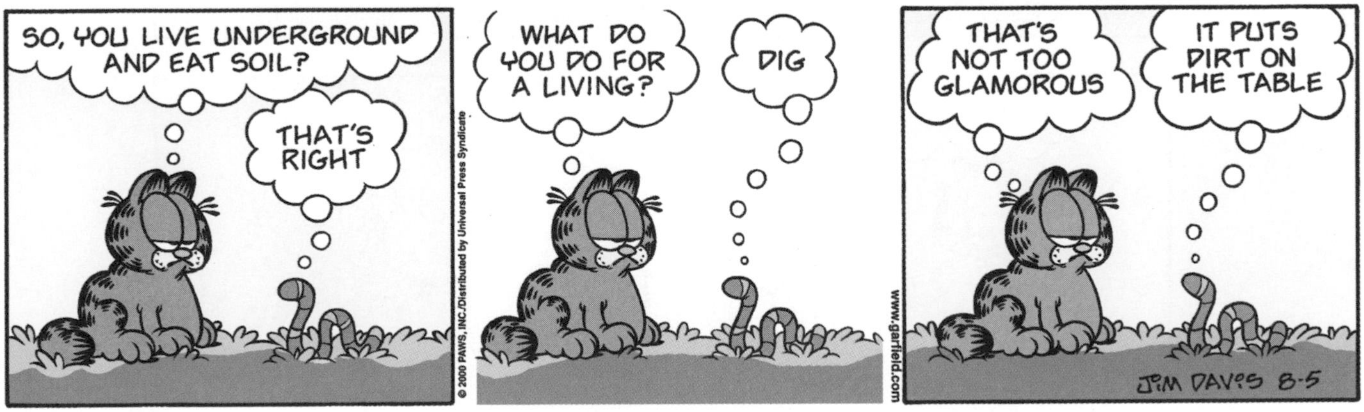
SO, YOU LIVE UNDERGROUND AND EAT SOIL?
THAT'S RIGHT
WHAT DO YOU DO FOR A LIVING?
DIG
THAT'S NOT TOO GLAMOROUS
IT PUTS DIRT ON THE TABLE
© 2000 PAWS, INC./Distributed by Universal Press Syndicate
www.garfield.com
JIM DAVIS 8-5

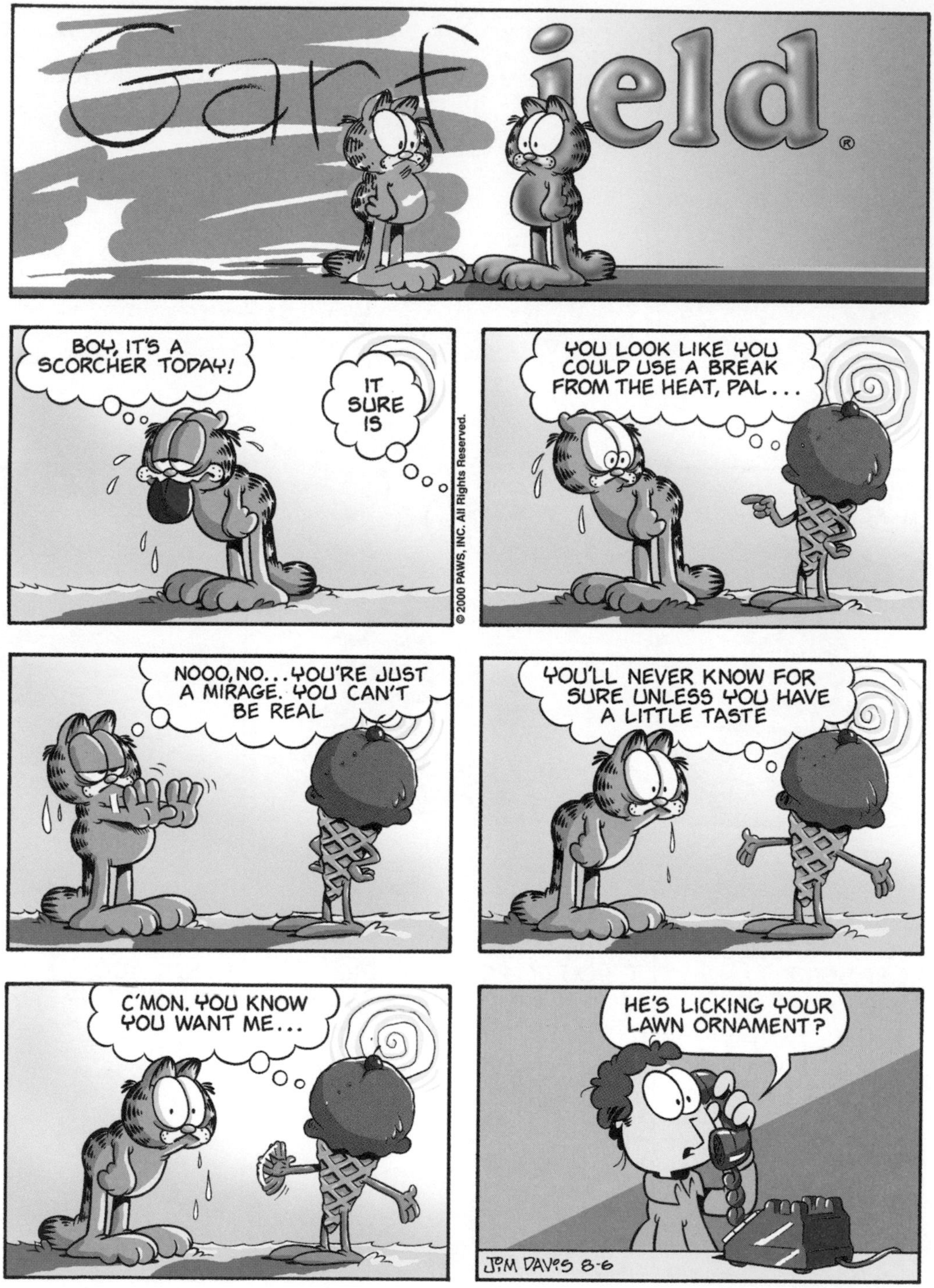
Garfield®
BOY, IT'S A SCORCHER TODAY!
IT SURE IS
© 2000 PAWS, INC. All Rights Reserved.
YOU LOOK LIKE YOU COULD USE A BREAK FROM THE HEAT, PAL...
NOOO, NO...YOU'RE JUST A MIRAGE. YOU CAN'T BE REAL
YOU'LL NEVER KNOW FOR SURE UNLESS YOU HAVE A LITTLE TASTE
C'MON. YOU KNOW YOU WANT ME...
HE'S LICKING YOUR LAWN ORNAMENT?
JIM DAVIS 8-6

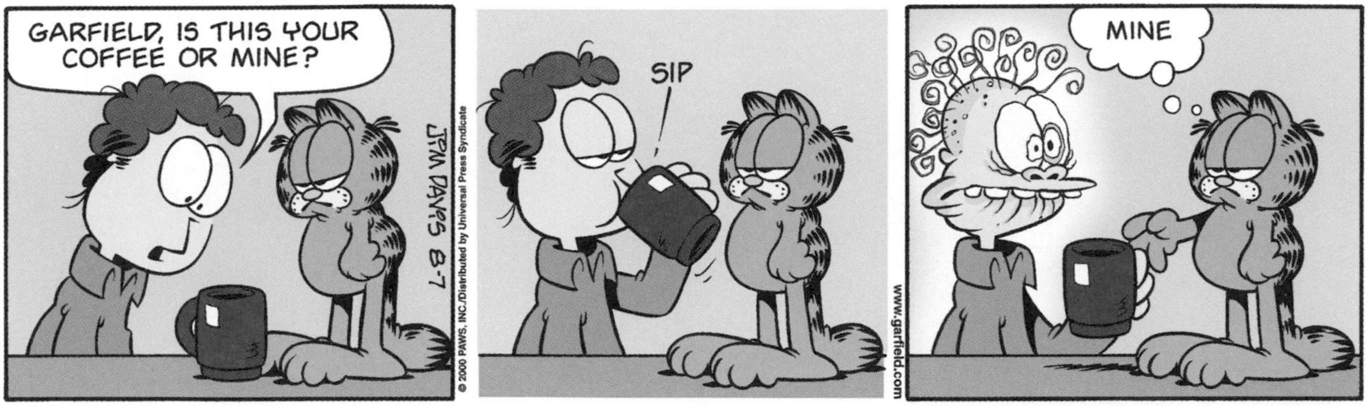
GARFIELD, IS THIS YOUR COFFEE OR MINE?
JIM DAVIS 8-7
SIP
© 2000 PAWS, INC./Distributed by Universal Press Syndicate
MINE
www.garfield.com

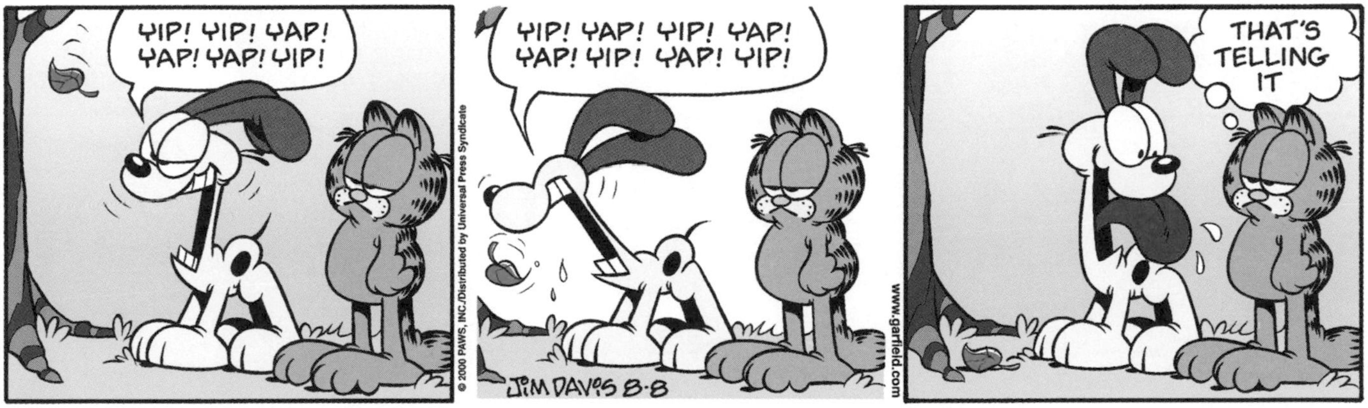
YIP! YIP! YAP! YAP! YAP! YIP!
YIP! YAP! YIP! YAP! YAP! YIP! YAP! YIP!
© 2000 PAWS, INC./Distributed by Universal Press Syndicate
JIM DAVIS 8-8
THAT'S TELLING IT
www.garfield.com

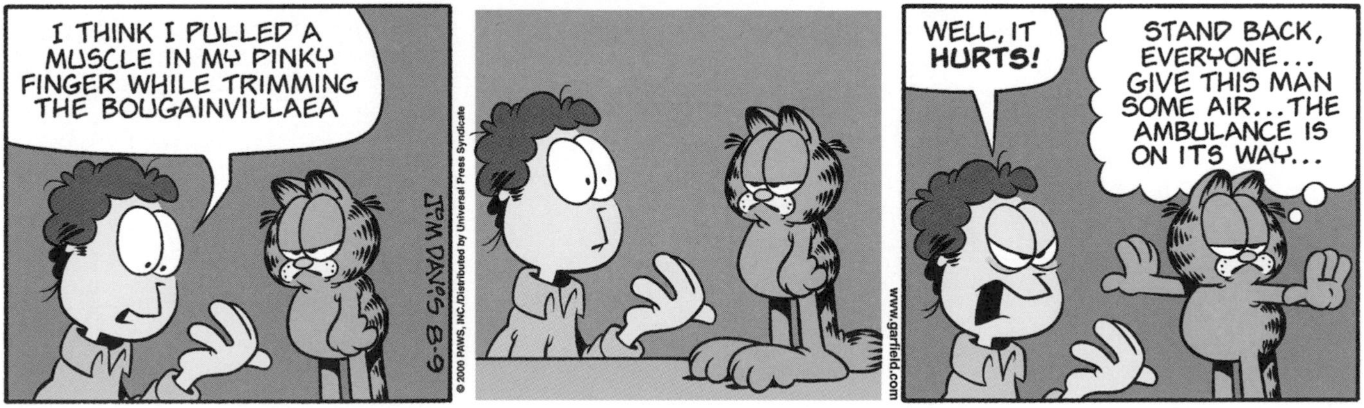
I THINK I PULLED A MUSCLE IN MY PINKY FINGER WHILE TRIMMING THE BOUGAINVILLAEA
JIM DAVIS 8-9
© 2000 PAWS, INC./Distributed by Universal Press Syndicate
WELL, IT **HURTS!**
STAND BACK, EVERYONE... GIVE THIS MAN SOME AIR...THE AMBULANCE IS ON ITS WAY...
www.garfield.com

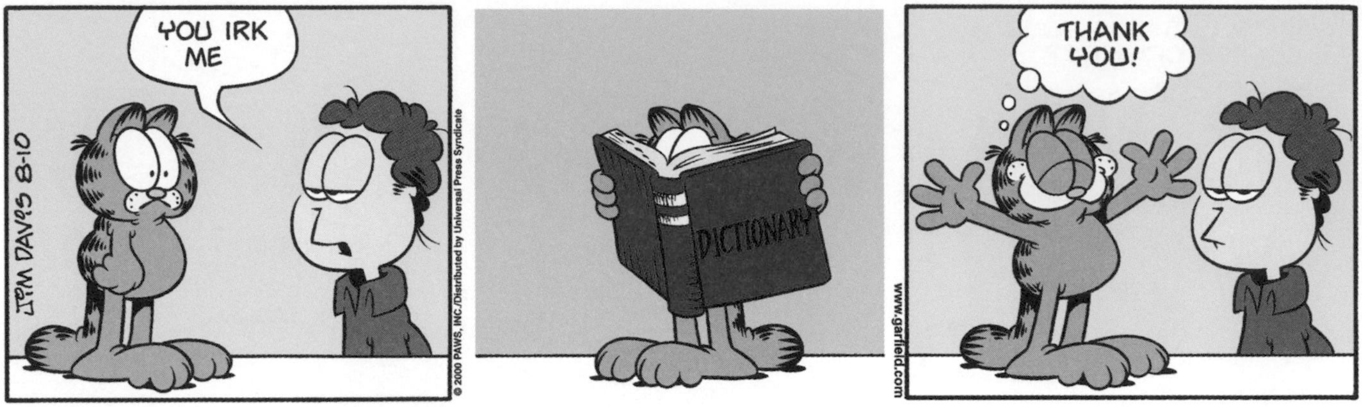
YOU IRK ME
JIM DAVIS 8-10
© 2000 PAWS, INC./Distributed by Universal Press Syndicate
DICTIONARY
www.garfield.com
THANK YOU!

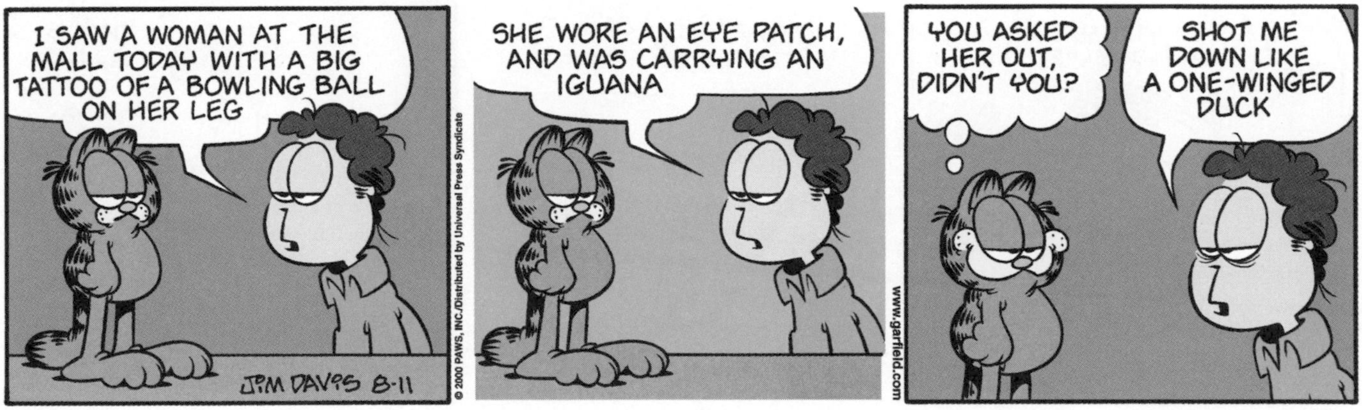
I SAW A WOMAN AT THE MALL TODAY WITH A BIG TATTOO OF A BOWLING BALL ON HER LEG
JIM DAVIS 8-11
© 2000 PAWS, INC./Distributed by Universal Press Syndicate
SHE WORE AN EYE PATCH, AND WAS CARRYING AN IGUANA
www.garfield.com
YOU ASKED HER OUT, DIDN'T YOU?
SHOT ME DOWN LIKE A ONE-WINGED DUCK

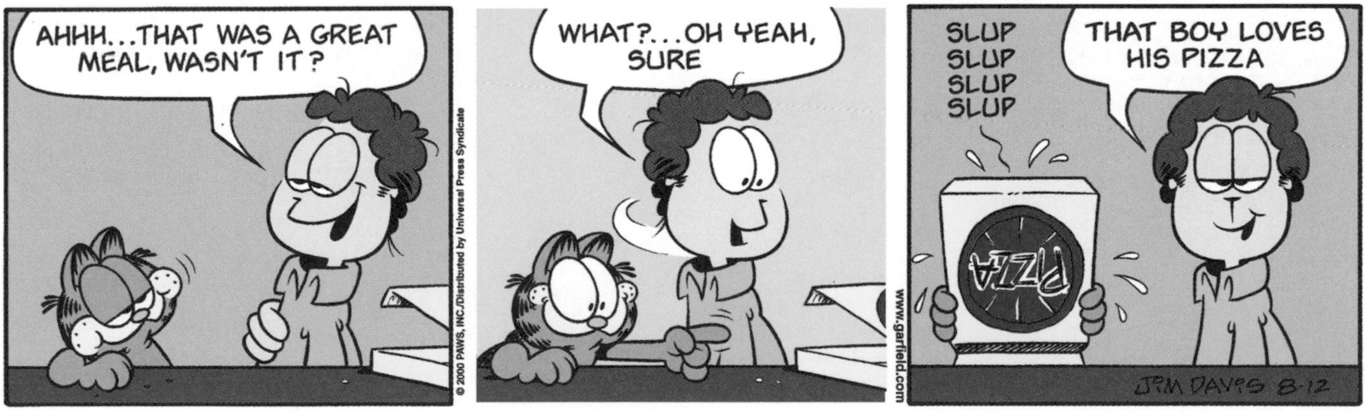
AHHH...THAT WAS A GREAT MEAL, WASN'T IT?
© 2000 PAWS, INC./Distributed by Universal Press Syndicate
WHAT?...OH YEAH, SURE
www.garfield.com
SLUP
SLUP
SLUP
SLUP
THAT BOY LOVES HIS PIZZA
JIM DAVIS 8-12

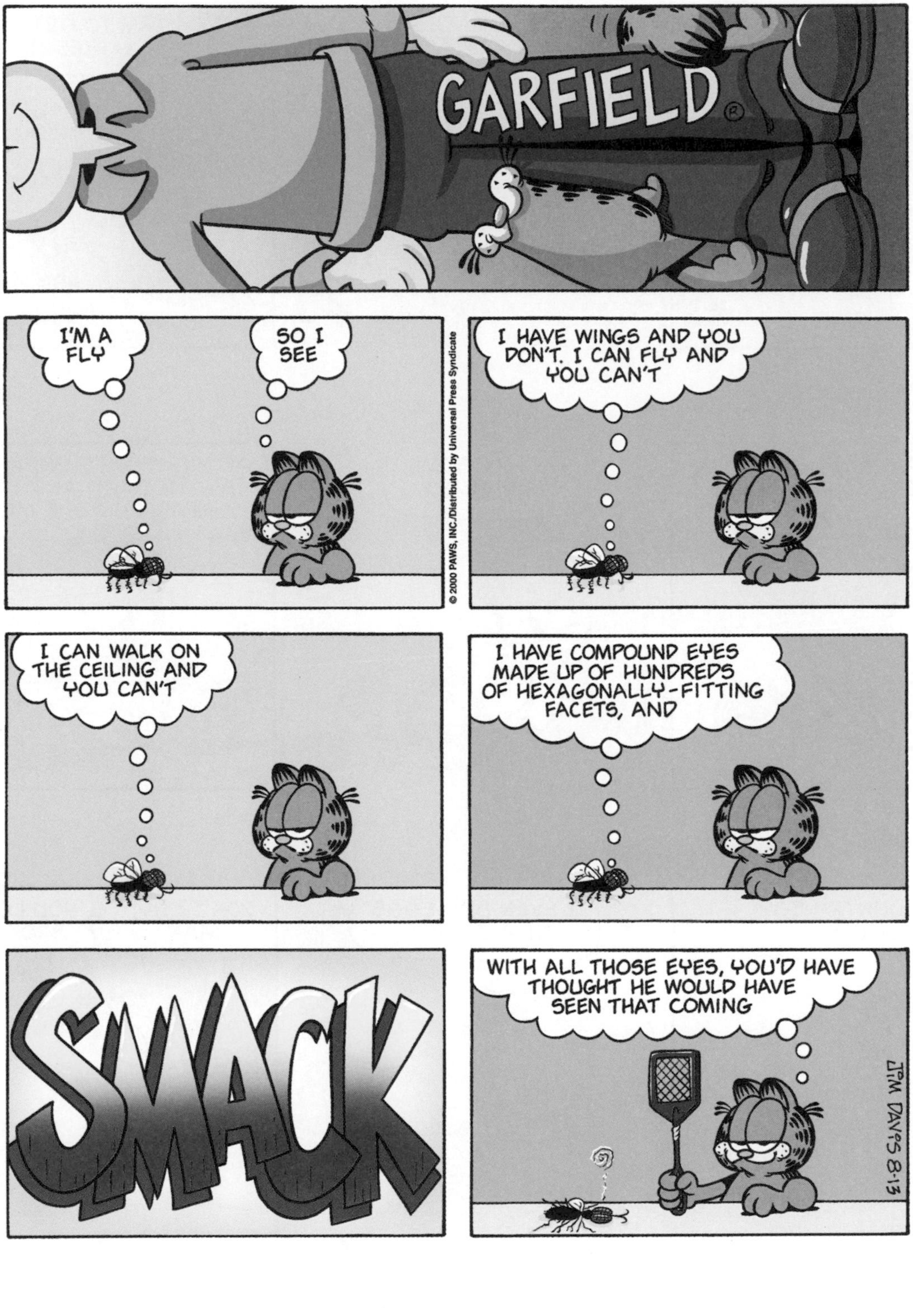
GARFIELD®
I'M A FLY
SO I SEE
© 2000 PAWS, INC./Distributed by Universal Press Syndicate
I HAVE WINGS AND YOU DON'T. I CAN FLY AND YOU CAN'T
I CAN WALK ON THE CEILING AND YOU CAN'T
I HAVE COMPOUND EYES MADE UP OF HUNDREDS OF HEXAGONALLY-FITTING FACETS, AND
SMACK
WITH ALL THOSE EYES, YOU'D HAVE THOUGHT HE WOULD HAVE SEEN THAT COMING
JIM DAVIS 8-13

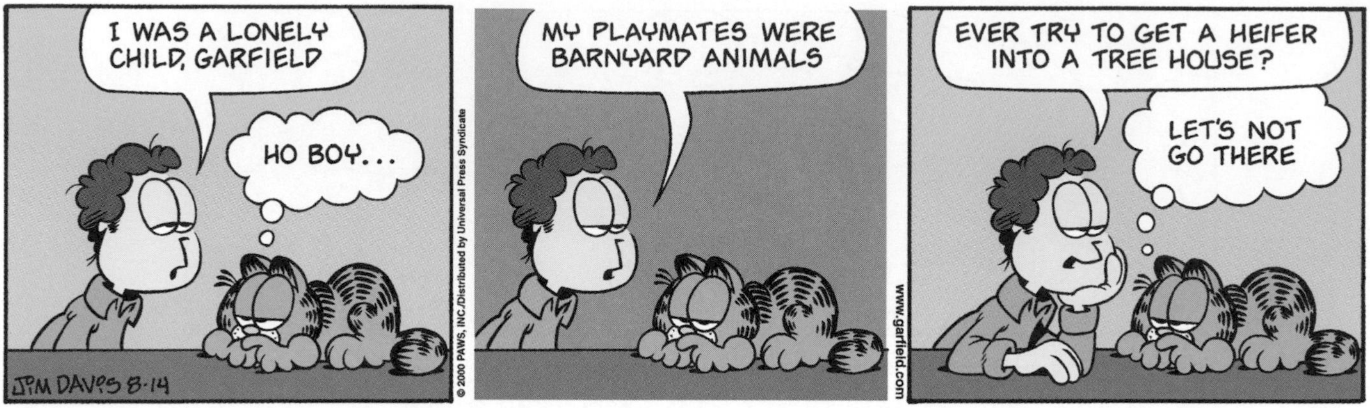
I WAS A LONELY CHILD, GARFIELD
HO BOY...
JIM DAVIS 8·14
© 2000 PAWS, INC./Distributed by Universal Press Syndicate
MY PLAYMATES WERE BARNYARD ANIMALS
www.garfield.com
EVER TRY TO GET A HEIFER INTO A TREE HOUSE?
LET'S NOT GO THERE

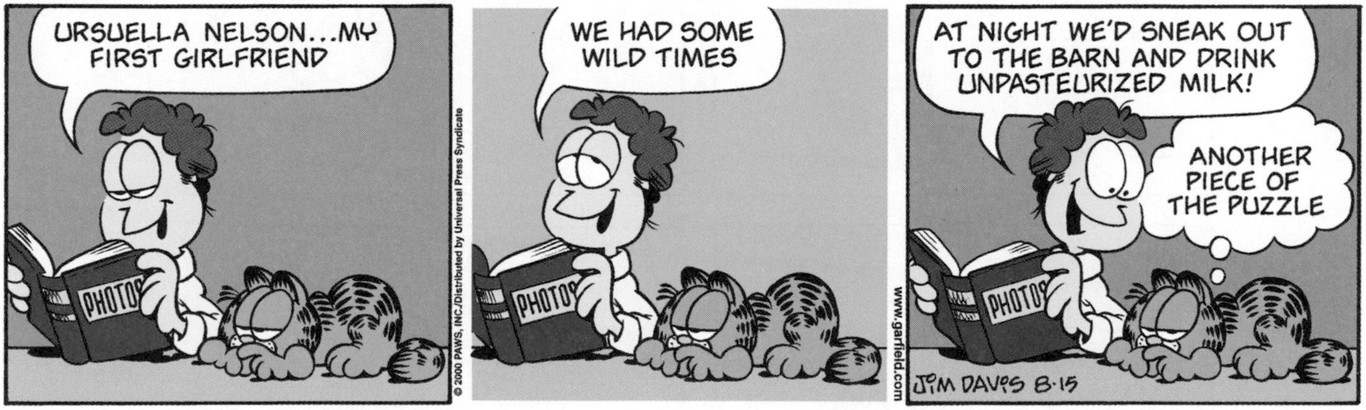
URSUELLA NELSON...MY FIRST GIRLFRIEND
PHOTOS
© 2000 PAWS, INC./Distributed by Universal Press Syndicate
WE HAD SOME WILD TIMES
PHOTOS
www.garfield.com
AT NIGHT WE'D SNEAK OUT TO THE BARN AND DRINK UNPASTEURIZED MILK!
ANOTHER PIECE OF THE PUZZLE
PHOTOS
JIM DAVIS 8·15

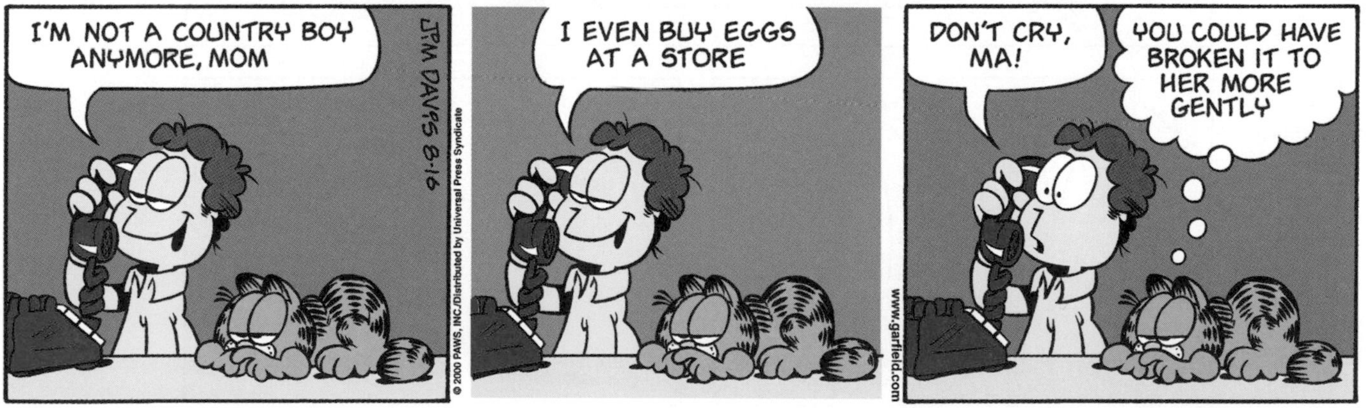
I'M NOT A COUNTRY BOY ANYMORE, MOM
JIM DAVIS 8·16
© 2000 PAWS, INC./Distributed by Universal Press Syndicate
I EVEN BUY EGGS AT A STORE
www.garfield.com
DON'T CRY, MA!
YOU COULD HAVE BROKEN IT TO HER MORE GENTLY

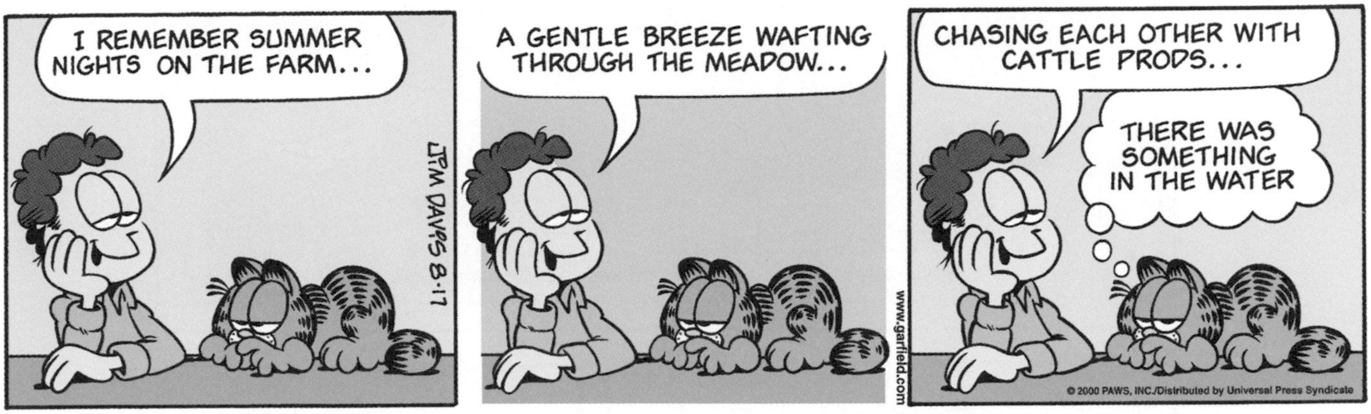
I REMEMBER SUMMER NIGHTS ON THE FARM...
JIM DAVIS 8-17
A GENTLE BREEZE WAFTING THROUGH THE MEADOW...
www.garfield.com
CHASING EACH OTHER WITH CATTLE PRODS...
THERE WAS SOMETHING IN THE WATER
© 2000 PAWS, INC./Distributed by Universal Press Syndicate

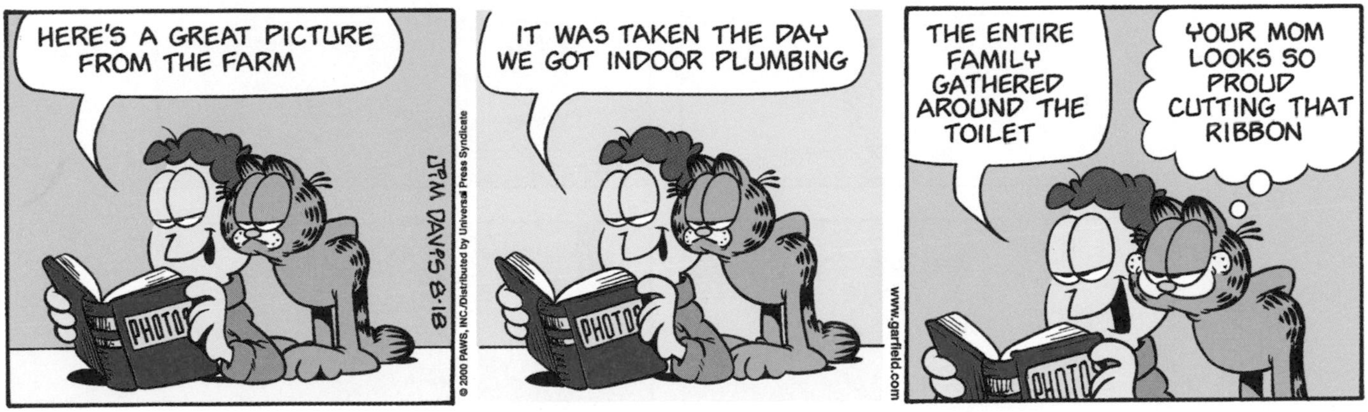
HERE'S A GREAT PICTURE FROM THE FARM
PHOTOS
JIM DAVIS 8-18
© 2000 PAWS, INC./Distributed by Universal Press Syndicate
IT WAS TAKEN THE DAY WE GOT INDOOR PLUMBING
www.garfield.com
THE ENTIRE FAMILY GATHERED AROUND THE TOILET
YOUR MOM LOOKS SO PROUD CUTTING THAT RIBBON

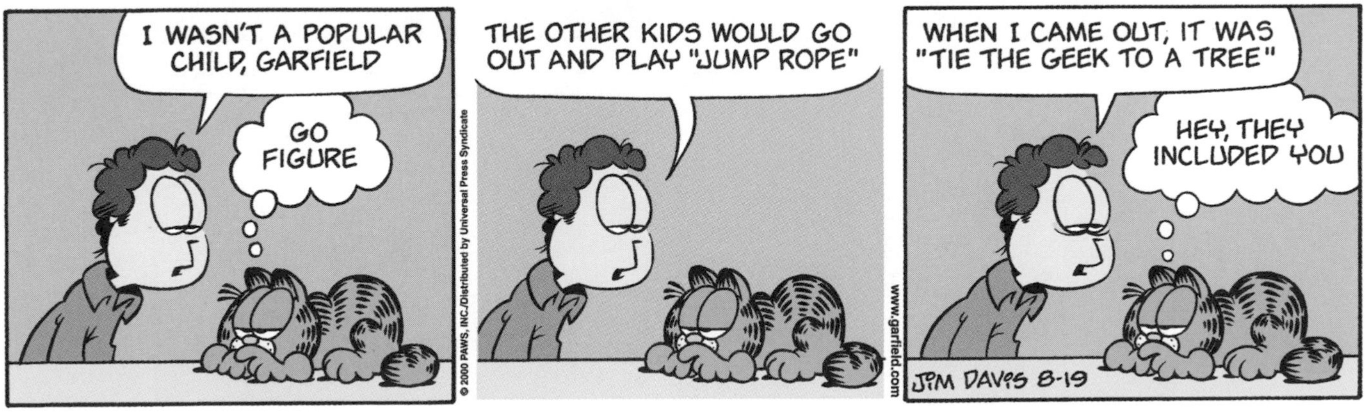
I WASN'T A POPULAR CHILD, GARFIELD
GO FIGURE
© 2000 PAWS, INC./Distributed by Universal Press Syndicate
THE OTHER KIDS WOULD GO OUT AND PLAY "JUMP ROPE"
www.garfield.com
WHEN I CAME OUT, IT WAS "TIE THE GEEK TO A TREE"
HEY, THEY INCLUDED YOU
JIM DAVIS 8-19

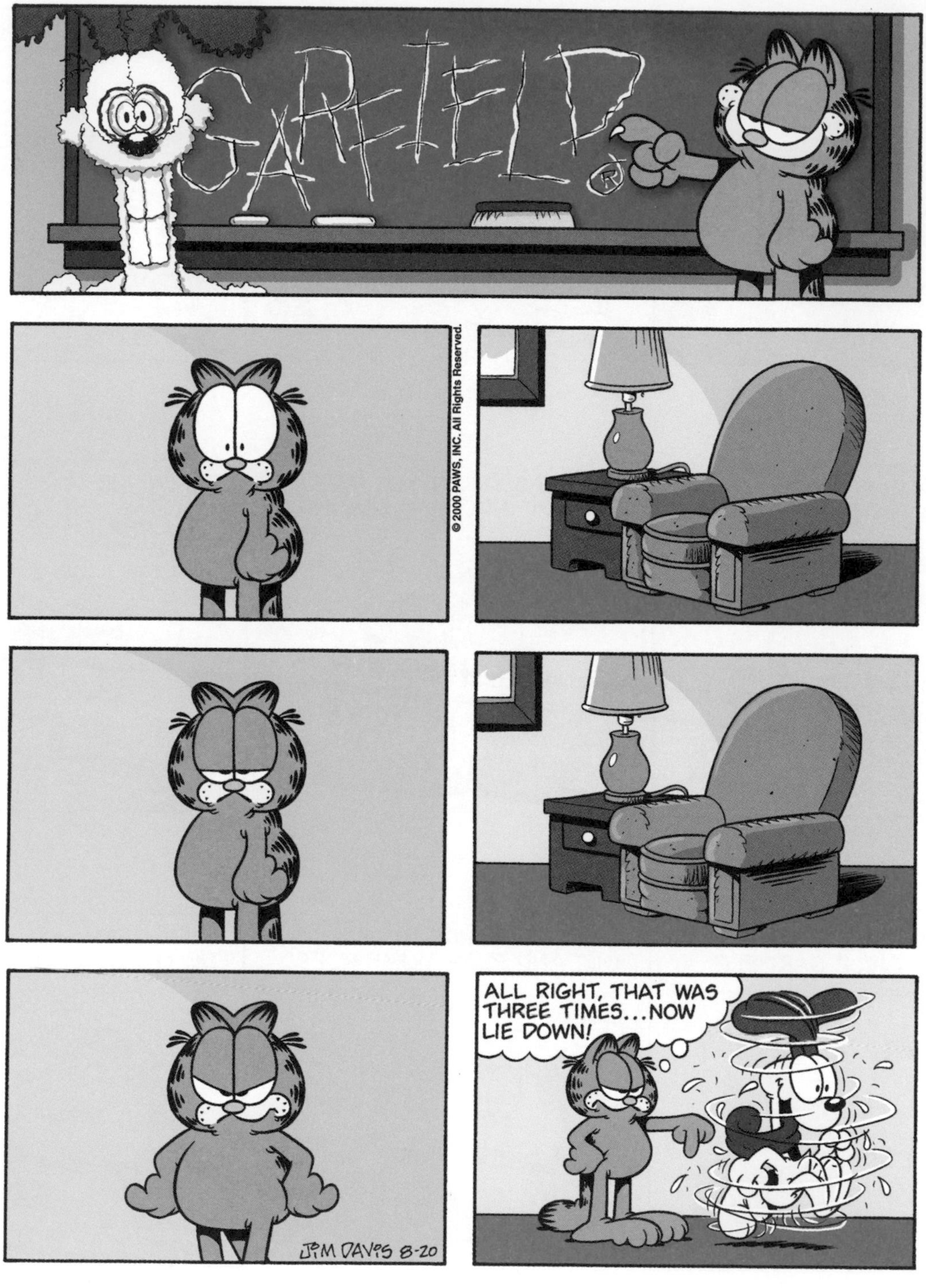
GARFIELD®
© 2000 PAWS, INC. All Rights Reserved.
JIM DAVIS 8-20
ALL RIGHT, THAT WAS THREE TIMES...NOW LIE DOWN!

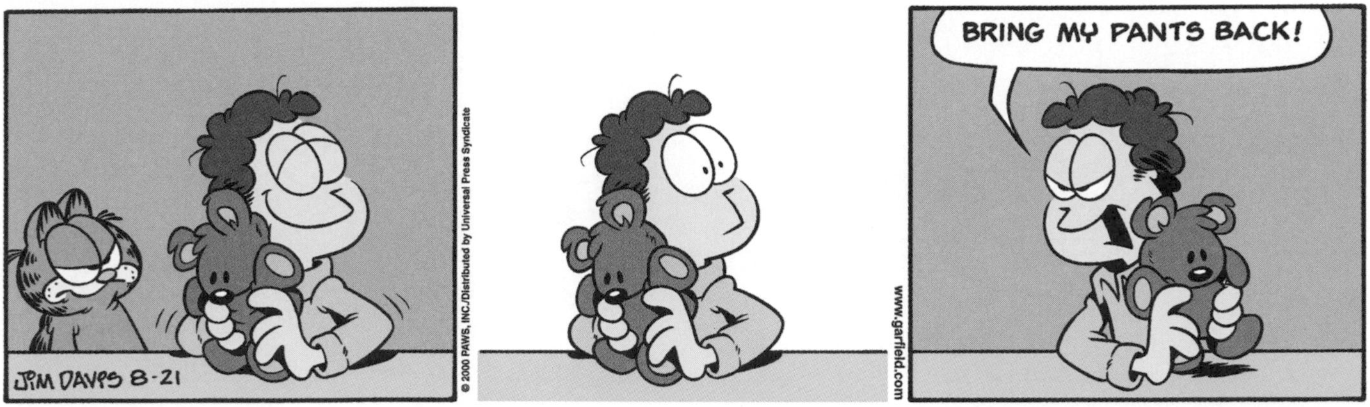
JIM DAVIS 8-21
© 2000 PAWS, INC./Distributed by Universal Press Syndicate
BRING MY PANTS BACK!
www.garfield.com

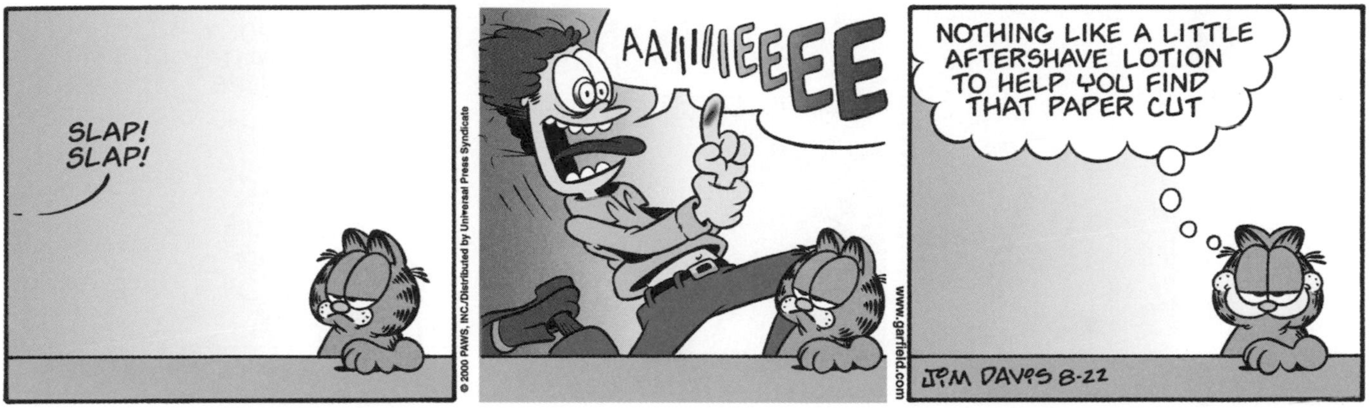
SLAP!
SLAP!
© 2000 PAWS, INC./Distributed by Universal Press Syndicate
AAIIIIIEEEEE
NOTHING LIKE A LITTLE AFTERSHAVE LOTION TO HELP YOU FIND THAT PAPER CUT
www.garfield.com
JIM DAVIS 8-22

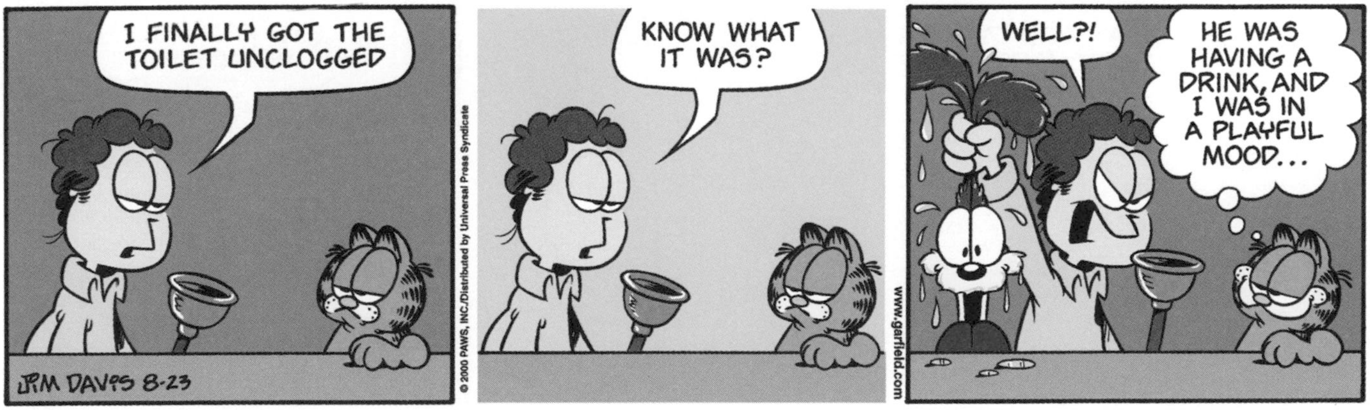
I FINALLY GOT THE TOILET UNCLOGGED
JIM DAVIS 8-23
© 2000 PAWS, INC./Distributed by Universal Press Syndicate
KNOW WHAT IT WAS?
WELL?!
HE WAS HAVING A DRINK, AND I WAS IN A PLAYFUL MOOD...
www.garfield.com

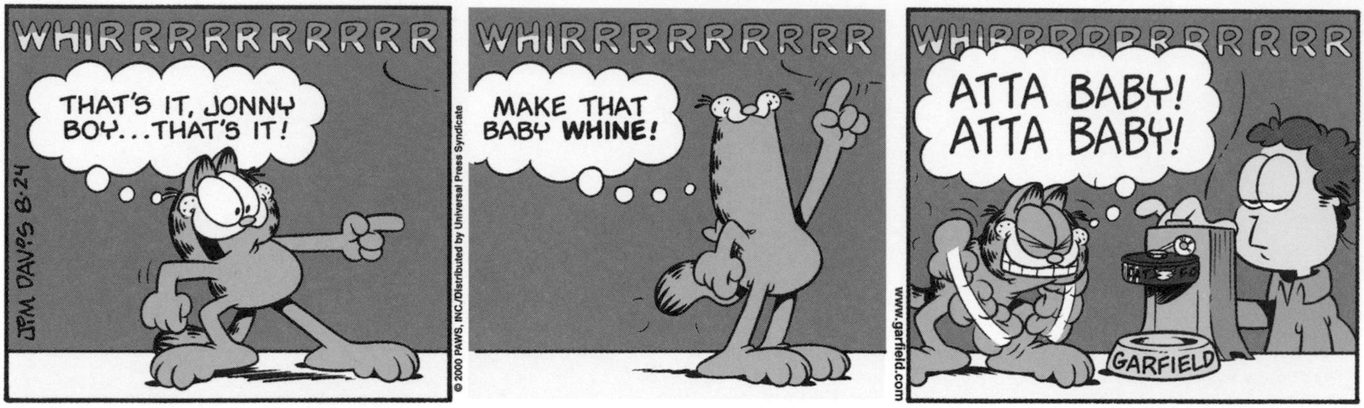
WHIRRRRRRRRRRR
THAT'S IT, JONNY BOY...THAT'S IT!
JIM DAVIS 8-24
WHIRRRRRRRRRRR
MAKE THAT BABY **WHINE**!
© 2000 PAWS, INC/Distributed by Universal Press Syndicate
WHIRRRRRRRRRRR
ATTA BABY! ATTA BABY!
GARFIELD
www.garfield.com

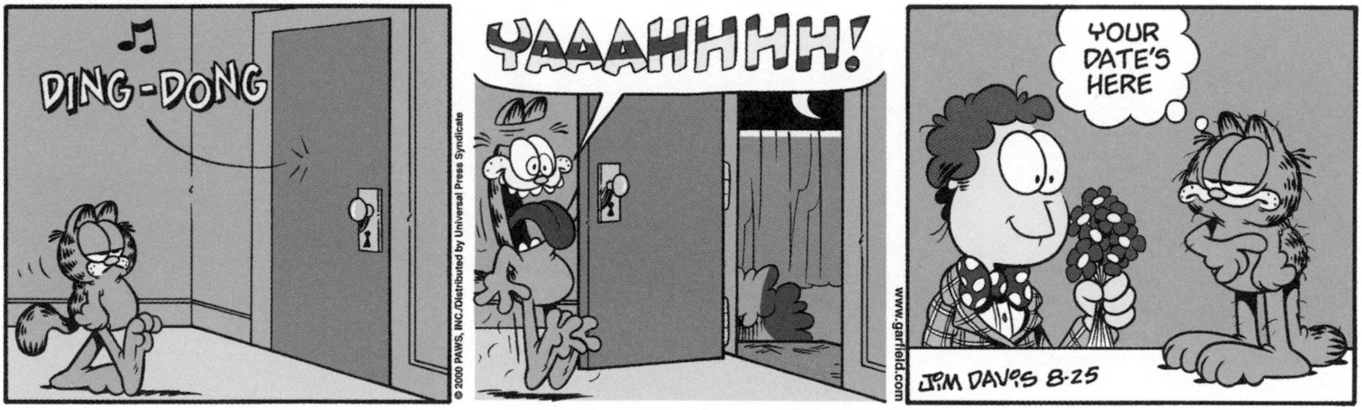
DING-DONG
YAAAHHHHH!
© 2000 PAWS, INC/Distributed by Universal Press Syndicate
YOUR DATE'S HERE
JIM DAVIS 8-25
www.garfield.com

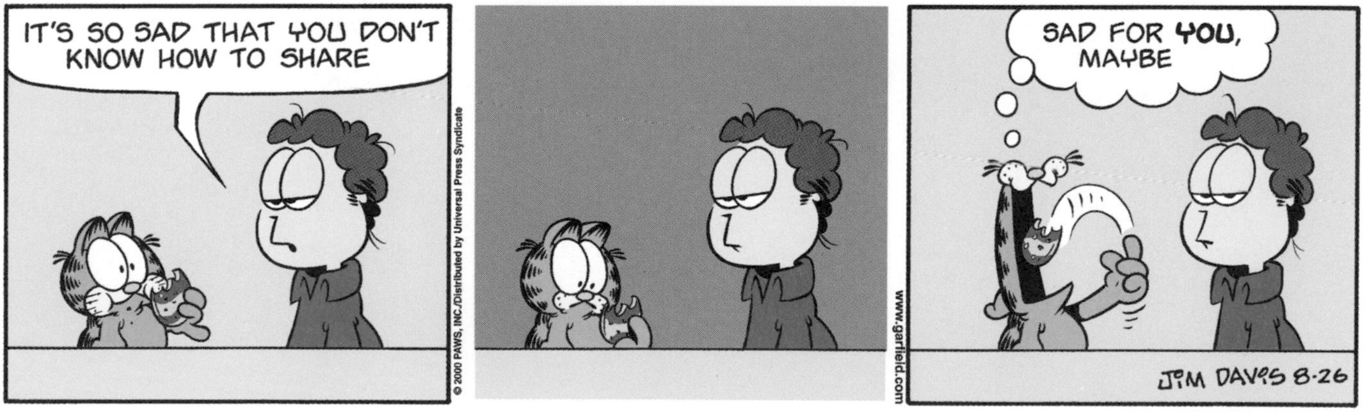
IT'S SO SAD THAT YOU DON'T KNOW HOW TO SHARE
© 2000 PAWS, INC/Distributed by Universal Press Syndicate
SAD FOR **YOU**, MAYBE
JIM DAVIS 8-26
www.garfield.com

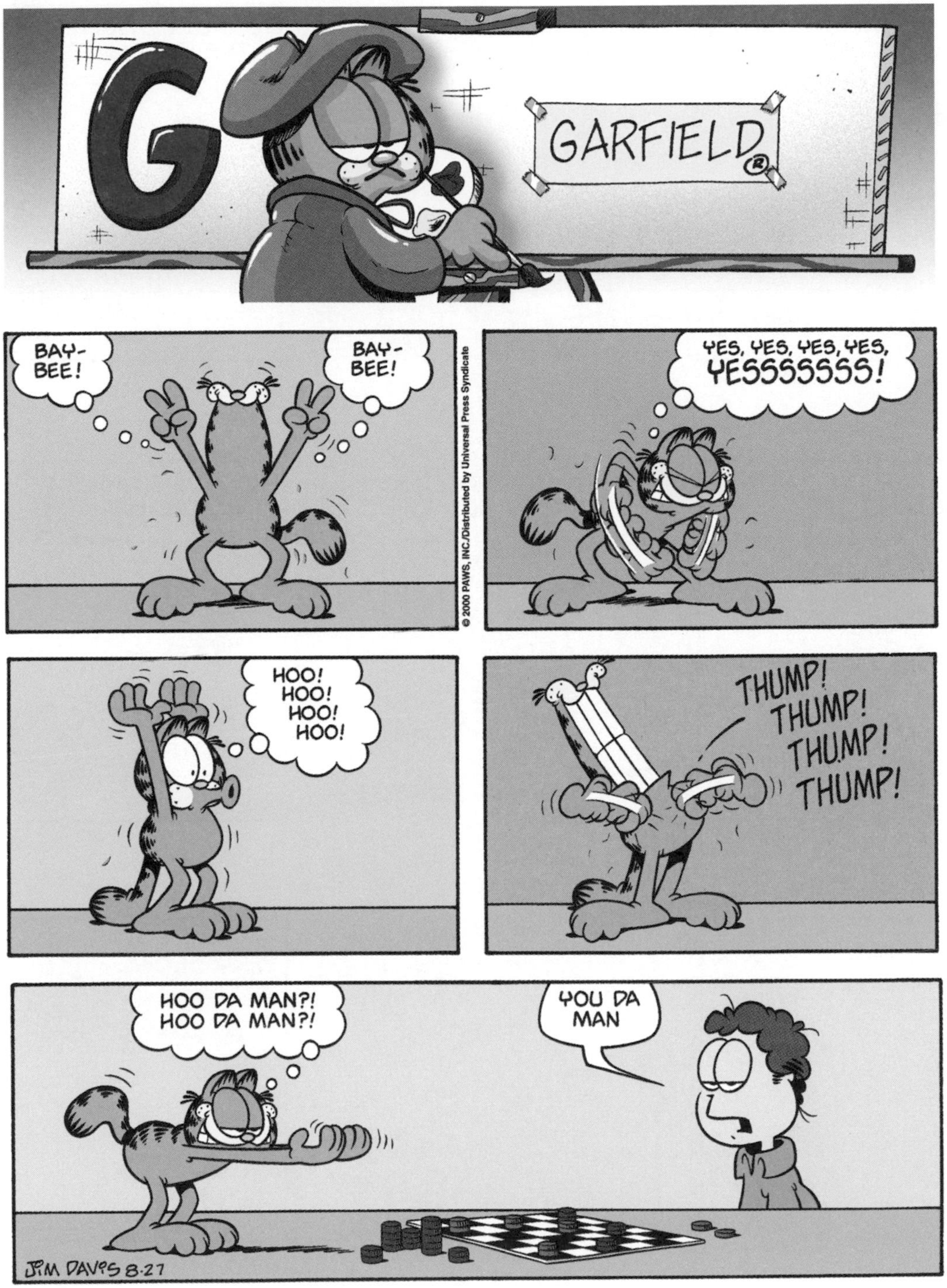
GARFIELD®
BAY-BEE!
BAY-BEE!
© 2000 PAWS, INC./Distributed by Universal Press Syndicate
YES, YES, YES, YES, YESSSSSSSS!
HOO! HOO! HOO! HOO!
THUMP! THUMP! THUMP! THUMP!
HOO DA MAN?! HOO DA MAN?!
YOU DA MAN
JIM DAVIS 8-27

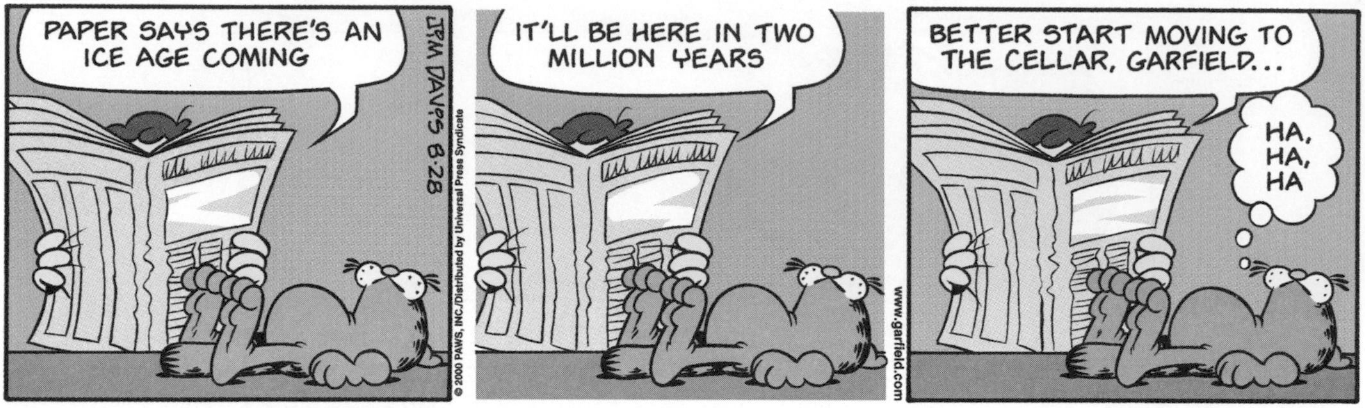
PAPER SAYS THERE'S AN ICE AGE COMING
JIM DAVIS 8-28
© 2000 PAWS, INC./Distributed by Universal Press Syndicate
IT'LL BE HERE IN TWO MILLION YEARS
www.garfield.com
BETTER START MOVING TO THE CELLAR, GARFIELD...
HA, HA, HA

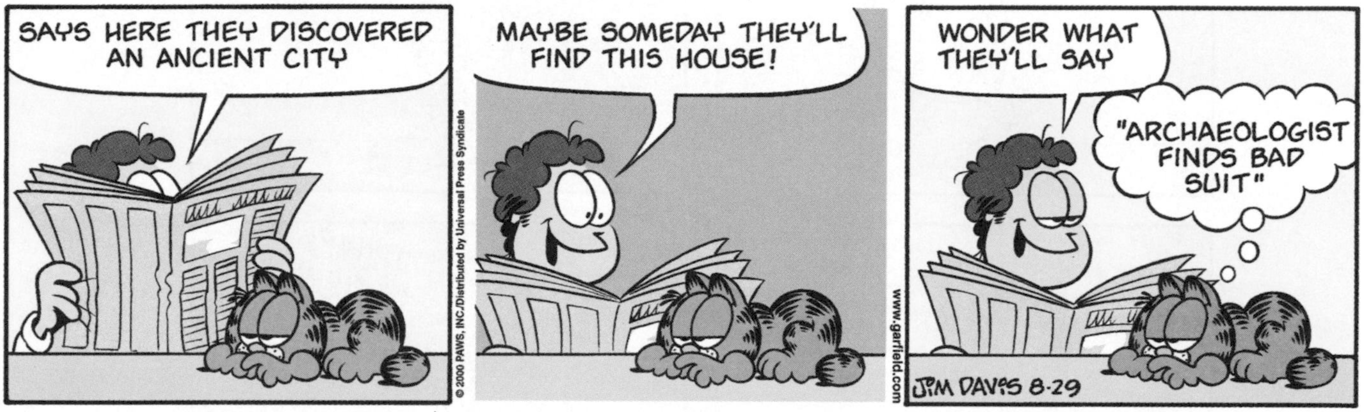
SAYS HERE THEY DISCOVERED AN ANCIENT CITY
© 2000 PAWS, INC./Distributed by Universal Press Syndicate
MAYBE SOMEDAY THEY'LL FIND THIS HOUSE!
www.garfield.com
WONDER WHAT THEY'LL SAY
"ARCHAEOLOGIST FINDS BAD SUIT"
JIM DAVIS 8-29

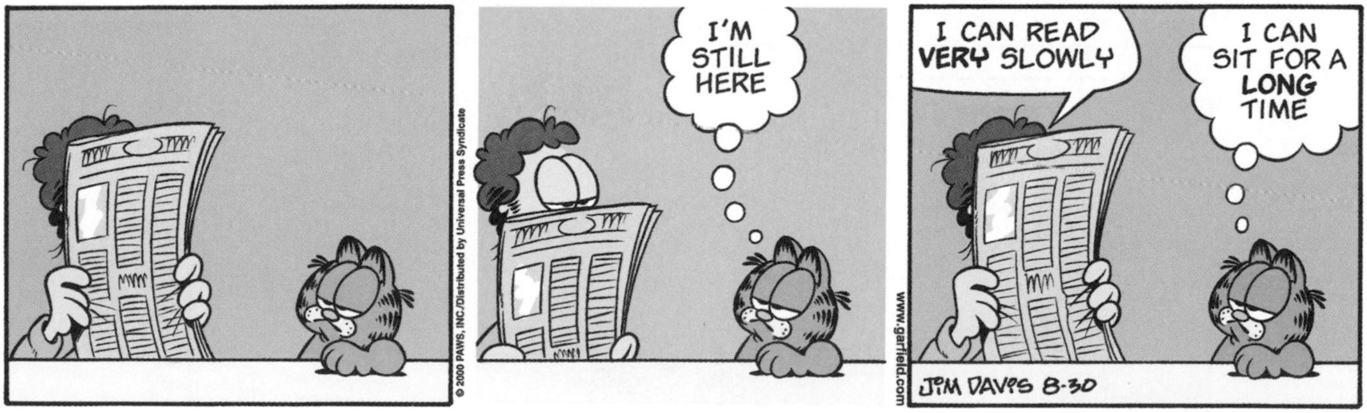
© 2000 PAWS, INC./Distributed by Universal Press Syndicate
I'M STILL HERE
www.garfield.com
I CAN READ **VERY** SLOWLY
I CAN SIT FOR A **LONG** TIME
JIM DAVIS 8-30

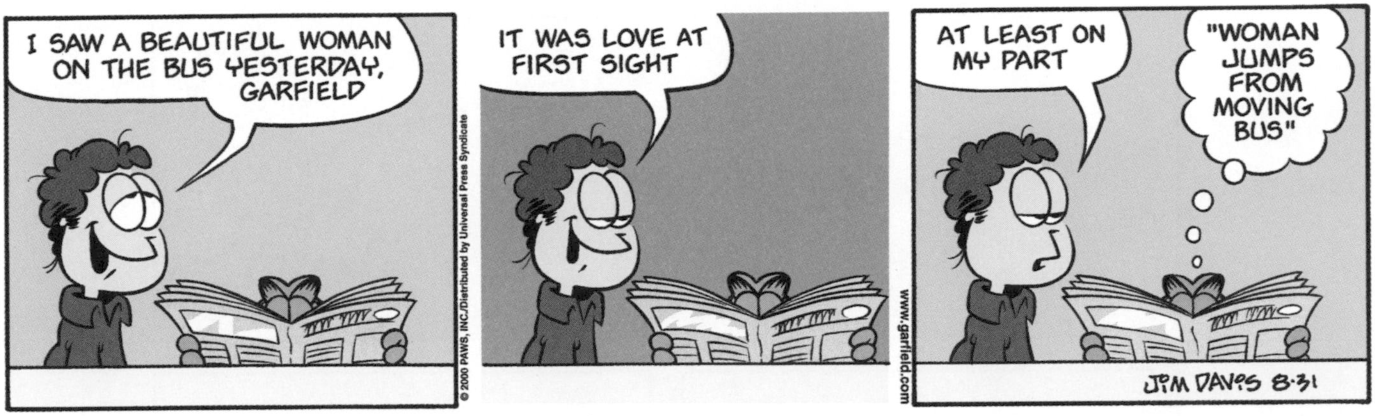
I SAW A BEAUTIFUL WOMAN ON THE BUS YESTERDAY, GARFIELD
IT WAS LOVE AT FIRST SIGHT
AT LEAST ON MY PART
"WOMAN JUMPS FROM MOVING BUS"
JIM DAVIS 8-31
© 2000 PAWS, INC./Distributed by Universal Press Syndicate
www.garfield.com

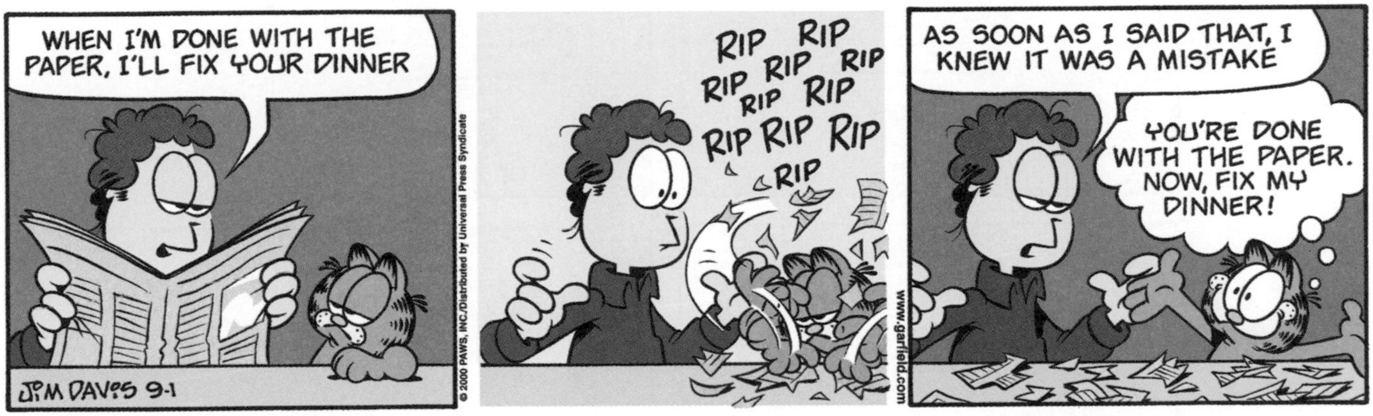
WHEN I'M DONE WITH THE PAPER, I'LL FIX YOUR DINNER
JIM DAVIS 9-1
RIP RIP RIP RIP RIP RIP RIP RIP RIP RIP RIP
AS SOON AS I SAID THAT, I KNEW IT WAS A MISTAKE
YOU'RE DONE WITH THE PAPER. NOW, FIX MY DINNER!
© 2000 PAWS, INC./Distributed by Universal Press Syndicate
www.garfield.com

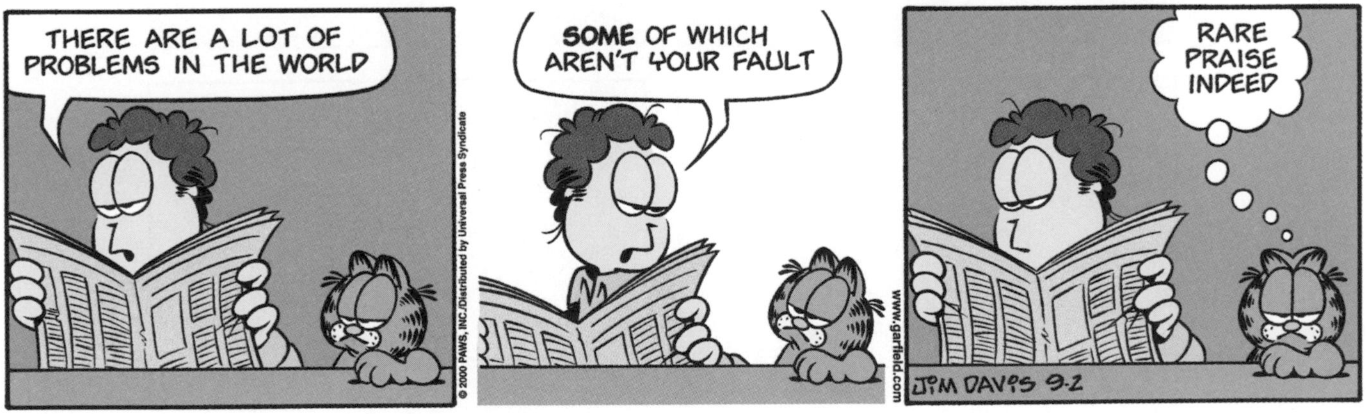
THERE ARE A LOT OF PROBLEMS IN THE WORLD
SOME OF WHICH AREN'T YOUR FAULT
RARE PRAISE INDEED
JIM DAVIS 9-2
© 2000 PAWS, INC./Distributed by Universal Press Syndicate
www.garfield.com

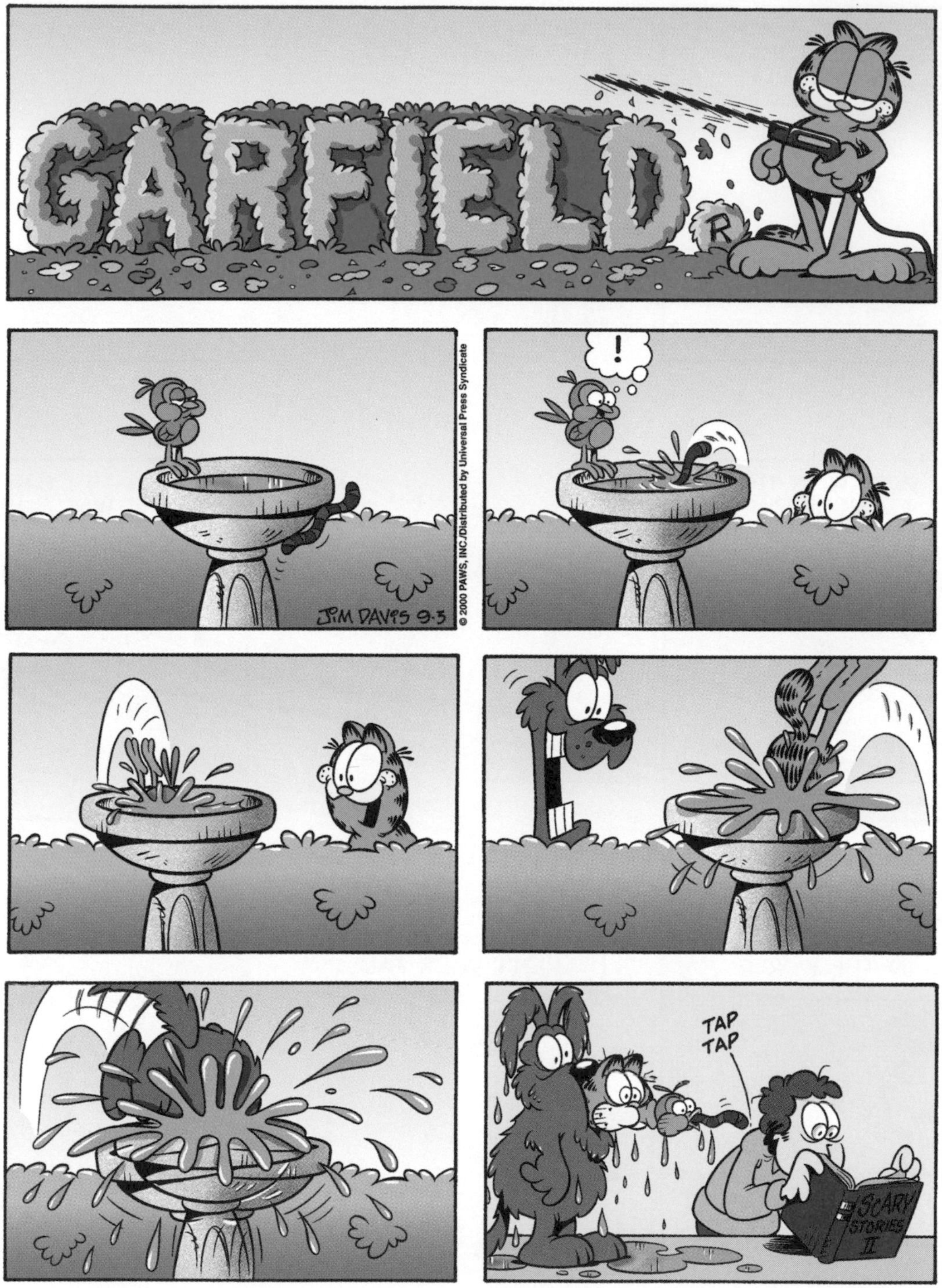
GARFIELD
JIM DAVIS 9-3
© 2000 PAWS, INC./Distributed by Universal Press Syndicate
!
TAP
TAP
SCARY STORIES II

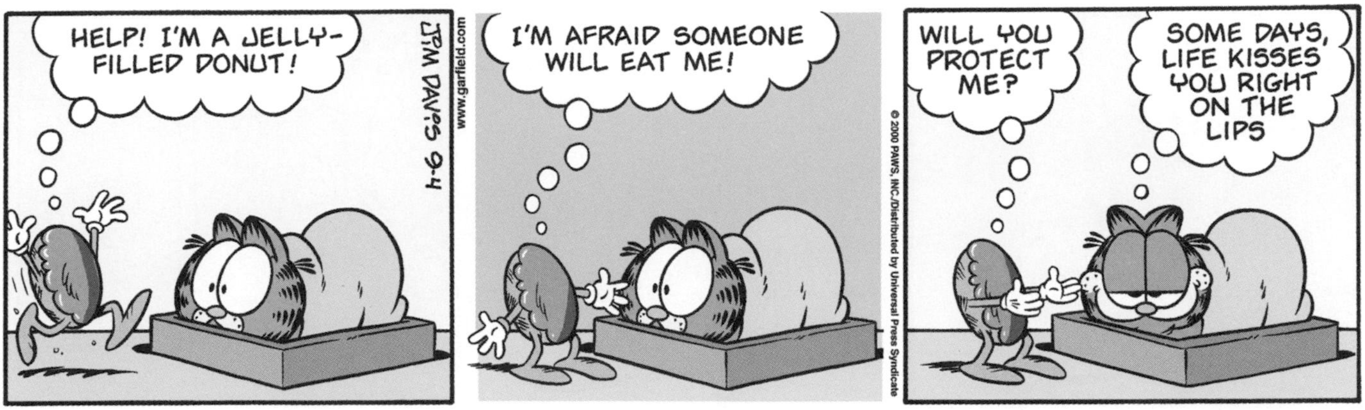
HELP! I'M A JELLY-FILLED DONUT!
JIM DAVIS 9-4
www.garfield.com
I'M AFRAID SOMEONE WILL EAT ME!
© 2000 PAWS, INC./Distributed by Universal Press Syndicate
WILL YOU PROTECT ME?
SOME DAYS, LIFE KISSES YOU RIGHT ON THE LIPS

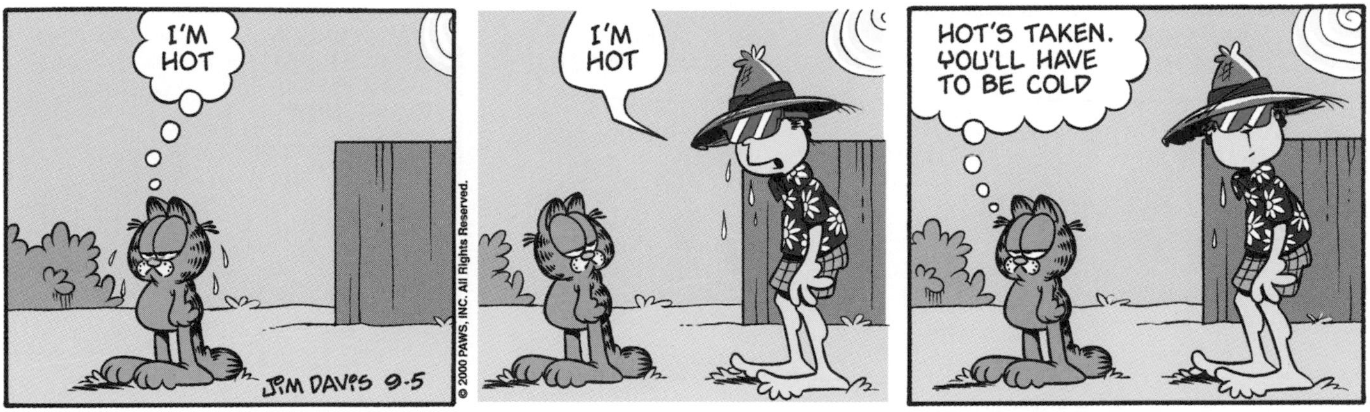
I'M HOT
JIM DAVIS 9-5
© 2000 PAWS, INC. All Rights Reserved.
I'M HOT
HOT'S TAKEN. YOU'LL HAVE TO BE COLD

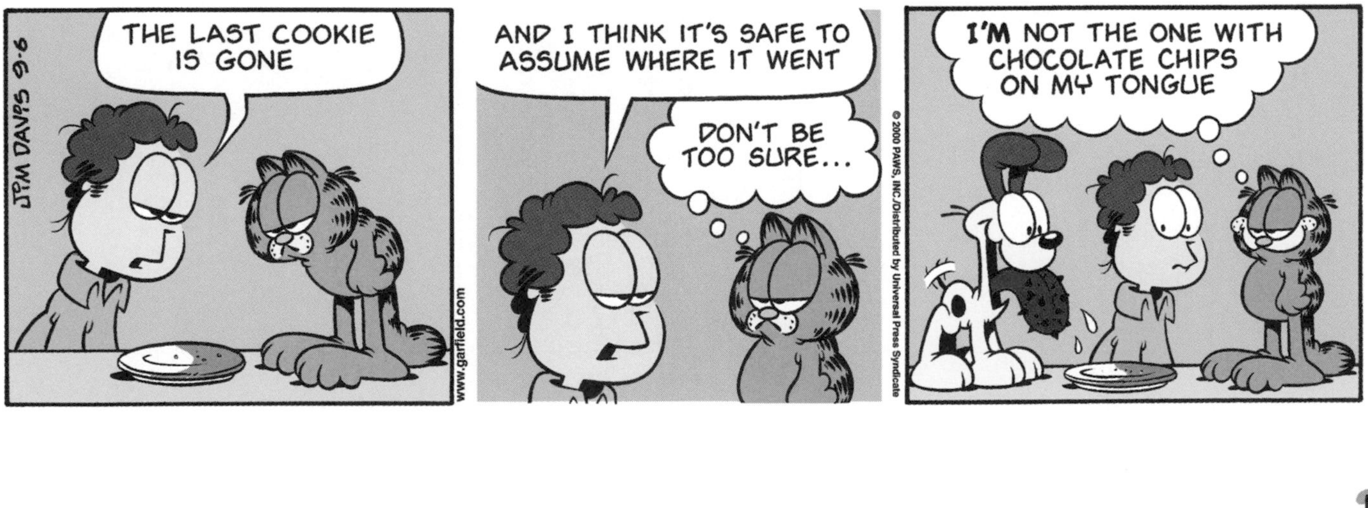
JIM DAVIS 9-6
THE LAST COOKIE IS GONE
www.garfield.com
AND I THINK IT'S SAFE TO ASSUME WHERE IT WENT
DON'T BE TOO SURE...
© 2000 PAWS, INC./Distributed by Universal Press Syndicate
I'M NOT THE ONE WITH CHOCOLATE CHIPS ON MY TONGUE

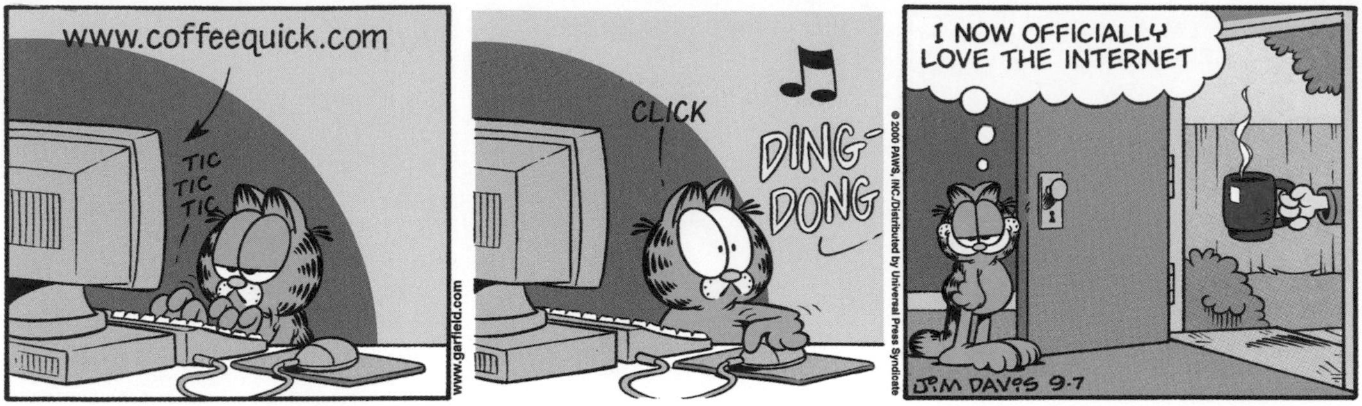
www.coffeequick.com
TIC TIC TIC
www.garfield.com
CLICK
DING-DONG
© 2000 PAWS, INC./Distributed by Universal Press Syndicate
I NOW OFFICIALLY LOVE THE INTERNET
JIM DAVIS 9-7

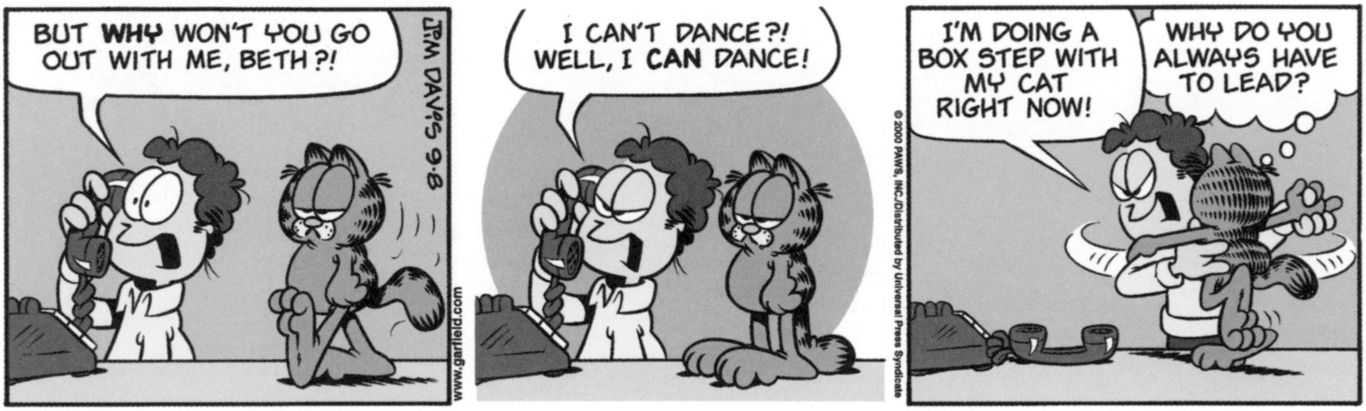
BUT **WHY** WON'T YOU GO OUT WITH ME, BETH?!
JIM DAVIS 9-8
www.garfield.com
I CAN'T DANCE?! WELL, I **CAN** DANCE!
© 2000 PAWS, INC./Distributed by Universal Press Syndicate
I'M DOING A BOX STEP WITH MY CAT RIGHT NOW!
WHY DO YOU ALWAYS HAVE TO LEAD?

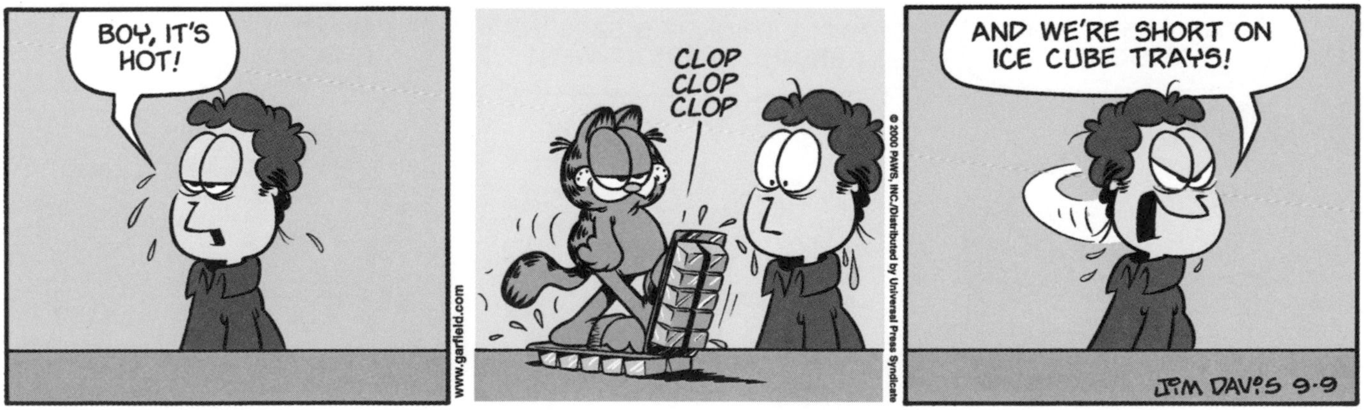
BOY, IT'S HOT!
www.garfield.com
CLOP CLOP CLOP
© 2000 PAWS, INC./Distributed by Universal Press Syndicate
AND WE'RE SHORT ON ICE CUBE TRAYS!
JIM DAVIS 9-9

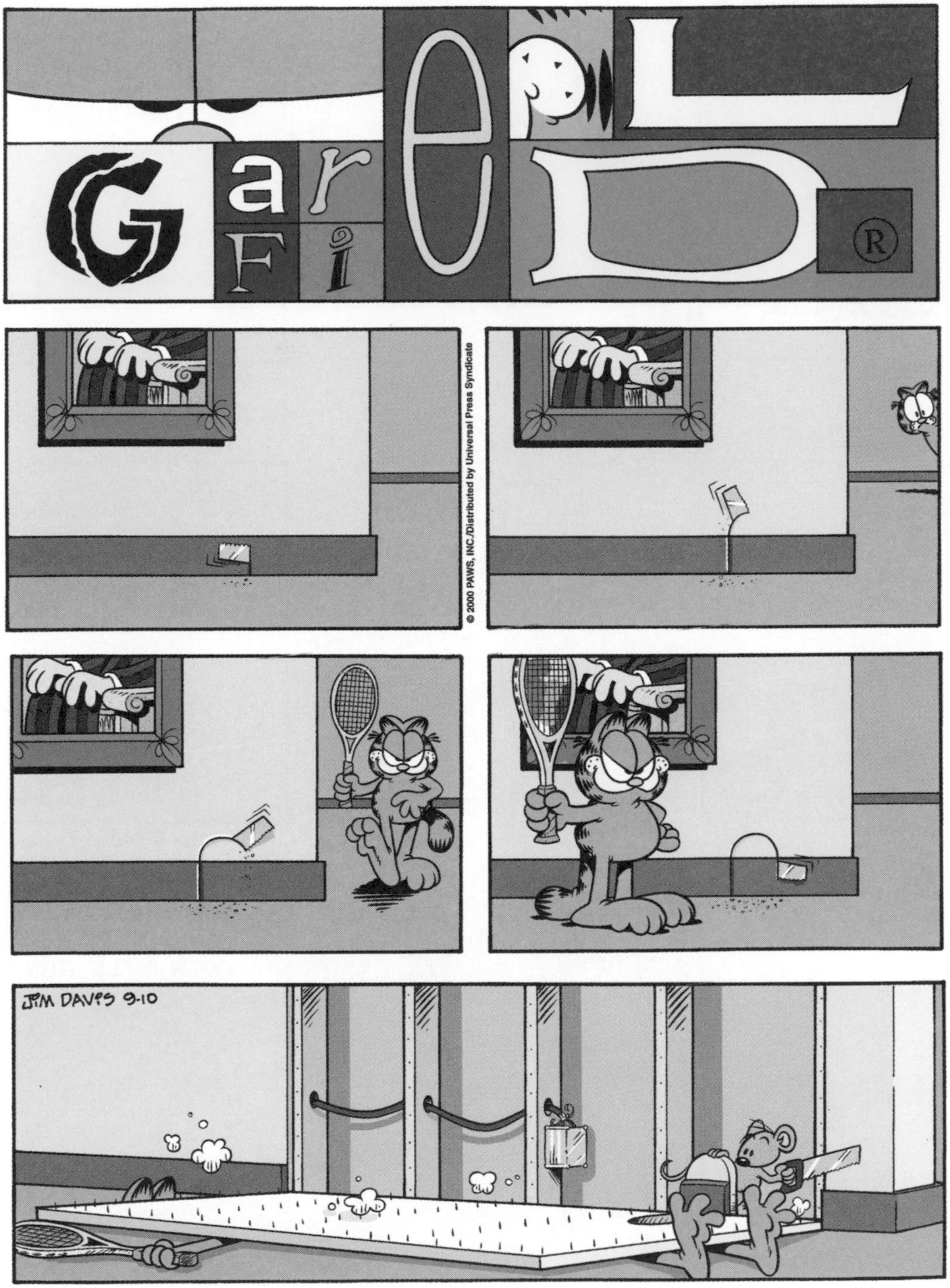
GarFieLD®
© 2000 PAWS, INC/Distributed by Universal Press Syndicate
JIM DAVIS 9-10

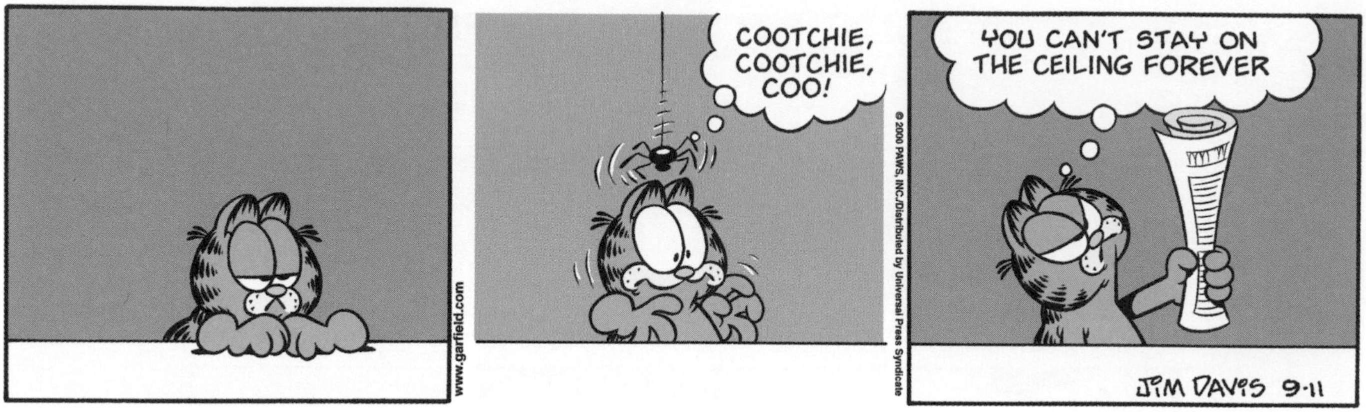
COOTCHIE, COOTCHIE, COO!
YOU CAN'T STAY ON THE CEILING FOREVER
JIM DAVIS 9-11
www.garfield.com
© 2000 PAWS, INC./Distributed by Universal Press Syndicate

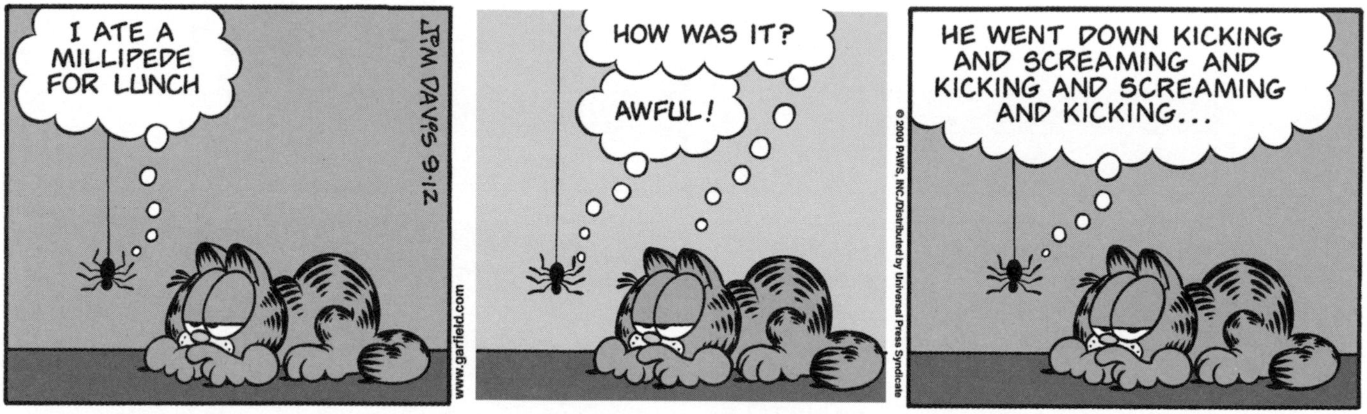
I ATE A MILLIPEDE FOR LUNCH
JIM DAVIS 9-12
HOW WAS IT?
AWFUL!
HE WENT DOWN KICKING AND SCREAMING AND KICKING AND SCREAMING AND KICKING...
www.garfield.com
© 2000 PAWS, INC./Distributed by Universal Press Syndicate

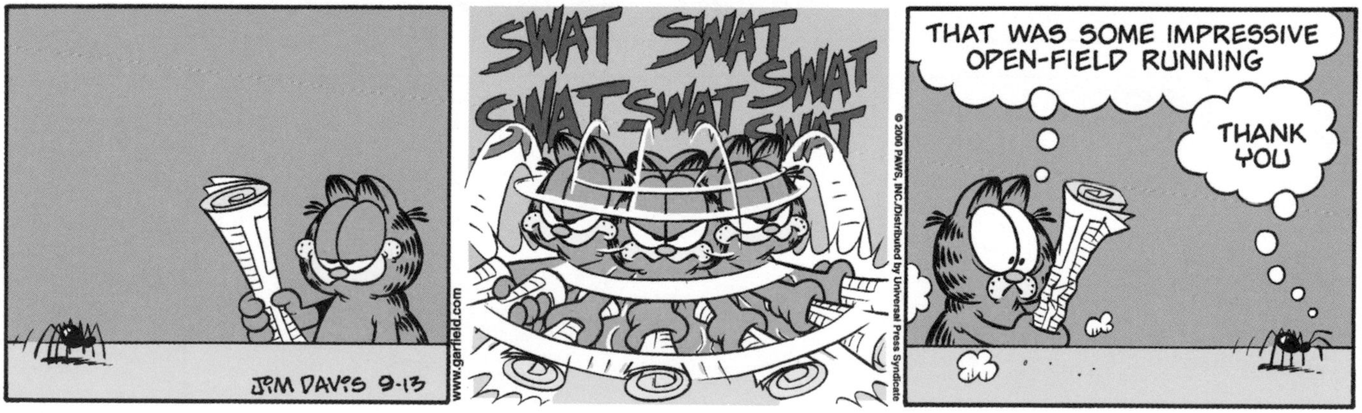
JIM DAVIS 9-13
SWAT SWAT SWAT SWAT SWAT SWAT
THAT WAS SOME IMPRESSIVE OPEN-FIELD RUNNING
THANK YOU
www.garfield.com
© 2000 PAWS, INC./Distributed by Universal Press Syndicate

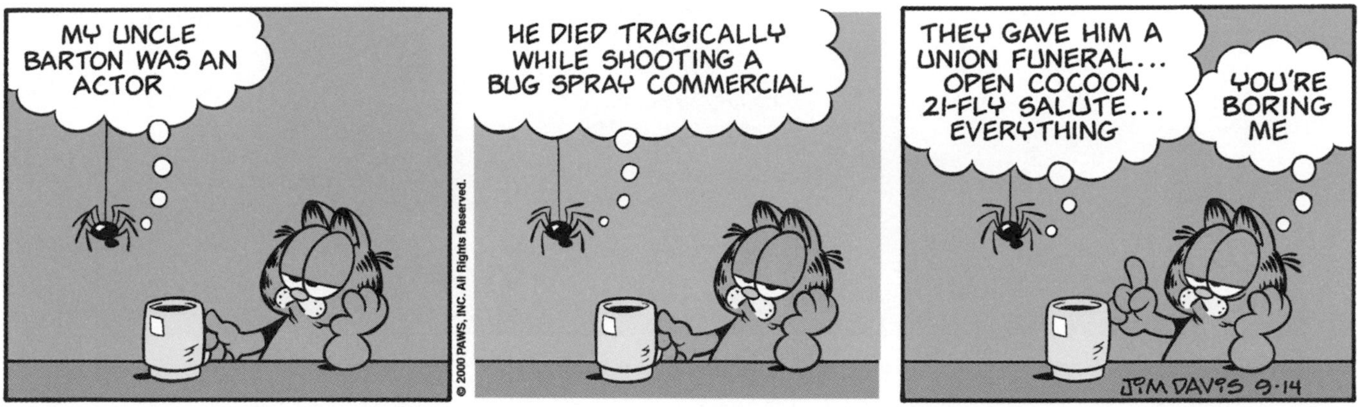
MY UNCLE BARTON WAS AN ACTOR
HE DIED TRAGICALLY WHILE SHOOTING A BUG SPRAY COMMERCIAL
THEY GAVE HIM A UNION FUNERAL... OPEN COCOON, 21-FLY SALUTE... EVERYTHING
YOU'RE BORING ME
JIM DAVIS 9-14

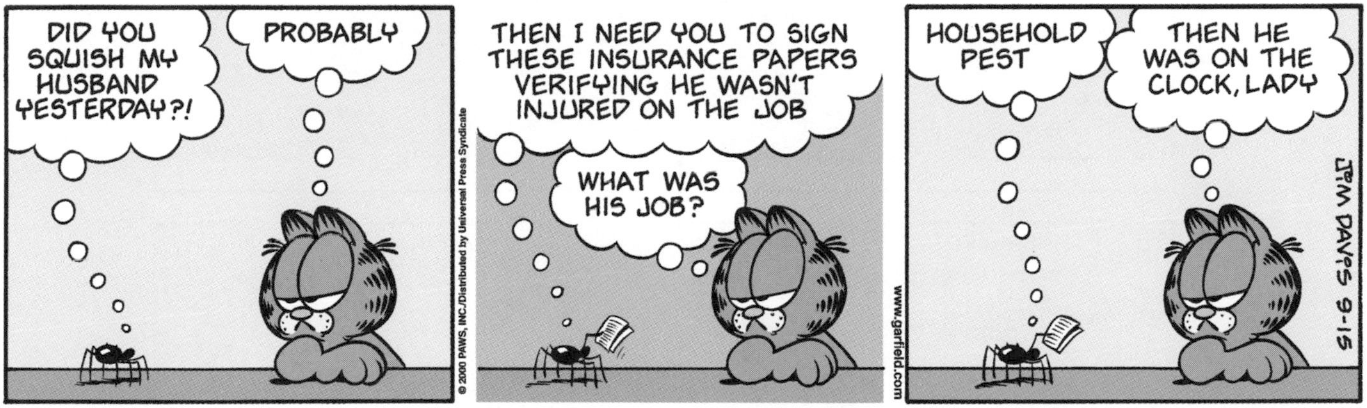
DID YOU SQUISH MY HUSBAND YESTERDAY?!
PROBABLY
THEN I NEED YOU TO SIGN THESE INSURANCE PAPERS VERIFYING HE WASN'T INJURED ON THE JOB
WHAT WAS HIS JOB?
HOUSEHOLD PEST
THEN HE WAS ON THE CLOCK, LADY
JIM DAVIS 9-15

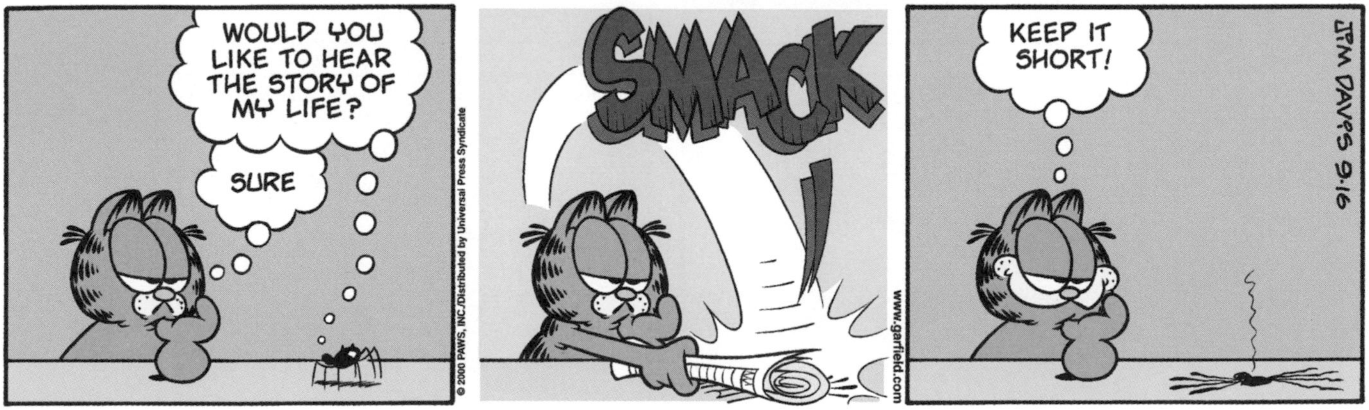
WOULD YOU LIKE TO HEAR THE STORY OF MY LIFE?
SURE
SMACK
KEEP IT SHORT!
JIM DAVIS 9-16

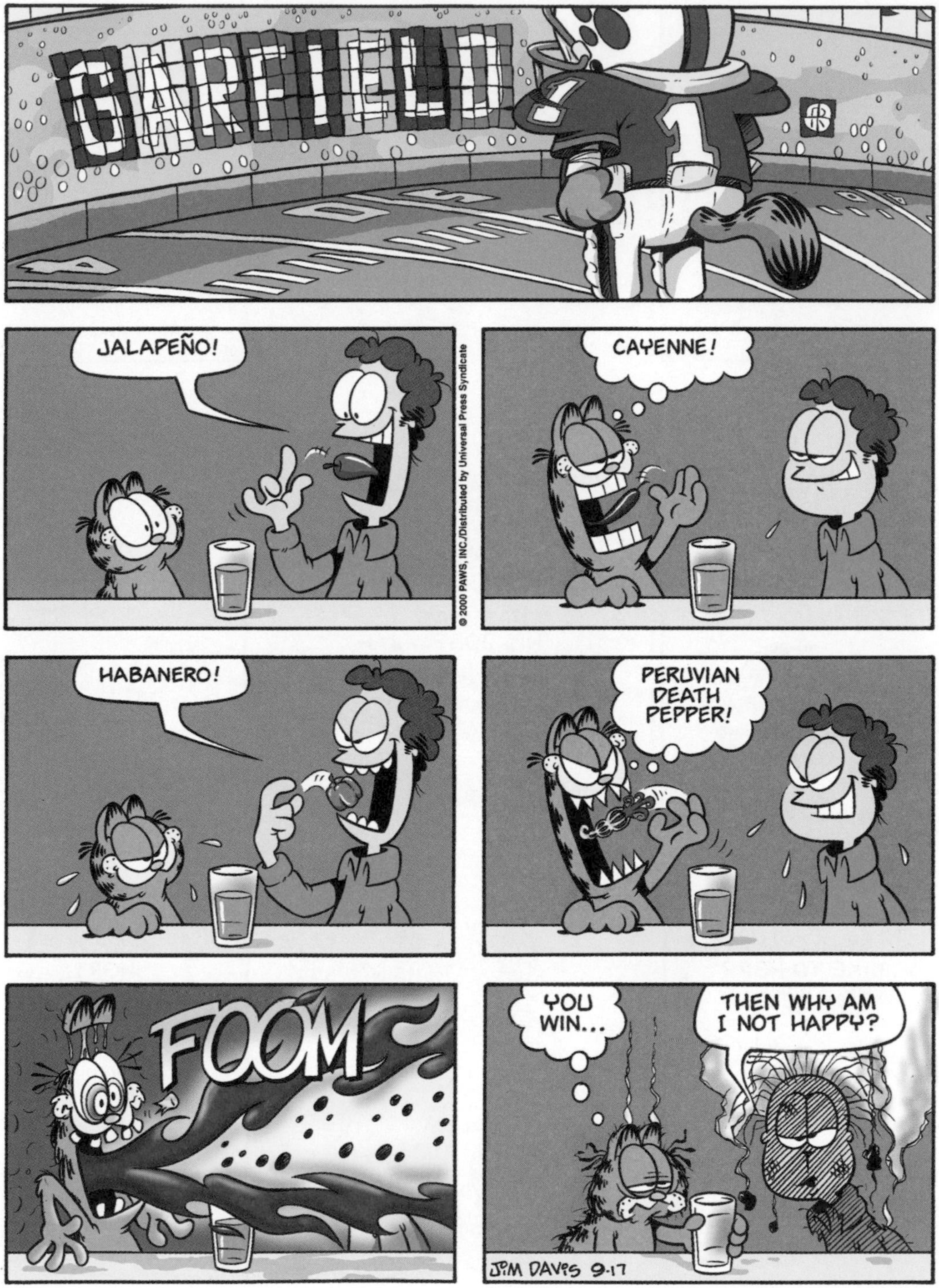
GARFIELD
© 2000 PAWS, INC./Distributed by Universal Press Syndicate
JALAPEÑO!
CAYENNE!
HABANERO!
PERUVIAN DEATH PEPPER!
FOOM
YOU WIN...
THEN WHY AM I NOT HAPPY?
JIM DAVIS 9-17

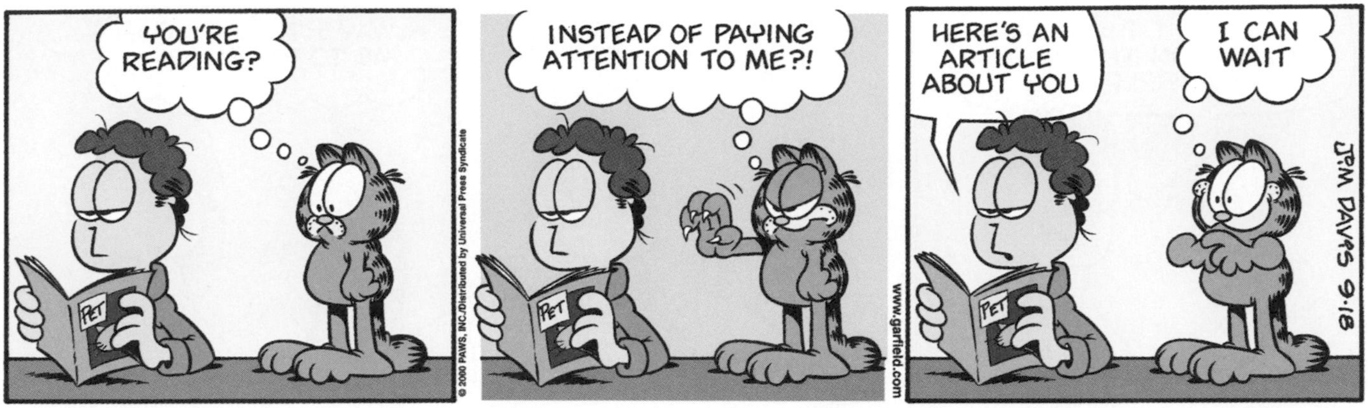
YOU'RE READING?
INSTEAD OF PAYING ATTENTION TO ME?!
HERE'S AN ARTICLE ABOUT YOU
I CAN WAIT
PET
JIM DAVIS 9.18
© 2000 PAWS, INC./Distributed by Universal Press Syndicate
www.garfield.com

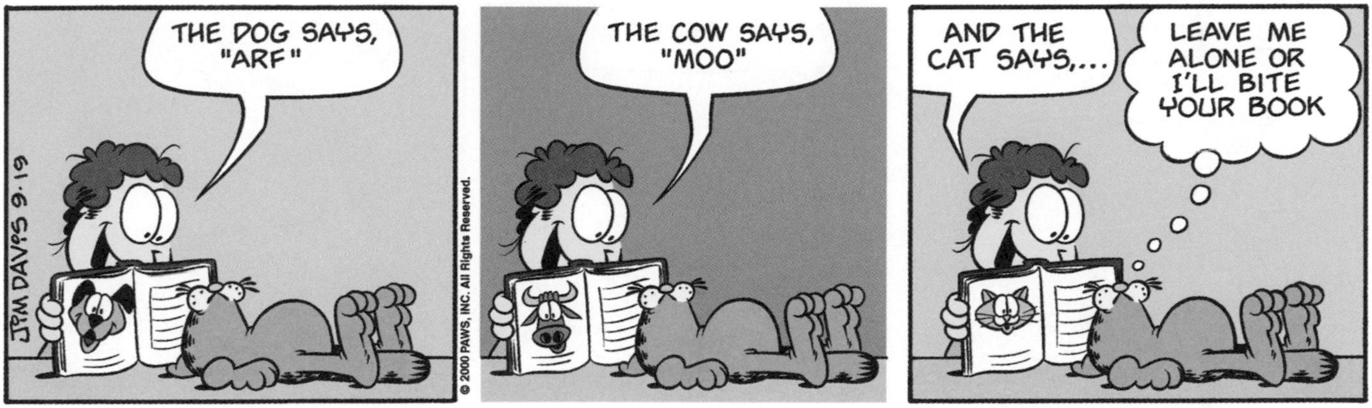
THE DOG SAYS, "ARF"
THE COW SAYS, "MOO"
AND THE CAT SAYS,...
LEAVE ME ALONE OR I'LL BITE YOUR BOOK
JIM DAVIS 9.19
© 2000 PAWS, INC. All Rights Reserved.

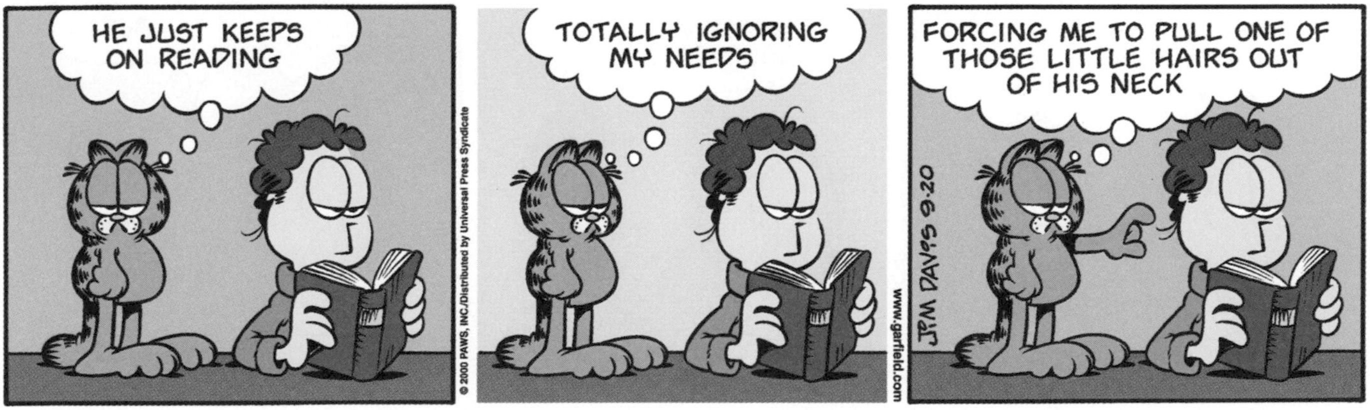
HE JUST KEEPS ON READING
TOTALLY IGNORING MY NEEDS
FORCING ME TO PULL ONE OF THOSE LITTLE HAIRS OUT OF HIS NECK
JIM DAVIS 9.20
© 2000 PAWS, INC./Distributed by Universal Press Syndicate
www.garfield.com

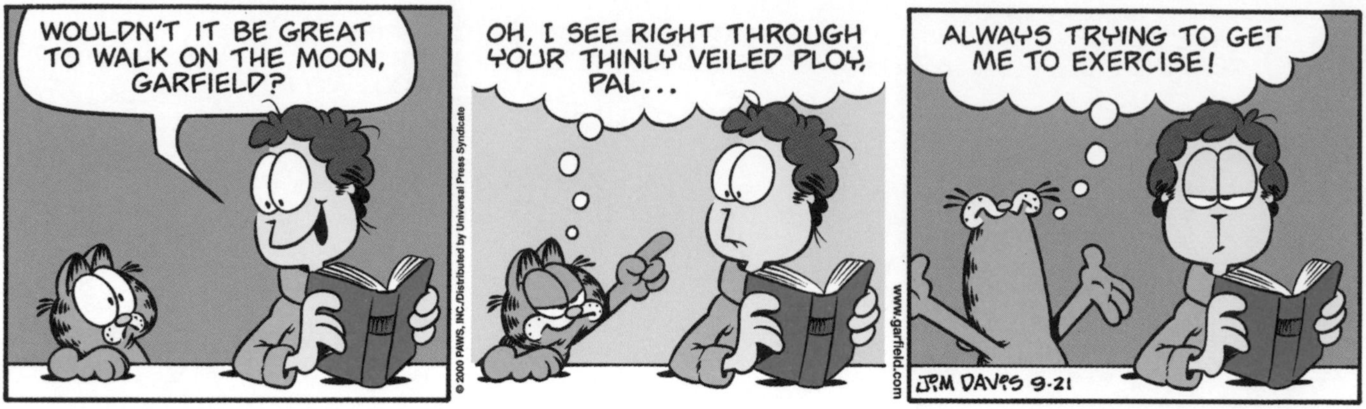
WOULDN'T IT BE GREAT TO WALK ON THE MOON, GARFIELD?
OH, I SEE RIGHT THROUGH YOUR THINLY VEILED PLOY, PAL...
ALWAYS TRYING TO GET ME TO EXERCISE!
JIM DAVIS 9-21
© 2000 PAWS, INC./Distributed by Universal Press Syndicate
www.garfield.com

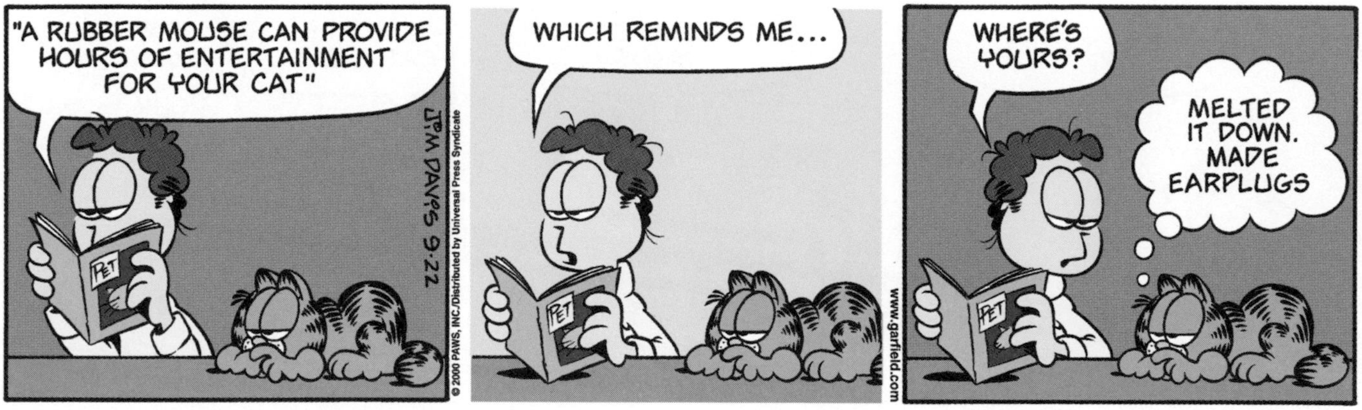
"A RUBBER MOUSE CAN PROVIDE HOURS OF ENTERTAINMENT FOR YOUR CAT"
PET
JIM DAVIS 9-22
WHICH REMINDS ME...
WHERE'S YOURS?
MELTED IT DOWN. MADE EARPLUGS
© 2000 PAWS, INC./Distributed by Universal Press Syndicate
www.garfield.com

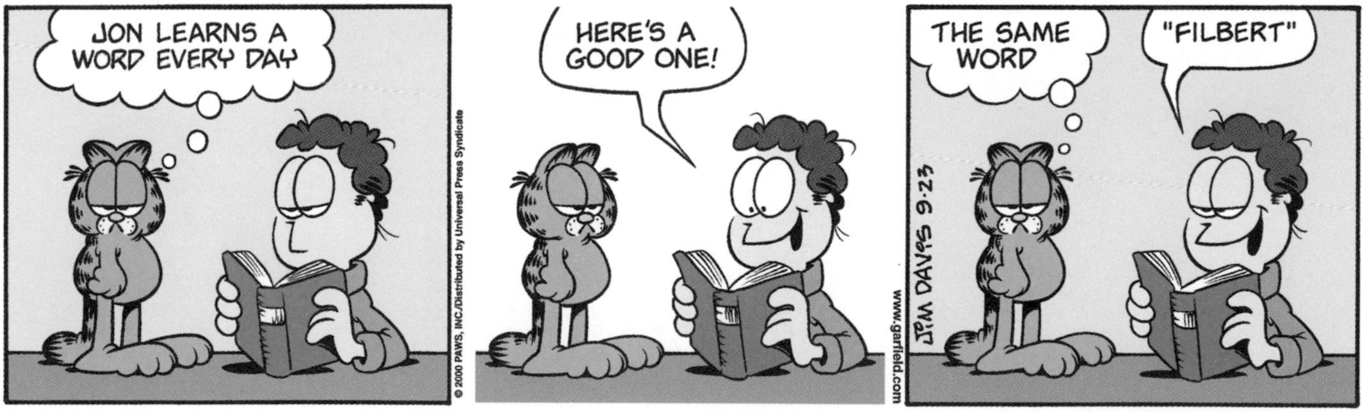
JON LEARNS A WORD EVERY DAY
HERE'S A GOOD ONE!
THE SAME WORD
"FILBERT"
JIM DAVIS 9-23
© 2000 PAWS, INC./Distributed by Universal Press Syndicate
www.garfield.com

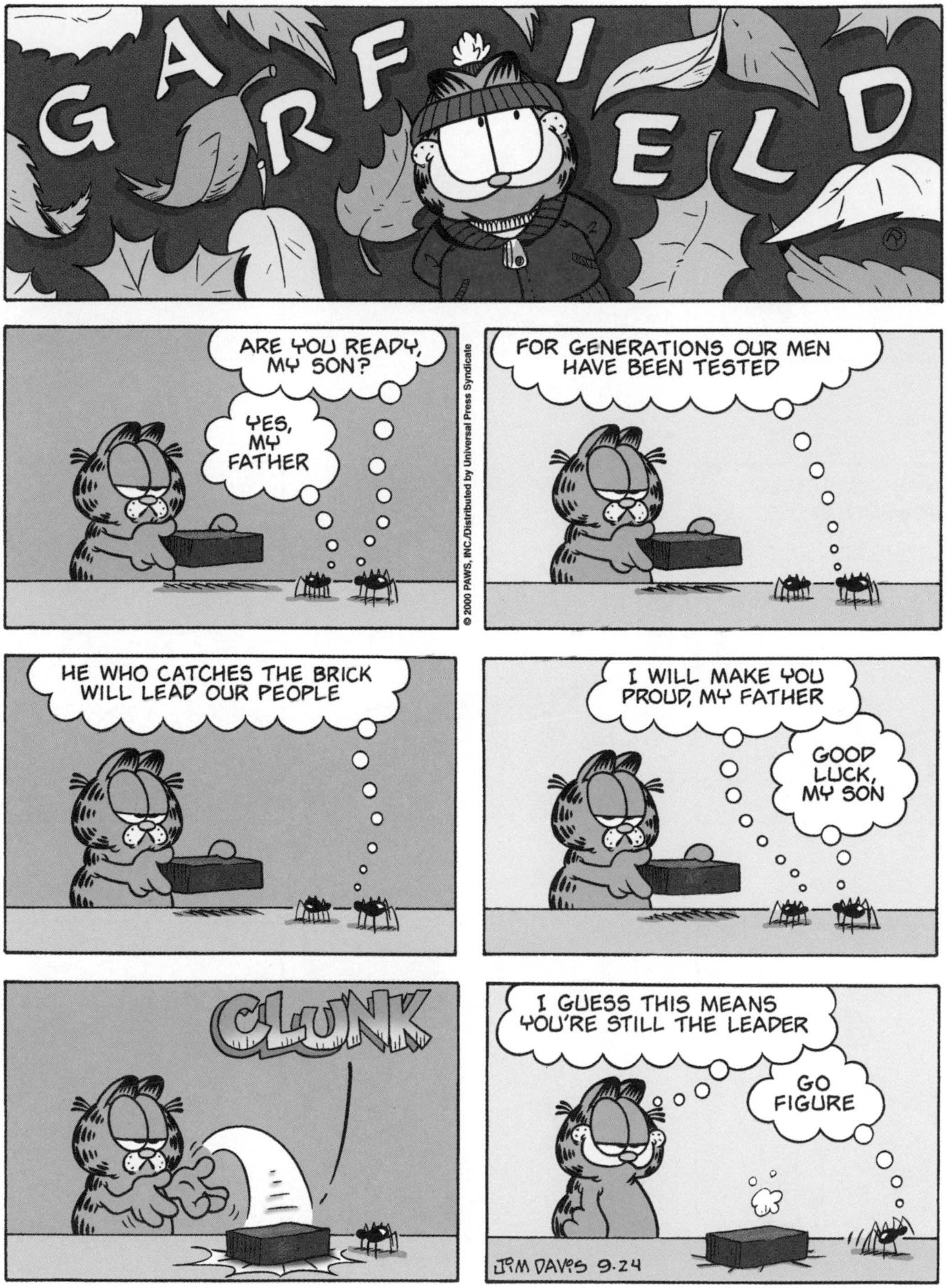

GARFIELD
ARE YOU READY, MY SON?
YES, MY FATHER
© 2000 PAWS, INC./Distributed by Universal Press Syndicate
FOR GENERATIONS OUR MEN HAVE BEEN TESTED
HE WHO CATCHES THE BRICK WILL LEAD OUR PEOPLE
I WILL MAKE YOU PROUD, MY FATHER
GOOD LUCK, MY SON
CLUNK
I GUESS THIS MEANS YOU'RE STILL THE LEADER
GO FIGURE
JIM DAVIS 9.24

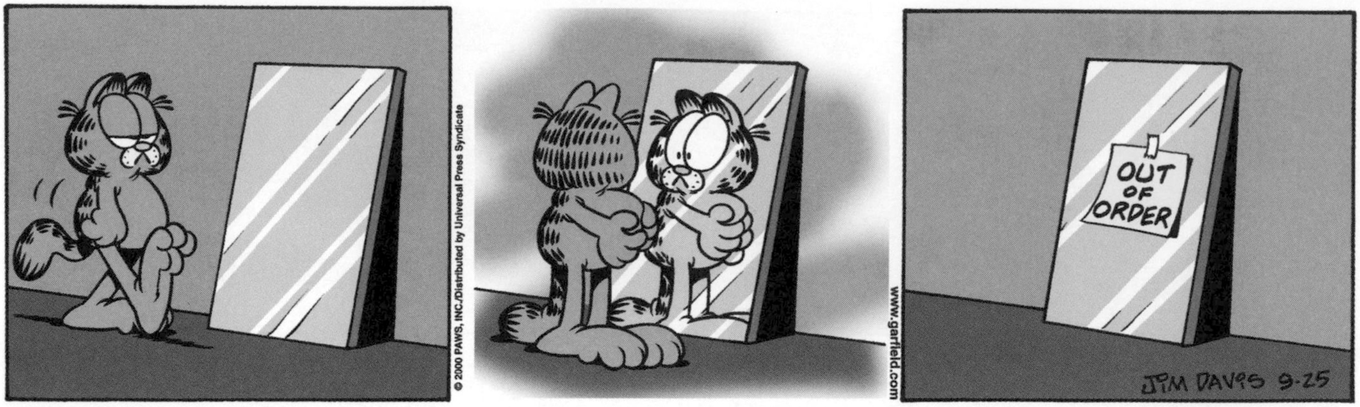
© 2000 PAWS, INC./Distributed by Universal Press Syndicate
www.garfield.com
OUT OF ORDER
JIM DAVIS 9-25

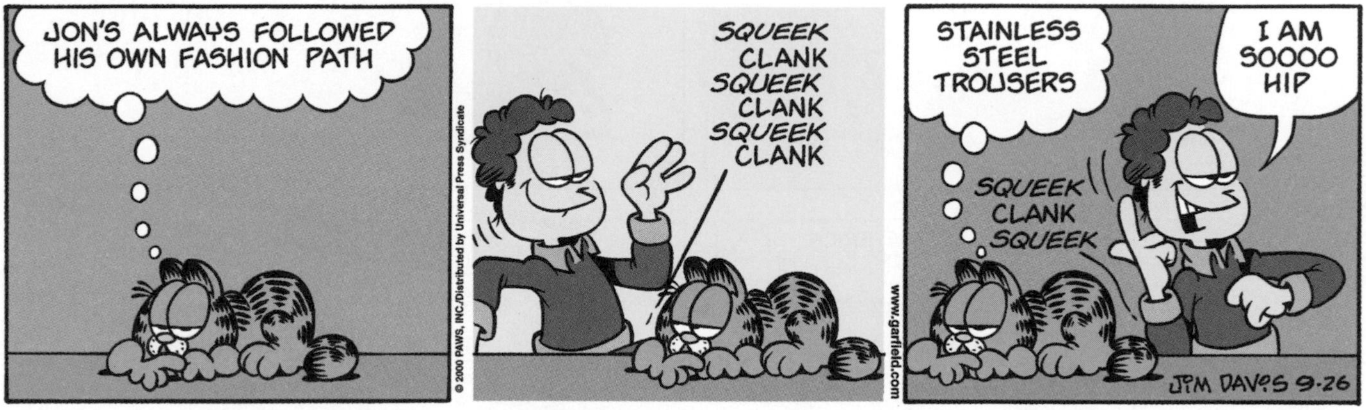
JON'S ALWAYS FOLLOWED HIS OWN FASHION PATH
© 2000 PAWS, INC./Distributed by Universal Press Syndicate
SQUEEK CLANK SQUEEK CLANK SQUEEK CLANK
www.garfield.com
STAINLESS STEEL TROUSERS
SQUEEK CLANK SQUEEK
I AM SOOOO HIP
JIM DAVIS 9-26

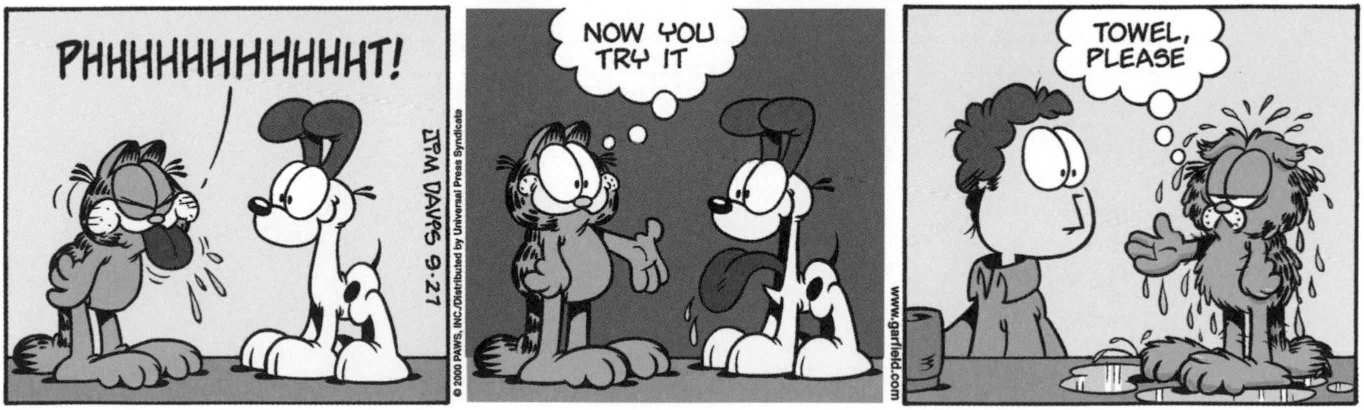
PHHHHHHHHHHHT!
JIM DAVIS 9-27
© 2000 PAWS, INC./Distributed by Universal Press Syndicate
NOW YOU TRY IT
www.garfield.com
TOWEL, PLEASE

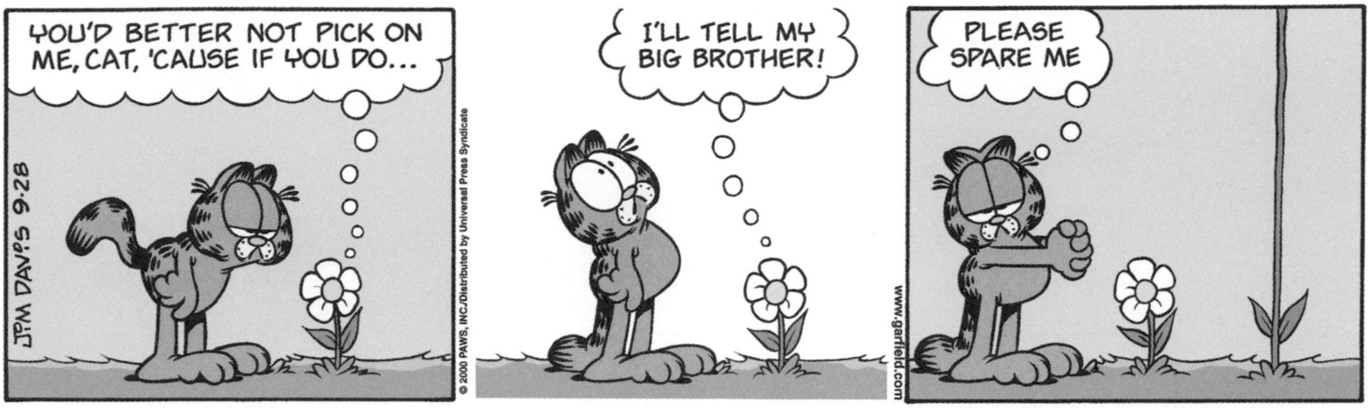
YOU'D BETTER NOT PICK ON ME, CAT, 'CAUSE IF YOU DO...
JIM DAVIS 9-28
I'LL TELL MY BIG BROTHER!
© 2000 PAWS, INC./Distributed by Universal Press Syndicate
PLEASE SPARE ME
www.garfield.com

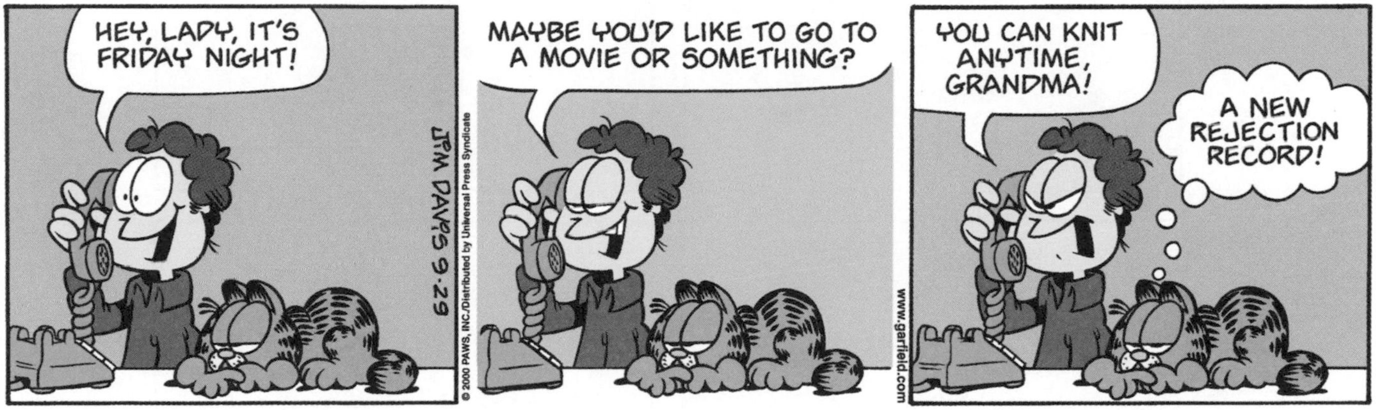
HEY, LADY, IT'S FRIDAY NIGHT!
JIM DAVIS 9-29
MAYBE YOU'D LIKE TO GO TO A MOVIE OR SOMETHING?
© 2000 PAWS, INC./Distributed by Universal Press Syndicate
YOU CAN KNIT ANYTIME, GRANDMA!
A NEW REJECTION RECORD!
www.garfield.com

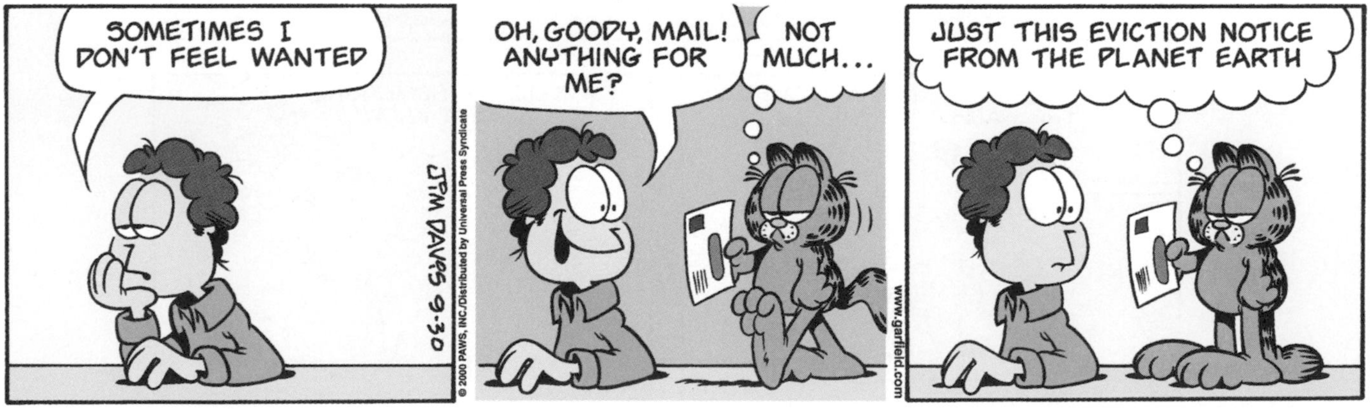
SOMETIMES I DON'T FEEL WANTED
JIM DAVIS 9-30
OH, GOODY, MAIL! ANYTHING FOR ME?
NOT MUCH...
© 2000 PAWS, INC./Distributed by Universal Press Syndicate
JUST THIS EVICTION NOTICE FROM THE PLANET EARTH
www.garfield.com

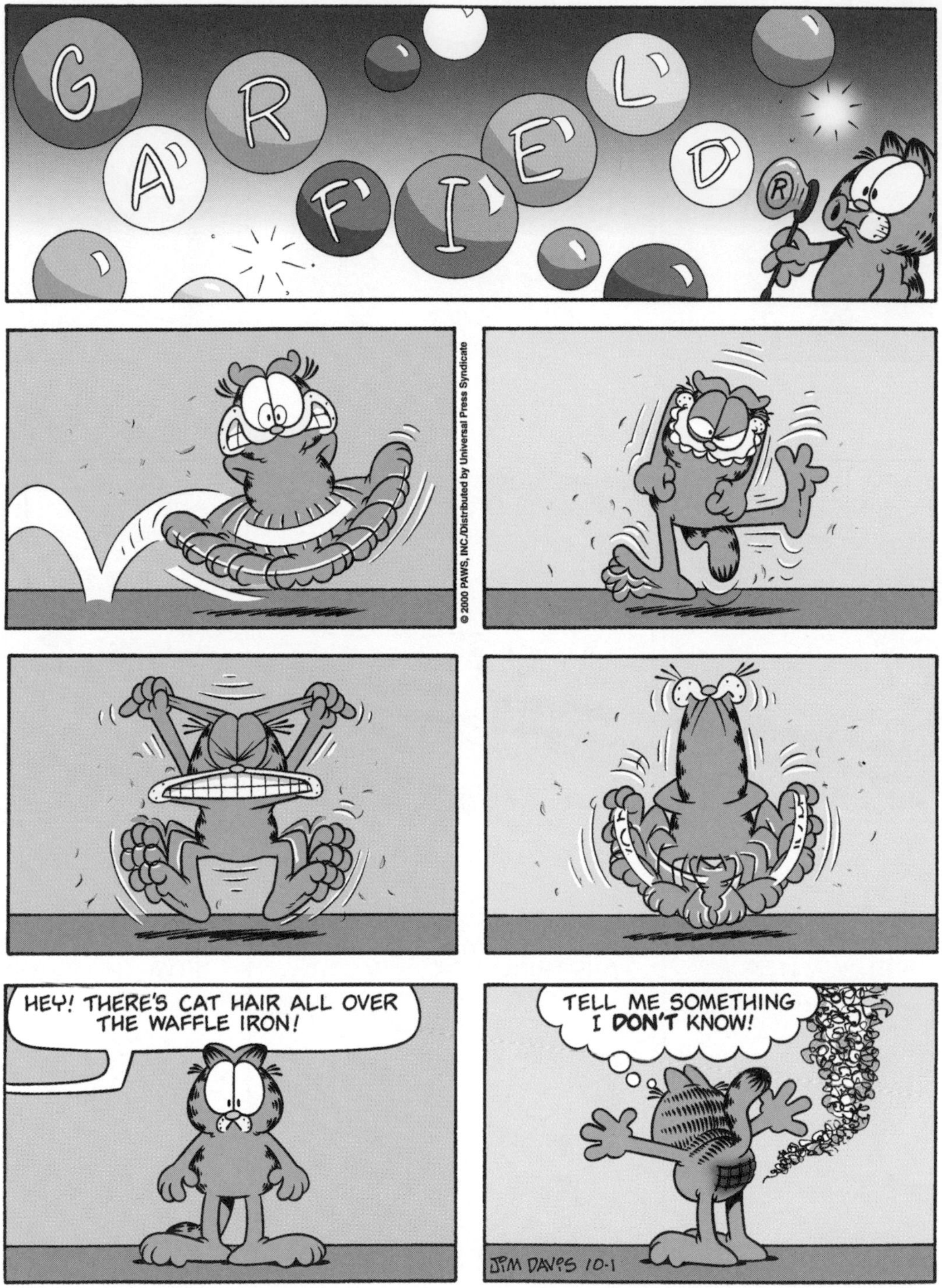
GARFIELD
®
© 2000 PAWS, INC./Distributed by Universal Press Syndicate
HEY! THERE'S CAT HAIR ALL OVER THE WAFFLE IRON!
TELL ME SOMETHING I **DON'T** KNOW!
JIM DAVIS 10-1

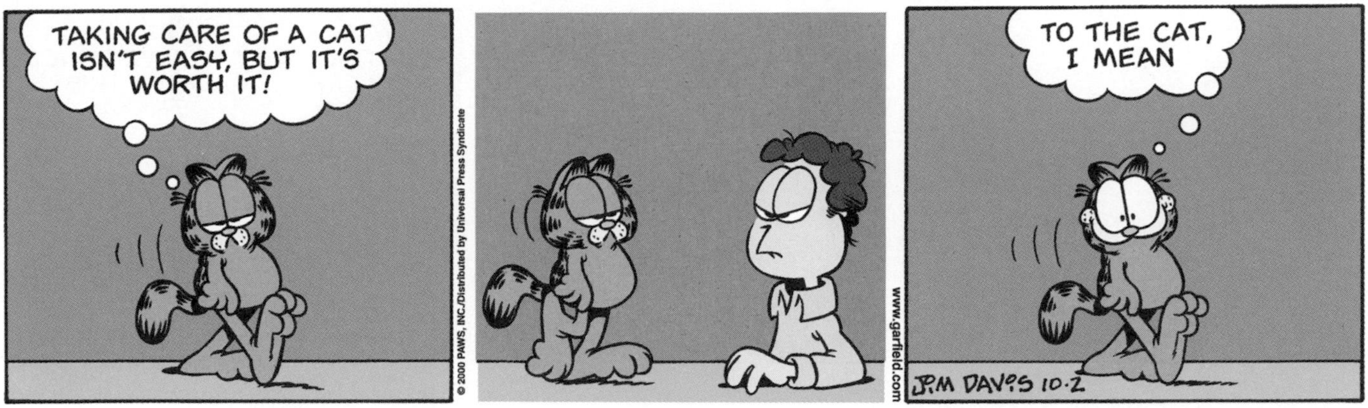
TAKING CARE OF A CAT ISN'T EASY, BUT IT'S WORTH IT!
© 2000 PAWS, INC./Distributed by Universal Press Syndicate
www.garfield.com
TO THE CAT, I MEAN
JIM DAVIS 10-2

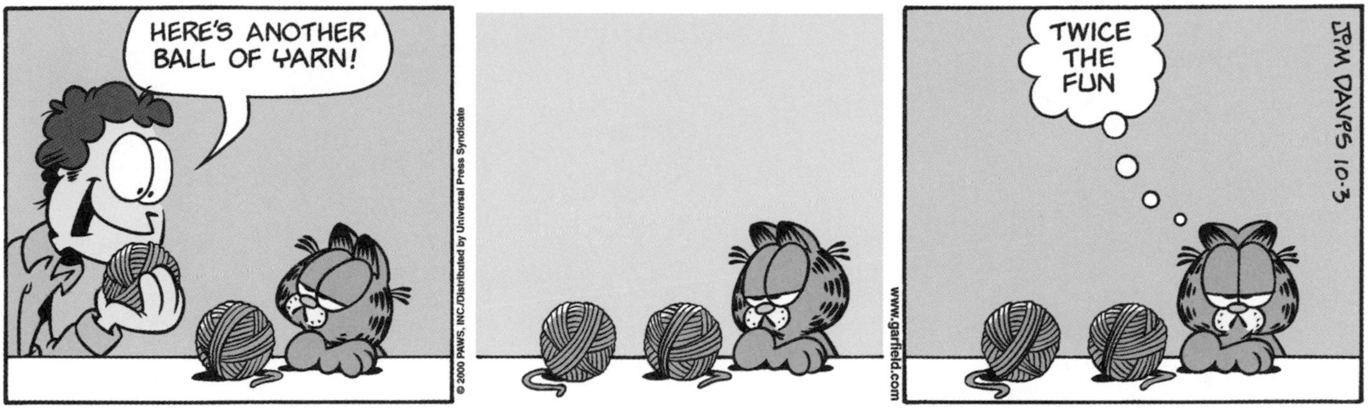
HERE'S ANOTHER BALL OF YARN!
© 2000 PAWS, INC./Distributed by Universal Press Syndicate
www.garfield.com
TWICE THE FUN
JIM DAVIS 10-3

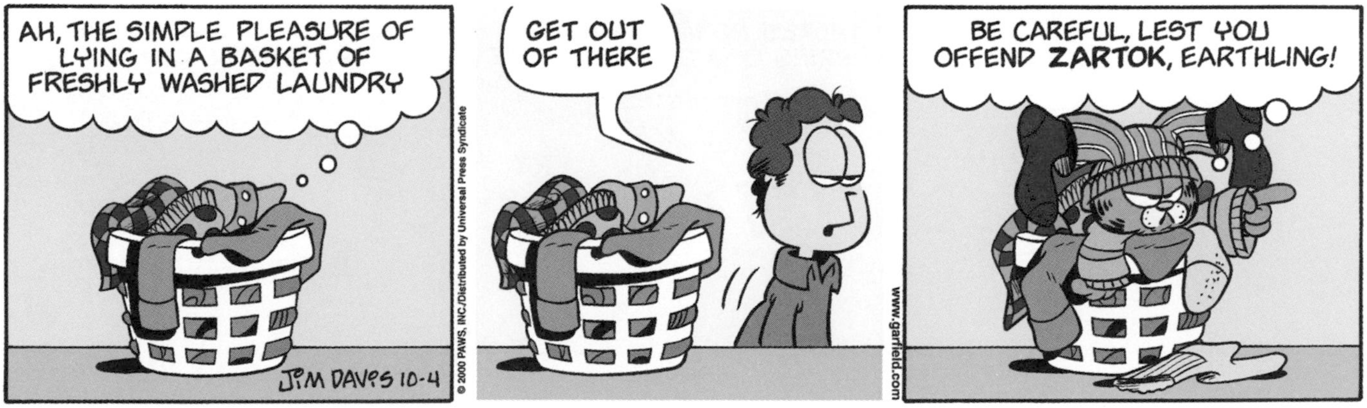
AH, THE SIMPLE PLEASURE OF LYING IN A BASKET OF FRESHLY WASHED LAUNDRY
JIM DAVIS 10-4
© 2000 PAWS, INC./Distributed by Universal Press Syndicate
GET OUT OF THERE
www.garfield.com
BE CAREFUL, LEST YOU OFFEND **ZARTOK**, EARTHLING!

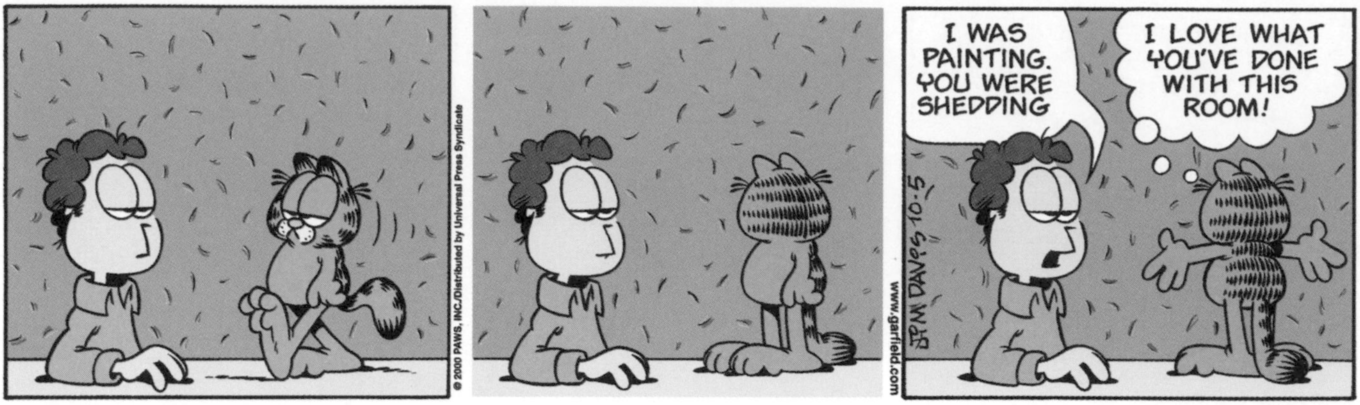
I WAS PAINTING. YOU WERE SHEDDING
I LOVE WHAT YOU'VE DONE WITH THIS ROOM!
© 2000 PAWS, INC./Distributed by Universal Press Syndicate
www.garfield.com
JIM DAVIS 10-5

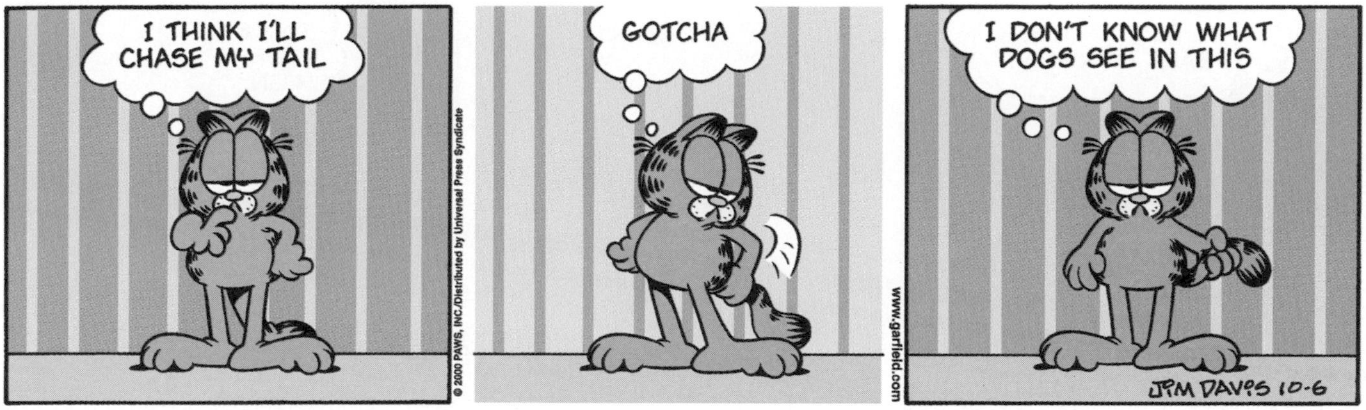
I THINK I'LL CHASE MY TAIL
GOTCHA
I DON'T KNOW WHAT DOGS SEE IN THIS
© 2000 PAWS, INC./Distributed by Universal Press Syndicate
www.garfield.com
JIM DAVIS 10-6

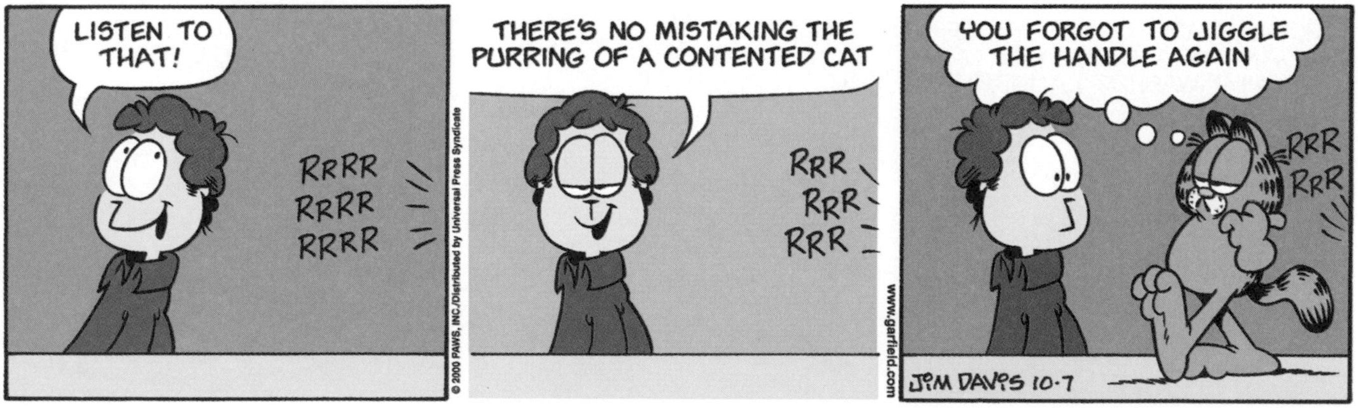
LISTEN TO THAT!
RRRR RRRR RRRR
THERE'S NO MISTAKING THE PURRING OF A CONTENTED CAT
RRR RRR RRR
YOU FORGOT TO JIGGLE THE HANDLE AGAIN
RRR RRR
© 2000 PAWS, INC./Distributed by Universal Press Syndicate
www.garfield.com
JIM DAVIS 10-7

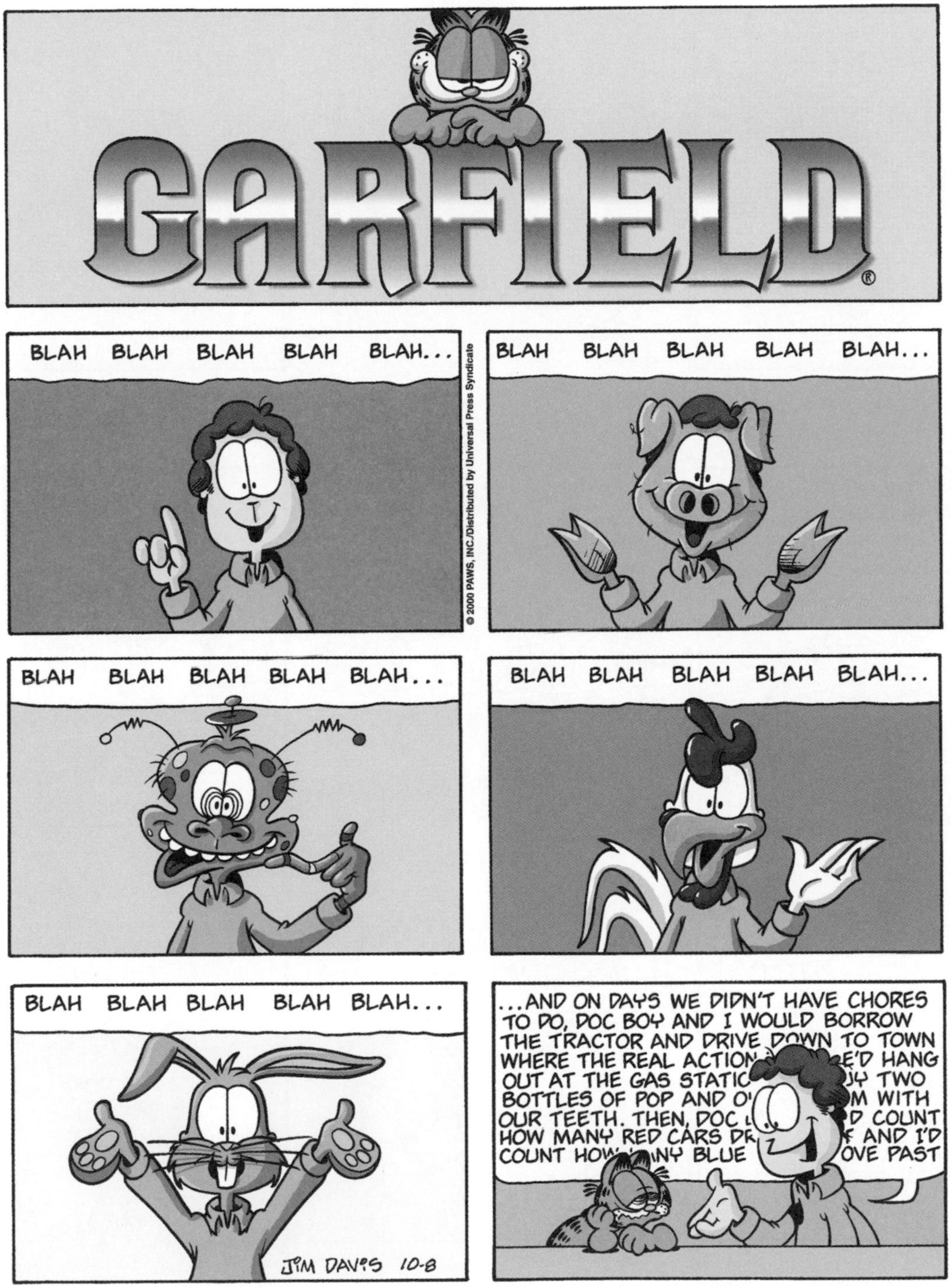
GARFIELD®
© 2000 PAWS, INC./Distributed by Universal Press Syndicate
BLAH BLAH BLAH BLAH BLAH...
BLAH BLAH BLAH BLAH BLAH...
BLAH BLAH BLAH BLAH BLAH...
BLAH BLAH BLAH BLAH BLAH...
BLAH BLAH BLAH BLAH BLAH...
JIM DAVIS 10-8

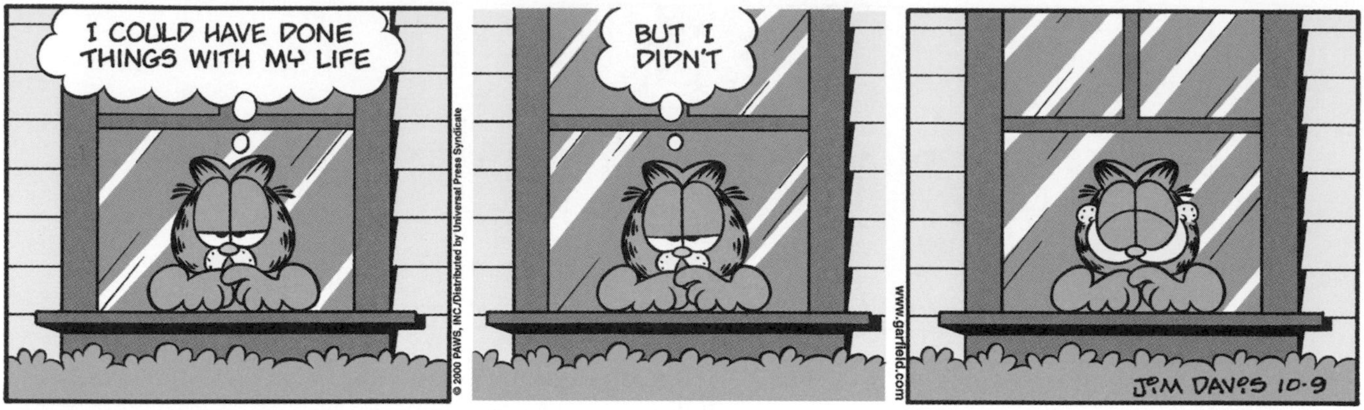
I COULD HAVE DONE THINGS WITH MY LIFE
BUT I DIDN'T
© 2000 PAWS, INC./Distributed by Universal Press Syndicate
www.garfield.com
JIM DAVIS 10-9

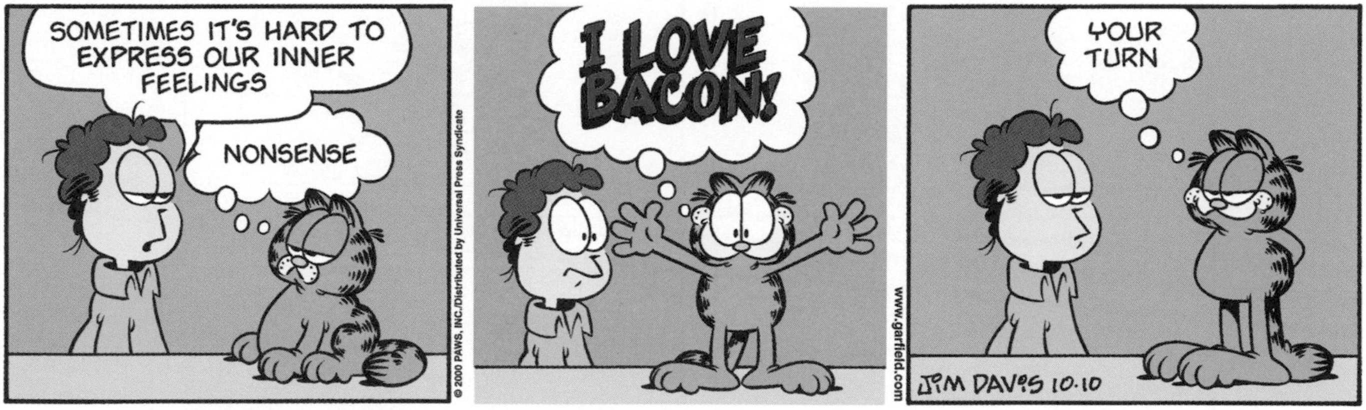
SOMETIMES IT'S HARD TO EXPRESS OUR INNER FEELINGS
NONSENSE
I LOVE BACON!
YOUR TURN
© 2000 PAWS, INC./Distributed by Universal Press Syndicate
www.garfield.com
JIM DAVIS 10.10

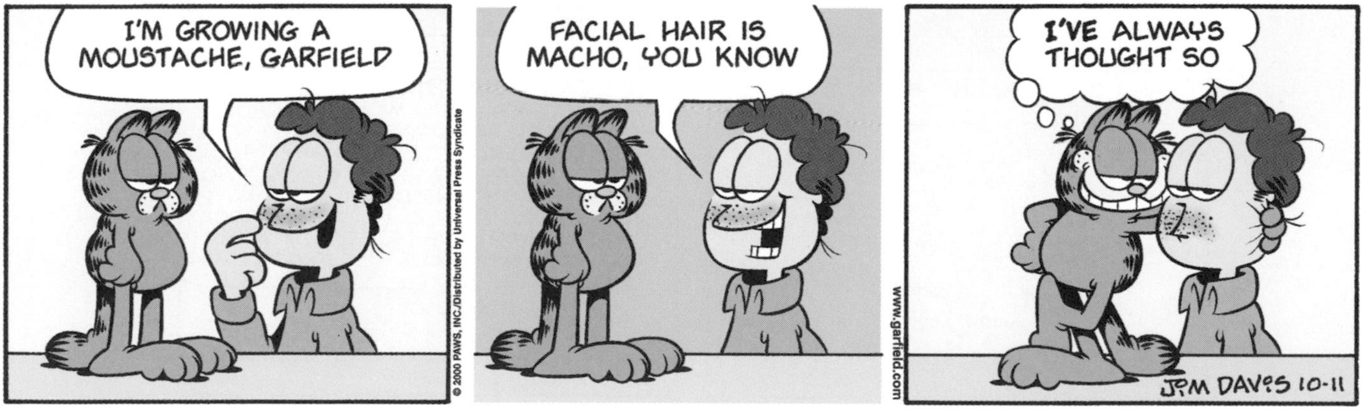
I'M GROWING A MOUSTACHE, GARFIELD
FACIAL HAIR IS MACHO, YOU KNOW
I'VE ALWAYS THOUGHT SO
© 2000 PAWS, INC./Distributed by Universal Press Syndicate
www.garfield.com
JIM DAVIS 10-11

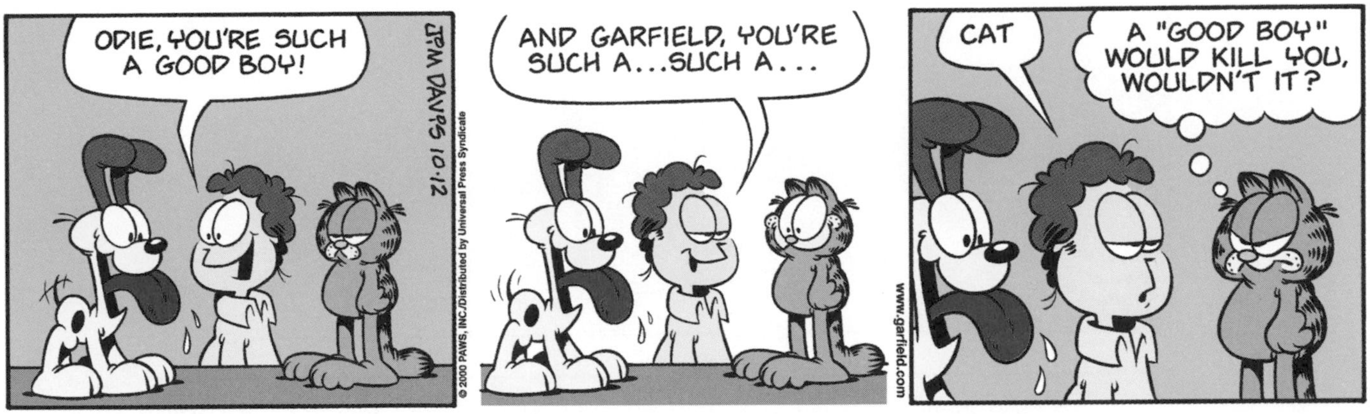
ODIE, YOU'RE SUCH A GOOD BOY!
JIM DAVIS 10-12
© 2000 PAWS, INC./Distributed by Universal Press Syndicate
AND GARFIELD, YOU'RE SUCH A...SUCH A...
www.garfield.com
CAT
A "GOOD BOY" WOULD KILL YOU, WOULDN'T IT?

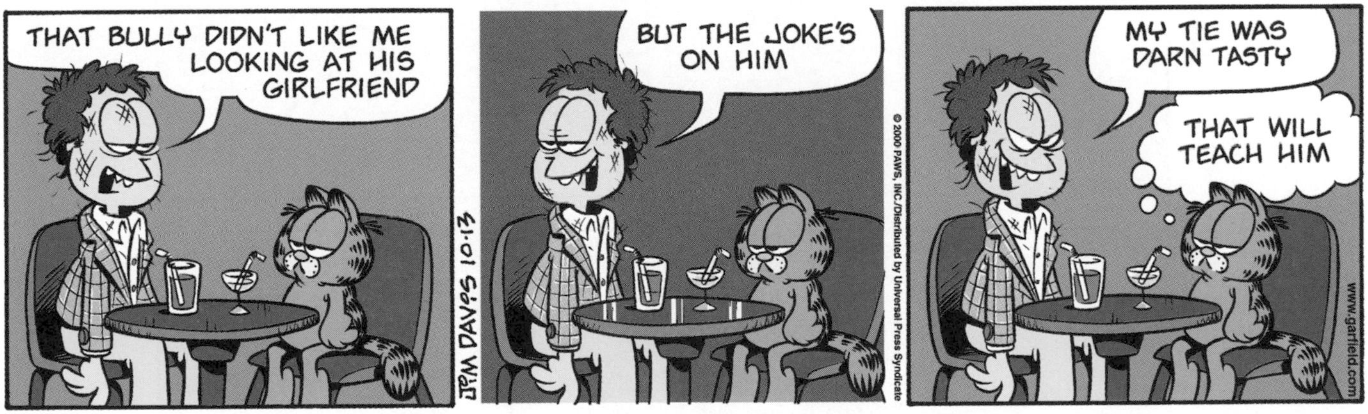
THAT BULLY DIDN'T LIKE ME LOOKING AT HIS GIRLFRIEND
JIM DAVIS 10-13
BUT THE JOKE'S ON HIM
© 2000 PAWS, INC./Distributed by Universal Press Syndicate
MY TIE WAS DARN TASTY
THAT WILL TEACH HIM
www.garfield.com

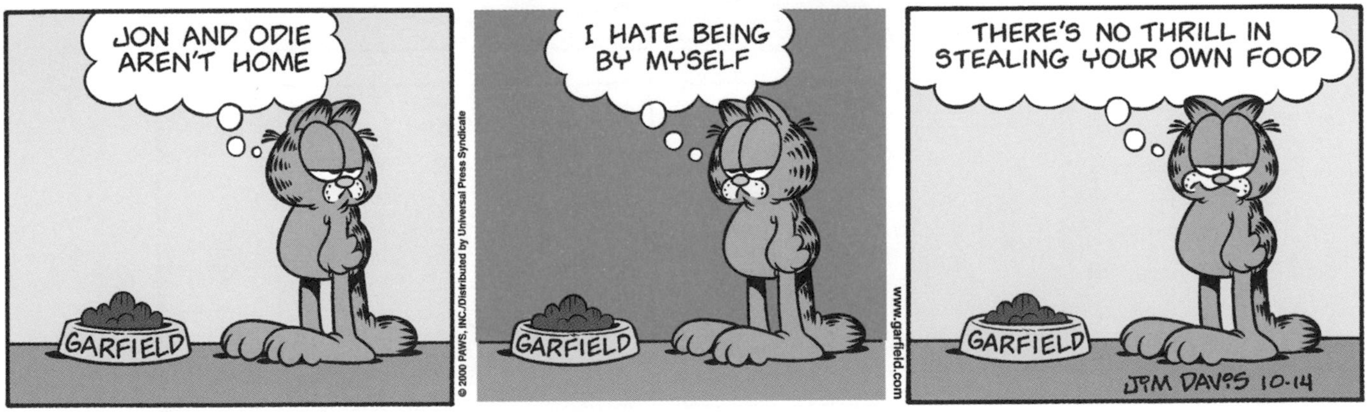
JON AND ODIE AREN'T HOME
GARFIELD
© 2000 PAWS, INC./Distributed by Universal Press Syndicate
I HATE BEING BY MYSELF
GARFIELD
www.garfield.com
THERE'S NO THRILL IN STEALING YOUR OWN FOOD
GARFIELD
JIM DAVIS 10-14

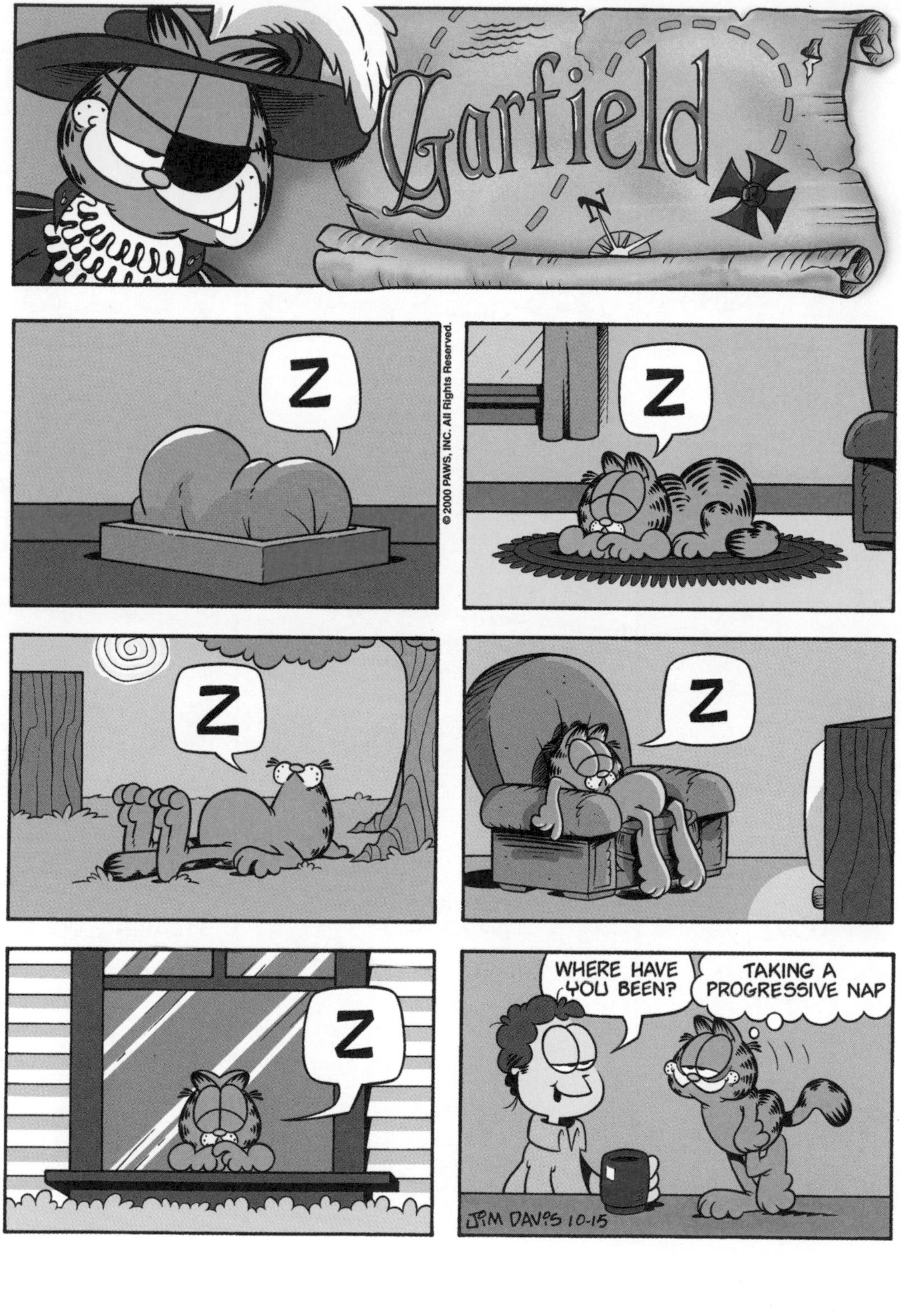
Garfield
N
© 2000 PAWS, INC. All Rights Reserved.
Z
Z
Z
Z
Z
WHERE HAVE YOU BEEN?
TAKING A PROGRESSIVE NAP
JIM DAVIS 10-15

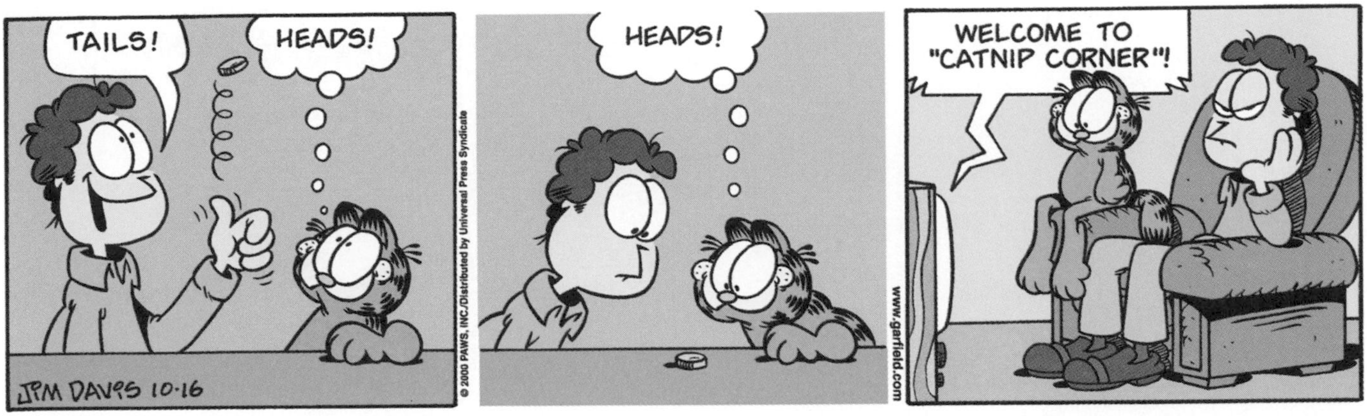
TAILS!
HEADS!
JIM DAVIS 10-16
© 2000 PAWS, INC./Distributed by Universal Press Syndicate
HEADS!
www.garfield.com
WELCOME TO "CATNIP CORNER"!

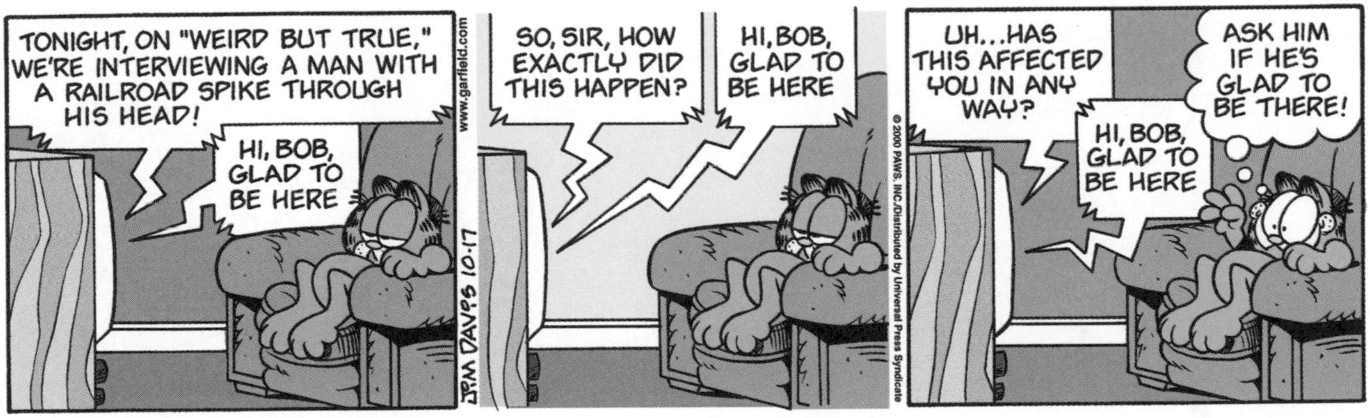
TONIGHT, ON "WEIRD BUT TRUE," WE'RE INTERVIEWING A MAN WITH A RAILROAD SPIKE THROUGH HIS HEAD!
HI, BOB, GLAD TO BE HERE
www.garfield.com
JIM DAVIS 10-17
SO, SIR, HOW EXACTLY DID THIS HAPPEN?
HI, BOB, GLAD TO BE HERE
© 2000 PAWS, INC./Distributed by Universal Press Syndicate
UH...HAS THIS AFFECTED YOU IN ANY WAY?
HI, BOB, GLAD TO BE HERE
ASK HIM IF HE'S GLAD TO BE THERE!

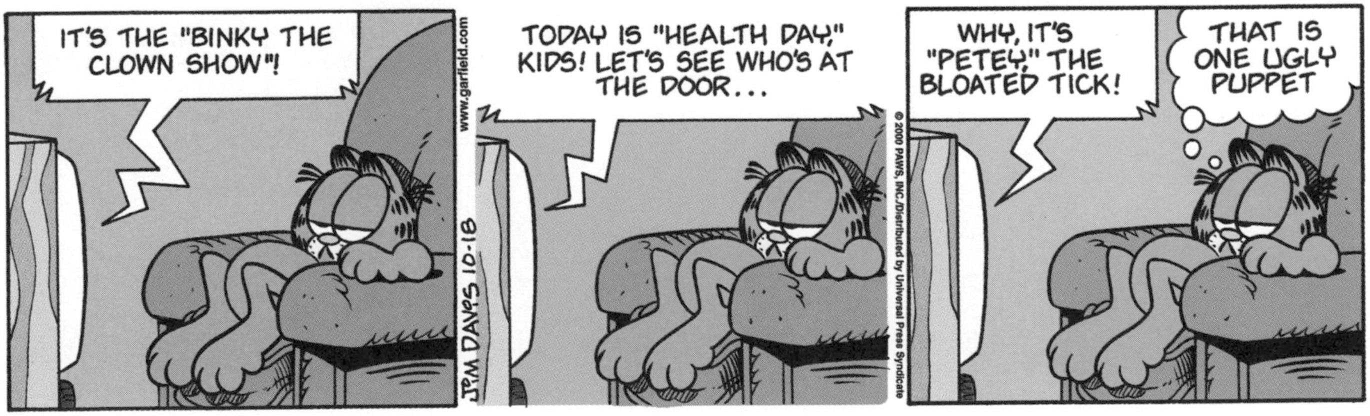
IT'S THE "BINKY THE CLOWN SHOW"!
www.garfield.com
JIM DAVIS 10-18
TODAY IS "HEALTH DAY," KIDS! LET'S SEE WHO'S AT THE DOOR...
© 2000 PAWS, INC./Distributed by Universal Press Syndicate
WHY, IT'S "PETEY," THE BLOATED TICK!
THAT IS ONE UGLY PUPPET

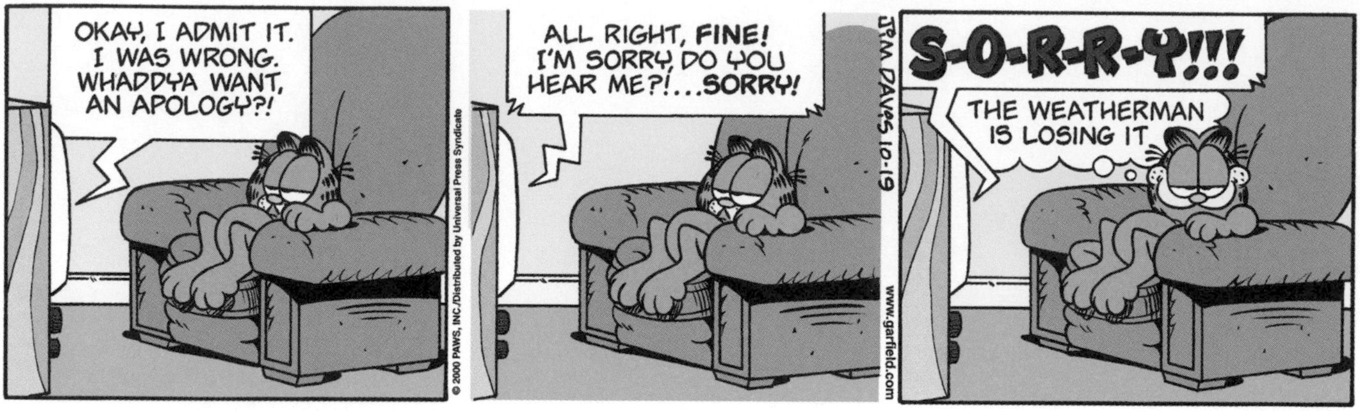
OKAY, I ADMIT IT. I WAS WRONG. WHADDYA WANT, AN APOLOGY?!
ALL RIGHT, FINE! I'M SORRY, DO YOU HEAR ME?!...SORRY!
JIM DAVIS 10-19
© 2000 PAWS, INC./Distributed by Universal Press Syndicate
www.garfield.com
S-O-R-R-Y!!!
THE WEATHERMAN IS LOSING IT

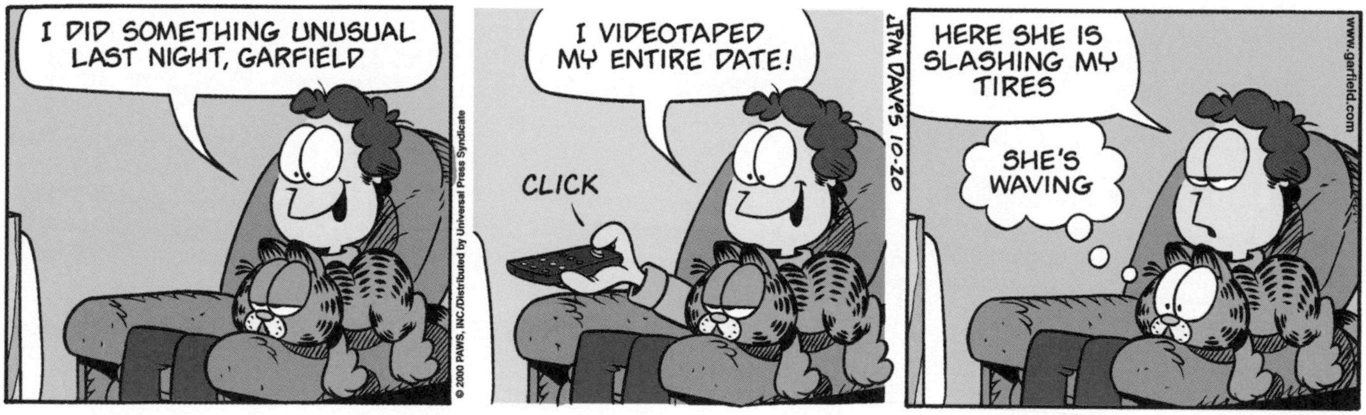
I DID SOMETHING UNUSUAL LAST NIGHT, GARFIELD
© 2000 PAWS, INC./Distributed by Universal Press Syndicate
I VIDEOTAPED MY ENTIRE DATE!
CLICK
JIM DAVIS 10-20
HERE SHE IS SLASHING MY TIRES
SHE'S WAVING
www.garfield.com

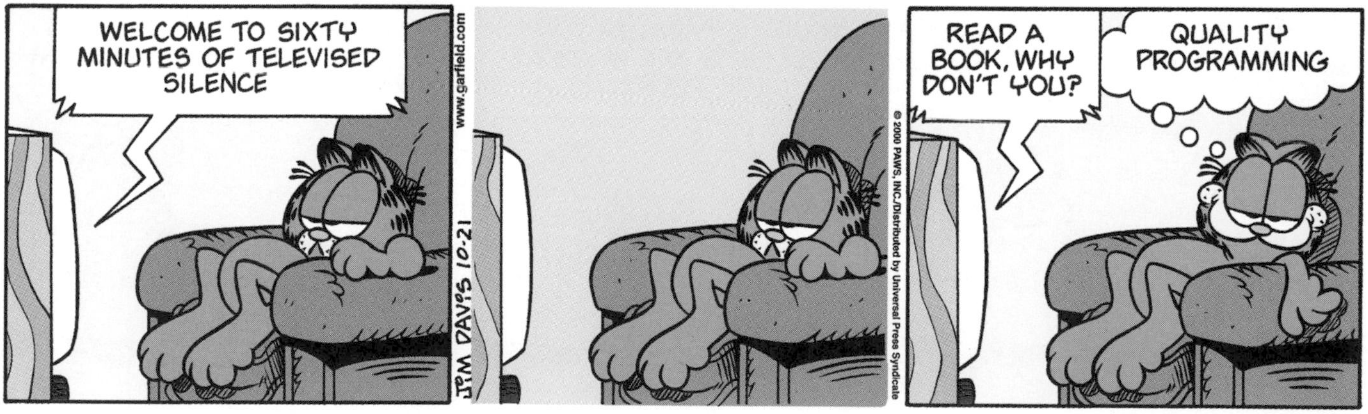
WELCOME TO SIXTY MINUTES OF TELEVISED SILENCE
JIM DAVIS 10-21
www.garfield.com
© 2000 PAWS, INC./Distributed by Universal Press Syndicate
READ A BOOK, WHY DON'T YOU?
QUALITY PROGRAMMING

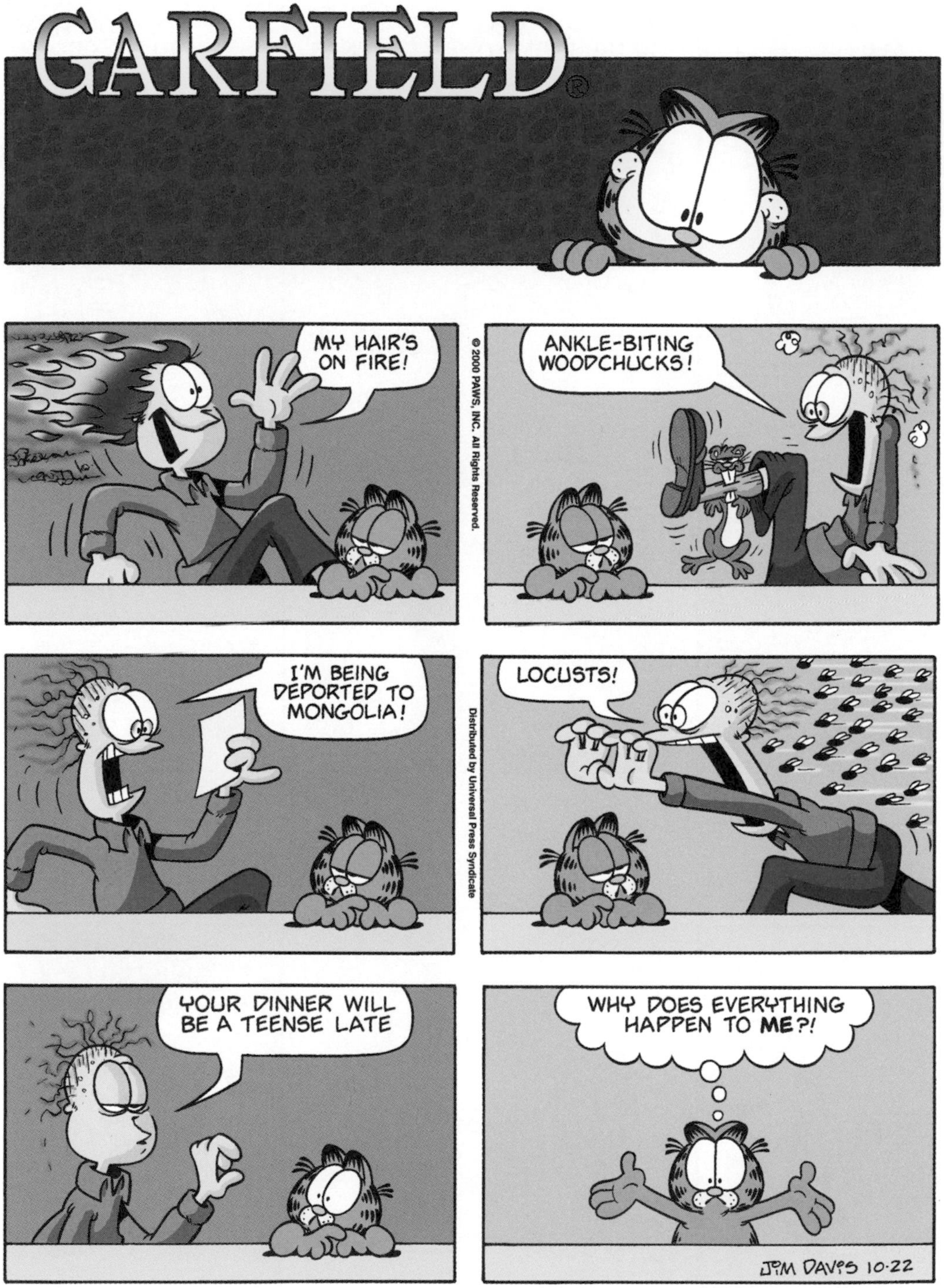
GARFIELD®
MY HAIR'S ON FIRE!
© 2000 PAWS, INC. All Rights Reserved.
ANKLE-BITING WOODCHUCKS!
I'M BEING DEPORTED TO MONGOLIA!
Distributed by Universal Press Syndicate
LOCUSTS!
YOUR DINNER WILL BE A TEENSE LATE
WHY DOES EVERYTHING HAPPEN TO **ME**?!
JIM DAVIS 10-22

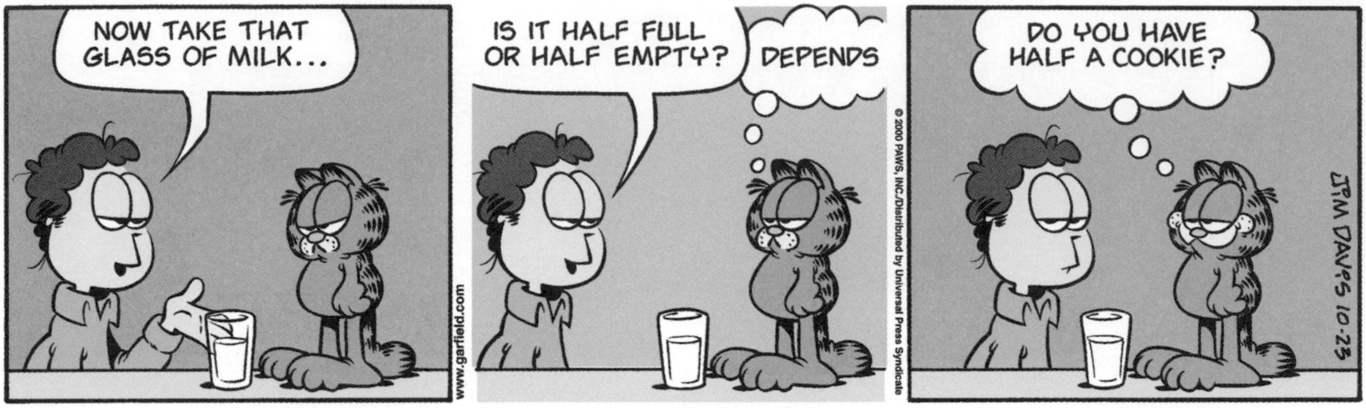
NOW TAKE THAT GLASS OF MILK...
IS IT HALF FULL OR HALF EMPTY?
DEPENDS
DO YOU HAVE HALF A COOKIE?
JIM DAVIS 10-23
www.garfield.com
© 2000 PAWS, INC./Distributed by Universal Press Syndicate

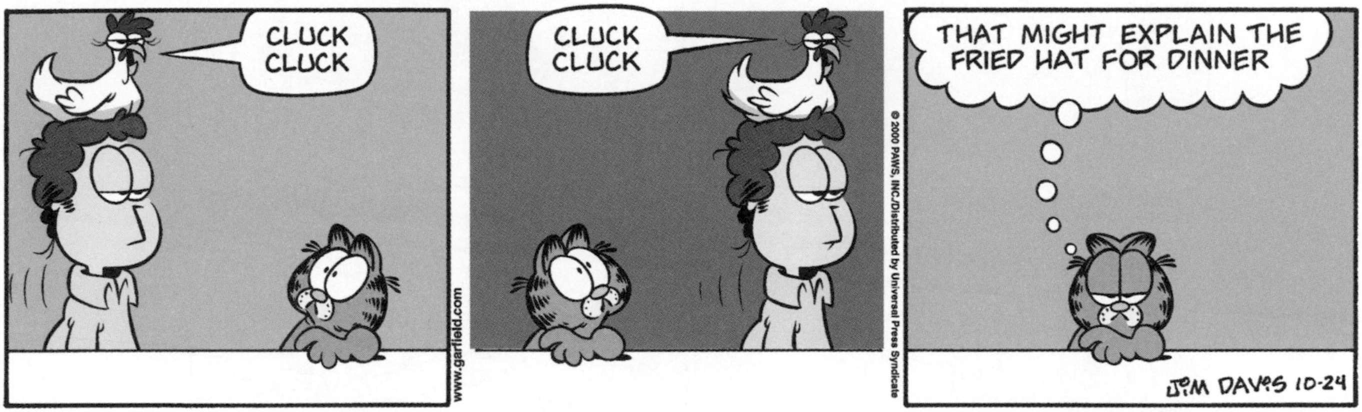
CLUCK CLUCK
CLUCK CLUCK
THAT MIGHT EXPLAIN THE FRIED HAT FOR DINNER
JIM DAVIS 10-24
www.garfield.com
© 2000 PAWS, INC./Distributed by Universal Press Syndicate

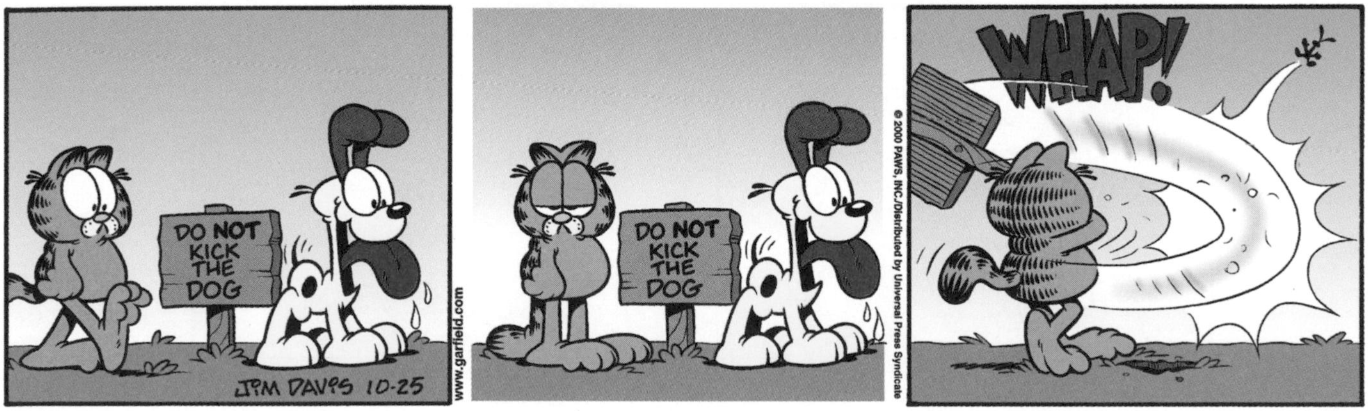
DO NOT KICK THE DOG
DO NOT KICK THE DOG
WHAP!
JIM DAVIS 10-25
www.garfield.com
© 2000 PAWS, INC./Distributed by Universal Press Syndicate

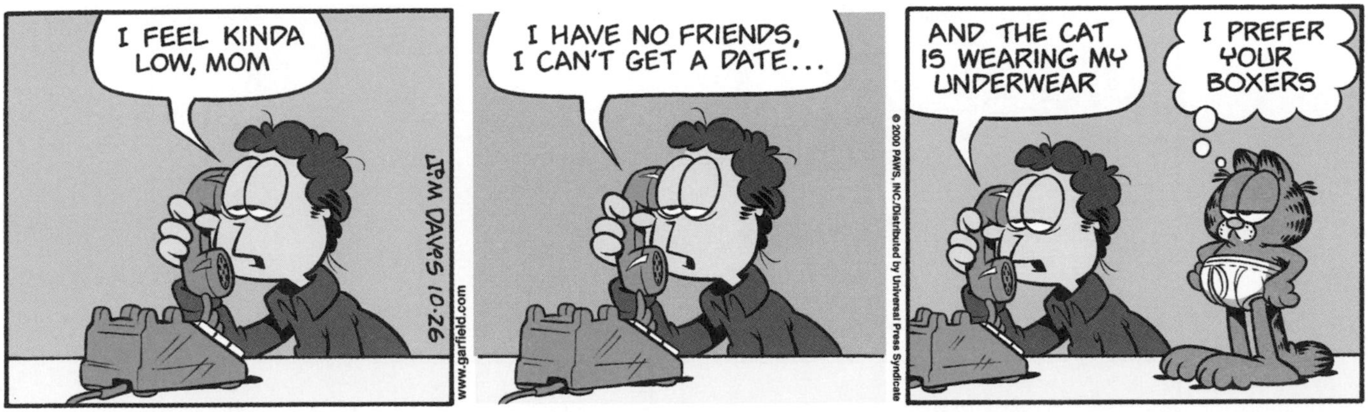
I FEEL KINDA LOW, MOM
JIM DAVIS 10-26
www.garfield.com
I HAVE NO FRIENDS, I CAN'T GET A DATE...
© 2000 PAWS, INC./Distributed by Universal Press Syndicate
AND THE CAT IS WEARING MY UNDERWEAR
I PREFER YOUR BOXERS

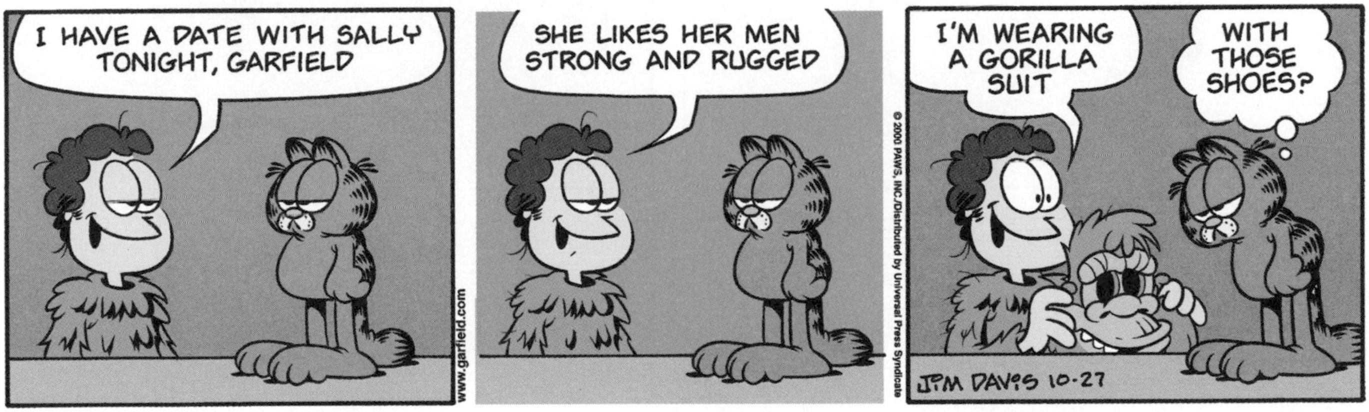
I HAVE A DATE WITH SALLY TONIGHT, GARFIELD
www.garfield.com
SHE LIKES HER MEN STRONG AND RUGGED
© 2000 PAWS, INC./Distributed by Universal Press Syndicate
I'M WEARING A GORILLA SUIT
WITH THOSE SHOES?
JIM DAVIS 10-27

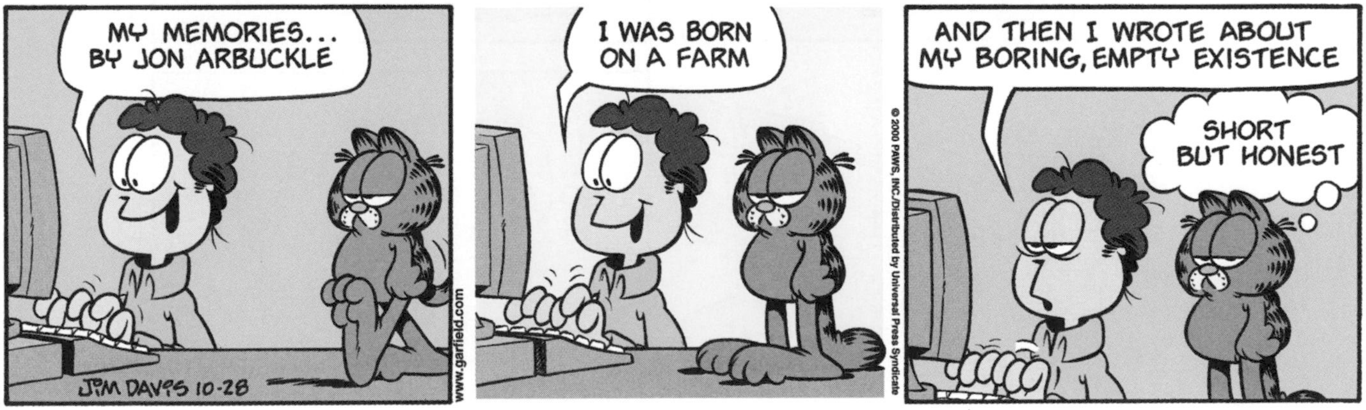
MY MEMORIES... BY JON ARBUCKLE
JIM DAVIS 10-28
www.garfield.com
I WAS BORN ON A FARM
© 2000 PAWS, INC./Distributed by Universal Press Syndicate
AND THEN I WROTE ABOUT MY BORING, EMPTY EXISTENCE
SHORT BUT HONEST

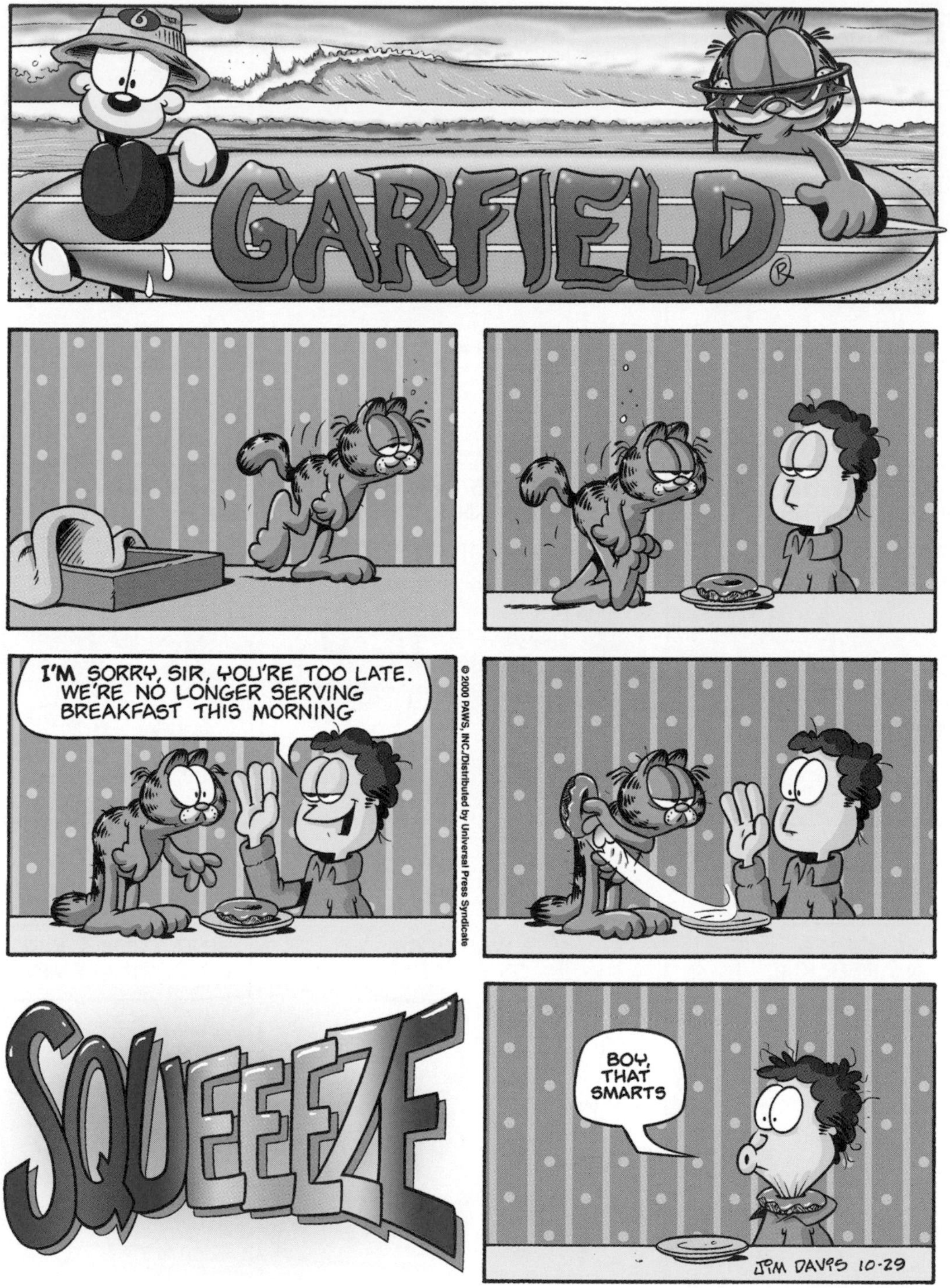

GARFIELD®
I'M SORRY, SIR, YOU'RE TOO LATE. WE'RE NO LONGER SERVING BREAKFAST THIS MORNING
SQUEEEEZE
BOY, THAT SMARTS
JIM DAVIS 10-29

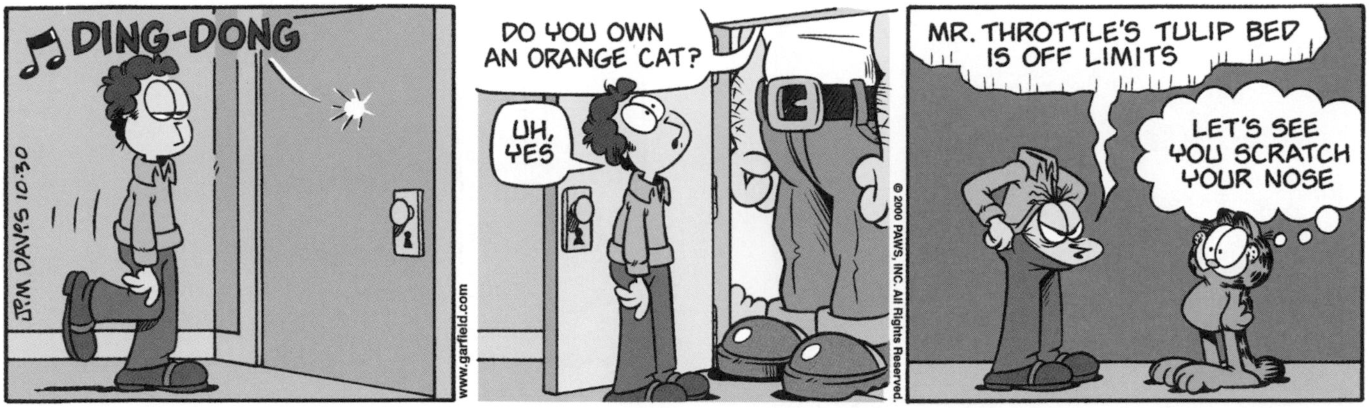
DING-DONG
JPM DAVPS 10·30
www.garfield.com
DO YOU OWN AN ORANGE CAT?
UH, YES
© 2000 PAWS, INC. All Rights Reserved.
MR. THROTTLE'S TULIP BED IS OFF LIMITS
LET'S SEE YOU SCRATCH YOUR NOSE

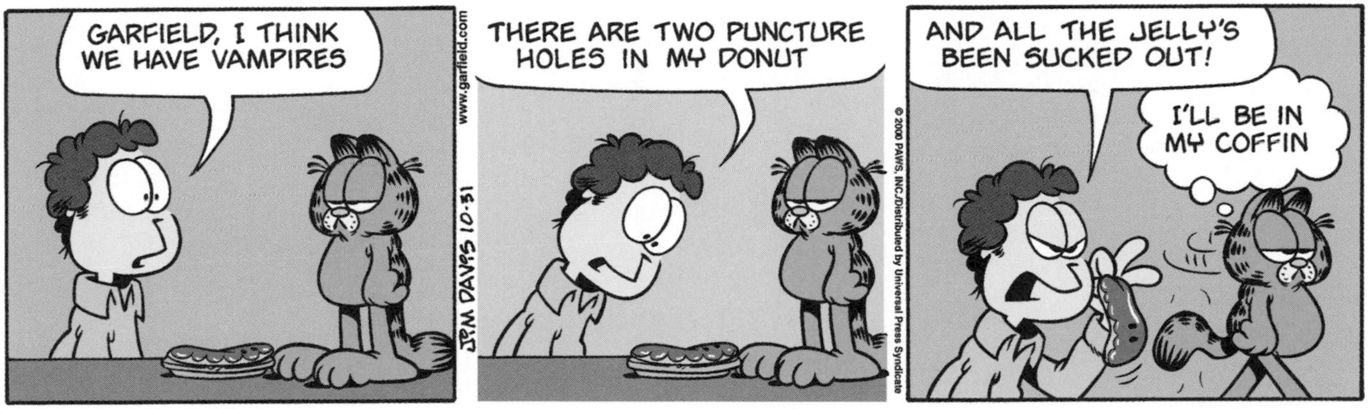
GARFIELD, I THINK WE HAVE VAMPIRES
www.garfield.com
JPM DAVPS 10·31
THERE ARE TWO PUNCTURE HOLES IN MY DONUT
© 2000 PAWS, INC./Distributed by Universal Press Syndicate
AND ALL THE JELLY'S BEEN SUCKED OUT!
I'LL BE IN MY COFFIN

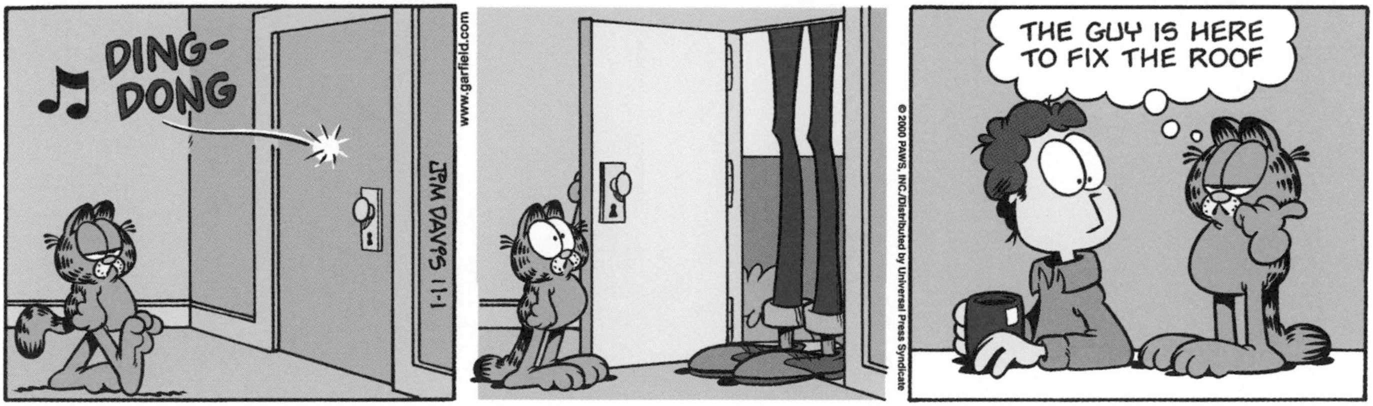
DING-DONG
JPM DAVPS 11·1
www.garfield.com
© 2000 PAWS, INC./Distributed by Universal Press Syndicate
THE GUY IS HERE TO FIX THE ROOF

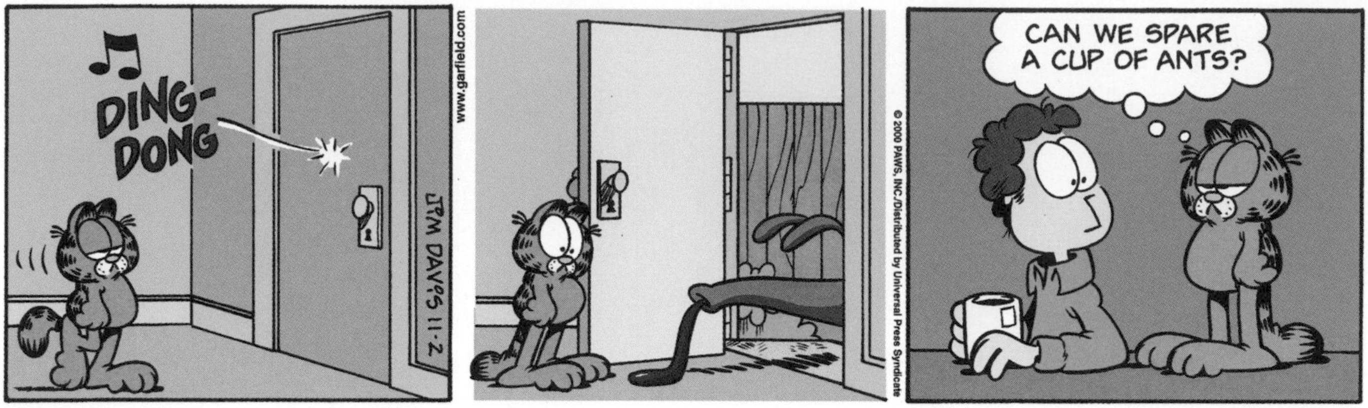
DING-DONG
www.garfield.com
JIM DAVIS 11-2
© 2000 PAWS, INC./Distributed by Universal Press Syndicate
CAN WE SPARE A CUP OF ANTS?

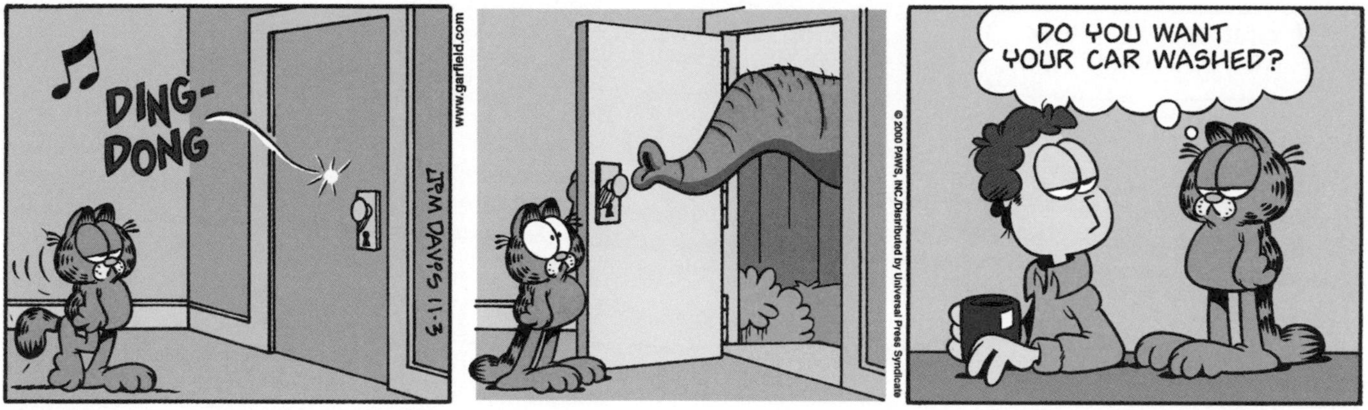
DING-DONG
www.garfield.com
JIM DAVIS 11-3
© 2000 PAWS, INC./Distributed by Universal Press Syndicate
DO YOU WANT YOUR CAR WASHED?

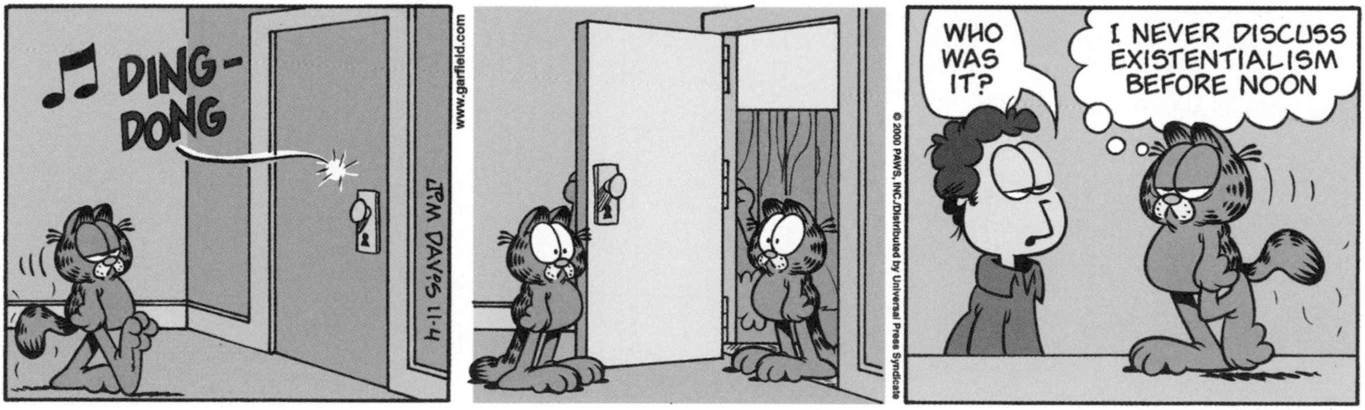
DING-DONG
www.garfield.com
JIM DAVIS 11-4
© 2000 PAWS, INC./Distributed by Universal Press Syndicate
WHO WAS IT?
I NEVER DISCUSS EXISTENTIALISM BEFORE NOON

TAKE THE GARFIELD TRIVIA CHALLENGE!

1 According to Garfield, there's nothing worse than a clever _____.

A. Canine
B. Arachnid
C. Armadillo
D. Insurance adjuster

2 What was the really, really hairy spider doing in Jon's bathroom?

A. Waxing its legs
B. Using Jon's comb
C. Unwinding with a hot bath
D. Using up all Jon's styling gel

3 In high school, Jon was voted Most Likely to ____.

A. Become the Tri-County Polka King
B. Date a kitchen appliance
C. Become a figure skater
D. Bring his mother to the prom

4 What did Garfield, Odie and Jon win in the TV special "Garfield Goes Hollywood"?

A. A year's supply of jumbo paper clips
B. A boat
C. A "certified pre-owned" electric toothbrush
D. An evening with Ed McMahon

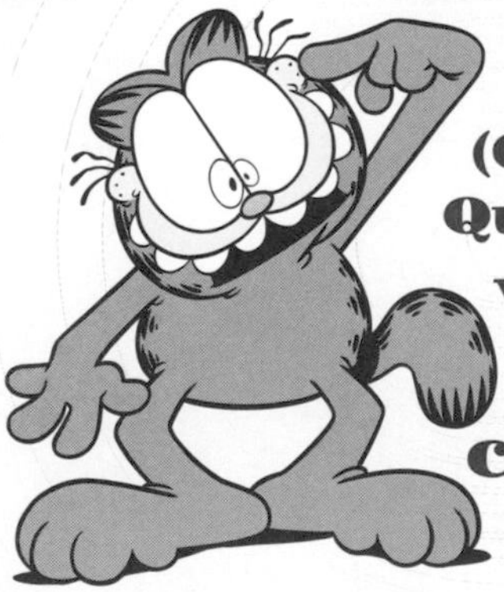

Test your GQ (Garfield Quotient) with our brain-crunching quiz!

5 In the Garfield Christmas TV special, what gift did Garfield give Grandma?

A. A hairball shaped like a reindeer
B. Old love letters from her husband
C. Cash
D. An autographed photo of Wilford Brimley

6 What did Garfield have tattooed on his chest?

A. "Born to eat bacon"
B. "My owner's a dork"
C. "Caution: Wide Load"
D. "USDA Choice"

7 What does Jon do on the first day of spring?

A. Dress up as a bunny and hop around the living room
B. Dress up as a flower and say, "Hello, Mister Springtime!"
C. Dress up as one of Gladys Knight's Pips
D. Dress up as a lawn sprinkler and spit on the backyard

8 When on the farm, what game do Jon and Doc Boy play?

A. Hide the Heifer
B. Touch the Udder
C. Whack the Hoe
D. Grease the Goose

ANSWERS:
1. B 2. B 3. B 4. B
5. B 6. B 7. B 8. B

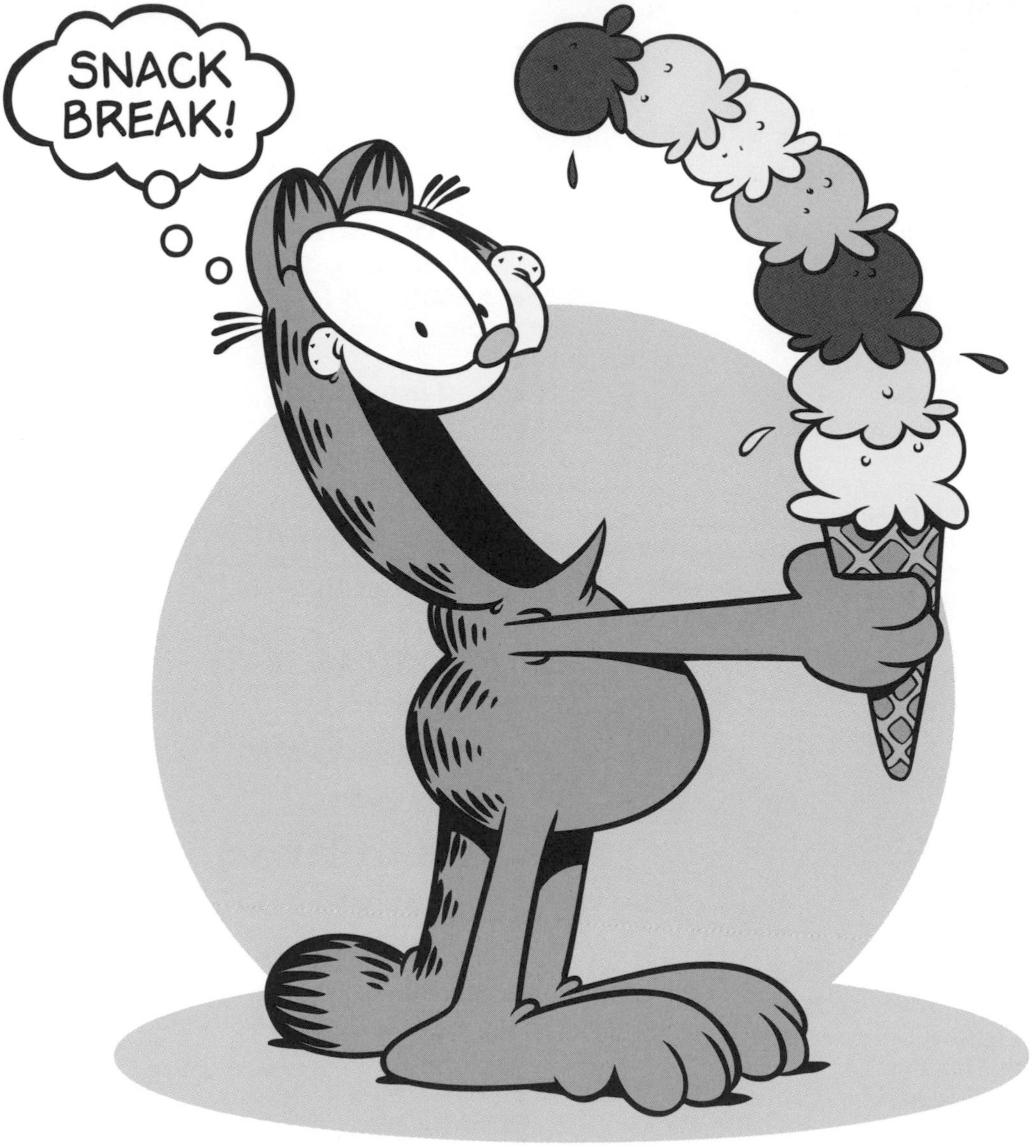
SNACK BREAK!

Garfield Eats Crow

BY JIM DAVIS

Ballantine Books • **New York**

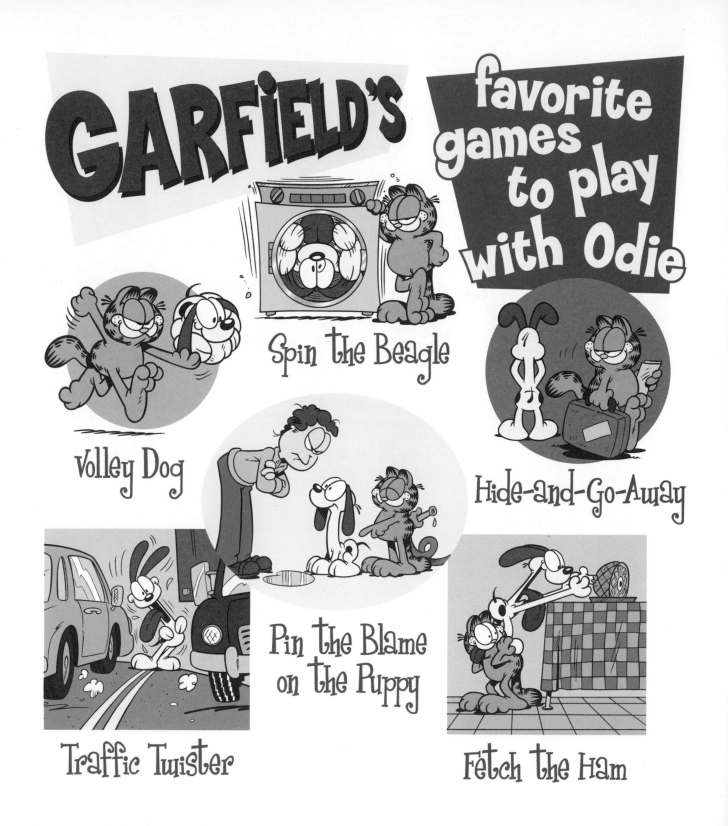

GARFIELD'S favorite games to play with Odie

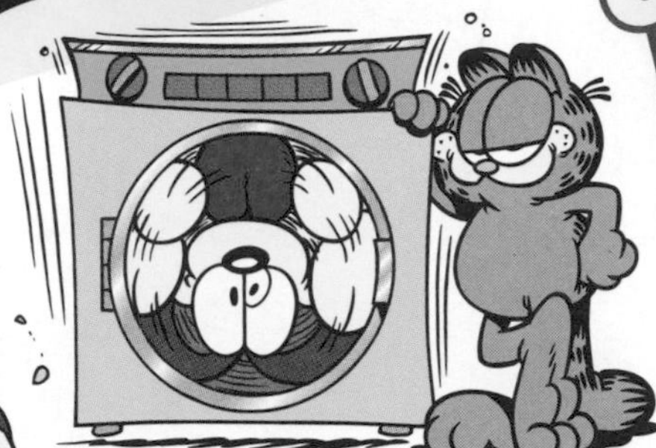

Spin the Beagle

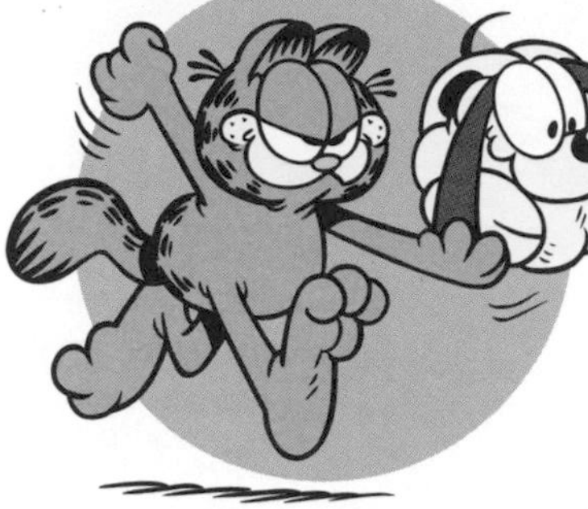

Volley Dog

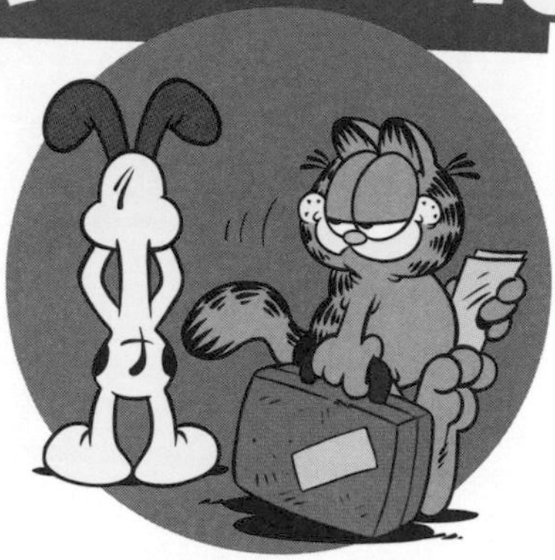

Hide-and-Go-Away

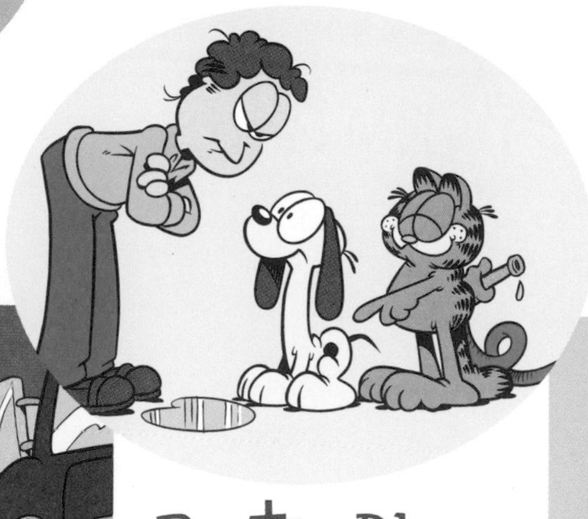

Pin the Blame on the Puppy

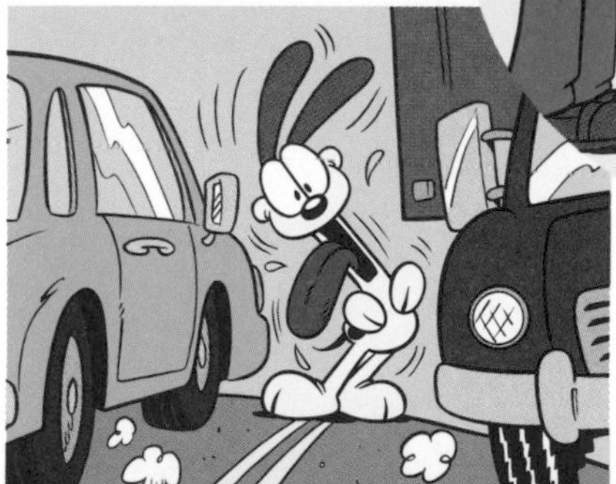

Traffic Twister

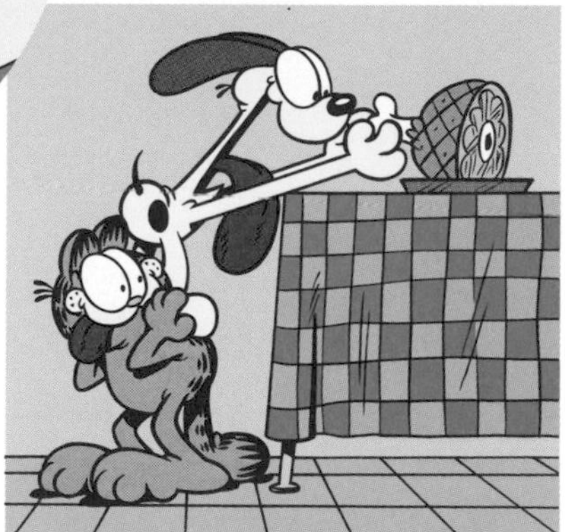

Fetch the Ham

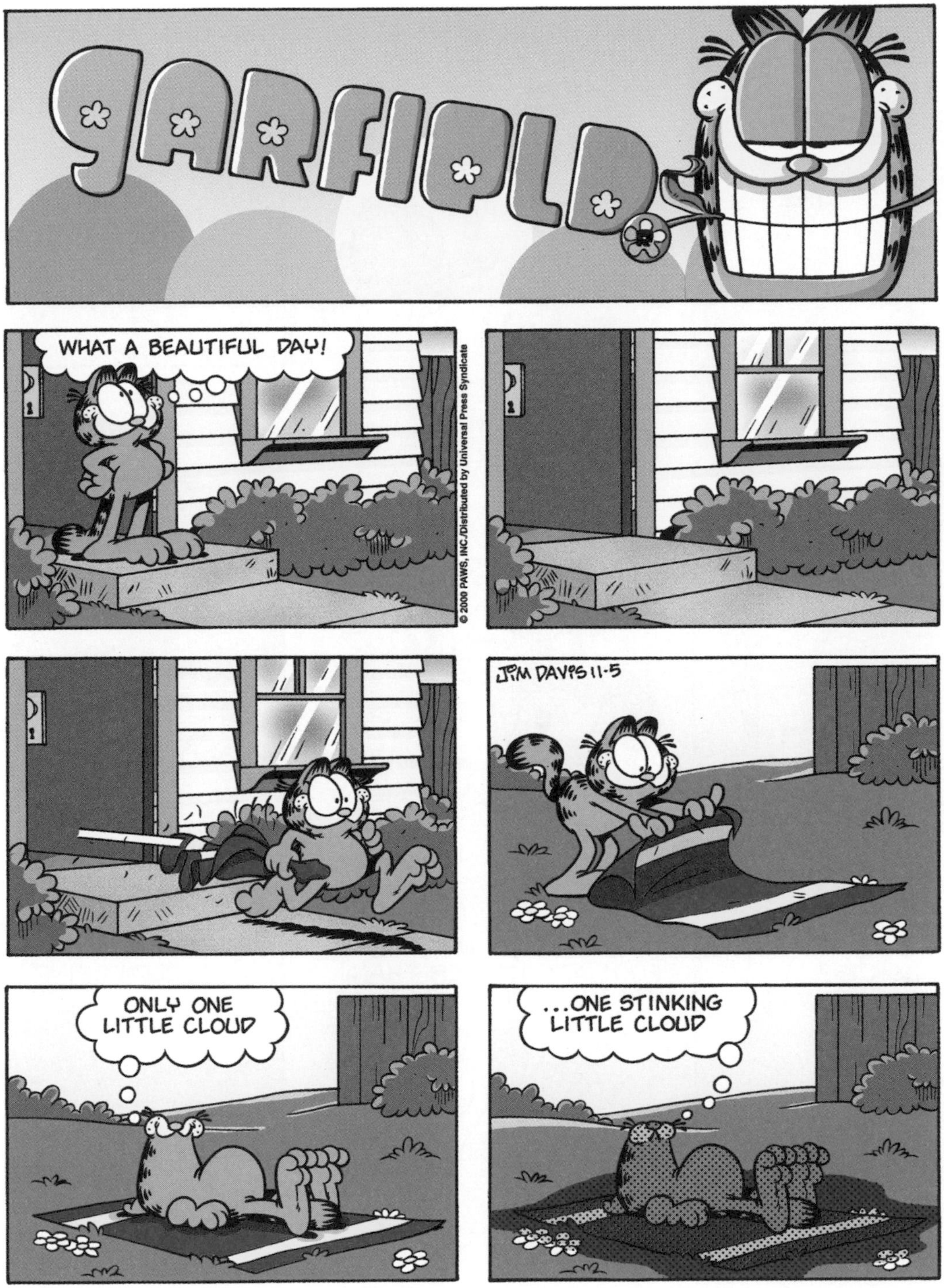
GARFIELD
WHAT A BEAUTIFUL DAY!
© 2000 PAWS, INC./Distributed by Universal Press Syndicate
JIM DAVIS 11-5
ONLY ONE LITTLE CLOUD
...ONE STINKING LITTLE CLOUD

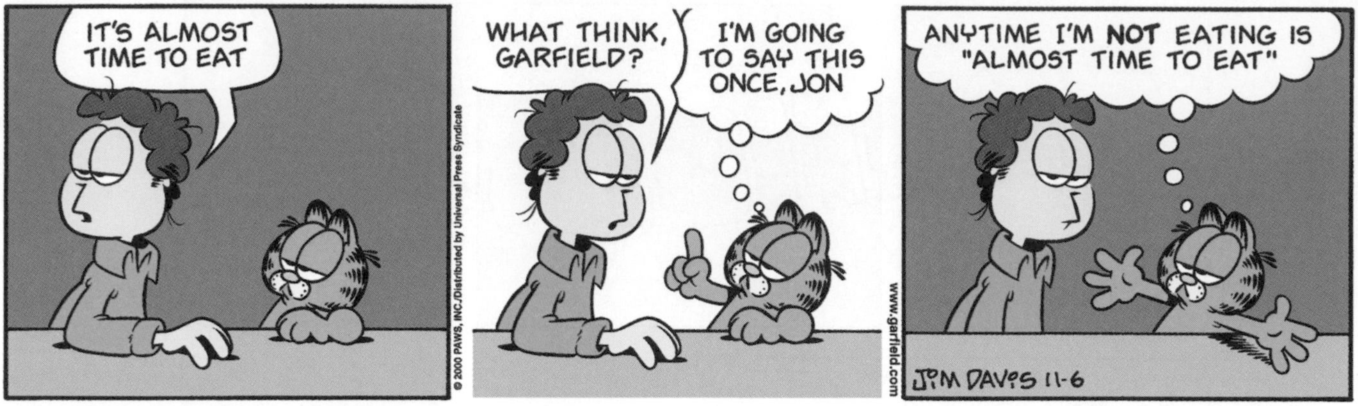
IT'S ALMOST TIME TO EAT
WHAT THINK, GARFIELD?
I'M GOING TO SAY THIS ONCE, JON
ANYTIME I'M **NOT** EATING IS "ALMOST TIME TO EAT"
© 2000 PAWS, INC./Distributed by Universal Press Syndicate
www.garfield.com
JIM DAVIS 11-6

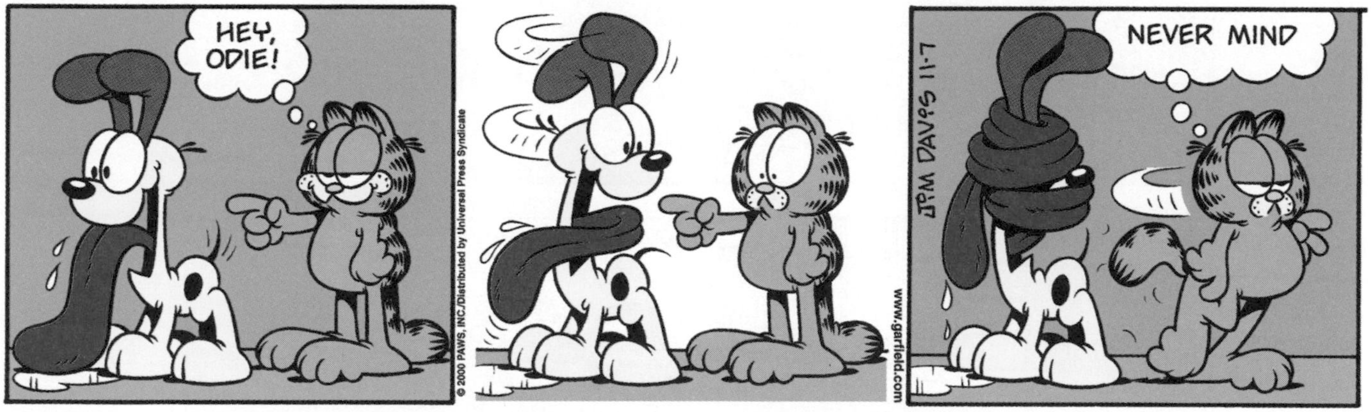
HEY, ODIE!
NEVER MIND
© 2000 PAWS, INC./Distributed by Universal Press Syndicate
www.garfield.com
JIM DAVIS 11-7

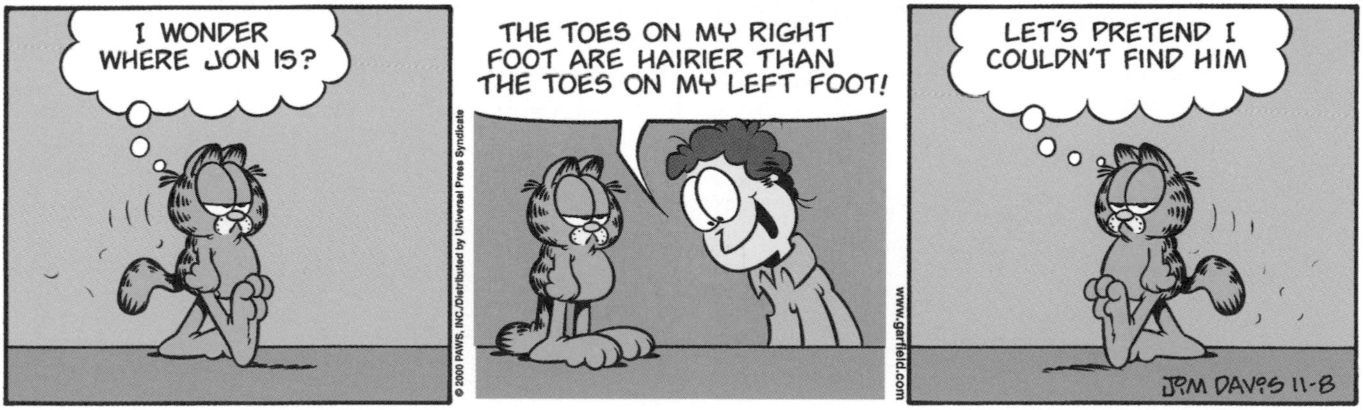
I WONDER WHERE JON IS?
THE TOES ON MY RIGHT FOOT ARE HAIRIER THAN THE TOES ON MY LEFT FOOT!
LET'S PRETEND I COULDN'T FIND HIM
© 2000 PAWS, INC./Distributed by Universal Press Syndicate
www.garfield.com
JIM DAVIS 11-8

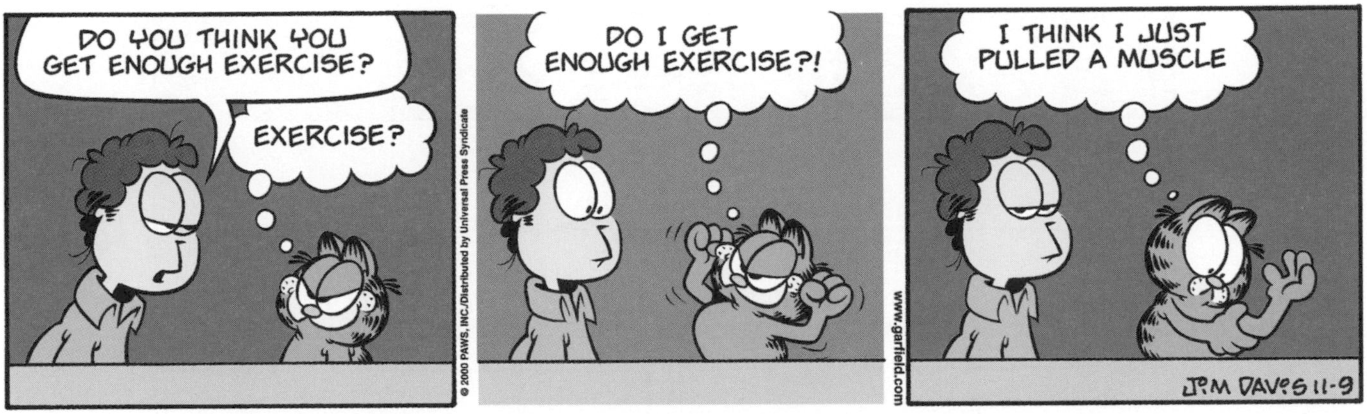
DO YOU THINK YOU GET ENOUGH EXERCISE?
EXERCISE?
DO I GET ENOUGH EXERCISE?!
I THINK I JUST PULLED A MUSCLE
JIM DAVIS 11-9
© 2000 PAWS, INC./Distributed by Universal Press Syndicate
www.garfield.com

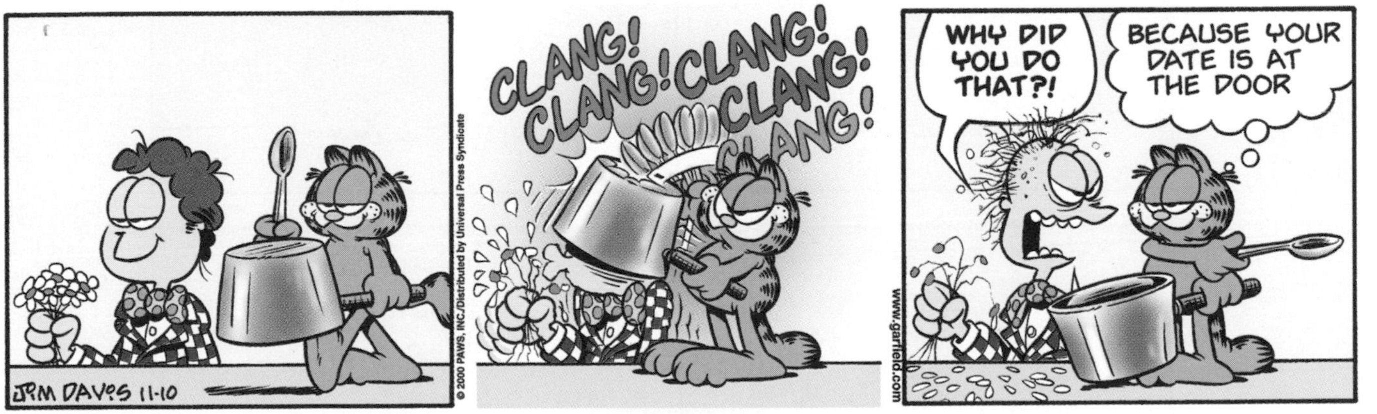
JIM DAVIS 11-10
CLANG! CLANG! CLANG! CLANG! CLANG! CLANG!
WHY DID YOU DO THAT?!
BECAUSE YOUR DATE IS AT THE DOOR
© 2000 PAWS, INC./Distributed by Universal Press Syndicate
www.garfield.com

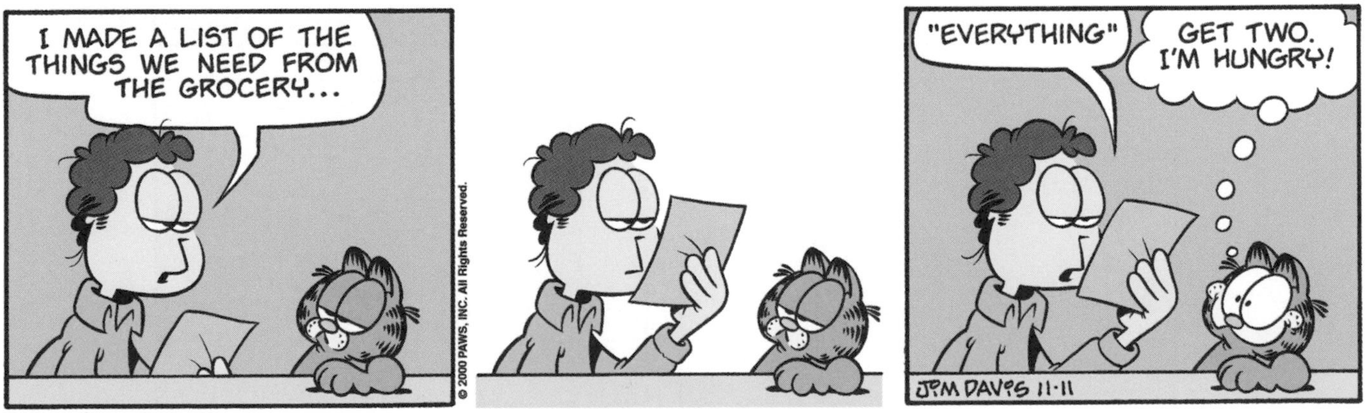
I MADE A LIST OF THE THINGS WE NEED FROM THE GROCERY...
"EVERYTHING"
GET TWO. I'M HUNGRY!
JIM DAVIS 11-11
© 2000 PAWS, INC. All Rights Reserved.

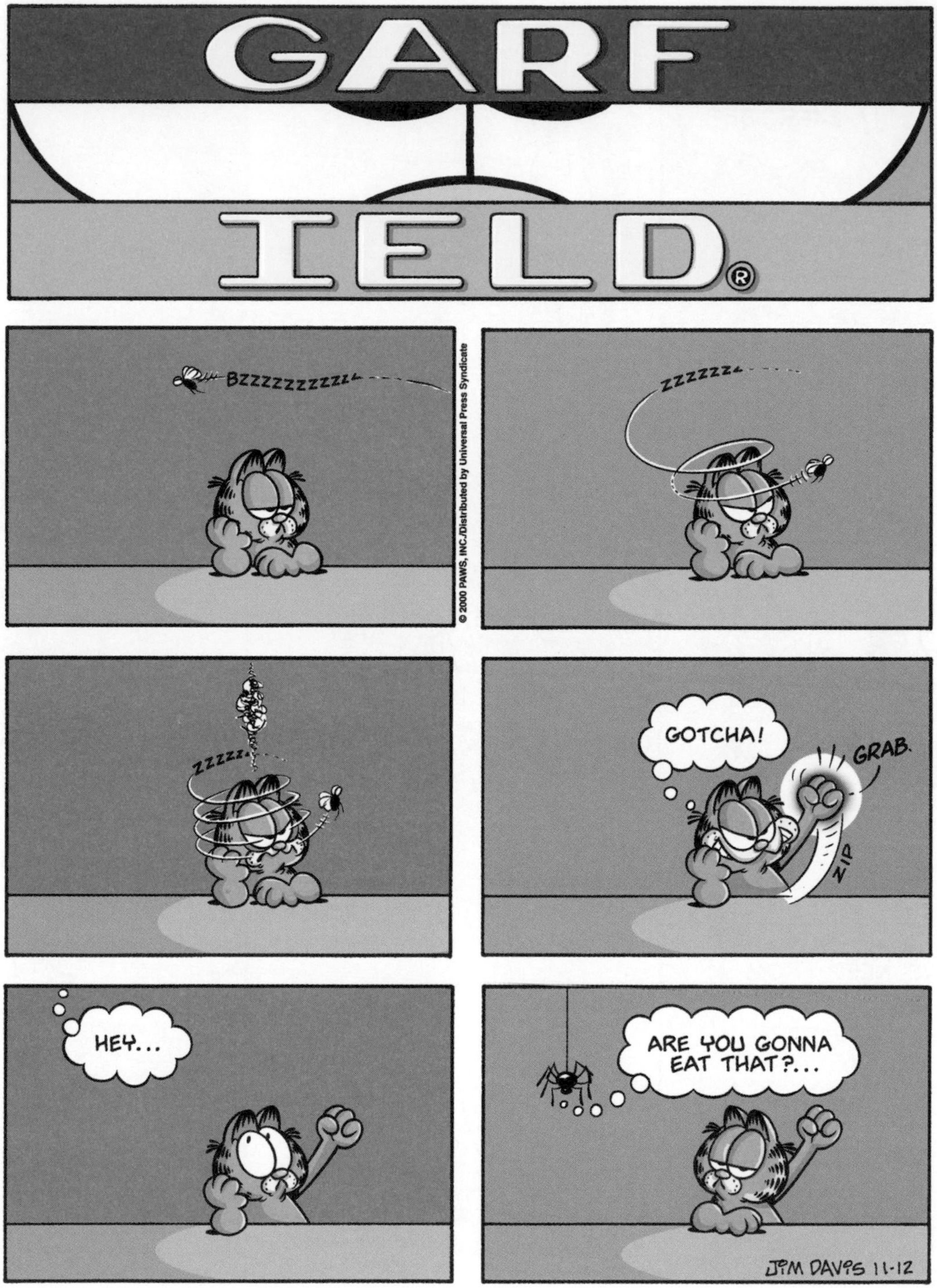
GARFIELD®
BZZZZZZZZZZZ
© 2000 PAWS, INC./Distributed by Universal Press Syndicate
ZZZZZZ
ZZZZZ
GOTCHA!
GRAB
ZIP
HEY...
ARE YOU GONNA EAT THAT?...
JIM DAVIS 11-12

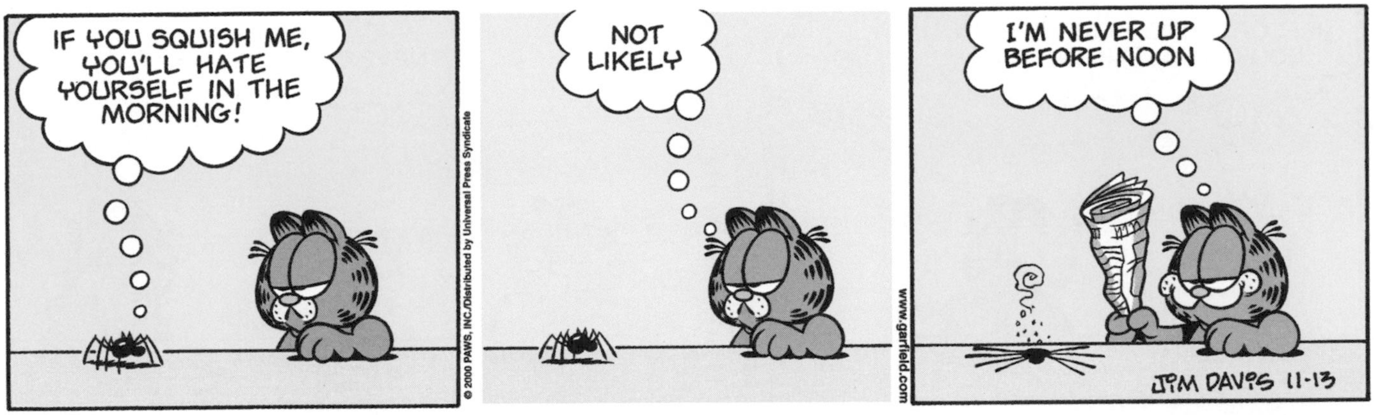
IF YOU SQUISH ME, YOU'LL HATE YOURSELF IN THE MORNING!
© 2000 PAWS, INC./Distributed by Universal Press Syndicate
NOT LIKELY
www.garfield.com
I'M NEVER UP BEFORE NOON
JIM DAVIS 11-13

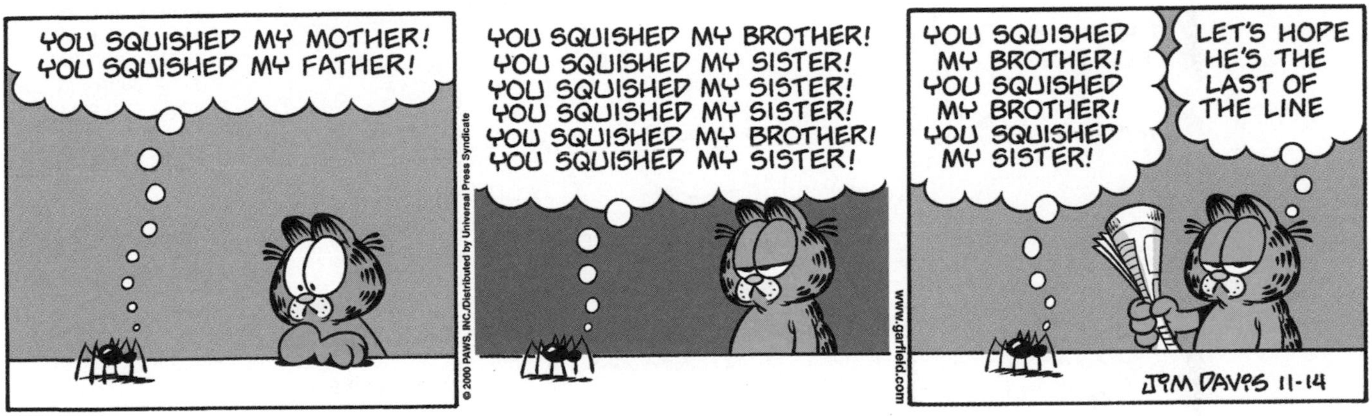
YOU SQUISHED MY MOTHER! YOU SQUISHED MY FATHER!
© 2000 PAWS, INC./Distributed by Universal Press Syndicate
YOU SQUISHED MY BROTHER! YOU SQUISHED MY SISTER! YOU SQUISHED MY SISTER! YOU SQUISHED MY SISTER! YOU SQUISHED MY BROTHER! YOU SQUISHED MY SISTER!
www.garfield.com
YOU SQUISHED MY BROTHER! YOU SQUISHED MY BROTHER! YOU SQUISHED MY SISTER!
LET'S HOPE HE'S THE LAST OF THE LINE
JIM DAVIS 11-14

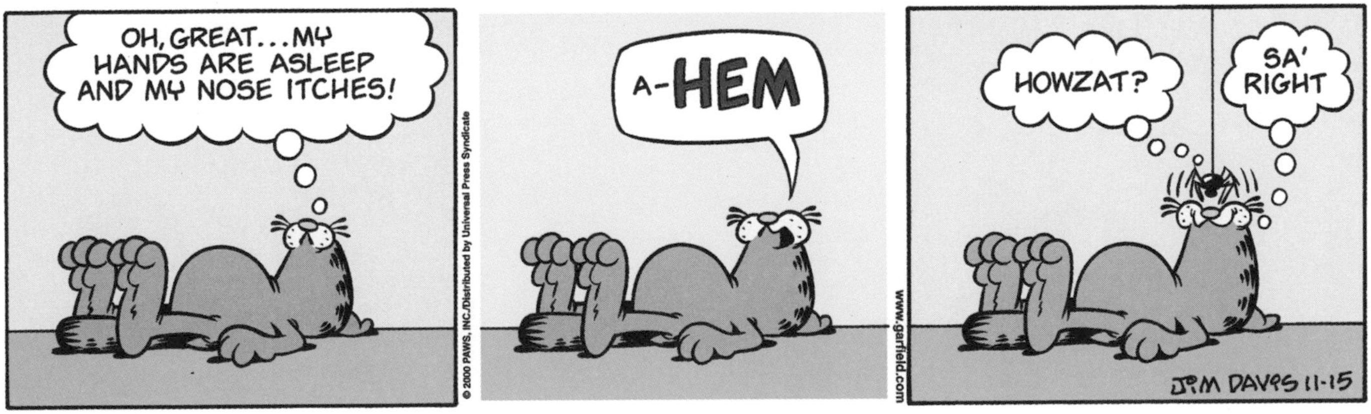
OH, GREAT...MY HANDS ARE ASLEEP AND MY NOSE ITCHES!
© 2000 PAWS, INC./Distributed by Universal Press Syndicate
A-HEM
www.garfield.com
HOWZAT?
SA' RIGHT
JIM DAVIS 11-15

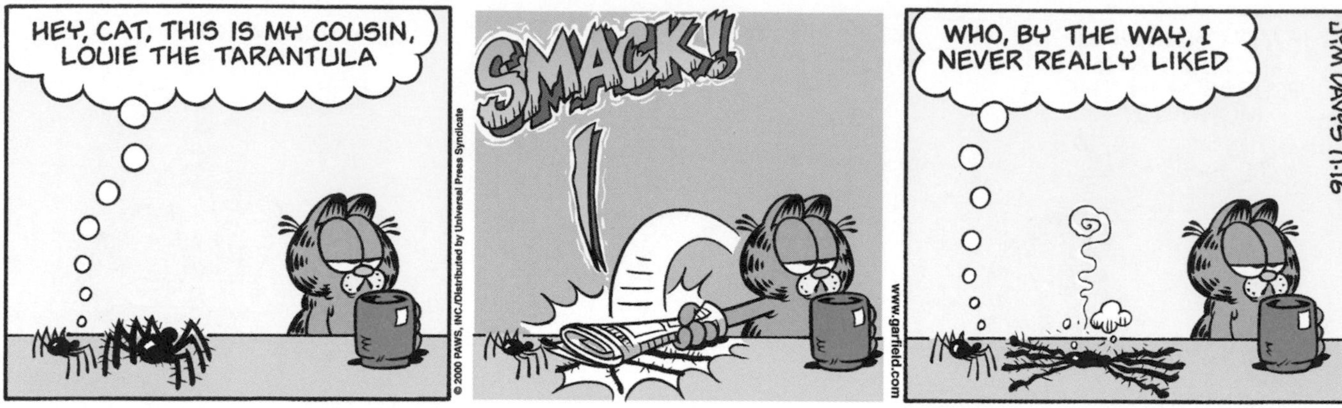
HEY, CAT, THIS IS MY COUSIN, LOUIE THE TARANTULA
SMACK!
WHO, BY THE WAY, I NEVER REALLY LIKED
JIM DAVIS 11-16
© 2000 PAWS, INC./Distributed by Universal Press Syndicate
www.garfield.com

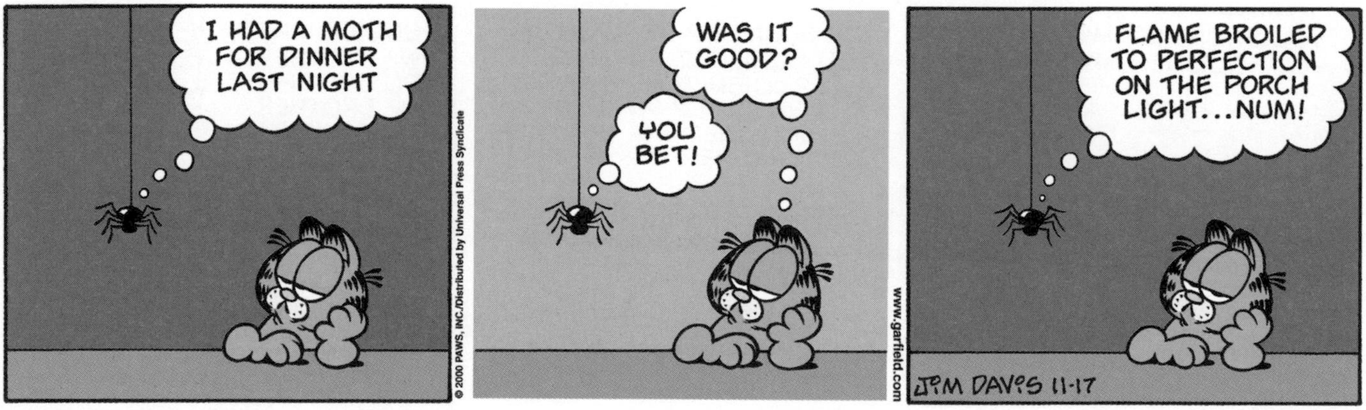
I HAD A MOTH FOR DINNER LAST NIGHT
WAS IT GOOD?
YOU BET!
FLAME BROILED TO PERFECTION ON THE PORCH LIGHT...NUM!
JIM DAVIS 11-17
© 2000 PAWS, INC./Distributed by Universal Press Syndicate
www.garfield.com

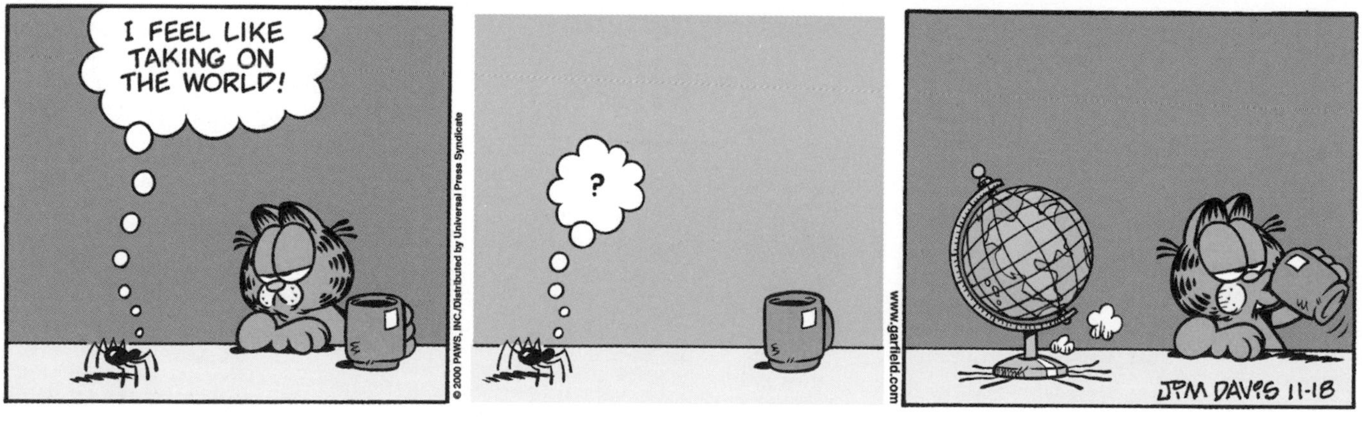
I FEEL LIKE TAKING ON THE WORLD!
?
JIM DAVIS 11-18
© 2000 PAWS, INC./Distributed by Universal Press Syndicate
www.garfield.com

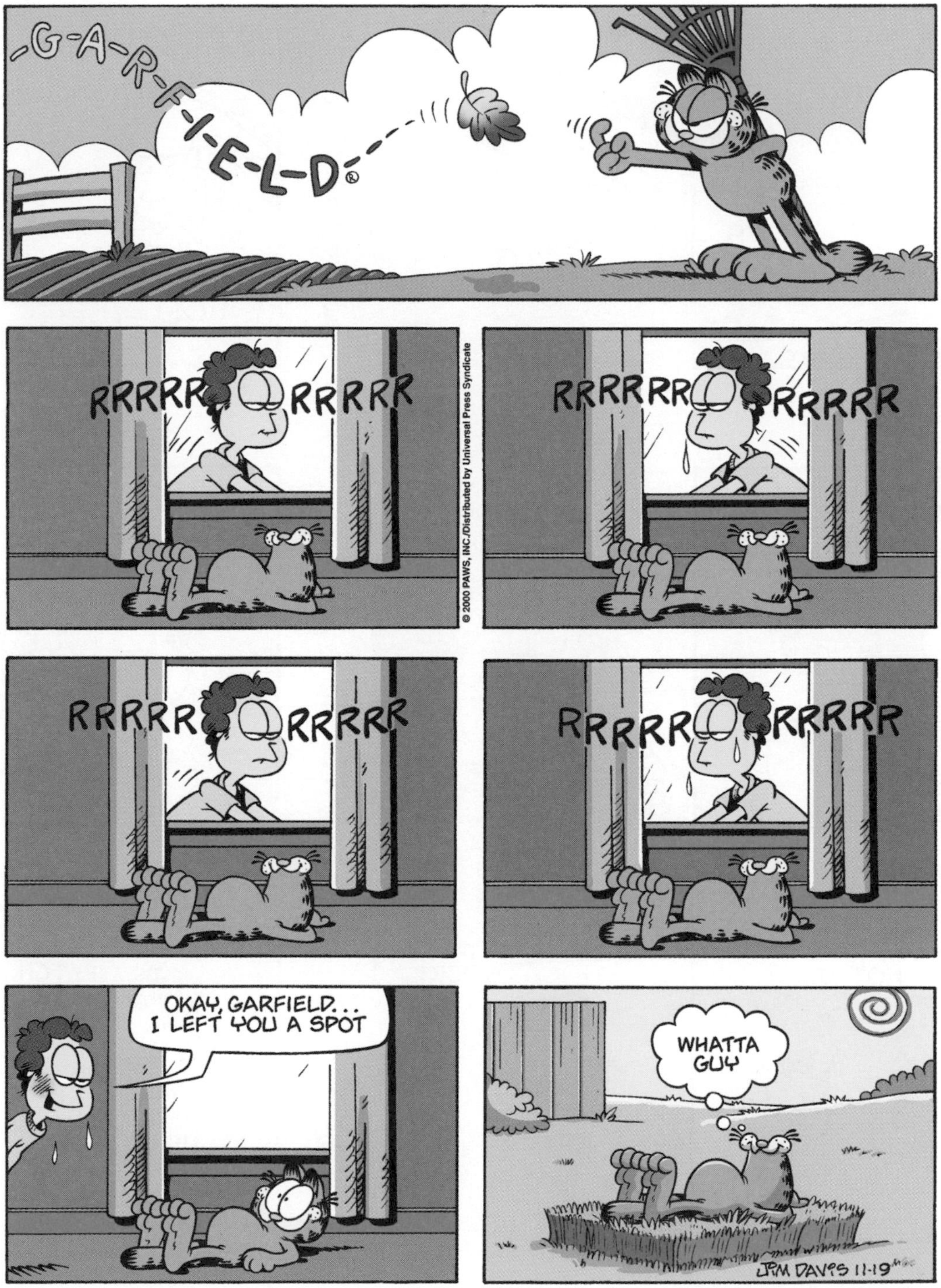

-G-A-R-F-I-E-L-D®
© 2000 PAWS, INC./Distributed by Universal Press Syndicate
RRRRR RRRRR
RRRRRR RRRRR
RRRRR RRRRR
RRRRR RRRRR
OKAY, GARFIELD...
I LEFT YOU A SPOT
WHATTA GUY
JIM DAVIS 11-19

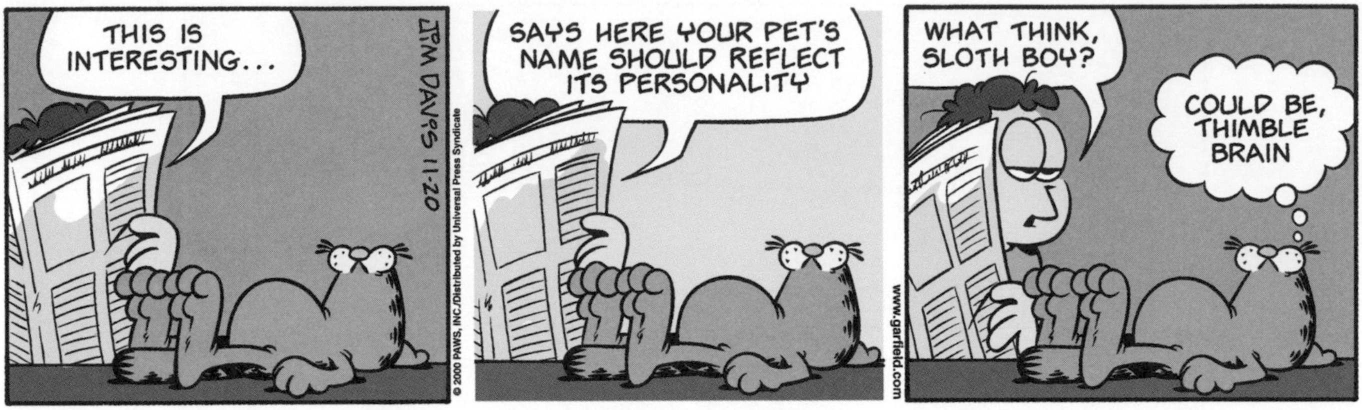
THIS IS INTERESTING...
SAYS HERE YOUR PET'S NAME SHOULD REFLECT ITS PERSONALITY
WHAT THINK, SLOTH BOY?
COULD BE, THIMBLE BRAIN
JIM DAVIS 11-20
© 2000 PAWS, INC./Distributed by Universal Press Syndicate
www.garfield.com

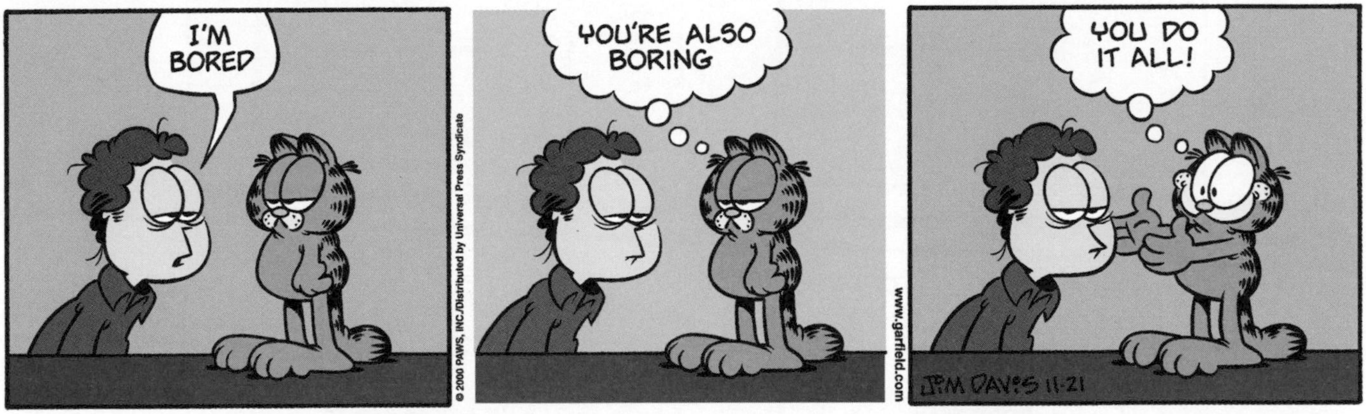
I'M BORED
YOU'RE ALSO BORING
YOU DO IT ALL!
JIM DAVIS 11-21
© 2000 PAWS, INC./Distributed by Universal Press Syndicate
www.garfield.com

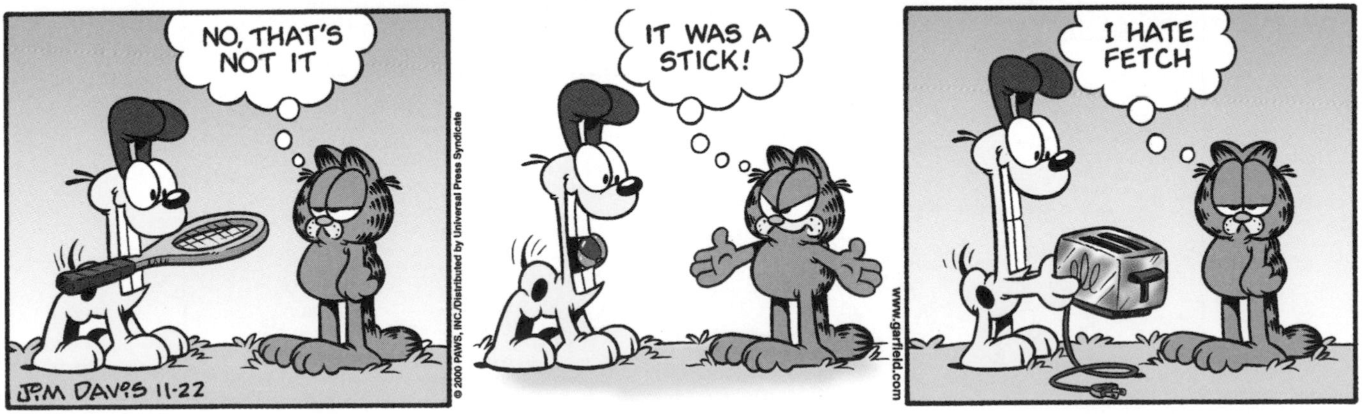
NO, THAT'S NOT IT
IT WAS A STICK!
I HATE FETCH
JIM DAVIS 11-22
© 2000 PAWS, INC./Distributed by Universal Press Syndicate
www.garfield.com

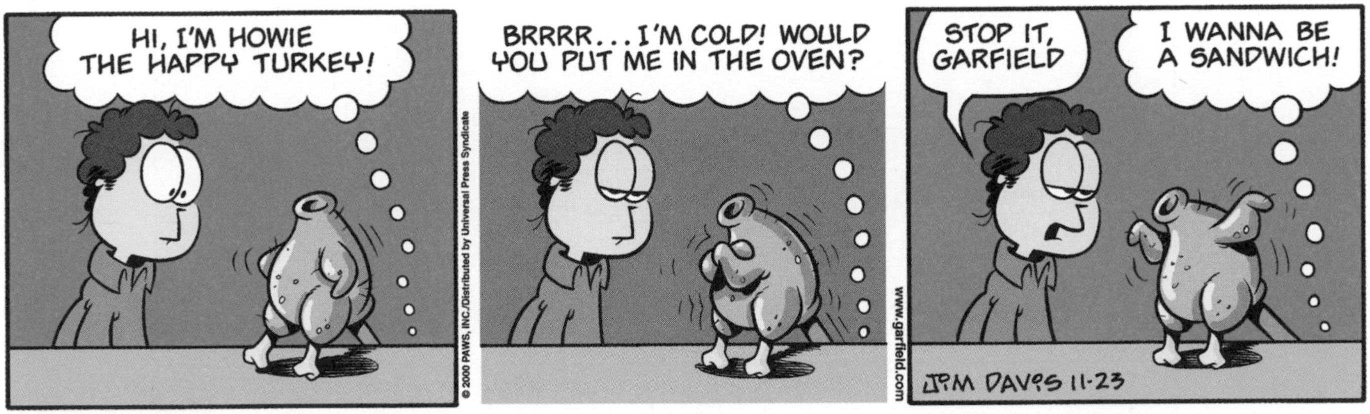
HI, I'M HOWIE THE HAPPY TURKEY!
BRRRR... I'M COLD! WOULD YOU PUT ME IN THE OVEN?
STOP IT, GARFIELD
I WANNA BE A SANDWICH!
JIM DAVIS 11-23
© 2000 PAWS, INC./Distributed by Universal Press Syndicate
www.garfield.com

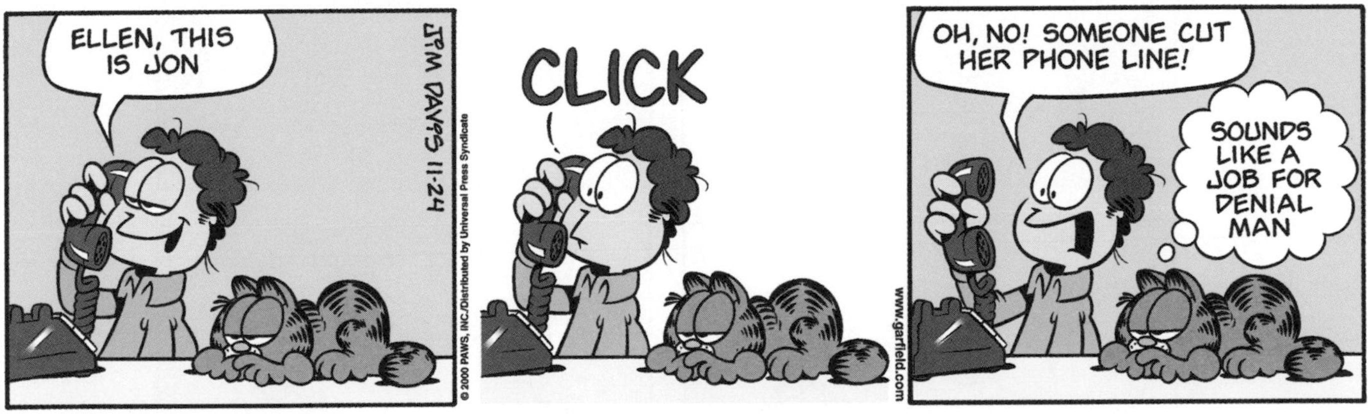
ELLEN, THIS IS JON
JIM DAVIS 11-24
CLICK
OH, NO! SOMEONE CUT HER PHONE LINE!
SOUNDS LIKE A JOB FOR DENIAL MAN
© 2000 PAWS, INC./Distributed by Universal Press Syndicate
www.garfield.com

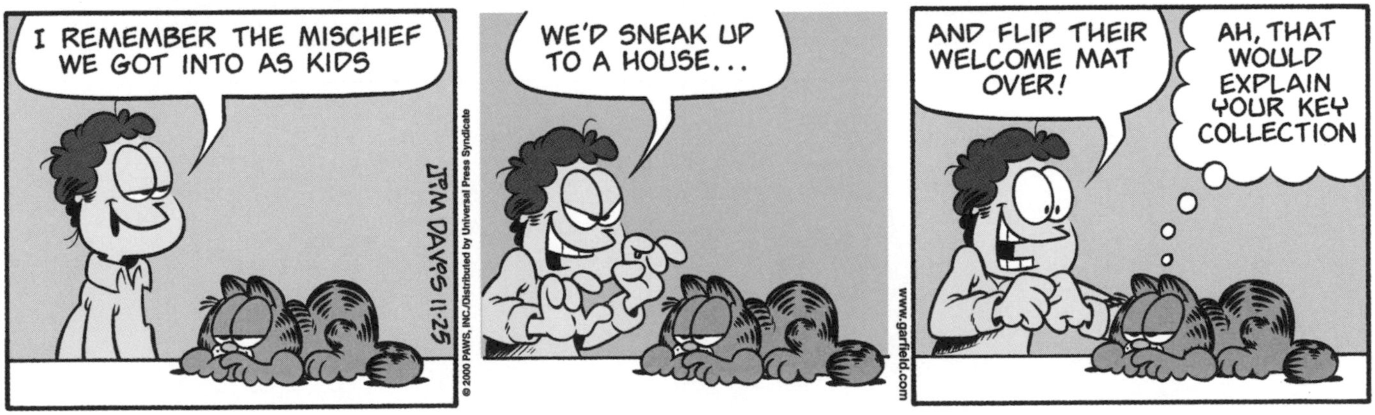
I REMEMBER THE MISCHIEF WE GOT INTO AS KIDS
JIM DAVIS 11-25
WE'D SNEAK UP TO A HOUSE...
AND FLIP THEIR WELCOME MAT OVER!
AH, THAT WOULD EXPLAIN YOUR KEY COLLECTION
© 2000 PAWS, INC./Distributed by Universal Press Syndicate
www.garfield.com

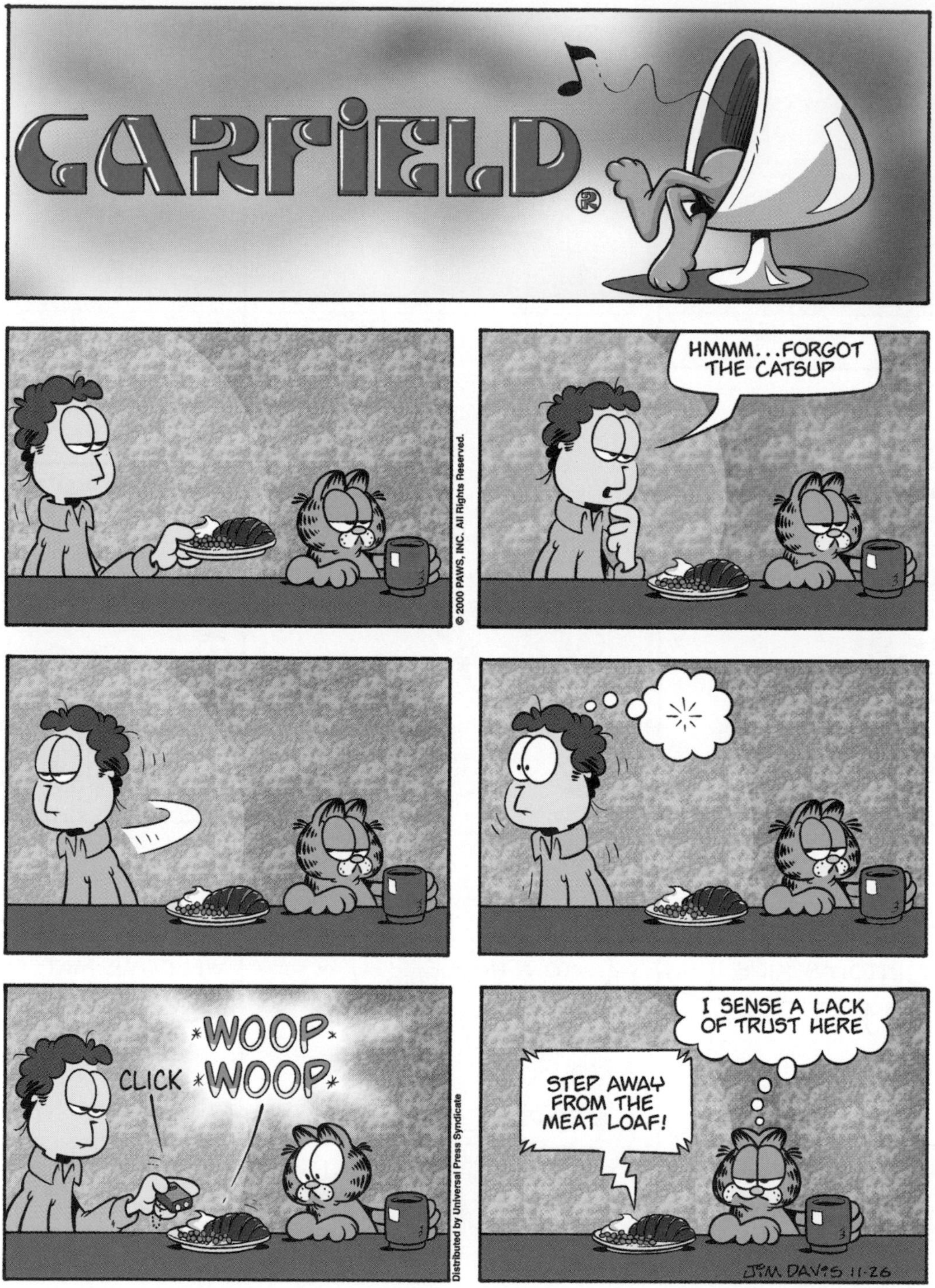
GARFIELD
HMMM...FORGOT THE CATSUP
CLICK
WOOP WOOP
STEP AWAY FROM THE MEAT LOAF!
I SENSE A LACK OF TRUST HERE
JIM DAVIS 11-26

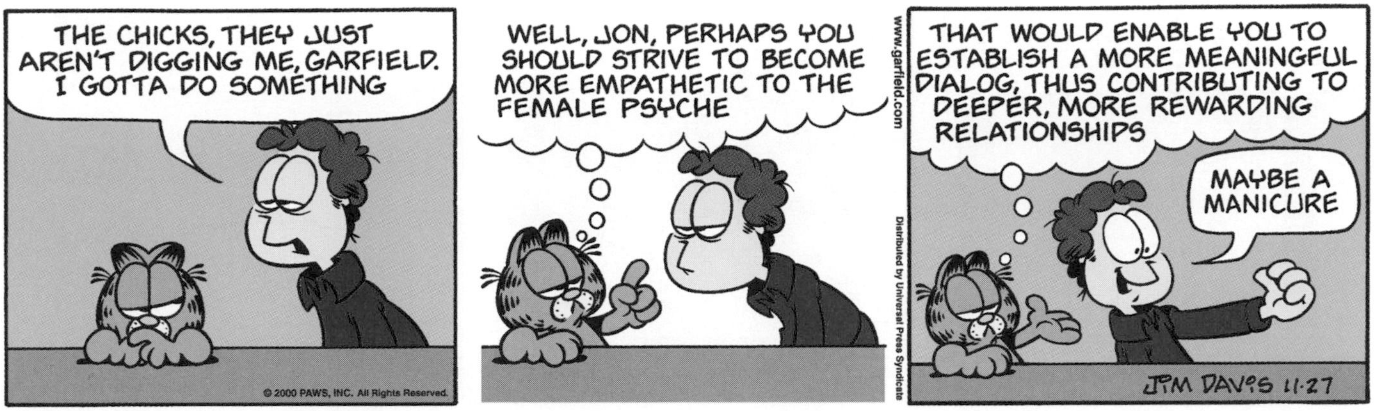
THE CHICKS, THEY JUST AREN'T DIGGING ME, GARFIELD. I GOTTA DO SOMETHING
© 2000 PAWS, INC. All Rights Reserved.
WELL, JON, PERHAPS YOU SHOULD STRIVE TO BECOME MORE EMPATHETIC TO THE FEMALE PSYCHE
www.garfield.com
Distributed by Universal Press Syndicate
THAT WOULD ENABLE YOU TO ESTABLISH A MORE MEANINGFUL DIALOG, THUS CONTRIBUTING TO DEEPER, MORE REWARDING RELATIONSHIPS
MAYBE A MANICURE
JIM DAVIS 11-27

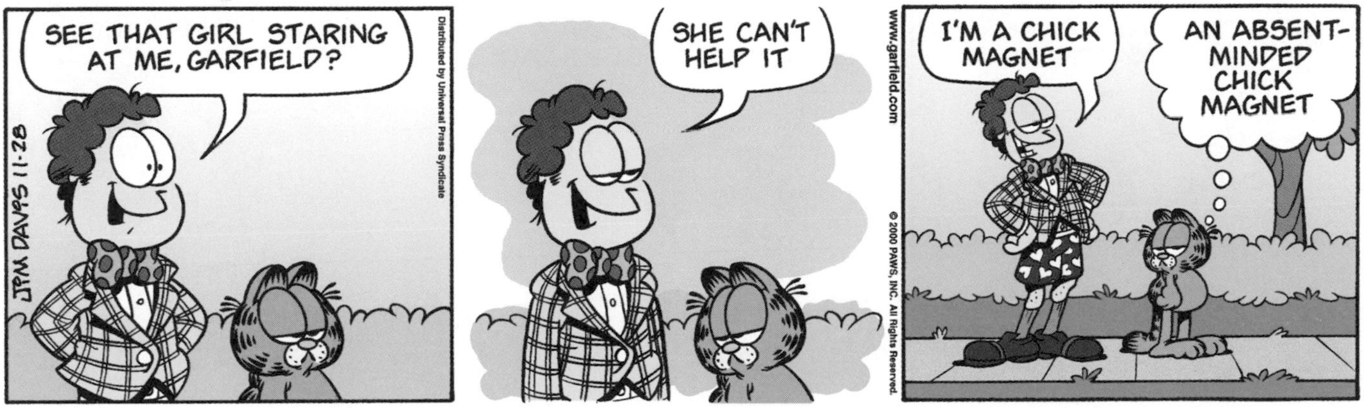
SEE THAT GIRL STARING AT ME, GARFIELD?
JIM DAVIS 11-28
Distributed by Universal Press Syndicate
SHE CAN'T HELP IT
www.garfield.com
© 2000 PAWS, INC. All Rights Reserved.
I'M A CHICK MAGNET
AN ABSENT-MINDED CHICK MAGNET

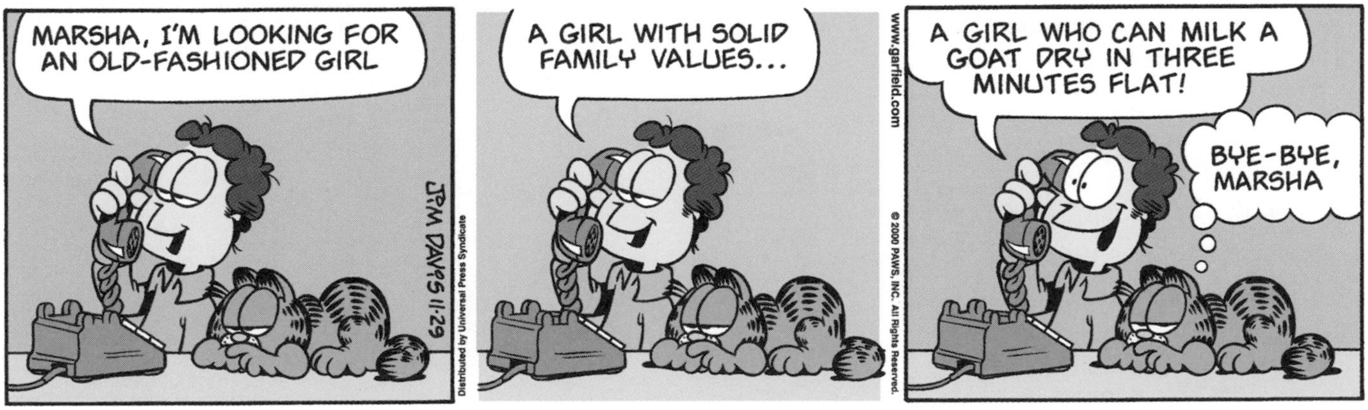
MARSHA, I'M LOOKING FOR AN OLD-FASHIONED GIRL
JIM DAVIS 11-29
Distributed by Universal Press Syndicate
A GIRL WITH SOLID FAMILY VALUES...
www.garfield.com
© 2000 PAWS, INC. All Rights Reserved.
A GIRL WHO CAN MILK A GOAT DRY IN THREE MINUTES FLAT!
BYE-BYE, MARSHA

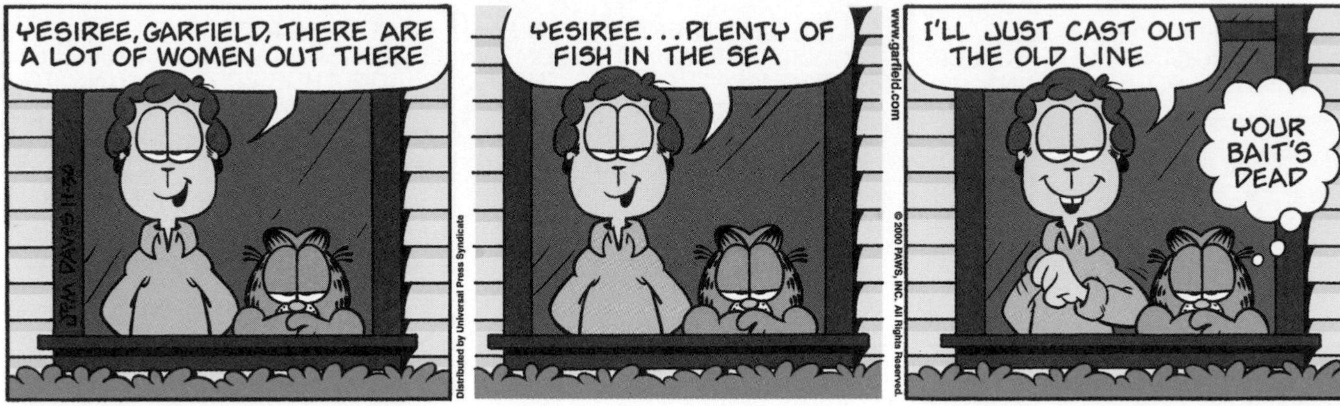
YESIREE, GARFIELD, THERE ARE A LOT OF WOMEN OUT THERE
YESIREE... PLENTY OF FISH IN THE SEA
I'LL JUST CAST OUT THE OLD LINE
YOUR BAIT'S DEAD
JIM DAVIS 11-30
Distributed by Universal Press Syndicate
www.garfield.com
© 2000 PAWS, INC. All Rights Reserved.

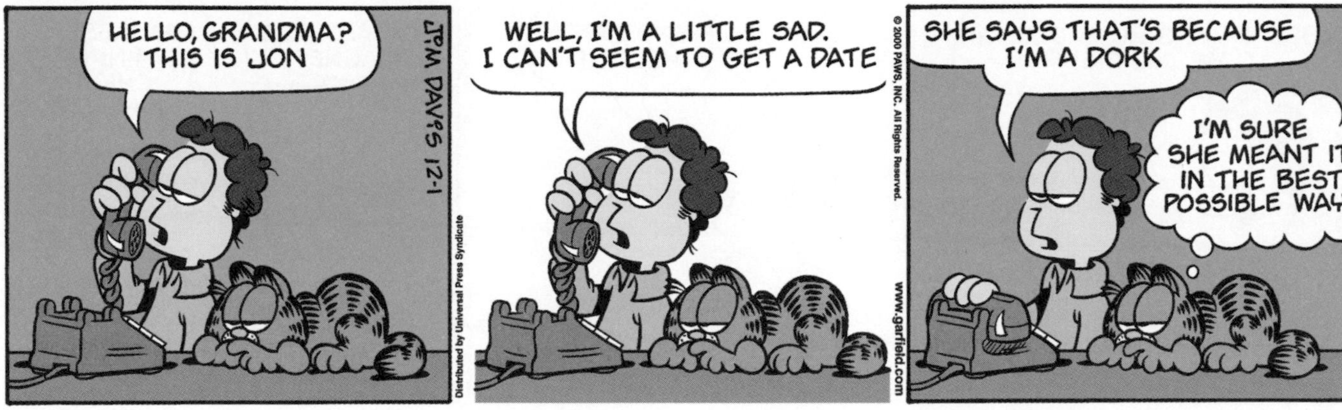
HELLO, GRANDMA? THIS IS JON
WELL, I'M A LITTLE SAD. I CAN'T SEEM TO GET A DATE
SHE SAYS THAT'S BECAUSE I'M A DORK
I'M SURE SHE MEANT IT IN THE BEST POSSIBLE WAY
JIM DAVIS 12-1
Distributed by Universal Press Syndicate
© 2000 PAWS, INC. All Rights Reserved.
www.garfield.com

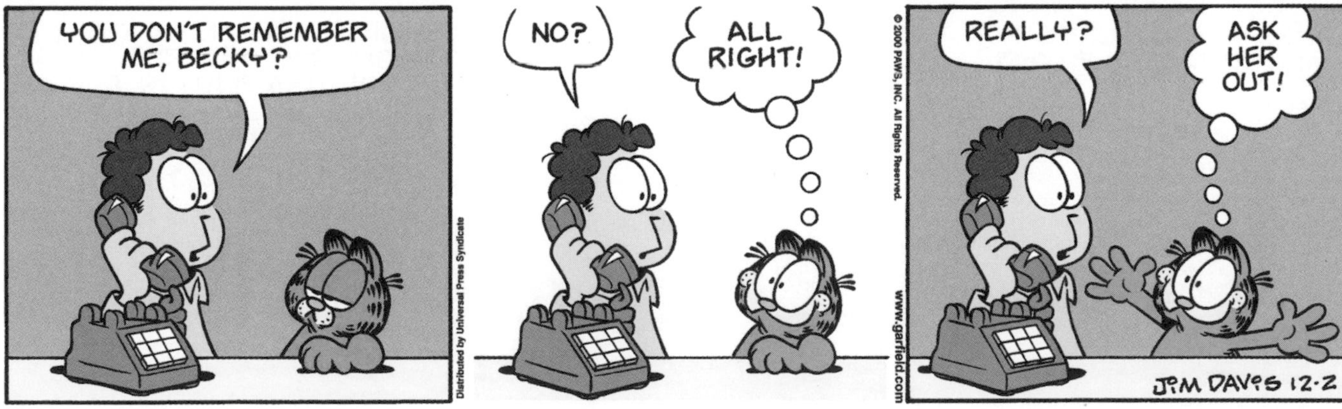
YOU DON'T REMEMBER ME, BECKY?
NO?
ALL RIGHT!
REALLY?
ASK HER OUT!
JIM DAVIS 12-2
Distributed by Universal Press Syndicate
© 2000 PAWS, INC. All Rights Reserved.
www.garfield.com

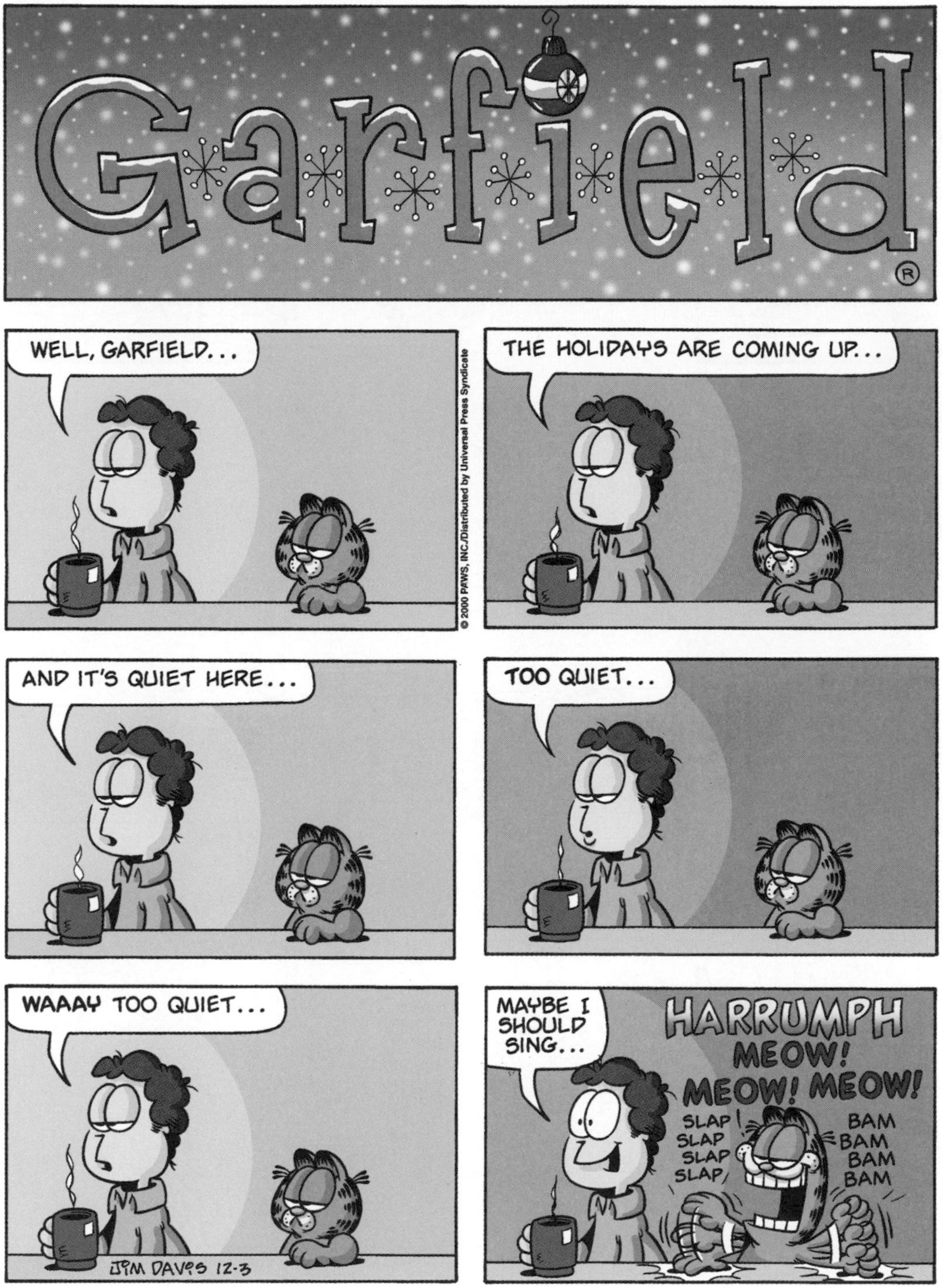
Garfield
WELL, GARFIELD...
© 2000 PAWS, INC/Distributed by Universal Press Syndicate
THE HOLIDAYS ARE COMING UP...
AND IT'S QUIET HERE...
TOO QUIET...
WAAAY TOO QUIET...
JIM DAVIS 12-3
MAYBE I SHOULD SING...
HARRUMPH
MEOW!
MEOW! MEOW!
SLAP! SLAP SLAP SLAP
BAM BAM BAM BAM

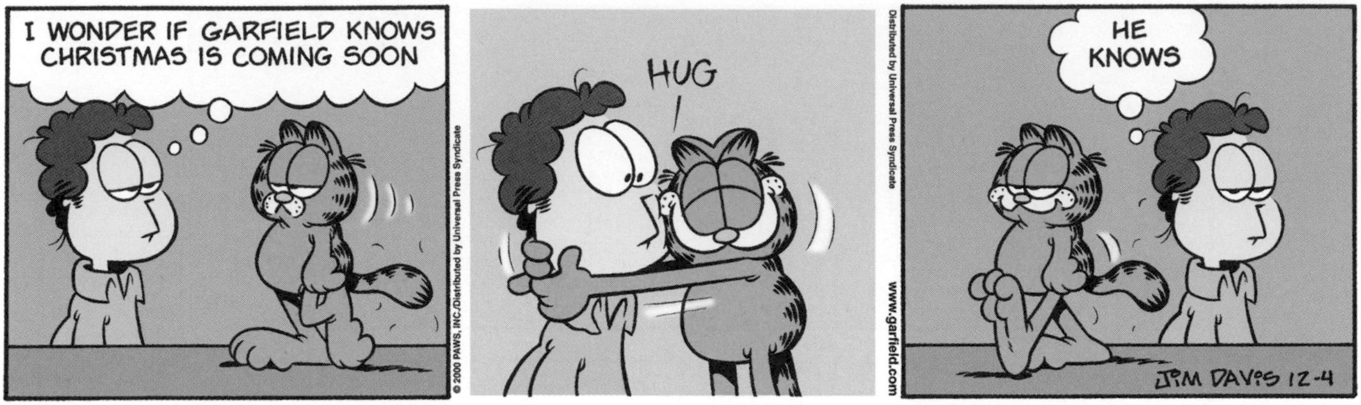
I WONDER IF GARFIELD KNOWS CHRISTMAS IS COMING SOON
HUG
HE KNOWS
© 2000 PAWS, INC./Distributed by Universal Press Syndicate
Distributed by Universal Press Syndicate
www.garfield.com
JIM DAVIS 12-4

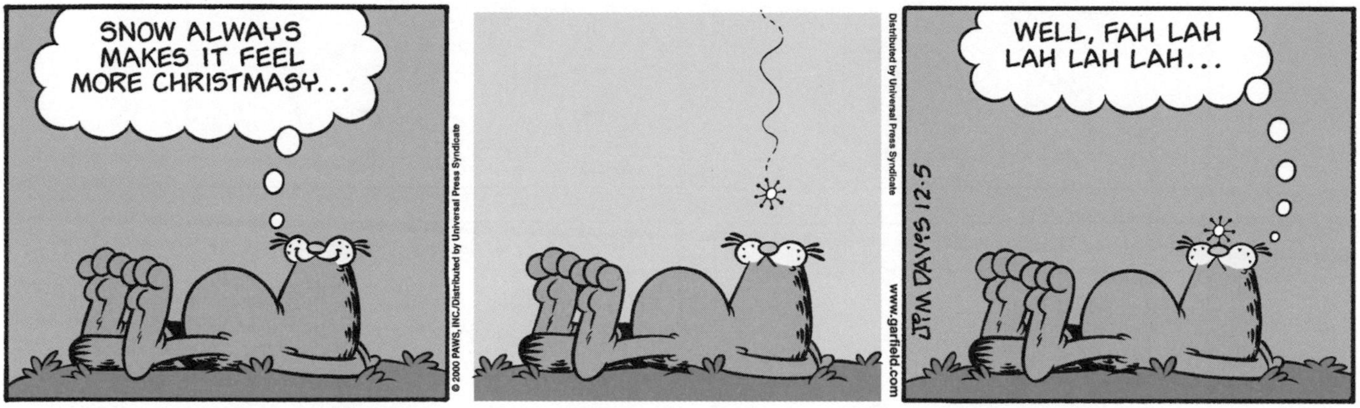
SNOW ALWAYS MAKES IT FEEL MORE CHRISTMASY...
WELL, FAH LAH LAH LAH LAH...
© 2000 PAWS, INC./Distributed by Universal Press Syndicate
Distributed by Universal Press Syndicate
www.garfield.com
JIM DAVIS 12-5

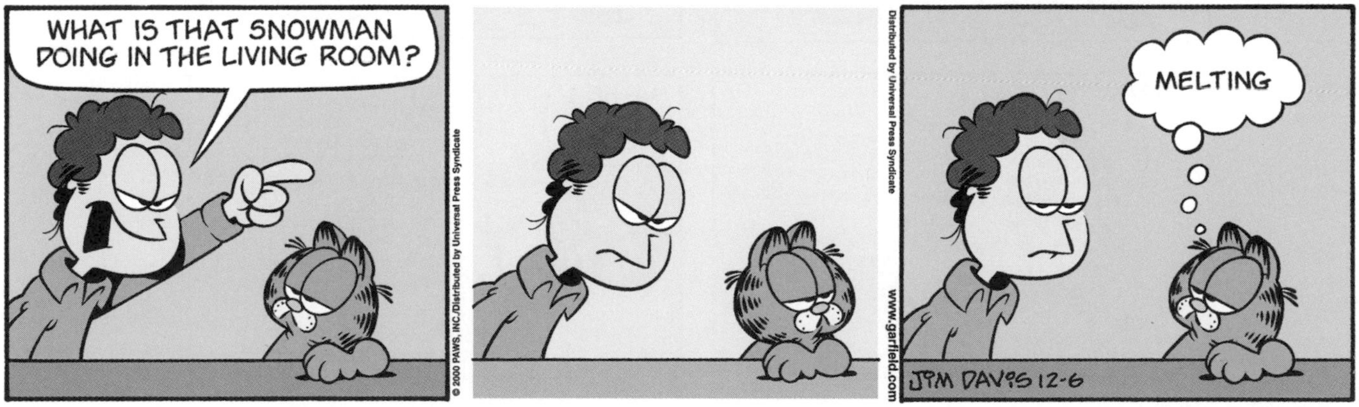
WHAT IS THAT SNOWMAN DOING IN THE LIVING ROOM?
MELTING
© 2000 PAWS, INC./Distributed by Universal Press Syndicate
Distributed by Universal Press Syndicate
www.garfield.com
JIM DAVIS 12-6

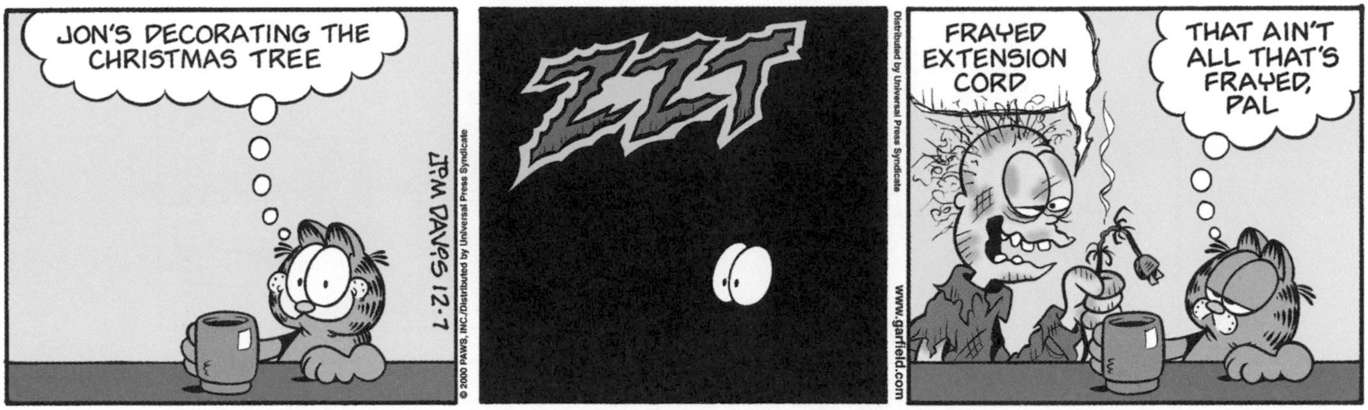
JON'S DECORATING THE CHRISTMAS TREE
JIM DAVIS 12-7
© 2000 PAWS, INC./Distributed by Universal Press Syndicate
ZZZT
Distributed by Universal Press Syndicate
www.garfield.com
FRAYED EXTENSION CORD
THAT AIN'T ALL THAT'S FRAYED, PAL

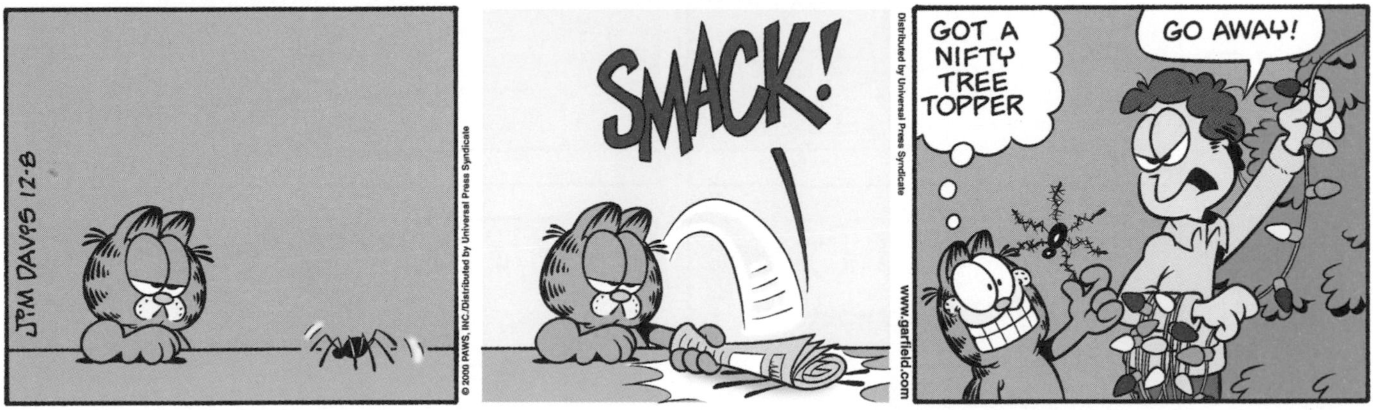
JIM DAVIS 12-8
© 2000 PAWS, INC./Distributed by Universal Press Syndicate
SMACK!
Distributed by Universal Press Syndicate
www.garfield.com
GOT A NIFTY TREE TOPPER
GO AWAY!

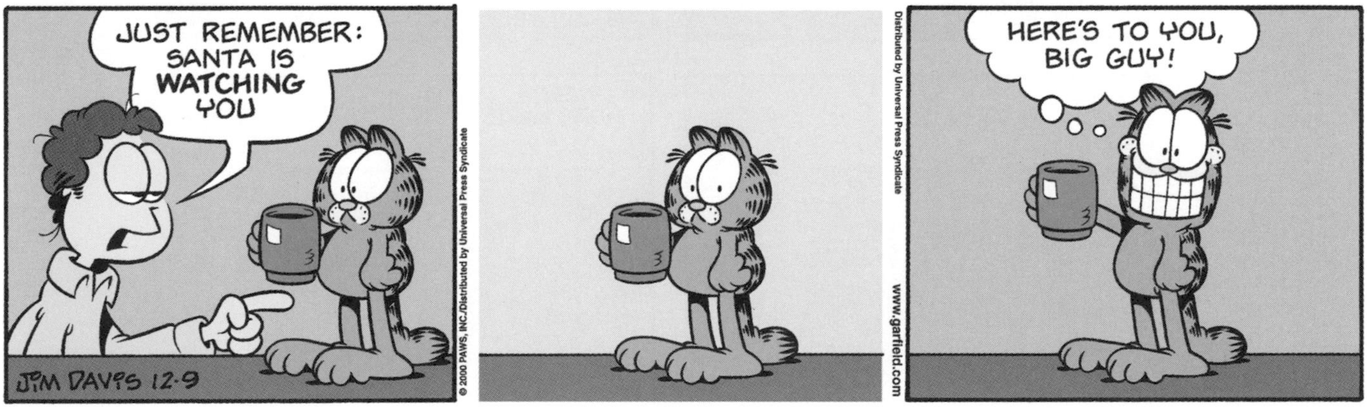
JUST REMEMBER: SANTA IS **WATCHING** YOU
JIM DAVIS 12-9
© 2000 PAWS, INC./Distributed by Universal Press Syndicate
Distributed by Universal Press Syndicate
www.garfield.com
HERE'S TO YOU, BIG GUY!

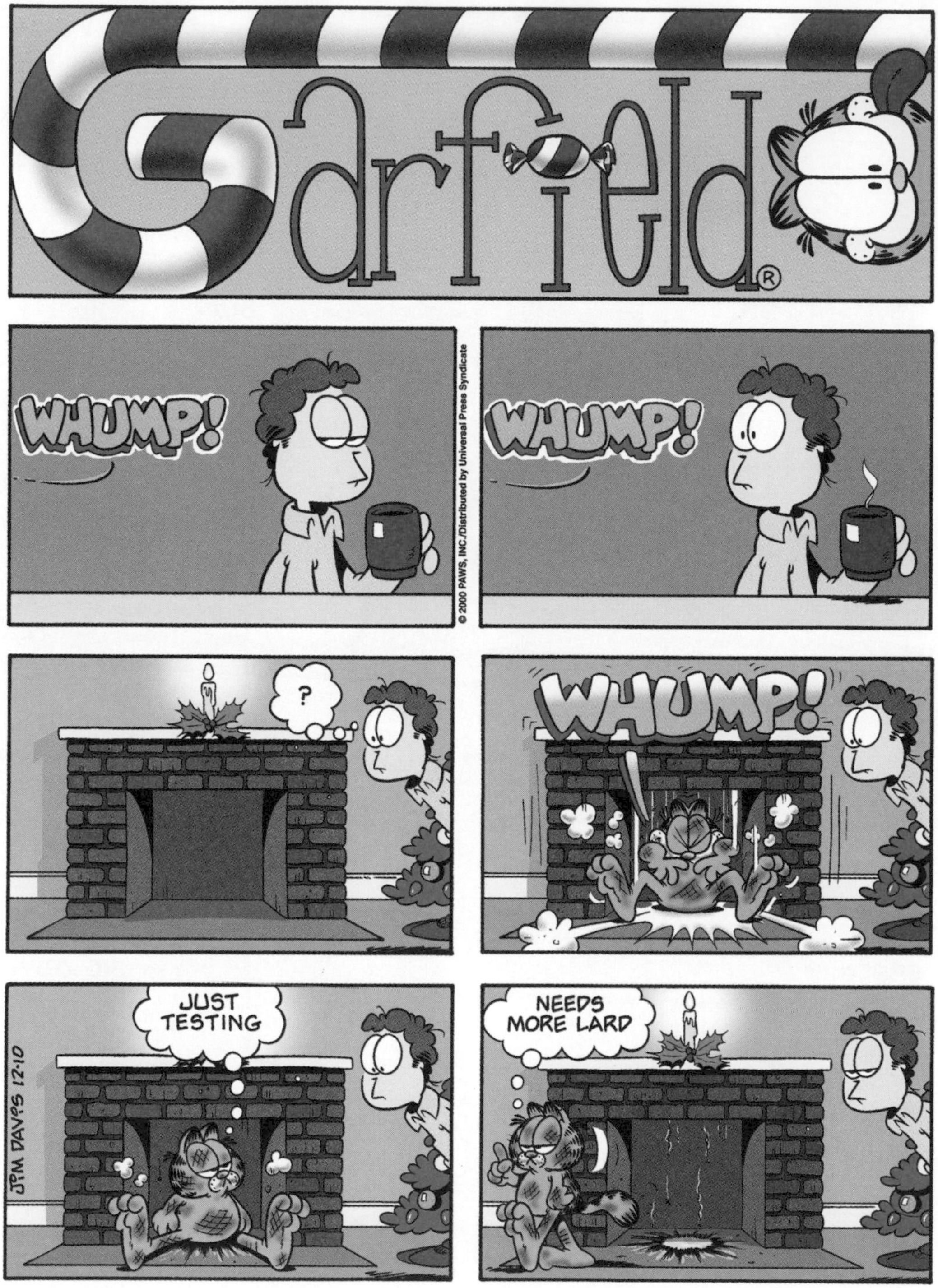
Garfield®
© 2000 PAWS, INC./Distributed by Universal Press Syndicate
WHUMP!
WHUMP!
?
WHUMP!
JUST TESTING
JPM DAVPS 12·10
NEEDS MORE LARD

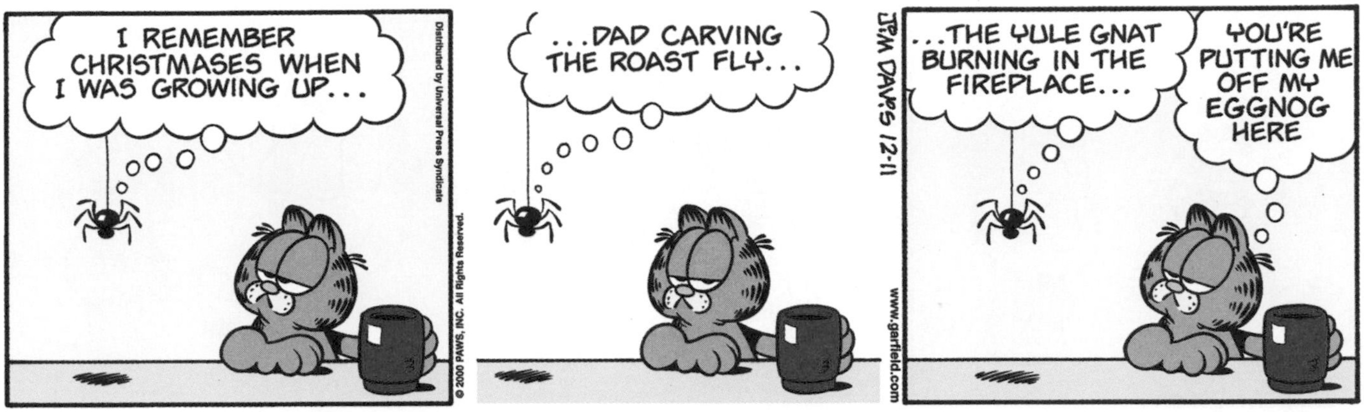
I REMEMBER CHRISTMASES WHEN I WAS GROWING UP...
...DAD CARVING THE ROAST FLY...
...THE YULE GNAT BURNING IN THE FIREPLACE...
YOU'RE PUTTING ME OFF MY EGGNOG HERE
JIM DAVIS 12-11
Distributed by Universal Press Syndicate
© 2000 PAWS, INC. All Rights Reserved.
www.garfield.com

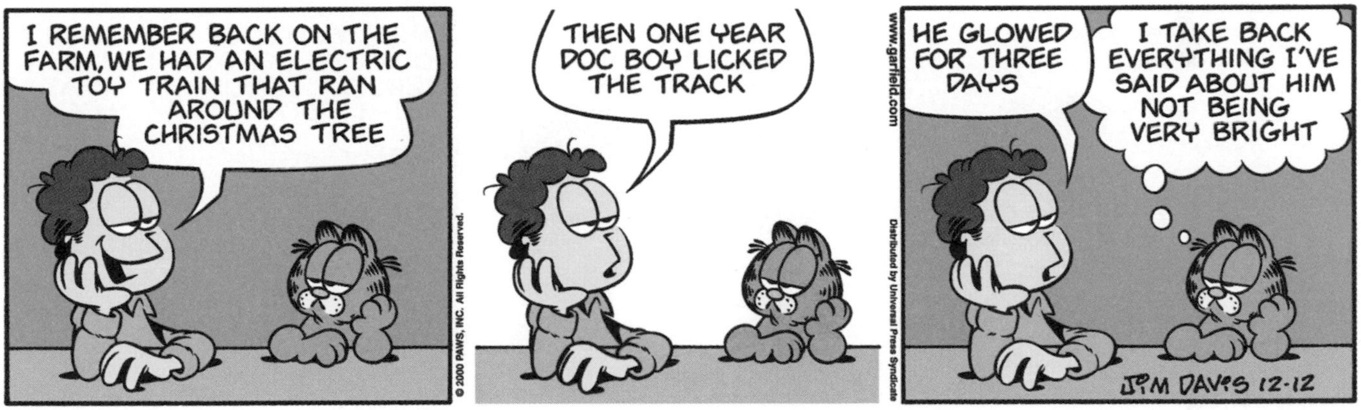
I REMEMBER BACK ON THE FARM, WE HAD AN ELECTRIC TOY TRAIN THAT RAN AROUND THE CHRISTMAS TREE
THEN ONE YEAR DOC BOY LICKED THE TRACK
HE GLOWED FOR THREE DAYS
I TAKE BACK EVERYTHING I'VE SAID ABOUT HIM NOT BEING VERY BRIGHT
JIM DAVIS 12-12
© 2000 PAWS, INC. All Rights Reserved.
www.garfield.com
Distributed by Universal Press Syndicate

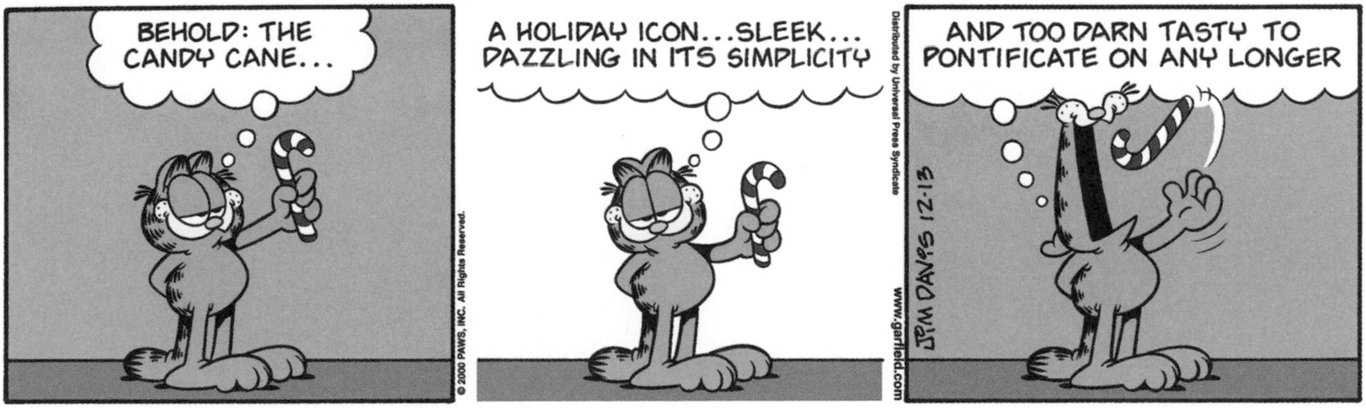
BEHOLD: THE CANDY CANE...
A HOLIDAY ICON...SLEEK... DAZZLING IN ITS SIMPLICITY
AND TOO DARN TASTY TO PONTIFICATE ON ANY LONGER
JIM DAVIS 12-13
© 2000 PAWS, INC. All Rights Reserved.
Distributed by Universal Press Syndicate
www.garfield.com

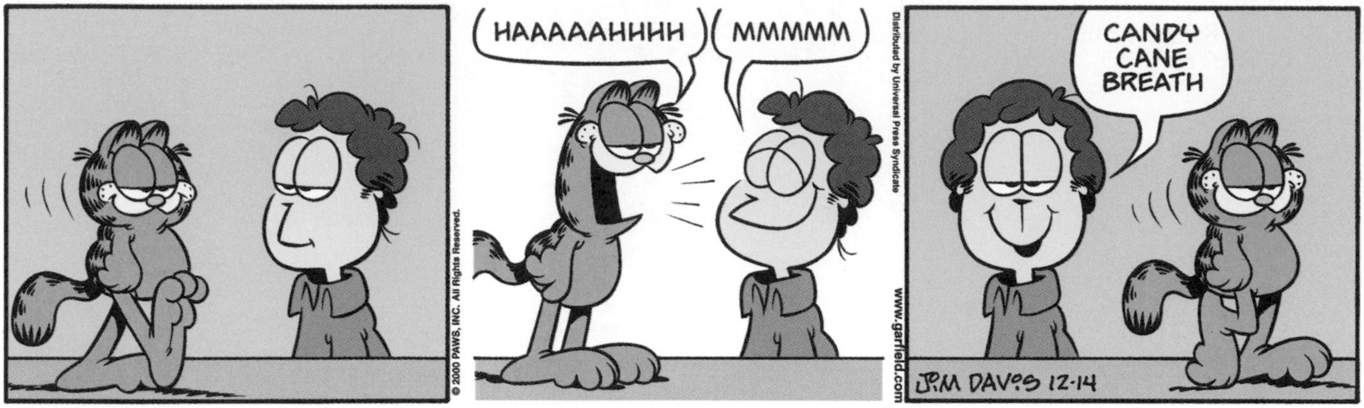
HAAAAAHHHH
MMMMM
CANDY CANE BREATH
JIM DAVIS 12-14
© 2000 PAWS, INC. All Rights Reserved.
Distributed by Universal Press Syndicate
www.garfield.com

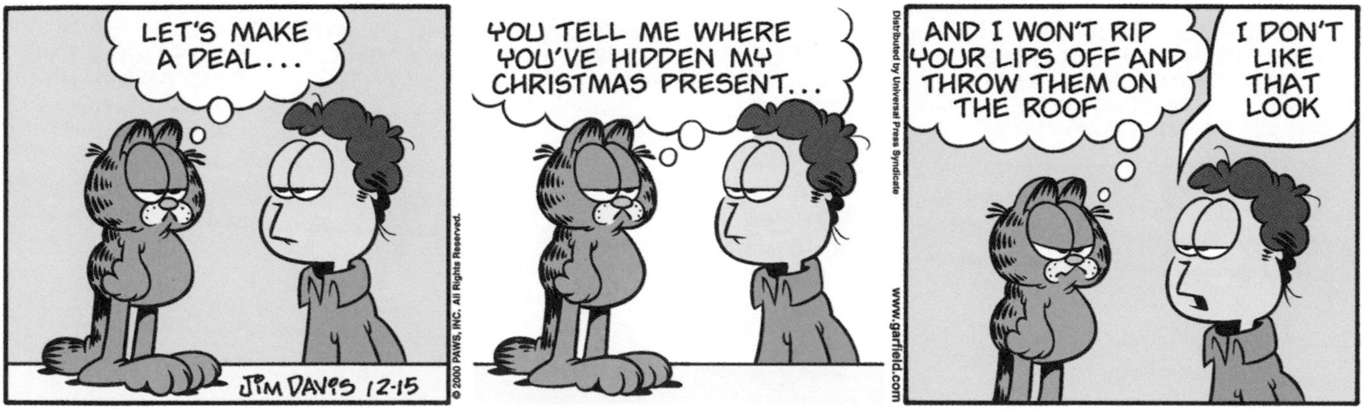
LET'S MAKE A DEAL...
JIM DAVIS 12-15
YOU TELL ME WHERE YOU'VE HIDDEN MY CHRISTMAS PRESENT...
AND I WON'T RIP YOUR LIPS OFF AND THROW THEM ON THE ROOF
I DON'T LIKE THAT LOOK
© 2000 PAWS, INC. All Rights Reserved.
Distributed by Universal Press Syndicate
www.garfield.com

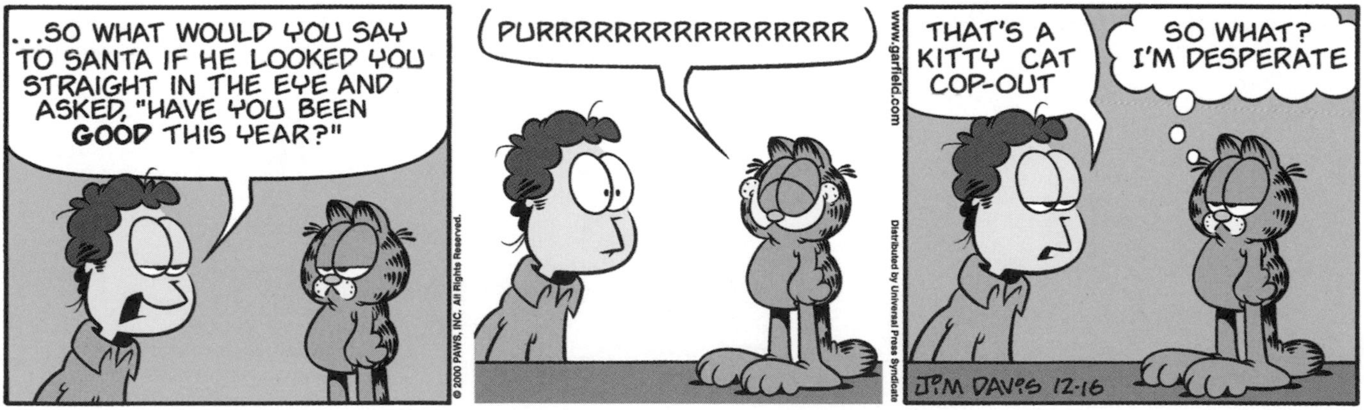
...SO WHAT WOULD YOU SAY TO SANTA IF HE LOOKED YOU STRAIGHT IN THE EYE AND ASKED, "HAVE YOU BEEN **GOOD** THIS YEAR?"
PURRRRRRRRRRRRRRRR
THAT'S A KITTY CAT COP-OUT
SO WHAT? I'M DESPERATE
JIM DAVIS 12-16
© 2000 PAWS, INC. All Rights Reserved.
www.garfield.com
Distributed by Universal Press Syndicate

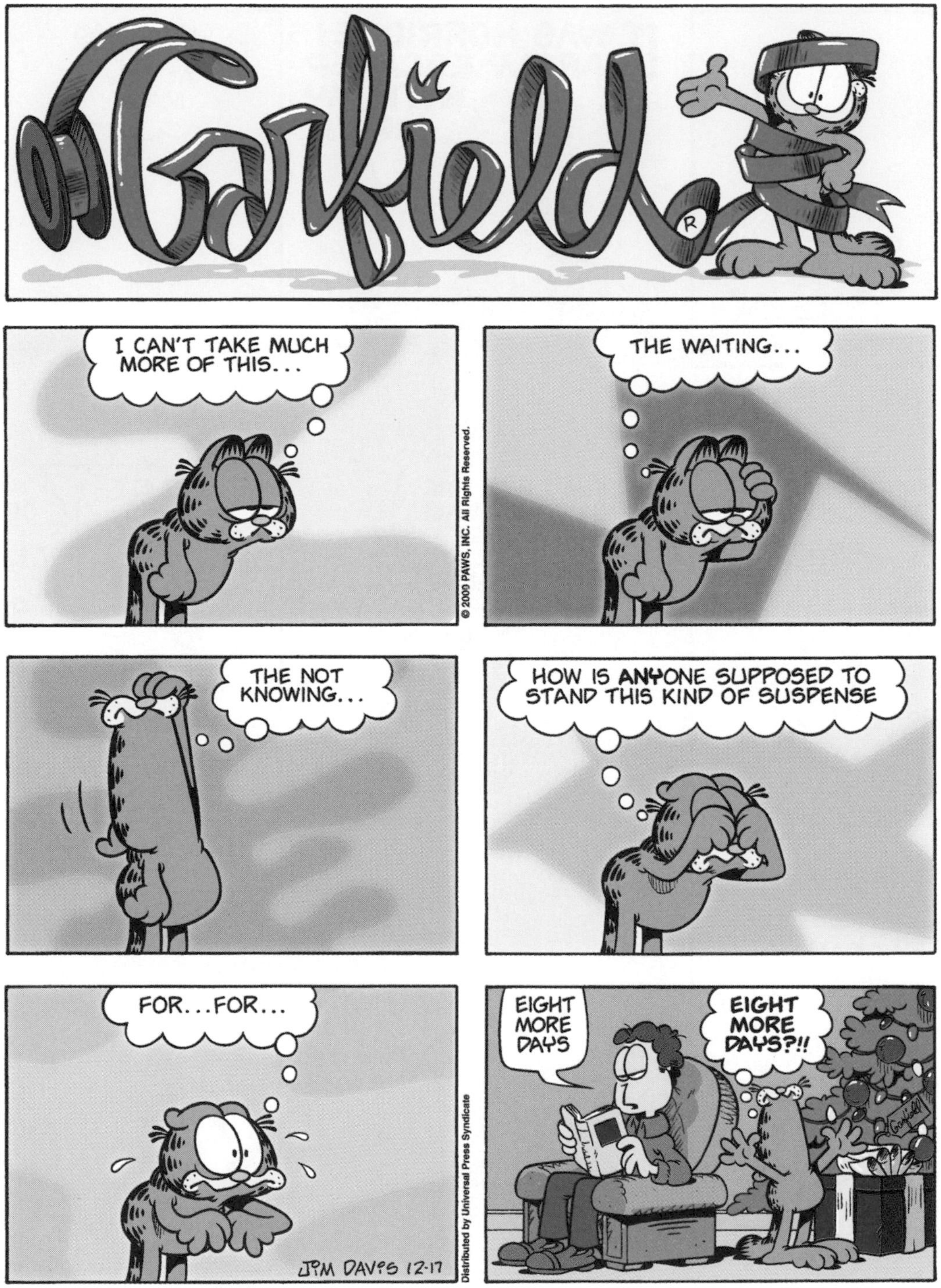
Garfield
I CAN'T TAKE MUCH MORE OF THIS...
THE WAITING...
THE NOT KNOWING...
HOW IS ANYONE SUPPOSED TO STAND THIS KIND OF SUSPENSE
FOR...FOR...
JIM DAVIS 12-17
EIGHT MORE DAYS
EIGHT MORE DAYS?!!
© 2000 PAWS, INC. All Rights Reserved.
Distributed by Universal Press Syndicate

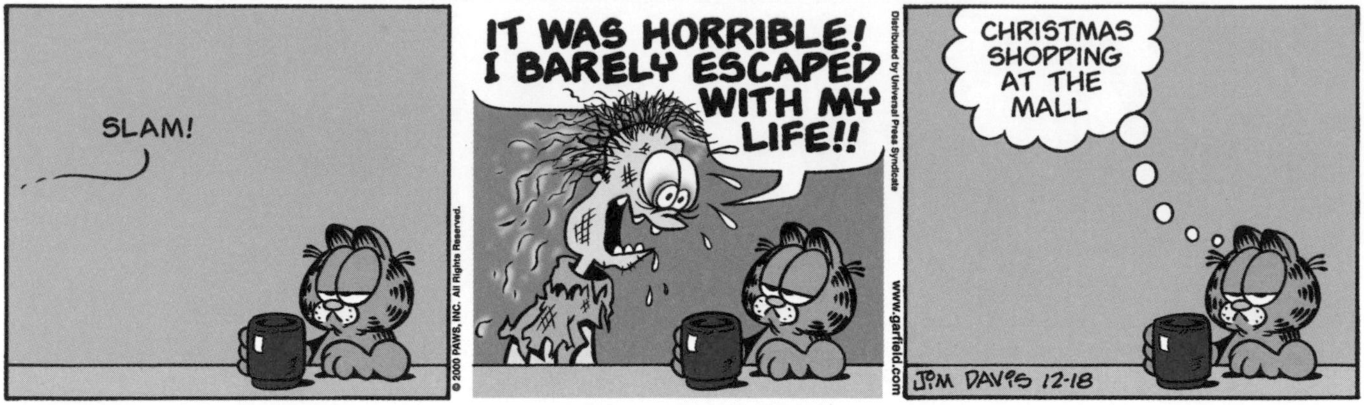
SLAM!
IT WAS HORRIBLE! I BARELY ESCAPED WITH MY LIFE!!
CHRISTMAS SHOPPING AT THE MALL
© 2000 PAWS, INC. All Rights Reserved.
Distributed by Universal Press Syndicate
www.garfield.com
JIM DAVIS 12-18

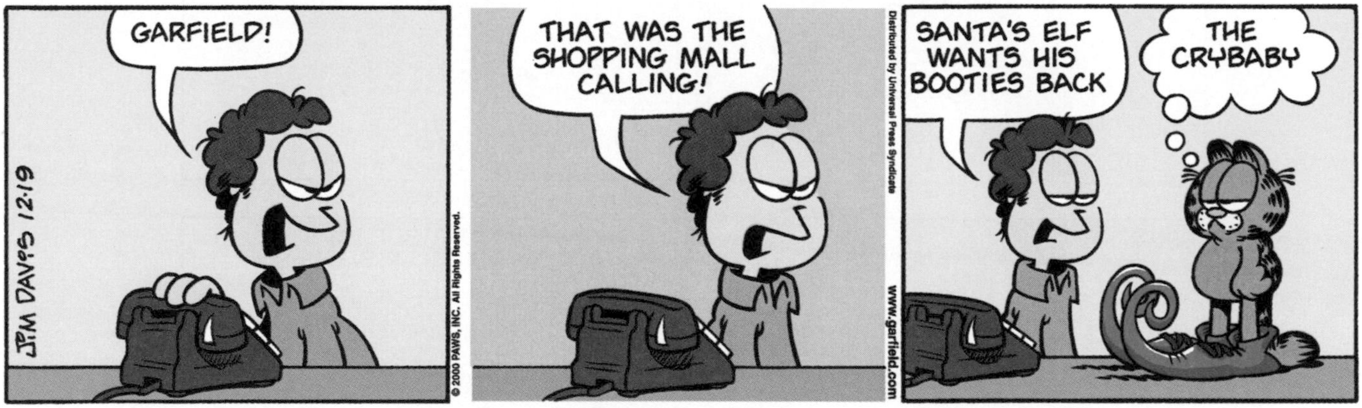
GARFIELD!
THAT WAS THE SHOPPING MALL CALLING!
SANTA'S ELF WANTS HIS BOOTIES BACK
THE CRYBABY
JIM DAVIS 12-19
© 2000 PAWS, INC. All Rights Reserved.
Distributed by Universal Press Syndicate
www.garfield.com

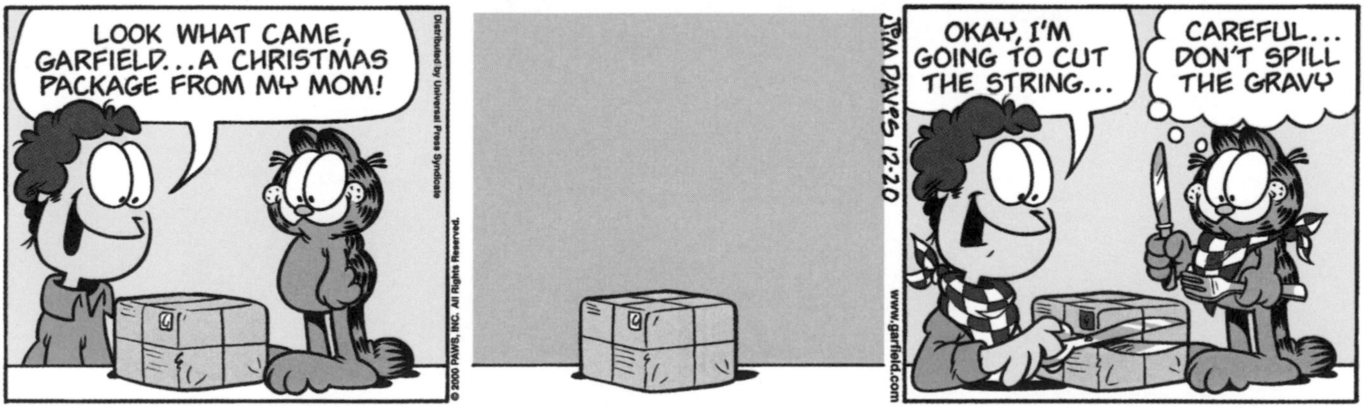
LOOK WHAT CAME, GARFIELD...A CHRISTMAS PACKAGE FROM MY MOM!
OKAY, I'M GOING TO CUT THE STRING...
CAREFUL... DON'T SPILL THE GRAVY
Distributed by Universal Press Syndicate
© 2000 PAWS, INC. All Rights Reserved.
JIM DAVIS 12-20
www.garfield.com

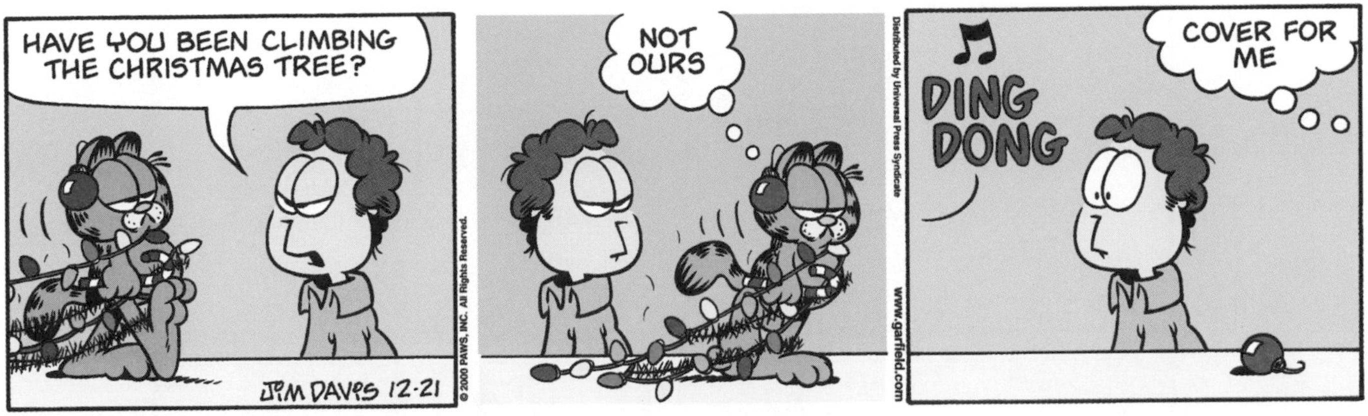
HAVE YOU BEEN CLIMBING THE CHRISTMAS TREE?
JIM DAVIS 12-21
© 2000 PAWS, INC. All Rights Reserved.
NOT OURS
Distributed by Universal Press Syndicate
www.garfield.com
DING DONG
COVER FOR ME

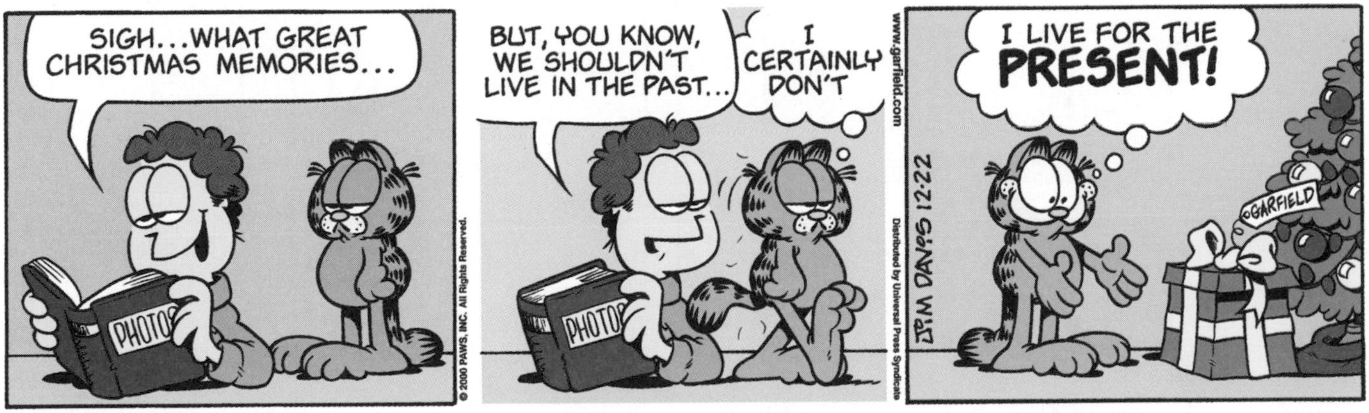
SIGH...WHAT GREAT CHRISTMAS MEMORIES...
PHOTOS
© 2000 PAWS, INC. All Rights Reserved.
BUT, YOU KNOW, WE SHOULDN'T LIVE IN THE PAST...
I CERTAINLY DON'T
www.garfield.com
JIM DAVIS 12-22
Distributed by Universal Press Syndicate
I LIVE FOR THE PRESENT!
GARFIELD

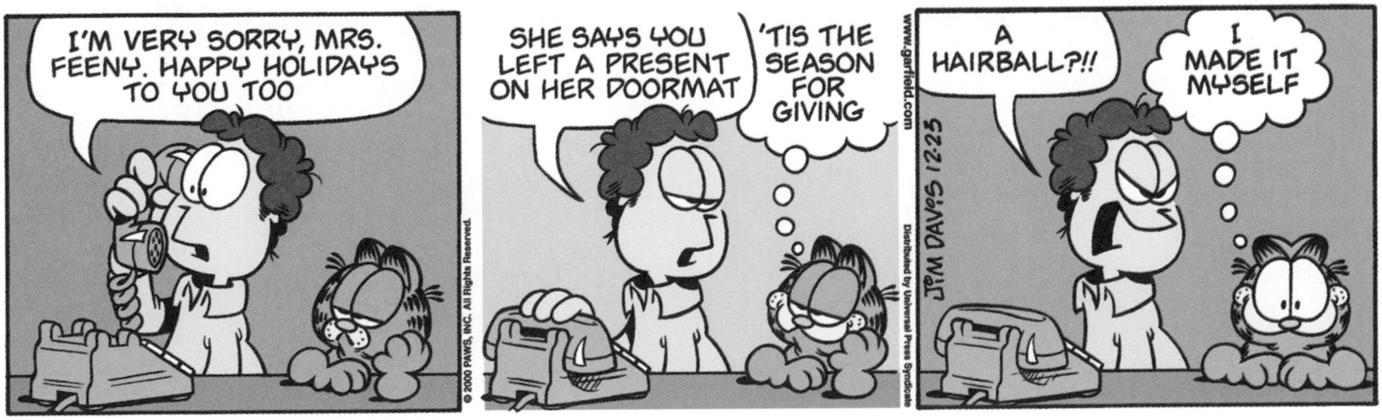
I'M VERY SORRY, MRS. FEENY. HAPPY HOLIDAYS TO YOU TOO
© 2000 PAWS, INC. All Rights Reserved.
SHE SAYS YOU LEFT A PRESENT ON HER DOORMAT
'TIS THE SEASON FOR GIVING
www.garfield.com
JIM DAVIS 12-23
Distributed by Universal Press Syndicate
A HAIRBALL?!!
I MADE IT MYSELF

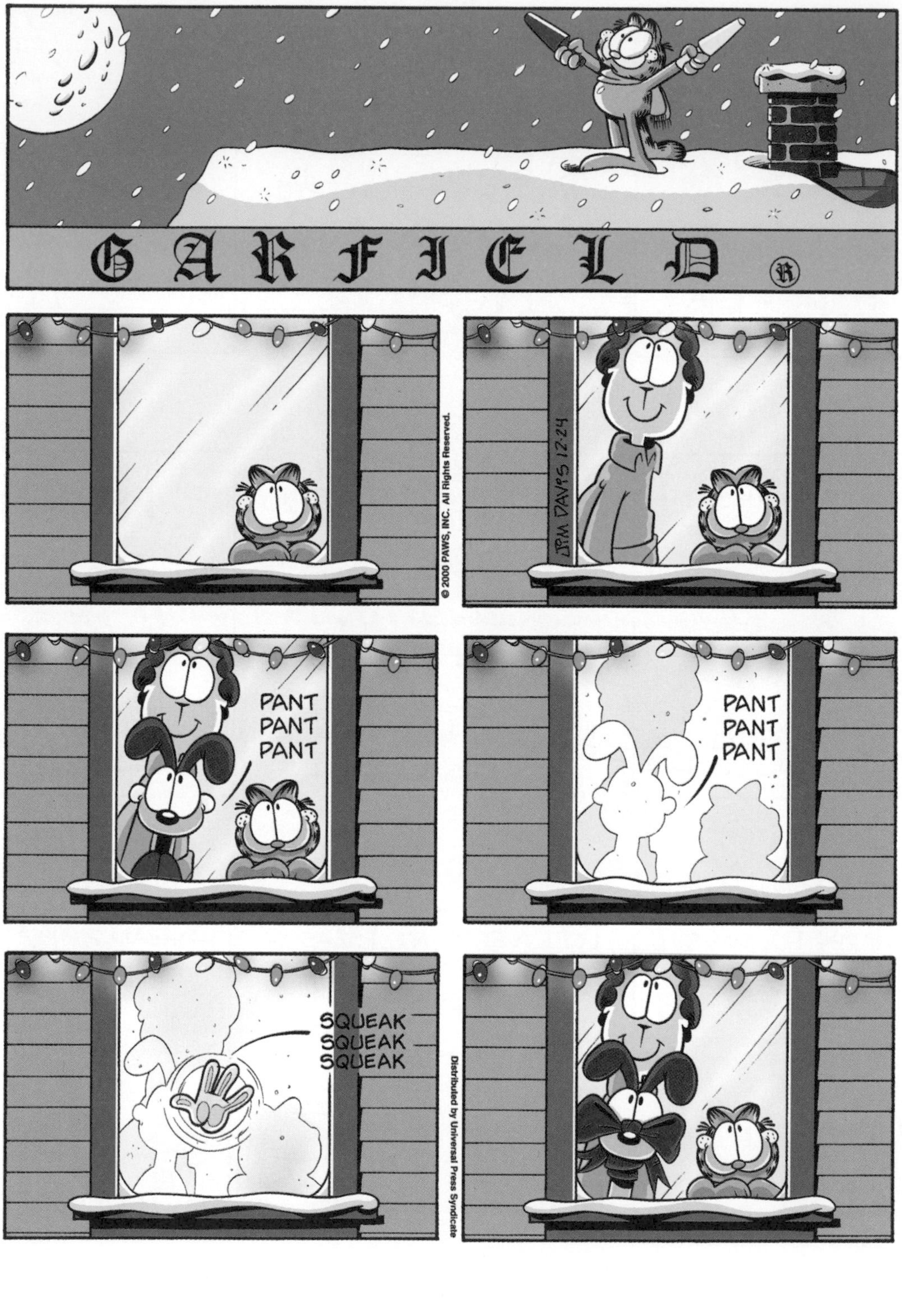
GARFIELD
JIM DAVIS 12-24
PANT
PANT
PANT
PANT
PANT
PANT
SQUEAK
SQUEAK
SQUEAK

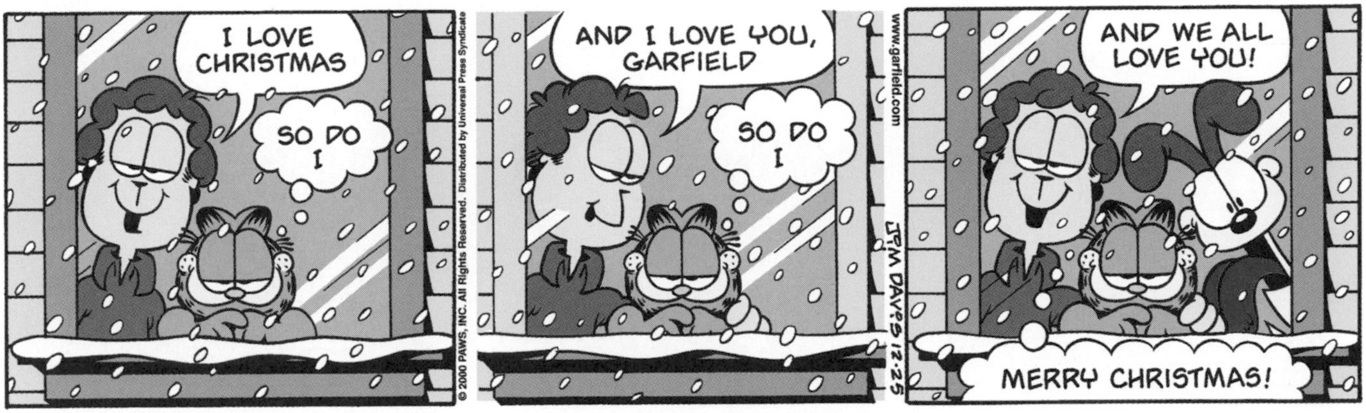
I LOVE CHRISTMAS
SO DO I
© 2000 PAWS, INC. All Rights Reserved. Distributed by Universal Press Syndicate
AND I LOVE YOU, GARFIELD
SO DO I
www.garfield.com
JIM DAVIS 12-25
AND WE ALL LOVE YOU!
MERRY CHRISTMAS!

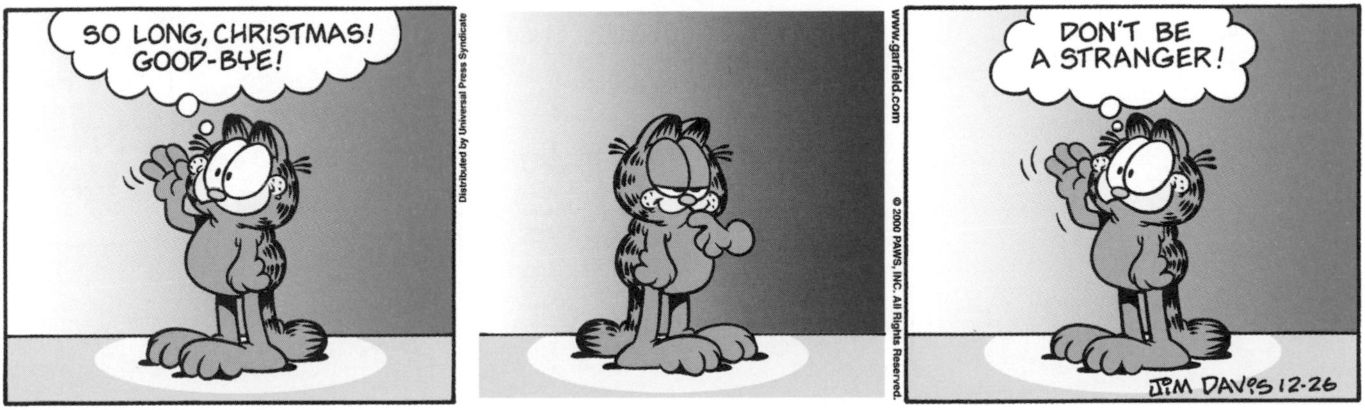
SO LONG, CHRISTMAS! GOOD-BYE!
Distributed by Universal Press Syndicate
www.garfield.com
© 2000 PAWS, INC. All Rights Reserved.
DON'T BE A STRANGER!
JIM DAVIS 12-26

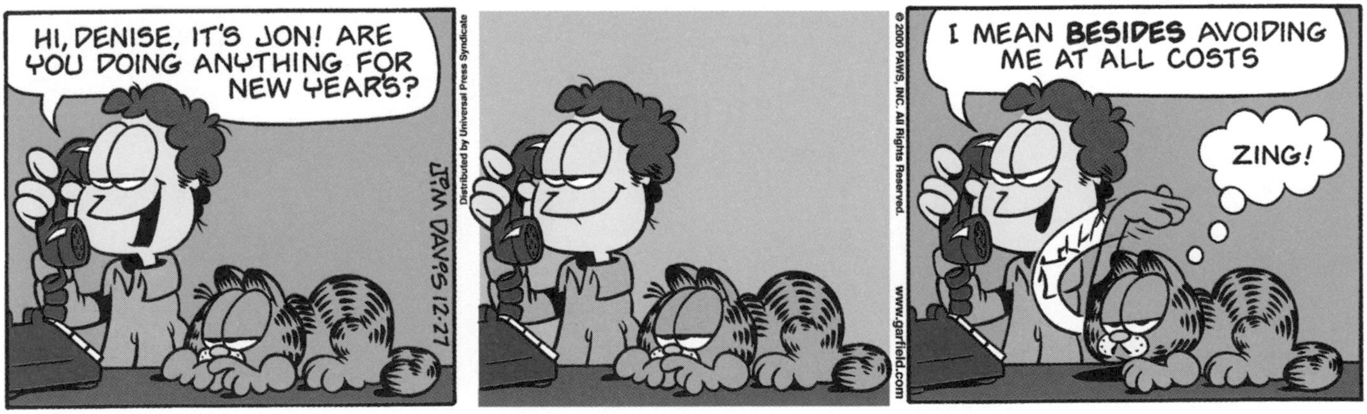
HI, DENISE, IT'S JON! ARE YOU DOING ANYTHING FOR NEW YEAR'S?
JIM DAVIS 12-27
Distributed by Universal Press Syndicate
© 2000 PAWS, INC. All Rights Reserved.
www.garfield.com
I MEAN **BESIDES** AVOIDING ME AT ALL COSTS
ZING!

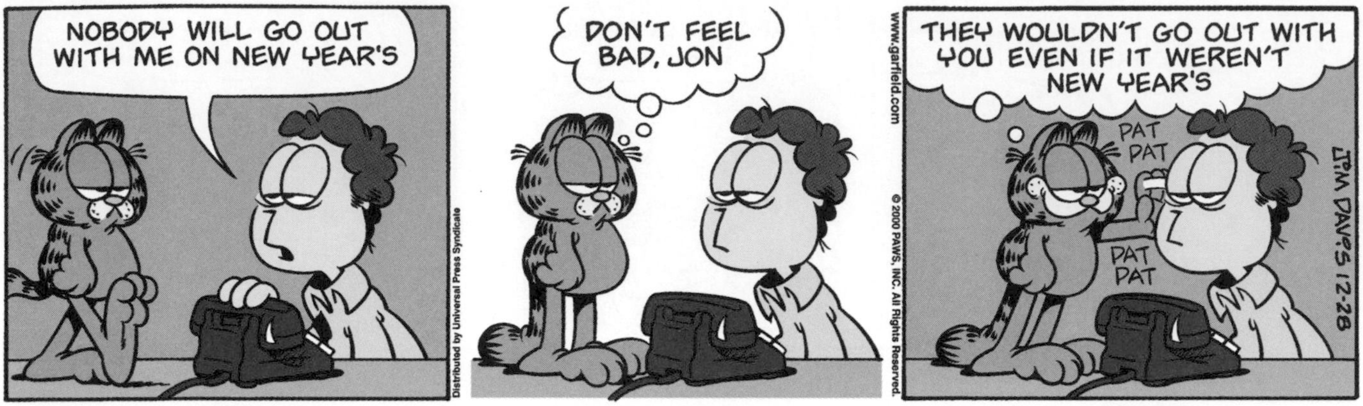
NOBODY WILL GO OUT WITH ME ON NEW YEAR'S
Distributed by Universal Press Syndicate
DON'T FEEL BAD, JON
www.garfield.com
© 2000 PAWS, INC. All Rights Reserved.
THEY WOULDN'T GO OUT WITH YOU EVEN IF IT WEREN'T NEW YEAR'S
PAT PAT
PAT PAT
JIM DAVIS 12-28

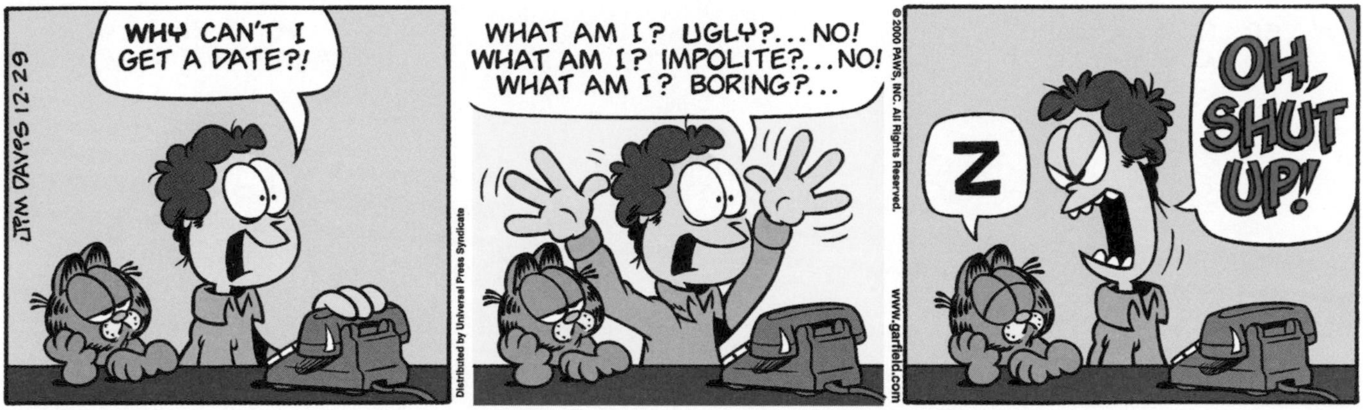
JIM DAVIS 12-29
WHY CAN'T I GET A DATE?!
Distributed by Universal Press Syndicate
WHAT AM I? UGLY?...NO!
WHAT AM I? IMPOLITE?...NO!
WHAT AM I? BORING?...
© 2000 PAWS, INC. All Rights Reserved.
www.garfield.com
Z
OH, SHUT UP!

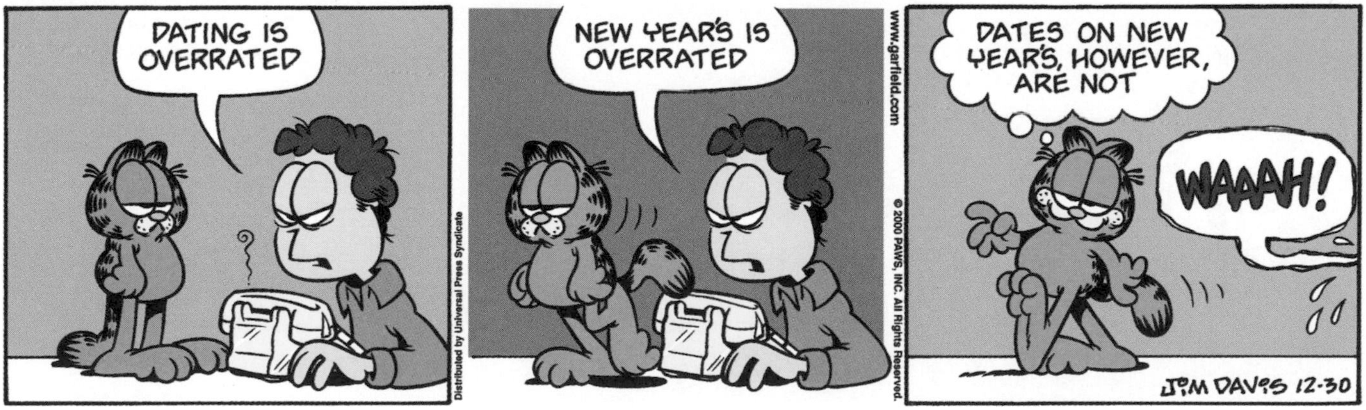
DATING IS OVERRATED
Distributed by Universal Press Syndicate
NEW YEAR'S IS OVERRATED
www.garfield.com
© 2000 PAWS, INC. All Rights Reserved.
DATES ON NEW YEAR'S, HOWEVER, ARE NOT
WAAAH!
JIM DAVIS 12-30

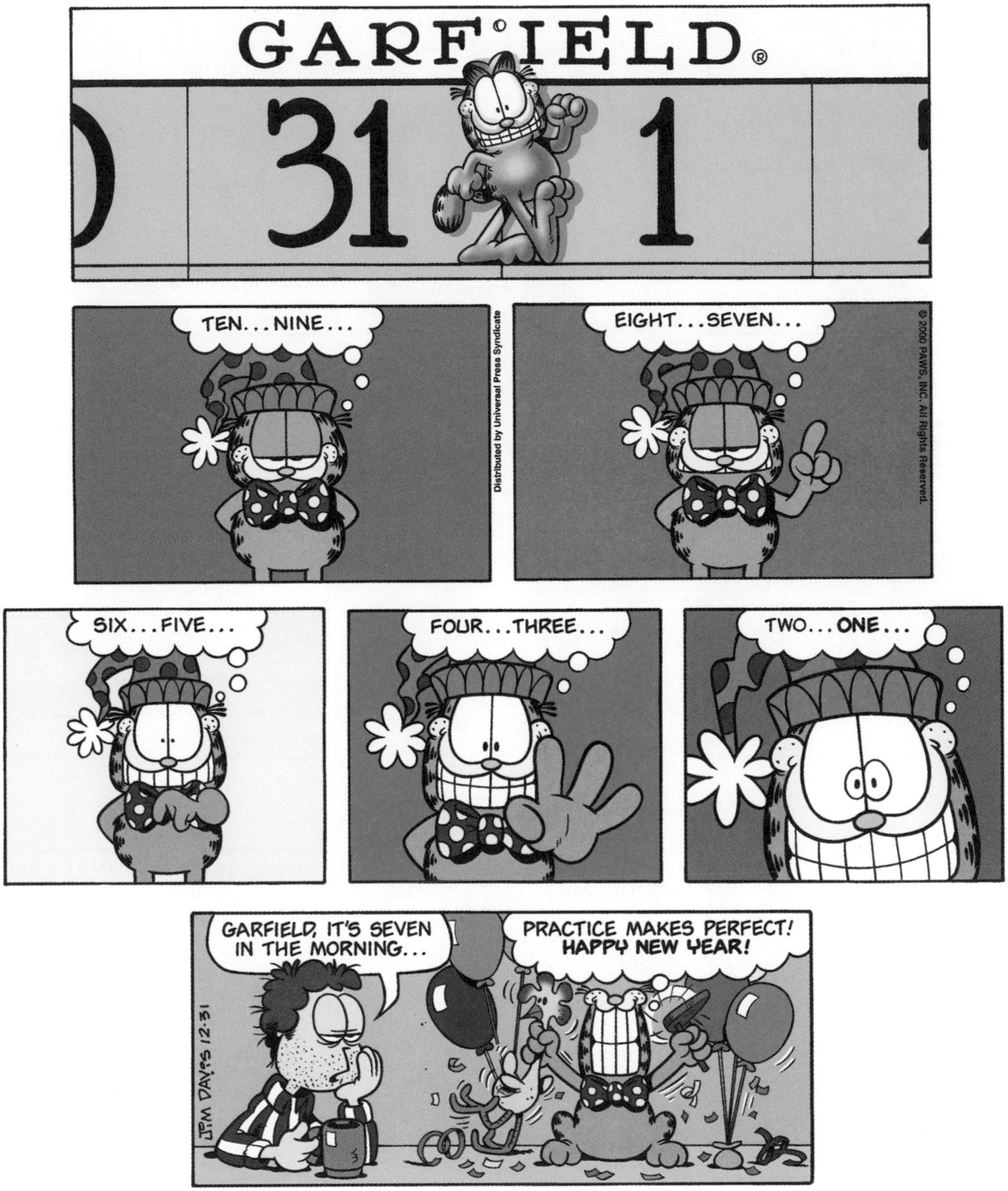
GARFIELD®
31
1
TEN... NINE...
Distributed by Universal Press Syndicate
EIGHT... SEVEN...
© 2000 PAWS, INC. All Rights Reserved.
SIX... FIVE...
FOUR... THREE...
TWO... ONE...
GARFIELD, IT'S SEVEN IN THE MORNING...
PRACTICE MAKES PERFECT! HAPPY NEW YEAR!
JPM DAVIS 12-31

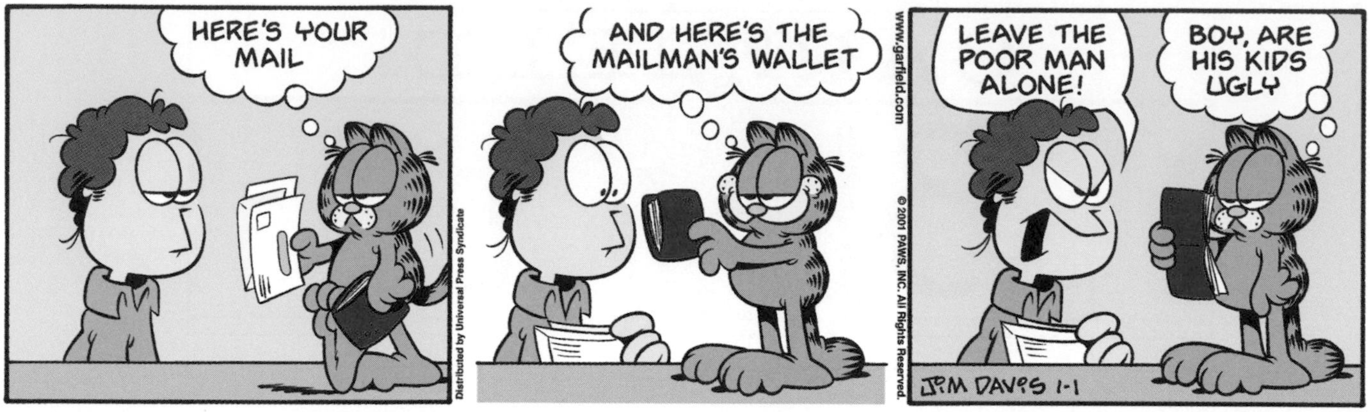
HERE'S YOUR MAIL
Distributed by Universal Press Syndicate
AND HERE'S THE MAILMAN'S WALLET
www.garfield.com
© 2001 PAWS, INC. All Rights Reserved.
LEAVE THE POOR MAN ALONE!
BOY, ARE HIS KIDS UGLY
JIM DAVIS 1-1

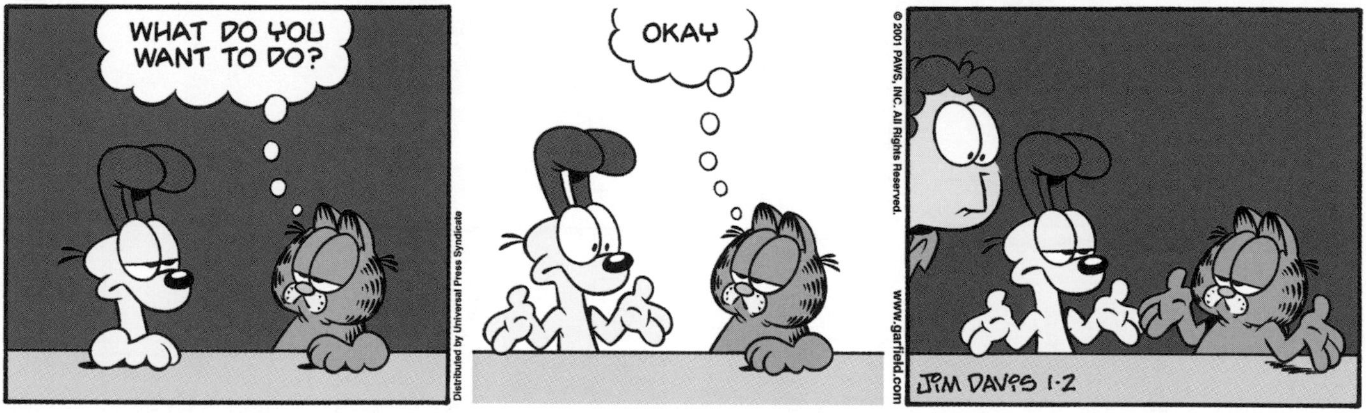
WHAT DO YOU WANT TO DO?
Distributed by Universal Press Syndicate
OKAY
© 2001 PAWS, INC. All Rights Reserved.
www.garfield.com
JIM DAVIS 1-2

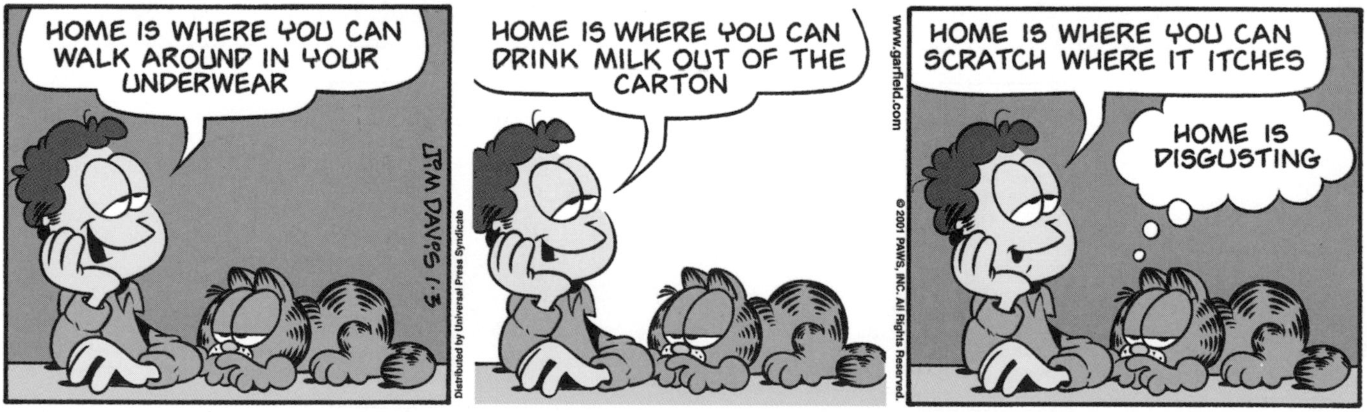
HOME IS WHERE YOU CAN WALK AROUND IN YOUR UNDERWEAR
JIM DAVIS 1-3
Distributed by Universal Press Syndicate
HOME IS WHERE YOU CAN DRINK MILK OUT OF THE CARTON
www.garfield.com
© 2001 PAWS, INC. All Rights Reserved.
HOME IS WHERE YOU CAN SCRATCH WHERE IT ITCHES
HOME IS DISGUSTING

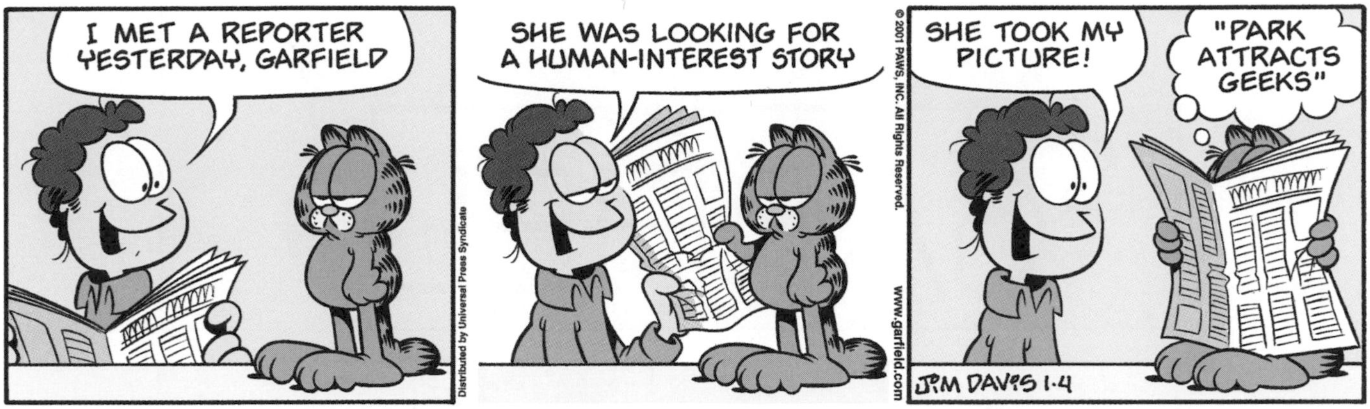
I MET A REPORTER YESTERDAY, GARFIELD
SHE WAS LOOKING FOR A HUMAN-INTEREST STORY
SHE TOOK MY PICTURE!
"PARK ATTRACTS GEEKS"
JIM DAVIS 1-4
Distributed by Universal Press Syndicate
© 2001 PAWS, INC. All Rights Reserved.
www.garfield.com

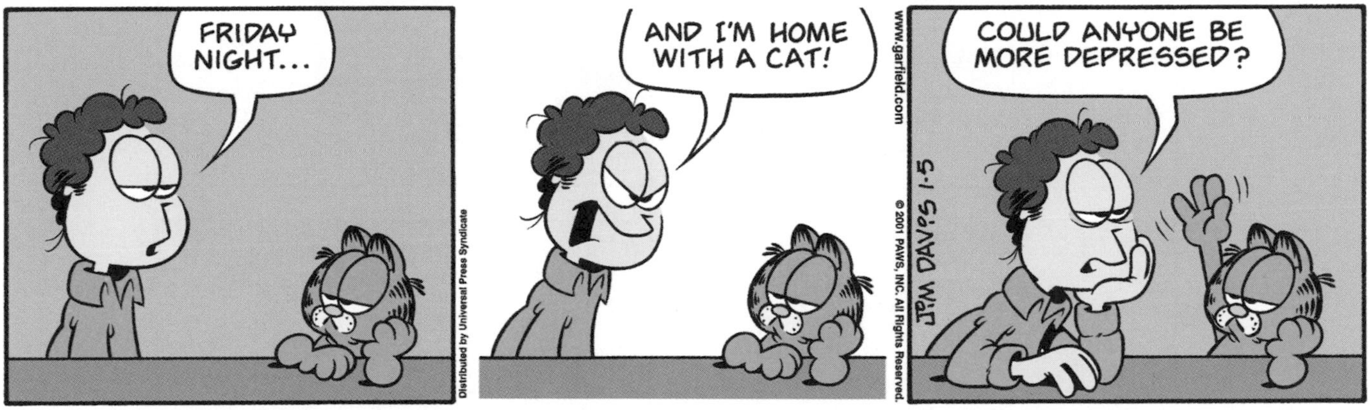
FRIDAY NIGHT...
AND I'M HOME WITH A CAT!
COULD ANYONE BE MORE DEPRESSED?
JIM DAVIS 1-5
Distributed by Universal Press Syndicate
© 2001 PAWS, INC. All Rights Reserved.
www.garfield.com

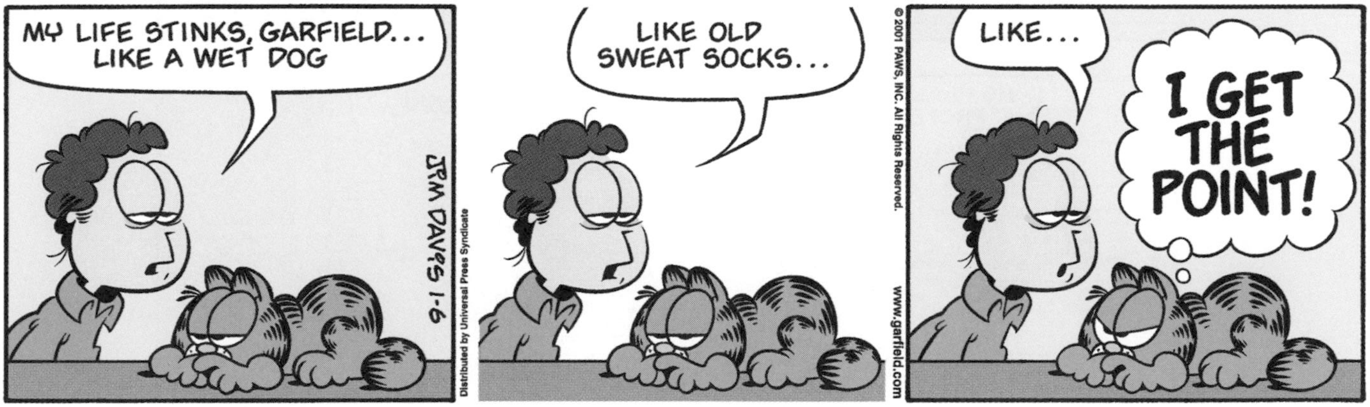
MY LIFE STINKS, GARFIELD... LIKE A WET DOG
LIKE OLD SWEAT SOCKS...
LIKE...
I GET THE POINT!
JIM DAVIS 1-6
Distributed by Universal Press Syndicate
© 2001 PAWS, INC. All Rights Reserved.
www.garfield.com

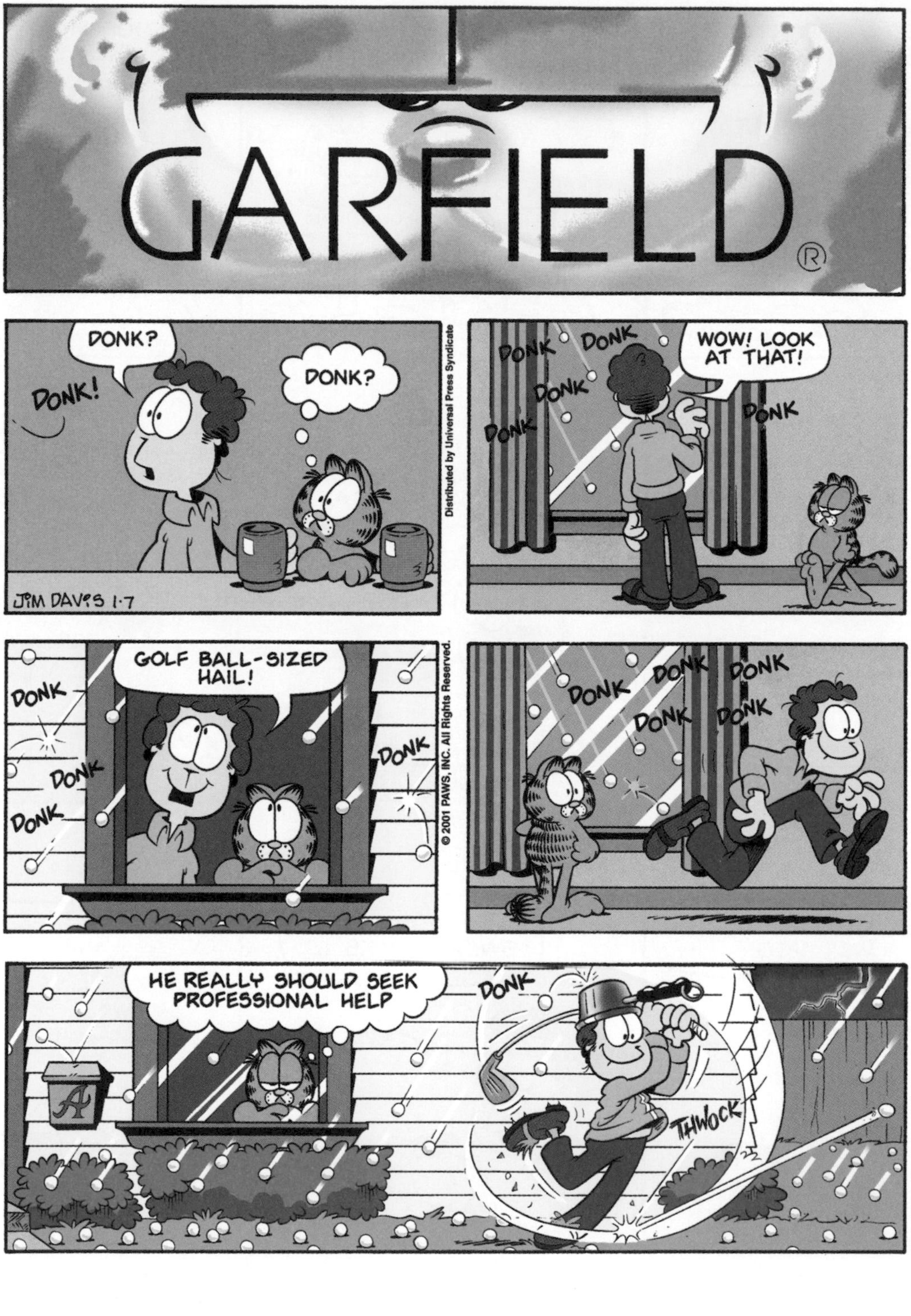
GARFIELD®
DONK!
DONK?
DONK?
JIM DAVIS 1-7
Distributed by Universal Press Syndicate
DONK
DONK
DONK
DONK
WOW! LOOK AT THAT!
DONK
GOLF BALL-SIZED HAIL!
DONK
DONK
DONK
DONK
© 2001 PAWS, INC. All Rights Reserved.
DONK
DONK
DONK
DONK
DONK
HE REALLY SHOULD SEEK PROFESSIONAL HELP
DONK
THWOCK

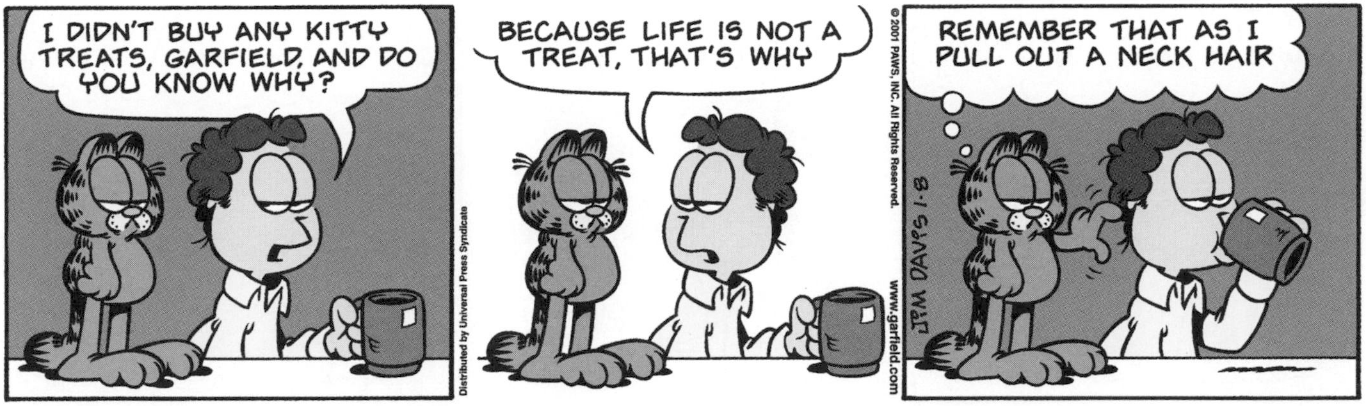
I DIDN'T BUY ANY KITTY TREATS, GARFIELD, AND DO YOU KNOW WHY?
BECAUSE LIFE IS NOT A TREAT, THAT'S WHY
REMEMBER THAT AS I PULL OUT A NECK HAIR
JIM DAVIS 1-8
Distributed by Universal Press Syndicate
© 2001 PAWS, INC. All Rights Reserved.
www.garfield.com

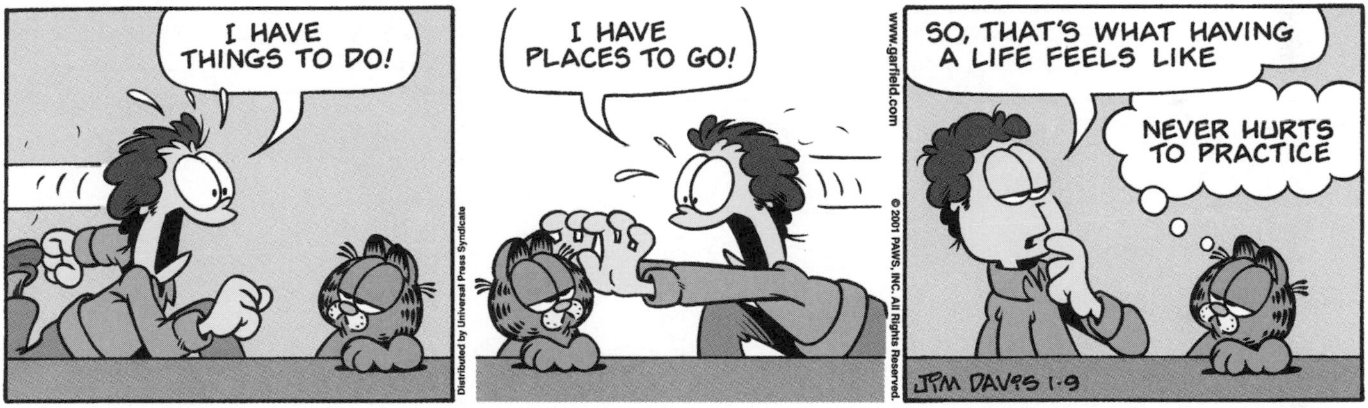
I HAVE THINGS TO DO!
I HAVE PLACES TO GO!
SO, THAT'S WHAT HAVING A LIFE FEELS LIKE
NEVER HURTS TO PRACTICE
JIM DAVIS 1-9
Distributed by Universal Press Syndicate
www.garfield.com
© 2001 PAWS, INC. All Rights Reserved.

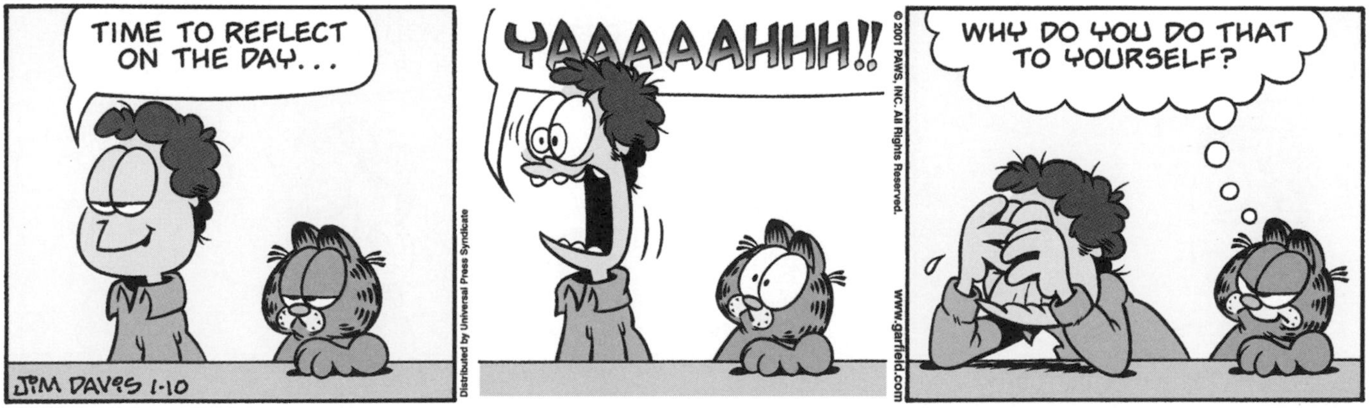
TIME TO REFLECT ON THE DAY...
YAAAAAHHH!!
WHY DO YOU DO THAT TO YOURSELF?
JIM DAVIS 1-10
Distributed by Universal Press Syndicate
© 2001 PAWS, INC. All Rights Reserved.
www.garfield.com

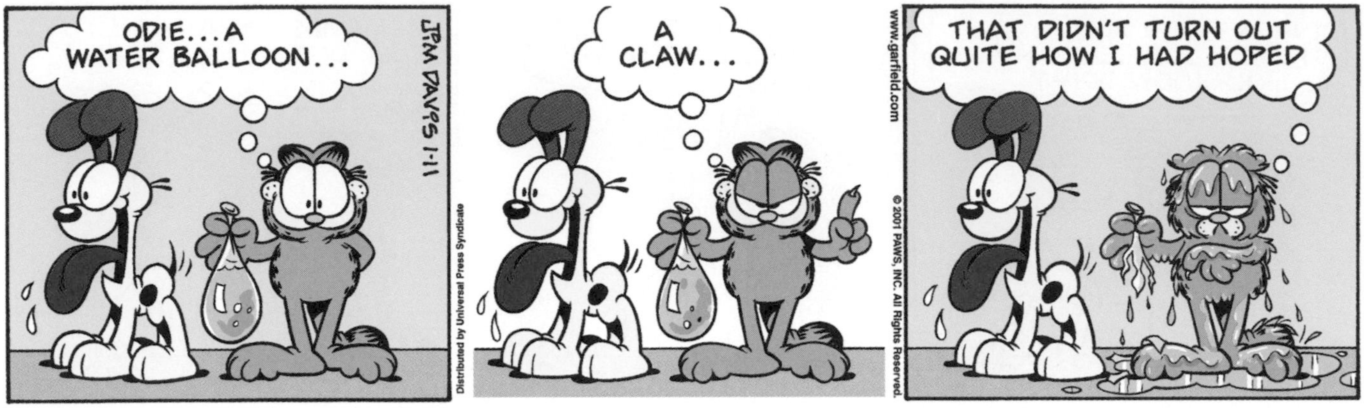
ODIE...A WATER BALLOON...
JPM DAVPS 1-11
Distributed by Universal Press Syndicate
A CLAW...
www.garfield.com
© 2001 PAWS, INC. All Rights Reserved.
THAT DIDN'T TURN OUT QUITE HOW I HAD HOPED

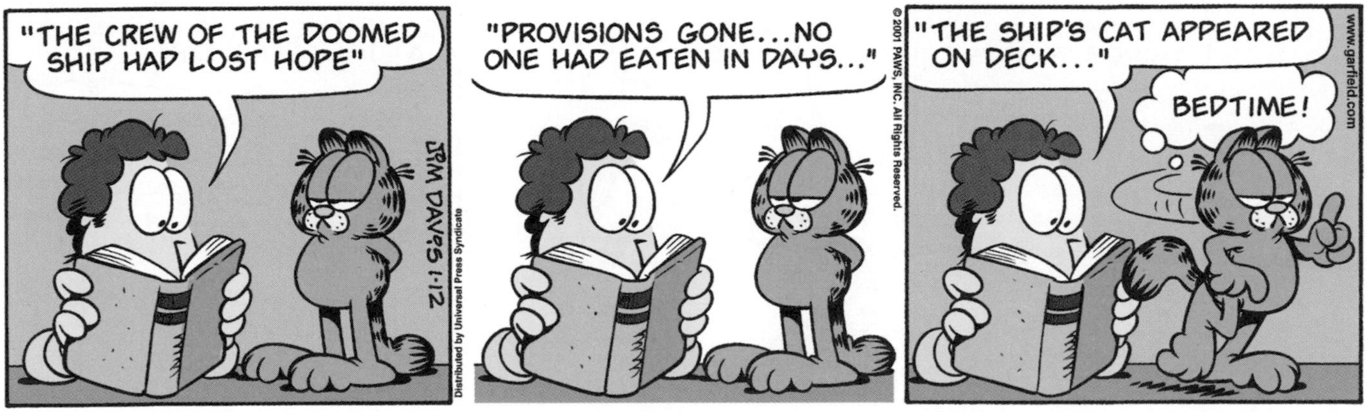
"THE CREW OF THE DOOMED SHIP HAD LOST HOPE"
JPM DAVPS 1-12
Distributed by Universal Press Syndicate
"PROVISIONS GONE...NO ONE HAD EATEN IN DAYS..."
© 2001 PAWS, INC. All Rights Reserved.
"THE SHIP'S CAT APPEARED ON DECK..."
BEDTIME!
www.garfield.com

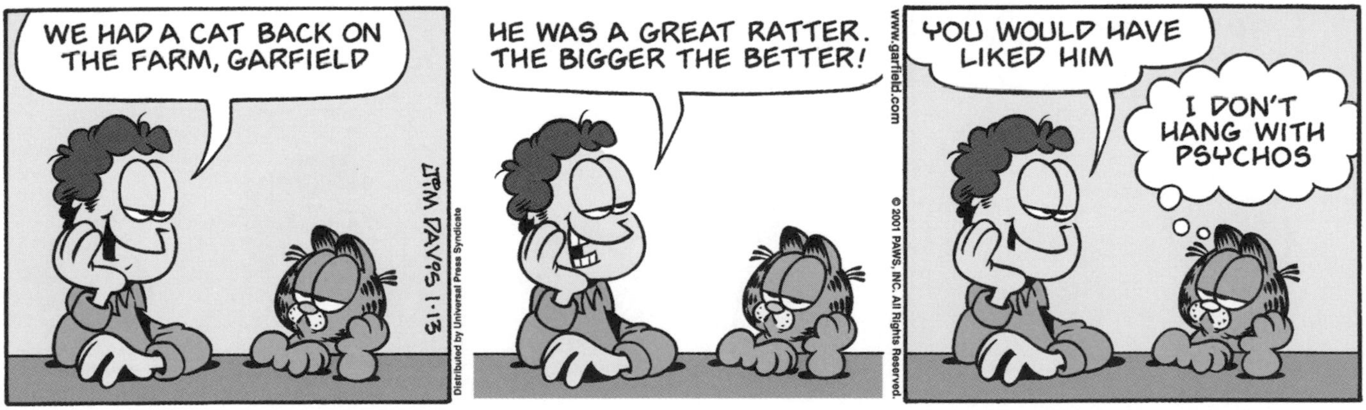
WE HAD A CAT BACK ON THE FARM, GARFIELD
JPM DAVPS 1-13
Distributed by Universal Press Syndicate
HE WAS A GREAT RATTER. THE BIGGER THE BETTER!
www.garfield.com
© 2001 PAWS, INC. All Rights Reserved.
YOU WOULD HAVE LIKED HIM
I DON'T HANG WITH PSYCHOS

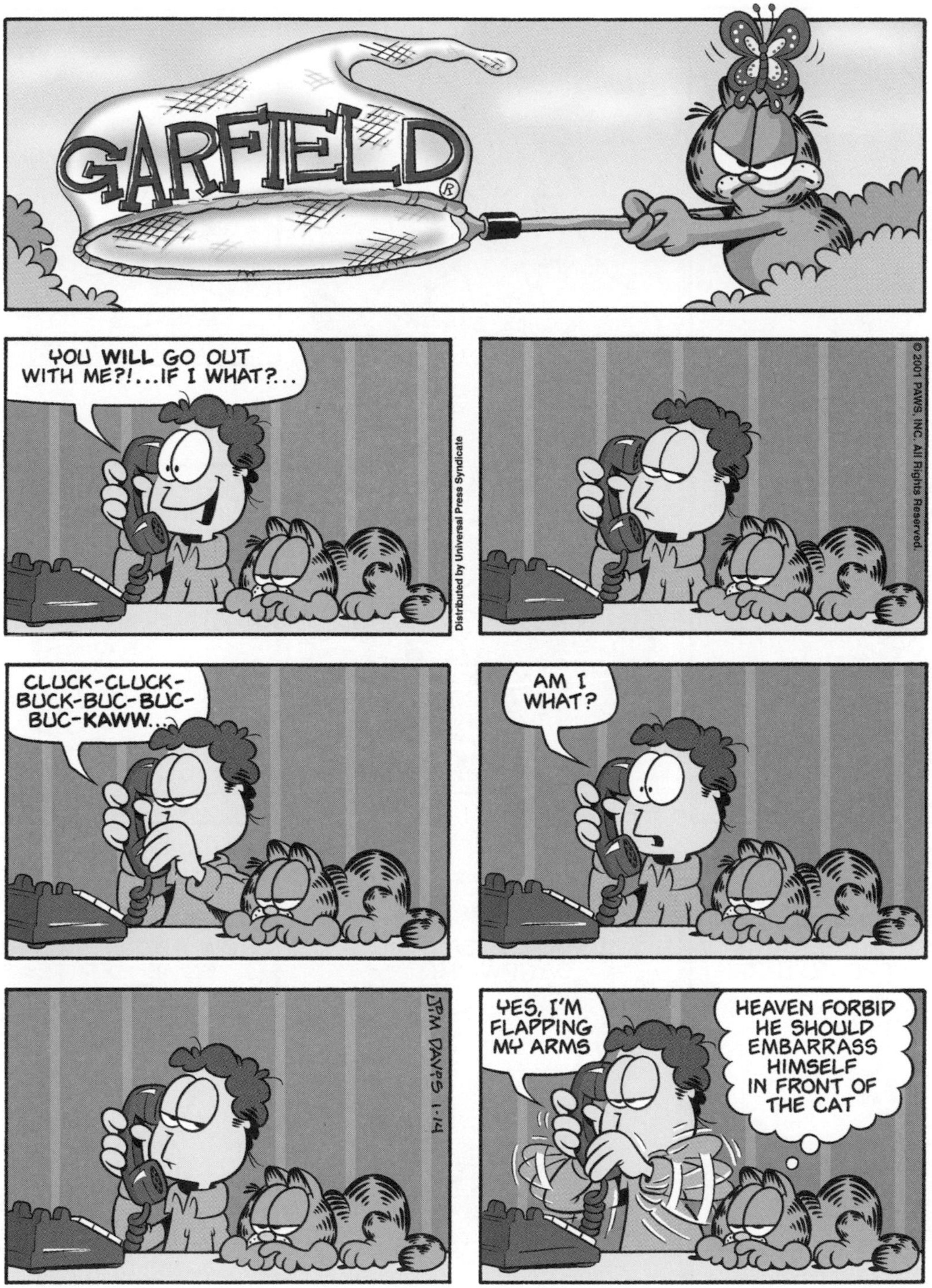
GARFIELD®
YOU WILL GO OUT WITH ME?!...IF I WHAT?...
Distributed by Universal Press Syndicate
© 2001 PAWS, INC. All Rights Reserved.
CLUCK-CLUCK-BUCK-BUC-BUC-BUC-KAWW...
AM I WHAT?
JIM DAVIS 1-14
YES, I'M FLAPPING MY ARMS
HEAVEN FORBID HE SHOULD EMBARRASS HIMSELF IN FRONT OF THE CAT

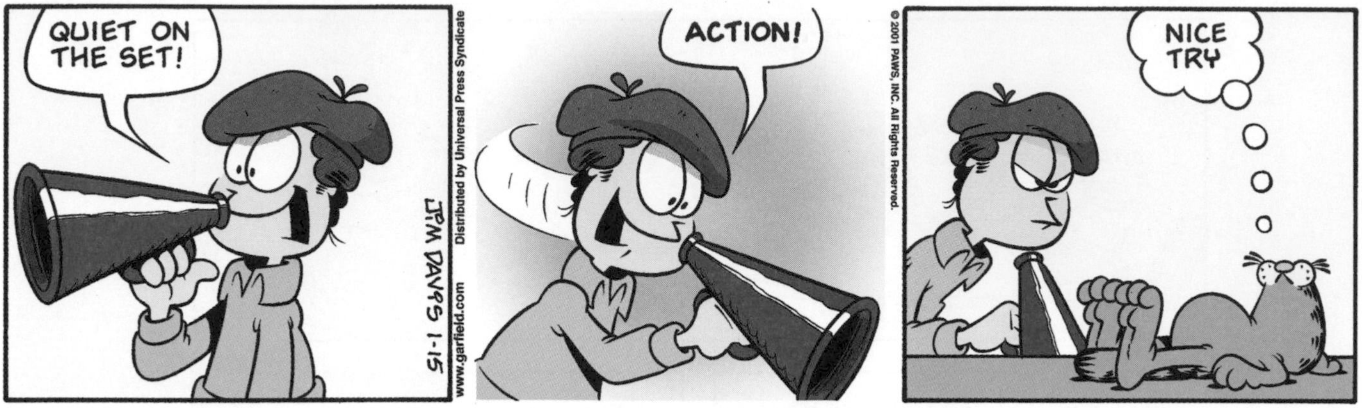
QUIET ON THE SET!
JIM DAVIS 1-15
www.garfield.com
Distributed by Universal Press Syndicate
ACTION!
© 2001 PAWS, INC. All Rights Reserved.
NICE TRY

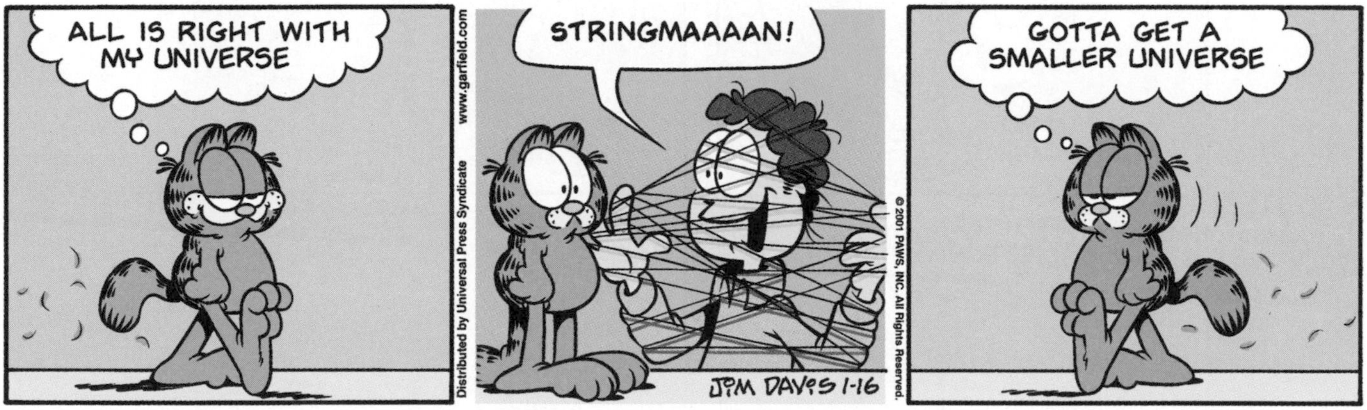
ALL IS RIGHT WITH MY UNIVERSE
www.garfield.com
Distributed by Universal Press Syndicate
STRINGMAAAAN!
JIM DAVIS 1-16
© 2001 PAWS, INC. All Rights Reserved.
GOTTA GET A SMALLER UNIVERSE

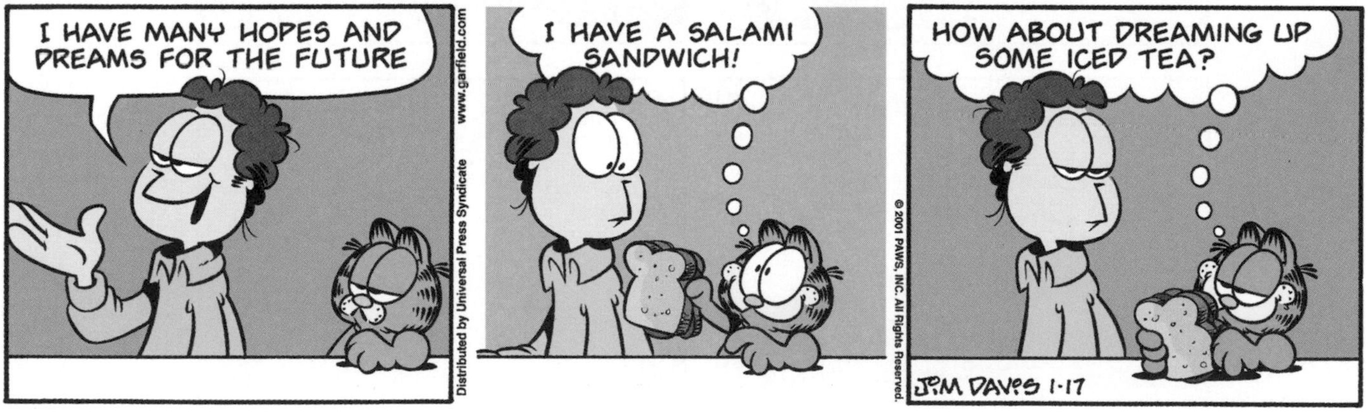
I HAVE MANY HOPES AND DREAMS FOR THE FUTURE
www.garfield.com
Distributed by Universal Press Syndicate
I HAVE A SALAMI SANDWICH!
© 2001 PAWS, INC. All Rights Reserved.
HOW ABOUT DREAMING UP SOME ICED TEA?
JIM DAVIS 1-17

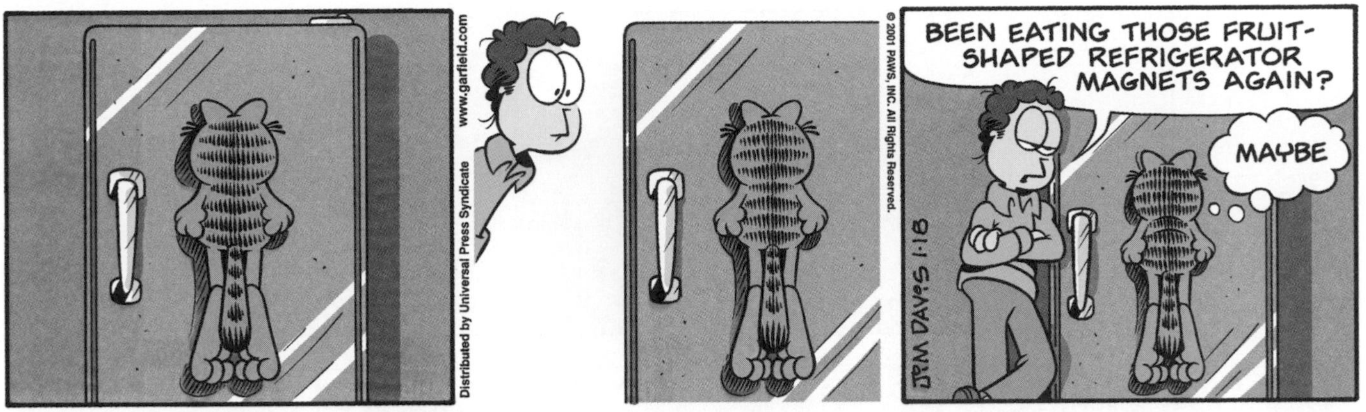
www.garfield.com
Distributed by Universal Press Syndicate
© 2001 PAWS, INC. All Rights Reserved.
BEEN EATING THOSE FRUIT-SHAPED REFRIGERATOR MAGNETS AGAIN?
MAYBE
JIM DAVIS 1-18

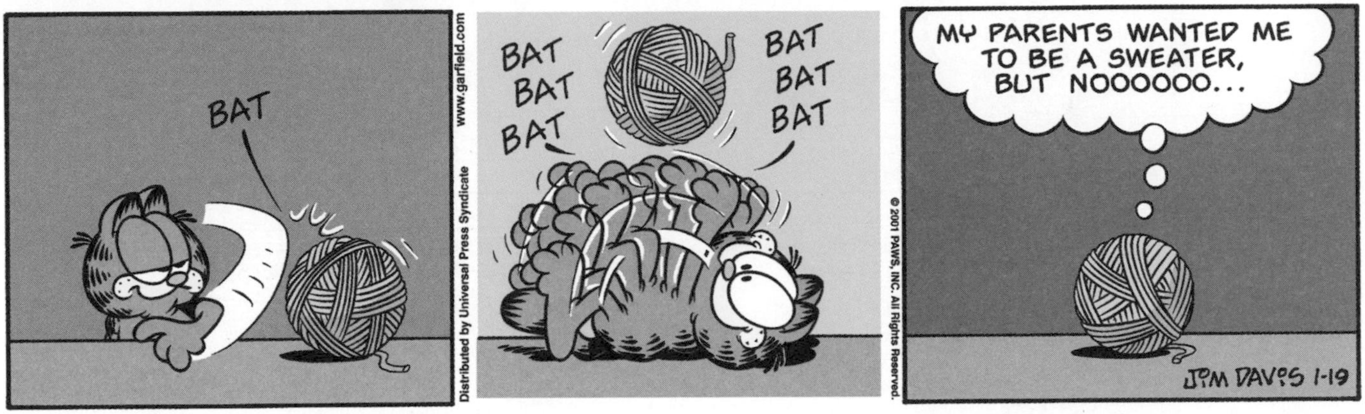
BAT
www.garfield.com
Distributed by Universal Press Syndicate
BAT BAT BAT
BAT BAT BAT
© 2001 PAWS, INC. All Rights Reserved.
MY PARENTS WANTED ME TO BE A SWEATER, BUT NOOOOOO...
JIM DAVIS 1-19

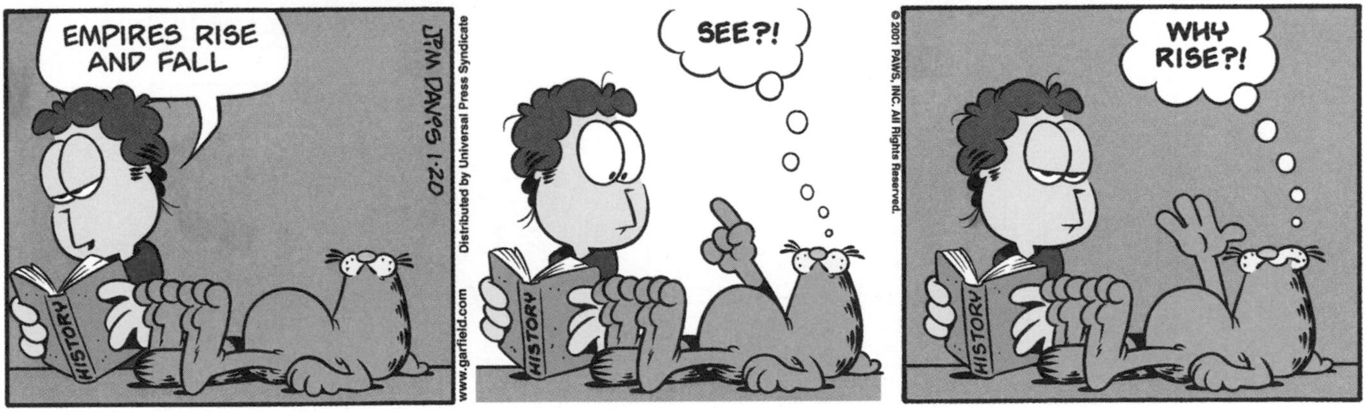
EMPIRES RISE AND FALL
HISTORY
JIM DAVIS 1-20
Distributed by Universal Press Syndicate
www.garfield.com
SEE?!
HISTORY
© 2001 PAWS, INC. All Rights Reserved.
WHY RISE?!
HISTORY

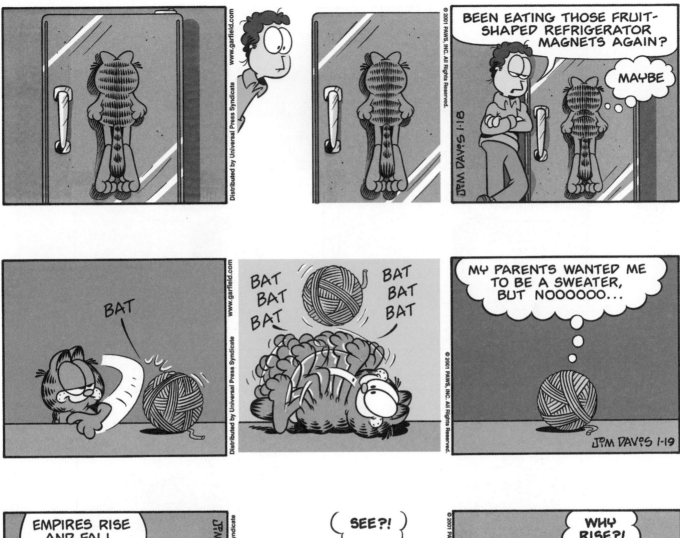

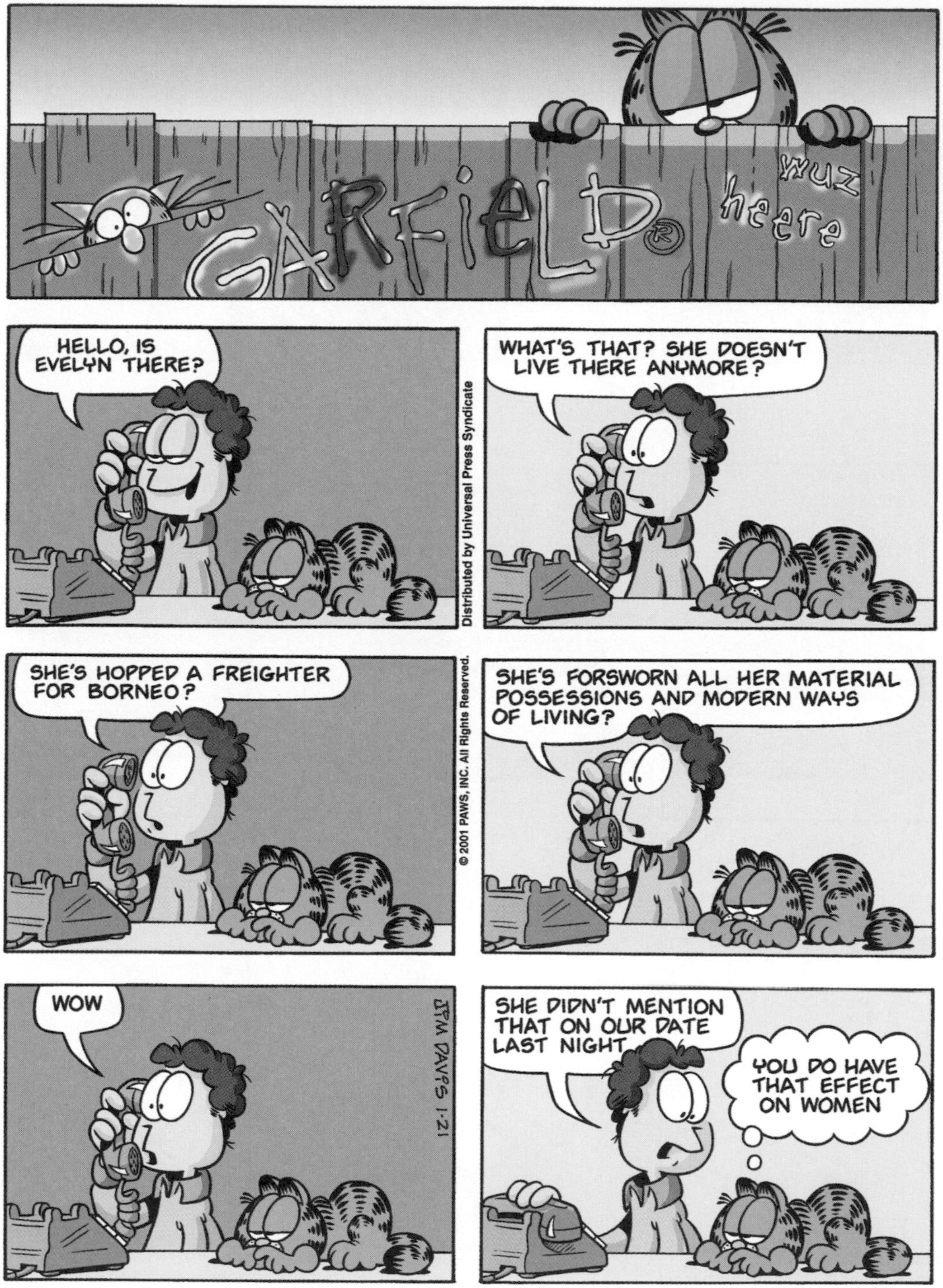
GARFIELD®
wuz heere
HELLO, IS EVELYN THERE?
WHAT'S THAT? SHE DOESN'T LIVE THERE ANYMORE?
SHE'S HOPPED A FREIGHTER FOR BORNEO?
SHE'S FORSWORN ALL HER MATERIAL POSSESSIONS AND MODERN WAYS OF LIVING?
WOW
JIM DAVIS 1-21
SHE DIDN'T MENTION THAT ON OUR DATE LAST NIGHT
YOU DO HAVE THAT EFFECT ON WOMEN
© 2001 PAWS, INC. All Rights Reserved. Distributed by Universal Press Syndicate

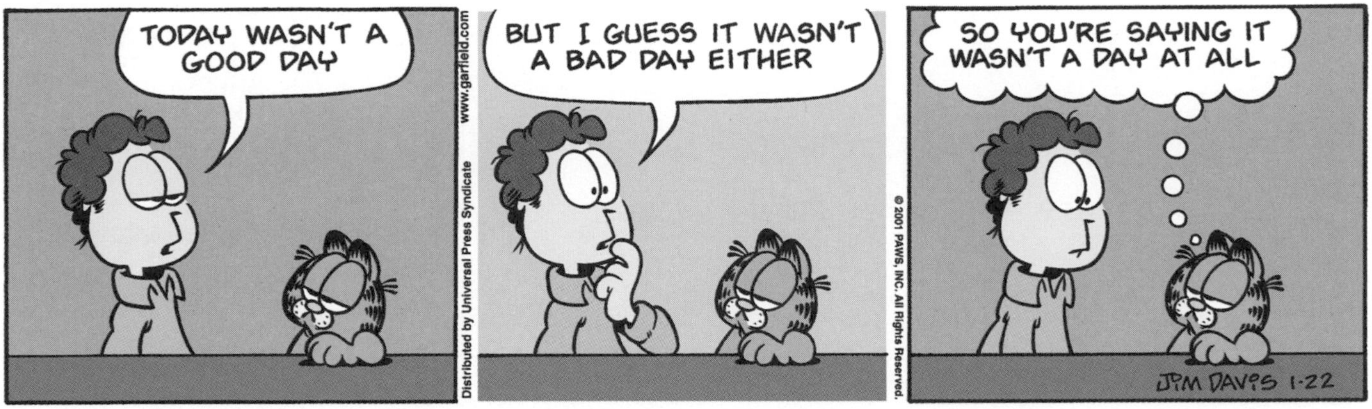
TODAY WASN'T A GOOD DAY
Distributed by Universal Press Syndicate www.garfield.com
BUT I GUESS IT WASN'T A BAD DAY EITHER
© 2001 PAWS, INC. All Rights Reserved.
SO YOU'RE SAYING IT WASN'T A DAY AT ALL
JIM DAVIS 1-22

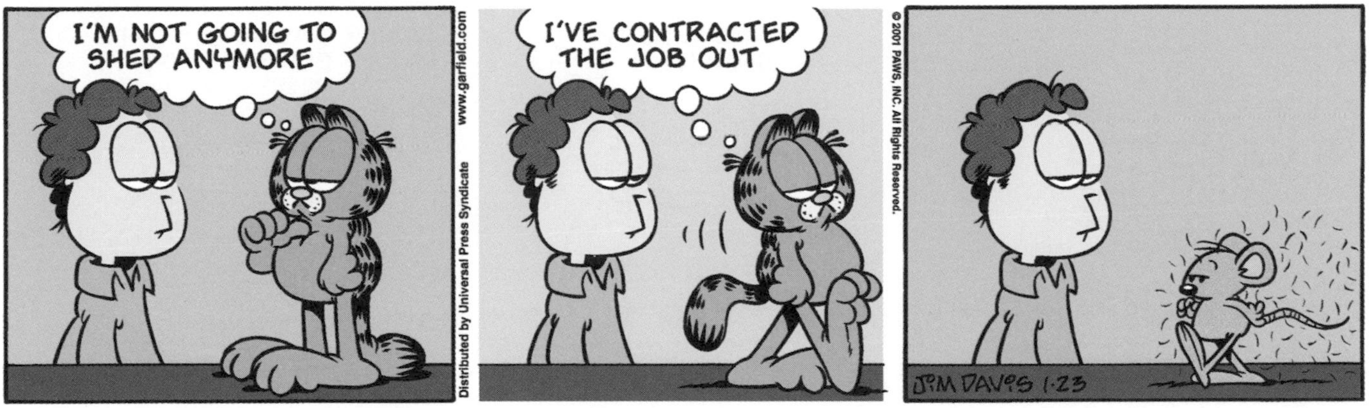
I'M NOT GOING TO SHED ANYMORE
Distributed by Universal Press Syndicate www.garfield.com
I'VE CONTRACTED THE JOB OUT
© 2001 PAWS, INC. All Rights Reserved.
JIM DAVIS 1-23

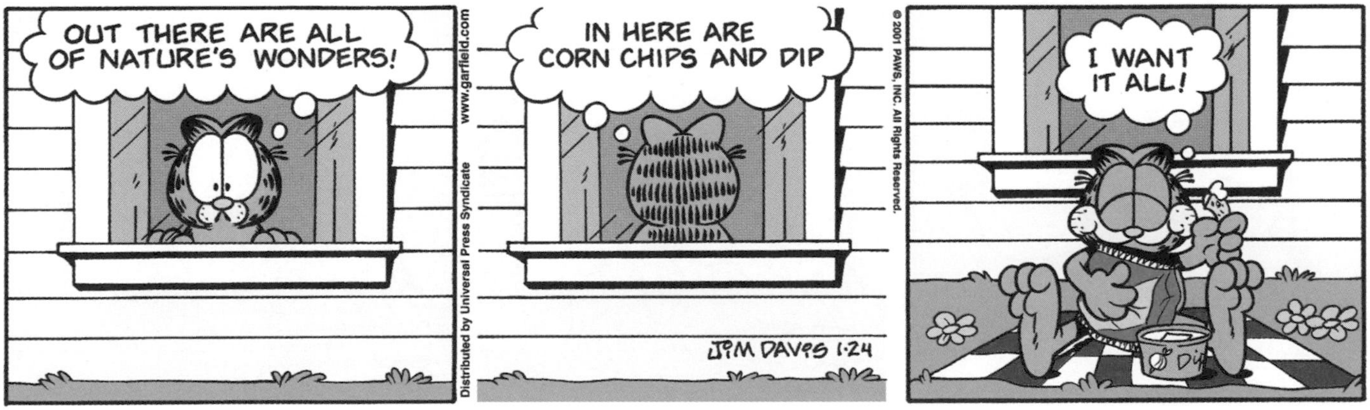
OUT THERE ARE ALL OF NATURE'S WONDERS!
Distributed by Universal Press Syndicate www.garfield.com
IN HERE ARE CORN CHIPS AND DIP
JIM DAVIS 1-24
© 2001 PAWS, INC. All Rights Reserved.
I WANT IT ALL!

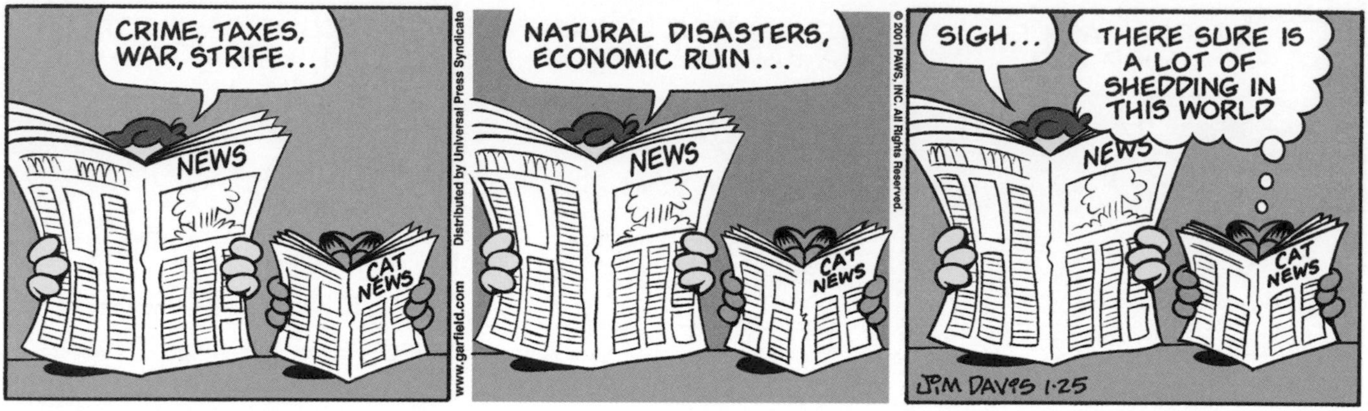
CRIME, TAXES, WAR, STRIFE...
NEWS
CAT NEWS
www.garfield.com Distributed by Universal Press Syndicate
NATURAL DISASTERS, ECONOMIC RUIN...
NEWS
CAT NEWS
© 2001 PAWS, INC. All Rights Reserved.
SIGH...
THERE SURE IS A LOT OF SHEDDING IN THIS WORLD
NEWS
CAT NEWS
JIM DAVIS 1-25

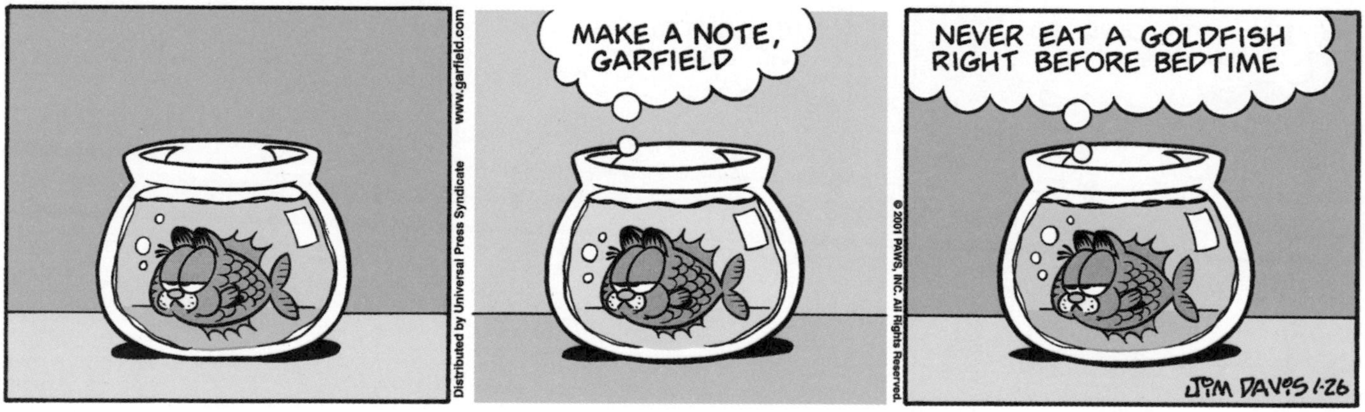
Distributed by Universal Press Syndicate www.garfield.com
MAKE A NOTE, GARFIELD
© 2001 PAWS, INC. All Rights Reserved.
NEVER EAT A GOLDFISH RIGHT BEFORE BEDTIME
JIM DAVIS 1-26

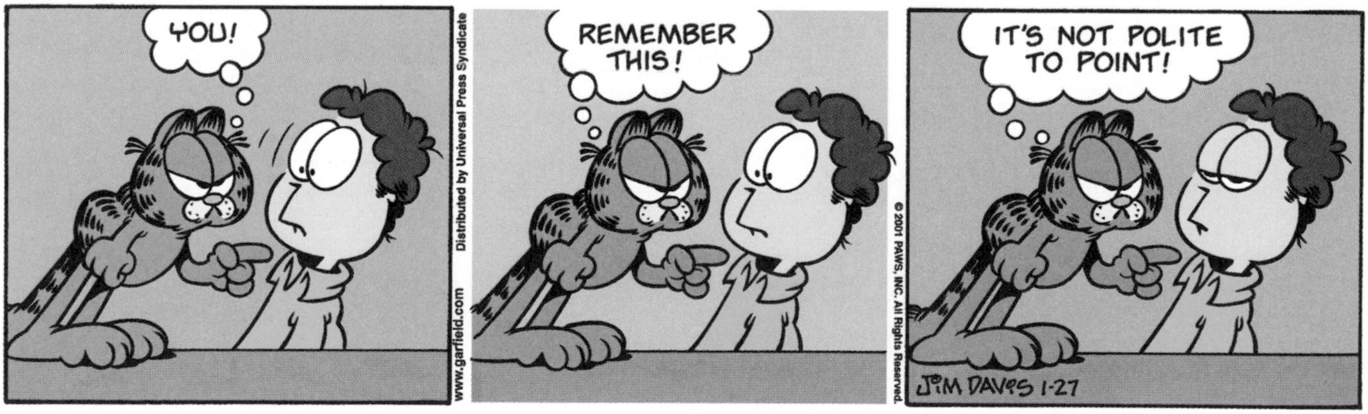
YOU!
www.garfield.com Distributed by Universal Press Syndicate
REMEMBER THIS!
© 2001 PAWS, INC. All Rights Reserved.
IT'S NOT POLITE TO POINT!
JIM DAVIS 1-27

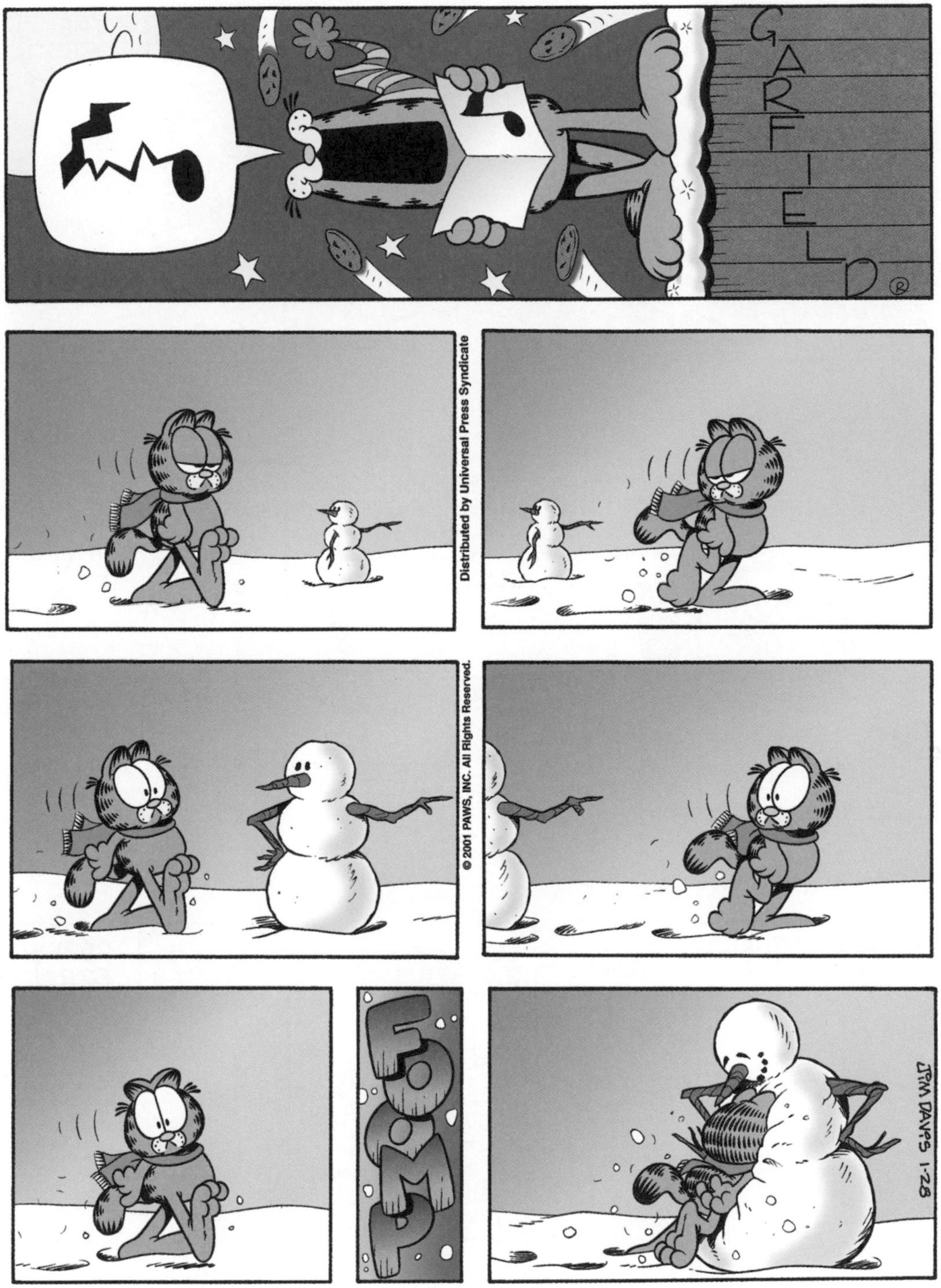
GARFIELD
Distributed by Universal Press Syndicate
© 2001 PAWS, INC. All Rights Reserved.
FOMP
JIM DAVIS 1-28

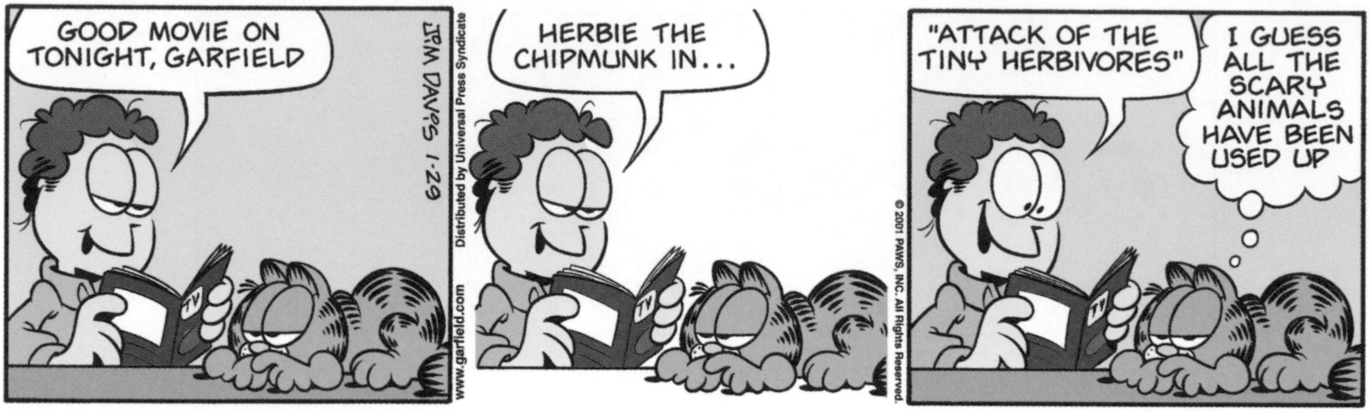
GOOD MOVIE ON TONIGHT, GARFIELD
JIM DAVIS 1-29
Distributed by Universal Press Syndicate
www.garfield.com
HERBIE THE CHIPMUNK IN...
"ATTACK OF THE TINY HERBIVORES"
I GUESS ALL THE SCARY ANIMALS HAVE BEEN USED UP
© 2001 PAWS, INC. All Rights Reserved.
TV

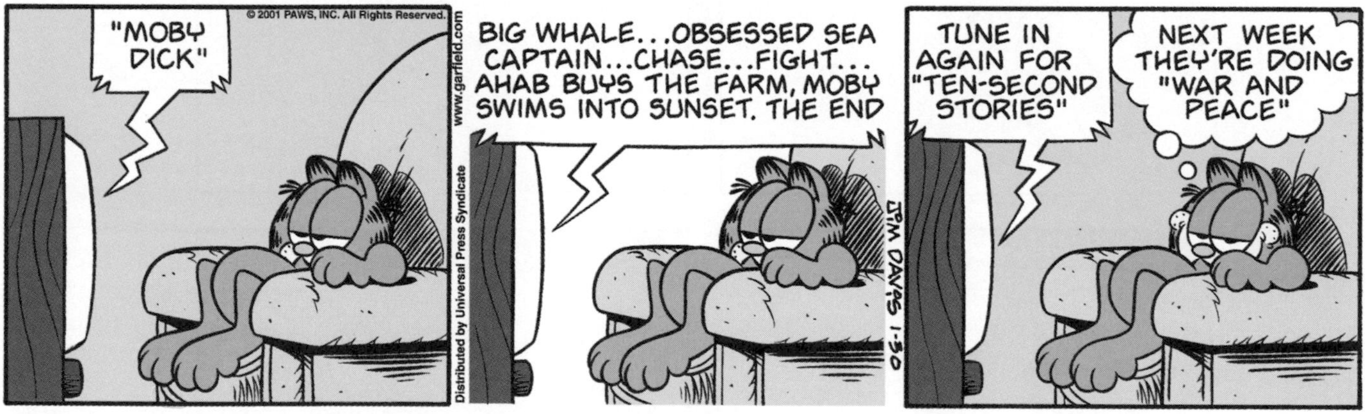
"MOBY DICK"
© 2001 PAWS, INC. All Rights Reserved.
www.garfield.com
Distributed by Universal Press Syndicate
BIG WHALE...OBSESSED SEA CAPTAIN...CHASE...FIGHT... AHAB BUYS THE FARM, MOBY SWIMS INTO SUNSET. THE END
JIM DAVIS 1-30
TUNE IN AGAIN FOR "TEN-SECOND STORIES"
NEXT WEEK THEY'RE DOING "WAR AND PEACE"

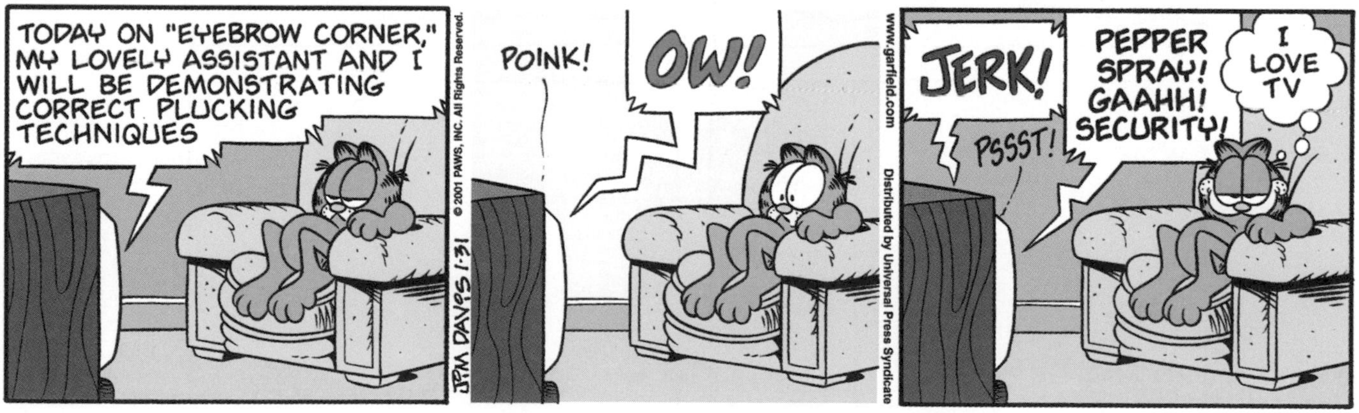
TODAY ON "EYEBROW CORNER," MY LOVELY ASSISTANT AND I WILL BE DEMONSTRATING CORRECT PLUCKING TECHNIQUES
© 2001 PAWS, INC. All Rights Reserved.
JIM DAVIS 1-31
POINK!
OW!
www.garfield.com
Distributed by Universal Press Syndicate
JERK!
PSSST!
PEPPER SPRAY! GAAHH! SECURITY!
I LOVE TV

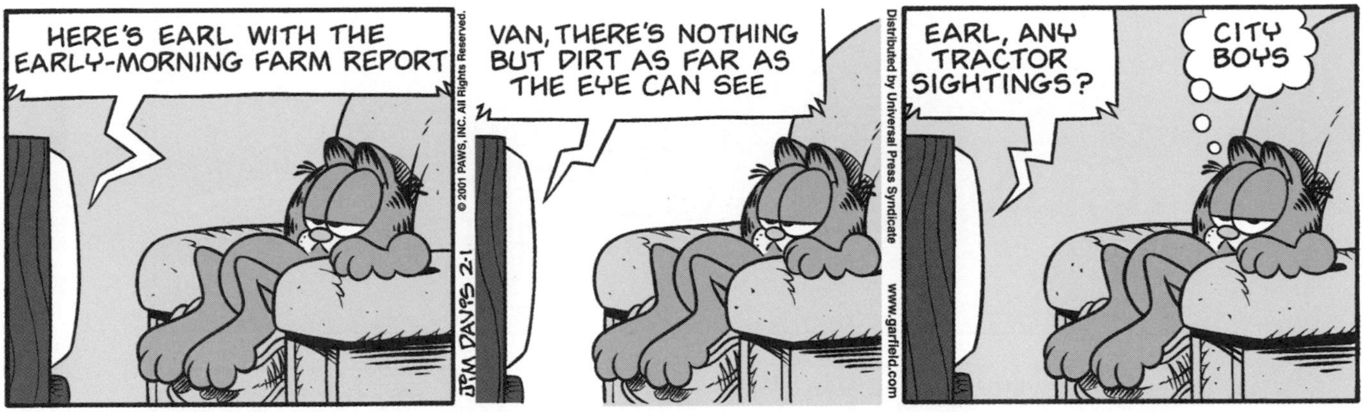
HERE'S EARL WITH THE EARLY-MORNING FARM REPORT
VAN, THERE'S NOTHING BUT DIRT AS FAR AS THE EYE CAN SEE
EARL, ANY TRACTOR SIGHTINGS?
CITY BOYS
JPM DAVPS 2·1
© 2001 PAWS, INC. All Rights Reserved.
Distributed by Universal Press Syndicate
www.garfield.com

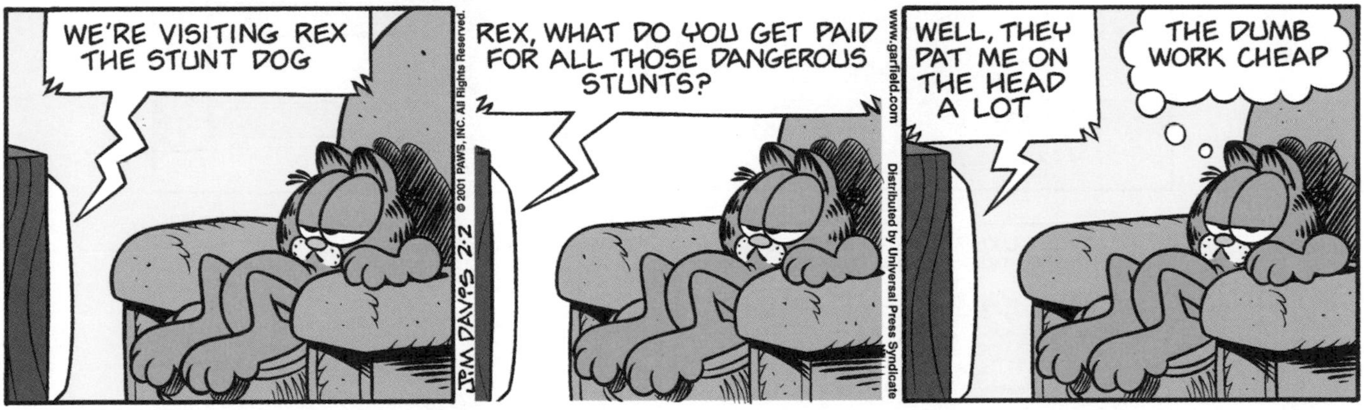
WE'RE VISITING REX THE STUNT DOG
REX, WHAT DO YOU GET PAID FOR ALL THOSE DANGEROUS STUNTS?
WELL, THEY PAT ME ON THE HEAD A LOT
THE DUMB WORK CHEAP
JPM DAVPS 2·2
© 2001 PAWS, INC. All Rights Reserved.
Distributed by Universal Press Syndicate
www.garfield.com

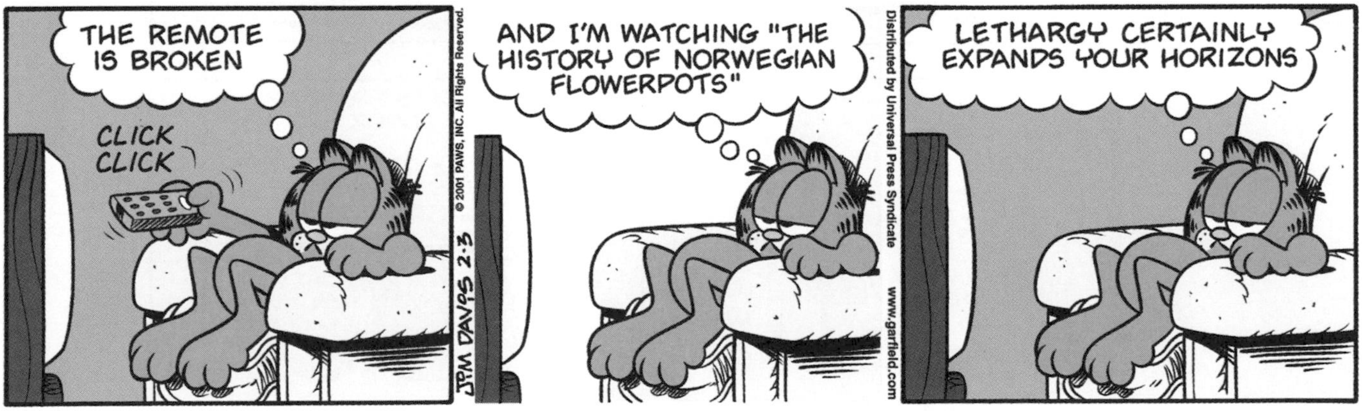
THE REMOTE IS BROKEN
CLICK CLICK
AND I'M WATCHING "THE HISTORY OF NORWEGIAN FLOWERPOTS"
LETHARGY CERTAINLY EXPANDS YOUR HORIZONS
JPM DAVPS 2·3
© 2001 PAWS, INC. All Rights Reserved.
Distributed by Universal Press Syndicate
www.garfield.com

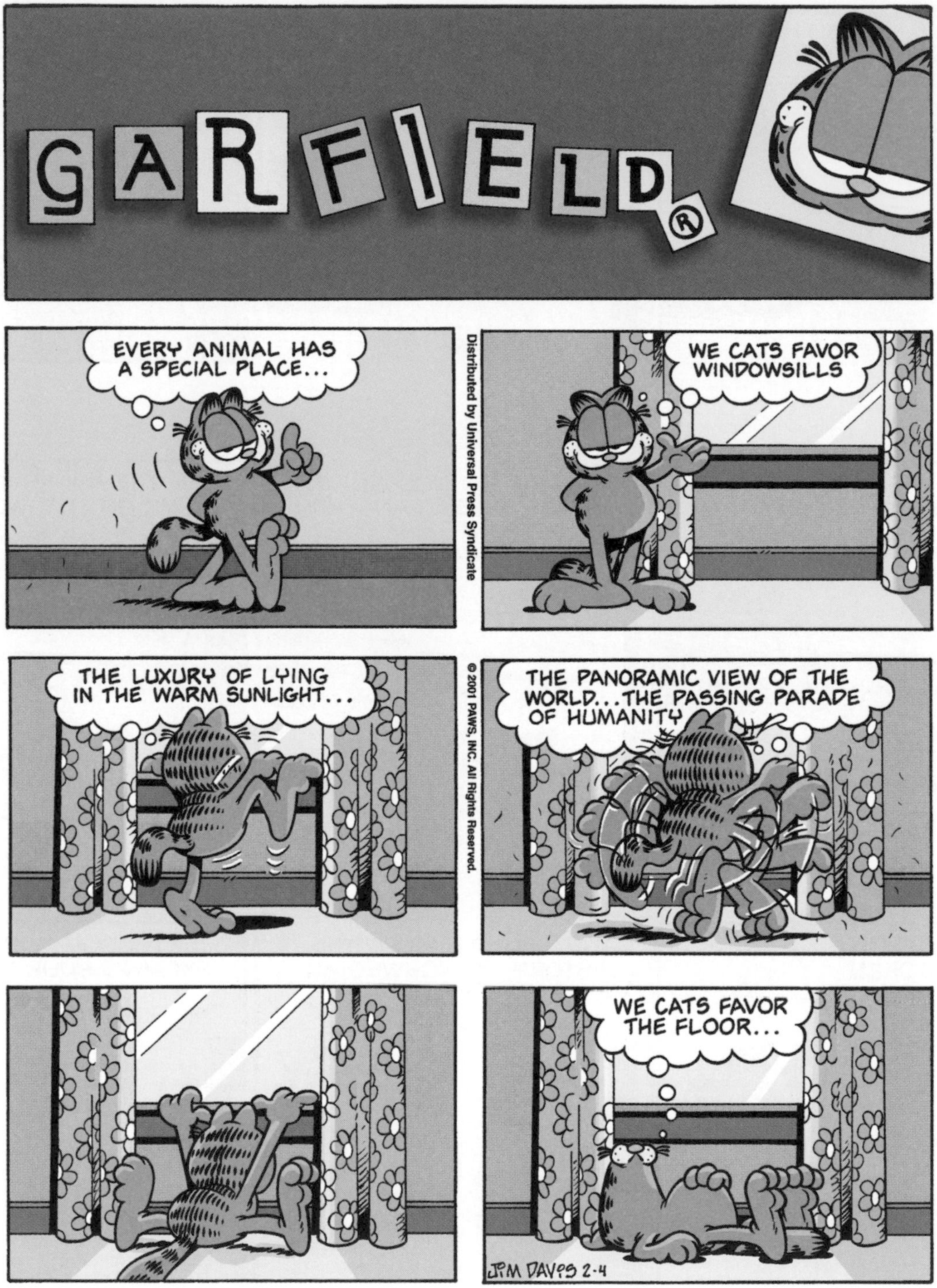
GARFIELD®
EVERY ANIMAL HAS A SPECIAL PLACE...
WE CATS FAVOR WINDOWSILLS
THE LUXURY OF LYING IN THE WARM SUNLIGHT...
THE PANORAMIC VIEW OF THE WORLD...THE PASSING PARADE OF HUMANITY
WE CATS FAVOR THE FLOOR...
JIM DAVIS 2-4
Distributed by Universal Press Syndicate
© 2001 PAWS, INC. All Rights Reserved.

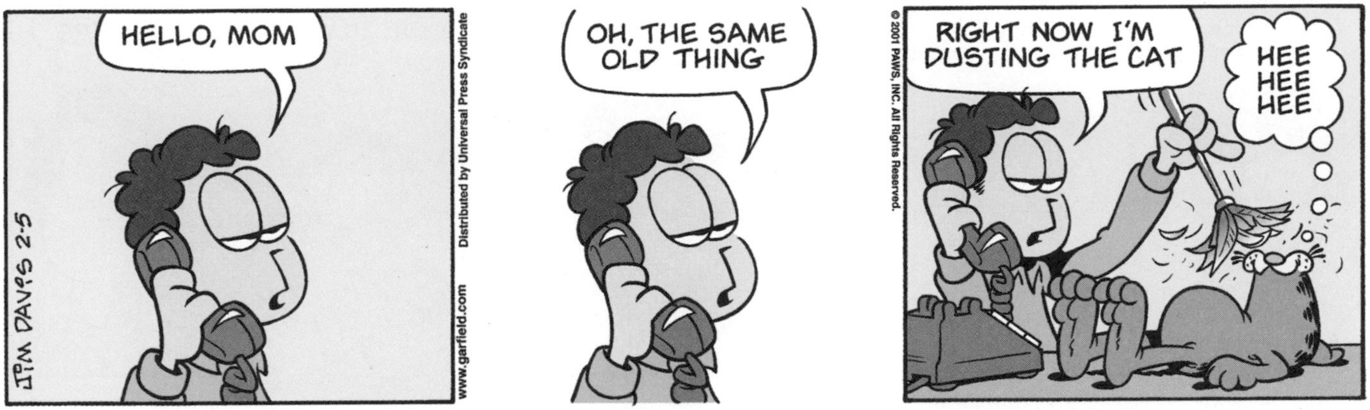
HELLO, MOM
OH, THE SAME OLD THING
RIGHT NOW I'M DUSTING THE CAT
HEE HEE HEE
JIM DAVIS 2-5
Distributed by Universal Press Syndicate www.garfield.com
© 2001 PAWS, INC. All Rights Reserved.

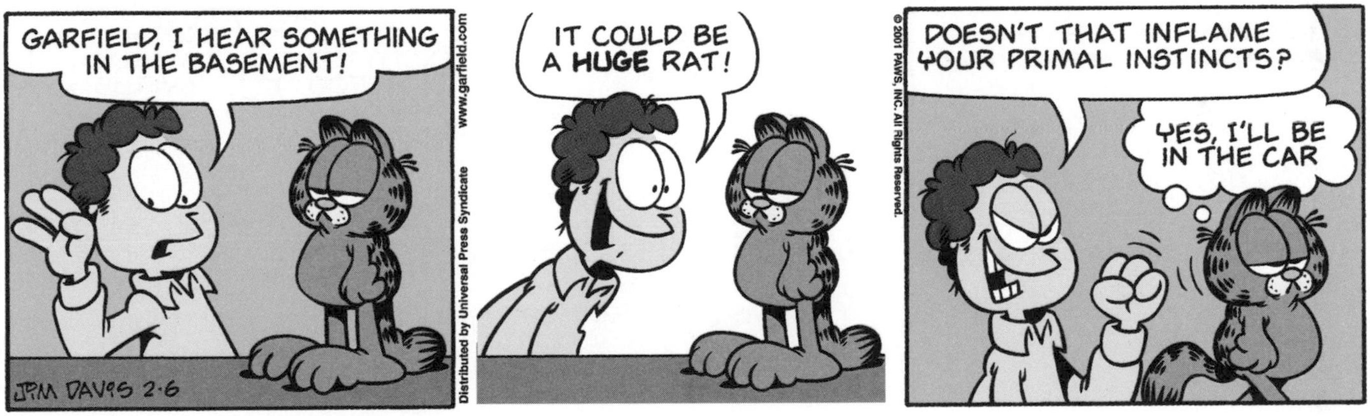
GARFIELD, I HEAR SOMETHING IN THE BASEMENT!
IT COULD BE A **HUGE** RAT!
DOESN'T THAT INFLAME YOUR PRIMAL INSTINCTS?
YES, I'LL BE IN THE CAR
JIM DAVIS 2-6
Distributed by Universal Press Syndicate www.garfield.com
© 2001 PAWS, INC. All Rights Reserved.

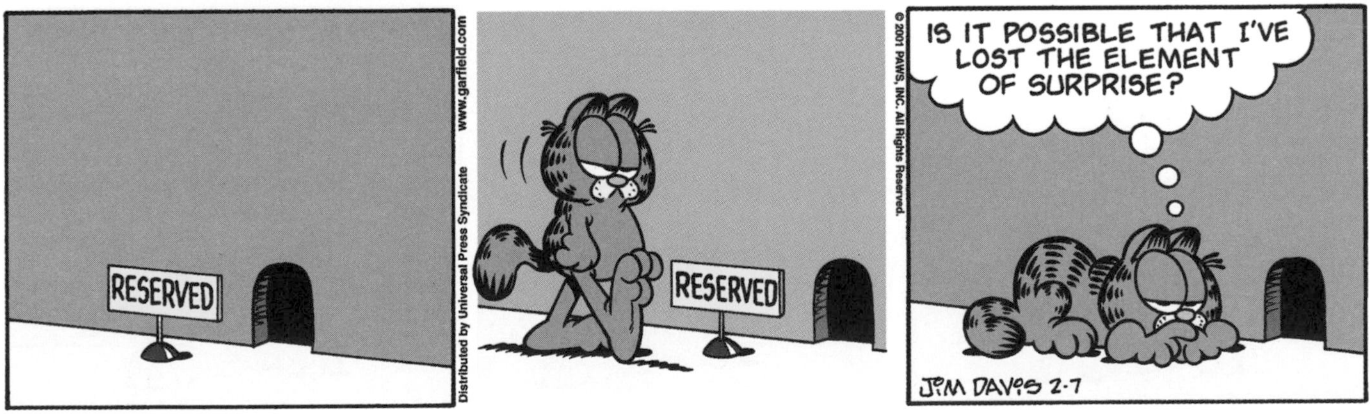
RESERVED
RESERVED
IS IT POSSIBLE THAT I'VE LOST THE ELEMENT OF SURPRISE?
JIM DAVIS 2-7
Distributed by Universal Press Syndicate www.garfield.com
© 2001 PAWS, INC. All Rights Reserved.

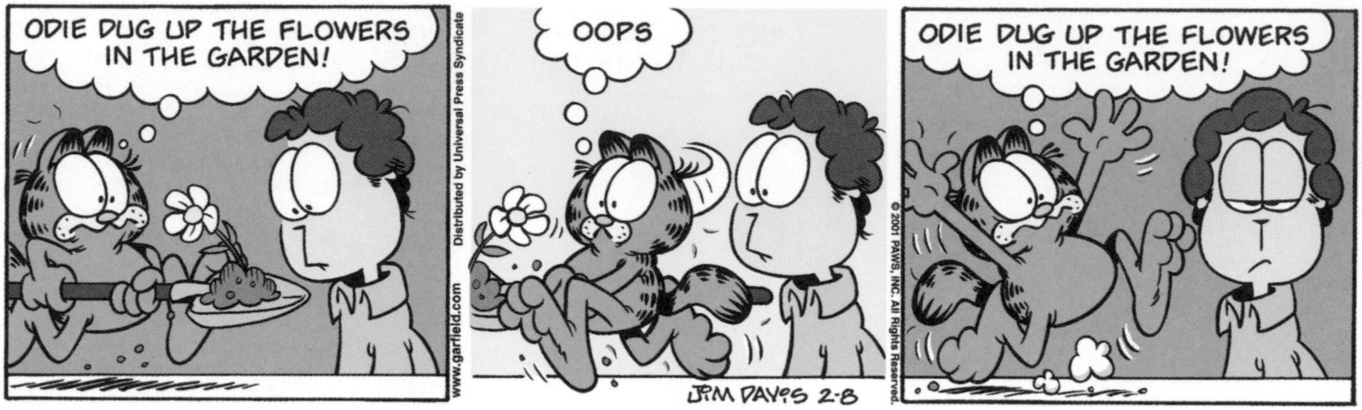
ODIE DUG UP THE FLOWERS IN THE GARDEN!
OOPS
ODIE DUG UP THE FLOWERS IN THE GARDEN!
JIM DAVIS 2-8
www.garfield.com Distributed by Universal Press Syndicate
© 2001 PAWS, INC. All Rights Reserved.

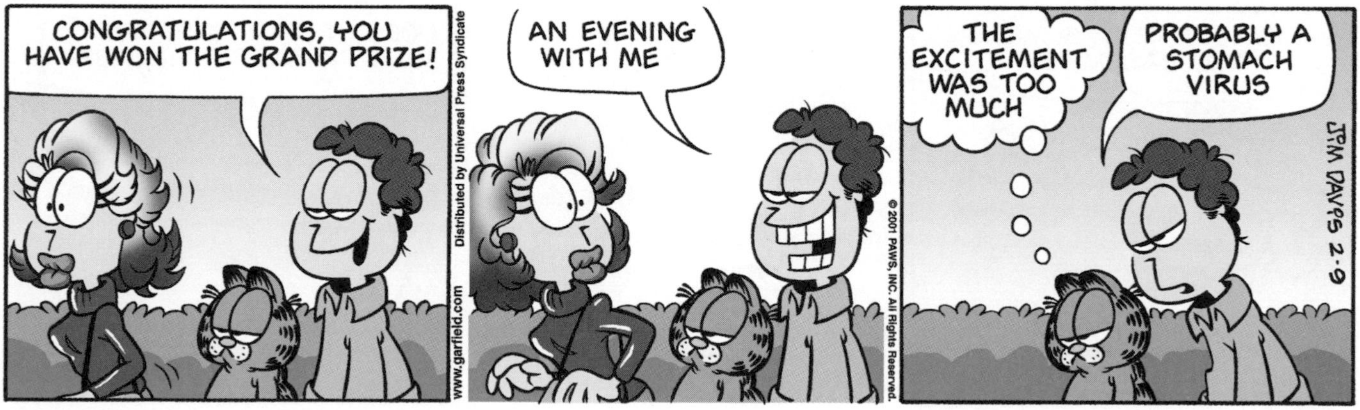
CONGRATULATIONS, YOU HAVE WON THE GRAND PRIZE!
AN EVENING WITH ME
THE EXCITEMENT WAS TOO MUCH
PROBABLY A STOMACH VIRUS
JIM DAVIS 2-9
www.garfield.com Distributed by Universal Press Syndicate
© 2001 PAWS, INC. All Rights Reserved.

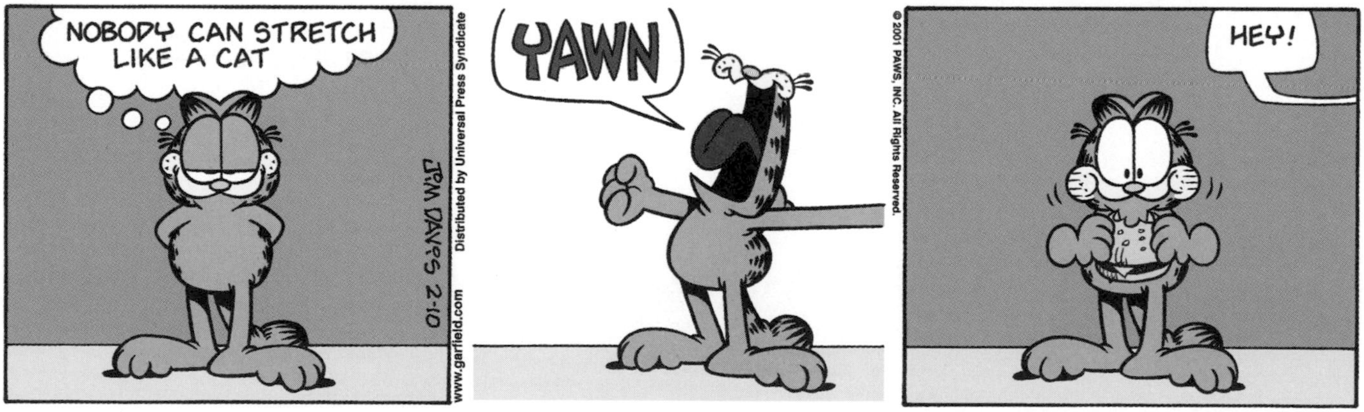
NOBODY CAN STRETCH LIKE A CAT
JIM DAVIS 2-10
YAWN
HEY!
www.garfield.com Distributed by Universal Press Syndicate
© 2001 PAWS, INC. All Rights Reserved.

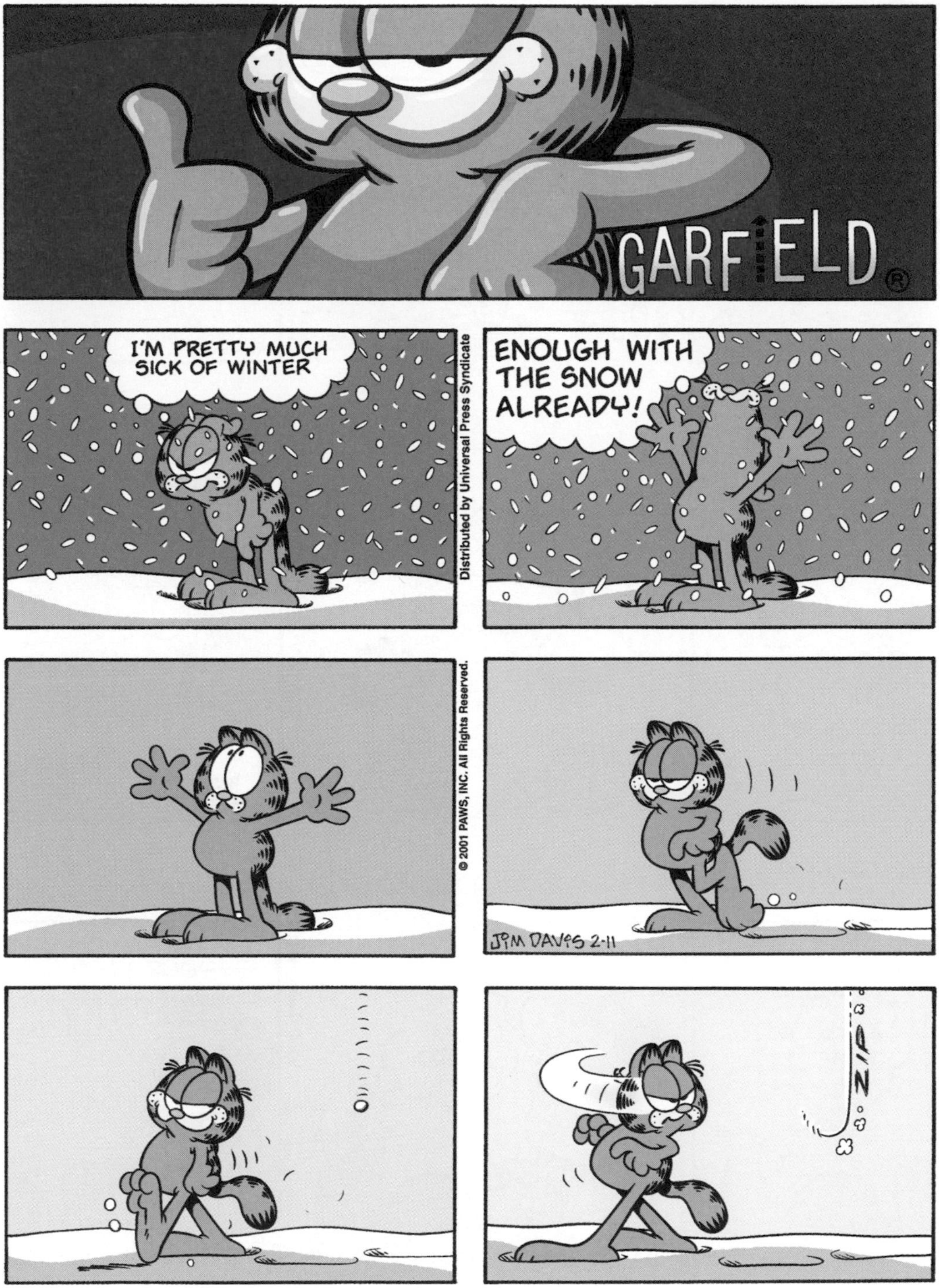
GARFIELD®
I'M PRETTY MUCH SICK OF WINTER
Distributed by Universal Press Syndicate
ENOUGH WITH THE SNOW ALREADY!
© 2001 PAWS, INC. All Rights Reserved.
JIM DAVIS 2-11
ZIP

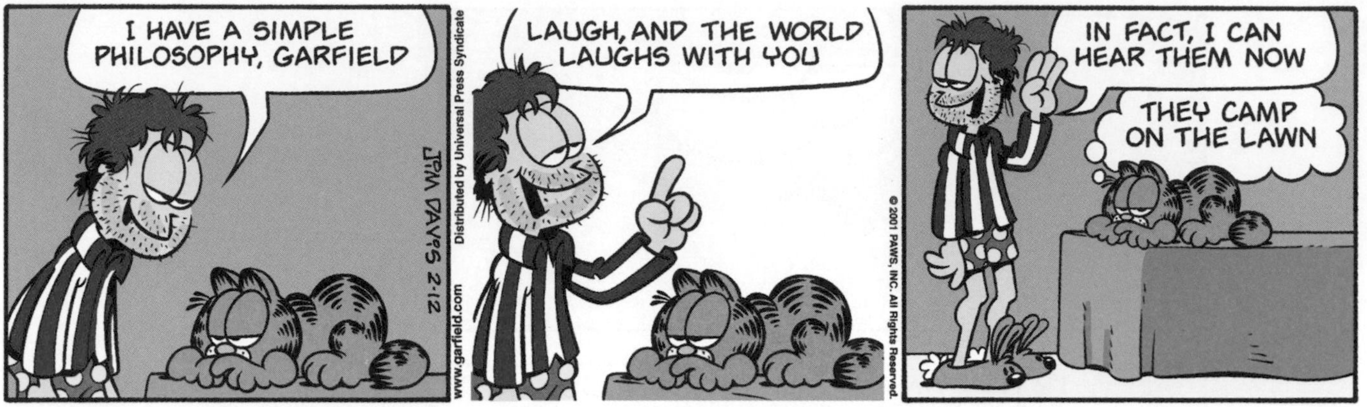
I HAVE A SIMPLE PHILOSOPHY, GARFIELD
JIM DAVIS 2-12
Distributed by Universal Press Syndicate
www.garfield.com
LAUGH, AND THE WORLD LAUGHS WITH YOU
© 2001 PAWS, INC. All Rights Reserved.
IN FACT, I CAN HEAR THEM NOW
THEY CAMP ON THE LAWN

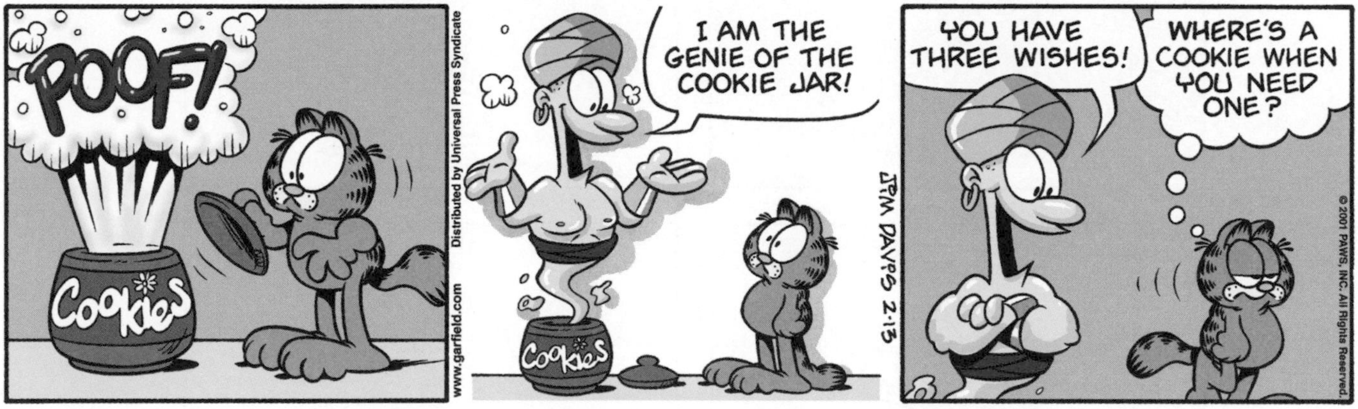
POOF!
COOKIES
Distributed by Universal Press Syndicate
www.garfield.com
I AM THE GENIE OF THE COOKIE JAR!
COOKIES
JIM DAVIS 2-13
YOU HAVE THREE WISHES!
WHERE'S A COOKIE WHEN YOU NEED ONE?
© 2001 PAWS, INC. All Rights Reserved.

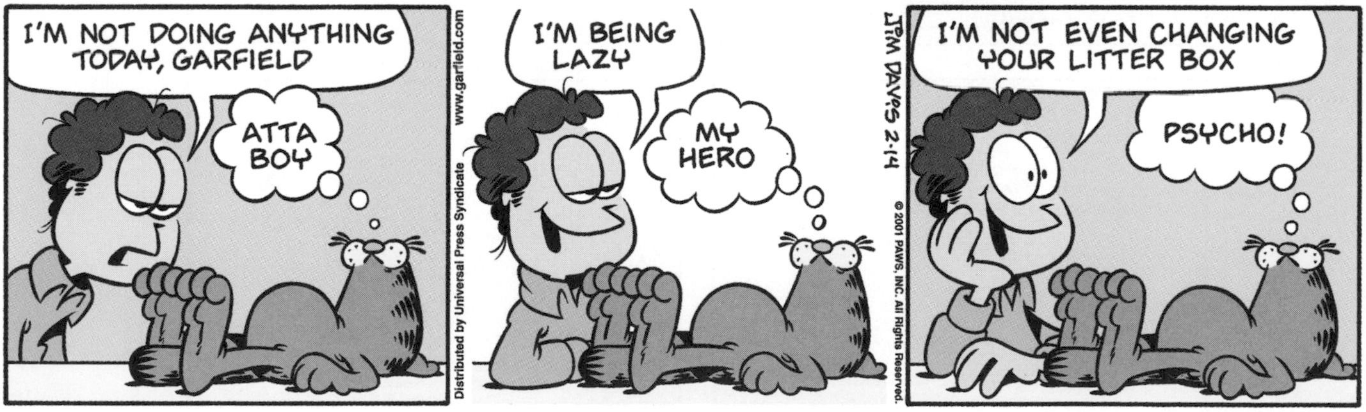
I'M NOT DOING ANYTHING TODAY, GARFIELD
ATTA BOY
www.garfield.com
Distributed by Universal Press Syndicate
I'M BEING LAZY
MY HERO
JIM DAVIS 2-14
© 2001 PAWS, INC. All Rights Reserved.
I'M NOT EVEN CHANGING YOUR LITTER BOX
PSYCHO!

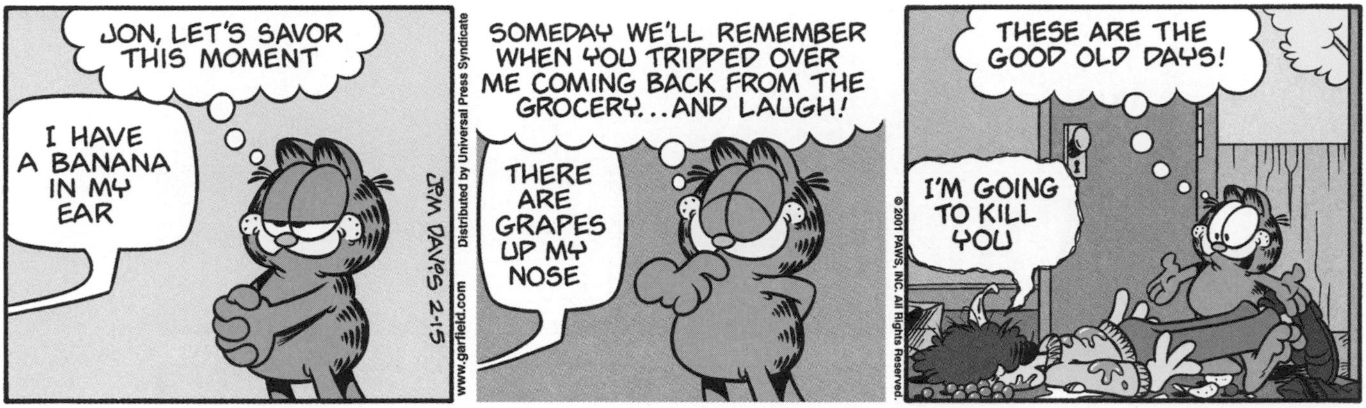
JON, LET'S SAVOR THIS MOMENT
I HAVE A BANANA IN MY EAR
JIM DAVIS 2-15
www.garfield.com Distributed by Universal Press Syndicate
SOMEDAY WE'LL REMEMBER WHEN YOU TRIPPED OVER ME COMING BACK FROM THE GROCERY...AND LAUGH!
THERE ARE GRAPES UP MY NOSE
THESE ARE THE GOOD OLD DAYS!
I'M GOING TO KILL YOU
© 2001 PAWS, INC. All Rights Reserved.

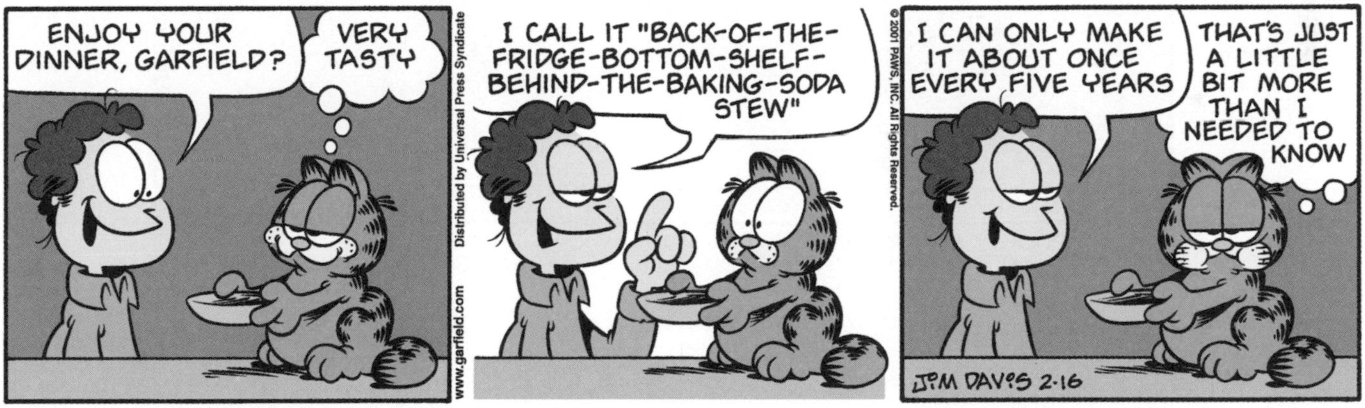
ENJOY YOUR DINNER, GARFIELD?
VERY TASTY
www.garfield.com Distributed by Universal Press Syndicate
I CALL IT "BACK-OF-THE-FRIDGE-BOTTOM-SHELF-BEHIND-THE-BAKING-SODA STEW"
© 2001 PAWS, INC. All Rights Reserved.
I CAN ONLY MAKE IT ABOUT ONCE EVERY FIVE YEARS
THAT'S JUST A LITTLE BIT MORE THAN I NEEDED TO KNOW
JIM DAVIS 2-16

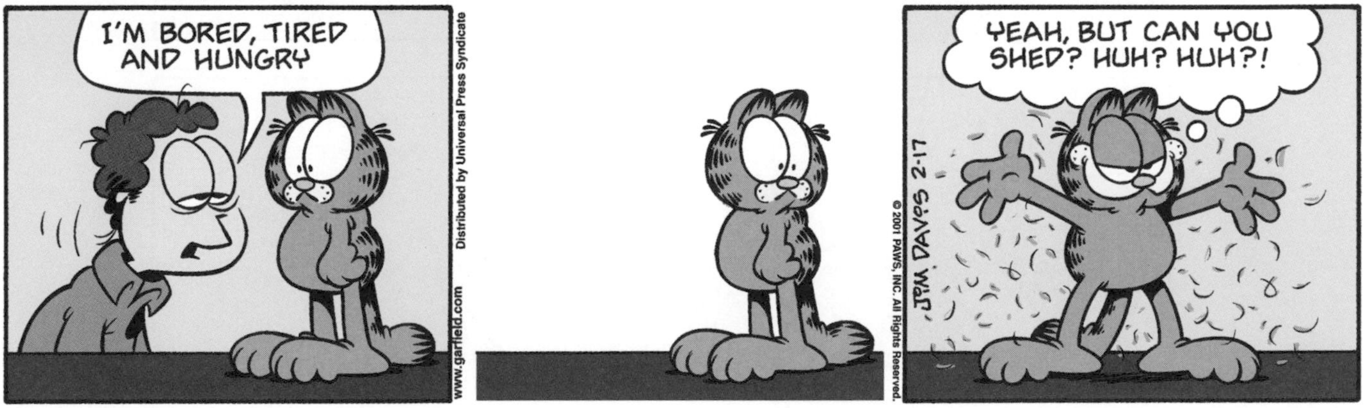
I'M BORED, TIRED AND HUNGRY
www.garfield.com Distributed by Universal Press Syndicate
JIM DAVIS 2-17
© 2001 PAWS, INC. All Rights Reserved.
YEAH, BUT CAN YOU SHED? HUH? HUH?!

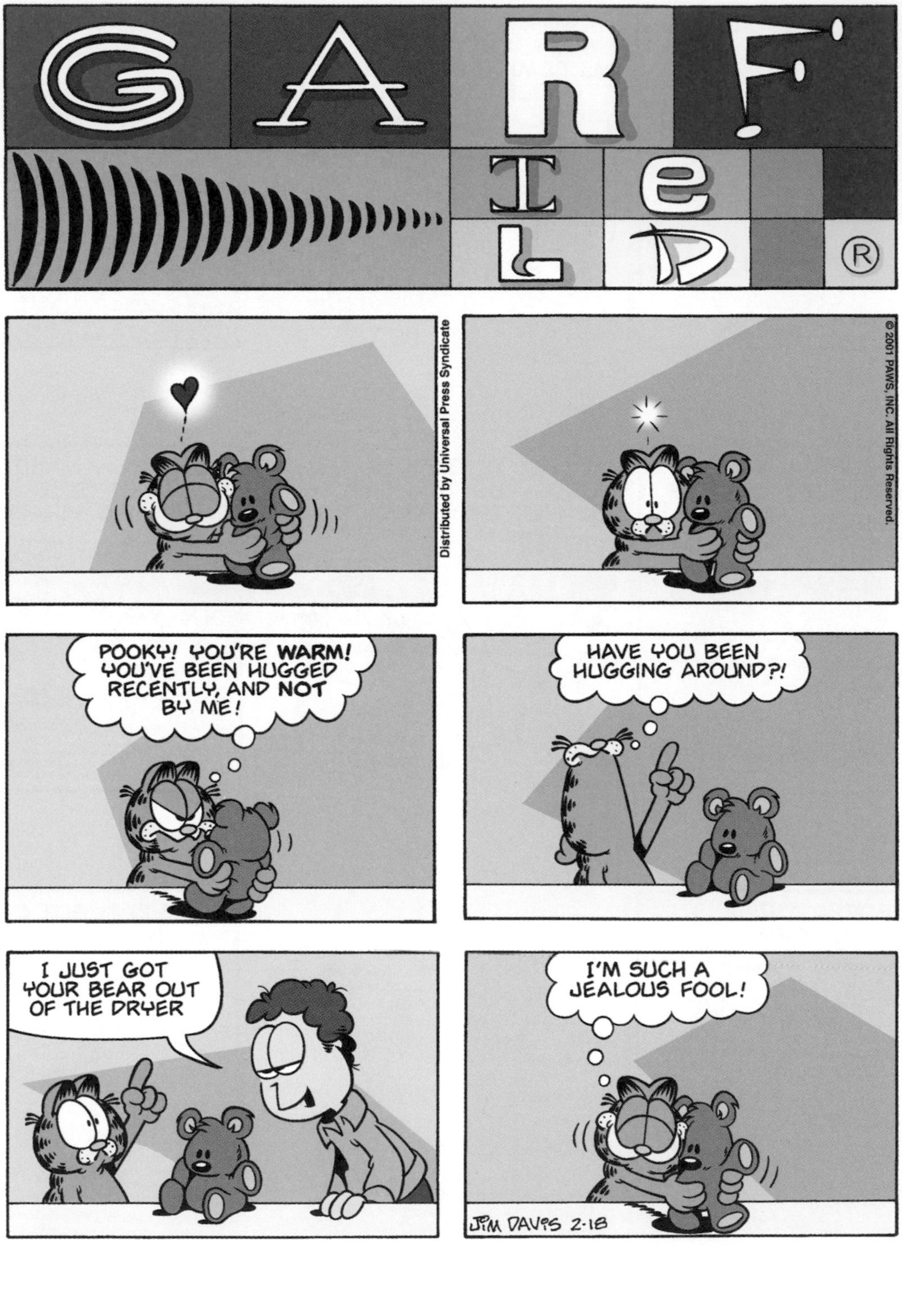
GARFIELD
Distributed by Universal Press Syndicate
© 2001 PAWS, INC. All Rights Reserved.
POOKY! YOU'RE WARM! YOU'VE BEEN HUGGED RECENTLY, AND NOT BY ME!
HAVE YOU BEEN HUGGING AROUND?!
I JUST GOT YOUR BEAR OUT OF THE DRYER
I'M SUCH A JEALOUS FOOL!
JIM DAVIS 2-18

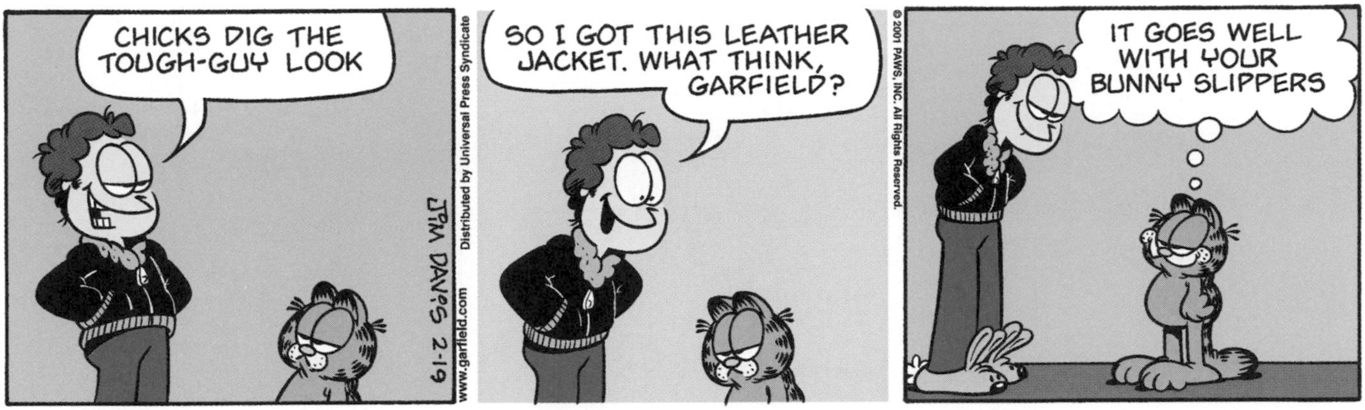
CHICKS DIG THE TOUGH-GUY LOOK
JIM DAVIS 2-19
www.garfield.com Distributed by Universal Press Syndicate
SO I GOT THIS LEATHER JACKET. WHAT THINK, GARFIELD?
© 2001 PAWS, INC. All Rights Reserved.
IT GOES WELL WITH YOUR BUNNY SLIPPERS

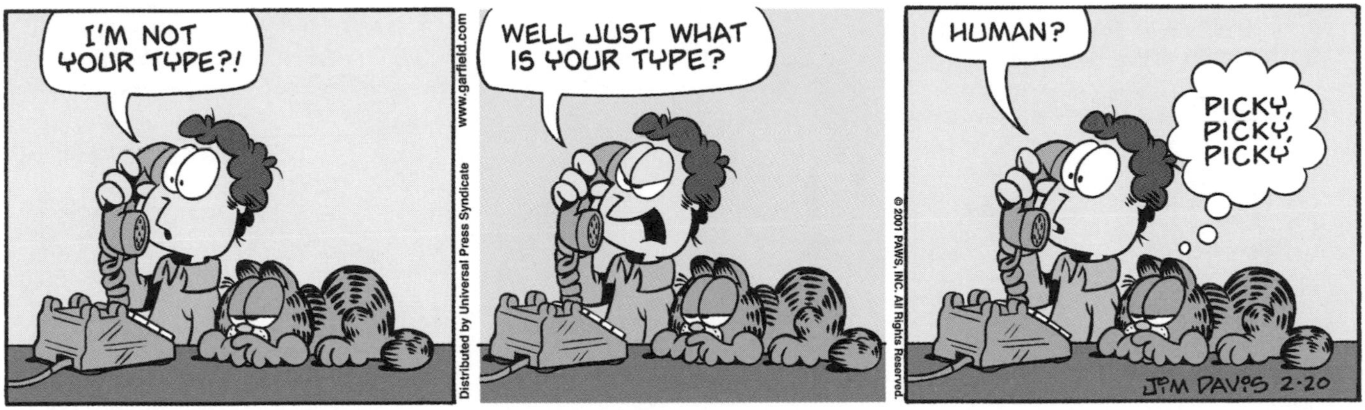
I'M NOT YOUR TYPE?!
www.garfield.com Distributed by Universal Press Syndicate
WELL JUST WHAT IS YOUR TYPE?
© 2001 PAWS, INC. All Rights Reserved.
HUMAN?
PICKY, PICKY, PICKY
JIM DAVIS 2-20

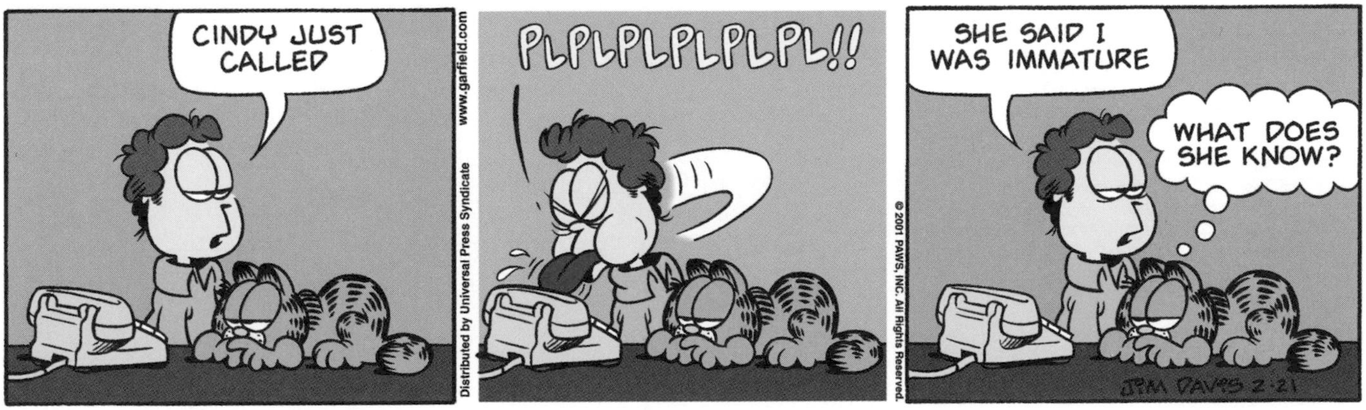
CINDY JUST CALLED
www.garfield.com Distributed by Universal Press Syndicate
PLPLPLPLPLPLPL!!
© 2001 PAWS, INC. All Rights Reserved.
SHE SAID I WAS IMMATURE
WHAT DOES SHE KNOW?
JIM DAVIS 2-21

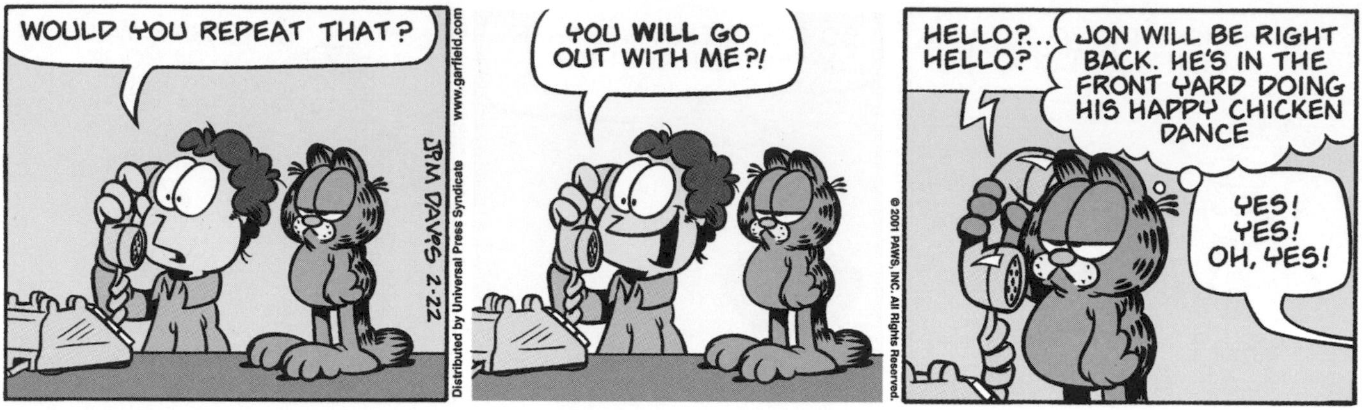
WOULD YOU REPEAT THAT?
JIM DAVIS 2-22
Distributed by Universal Press Syndicate www.garfield.com
YOU **WILL** GO OUT WITH ME?!
© 2001 PAWS, INC. All Rights Reserved.
HELLO?... HELLO?
JON WILL BE RIGHT BACK. HE'S IN THE FRONT YARD DOING HIS HAPPY CHICKEN DANCE
YES! YES! OH, YES!

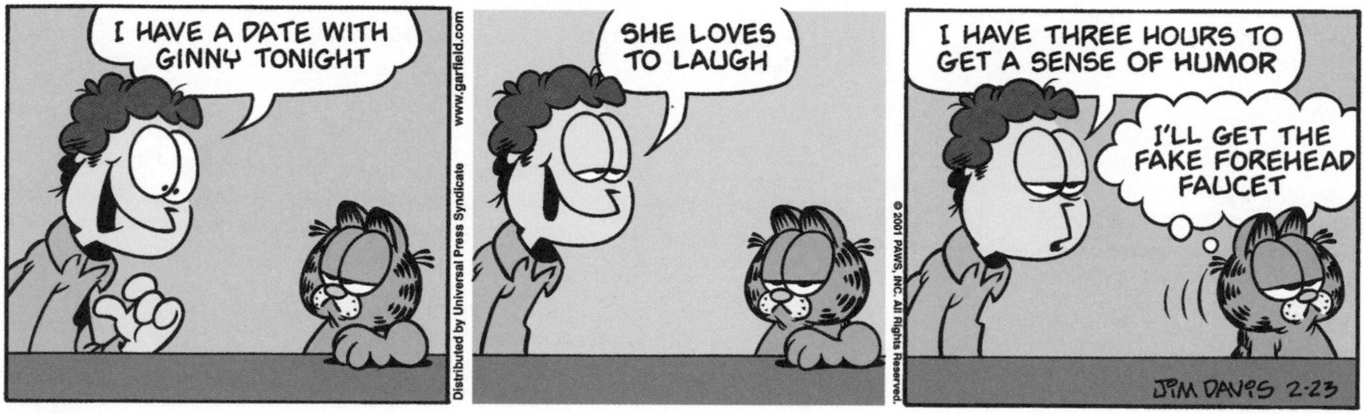
I HAVE A DATE WITH GINNY TONIGHT
Distributed by Universal Press Syndicate www.garfield.com
SHE LOVES TO LAUGH
© 2001 PAWS, INC. All Rights Reserved.
I HAVE THREE HOURS TO GET A SENSE OF HUMOR
I'LL GET THE FAKE FOREHEAD FAUCET
JIM DAVIS 2-23

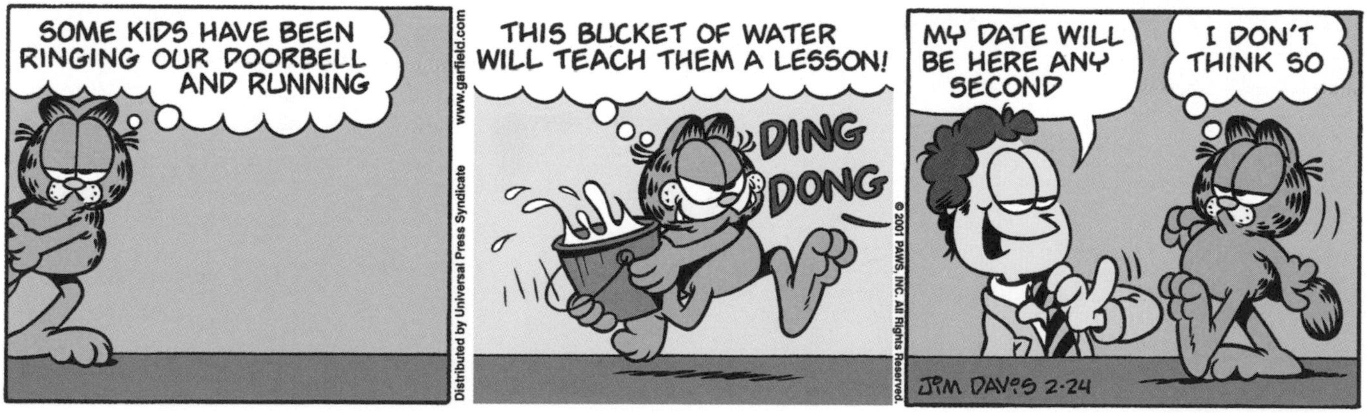
SOME KIDS HAVE BEEN RINGING OUR DOORBELL AND RUNNING
Distributed by Universal Press Syndicate www.garfield.com
THIS BUCKET OF WATER WILL TEACH THEM A LESSON!
DING
DONG
© 2001 PAWS, INC. All Rights Reserved.
MY DATE WILL BE HERE ANY SECOND
I DON'T THINK SO
JIM DAVIS 2-24

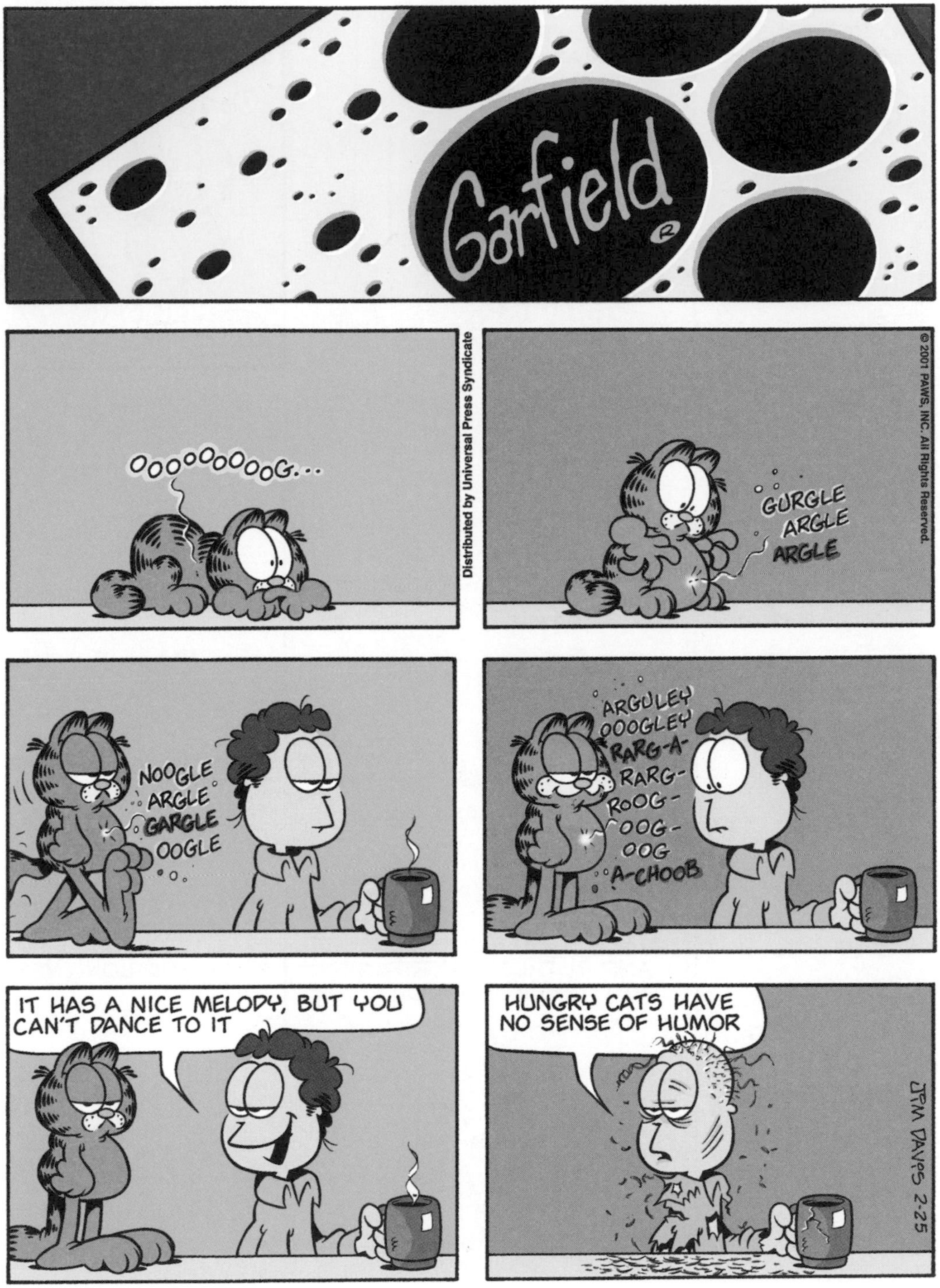
Garfield®
OOOOOOOOOG...
Distributed by Universal Press Syndicate
© 2001 PAWS, INC. All Rights Reserved.
GURGLE ARGLE ARGLE
NOOGLE ARGLE GARGLE OOGLE
ARGULEY OOOGLEY RARG-A-RARG-ROOG-OOG-OOG A-CHOOB
IT HAS A NICE MELODY, BUT YOU CAN'T DANCE TO IT
HUNGRY CATS HAVE NO SENSE OF HUMOR
JIM DAVIS 2-25

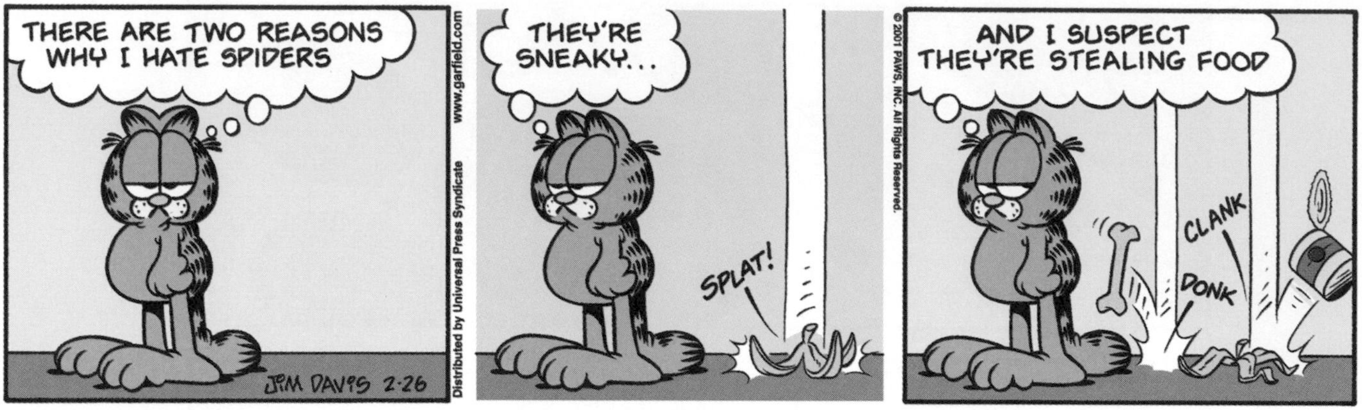
THERE ARE TWO REASONS WHY I HATE SPIDERS
JIM DAVIS 2·26
www.garfield.com Distributed by Universal Press Syndicate
THEY'RE SNEAKY...
SPLAT!
© 2001 PAWS, INC. All Rights Reserved.
AND I SUSPECT THEY'RE STEALING FOOD
CLANK
DONK

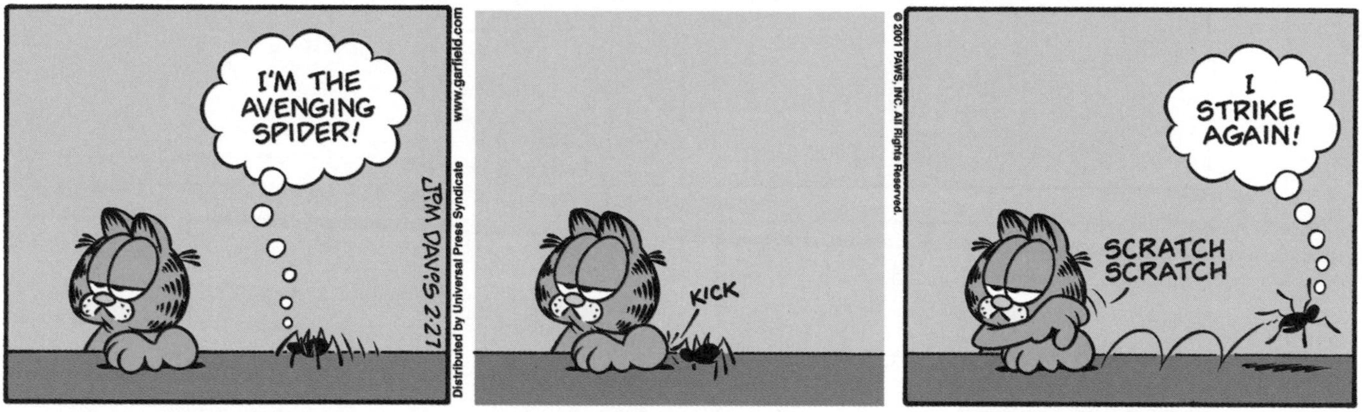
I'M THE AVENGING SPIDER!
JIM DAVIS 2·27
www.garfield.com Distributed by Universal Press Syndicate
KICK
© 2001 PAWS, INC. All Rights Reserved.
SCRATCH SCRATCH
I STRIKE AGAIN!

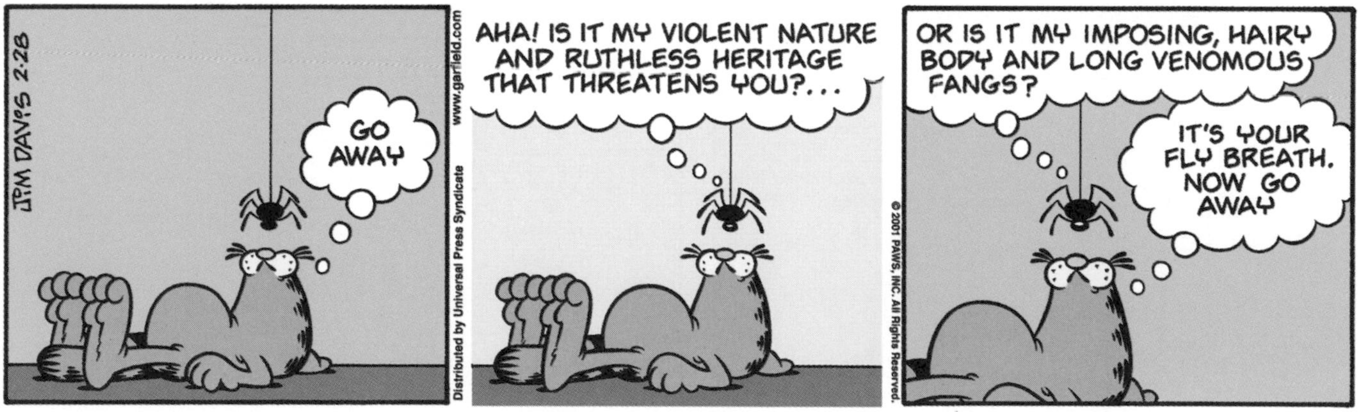
JIM DAVIS 2·28
GO AWAY
www.garfield.com Distributed by Universal Press Syndicate
AHA! IS IT MY VIOLENT NATURE AND RUTHLESS HERITAGE THAT THREATENS YOU?...
© 2001 PAWS, INC. All Rights Reserved.
OR IS IT MY IMPOSING, HAIRY BODY AND LONG VENOMOUS FANGS?
IT'S YOUR FLY BREATH. NOW GO AWAY

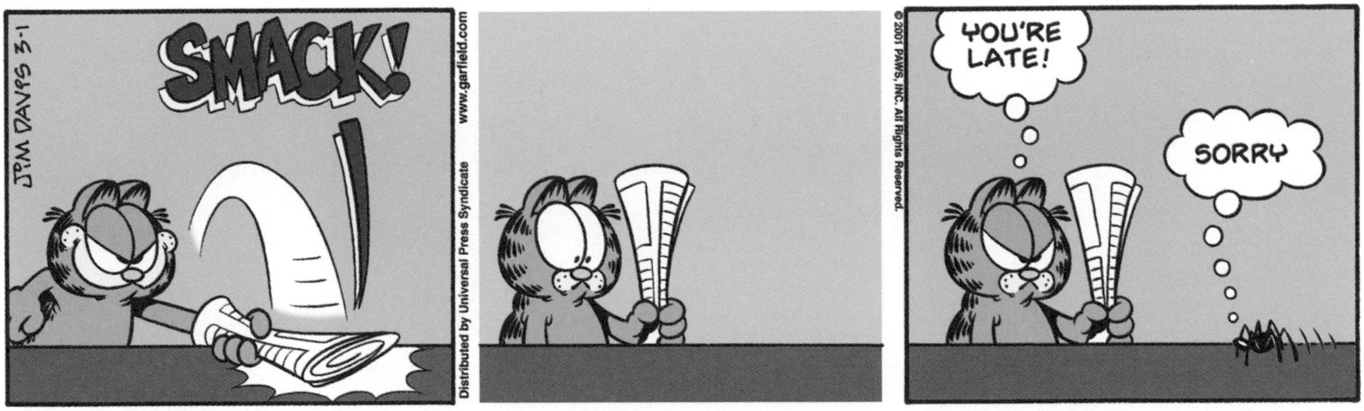
JIM DAVIS 3-1
SMACK!
Distributed by Universal Press Syndicate www.garfield.com
© 2001 PAWS, INC. All Rights Reserved.
YOU'RE LATE!
SORRY

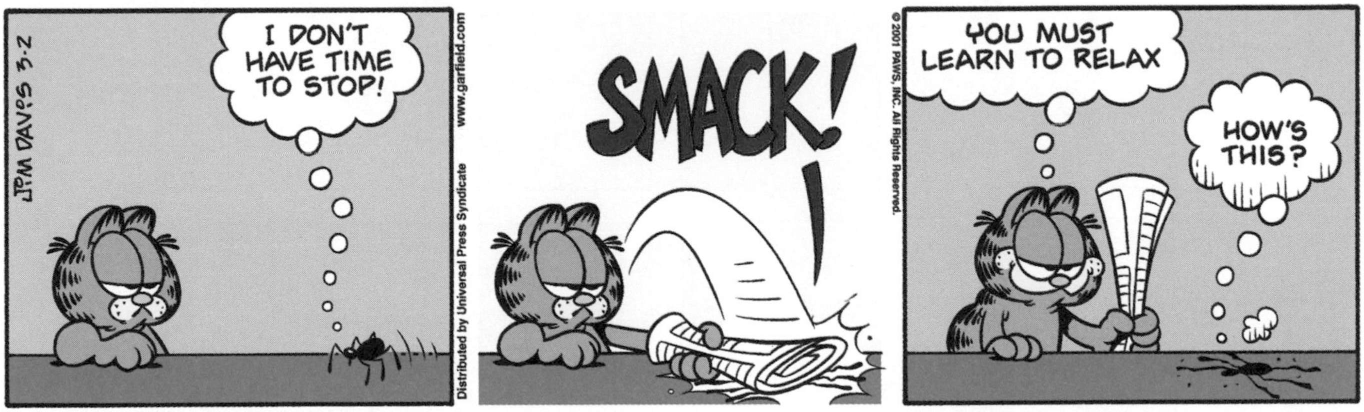
JIM DAVIS 3-2
I DON'T HAVE TIME TO STOP!
Distributed by Universal Press Syndicate www.garfield.com
SMACK!
© 2001 PAWS, INC. All Rights Reserved.
YOU MUST LEARN TO RELAX
HOW'S THIS?

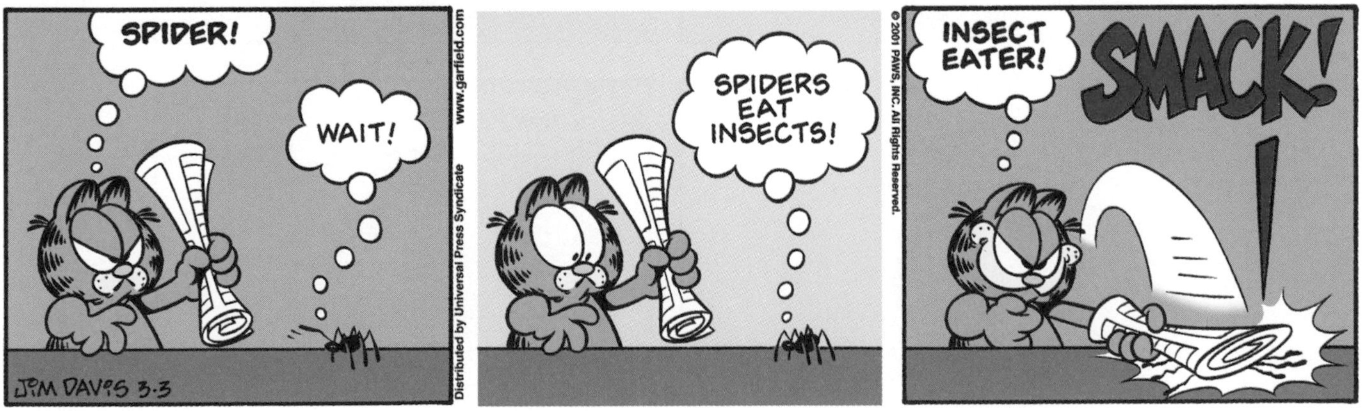
SPIDER!
WAIT!
JIM DAVIS 3-3
Distributed by Universal Press Syndicate www.garfield.com
SPIDERS EAT INSECTS!
© 2001 PAWS, INC. All Rights Reserved.
INSECT EATER!
SMACK!

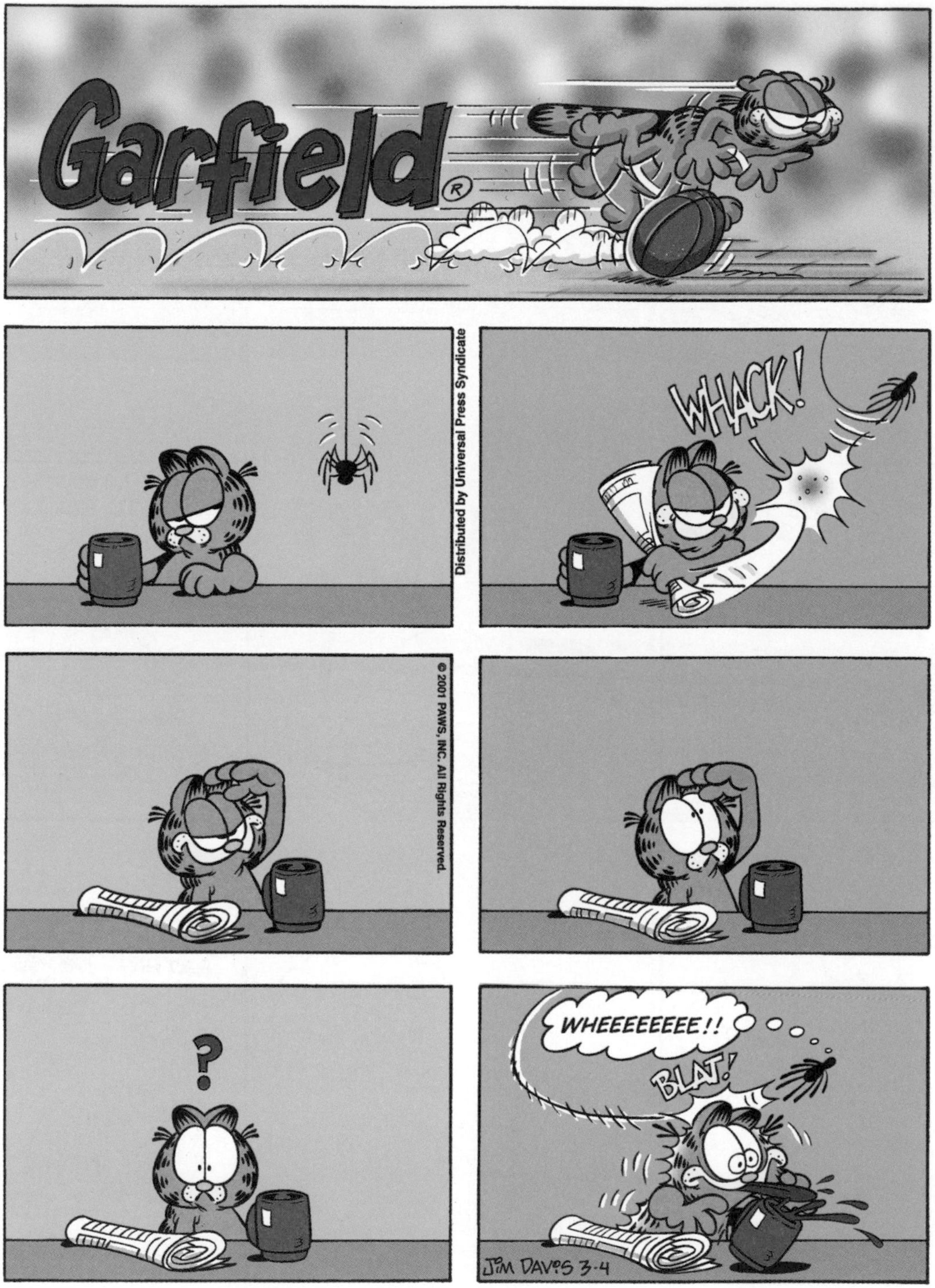
Garfield®
Distributed by Universal Press Syndicate
WHACK!
© 2001 PAWS, INC. All Rights Reserved.
?
WHEEEEEEEE!!
BLAT!
JIM DAVIS 3-4

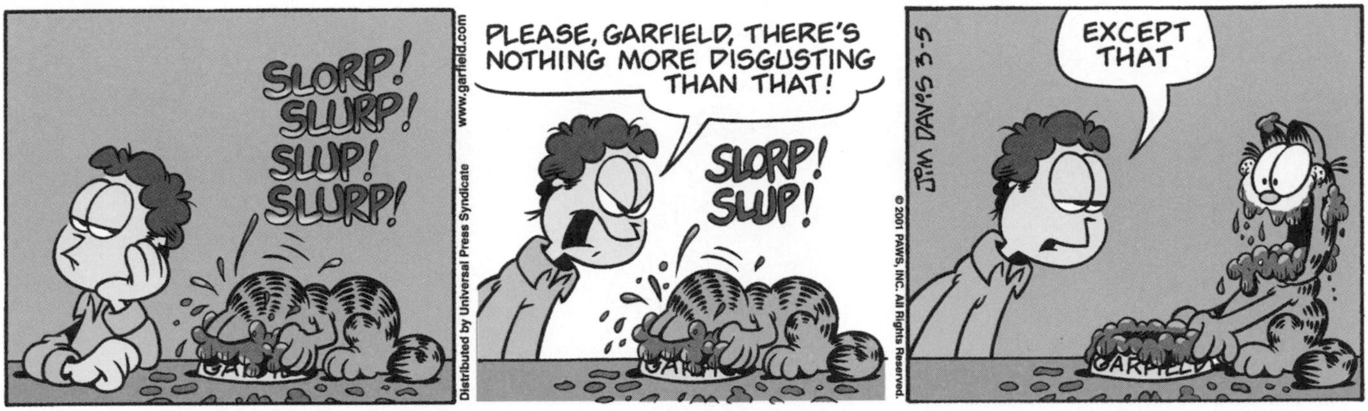
SLORP! SLURP! SLUP! SLURP!
Distributed by Universal Press Syndicate www.garfield.com
PLEASE, GARFIELD, THERE'S NOTHING MORE DISGUSTING THAN THAT!
SLORP! SLUP!
© 2001 PAWS, INC. All Rights Reserved.
JIM DAVIS 3-5
EXCEPT THAT
GARFIELD

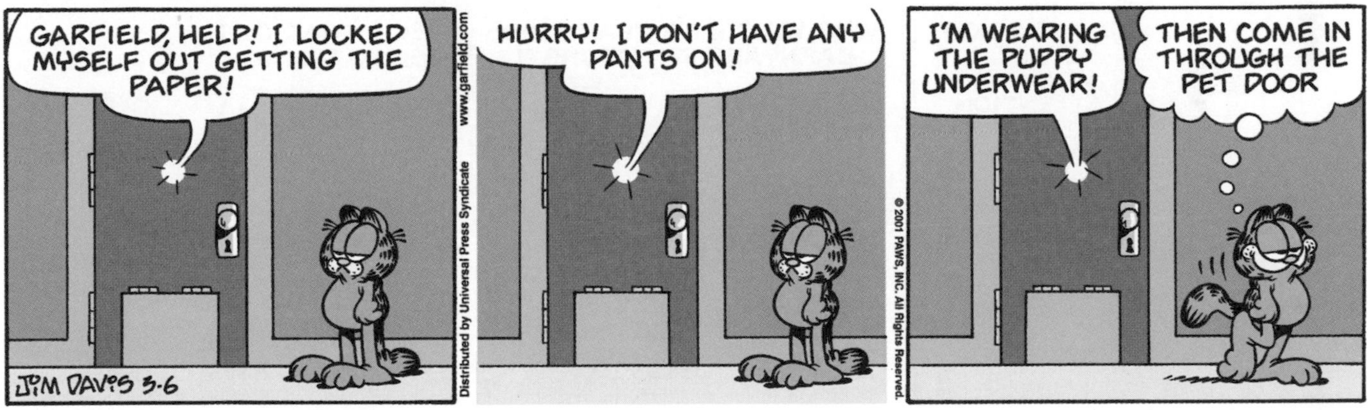
GARFIELD, HELP! I LOCKED MYSELF OUT GETTING THE PAPER!
JIM DAVIS 3-6
Distributed by Universal Press Syndicate www.garfield.com
HURRY! I DON'T HAVE ANY PANTS ON!
© 2001 PAWS, INC. All Rights Reserved.
I'M WEARING THE PUPPY UNDERWEAR!
THEN COME IN THROUGH THE PET DOOR

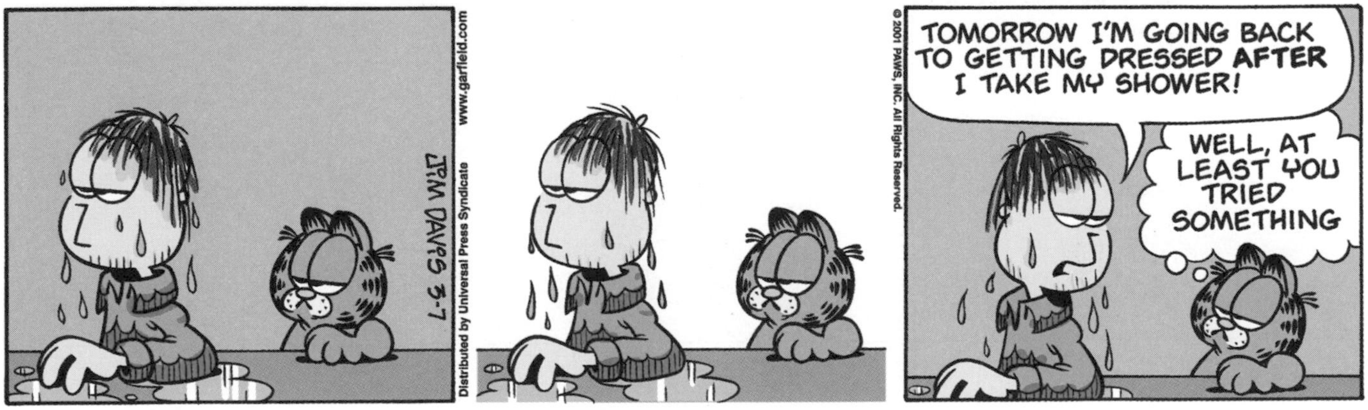
JIM DAVIS 3-7
Distributed by Universal Press Syndicate www.garfield.com
© 2001 PAWS, INC. All Rights Reserved.
TOMORROW I'M GOING BACK TO GETTING DRESSED **AFTER** I TAKE MY SHOWER!
WELL, AT LEAST YOU TRIED SOMETHING

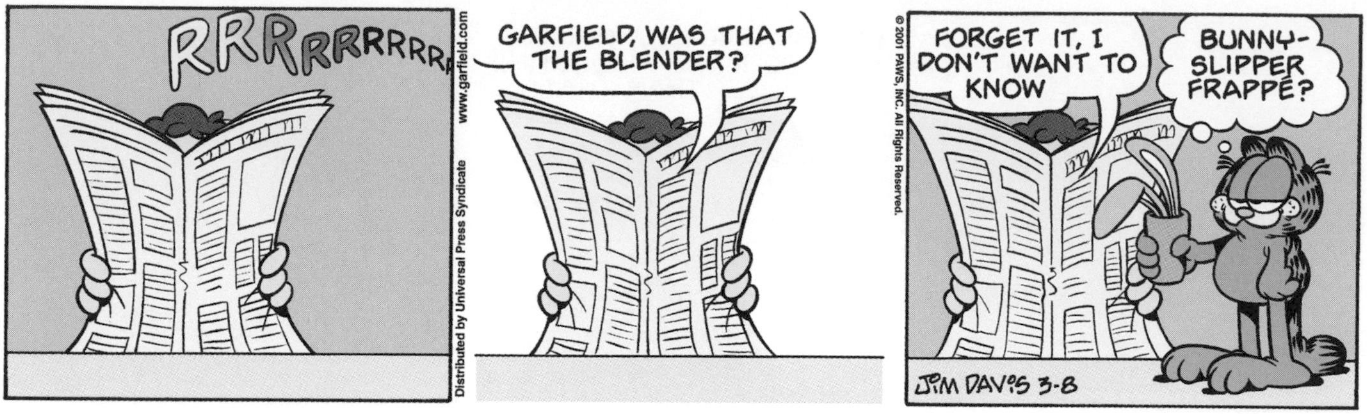
RRRRRRRRRR
www.garfield.com
Distributed by Universal Press Syndicate
GARFIELD, WAS THAT THE BLENDER?
© 2001 PAWS, INC. All Rights Reserved.
FORGET IT, I DON'T WANT TO KNOW
BUNNY-SLIPPER FRAPPÉ?
JIM DAVIS 3-8

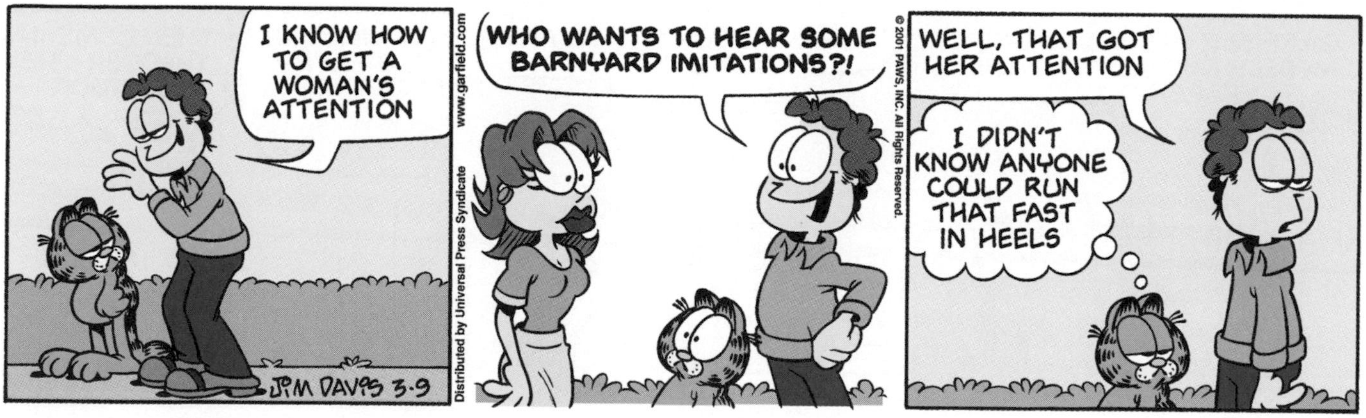
I KNOW HOW TO GET A WOMAN'S ATTENTION
JIM DAVIS 3-9
www.garfield.com
Distributed by Universal Press Syndicate
WHO WANTS TO HEAR SOME BARNYARD IMITATIONS?!
© 2001 PAWS, INC. All Rights Reserved.
WELL, THAT GOT HER ATTENTION
I DIDN'T KNOW ANYONE COULD RUN THAT FAST IN HEELS

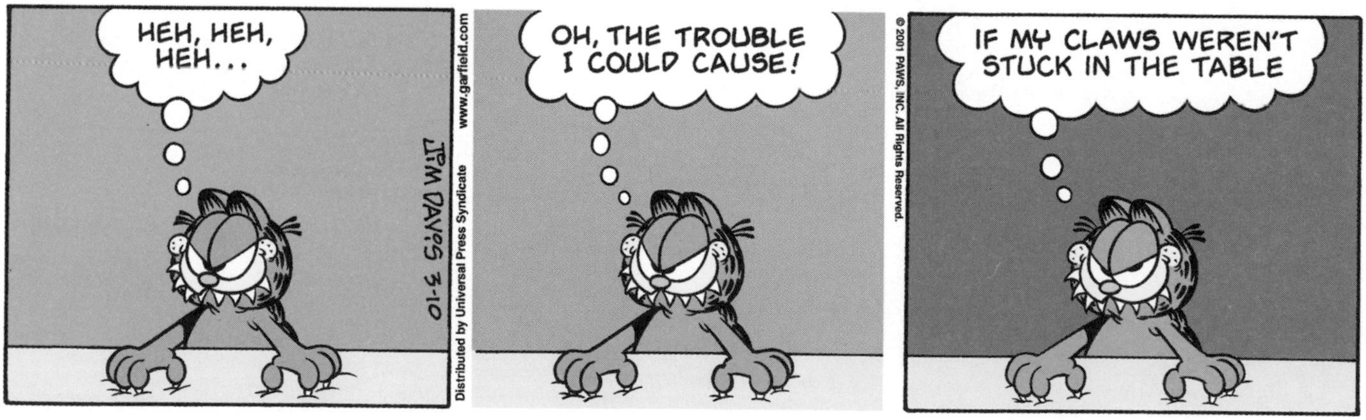
HEH, HEH, HEH...
JIM DAVIS 3-10
www.garfield.com
Distributed by Universal Press Syndicate
OH, THE TROUBLE I COULD CAUSE!
© 2001 PAWS, INC. All Rights Reserved.
IF MY CLAWS WEREN'T STUCK IN THE TABLE

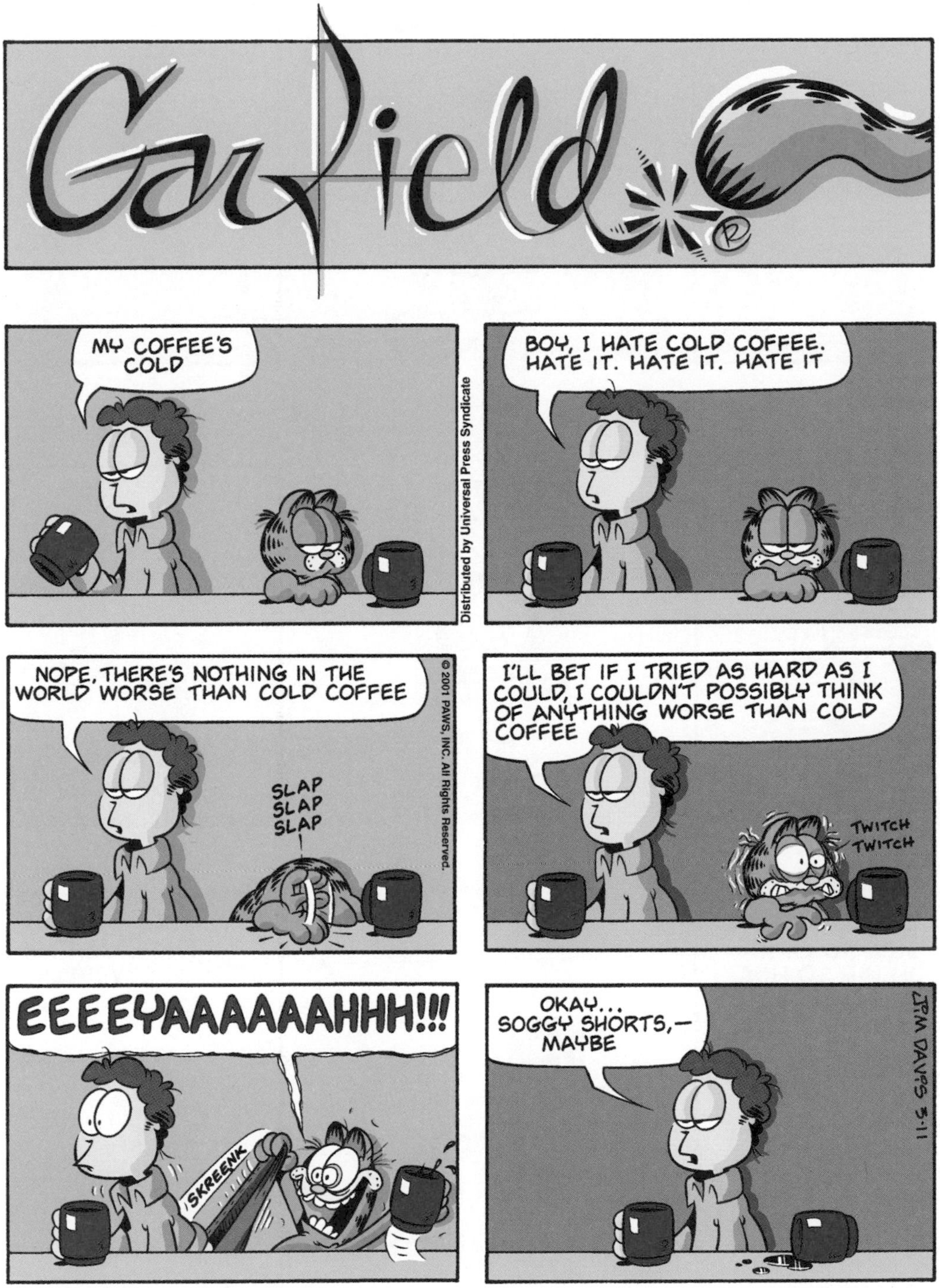
Garfield
MY COFFEE'S COLD
Distributed by Universal Press Syndicate
BOY, I HATE COLD COFFEE. HATE IT. HATE IT. HATE IT
NOPE, THERE'S NOTHING IN THE WORLD WORSE THAN COLD COFFEE
SLAP SLAP SLAP
© 2001 PAWS, INC. All Rights Reserved.
I'LL BET IF I TRIED AS HARD AS I COULD, I COULDN'T POSSIBLY THINK OF ANYTHING WORSE THAN COLD COFFEE
TWITCH TWITCH
EEEEYAAAAAAHHH!!!
SKREENK
OKAY... SOGGY SHORTS,— MAYBE
JIM DAVIS 3-11

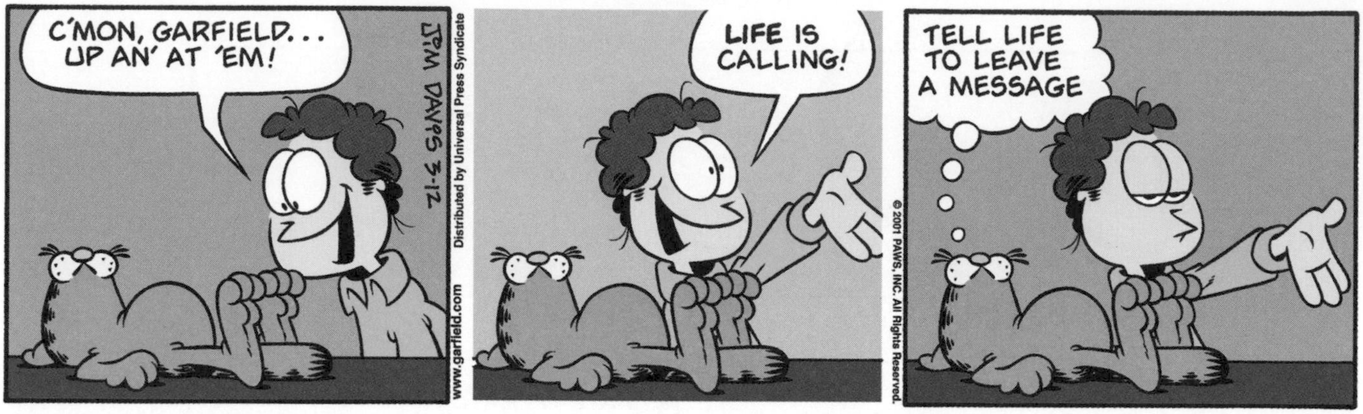
C'MON, GARFIELD...
UP AN' AT 'EM!
JIM DAVIS 3-12
www.garfield.com
Distributed by Universal Press Syndicate
LIFE IS CALLING!
© 2001 PAWS, INC. All Rights Reserved.
TELL LIFE TO LEAVE A MESSAGE

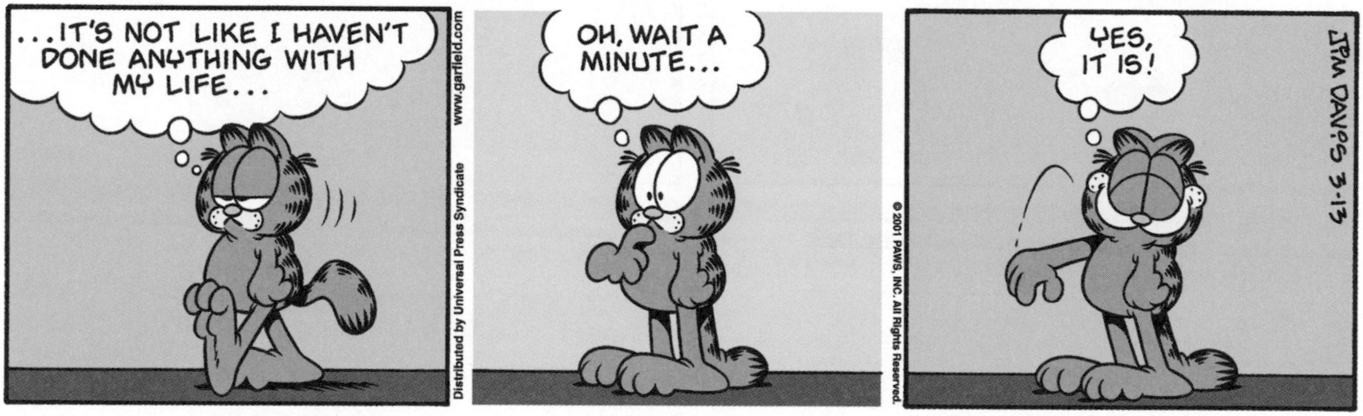
...IT'S NOT LIKE I HAVEN'T DONE ANYTHING WITH MY LIFE...
www.garfield.com
Distributed by Universal Press Syndicate
OH, WAIT A MINUTE...
© 2001 PAWS, INC. All Rights Reserved.
YES, IT IS!
JIM DAVIS 3-13

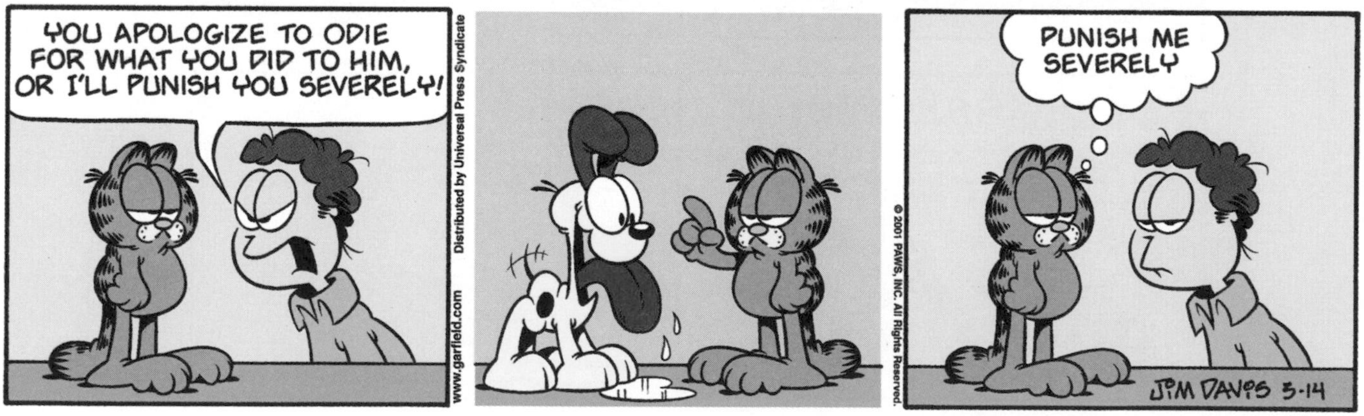
YOU APOLOGIZE TO ODIE FOR WHAT YOU DID TO HIM, OR I'LL PUNISH YOU SEVERELY!
Distributed by Universal Press Syndicate
www.garfield.com
© 2001 PAWS, INC. All Rights Reserved.
PUNISH ME SEVERELY
JIM DAVIS 3-14

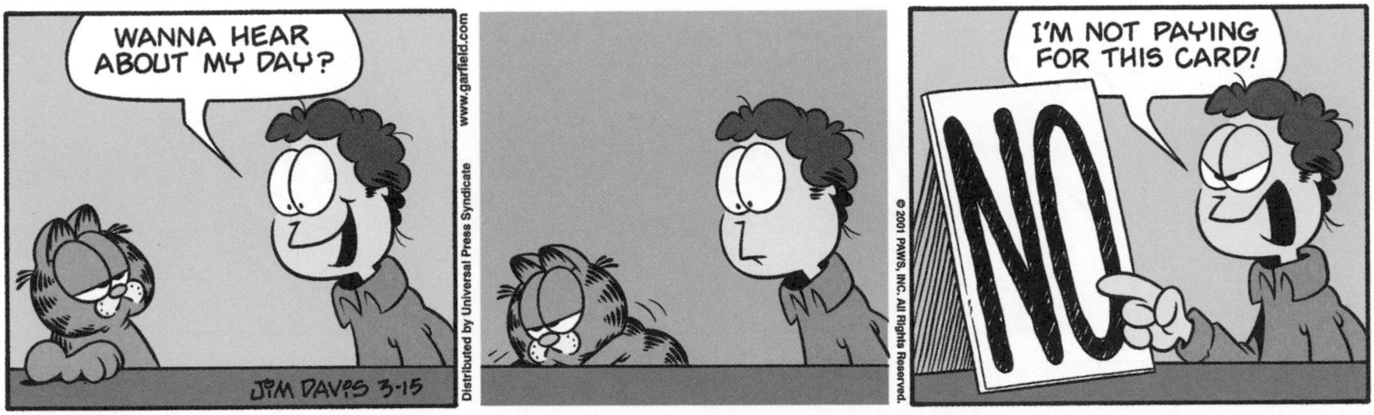
WANNA HEAR ABOUT MY DAY?
JIM DAVIS 3-15
Distributed by Universal Press Syndicate www.garfield.com
© 2001 PAWS, INC. All Rights Reserved.
I'M NOT PAYING FOR THIS CARD!
NO

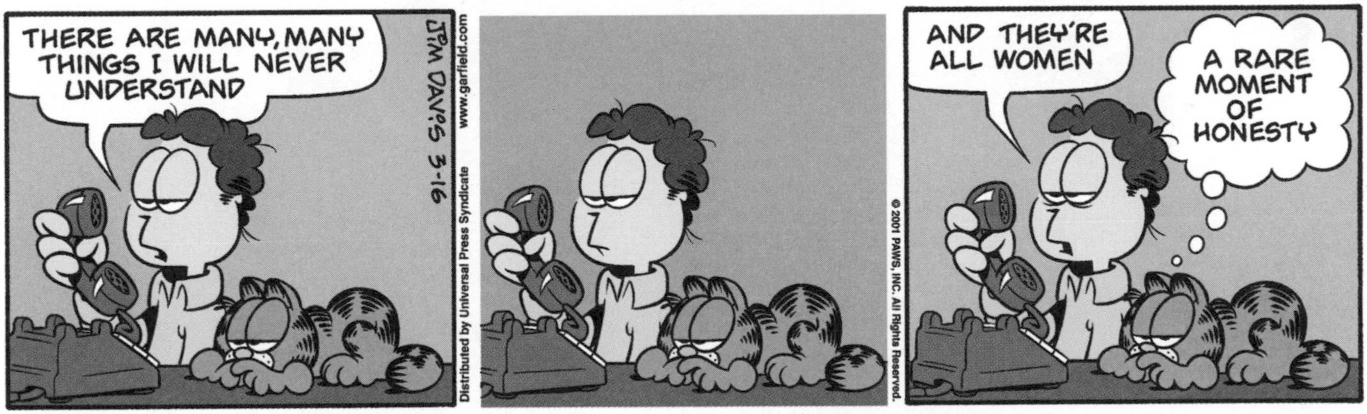
THERE ARE MANY, MANY THINGS I WILL NEVER UNDERSTAND
JIM DAVIS 3-16
Distributed by Universal Press Syndicate www.garfield.com
© 2001 PAWS, INC. All Rights Reserved.
AND THEY'RE ALL WOMEN
A RARE MOMENT OF HONESTY

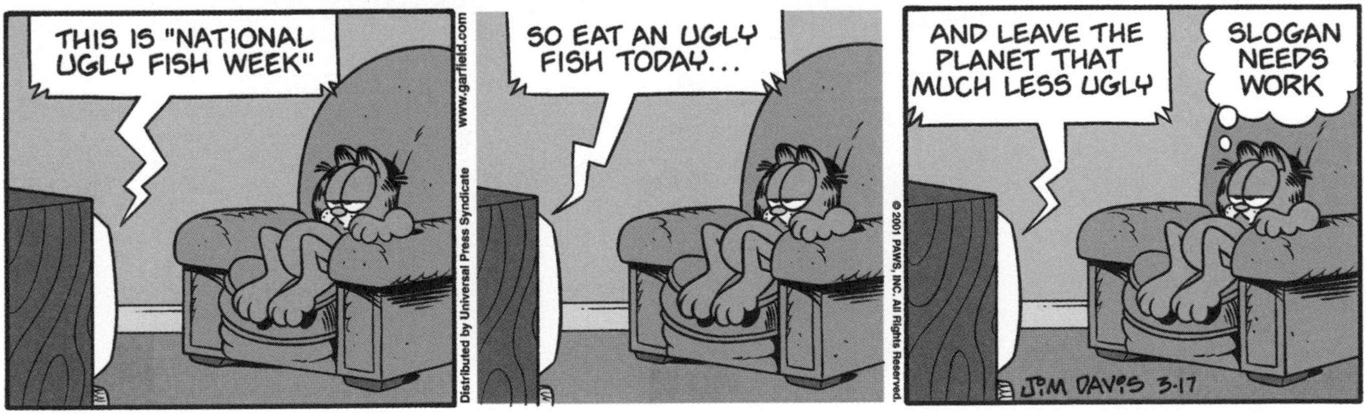
THIS IS "NATIONAL UGLY FISH WEEK"
Distributed by Universal Press Syndicate www.garfield.com
SO EAT AN UGLY FISH TODAY...
© 2001 PAWS, INC. All Rights Reserved.
AND LEAVE THE PLANET THAT MUCH LESS UGLY
SLOGAN NEEDS WORK
JIM DAVIS 3-17

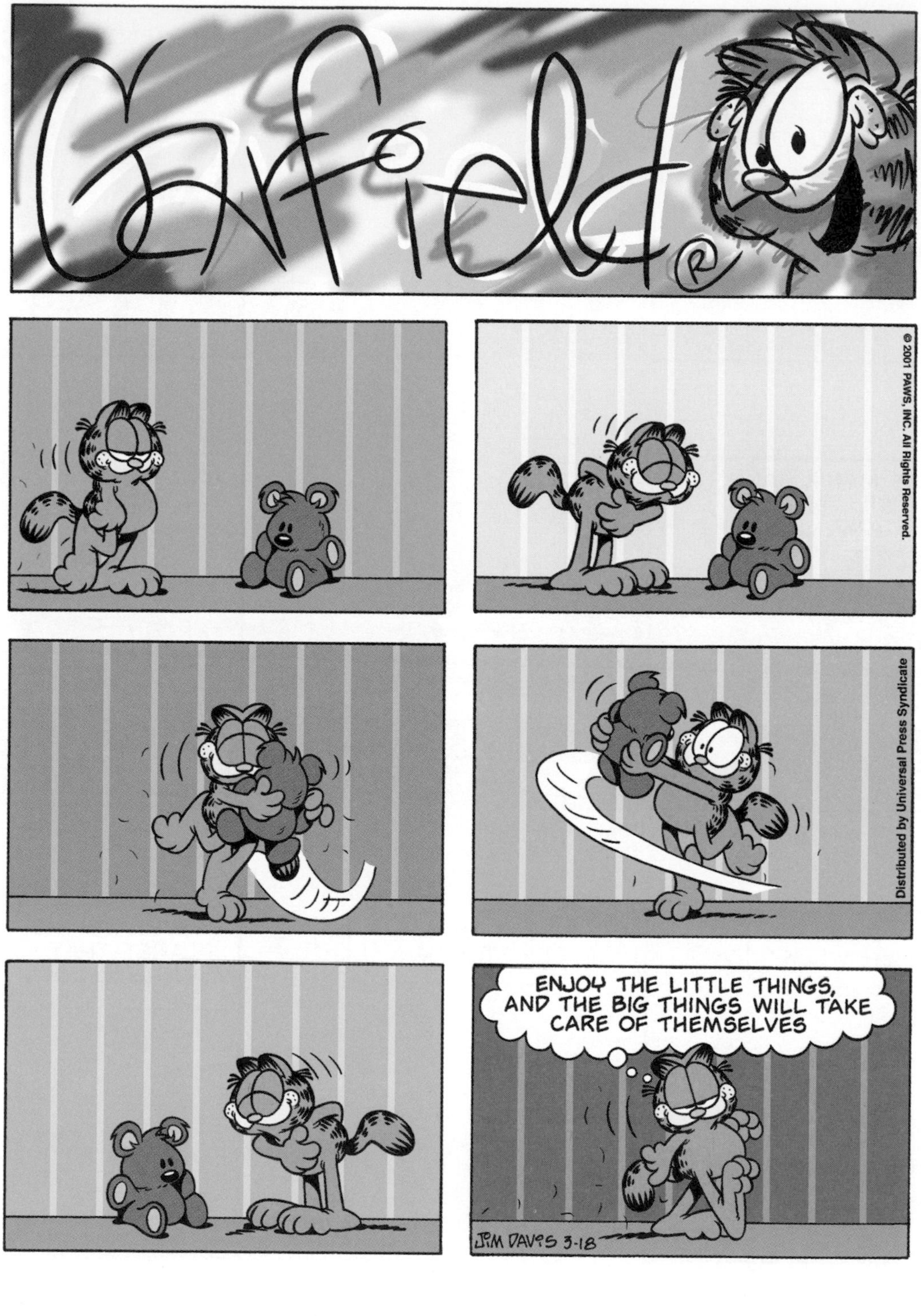
Garfield®
© 2001 PAWS, INC. All Rights Reserved.
Distributed by Universal Press Syndicate
ENJOY THE LITTLE THINGS, AND THE BIG THINGS WILL TAKE CARE OF THEMSELVES
JIM DAVIS 3-18

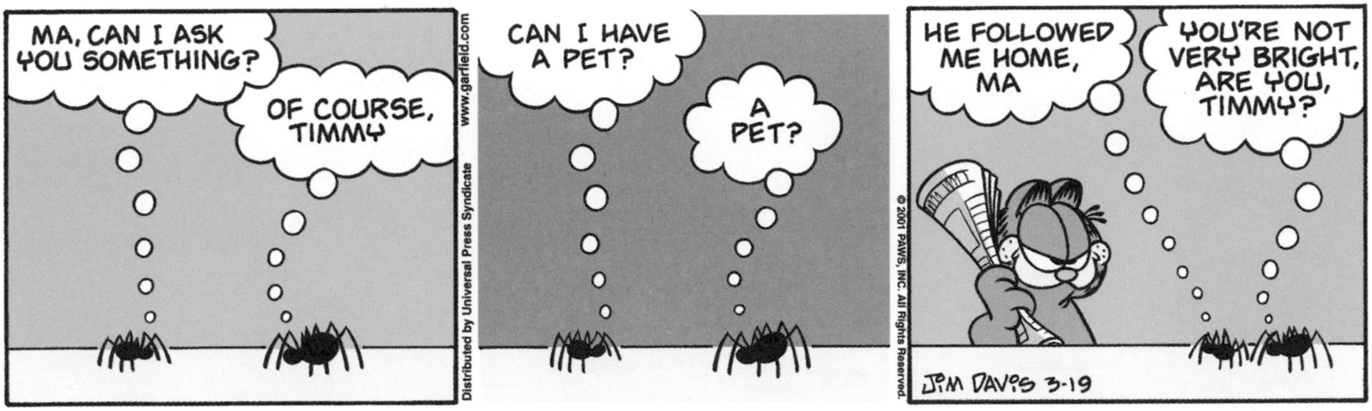
MA, CAN I ASK YOU SOMETHING?
OF COURSE, TIMMY
CAN I HAVE A PET?
A PET?
HE FOLLOWED ME HOME, MA
YOU'RE NOT VERY BRIGHT, ARE YOU, TIMMY?
JIM DAVIS 3-19
www.garfield.com
Distributed by Universal Press Syndicate
© 2001 PAWS, INC. All Rights Reserved.

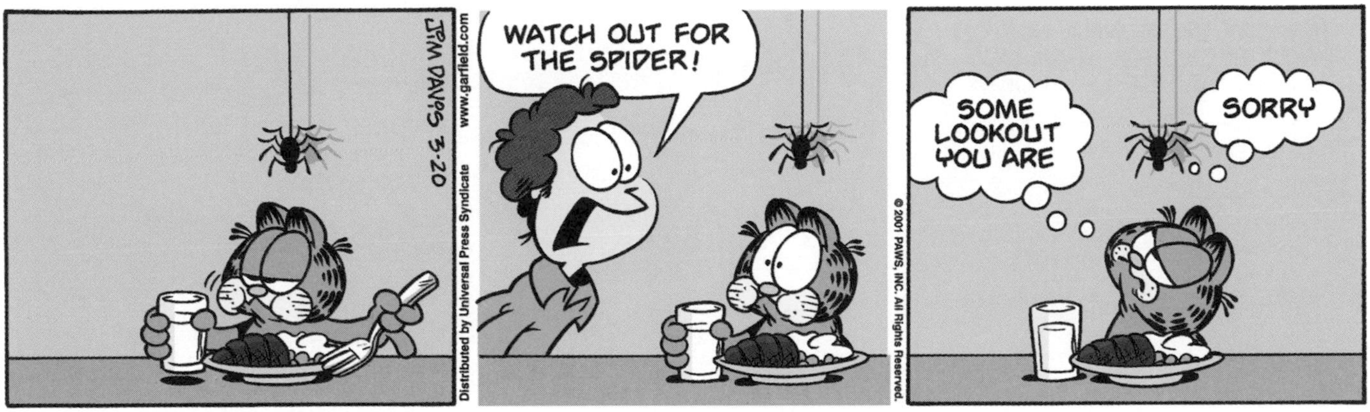
JIM DAVIS 3-20
WATCH OUT FOR THE SPIDER!
SOME LOOKOUT YOU ARE
SORRY
www.garfield.com
Distributed by Universal Press Syndicate
© 2001 PAWS, INC. All Rights Reserved.

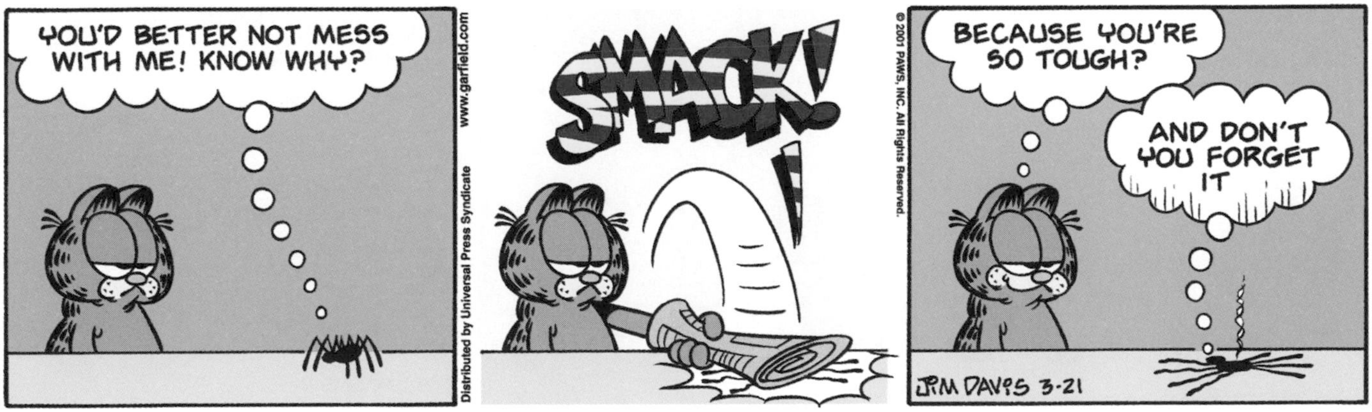
YOU'D BETTER NOT MESS WITH ME! KNOW WHY?
SMACK!
BECAUSE YOU'RE SO TOUGH?
AND DON'T YOU FORGET IT
JIM DAVIS 3-21
www.garfield.com
Distributed by Universal Press Syndicate
© 2001 PAWS, INC. All Rights Reserved.

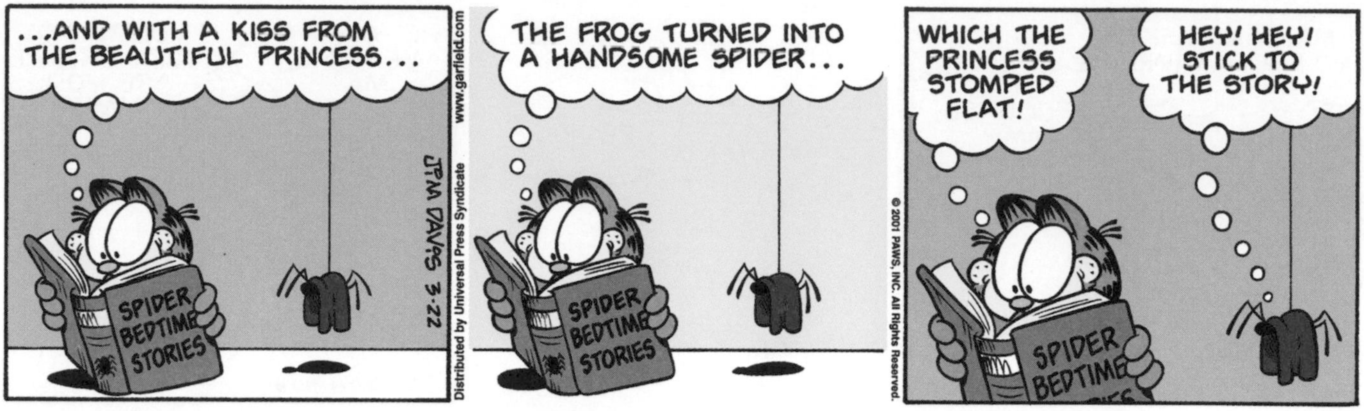
...AND WITH A KISS FROM THE BEAUTIFUL PRINCESS...
SPIDER BEDTIME STORIES
JIM DAVIS 3-22
www.garfield.com
Distributed by Universal Press Syndicate
THE FROG TURNED INTO A HANDSOME SPIDER...
SPIDER BEDTIME STORIES
© 2001 PAWS, INC. All Rights Reserved.
WHICH THE PRINCESS STOMPED FLAT!
HEY! HEY! STICK TO THE STORY!
SPIDER BEDTIME

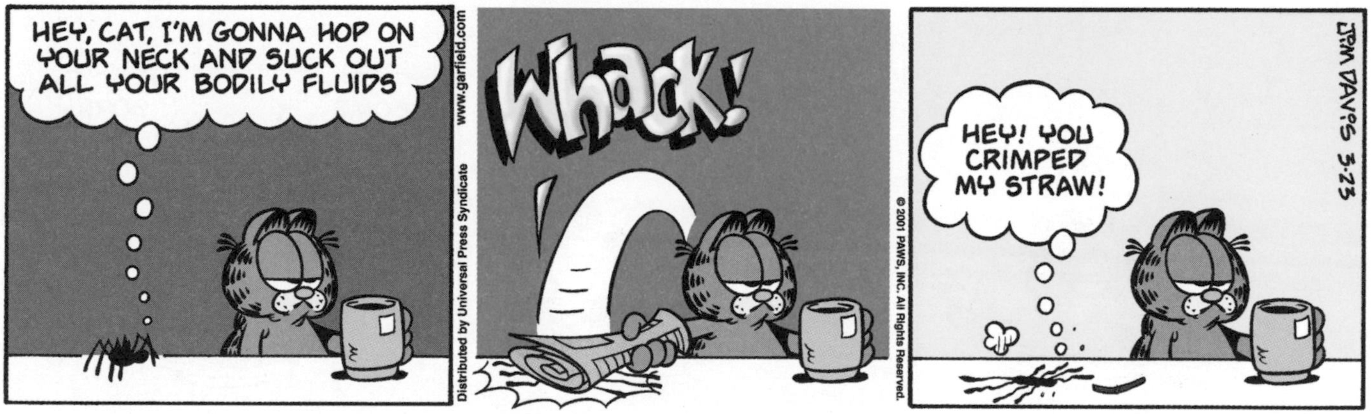
HEY, CAT, I'M GONNA HOP ON YOUR NECK AND SUCK OUT ALL YOUR BODILY FLUIDS
www.garfield.com
Distributed by Universal Press Syndicate
WHACK!
© 2001 PAWS, INC. All Rights Reserved.
HEY! YOU CRIMPED MY STRAW!
JIM DAVIS 3-23

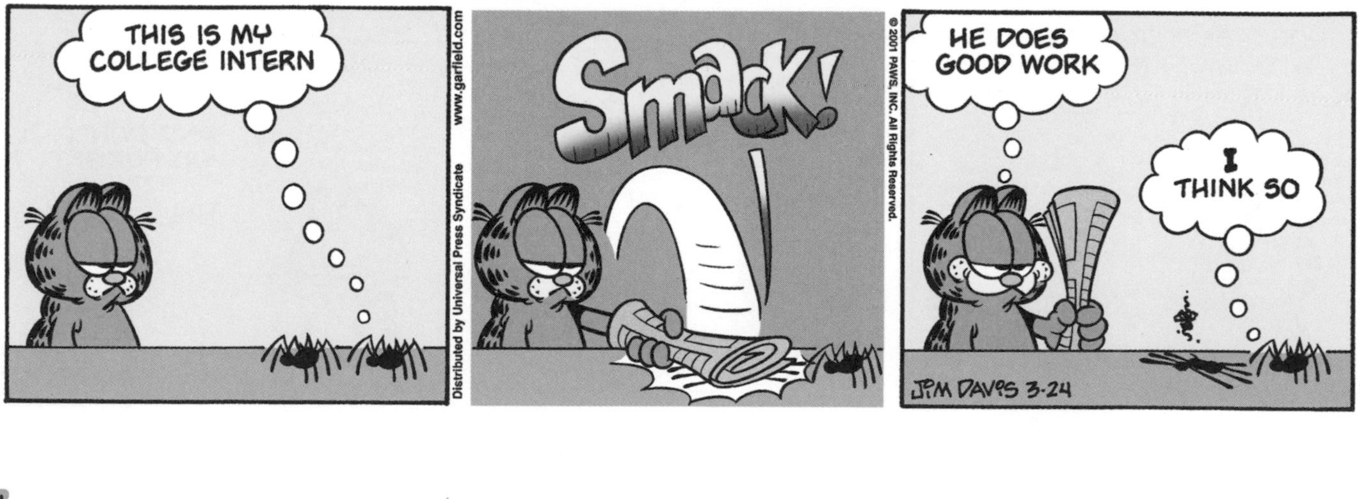
THIS IS MY COLLEGE INTERN
www.garfield.com
Distributed by Universal Press Syndicate
SMACK!
© 2001 PAWS, INC. All Rights Reserved.
HE DOES GOOD WORK
I THINK SO
JIM DAVIS 3-24

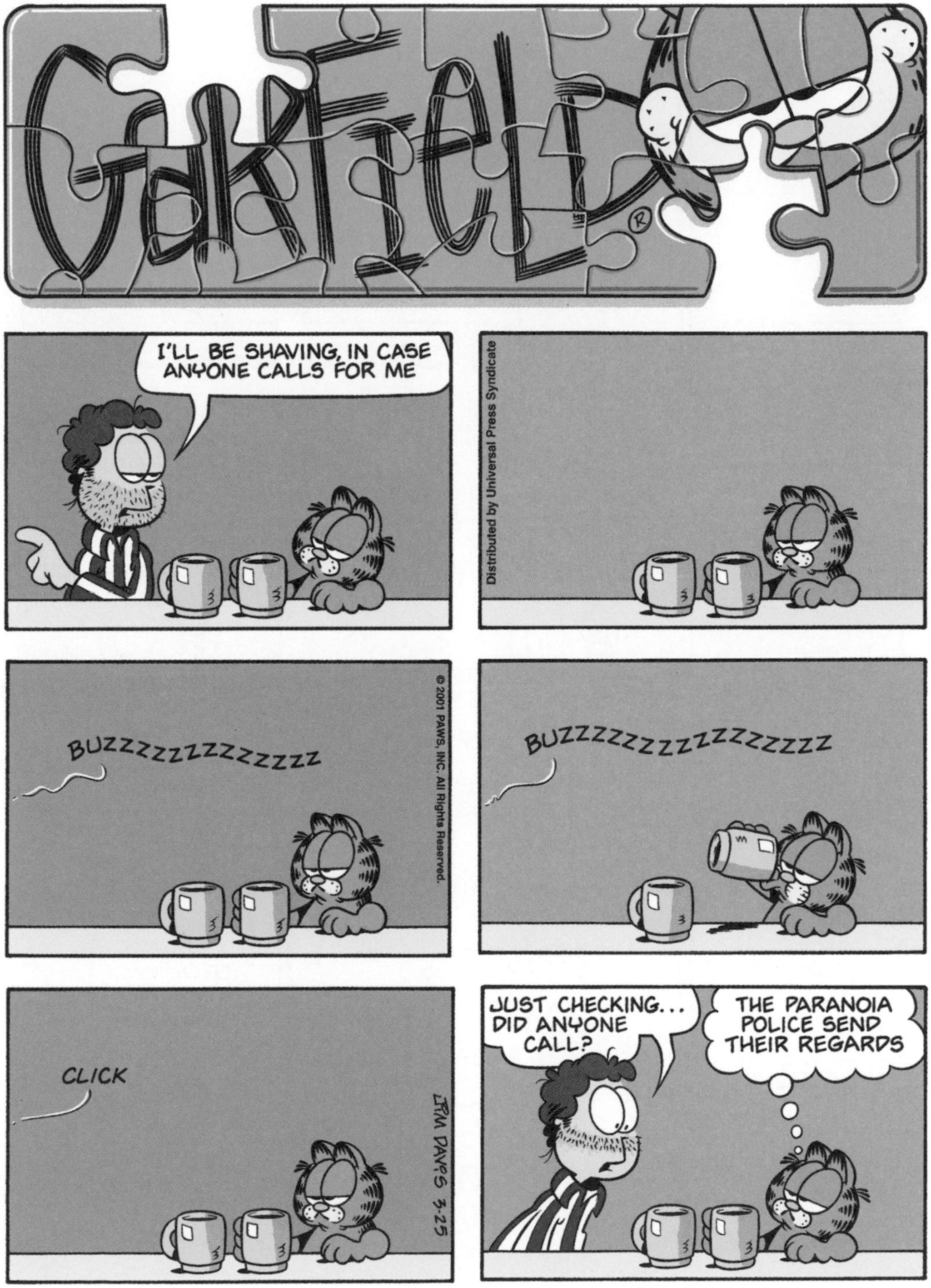
GARFIELD®
I'LL BE SHAVING, IN CASE ANYONE CALLS FOR ME
Distributed by Universal Press Syndicate
BUZZZZZZZZZZZZZ
© 2001 PAWS, INC. All Rights Reserved.
BUZZZZZZZZZZZZZZZZZ
CLICK
JIM DAVIS 3-25
JUST CHECKING... DID ANYONE CALL?
THE PARANOIA POLICE SEND THEIR REGARDS

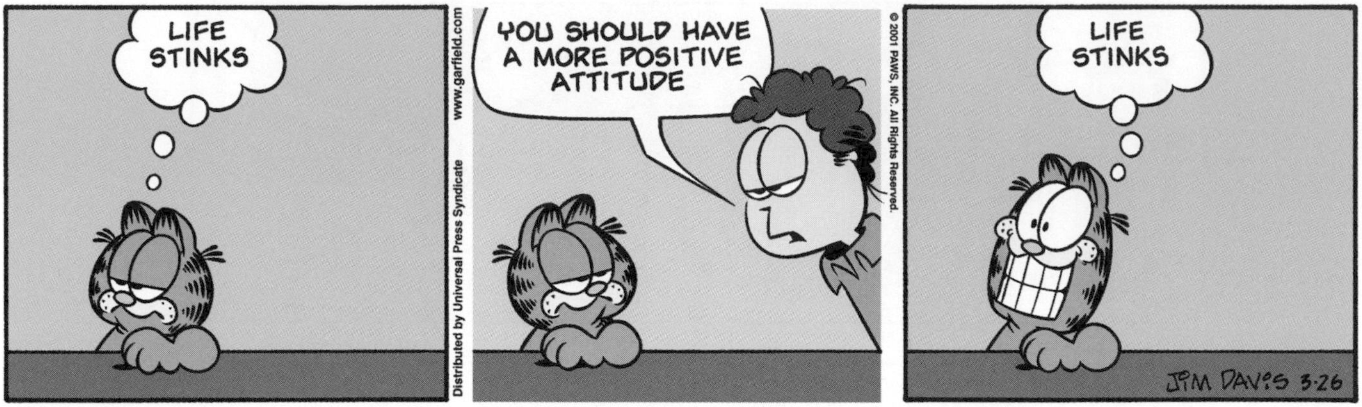
LIFE STINKS
Distributed by Universal Press Syndicate www.garfield.com
YOU SHOULD HAVE A MORE POSITIVE ATTITUDE
© 2001 PAWS, INC. All Rights Reserved.
LIFE STINKS
JIM DAVIS 3-26

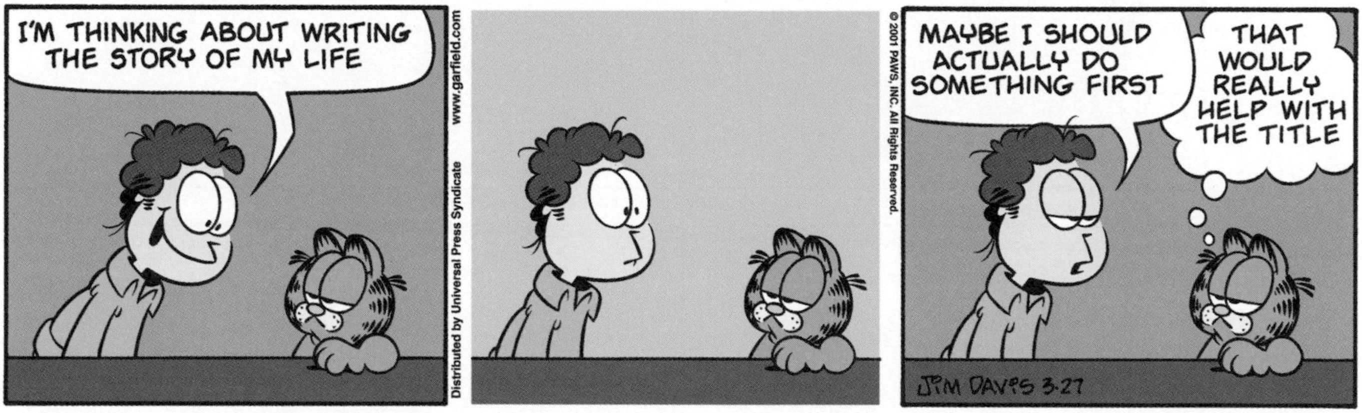
I'M THINKING ABOUT WRITING THE STORY OF MY LIFE
Distributed by Universal Press Syndicate www.garfield.com
© 2001 PAWS, INC. All Rights Reserved.
MAYBE I SHOULD ACTUALLY DO SOMETHING FIRST
THAT WOULD REALLY HELP WITH THE TITLE
JIM DAVIS 3-27

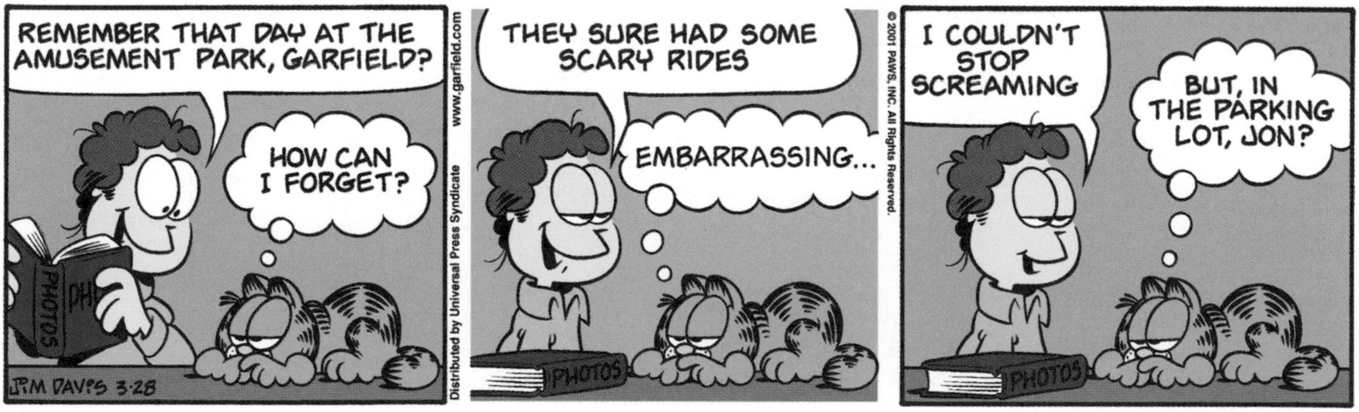
REMEMBER THAT DAY AT THE AMUSEMENT PARK, GARFIELD?
HOW CAN I FORGET?
PHOTOS
JIM DAVIS 3-28
Distributed by Universal Press Syndicate www.garfield.com
THEY SURE HAD SOME SCARY RIDES
EMBARRASSING...
PHOTOS
© 2001 PAWS, INC. All Rights Reserved.
I COULDN'T STOP SCREAMING
BUT, IN THE PARKING LOT, JON?
PHOTOS

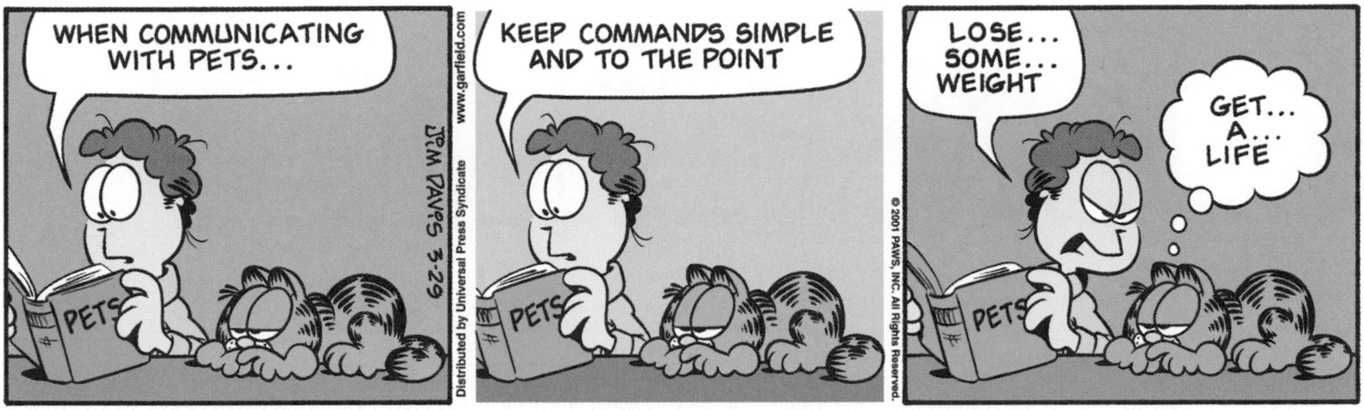
WHEN COMMUNICATING WITH PETS...
PETS
JIM DAVIS 3-29
www.garfield.com
Distributed by Universal Press Syndicate
KEEP COMMANDS SIMPLE AND TO THE POINT
PETS
© 2001 PAWS, INC. All Rights Reserved.
LOSE... SOME... WEIGHT
GET... A... LIFE
PETS

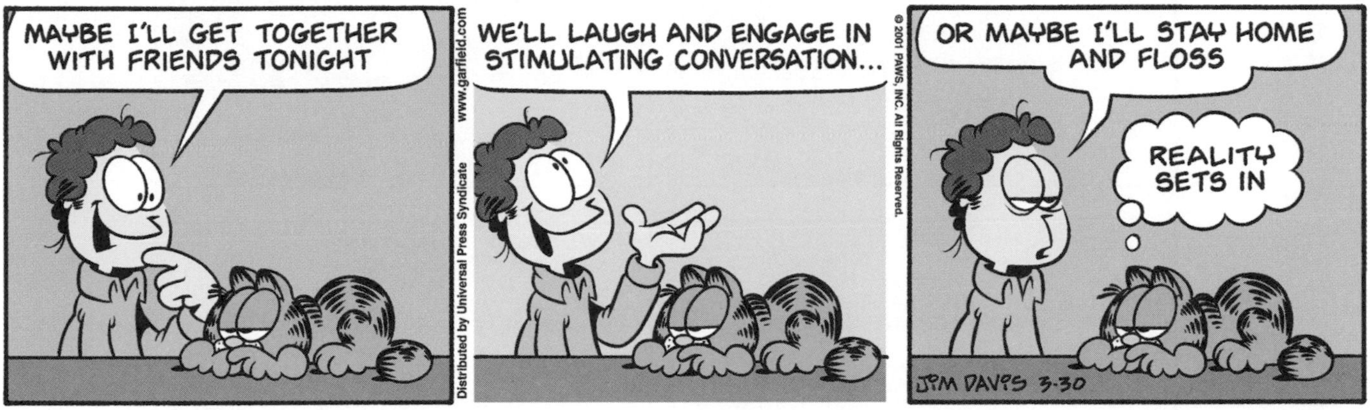
MAYBE I'LL GET TOGETHER WITH FRIENDS TONIGHT
www.garfield.com
Distributed by Universal Press Syndicate
WE'LL LAUGH AND ENGAGE IN STIMULATING CONVERSATION...
© 2001 PAWS, INC. All Rights Reserved.
OR MAYBE I'LL STAY HOME AND FLOSS
REALITY SETS IN
JIM DAVIS 3-30

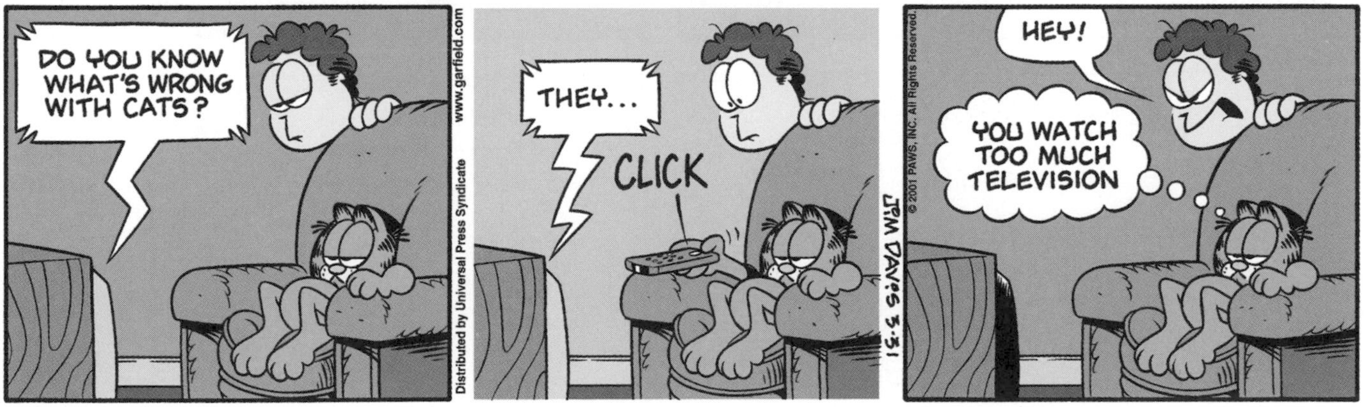
DO YOU KNOW WHAT'S WRONG WITH CATS?
www.garfield.com
Distributed by Universal Press Syndicate
THEY...
CLICK
JIM DAVIS 3-31
© 2001 PAWS, INC. All Rights Reserved.
HEY!
YOU WATCH TOO MUCH TELEVISION

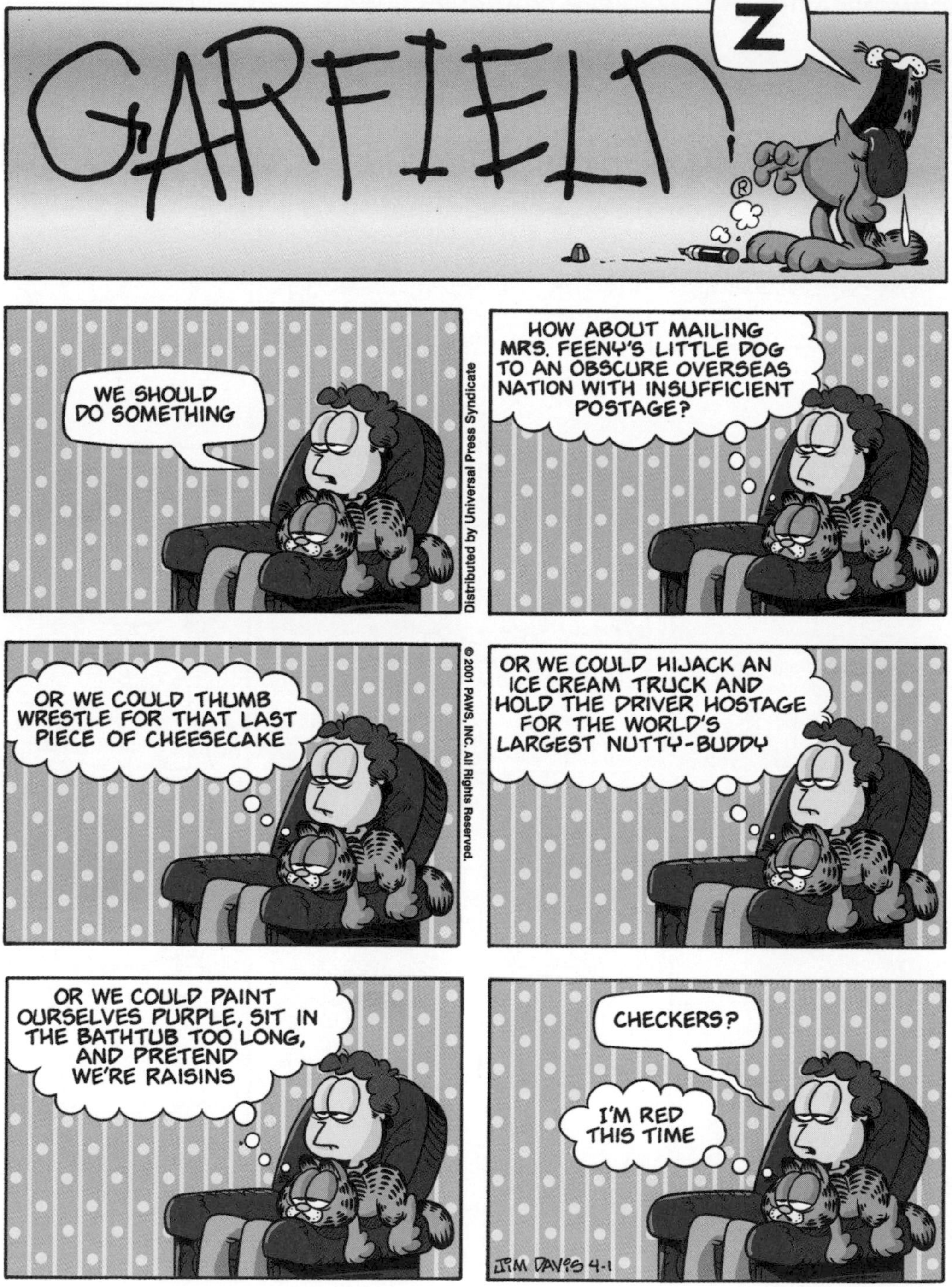
GARFIELD
Z
®
WE SHOULD DO SOMETHING
HOW ABOUT MAILING MRS. FEENY'S LITTLE DOG TO AN OBSCURE OVERSEAS NATION WITH INSUFFICIENT POSTAGE?
OR WE COULD THUMB WRESTLE FOR THAT LAST PIECE OF CHEESECAKE
OR WE COULD HIJACK AN ICE CREAM TRUCK AND HOLD THE DRIVER HOSTAGE FOR THE WORLD'S LARGEST NUTTY-BUDDY
OR WE COULD PAINT OURSELVES PURPLE, SIT IN THE BATHTUB TOO LONG, AND PRETEND WE'RE RAISINS
CHECKERS?
I'M RED THIS TIME
JIM DAVIS 4-1
Distributed by Universal Press Syndicate
© 2001 PAWS, INC. All Rights Reserved.

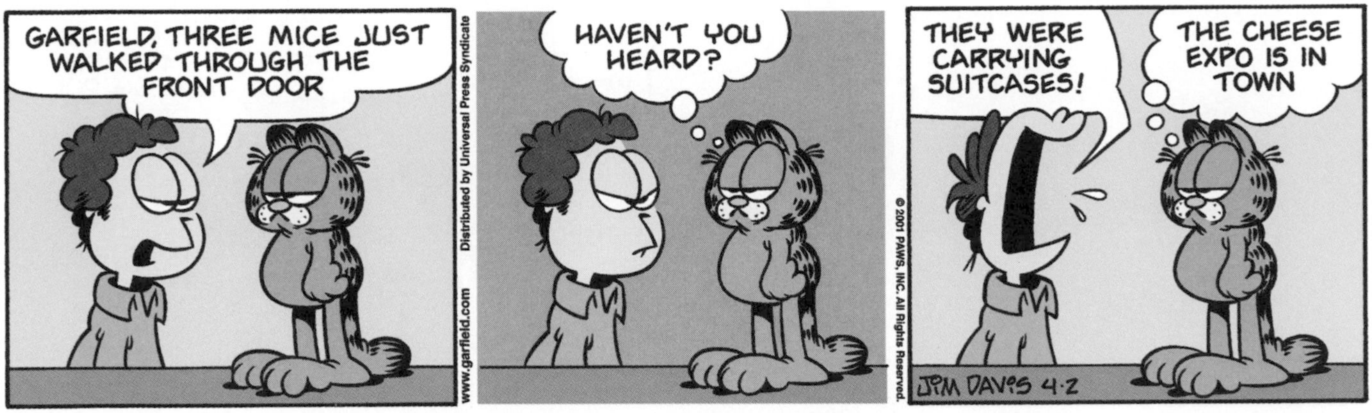
GARFIELD, THREE MICE JUST WALKED THROUGH THE FRONT DOOR
HAVEN'T YOU HEARD?
THEY WERE CARRYING SUITCASES!
THE CHEESE EXPO IS IN TOWN
JIM DAVIS 4·2
www.garfield.com
Distributed by Universal Press Syndicate
© 2001 PAWS, INC. All Rights Reserved.

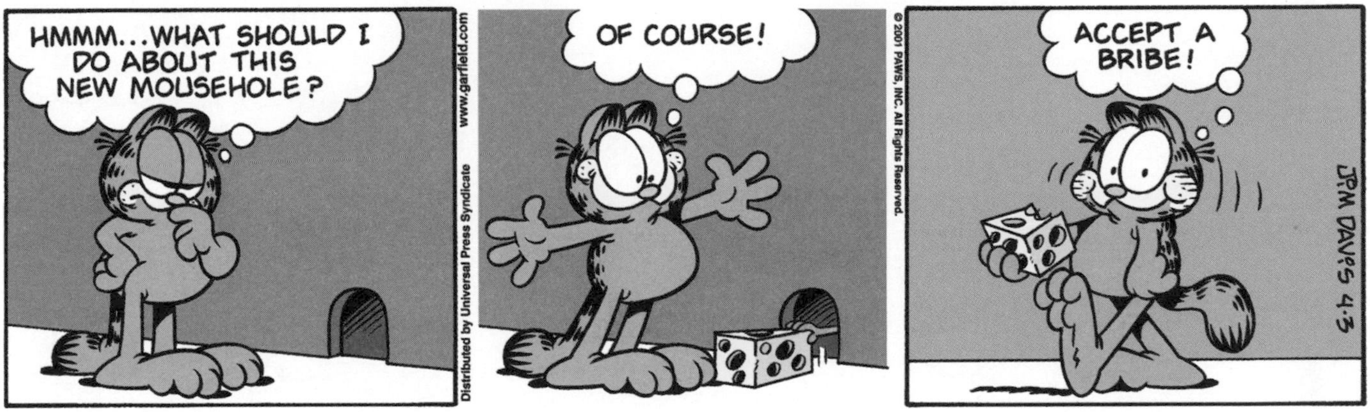
HMMM...WHAT SHOULD I DO ABOUT THIS NEW MOUSEHOLE?
OF COURSE!
ACCEPT A BRIBE!
JIM DAVIS 4·3
www.garfield.com
Distributed by Universal Press Syndicate
© 2001 PAWS, INC. All Rights Reserved.

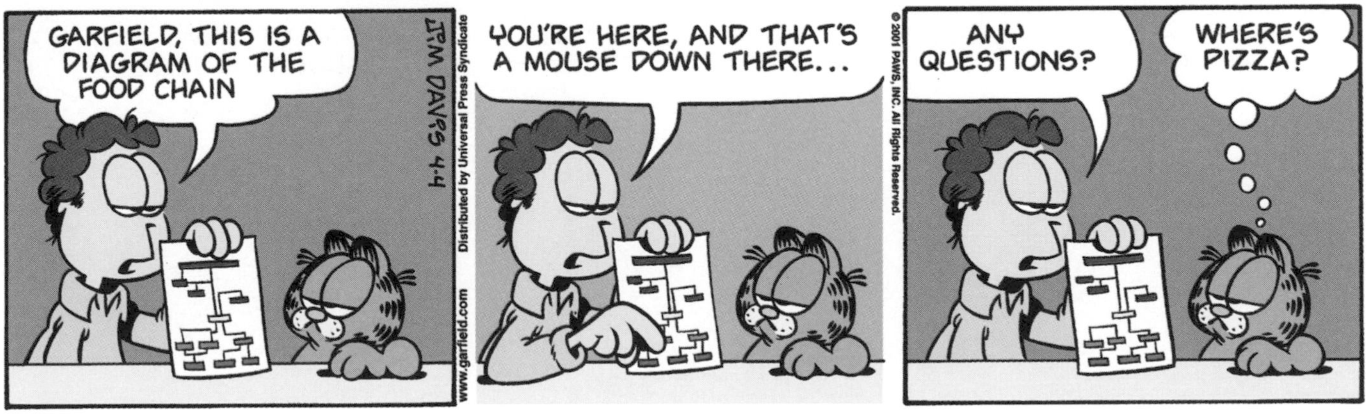
GARFIELD, THIS IS A DIAGRAM OF THE FOOD CHAIN
YOU'RE HERE, AND THAT'S A MOUSE DOWN THERE...
ANY QUESTIONS?
WHERE'S PIZZA?
JIM DAVIS 4·4
www.garfield.com
Distributed by Universal Press Syndicate
© 2001 PAWS, INC. All Rights Reserved.

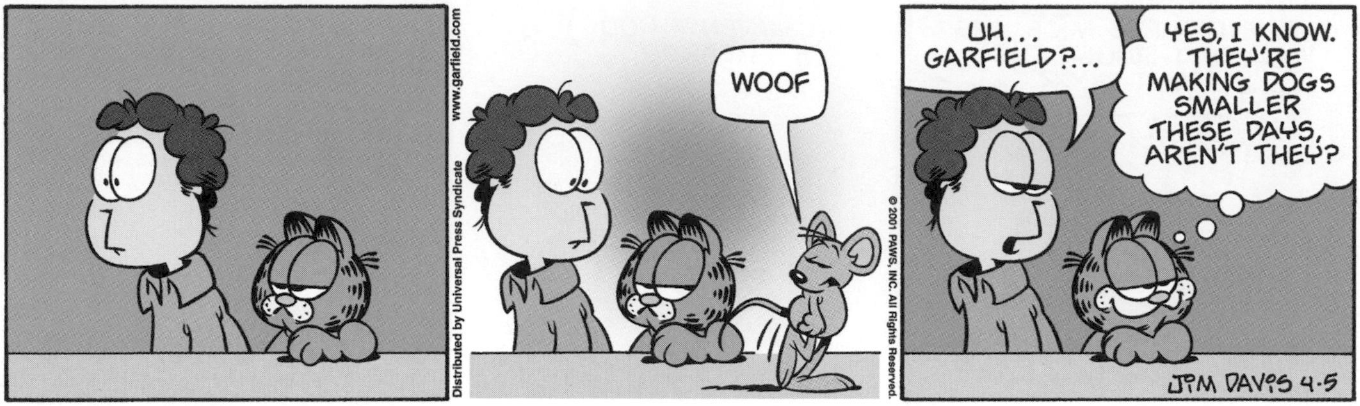
Distributed by Universal Press Syndicate www.garfield.com
WOOF
© 2001 PAWS, INC. All Rights Reserved.
UH... GARFIELD?...
YES, I KNOW. THEY'RE MAKING DOGS SMALLER THESE DAYS, AREN'T THEY?
JIM DAVIS 4-5

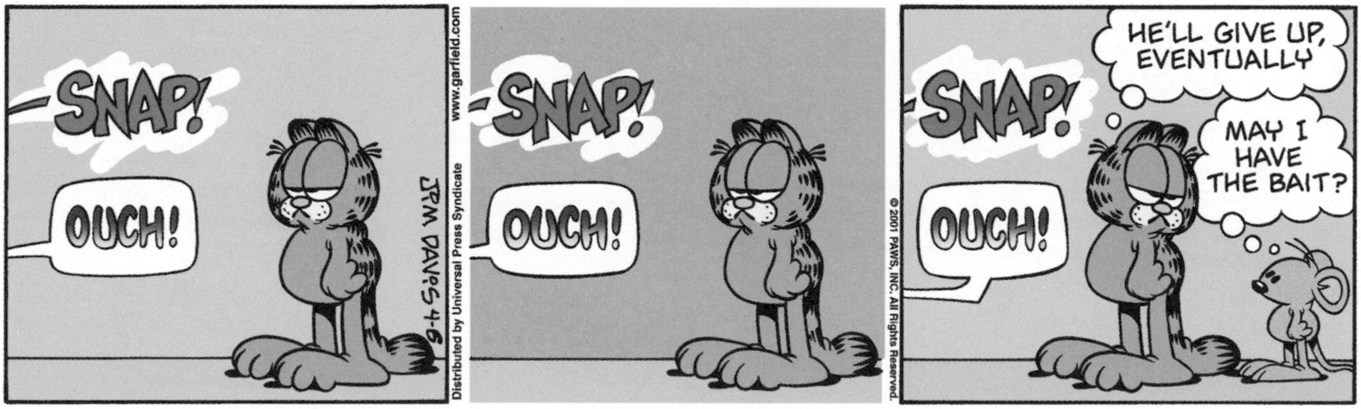
SNAP!
OUCH!
JIM DAVIS 4-6
Distributed by Universal Press Syndicate www.garfield.com
SNAP!
OUCH!
© 2001 PAWS, INC. All Rights Reserved.
SNAP!
OUCH!
HE'LL GIVE UP, EVENTUALLY
MAY I HAVE THE BAIT?

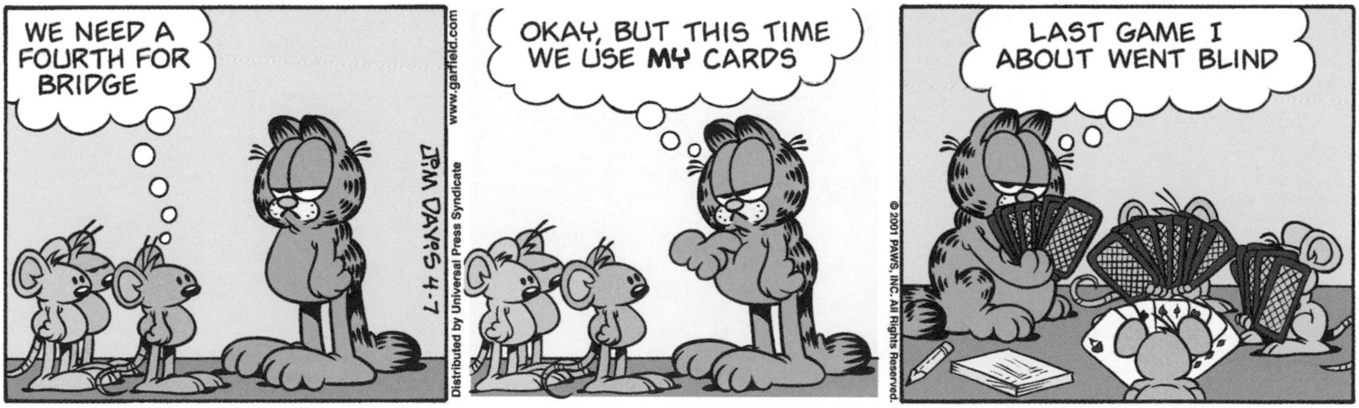
WE NEED A FOURTH FOR BRIDGE
JIM DAVIS 4-7
Distributed by Universal Press Syndicate www.garfield.com
OKAY, BUT THIS TIME WE USE MY CARDS
© 2001 PAWS, INC. All Rights Reserved.
LAST GAME I ABOUT WENT BLIND

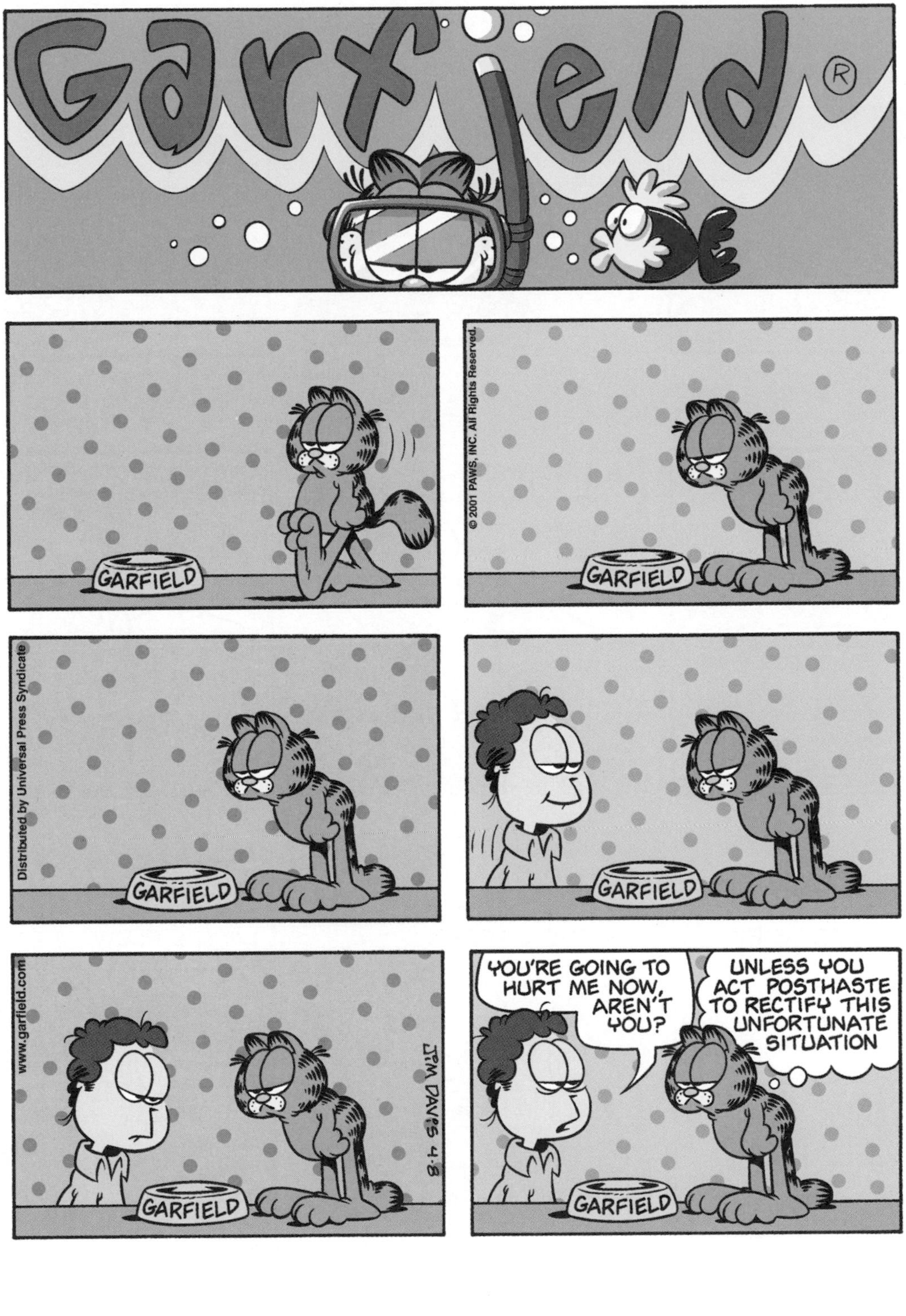
Garfield®
© 2001 PAWS, INC. All Rights Reserved.
Distributed by Universal Press Syndicate
www.garfield.com
GARFIELD
JIM DAVIS 4-8
YOU'RE GOING TO HURT ME NOW, AREN'T YOU?
UNLESS YOU ACT POSTHASTE TO RECTIFY THIS UNFORTUNATE SITUATION

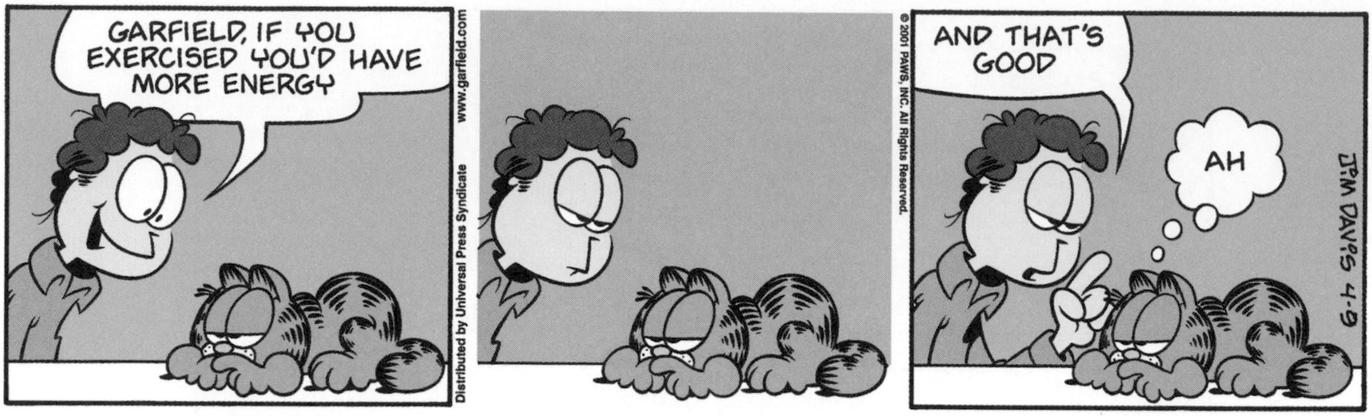
GARFIELD, IF YOU EXERCISED YOU'D HAVE MORE ENERGY
Distributed by Universal Press Syndicate www.garfield.com
© 2001 PAWS, INC. All Rights Reserved.
AND THAT'S GOOD
AH
JPM DAVIS 4-9

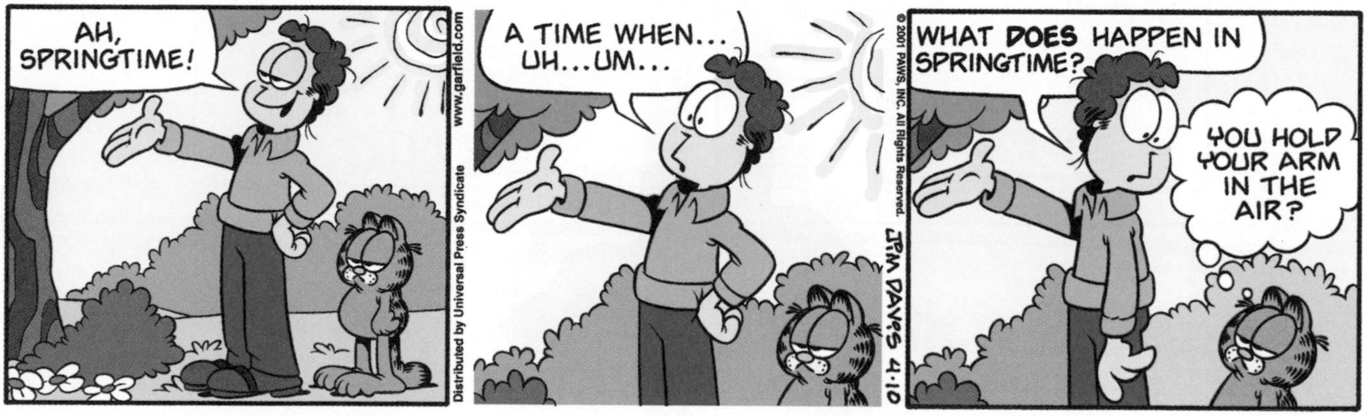
AH, SPRINGTIME!
Distributed by Universal Press Syndicate www.garfield.com
A TIME WHEN... UH...UM...
© 2001 PAWS, INC. All Rights Reserved.
JPM DAVIS 4-10
WHAT DOES HAPPEN IN SPRINGTIME?
YOU HOLD YOUR ARM IN THE AIR?

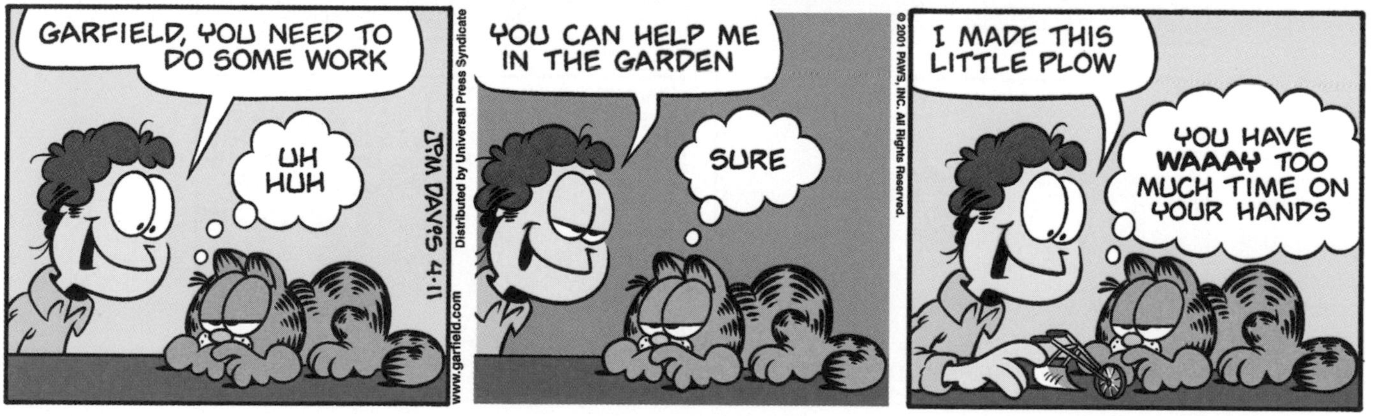
GARFIELD, YOU NEED TO DO SOME WORK
UH HUH
JPM DAVIS 4-11
Distributed by Universal Press Syndicate www.garfield.com
YOU CAN HELP ME IN THE GARDEN
SURE
© 2001 PAWS, INC. All Rights Reserved.
I MADE THIS LITTLE PLOW
YOU HAVE WAAAY TOO MUCH TIME ON YOUR HANDS

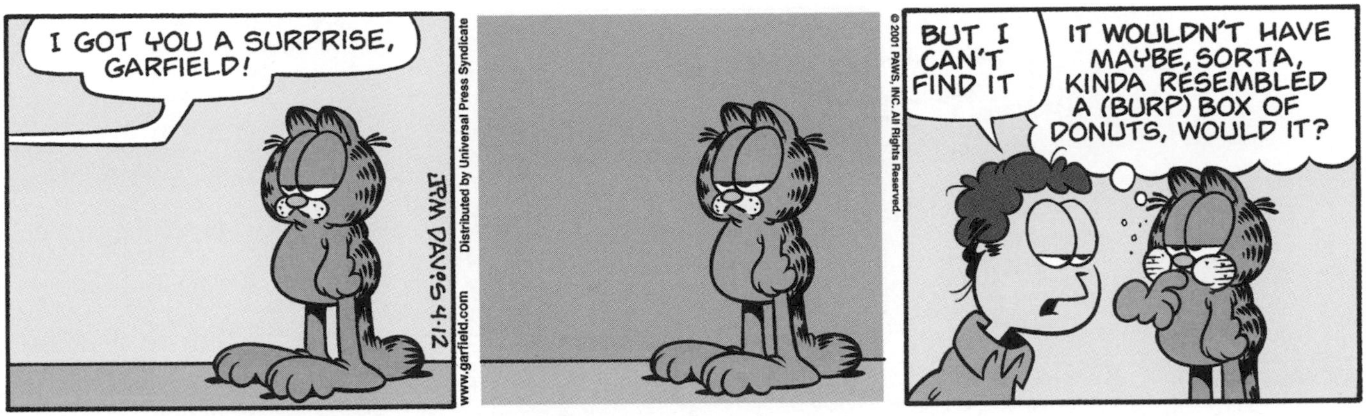
I GOT YOU A SURPRISE, GARFIELD!
JIM DAVIS 4-12
Distributed by Universal Press Syndicate
www.garfield.com
© 2001 PAWS, INC. All Rights Reserved.
BUT I CAN'T FIND IT
IT WOULDN'T HAVE MAYBE, SORTA, KINDA RESEMBLED A (BURP) BOX OF DONUTS, WOULD IT?

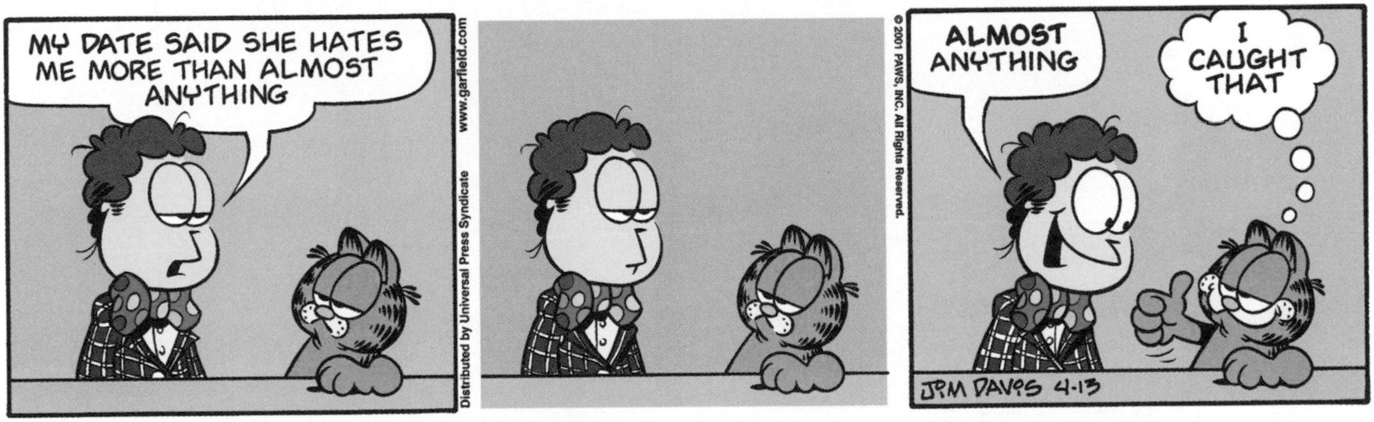
MY DATE SAID SHE HATES ME MORE THAN ALMOST ANYTHING
Distributed by Universal Press Syndicate
www.garfield.com
© 2001 PAWS, INC. All Rights Reserved.
ALMOST ANYTHING
I CAUGHT THAT
JIM DAVIS 4-13

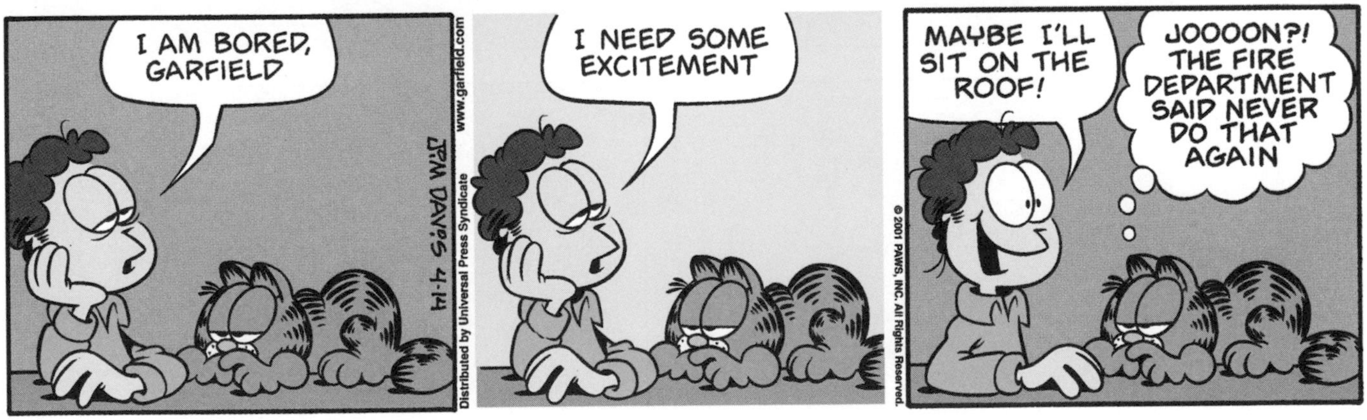
I AM BORED, GARFIELD
JIM DAVIS 4-14
www.garfield.com
Distributed by Universal Press Syndicate
I NEED SOME EXCITEMENT
© 2001 PAWS, INC. All Rights Reserved.
MAYBE I'LL SIT ON THE ROOF!
JOOOON?! THE FIRE DEPARTMENT SAID NEVER DO THAT AGAIN

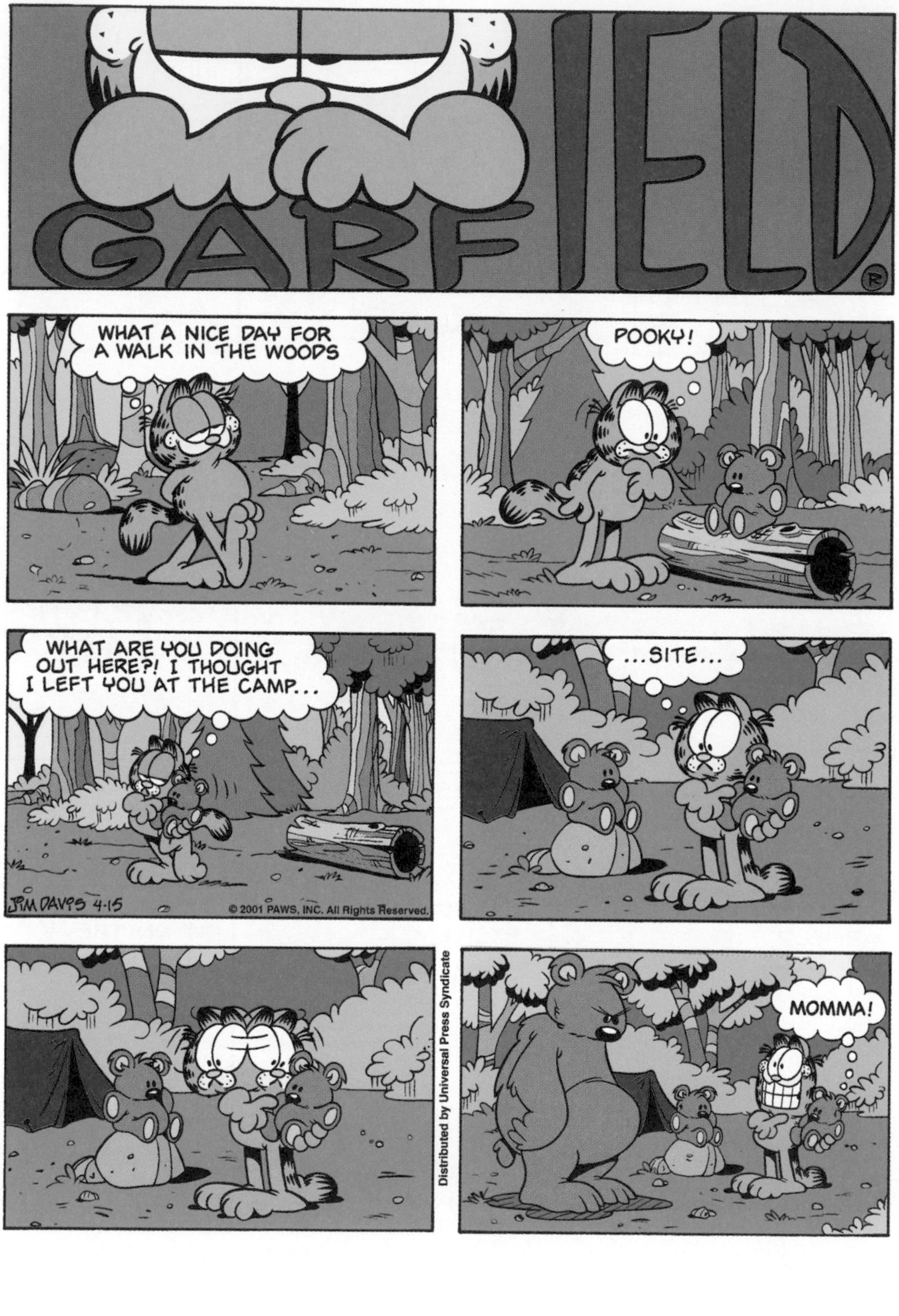
GARFIELD
WHAT A NICE DAY FOR A WALK IN THE WOODS
POOKY!
WHAT ARE YOU DOING OUT HERE?! I THOUGHT I LEFT YOU AT THE CAMP...
JIM DAVIS 4-15
© 2001 PAWS, INC. All Rights Reserved.
...SITE...
Distributed by Universal Press Syndicate
MOMMA!

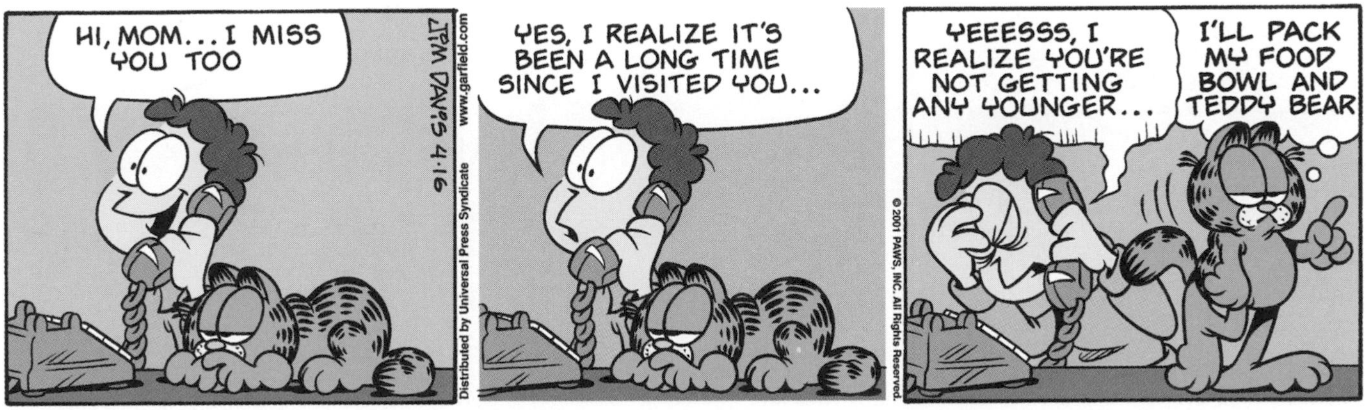
HI, MOM... I MISS YOU TOO
JPM DAVPS 4·16
www.garfield.com
Distributed by Universal Press Syndicate
YES, I REALIZE IT'S BEEN A LONG TIME SINCE I VISITED YOU...
© 2001 PAWS, INC. All Rights Reserved.
YEEEESSS, I REALIZE YOU'RE NOT GETTING ANY YOUNGER...
I'LL PACK MY FOOD BOWL AND TEDDY BEAR

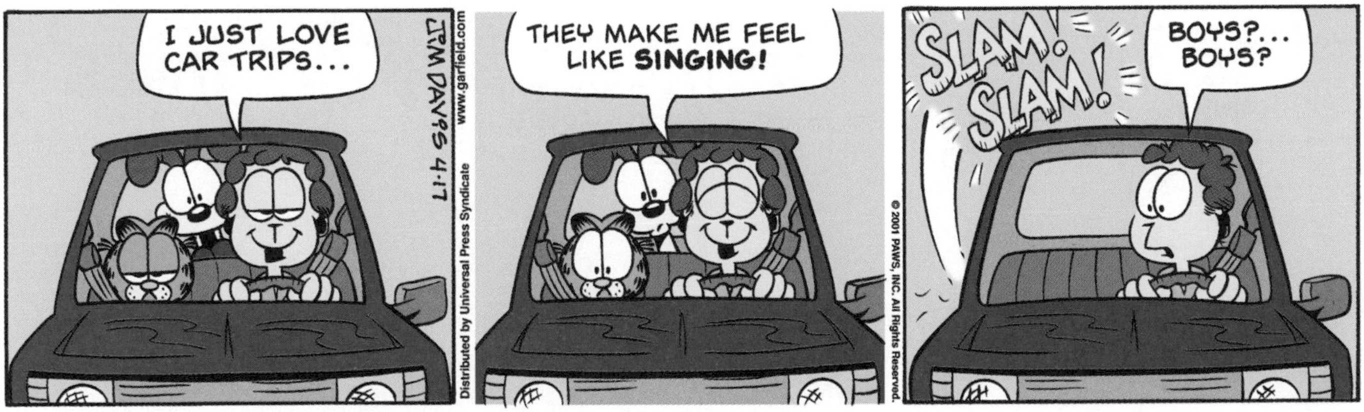
I JUST LOVE CAR TRIPS...
JPM DAVPS 4·17
www.garfield.com
Distributed by Universal Press Syndicate
THEY MAKE ME FEEL LIKE SINGING!
© 2001 PAWS, INC. All Rights Reserved.
SLAM! SLAM!
BOYS?... BOYS?

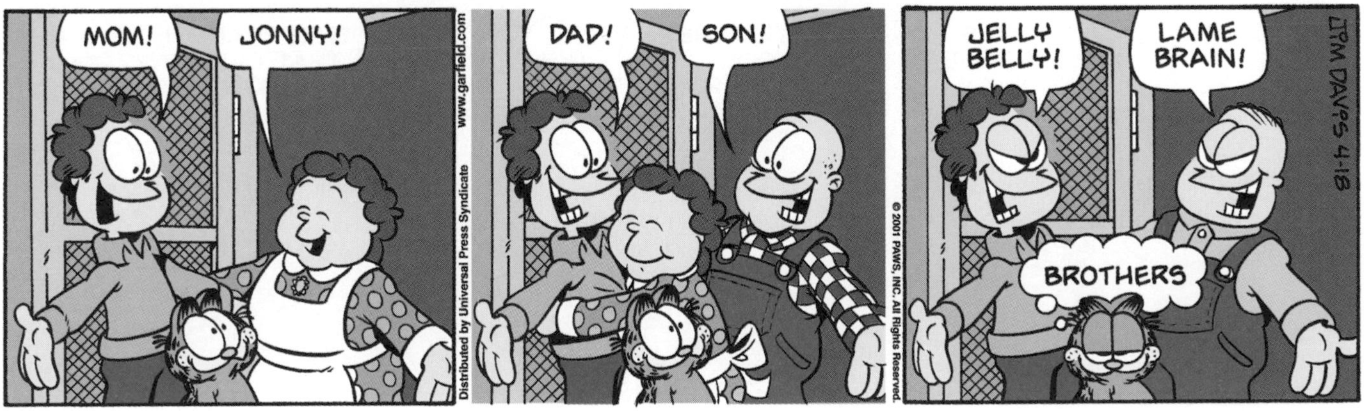
MOM!
JONNY!
www.garfield.com
Distributed by Universal Press Syndicate
DAD!
SON!
© 2001 PAWS, INC. All Rights Reserved.
JELLY BELLY!
LAME BRAIN!
BROTHERS
JPM DAVPS 4·18

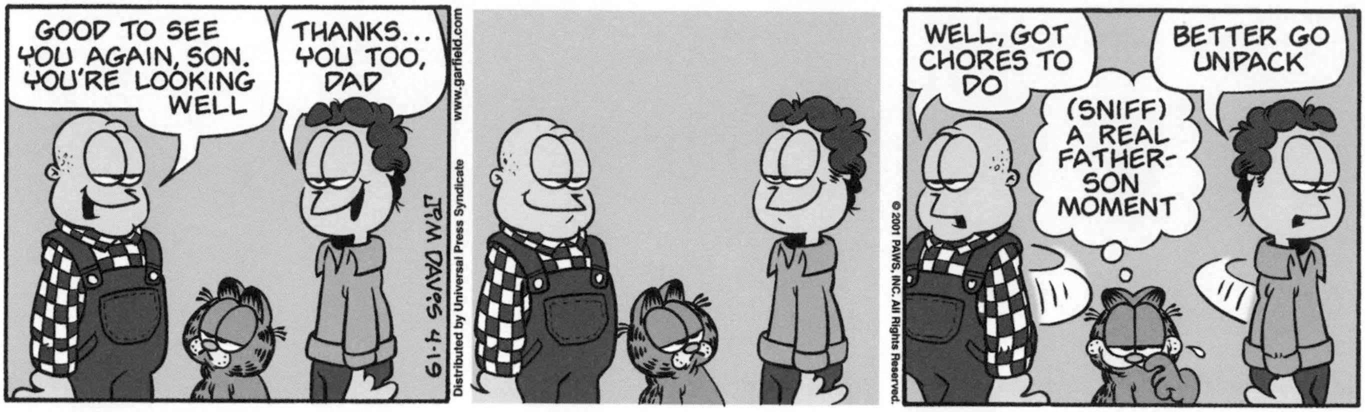
GOOD TO SEE YOU AGAIN, SON. YOU'RE LOOKING WELL
THANKS... YOU TOO, DAD
JIM DAVIS 4-19
www.garfield.com
Distributed by Universal Press Syndicate
© 2001 PAWS, INC. All Rights Reserved.
WELL, GOT CHORES TO DO
(SNIFF) A REAL FATHER-SON MOMENT
BETTER GO UNPACK

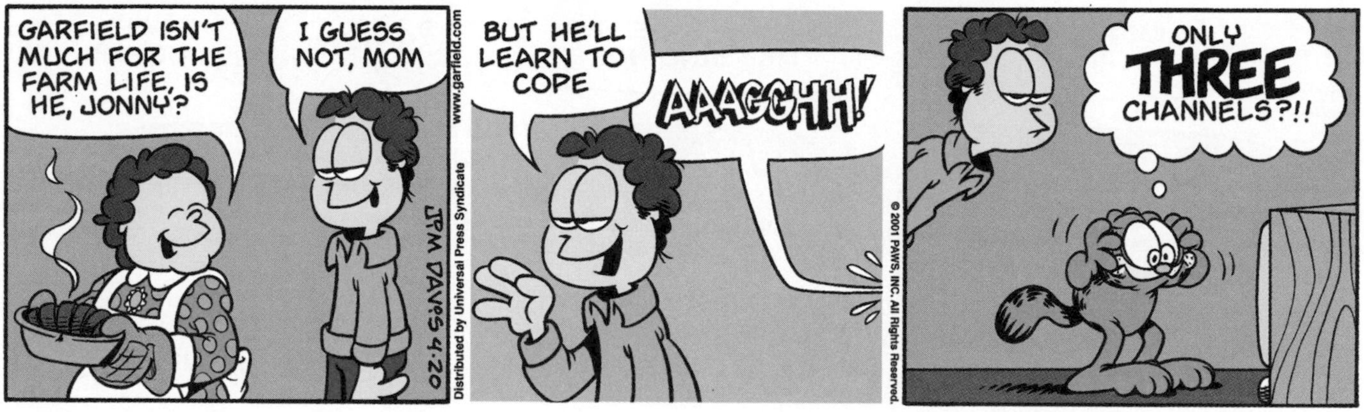
GARFIELD ISN'T MUCH FOR THE FARM LIFE, IS HE, JONNY?
I GUESS NOT, MOM
JIM DAVIS 4-20
www.garfield.com
Distributed by Universal Press Syndicate
BUT HE'LL LEARN TO COPE
AAAGGHH!
© 2001 PAWS, INC. All Rights Reserved.
ONLY THREE CHANNELS?!!

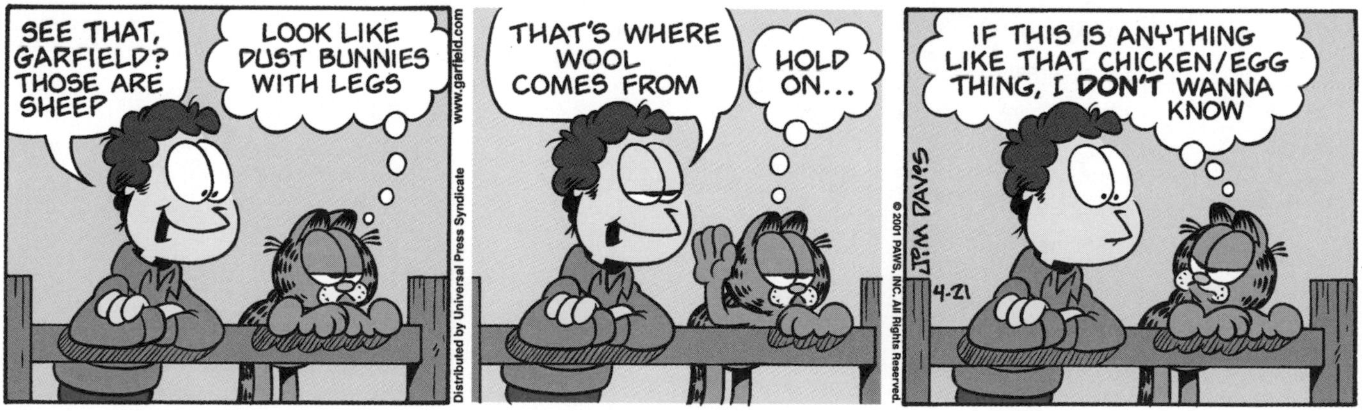
SEE THAT, GARFIELD? THOSE ARE SHEEP
LOOK LIKE DUST BUNNIES WITH LEGS
www.garfield.com
Distributed by Universal Press Syndicate
THAT'S WHERE WOOL COMES FROM
HOLD ON...
© 2001 PAWS, INC. All Rights Reserved.
JIM DAVIS 4-21
IF THIS IS ANYTHING LIKE THAT CHICKEN/EGG THING, I DON'T WANNA KNOW

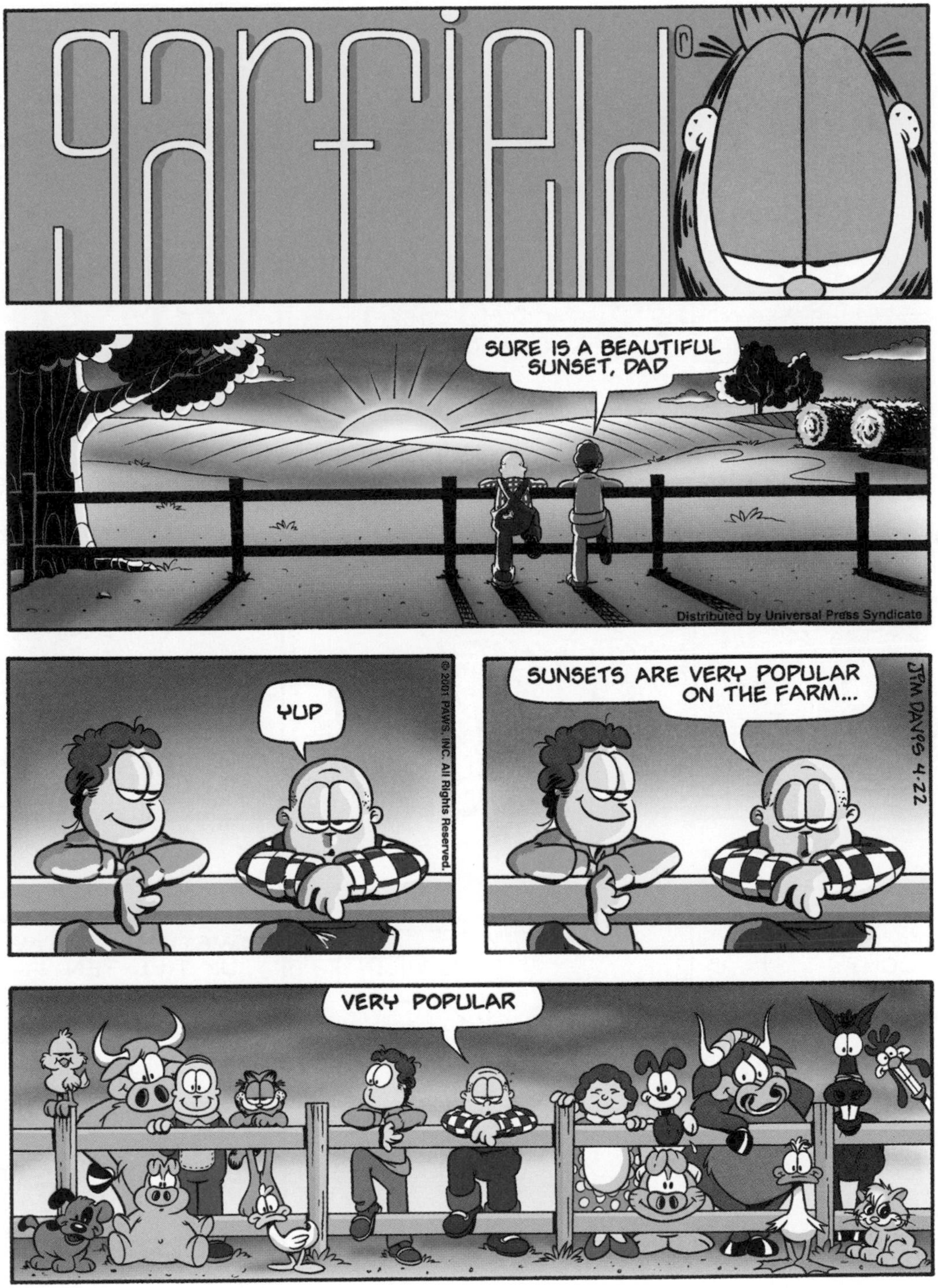
garfield®
SURE IS A BEAUTIFUL SUNSET, DAD
Distributed by Universal Press Syndicate
© 2001 PAWS, INC. All Rights Reserved.
YUP
SUNSETS ARE VERY POPULAR ON THE FARM...
JIM DAVIS 4-22
VERY POPULAR

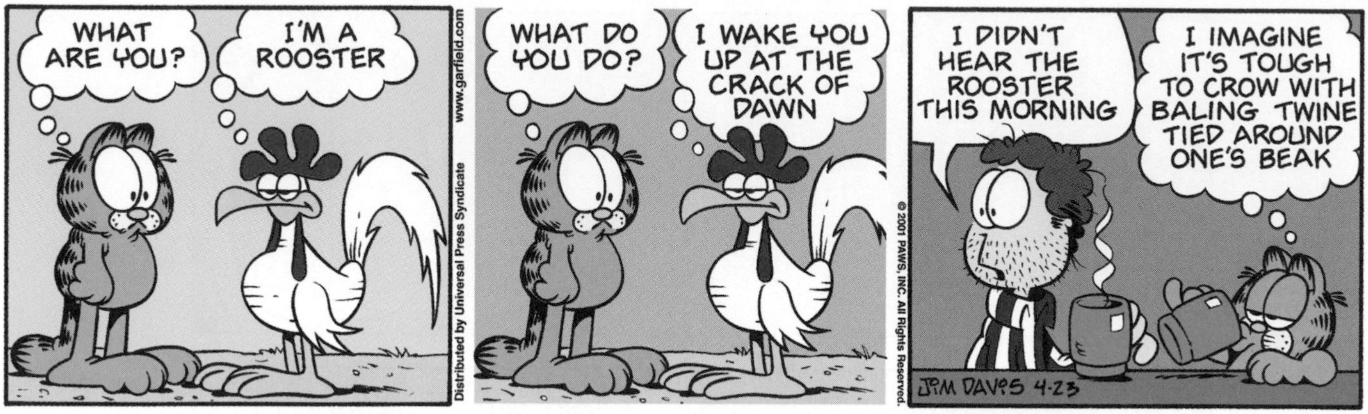
WHAT ARE YOU?
I'M A ROOSTER
WHAT DO YOU DO?
I WAKE YOU UP AT THE CRACK OF DAWN
I DIDN'T HEAR THE ROOSTER THIS MORNING
I IMAGINE IT'S TOUGH TO CROW WITH BALING TWINE TIED AROUND ONE'S BEAK
JIM DAVIS 4-23
www.garfield.com
Distributed by Universal Press Syndicate
© 2001 PAWS, INC. All Rights Reserved.

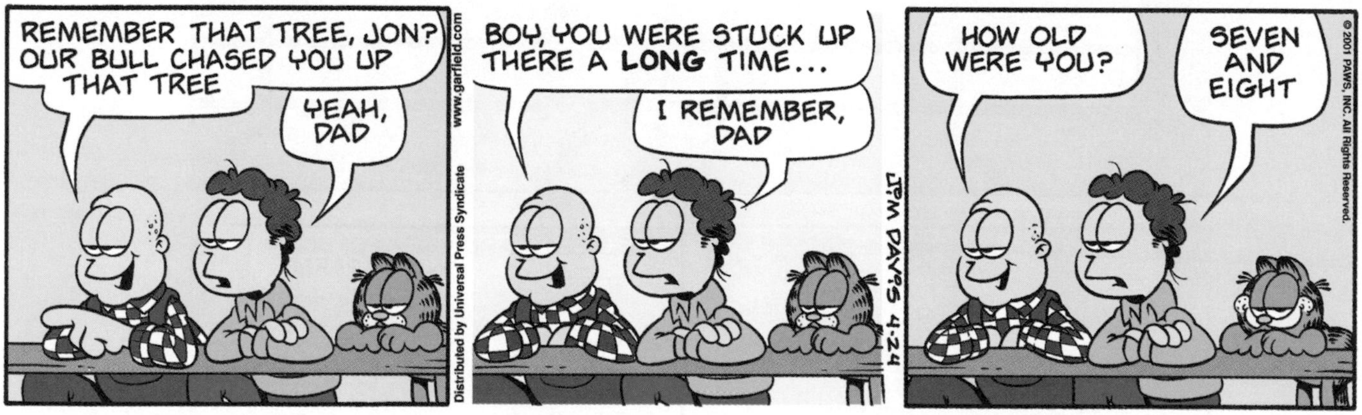
REMEMBER THAT TREE, JON? OUR BULL CHASED YOU UP THAT TREE
YEAH, DAD
BOY, YOU WERE STUCK UP THERE A **LONG** TIME...
I REMEMBER, DAD
HOW OLD WERE YOU?
SEVEN AND EIGHT
JIM DAVIS 4-24
www.garfield.com
Distributed by Universal Press Syndicate
© 2001 PAWS, INC. All Rights Reserved.

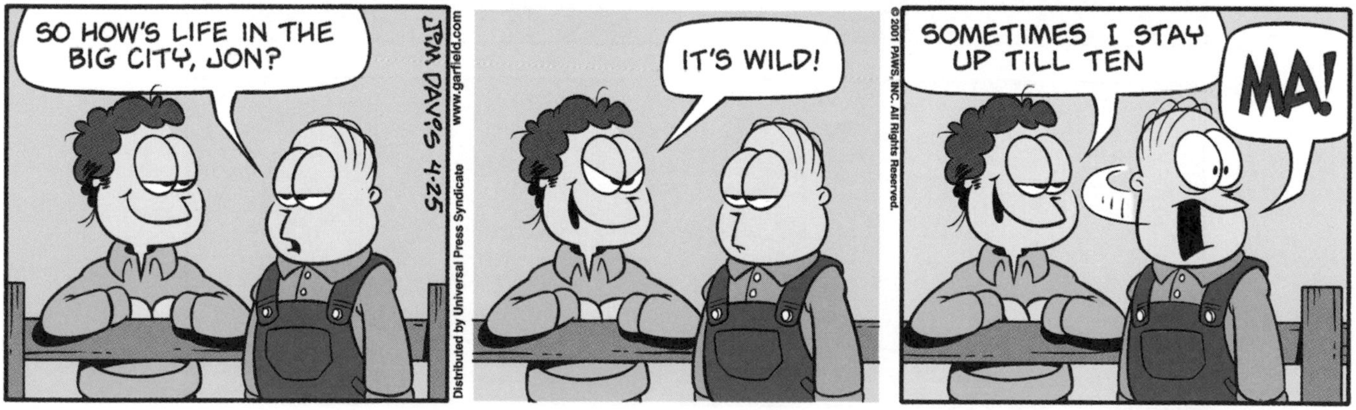
SO HOW'S LIFE IN THE BIG CITY, JON?
IT'S WILD!
SOMETIMES I STAY UP TILL TEN
MA!
JIM DAVIS 4-25
www.garfield.com
Distributed by Universal Press Syndicate
© 2001 PAWS, INC. All Rights Reserved.

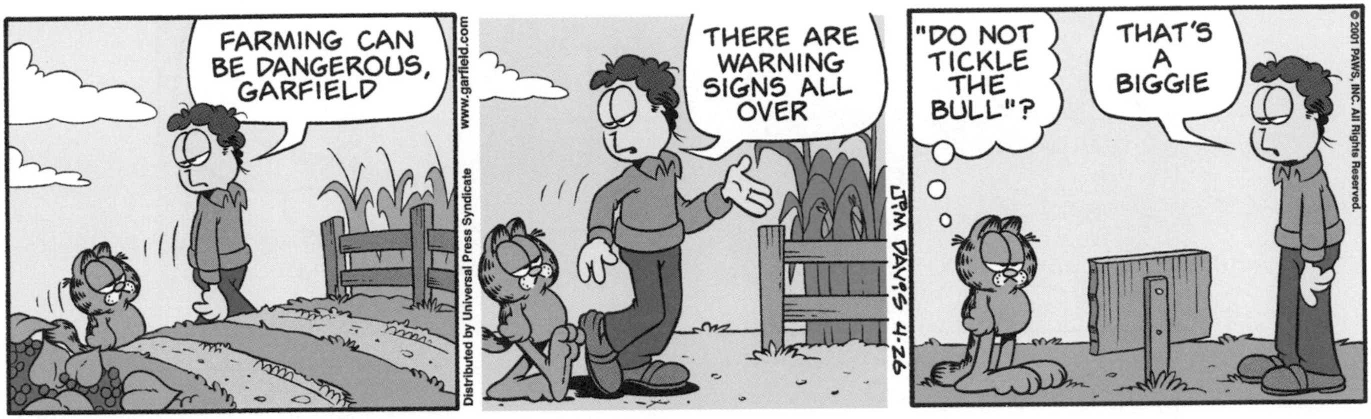
FARMING CAN BE DANGEROUS, GARFIELD
www.garfield.com
Distributed by Universal Press Syndicate
THERE ARE WARNING SIGNS ALL OVER
JIM DAVIS 4-26
"DO NOT TICKLE THE BULL"?
THAT'S A BIGGIE
© 2001 PAWS, INC. All Rights Reserved.

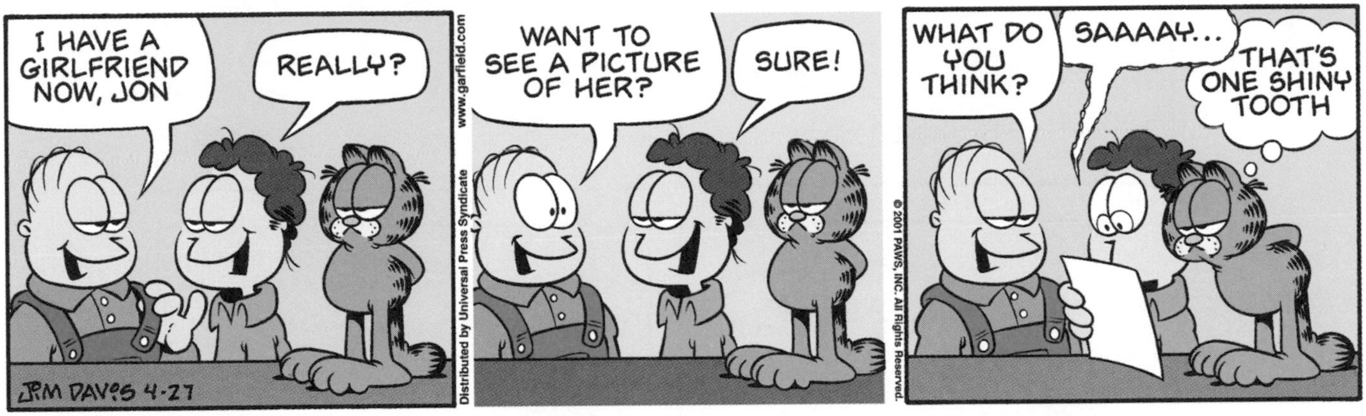
I HAVE A GIRLFRIEND NOW, JON
REALLY?
JIM DAVIS 4-27
www.garfield.com
Distributed by Universal Press Syndicate
WANT TO SEE A PICTURE OF HER?
SURE!
© 2001 PAWS, INC. All Rights Reserved.
WHAT DO YOU THINK?
SAAAAY...
THAT'S ONE SHINY TOOTH

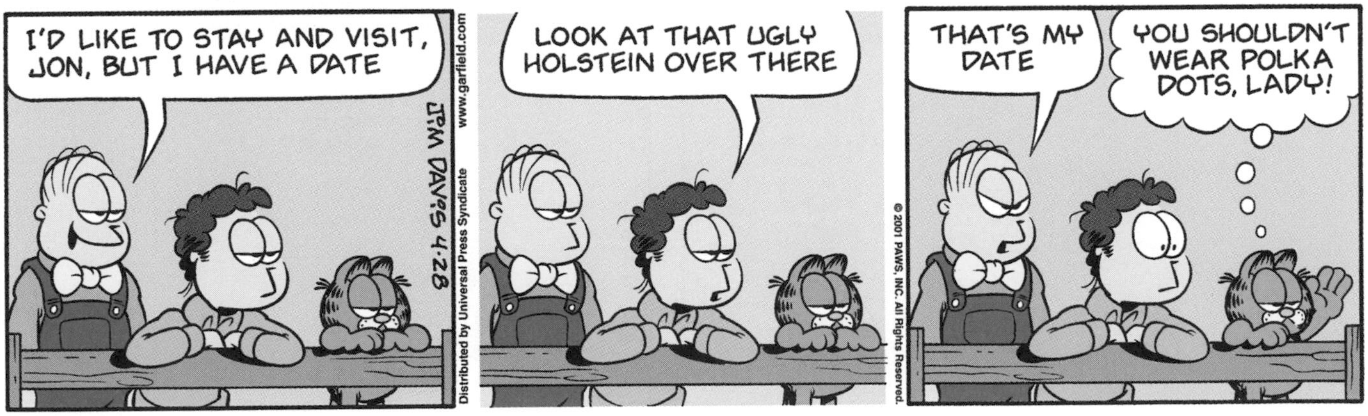
I'D LIKE TO STAY AND VISIT, JON, BUT I HAVE A DATE
JIM DAVIS 4-28
www.garfield.com
Distributed by Universal Press Syndicate
LOOK AT THAT UGLY HOLSTEIN OVER THERE
© 2001 PAWS, INC. All Rights Reserved.
THAT'S MY DATE
YOU SHOULDN'T WEAR POLKA DOTS, LADY!

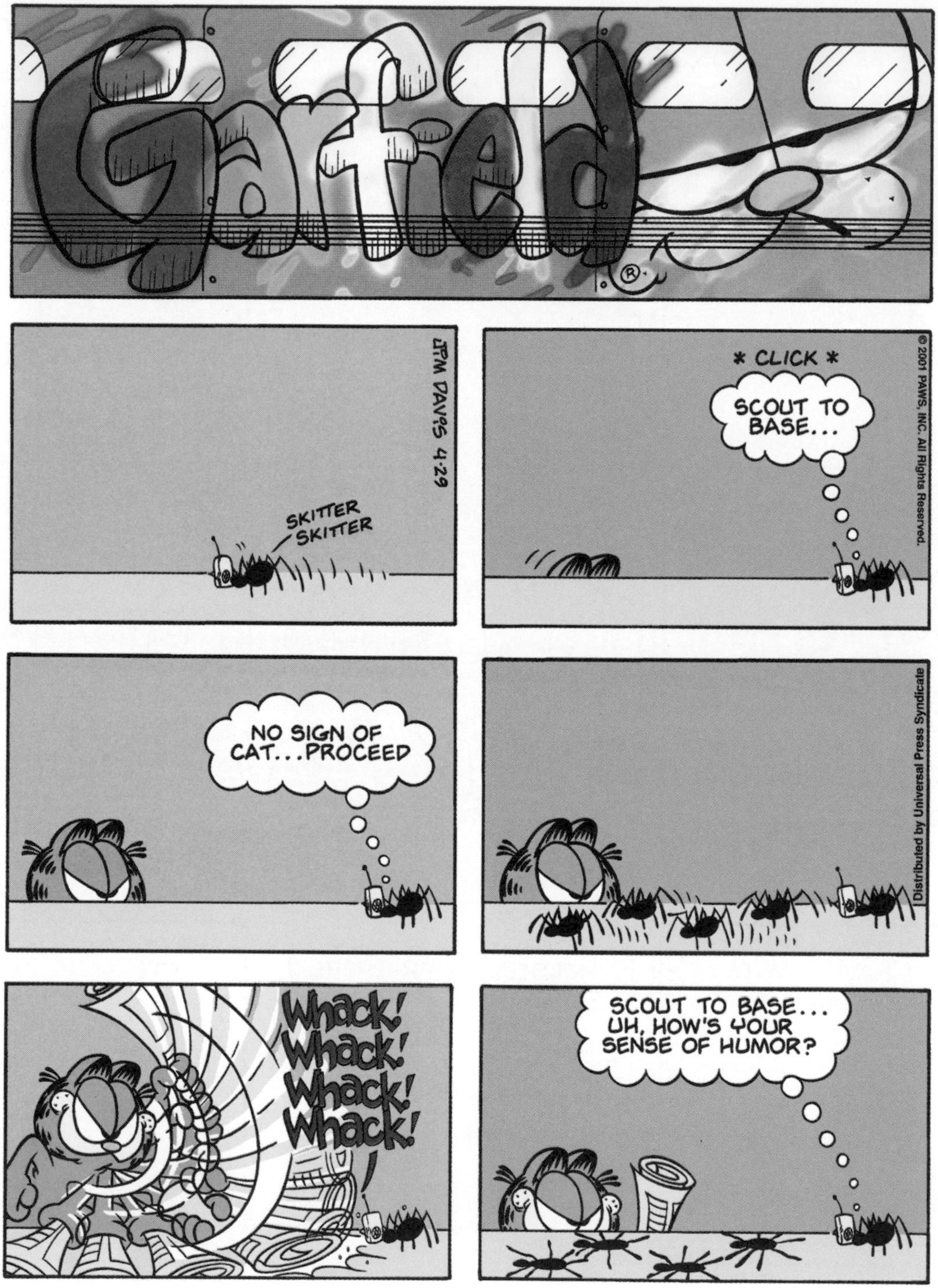
Garfield
JPM DAVPS 4·29
SKITTER SKITTER
© 2001 PAWS, INC. All Rights Reserved.
* CLICK *
SCOUT TO BASE...
NO SIGN OF CAT...PROCEED
Distributed by Universal Press Syndicate
Whack! Whack! Whack! Whack!
SCOUT TO BASE... UH, HOW'S YOUR SENSE OF HUMOR?

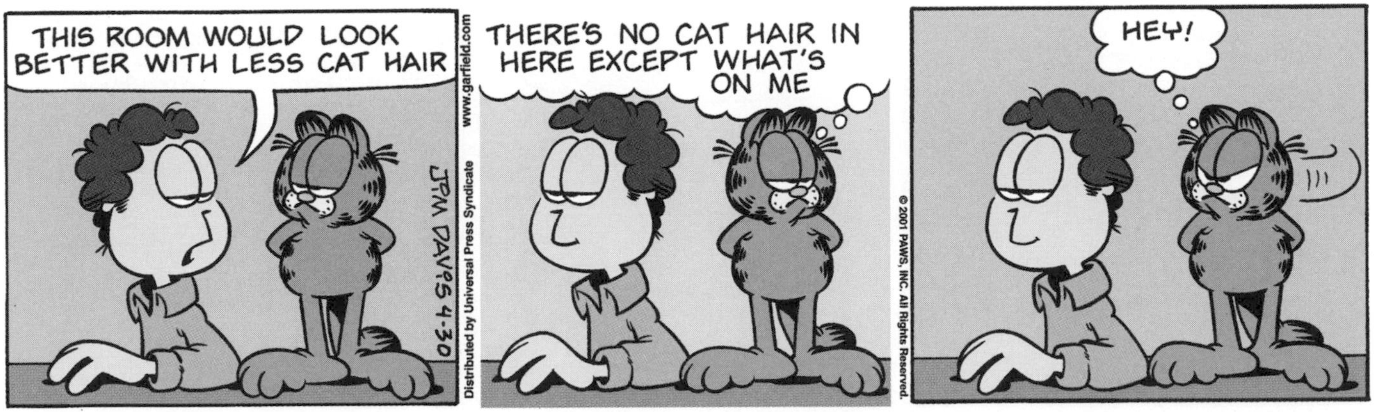
THIS ROOM WOULD LOOK BETTER WITH LESS CAT HAIR
JIM DAVIS 4-30
www.garfield.com
Distributed by Universal Press Syndicate
THERE'S NO CAT HAIR IN HERE EXCEPT WHAT'S ON ME
© 2001 PAWS, INC. All Rights Reserved.
HEY!

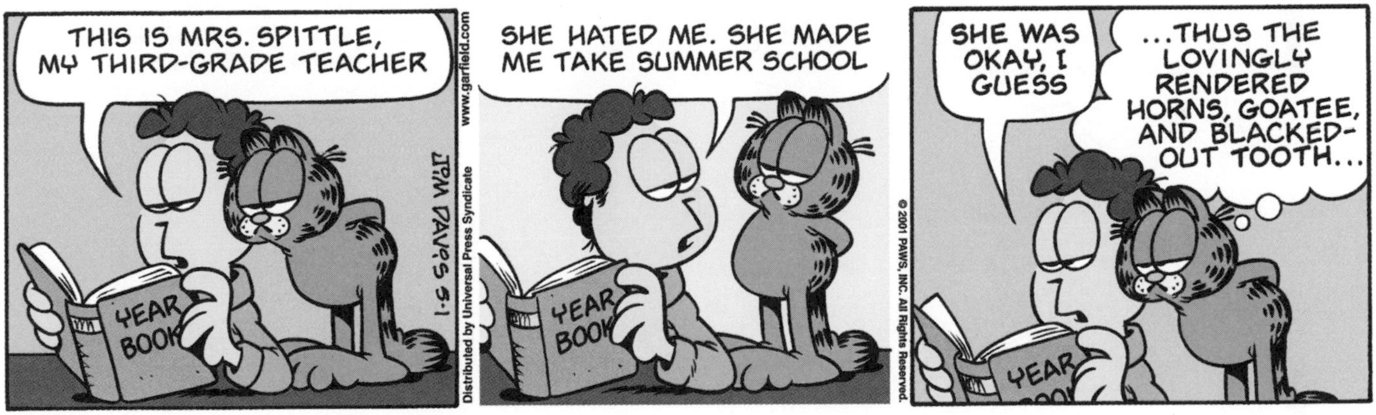
THIS IS MRS. SPITTLE, MY THIRD-GRADE TEACHER
YEAR BOOK
JIM DAVIS 5-1
www.garfield.com
Distributed by Universal Press Syndicate
SHE HATED ME. SHE MADE ME TAKE SUMMER SCHOOL
YEAR BOOK
© 2001 PAWS, INC. All Rights Reserved.
SHE WAS OKAY, I GUESS
...THUS THE LOVINGLY RENDERED HORNS, GOATEE, AND BLACKED-OUT TOOTH...

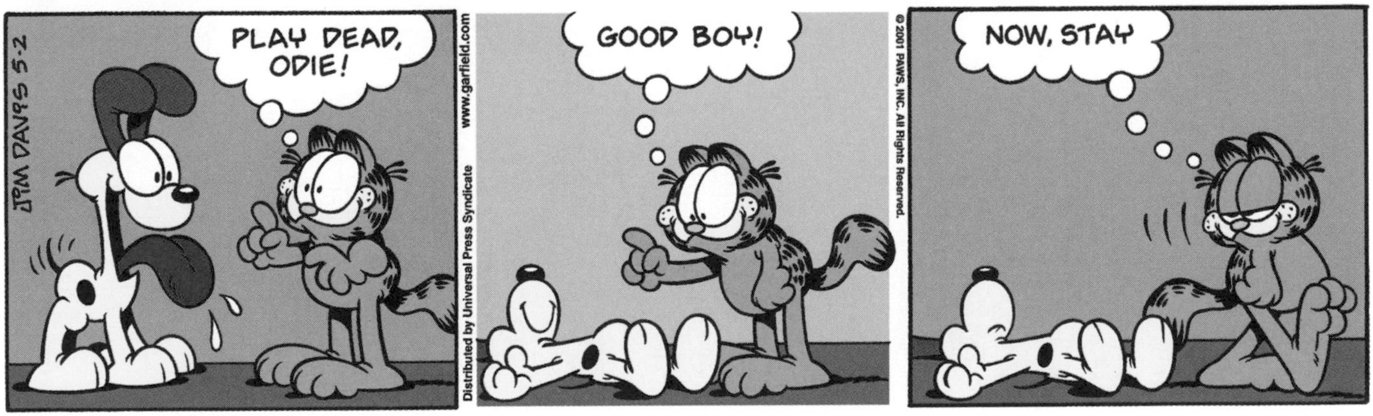
JIM DAVIS 5-2
PLAY DEAD, ODIE!
www.garfield.com
Distributed by Universal Press Syndicate
GOOD BOY!
© 2001 PAWS, INC. All Rights Reserved.
NOW, STAY

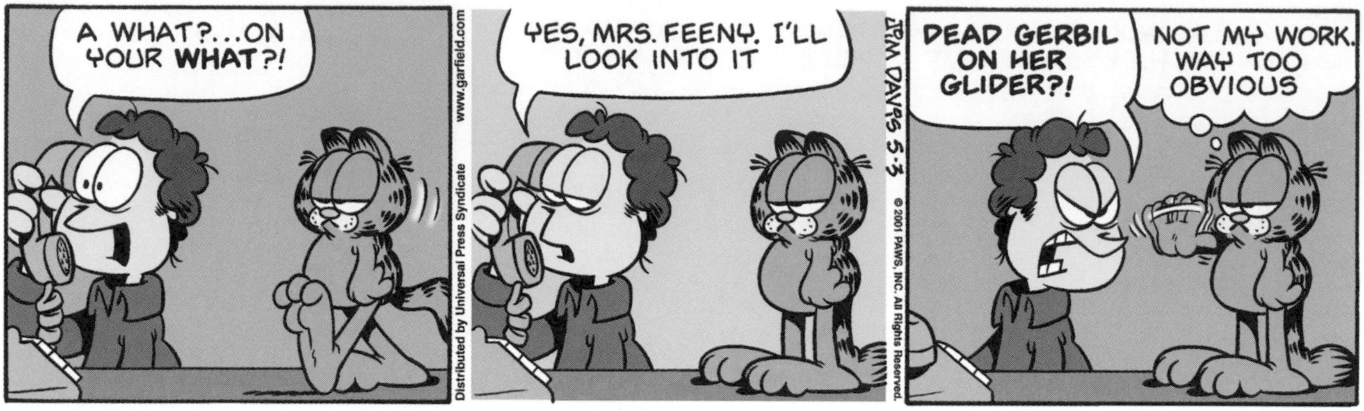
A WHAT?...ON YOUR **WHAT**?!
www.garfield.com
Distributed by Universal Press Syndicate
YES, MRS. FEENY. I'LL LOOK INTO IT
JIM DAVIS 5-3
© 2001 PAWS, INC. All Rights Reserved.
DEAD GERBIL ON HER GLIDER?!
NOT MY WORK. WAY TOO OBVIOUS

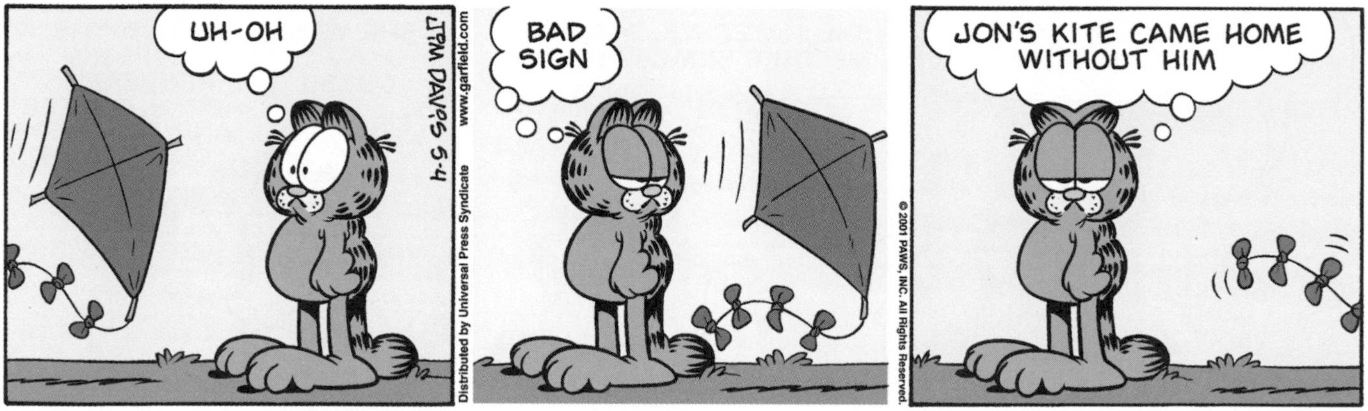
UH-OH
JIM DAVIS 5-4
www.garfield.com
Distributed by Universal Press Syndicate
BAD SIGN
© 2001 PAWS, INC. All Rights Reserved.
JON'S KITE CAME HOME WITHOUT HIM

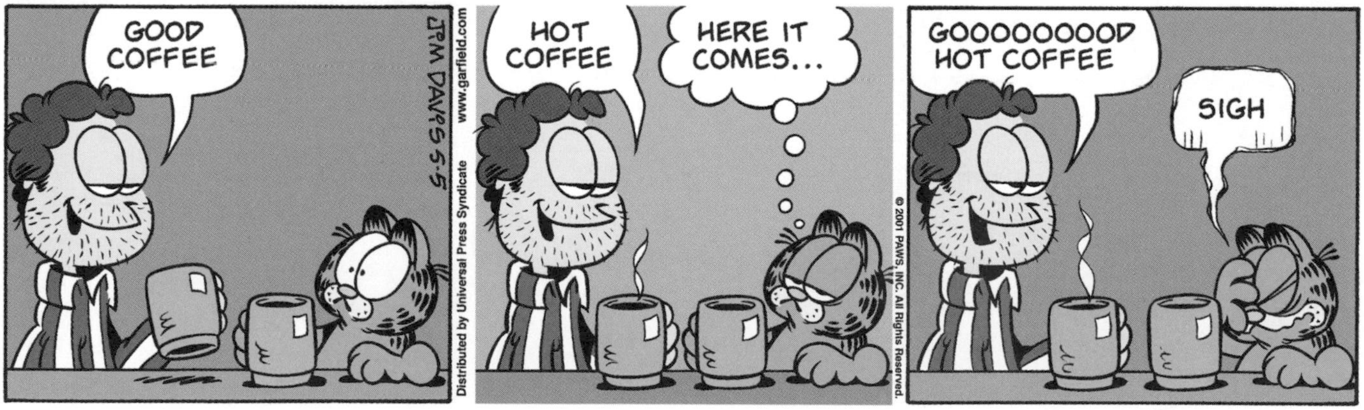
GOOD COFFEE
JIM DAVIS 5-5
www.garfield.com
Distributed by Universal Press Syndicate
HOT COFFEE
HERE IT COMES...
© 2001 PAWS, INC. All Rights Reserved.
GOOOOOOOOD HOT COFFEE
SIGH

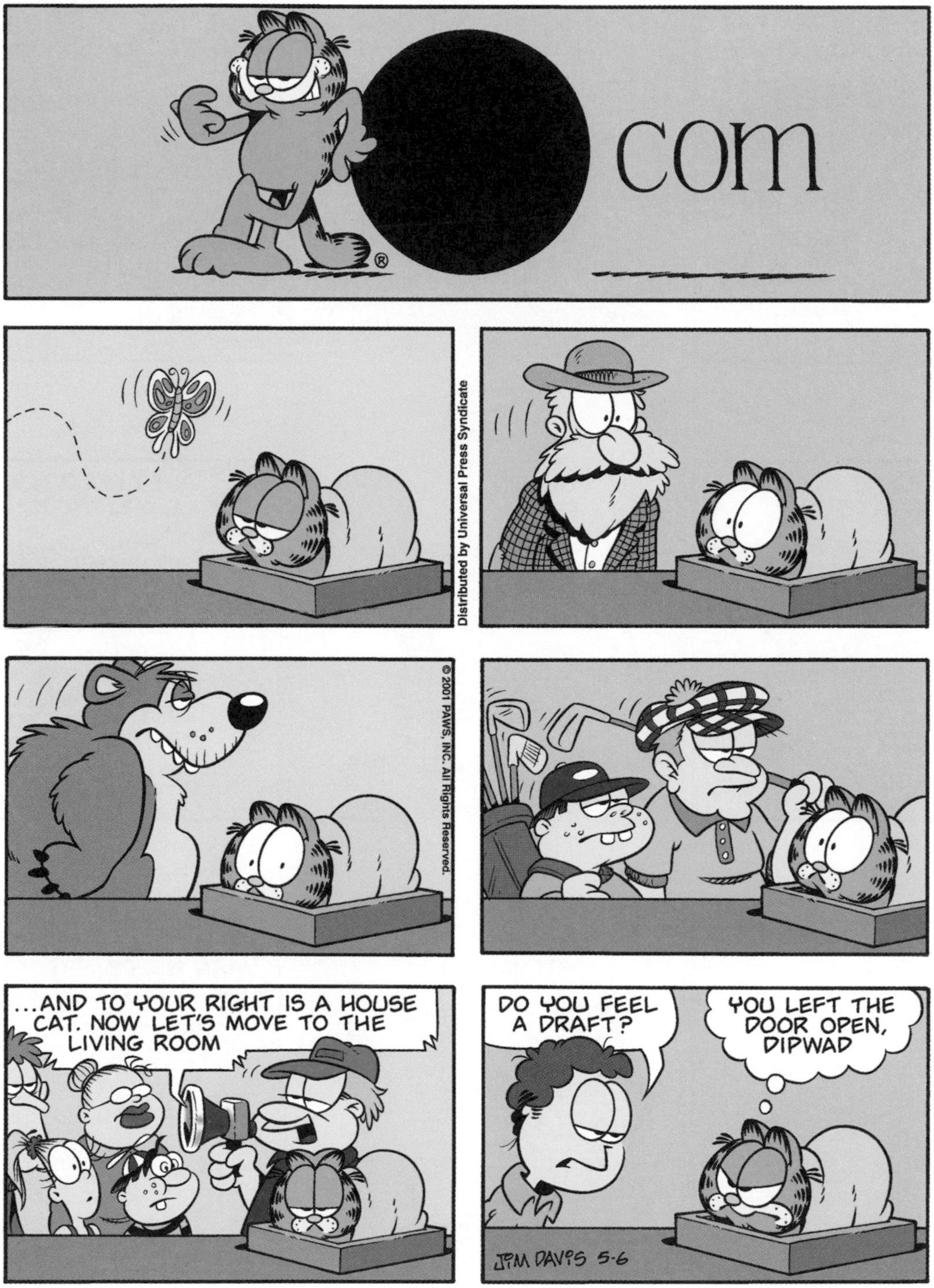
com
Distributed by Universal Press Syndicate
© 2001 PAWS, INC. All Rights Reserved.
...AND TO YOUR RIGHT IS A HOUSE CAT. NOW LET'S MOVE TO THE LIVING ROOM
DO YOU FEEL A DRAFT?
YOU LEFT THE DOOR OPEN, DIPWAD
JIM DAVIS 5-6

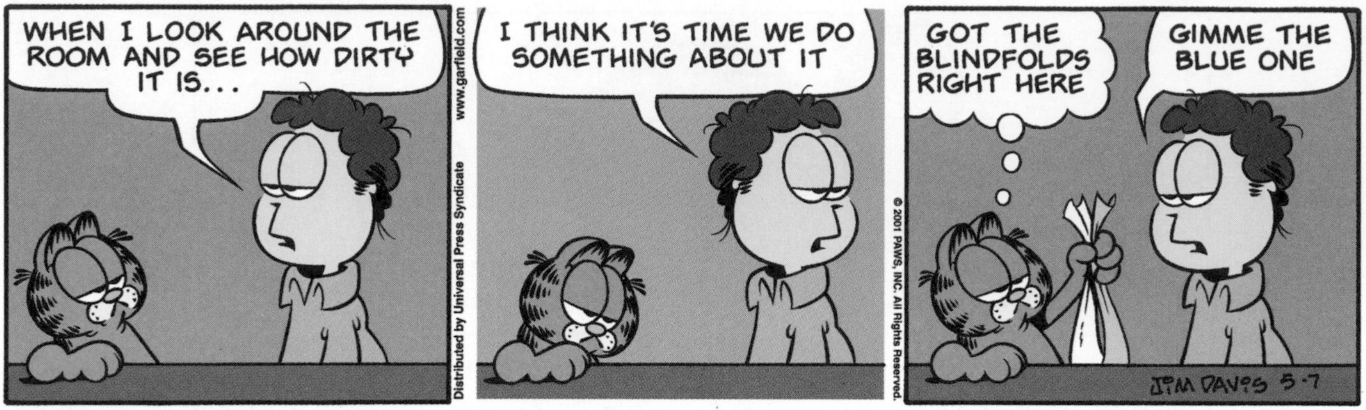
WHEN I LOOK AROUND THE ROOM AND SEE HOW DIRTY IT IS...
I THINK IT'S TIME WE DO SOMETHING ABOUT IT
GOT THE BLINDFOLDS RIGHT HERE
GIMME THE BLUE ONE
JIM DAVIS 5-7
www.garfield.com Distributed by Universal Press Syndicate
© 2001 PAWS, INC. All Rights Reserved.

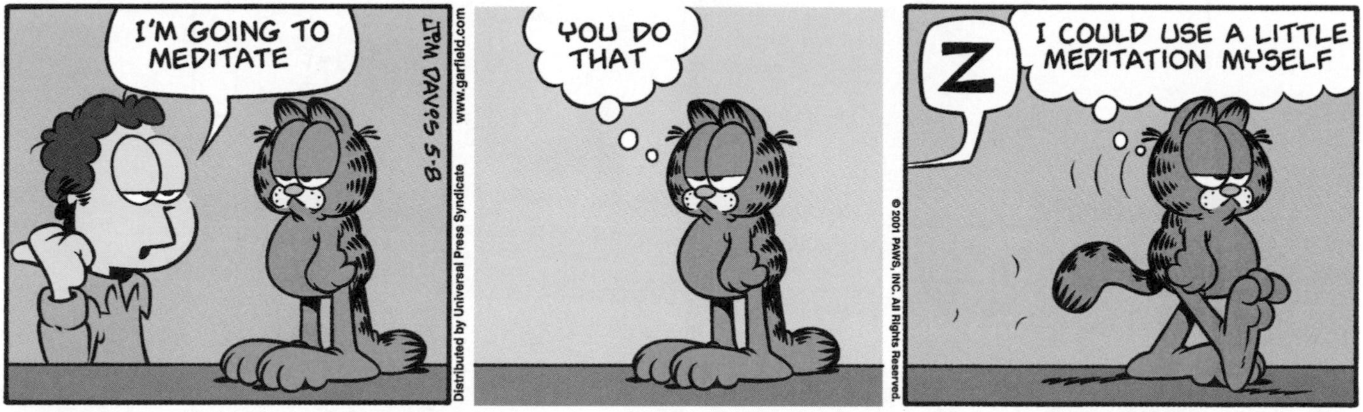
I'M GOING TO MEDITATE
JIM DAVIS 5-8
YOU DO THAT
Z
I COULD USE A LITTLE MEDITATION MYSELF
www.garfield.com Distributed by Universal Press Syndicate
© 2001 PAWS, INC. All Rights Reserved.

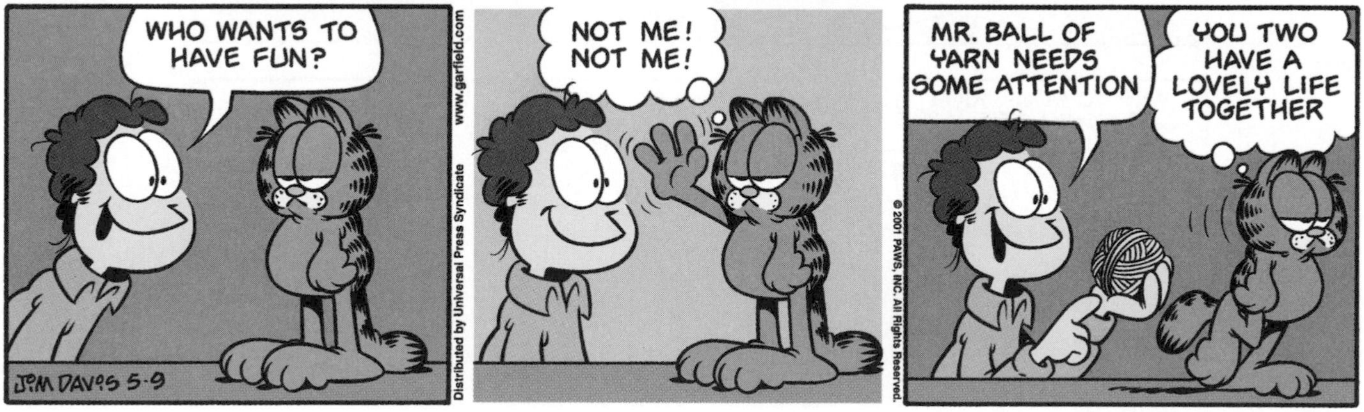
WHO WANTS TO HAVE FUN?
JIM DAVIS 5-9
NOT ME! NOT ME!
MR. BALL OF YARN NEEDS SOME ATTENTION
YOU TWO HAVE A LOVELY LIFE TOGETHER
www.garfield.com Distributed by Universal Press Syndicate
© 2001 PAWS, INC. All Rights Reserved.

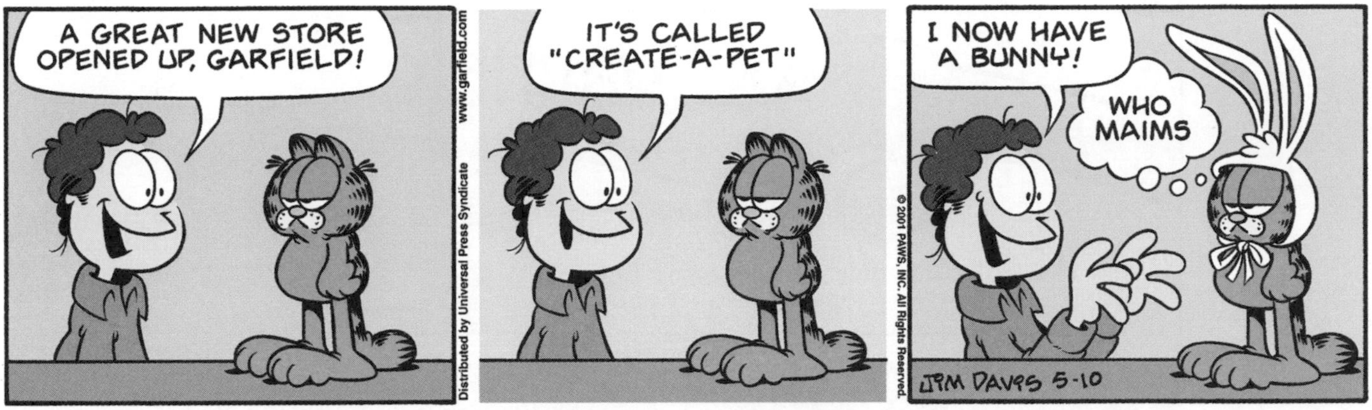
A GREAT NEW STORE OPENED UP, GARFIELD!
Distributed by Universal Press Syndicate www.garfield.com
IT'S CALLED "CREATE-A-PET"
© 2001 PAWS, INC. All Rights Reserved.
I NOW HAVE A BUNNY!
WHO MAIMS
JIM DAVIS 5-10

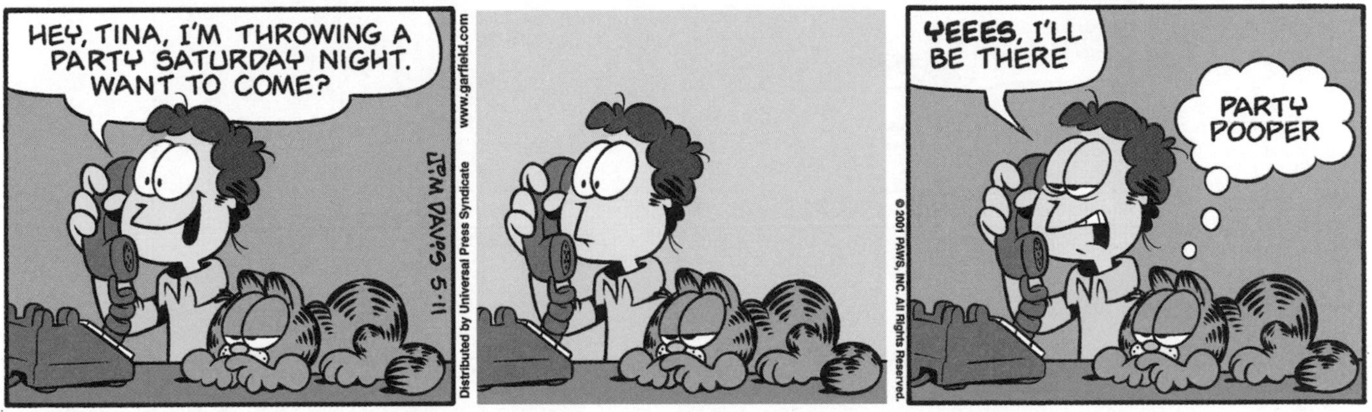
HEY, TINA, I'M THROWING A PARTY SATURDAY NIGHT. WANT TO COME?
JIM DAVIS 5-11
Distributed by Universal Press Syndicate www.garfield.com
© 2001 PAWS, INC. All Rights Reserved.
YEEES, I'LL BE THERE
PARTY POOPER

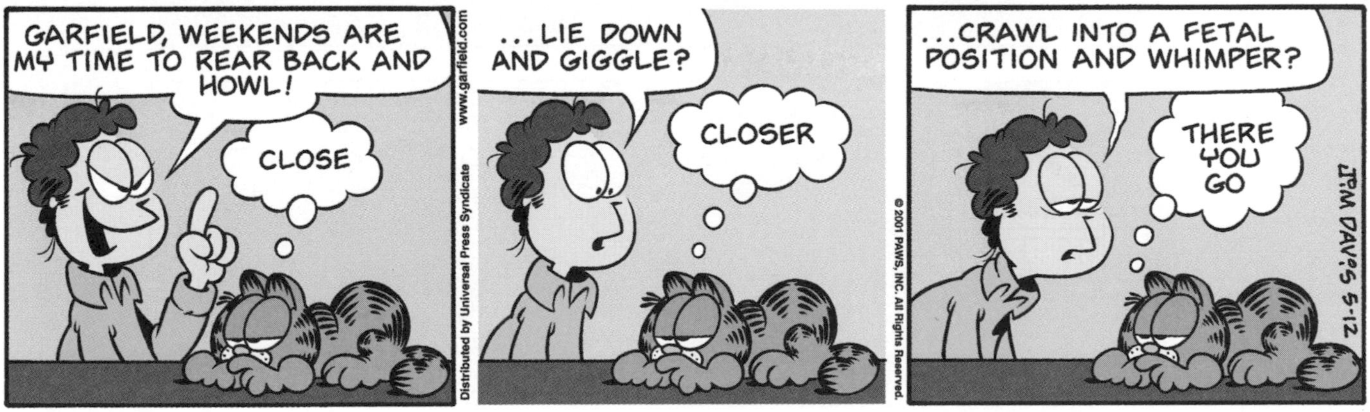
GARFIELD, WEEKENDS ARE MY TIME TO REAR BACK AND HOWL!
CLOSE
Distributed by Universal Press Syndicate www.garfield.com
...LIE DOWN AND GIGGLE?
CLOSER
© 2001 PAWS, INC. All Rights Reserved.
...CRAWL INTO A FETAL POSITION AND WHIMPER?
THERE YOU GO
JIM DAVIS 5-12

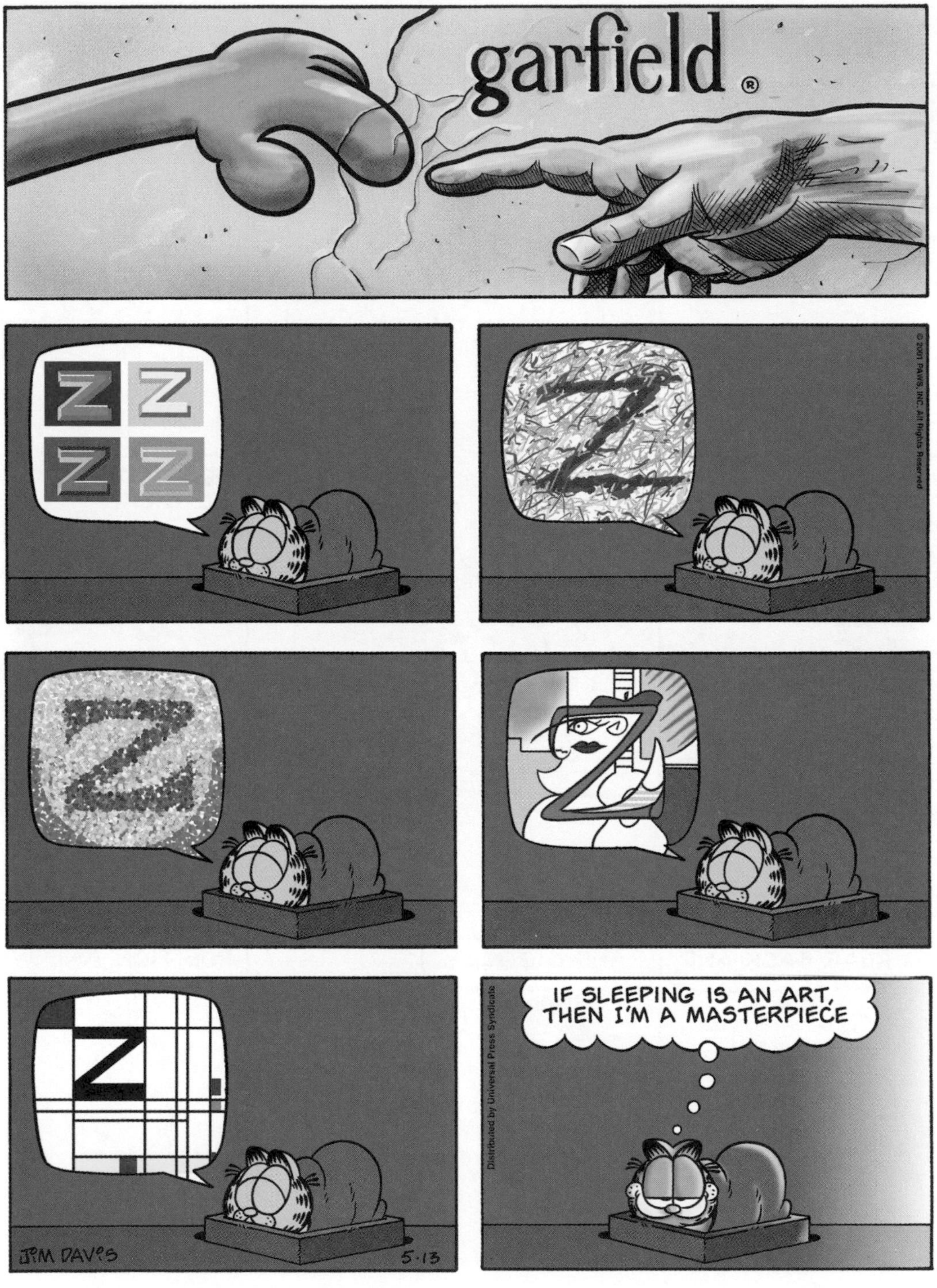
garfield®
© 2001 PAWS, INC. All Rights Reserved
Z Z Z Z
Z
Z
Z
Z
Distributed by Universal Press Syndicate
IF SLEEPING IS AN ART, THEN I'M A MASTERPIECE
JIM DAVIS
5-13

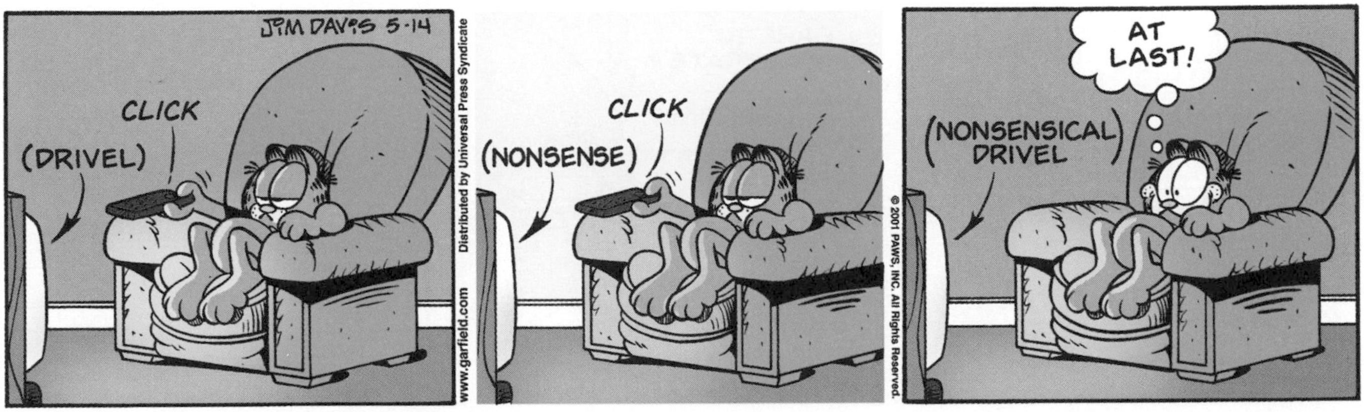
JIM DAVIS 5-14
CLICK
(DRIVEL)
www.garfield.com
Distributed by Universal Press Syndicate
CLICK
(NONSENSE)
© 2001 PAWS, INC. All Rights Reserved.
(NONSENSICAL DRIVEL)
AT LAST!

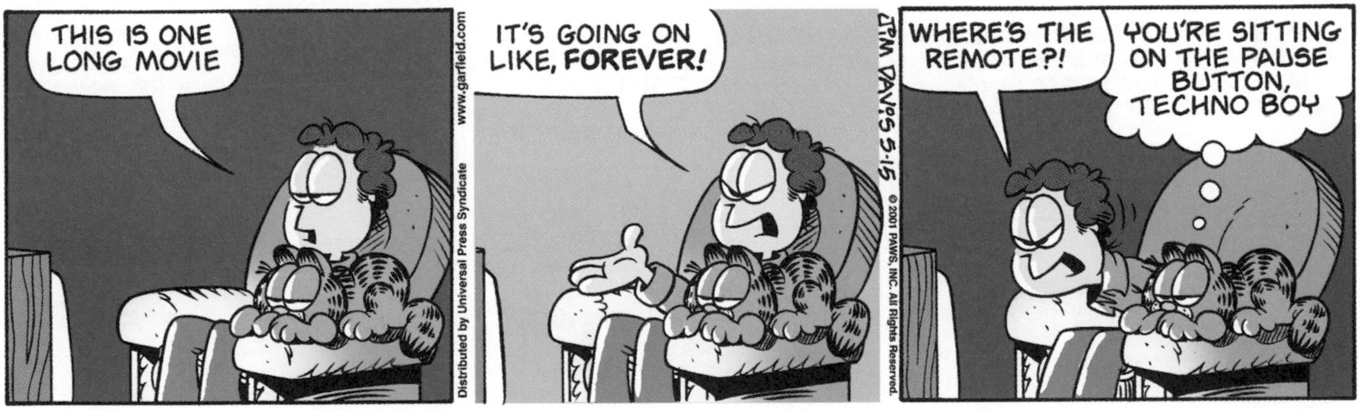
THIS IS ONE LONG MOVIE
www.garfield.com
Distributed by Universal Press Syndicate
IT'S GOING ON LIKE, **FOREVER!**
JIM DAVIS 5-15
© 2001 PAWS, INC. All Rights Reserved.
WHERE'S THE REMOTE?!
YOU'RE SITTING ON THE PAUSE BUTTON, TECHNO BOY

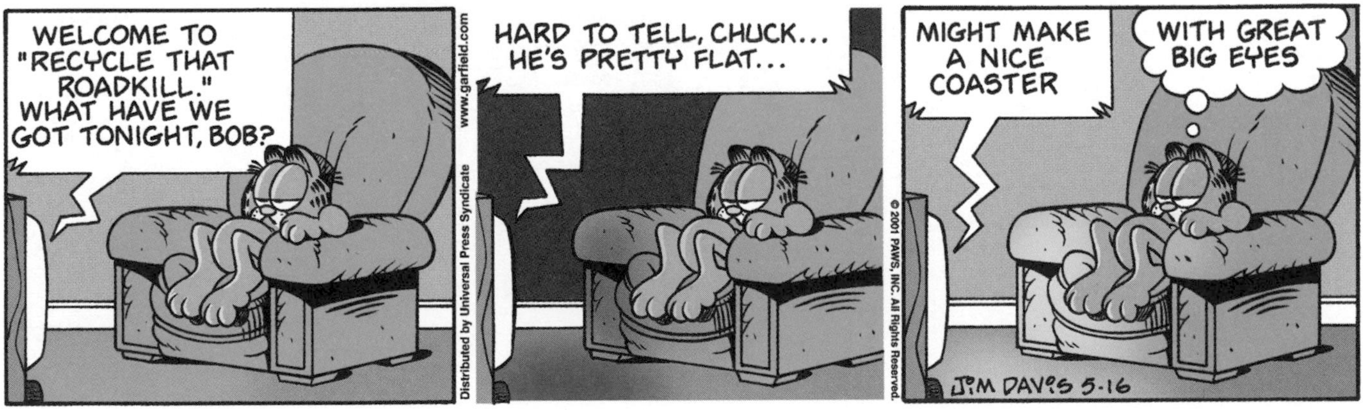
WELCOME TO "RECYCLE THAT ROADKILL." WHAT HAVE WE GOT TONIGHT, BOB?
www.garfield.com
Distributed by Universal Press Syndicate
HARD TO TELL, CHUCK... HE'S PRETTY FLAT...
© 2001 PAWS, INC. All Rights Reserved.
MIGHT MAKE A NICE COASTER
WITH GREAT BIG EYES
JIM DAVIS 5-16

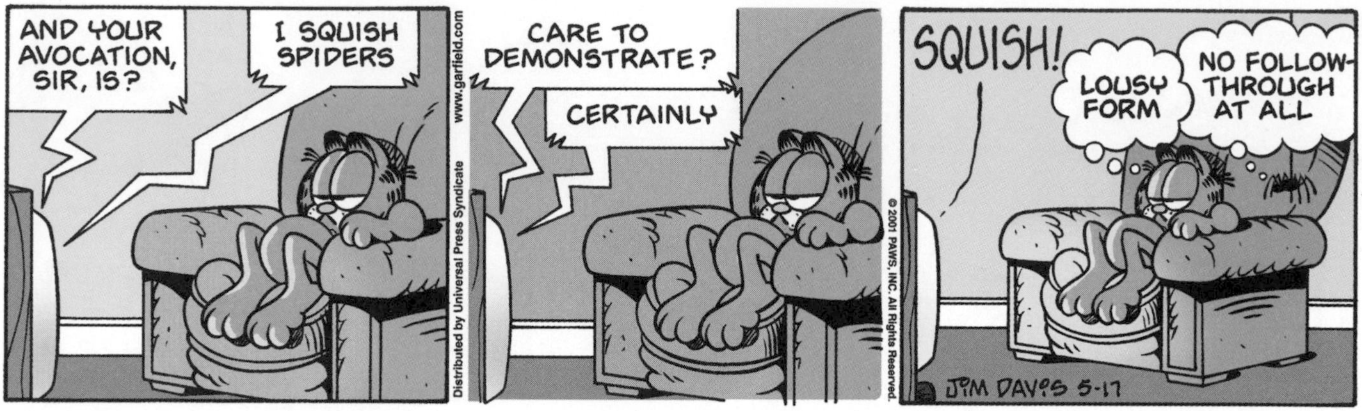
AND YOUR AVOCATION, SIR, IS?
I SQUISH SPIDERS
Distributed by Universal Press Syndicate www.garfield.com
CARE TO DEMONSTRATE?
CERTAINLY
© 2001 PAWS, INC. All Rights Reserved.
SQUISH!
LOUSY FORM
NO FOLLOW-THROUGH AT ALL
JIM DAVIS 5-17

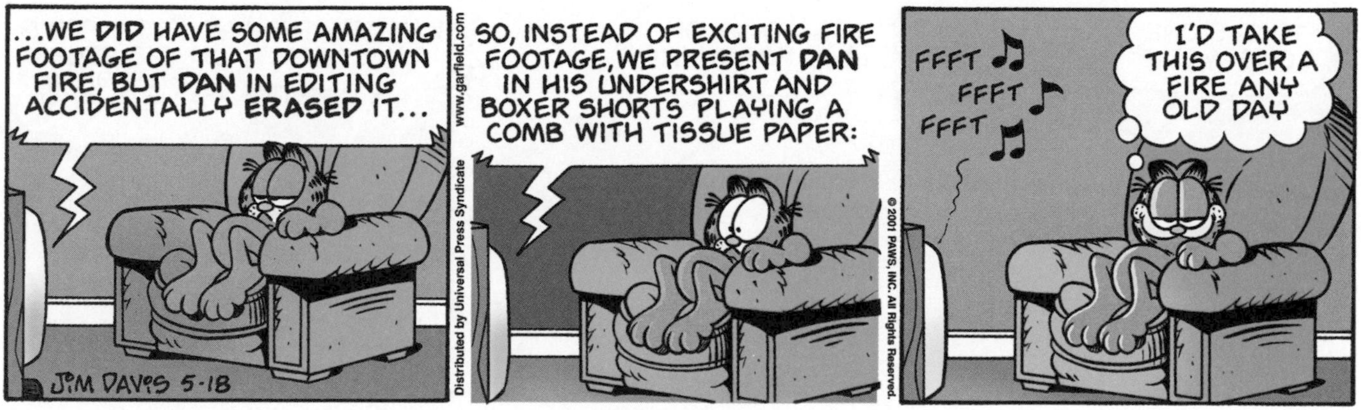
...WE DID HAVE SOME AMAZING FOOTAGE OF THAT DOWNTOWN FIRE, BUT DAN IN EDITING ACCIDENTALLY ERASED IT...
JIM DAVIS 5-18
Distributed by Universal Press Syndicate www.garfield.com
SO, INSTEAD OF EXCITING FIRE FOOTAGE, WE PRESENT DAN IN HIS UNDERSHIRT AND BOXER SHORTS PLAYING A COMB WITH TISSUE PAPER:
© 2001 PAWS, INC. All Rights Reserved.
FFFT
FFFT
FFFT
I'D TAKE THIS OVER A FIRE ANY OLD DAY

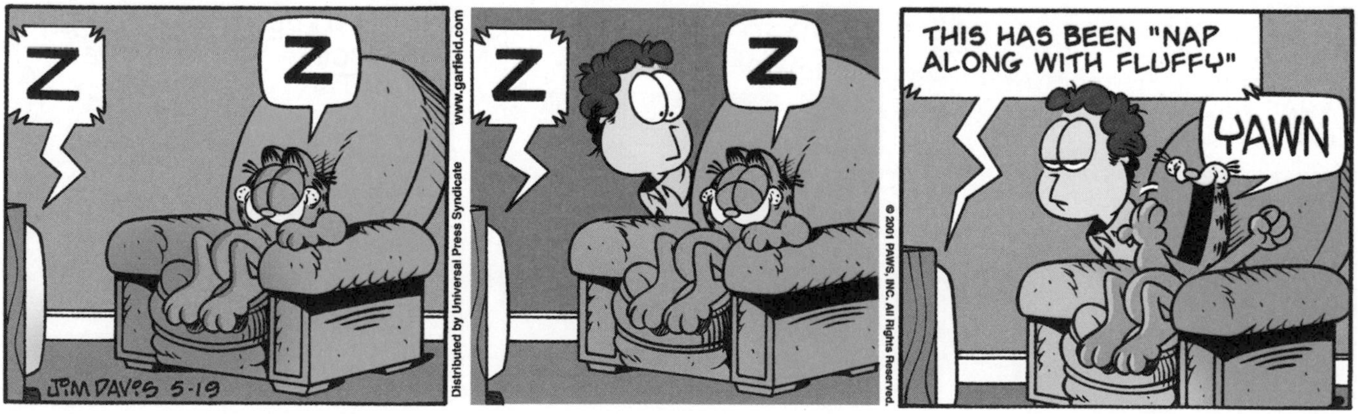
Z
Z
JIM DAVIS 5-19
Distributed by Universal Press Syndicate www.garfield.com
Z
Z
© 2001 PAWS, INC. All Rights Reserved.
THIS HAS BEEN "NAP ALONG WITH FLUFFY"
YAWN

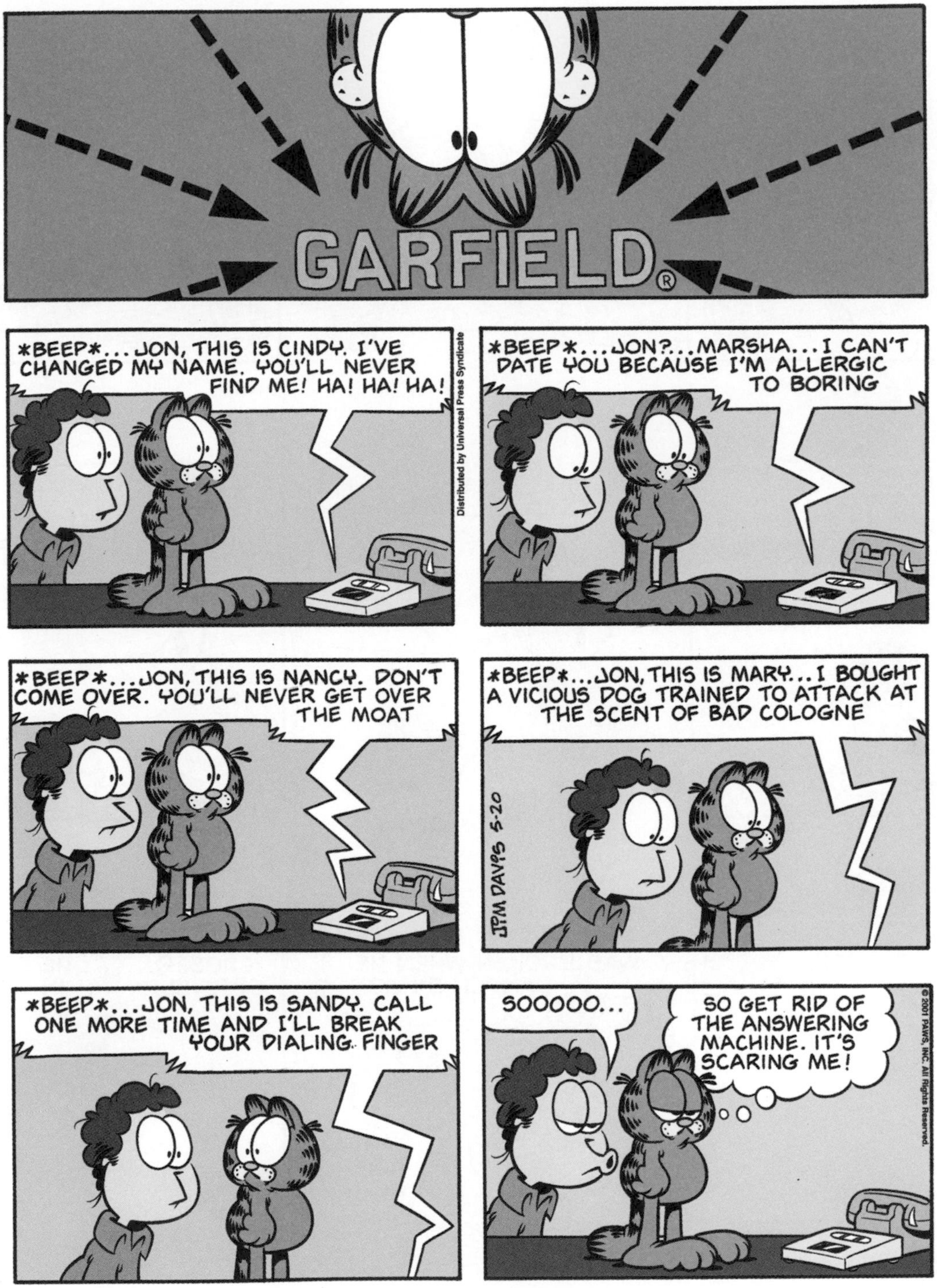
GARFIELD®
BEEP...JON, THIS IS CINDY. I'VE CHANGED MY NAME. YOU'LL NEVER FIND ME! HA! HA! HA!
Distributed by Universal Press Syndicate
BEEP...JON?...MARSHA...I CAN'T DATE YOU BECAUSE I'M ALLERGIC TO BORING
BEEP...JON, THIS IS NANCY. DON'T COME OVER. YOU'LL NEVER GET OVER THE MOAT
JPM DAVIS 5-20
BEEP...JON, THIS IS MARY...I BOUGHT A VICIOUS DOG TRAINED TO ATTACK AT THE SCENT OF BAD COLOGNE
BEEP...JON, THIS IS SANDY. CALL ONE MORE TIME AND I'LL BREAK YOUR DIALING FINGER
SOOOOO...
SO GET RID OF THE ANSWERING MACHINE. IT'S SCARING ME!
© 2001 PAWS, INC. All Rights Reserved.

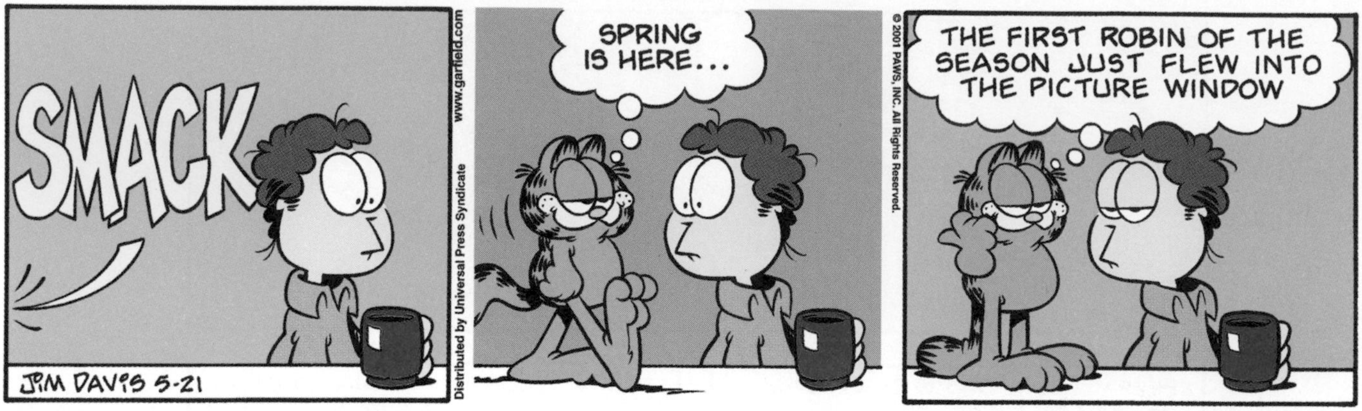
SMACK
JIM DAVIS 5-21
SPRING IS HERE...
THE FIRST ROBIN OF THE SEASON JUST FLEW INTO THE PICTURE WINDOW
www.garfield.com
Distributed by Universal Press Syndicate
© 2001 PAWS, INC. All Rights Reserved.

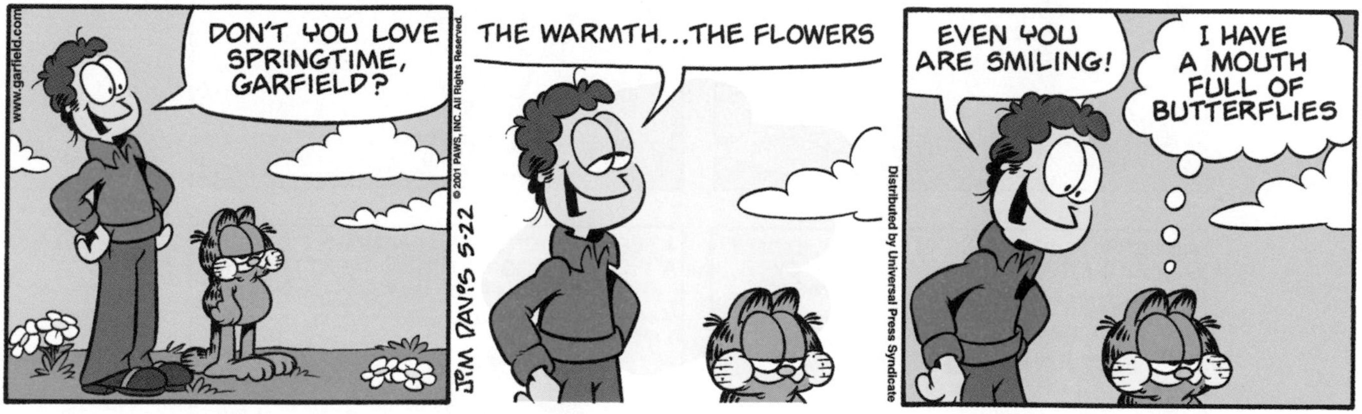
DON'T YOU LOVE SPRINGTIME, GARFIELD?
THE WARMTH...THE FLOWERS
EVEN YOU ARE SMILING!
I HAVE A MOUTH FULL OF BUTTERFLIES
JIM DAVIS 5-22
www.garfield.com
© 2001 PAWS, INC. All Rights Reserved.
Distributed by Universal Press Syndicate

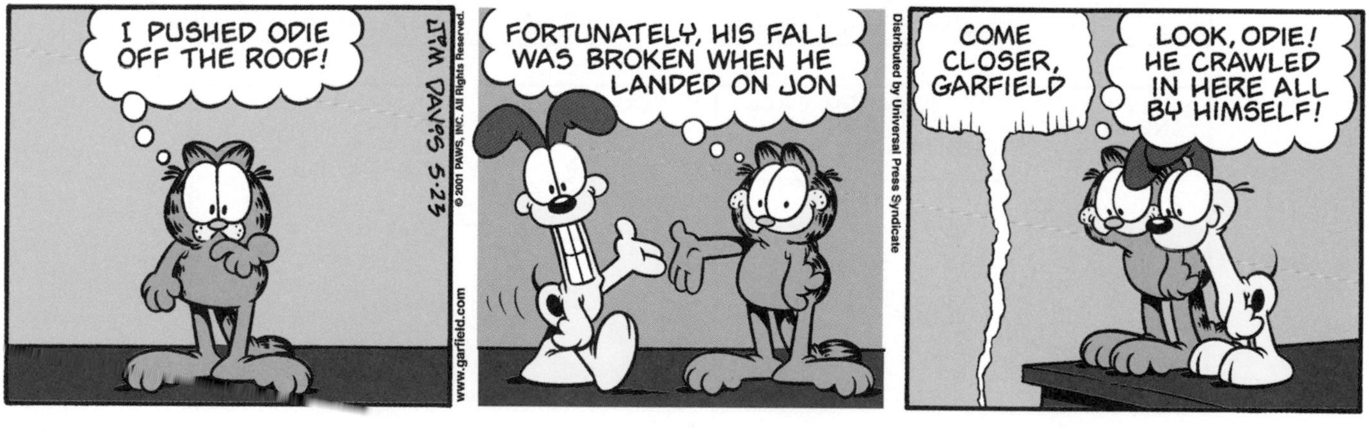
I PUSHED ODIE OFF THE ROOF!
FORTUNATELY, HIS FALL WAS BROKEN WHEN HE LANDED ON JON
COME CLOSER, GARFIELD
LOOK, ODIE! HE CRAWLED IN HERE ALL BY HIMSELF!
JIM DAVIS 5-23
© 2001 PAWS, INC. All Rights Reserved.
www.garfield.com
Distributed by Universal Press Syndicate

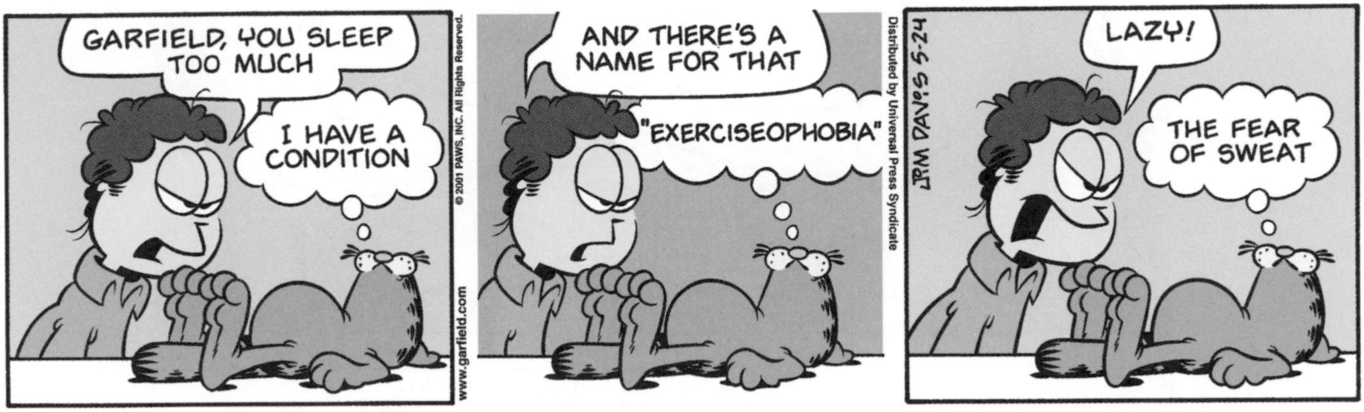
GARFIELD, YOU SLEEP TOO MUCH
I HAVE A CONDITION
© 2001 PAWS, INC. All Rights Reserved.
www.garfield.com
AND THERE'S A NAME FOR THAT
"EXERCISEOPHOBIA"
Distributed by Universal Press Syndicate
JIM DAVIS 5-24
LAZY!
THE FEAR OF SWEAT

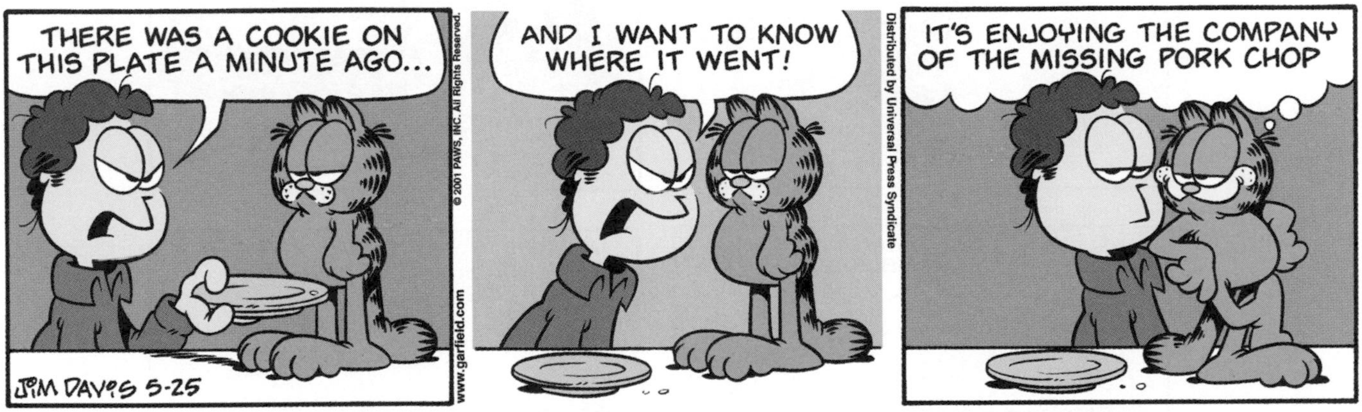
THERE WAS A COOKIE ON THIS PLATE A MINUTE AGO...
JIM DAVIS 5-25
© 2001 PAWS, INC. All Rights Reserved.
www.garfield.com
AND I WANT TO KNOW WHERE IT WENT!
Distributed by Universal Press Syndicate
IT'S ENJOYING THE COMPANY OF THE MISSING PORK CHOP

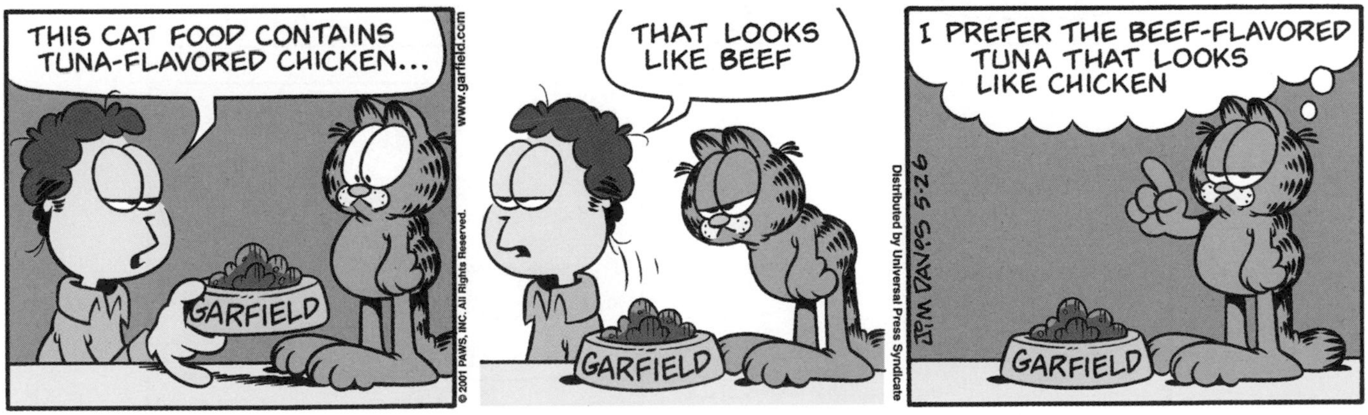
THIS CAT FOOD CONTAINS TUNA-FLAVORED CHICKEN...
GARFIELD
www.garfield.com
© 2001 PAWS, INC. All Rights Reserved.
THAT LOOKS LIKE BEEF
GARFIELD
Distributed by Universal Press Syndicate
JIM DAVIS 5-26
I PREFER THE BEEF-FLAVORED TUNA THAT LOOKS LIKE CHICKEN
GARFIELD

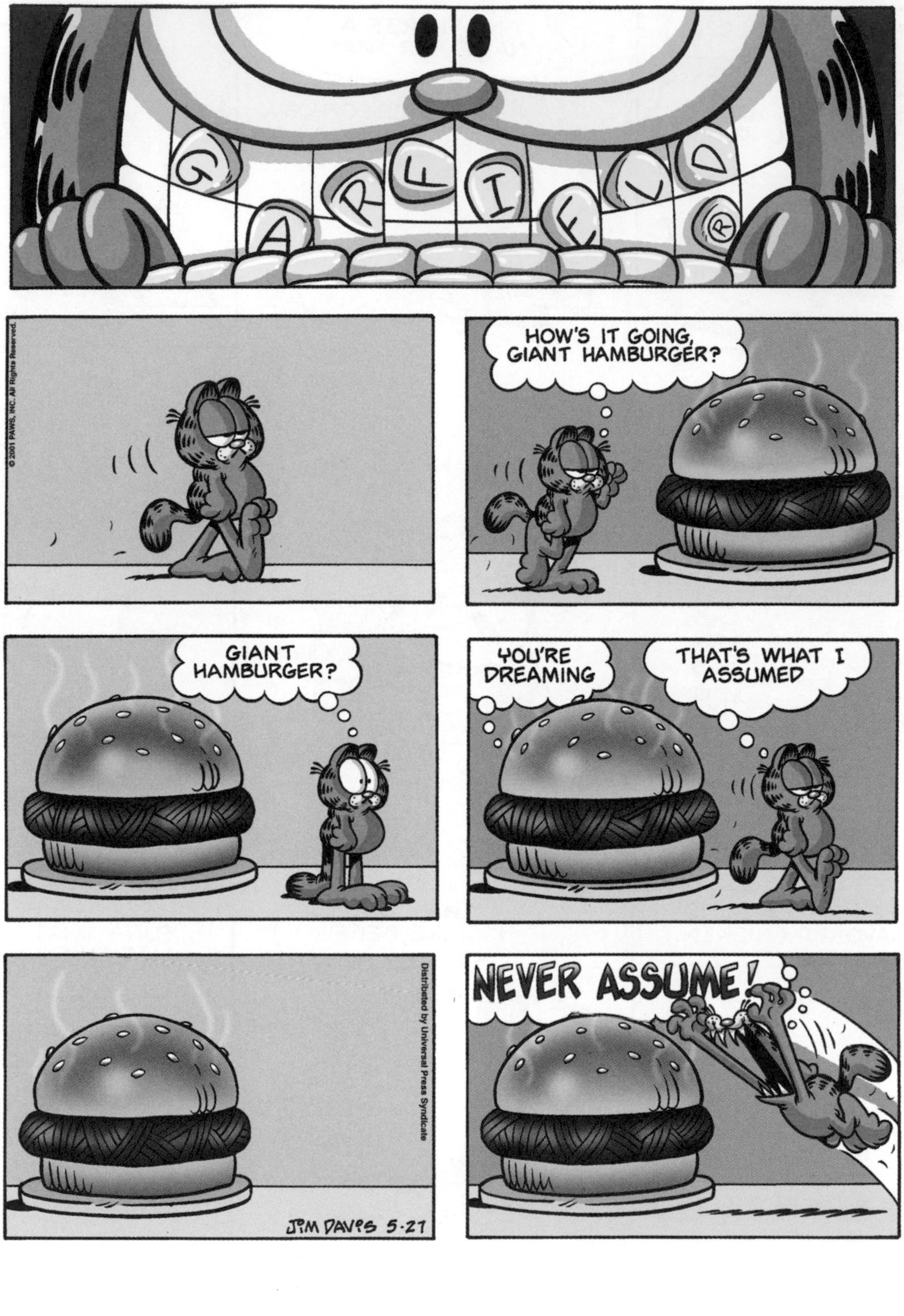
GARFIELD®
© 2001 PAWS, INC. All Rights Reserved.
HOW'S IT GOING, GIANT HAMBURGER?
GIANT HAMBURGER?
YOU'RE DREAMING
THAT'S WHAT I ASSUMED
Distributed by Universal Press Syndicate
JIM DAVIS 5-27
NEVER ASSUME!

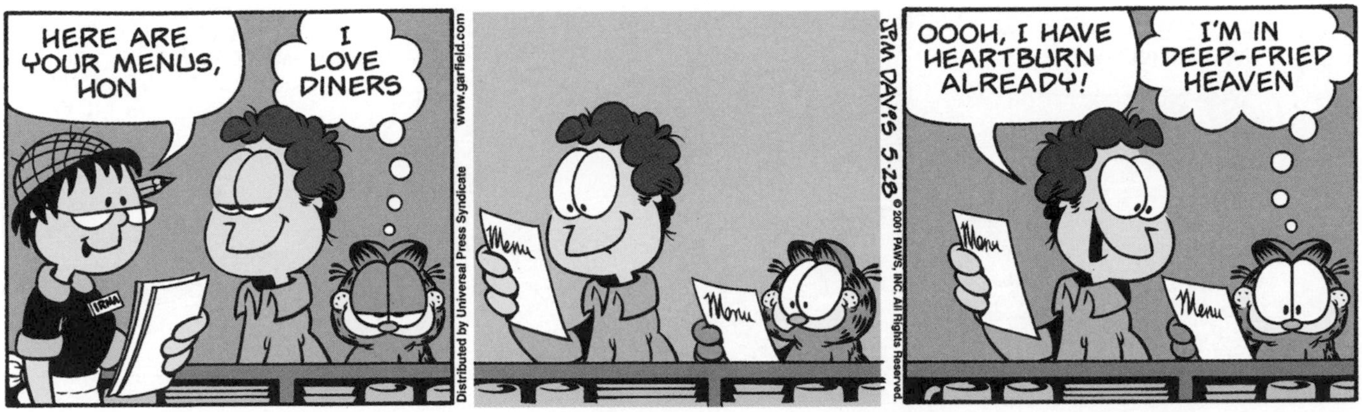
HERE ARE YOUR MENUS, HON
I LOVE DINERS
www.garfield.com
Distributed by Universal Press Syndicate
JIM DAVIS 5-28
© 2001 PAWS, INC. All Rights Reserved.
OOOH, I HAVE HEARTBURN ALREADY!
I'M IN DEEP-FRIED HEAVEN

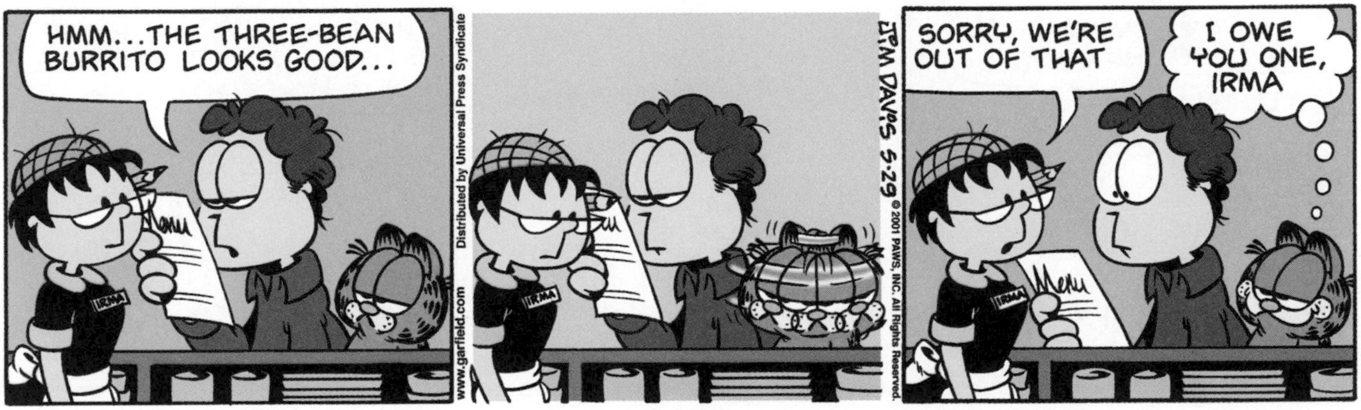
HMM...THE THREE-BEAN BURRITO LOOKS GOOD...
Distributed by Universal Press Syndicate
www.garfield.com
JIM DAVIS 5-29
© 2001 PAWS, INC. All Rights Reserved.
SORRY, WE'RE OUT OF THAT
I OWE YOU ONE, IRMA

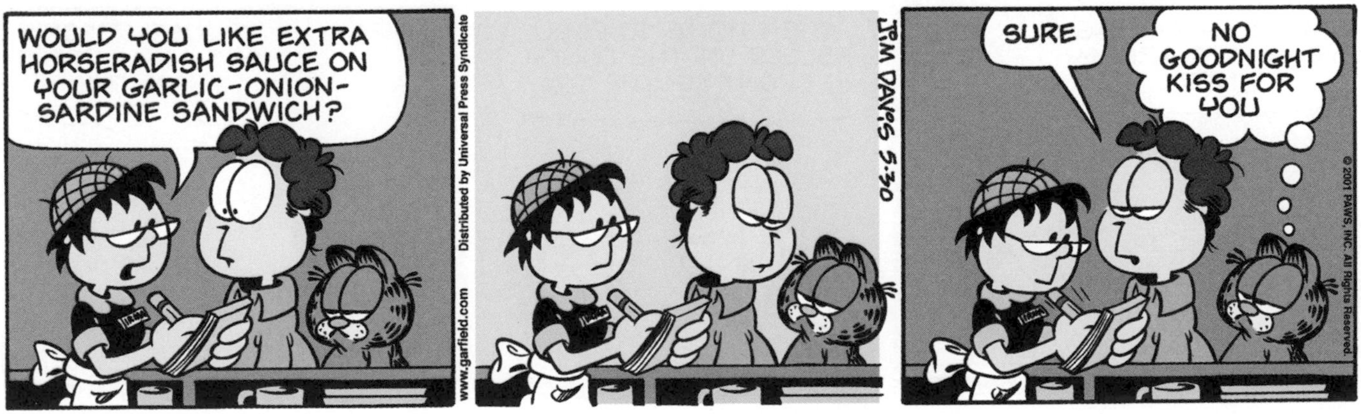
WOULD YOU LIKE EXTRA HORSERADISH SAUCE ON YOUR GARLIC-ONION-SARDINE SANDWICH?
Distributed by Universal Press Syndicate
www.garfield.com
JIM DAVIS 5-30
SURE
NO GOODNIGHT KISS FOR YOU
© 2001 PAWS, INC. All Rights Reserved.

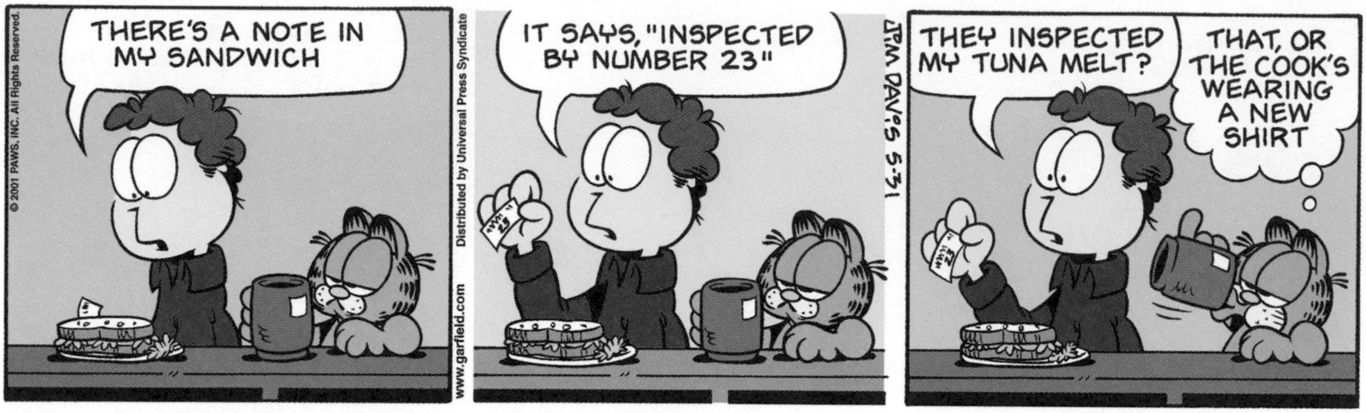
THERE'S A NOTE IN MY SANDWICH
IT SAYS, "INSPECTED BY NUMBER 23"
THEY INSPECTED MY TUNA MELT?
THAT, OR THE COOK'S WEARING A NEW SHIRT
JIM DAVIS 5-31
© 2001 PAWS, INC. All Rights Reserved.
Distributed by Universal Press Syndicate
www.garfield.com

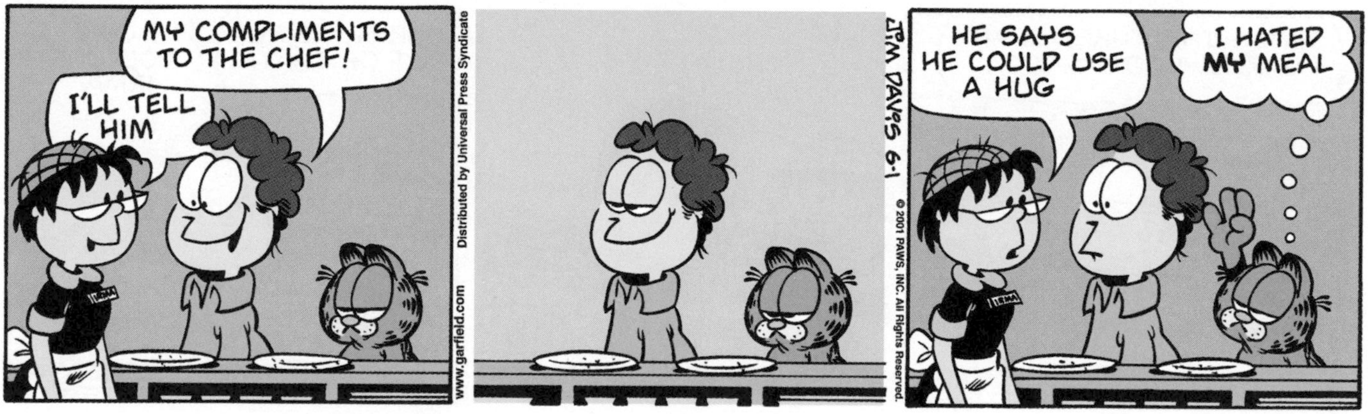
MY COMPLIMENTS TO THE CHEF!
I'LL TELL HIM
HE SAYS HE COULD USE A HUG
I HATED **MY** MEAL
JIM DAVIS 6-1
© 2001 PAWS, INC. All Rights Reserved.
Distributed by Universal Press Syndicate
www.garfield.com

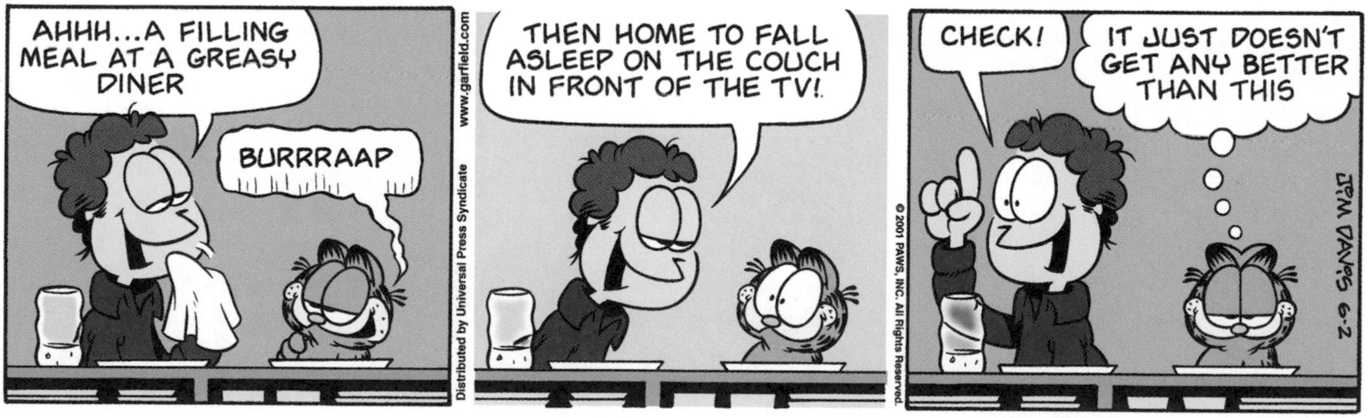
AHHH...A FILLING MEAL AT A GREASY DINER
BURRRAAP
THEN HOME TO FALL ASLEEP ON THE COUCH IN FRONT OF THE TV!
CHECK!
IT JUST DOESN'T GET ANY BETTER THAN THIS
JIM DAVIS 6-2
© 2001 PAWS, INC. All Rights Reserved.
Distributed by Universal Press Syndicate
www.garfield.com

YOU KNOW YOU'RE A NERD WHEN...

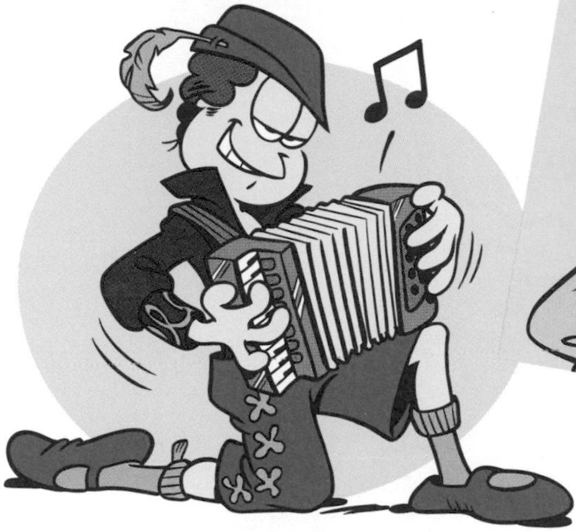

You think playing the accordion makes you look "hot"

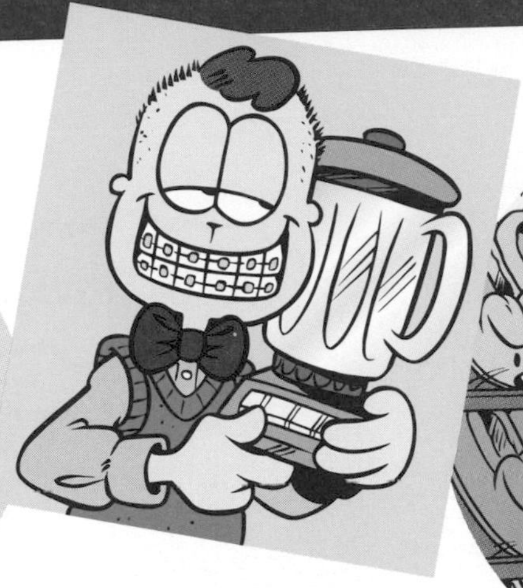

In school, you were voted "Most Likely to Marry a Kitchen Appliance"

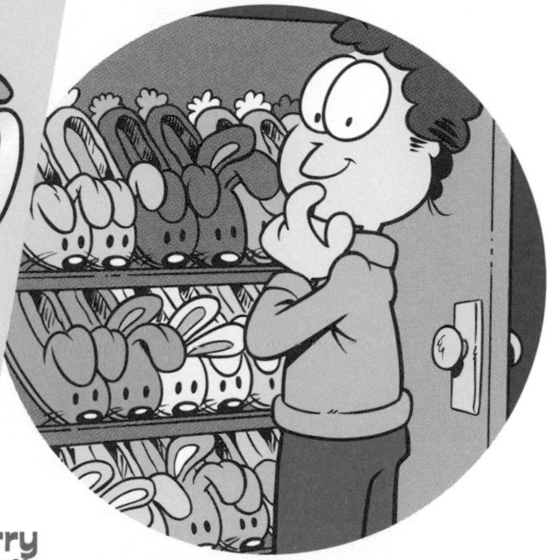

You own an extensive collection of bunny slippers

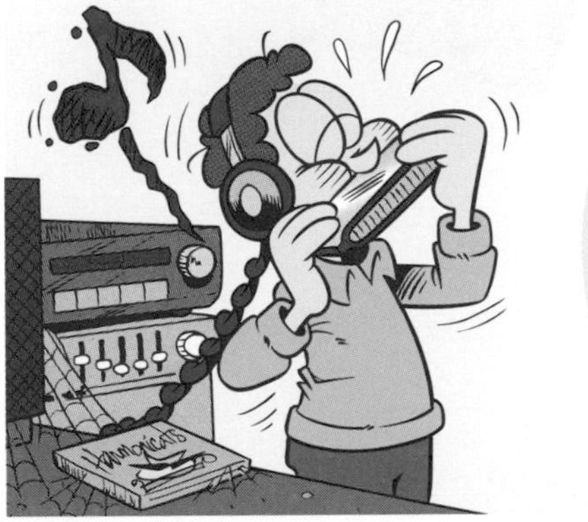

The last CD you bought was "Best of the Harmonicats"

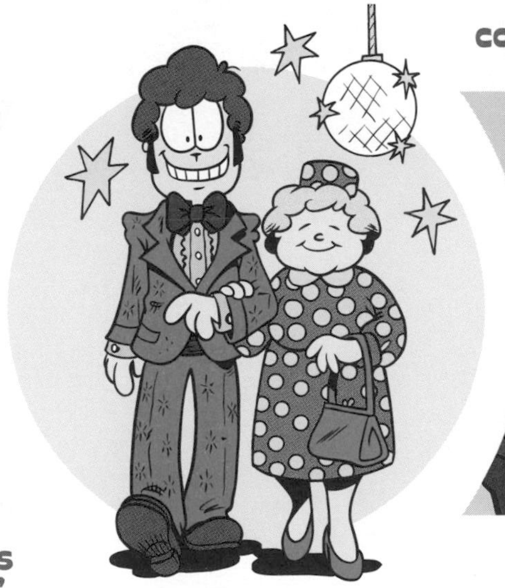

You take your mom to the prom

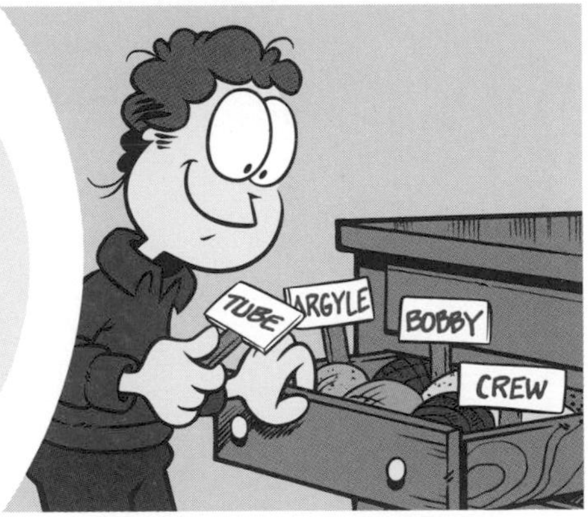
TUBE
ARGYLE
BOBBY
CREW

You alphabetize your sock drawer

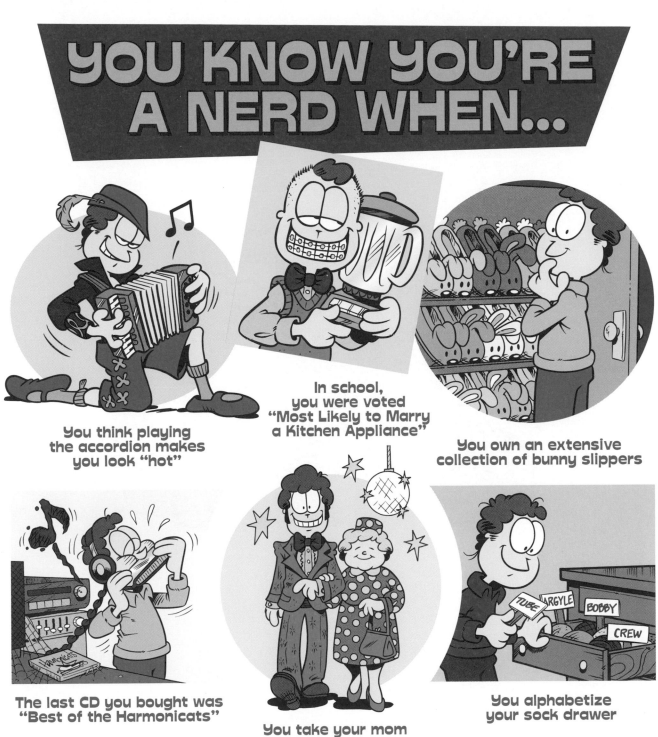

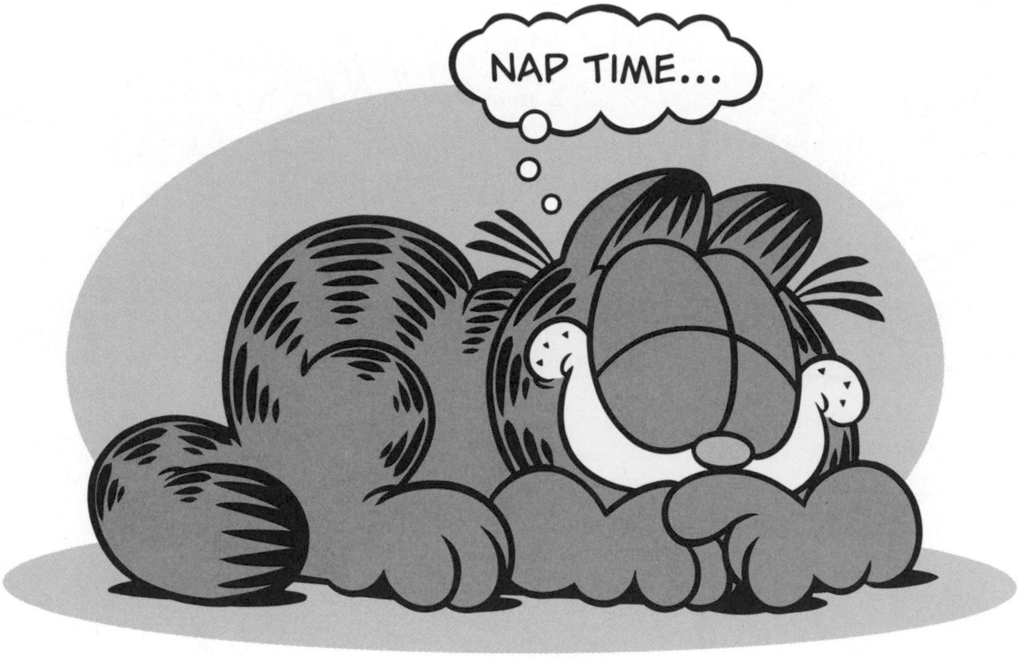
NAP TIME...